RELATIONSHIP MAINTENANCE

Relationship maintenance encompasses a wide range of activities that partners use to preserve their relationships. Despite the importance of these efforts, considerably more empirical focus has been devoted to starting (i.e. initiation) and ending (i.e. dissolution) relationships than on maintaining them. In this volume, internationally renowned scholars from a variety of disciplines describe diverse sets of relationship maintenance efforts in order to show why some relationships endure, whereas others falter. By focusing on 'what to do' rather than 'what not to do' in relationships, this book paints a more comprehensive picture of the forms, functions, and contexts of relationship maintenance. It is essential reading for scholars and students in psychology, communication, human development and family science, sociology, and couple/marriage and family therapy.

Brian G. Ogolsky is Director of Graduate Studies and Associate Professor of Human Development and Family Studies at the University of Illinois, Urbana-Champaign. He has won the International Association for Relationship Research's Book Award and several teaching awards for his mentorship and classroom teaching of statistics, methods, and intimate relationships.

J. Kale Monk is a fellow of the Center for Family Policy and Research and Assistant Professor of Human Development and Family Science at the University of Missouri. He has received awards for scholarship from the International Association for Relationship Research, the National Council on Family Relations, and the American Association for Marriage and Family Therapy.

Advances in Personal Relationships

Christopher R. Agnew
Purdue University

John P. Caughlin
University of Illinois at Urbana-Champaign

C. Raymond Knee
University of Houston

Terri L. Orbuch
Oakland University

Although scholars from a variety of disciplines have written and conversed about the importance of personal relationships for decades, the emergence of personal relationships as a field of study is relatively recent. *Advances in Personal Relationships* represents the culmination of years of multidisciplinary and interdisciplinary work on personal relationships. Sponsored by the International Association for Relationship Research, the series offers readers cutting-edge research and theory in the field. Contributing authors are internationally known scholars from a variety of disciplines, including social psychology, clinical psychology, communication, history, sociology, gerontology, and family studies. Volumes include integrative reviews, conceptual pieces, summaries of research programs, and major theoretical works. *Advances in Personal Relationships* presents first-rate scholarship that is both provocative and theoretically grounded. The theoretical and empirical work described by authors will stimulate readers and advance the field by offering new ideas and retooling old ones. The series will be of interest to upper-division undergraduate students, graduate students, researchers, and practitioners.

Other Books in the Series

Relationship Maintenance

Theory, Process, and Context

Edited by

Brian G. Ogolsky
University of Illinois at Urbana-Champaign

J. Kale Monk
University of Missouri

CAMBRIDGE
UNIVERSITY PRESS

University Printing House, Cambridge CB2 8BS, United Kingdom

One Liberty Plaza, 20th Floor, New York, NY 10006, USA

477 Williamstown Road, Port Melbourne, VIC 3207, Australia

314–321, 3rd Floor, Plot 3, Splendor Forum, Jasola District Centre,
New Delhi – 110025, India

79 Anson Road, #06–04/06, Singapore 079906

Cambridge University Press is part of the University of Cambridge.

It furthers the University's mission by disseminating knowledge in the pursuit of
education, learning, and research at the highest international levels of excellence.

www.cambridge.org
Information on this title: www.cambridge.org/9781108419857
DOI: 10.1017/9781108304320

© Brian G. Ogolsky and J. Kale Monk 2020

First published 2020

Printed in the United Kingdom by TJ International Ltd. Padstow Cornwall

A catalogue record for this publication is available from the British Library.

ISBN 978-1-108-41985-7 Hardback

CONTENTS

TABLES

FIGURES

CONTRIBUTORS

Christopher R. Agnew, *Department of Psychological Sciences, Purdue University, USA*

Arthur Aron, *Department of Psychology, Stony Brook University, USA*

Joyce Baptist, *School of Family Studies and Human Services, Kansas State University, USA*

Brian R.W. Baucom, *Department of Psychology, University of Utah, USA*

Donald H. Baucom, *Department of Psychology and Neuroscience, University of North Carolina Chapel Hill, USA*

John P. Caughlin, *Department of Communication, University of Illinois at Urbana-Champaign, USA*

Alexander Dugas, *Department of Psychology, Florida State University, USA*

Diane Felmlee, *Department of Sociology & Criminology, Pennsylvania State University, USA*

Nelli Ferenczi, *Regent's School of Psychotherapy & Psychology, Regent's University London, UK*

Katherine Fiori, *Gordon F. Derner School of Psychology, Adelphi University, USA*

R. Chris Fraley, *Department of Psychology, University of Illinois at Urbana-Champaign, USA*

Stanley O. Gaines, Jr., *Centre for Culture and Evolution, Brunel University London, UK*

Omri Gillath, *Department of Psychology, University of Kansas, USA*

Emily A. Impett, *Department of Psychology, University of Toronto Mississauga, Canada*

Jeremy Kanter, *Department of Family and Consumer Sciences, Illinois State University, USA*

Gery C. Karantzas, *School of Psychology, Deakin University, Australia*

Juwon Lee, *Department of Psychology, Carnegie Mellon University, USA*

Feea R. Leifker, *Department of Psychology, University of Utah, USA*

Edward P. Lemay, Jr., *Department of Psychology, University of Maryland, College Park, USA*

Karena Leo, *Department of Psychology, University of Utah, USA*

Gary Lewandowski Jr., *Department of Psychology, Monmouth University, USA*

Brandon McDaniel, *Health Services and Informatics Research, Parkview Research Center, USA*

James K. McNulty, *Department of Psychology, Florida State University, USA*

Shelby Messerschmitt-Coen, *Counselor Education and Supervision, Ohio State University, USA*

J. Kale Monk, *Department of Human Development and Family Science, University of Missouri, USA*

Amy Muise, *Department of Psychology, York University, Canada*

Brian G. Ogolsky, *Department of Human Development and Family Studies, University of Illinois at Urbana-Champaign, USA*

Daniel Perlman, *Department of Human Development and Family Studies, University of North Carolina at Greensboro, USA*

Christine Proulx, *Department of Human Development and Family Science, University of Missouri, USA*

Ashley K. Randall, *Counseling and Counseling Psychology, Arizona State University, USA*

Amy Rauer, *Department of Child and Family Studies, University of Tennessee, USA*

Natalie O. Rosen, *Departments of Psychology & Neuroscience and Obstetrics & Gynaecology, Dalhousie University, Canada*

Jeffry A. Simpson, *Department of Psychology, University of Minnesota, USA*

Susan Sprecher, *Department of Sociology & Anthropology, Illinois State University, USA*

Laura Stafford, *School of Media and Communication, Bowling Green State University, USA*

Jeffrey E. Stokes, *Department of Gerontology, University of Massachusetts Boston, USA*

Nadya Teneva, *Department of Psychology, University of Maryland, College Park, USA*

Jennifer A. Theiss, *School of Communication and Information, Rutgers University, USA*

Laura E. VanderDrift, *Department of Psychology, Syracuse University, USA*

Amber Vennum, *School of Family Studies and Human Services, Kansas State University, USA*

Ningxin Wang, *Department of Management and Organization, National University of Singapore, Singapore*

Xiaomeng Xu, *Department of Psychology, Idaho State University, USA*

Ethan S. Young, *Department of Psychology, University of Minnesota, USA*

PART I

INTRODUCTION

Maintaining the Literature on Relationship Maintenance

BRIAN G. OGOLSKY[1] AND J. KALE MONK[2]

Researchers use the term "relationship maintenance" to encompass the wide range of activities that partners use to preserve their romantic partnerships. Thus, relationship maintenance is distinct from attraction, relationship initiation, and relationship dissolution – topics that are beyond the scope of this volume. Ironically, considerably more research has been devoted to relationship initiation and dissolution than relationship maintenance, despite the fact that partners spend more of their time maintaining relationships than beginning or ending them. That said, the literature on relationship maintenance has rapidly expanded across many disciplines to incorporate an incredible diversity of strategies that take place in the context of relationships. Despite these advances in the study of relationship maintenance, there is limited consensus on the bounds of this construct. That is, the definition, process, context, and correlates of relationship maintenance vary considerably across disciplines. This book serves as a contemporary attempt to bring together the vast literature on relationship maintenance with contributions from scholars across different fields who study diverse facets of relationship maintenance.

We open the book with a brief chapter that is organized around the six most basic, yet critical questions that cut across all research: Who, What, When, Where, Why, and How. In the first section ("who"), we discuss the types of people who perform relationship maintenance as well as differences among individuals. The "what" section identifies the central definitional issues that continue to plague the field. The third section ("when") highlights the conditions under which people perform maintenance as well as the relationship challenges that prompt it. The "where" section identifies the small body of literature on geographic differences in relationship maintenance. The "why" section covers the principal theories that explain

[1] Department of Human Development and Family Studies, University of Illinois at Urbana-Champaign, bogolsky@illinois.edu
[2] Department of Human Development and Family Science, University of Missouri, monkj@missouri.edu

engagement in relationship maintenance activities. The final section comments on "how" maintenance activities sustain or enhance relationships. That is, it outlines the correlates, mediators, and moderators that explain the mechanisms by which maintenance operates. We conclude our chapter with a brief overview of the organization of the book.

WHO?

Relationship maintenance is considered a universal relationship process because it cuts across all types of relationships. Although this book focuses on the maintenance of romantic relationships, the broader literature on relationship maintenance has demonstrated its importance in the context of friendship (Labelle & Myers, 2016), family relationships (Harach & Kuczynski, 2004), employment (Xesha, Iwu, Slabbert, & Nduna, 2017), and even human–pet interactions (Zilcha-Mano, Mikulincer, & Shaver, 2011). Simply put, relationship maintenance is a necessary feature of every interpersonal (and sometimes interspecies) relationship.

Although relationship maintenance appears to be a universal relationship process, past research has shown that it is not identical for all people. One of the most frequently studied individual-difference variables is attachment. Relationship maintenance has been shown to vary as a function of both attachment anxiety and avoidance (e.g., Adams & Baptist, 2012; Lee, Karantzas, Gillath, & Fraley, Chapter 4). Although such associations vary across maintenance type, they are consistently in the negative direction, which indicates that anxiety and avoidance appear to be barriers to relationship maintenance. In addition to attachment, relationship maintenance also differs as a function of gender, and to a lesser degree, sex. In general, femininity demonstrates a stronger correlation with relationship maintenance than masculinity (e.g., Stafford, Dainton, & Haas, 2000). Sex differences also show that women perceive and report higher levels of relationship maintenance than men, although these differences are small in magnitude (Ogolsky & Bowers, 2013). In addition to sex and gender differences in maintenance, there is also variability in the motives, expression, function, and consequences of maintenance based on a number of other factors, including race (see Fiori & Rauer, Chapter 14) and age (see Rauer & Proulx, Chapter 17).

WHAT?

Over the past several decades, relationship maintenance scholars have attempted to define and explain key maintenance processes that serve to initiate and preserve romantic relationships. As we have observed in much of our past work (e.g., Ogolsky, Monk, Rice, Theisen, & Maniotes, 2017; Ogolsky & Monk, 2018), the definition of maintenance varies greatly across disciplines. For example, some scholars liken maintenance to a relationship state, falling between initiation and dissolution (see Perlman, Chapter 19), which characterizes maintenance as a discrete event or period rather than a dynamic process. Conversely, other scholars characterize maintenance as cognitive or behavioral efforts focused on continuing a relationship. Nearly 25 years ago, Dindia and Canary (1993) put forth four main definitions of relationship maintenance: (1) whether the relationship continues to exist, (2) keeping a relationship in a given form or state, (3) keeping the relationship satisfying, and (4) efforts to repair the relationship. Even still, relationship maintenance has also been considered a response to an interdependence dilemma (Agnew & VanderDrift, 2015) or the driving force behind threat mitigation aimed at sustaining the relationship (Ogolsky et al., 2017).

Although expansive definitions help capture relational processes that promote relationship persistence, conceptual inconsistencies create confusion and redundancies across studies. In a recent review of the literature, Ogolsky and colleagues (2017) identified more than 1,000 articles on the topic of relationship maintenance. Despite this pervasive coverage of the topic, the range of definitions (see Table 1.1 for example definitions) and the specific maintenance activities explored (see Perlman, Chapter 19; see also Ogolsky et al., 2017;

TABLE 1.1 *Exemplar definitions of relationship maintenance*

Key citation	Relationship maintenance definition
Acitelli (2001)	"to keep a relationship in a satisfying condition" (p. 153)
Agnew & VanderDrift (2015)	"processes that help to keep involved actors relatively interdependent with one another" (p. 581)
Alberts, Yoshimura, Rabby, & Loschiavo (2005)	"the preserving or sustaining of a desired relationship state or definition" (p. 304)
Ayers (1983)	Strategies used to keep a relationship in a stable state (i.e., "the basic patterns of exchange in the relationship are established and accepted" [p. 62] and "a given level of intimacy" [p. 62] is maintained)
Baxter & Dindia (1990)	"[Preventative and remedial] efforts to sustain a dynamic equilibrium in their relationship definition and satisfaction levels as they cope with the ebb and flow of everyday relating" (p. 188)
Baxter & Simon (1993)	"the process of sustaining a relationship's quality, particularly the satisfaction levels of the partners, in the presence of ongoing dialectical flux" (p. 226)
Bell, Daly, & Gonzalez (1987)	"enact lines of behavior ... to maintain and even enhance the affinity in their marriage" (p. 446)
Braiker & Kelley (1979)	"behaviors [primarily communication] engaged in by members of the couple to reduce costs and maximize

TABLE 1.1 *(cont.)*

Key citation	Relationship maintenance definition
	rewards from the relationship" (p. 151)... "the close communication of feelings and needs, and discussions directed at improving the relationship" (p. 156)
Burleson, Metts, & Kirch (2000)	"[Actions and tasks] associated with the maintenance, management, or repair of a relationship. These tasks focus on defining the relationship, establishing its parameters, managing its tensions, and dealing with threats to its integrity and endurance." (p. 248)
Canary & Stafford (1994)	"actions and activities used to sustain desired relational definitions" (p. 5)
Canary, Stafford, & Semic (2002)	"activities to repair, sustain, and thereby continue relationships in ways they want them to be" (p. 395)
Dainton & Aylor (2001) (see also Dindia & Canary, 1993)	"efforts to keep a relationship in a specified state or condition" (p. 176)
Dindia & Baxter (1987)	"strategies that are employed to stabilize the continuation of a relationship" (p. 145)
Duck (1994)	"area where relationships continue to exist between the point of their initial development...and their possible decline" (p. 45) "relational maintenance contains two elements, not one: the first is strategic planning for the continuance of the relationship; and the second is the breezy allowance of the relationship to continue by means of the everyday interactions and conversations that make the relationship what it is" (p. 46)
Gagné, Khan, Lydon, & To (2008)	"engage in various strategies to defend against the threat of meeting attractive alternatives to their dating partners" (p. 59)
Goldberg, Smith, & Kashy (2010)	"the practice of engaging in behaviors aimed at sustaining the quality and stability of the relationship" (p. 223)
Lambert & Fincham (2011)	"One way to maintain a relationship is to voice concerns to the partner so that appropriate adjustments can be made" (p. 53)
Ledbetter et al. (2010)	"communicative acts that foster perception of shared resources, identities, and perspectives" (p. 22)
McNulty, O'Mara, & Karney (2008)	"interpreting negative events in ways that allow each partner to maintain positive views of the relationship and of each other" (p. 631)
Roloff & Cloven (1994)	"individual or joint approaches intimates take to limit the relational harm that may result from prior or future conflicts and transgression" (p. 27) "maintenance approaches focus on preserving relationships, and may not otherwise benefit the individuals involved" (p. 29)
Rusbult, Olsen, Davis, & Hannon (2001)	"the specific means by which partners manage to sustain long-term, well-functioning relationships" (p. 96)

TABLE 1.1 *(cont.)*

Key citation	Relationship maintenance definition
Schoebi, Pagani, Luginbuehl, & Bradbury (2015)	"requires behavioral capacities that enable individuals to resolve conflicts and cope with stress in difficult times"... "motivational basis to preserve and sustain one's relationship throughout the challenges of daily life" (p. 160) ... "behaviors that maintain positive relationship qualities such as satisfaction, intimacy, and love [preventative aim], and... attempts to repair and strengthen a vulnerable relationship [intervention aim]" (p. 161)
Sigman (1991)	"relationship continuity constructional units, [or] pieces of behavior that precede, occur during, and succeed moments of relationship members' interactional nonengagement and serve to define the relationship as a continuous one despite the absence of face-to-face engagement" (p. 109)
Stafford & Canary (1991)	"communication strategies and routines that function to maintain relationships" (p. 218) "efforts expended to maintain the nature of the relationship to the actor's satisfaction" (p. 220)
Stafford, Dainton, & Haas (2000), p. 307	"[strategic behaviors] which individuals enact with the conscious intent of preserving or improving the relationship ... [and routine behaviors] that people perform that foster relational maintenance"

Note: For full references for articles cited in the table, see Ogolsky et al. (2017).

Ogolsky & Monk, 2018) in past research vary considerably. Some of the definitions set clear parameters on the specific criteria for maintenance activities. Others judge maintenance in terms of its correlation with known relationship outcomes (e.g., satisfaction). The remaining definitions refer to the processes that underlie maintenance (e.g., preservation of a current state). Of note, one of the chapters in this volume presents a novel and provocative definition of relationship maintenance as the process of growth (Stafford, Chapter 7). Taken together, it is clear that the research on the topic of relationship maintenance has grown considerably, yet definitional inconsistencies continue to pervade. Thus, crossing disciplinary boundaries and making implicit definitions of relationship maintenance more overt is the impetus for this volume.

WHEN?

The need for relationship maintenance comes online in the face of various relational experiences. Ogolsky and colleagues (2017) argue that there are two macromotives that undergird relationship maintenance processes: threat mitigation and relationship enhancement. Threat-mitigation strategies occur in order to stave off conditions that threaten the health of the relationship, such as partner transgressions (McNulty & Dugas, Chapter 8), or stress (Randall & Messerschmitt-Coen, Chapter 10). Relationship-enhancement strategies, however, encourage positive relationship outcomes void of any overt threat to the relationship. Relationship-enhancement strategies include behaviors such as generosity, social support, and joint leisure activity.

These macromotives also intersect with the definitions of relationship maintenance. Threat-mitigation strategies occur in reaction to specific relational threats, which suggests that they occur with the goal of keeping the relationship in a given state. That is, strategies such as derogating alternatives (VanderDrift & Agnew, Chapter 2; Young & Simpson, Chapter 3) or managing a conflict (Leo, Leifker, Baucom, & Baucom, Chapter 11) are done with the intent of moving the relationship back to a state of homeostasis. Relationship-enhancement strategies better align with definitions that involve moving the relationship forward. For example, routinely expressing gratitude (McNulty & Dugas, Chapter 8) or exhibiting responsiveness (Sprecher, Felmlee, Stokes, & McDaniel, Chapter 9) promotes a climate that allows partners to deepen their connection and reestablish relational goals. Many maintenance processes, such as sex and physical affection (see Impett, Muise, & Rosen, Chapter 12), for example, can both mitigate threat (e.g., motivated to have sex out of concern a partner will stray) and enhance a relationship (e.g., motivated to pleasure a partner or enhance the compassionate bond with a partner), depending on the motive. In addition to these motives dictating *when* maintenance is prompted, relationship maintenance can also occur at all points in the life course, although expression, function, and consequences can vary (see Rauer & Proulx, Chapter 17).

WHERE?

Of all the "W" questions addressed in this chapter, the "where" question has the smallest body of empirical support. Much of what we know about the location of maintenance comes from the limited work on cross-cultural variation (see Gaines & Ferenczi, Chapter 15). Work in this area has consistently shown that maintenance behavior is more similar than it is different cross-culturally. The most pronounced difference exists as a function of societal values. That is, individualistic countries like the USA put a higher premium on relationship-enhancement activities. Collectivist countries like Japan and South Korea, however, assign less value to relationship maintenance efforts, and as such, report lower levels than people in individualistic countries (e.g., Yum & Canary, 2009; see also Vennum, Kanter, & Baptist, Chapter 18). Within the same country, maintenance also occurs across different social locations (e.g., race, sexual orientation, sex, and gender) despite different stressors and barriers encountered by marginalized groups (e.g., discrimination; Fiori & Rauer, Chapter 14).

A second body of literature that shines some light on the location of relationship maintenance examines long-distance relationships. There are many situations that create a need or desire for relationship partners to live apart from each other (e.g., educational attainment, military deployment or other employment responsibilities). Research on partners in long-distance relationships routinely shows that they use a broader range of relationship maintenance strategies than do geographically proximal partners. These expanded strategies include the use of technology (e.g., Skype, text-messaging; Billedo, Kerkhof, & Finkenauer, 2015) and imagined interaction (Comfort, Grinstead, McCartney, Bourgois, & Knight, 2005; see Caughlin & Wang, Chapter 16, for a review of technology in relationships). Moreover, long-distance partners use more assurances (e.g., thinking or planning for the future) than do geographically close partners (see Ogolsky et al., 2017).

WHY?

The literature on relationship maintenance is rife with theories to explain why people engage in activities to promote their relationships. Among these theoretical explanations are models of early experiences such as attachment (Lee et al., Chapter 4) and evolution (Young & Simpson, Chapter 3), as well as models of relationship processes such as social exchange, interdependence, and equity (VanderDrift & Agnew, Chapter 2), uncertainty (Theiss, Chapter 5), and self-expansion (Xu, Lewandowski, & Aron, Chapter 6). The central difference between these two groups of theories is the relative weight of the individual versus the dyad.

Models of early experiences focus heavily on the individual nested within the broader family or evolutionary context. Attributions about relationship maintenance, therefore, stem from interactions between the individual and his or her caregiver (in the case of attachment) or from an evolutionary need to ensure successful reproduction (in the case of evolution). Models of relationship process tend to focus on the unique interaction between romantic partners as a catalyst for the promotion of relationship maintenance. Social exchange frameworks identify the relative balance of rewards and costs as a central determinant of maintenance. Uncertainty perspectives highlight the need for maintenance in response to the lack of clarity that stems from relationship transitions. Self-expansion argues that maintenance is best achieved through the use of novel activities that serve as a catalyst for physiological closeness. Despite the different explanations across a number of theories, there is consistency in the fact that people engage in relationship maintenance because it is important to the persistence of relationships (see Ogolsky et al., 2017). This fact is also why relationship maintenance is a salient focus in educational and therapeutic relationship intervention efforts (see Vennum et al., Chapter 18).

HOW?

The answer to the "How" question stems from the expansive work exploring the correlates of maintenance as well as examining the mediators and moderators of the associations between relationship maintenance and outcomes. Among the most common correlates of relationship maintenance are satisfaction and commitment. Numerous chapters in this volume even incorporate these correlates into the very definition of relationship maintenance. Nearly all of the maintenance strategies covered in the literature correlate with relationship satisfaction and/or commitment, and a meta-analysis of this work shows that these effects are moderate to large in magnitude (Ogolsky & Bowers, 2013).

In terms of mediation and moderation, the literature varies as a function of the specific maintenance strategy in question. Threat-mitigation strategies, in general, have a positive association with relationship outcomes, but this association is moderated by the severity of the threat and the frequency of the transgression. For example, the research on forgiveness has shown that it is beneficial to the relationship if the transgression is not severe (Fincham, Jackson, & Beach, 2005) and is not recurrent (McNulty, 2008). In the context of conflict, self-regulation serves a mediating role on relationship outcomes through a stress-buffering process (Finkel & Campbell, 2001). In the relationship-enhancement domain, individual dispositions appear to moderate associations with relationship outcomes. For example, partner-focused prayer is associated with relationship satisfaction among those who pray regularly (Beach, Fincham, Hurt, McNair, & Stanley, 2008). Humor is also beneficial to relationships, particularly among those who routinely use it (Hall, 2013). Across both macromotives, issues of biased perception also influence the impact of relationship maintenance activities (Lemay & Teneva, Chapter 13).

INTRODUCTION TO THE VOLUME

Our overview chapter is meant to set the scene for the research that follows. Each chapter elaborates on the core questions and research areas that we identified earlier. The book is organized around three major sections that highlight theory, process, and context. In each chapter, the authors provide an integrative review and critique of the existing literature as it pertains to the maintenance of close relationships. The book focuses heavily on recent research (e.g., within the last 10 years). The first section features five chapters that explore theoretical explanations of relationship maintenance. Each of these chapters examines a major theoretical framework and explains how it conceptualizes relationship maintenance. The second section contains seven chapters that focus on the various processes of relationship maintenance. Each of these chapters describe a specific maintenance activity (or set of activities) and identify the mechanisms by which those behaviors or strategies promote the development of relationships and how they impact broader relational processes. The third section of the book is dedicated to the diverse social contexts in which relationship maintenance is embedded. This section includes five chapters that explain the diversity of relationship maintenance across culture, context, race, sex, gender, and the life course. The final chapter in this section focuses on the practical implications of relationship mainte-nance in the lives of couples and families. The concluding chapter provides a discussion of the past, present, and future of relationship maintenance research by highlighting the critical gaps in the existing literature as well as opportunities for advancements in theoretical, empirical, and methodological work.

The book represents the most up-to-date, interdisciplinary research on relationship maintenance. This is not the first book to cover the topic of relationship maintenance, but it is unique in its attention to diverse perspec-tives on the definitions, processes, antecedents, and consequences of main-tenance activities. The research covered in this collection of chapters comes from all facets of the behavioral sciences and advances important new ideas about the ways in which people develop their relationships. This collaboration across disciplines is a vital step in order to advance the interdisciplinary area of relationship maintenance. Given that interpersonal relationships are cen-tral to our health and well-being, a comprehensive understanding of the maintenance of these relationships is essential. We believe this collection of chapters brings us ever closer to understanding the depth and breadth of our most important resources: each other.

REFERENCES

Adams, R. & Baptist, J. (2012). Relationship maintenance behavior and adult attachment: An analysis of the actor-partner interdependence model. *The American Journal of Family Therapy*, *40*, 203–244.

Agnew, C. R., & VanderDrift, L. E. (2015). Relationship maintenance and dissolution. In M. Mikulincer & P. R. Shaver (Eds.), *APA handbook of personality and social psychology: Vol. 3. Interpersonal relations* (pp. 581–604). Washington, DC: APA.

Beach, S. R., Fincham, F. D., Hurt, T. R., McNair, L. M., & Stanley, S. M. (2008). Prayer and marital intervention: A conceptual framework. *Journal of Social and Clinical Psychology*, *27*, 641–669. doi:10.1521/jscp.2008.27.7.641

Billedo, C. J., Kerkhof, P., & Finkenauer, C. (2015). The use of social networking sites for relationship maintenance in long-distance and geographically close romantic relationships. *Cyberpsychology, Behavior, and Social Networking*, *18*, 152–157. doi:10.1089/cyber.2014.0469

Comfort, M., Grinstead, O., McCartney, K., Bourgois, P., & Knight, K. (2005). "You can't do nothing in this damn place": Sex and intimacy among couples with an incarcerated male partner. *The Journal of Sex Research, 42*, 3–12. doi:10.1080/00224490509552251

Dindia, K., & Canary, D. J. (1993). Definitions and theoretical perspectives on maintaining relationships. *Journal of Social and Personal Relationships, 10*, 163–173.

Fincham, F. D., Jackson, H., & Beach, S. R. (2005). Transgression severity and forgiveness: Different moderators for objective and subjective severity. *Journal of Social and Clinical Psychology, 24*, 860–875. doi:10.1521/jscp.2005.24.6.860

Finkel, E. J., & Campbell, W. (2001). Self-control and accommodation in close relationships: An interdependence analysis. *Journal of Personality and Social Psychology, 81*, 263–277.

Hall, J. A. (2013). Humor in long-term romantic relationships: The association of general humor styles and relationship-specific functions with relationship satisfaction. *Western Journal of Communication, 77*, 272–292.

Harach, L., & Kuczynski, L. (2004). Construction and maintenance of parent-child relationships: Bidirectional contributions from the perspective of parents. *Infant and Child Development, 14*, 327–343.

Labelle, S., & Myers, S. (2016). The use of relational maintenance behaviors in sustained adult friendships. *Communication Research Reports, 33*, 310–316.

McNulty, J. K. (2008). Forgiveness in marriage: Putting the benefits into context. *Journal of Family Psychology, 22*, 171–175. doi:10.1037/0893-3200.22.1.171

Ogolsky, B., & Bowers, J. (2013). A meta-analytic review of relationship maintenance and its correlates. *Journal of Social and Personal Relationships, 30*, 343–367. doi:10.1177/0265407512463338

Ogolsky, B., & Monk, J. (2018). Maintaining relationships. In A. Vangelisti & D. Perlman (Eds.), *Cambridge handbook of personal relationships* (523–537). New York: Cambridge.

Ogolsky, B., Monk, J., Rice, T., Theisen, J., & Maniotes, C. (2017). Relationship maintenance: A review of research on romantic relationships. *Family Theory and Review, 9*, 275–306.

Stafford, L., Dainton, M., & Haas, S. (2000). Measuring routine and strategic relational maintenance: Scale revision, sex versus gender roles, and prediction of relational characteristics. *Communication Monographs, 67*, 306–323.

Xesha, D., Iwu, C., Slabbert, A., & Nduna, J. (2017). The impact of employer-employee relationships on business growth. *Journal of Economics, 5*, 313–324.

Yum, Y. O., & Canary, D. J. (2009). Cultural differences in equity theory predictions of relational maintenance strategies. *Human Communication Research, 35*(3), 384–406.

Zilcha-Mano, S., Mikulincer, M., & Shaver, P. (2011). An attachment perspective on human-pet relationships: Conceptualization and assessment of pet attachment orientations. *Journal of Research in Personality, 45*, 345–357.

PART II

THEORIES OF RELATIONSHIP MAINTENANCE

Interdependence Perspectives on Relationship Maintenance

LAURA E. VANDERDRIFT[1] AND CHRISTOPHER R. AGNEW[2]

Humans are among the most social, cooperative species in existence, and perhaps nothing exemplifies this more than the fundamental nature of their close relationships (Van Lange, Balliet, Parks, & Van Vugt, 2014). As humans, we demonstrate a need to belong – to have close, connected relationships with others – that permeates our motivations and action. Under most conditions, we form social attachments readily and resist dissolving existing bonds (Baumeister & Leary, 1995). Lacking such attachments, we experience ill effects to our mental health, physical health, and overall well-being (see White, VanderDrift, & Heffernan, 2015). Beyond simply having *any* attachments, having *high-quality* attachments has been found to lower the risk for all-cause mortality and disease morbidity at rates on a par with or greater than the other largest known contributors to poor health (e.g., smoking, obesity; Holt-Lunstad, Robles, & Sbarra, 2017). Together, the evidence overwhelmingly supports the notion that close relationships with others are necessary.

The necessity of relationships stems from the fact that they are a primary source of fulfillment of a variety of fundamental needs, from the inherently relational (e.g., needs for belonging, caregiving, and companionship) to the more general (e.g., needs for autonomy, competence, and self-expansion). According to Interdependence Theory (IT), need fulfillment provides two general types of outcomes: direct and indirect (Rusbult & Van Lange, 2003; VanderDrift & Agnew, 2012). Direct outcomes are the experiences of pleasure (or pain) that result from a need being sated (or not sated). By way of metaphor, the relief that a sip of water provides when thirsty is akin to the satisfaction that companionship yields when lonely. Additionally, need fulfillment provides indirect outcomes, which rest on the broader implications of an interaction. Extending our metaphor, the security conferred by knowing one has a reliable well from which to obtain water is akin to the security

[1] Department of Psychology, Syracuse University, lvanderd@syr.edu
[2] Department of Psychological Sciences, Purdue University, agnew@purdue.edu

provided by the sense that a partner is available to provide support when such support is needed.

Despite the beneficial fulfillment of important needs, relationships do not come without costs. From the perspective of IT, relationships represent a unique situational problem, in which two actors' best individual interests and preferred options are not necessarily congruent (Kelley & Thibaut, 1978; Thibaut & Kelley, 1959). Nevertheless, the nature of dyadic interdependence means they must solve the problem. The term "relationship maintenance" refers to the set of processes – behavioral and cognitive – that help keep interdependent relationships intact despite the fact that situational actors must adapt to constantly changing situations. Prior to discussing maintenance processes in detail, it is important to review IT to understand why relationship maintenance is required at all.

INTERDEPENDENCE THEORY

IT, as originally articulated by Thibaut and Kelley (1959), was not strictly a theory concerned with how relationships are maintained. Rather, it was formulated to help explain how people represent and consider situations of interdependence with respect to choosing among potential courses of action. Courses of action here include stay–leave decisions: is this situation of interdependence one that should be continued or dissolved? Consistent with this traditional conceptualization of IT, the primary concerns of relationship partners with respect to maintaining their relationships are whether to cooperate (stay) or defect (leave) in the face of individual interdependence problems (Kelley & Thibaut, 1978). Cumulatively, across all the choices partners make (dozens of them, daily), relationships develop particular sets of expectations and patterns of behavior that are unique to that relationship, which contemporary IT theorists have used as the basis for understanding relationship maintenance (Kelley, 1984). Prior to delving into consideration of specific relationship maintenance processes, it is important to understand the building blocks of such expectations and also the impetus that makes maintenance necessary: interdependence problems.

Interdependence problems. Within IT, *interdependence problems* are broadly defined as situations that involve (at least) two individuals – each with their own needs, motives, and cognitions – interacting in specific social contexts. The title of "problems" may be a bit misleading, as not all interdependence problems create turmoil for the relationship. It simply refers to the fact that all such situations require solving (i.e., making choices as to how to proceed). Sometimes problems can be easily solved, when interacting partners' needs, motives, and cognitions all align, and their behaviors coordinate to ensure all receive their optimal outcomes. Other times, however, problems produce conflicts that must be resolved. These problems take various forms, but among the most common variants are those problems that are inherent in *outcome patterns* and those that arise from *coordination problems*.

Outcome patterns specify the projected payoff (or benefit) for each member of an interaction. For example, consider John and Mary, a hypothetical couple. Perhaps John and Mary have just had a baby who, as babies do, requires regular nighttime bottle feedings. John and Mary both agree that they must feed her, and that only one of them should get up to feed her each night. They disagree, however, about who it should be. This outcome pattern can be depicted in a matrix, which is a tool commonly used by IT theorists. The numbers included in such matrices are somewhat arbitrary with respect to units they represent but meaningful with respect to relative magnitudes between them (such that, e.g., "2" is twice as good an outcome as "1"):

		Mary	
		Feeding	Sleeping
John	Feeding	−6 / −6	1 / 8
	Sleeping	8 / 1	−10 / −10

TABLE 2.1   Interdependence problems matrix

As this matrix depicts (see Table 2.1), both John and Mary have two options: Feeding or Sleeping. The outcomes each obtains for their choice, depicted below the diagonal in each cell for John and above the diagonal for Mary, depend not only on their own actions but also on the actions of their partner. For both, the worst option is the lower right-hand corner; both of them sleeping while their child needs to be fed is a highly undesirable option for both of them (each receives outcomes valuing −10, reflecting, among other things, their love for their child and desire to keep him/her healthy and happy). Also for both, the second worst option is the upper left-hand corner; both of them foregoing sleep to feed their baby is undesirable, perhaps for its inefficiency (−6 for each). Thus, in this situation depicting an interdependence problem, there are essentially two non-negative options for the couple members to choose between: either Mary sleeps and John feeds (i.e., the top right-hand corner) or John sleeps and Mary feeds (i.e., the bottom left-hand corner). Sleeping produces higher outcomes for both (8) than feeding does (1), and there is not an obviously "correct" choice in this payoff matrix (the structure of which resembles a variant of the Prisoner's Dilemma game). How John and Mary solve this interdependence problem is relationship maintenance (or lack thereof), and we will discuss their options and likely cognitions in this situation later.

Relatedly, outcome problems also exist when what is rewarding immediately is not what is rewarding over time. To explain this, IT uses what are referred to as "transition lists," which detail not only the behavioral options and outcomes for the partners in one situation but also the means by which they proceed from one pattern of interdependence to another (Kelley, 1984). The partners might not simply be interdependent in one situation but might be so in their pursuit of temporally extended outcomes and in their ability to move from situation to situation (Rusbult & Van Lange, 2003). In this way, the option an individual selects in a given situation is not simply dictated by their outcomes at that time but potentially also by consideration of more temporally distal outcomes.

In the following is a transition list that demonstrates a series of problems that make up what IT calls an "Investment Situation" (Kelley et al., 2003) (see Table 2.2). In this situation, partners can arrive at a very desirable payoff situation (Juncture N), but it requires both investing resources in a series of preliminary junctures (Junctures J, K, L, and M). If both partners choose to invest at each juncture, they continue through the list and eventually reach the desirable Juncture N. However, if either partner chooses not to invest at a given Juncture, then the relationship is exited (Juncture X; not represented as a row in this list), all previous investment is lost, and the possibility of arriving at Juncture N is gone. As such, individuals may choose to keep selecting seemingly undesirable options in the short run (with outcomes valued at −2 in each instance), but this is in the service of a positive long-term outcome (in this case, +16).

Other interdependence problems exist because relationship partners do not have direct access to each other's needs, motives, and cognitions (and they certainly do not have them in matrix form, with payoffs and response options clearly delineated, and a transition list specified in advance!). In real interactions, it is common to experience *noise*, or discrepancies between the outcomes an actor intends to cause and the outcomes the other actually experiences. Noise can reduce cooperation, as it makes the partner's motives unclear and makes cooperating riskier (Van Lange, Ouwerkerk, & Tazelaar, 2002). It is also common to experience *coordination problems*, in which partners must coordinate their behavior, consider the temporal nature of their relationship, and correctly discern each other's motives in order for a situation to be optimally solved (see Theiss, Chapter 5, for a more detailed description of uncertainty). With such problems, the chance of obtaining optimal outcomes is especially influenced by relationship dynamics, to which we turn our attention now.

Beyond cooperation/defection: Relationship dynamics. More contemporary interpretations of IT have noted that other decisions can be examined

TABLE 2.2 *Investment situation transition list*

Juncture	Options	Possible selections	Outcomes for A and B	Transition to next juncture
J	(a1, a2)	a1b1	−2, −2	K
	(b1, b2)	a1b2	−2, 0	X
		a2b1	0, −2	X
		a2b2	0, 0	X
K	(a1, a2)	a1b1	−2, −2	L
	(b1, b2)	a1b2	−2, 0	X
		a2b1	0, −2	X
		a2b2	0, 0	X
L	(a1, a2)	a1b1	−2, −2	M
	(b1, b2)	a1b2	−2, 0	X
		a2b1	0, −2	X
		a2b2	0, 0	X
M	(a1, a2)	a1b1	−2, −2	N
	(b1, b2)	a1b2	−2, 0	X
		a2b1	0, −2	X
		a2b2	0, 0	X
N	(a3, a4)	a3b3	+16, +16	N
	(b3, b4)	a3b4	+16, +16	N
		a4b3	+16, +16	N
		a4b4	+16, +16	N

within interdependent situations, beyond just whether to stay or go, or to cooperate or defect. Put most succinctly by Rusbult and colleagues, "of course, persistence is a rather minimal requirement for maintenance" (Rusbult, Martz, & Agnew, 1998, p. 361). When partners confront interdependence problems, they do not only solve the particular situation, but they develop stable response patterns over time. What type of response pattern they stably adopt has important implications for how the relationship is maintained. When individuals always seek to maximize their own self-interest in response to interdependent problems, the relationship is unlikely to persist. Partners who seek to maximize joint outcomes (i.e., the combined outcomes of both self and partner), on the other hand, are likely to experience a continued relationship.

Although not historically considered an IT-relevant concept, the notion of equity may be salient for some individuals when solving problems (Walster, Walster, & Berscheid, 1978). Equity Theory, like IT, holds that individuals try to maximize their outcomes. From the perspective of Equity Theory, however, for individuals to maximize outcomes, society should accept systems that ensure equity and reward those who adhere to these systems. When individuals find themselves in inequitable systems, they experience distress and try to eliminate the distress by restoring equity (Walster et al., 1978). These tenets have been found to apply stably to "exchange" relationships, in which concerns regarding fairness are paramount (Clark & Mills, 1979). However, in "communal" relationships, or ones in which the partners have a mutual concern for each other's well-being, individuals do not always choose to balance their individual outcomes with their partner's, but instead choose to maximize their joint outcomes (Clark, Mills, & Powell, 1986). One reason why partners may or may not choose to maximize joint outcomes, according to IT, is their psychological state of commitment toward a given relationship (Rusbult et al., 1998).

COMMITMENT AND RELATIONSHIP MAINTENANCE

Without question, a driving force behind humans' participation in close romantic relationships is the abundance of positive emotion – of love – that is attached to them. Pop culture, and romantic partners themselves, point to love as the reason relationships thrive, are desirable, and survive. IT departs from the mainstream by not focusing on love. When facing interdependence problems, when it might be expected that positive emotion is hardly salient, love is not what promotes relationship maintenance. From an IT perspective, love encapsulates all the positivity that draws individuals together (e.g., positive emotion experienced from a particular relationship), whereas *commitment* to a relationship serves to promote and maintain interaction between individuals (Kelley, 1983). Commitment, conceptualized as consisting of a long-term orientation, a motivation to persist, and an affective connection to a partner (Arriaga & Agnew, 2001), fuels individuals' expectations that they will persist "through thick and thin." More concretely, being committed means engaging in consistent pro-relationship activities when confronted with changing and challenging situations (Becker, 1960).

   Numerous factors have been identified as giving rise to a sense of commitment. On one side are all the elements that serve to push two individuals together, including love, desirable activities, and status, and the cost that would be incurred if they were to leave. Collectively, these pushing factors are the "pros" of remaining in the relationship. On the other side are all the elements that serve to pull two individuals apart, including the psychological costs (anxiety, effort) that are experienced with the partner and high-quality alternatives that must be foregone in order to remain in a given relationship. Collectively, the pulling factors are the "cons" of remaining in the relationship (Arriaga & Agnew, 2001; Kelley, 1983; Rusbult et al., 1998). In the simplest sense, an individual experiences commitment when the pros outweigh the cons. Of course, pros and cons vacillate – needs and their fulfillment wax and wane, work stress comes and goes, alternatives appear and disappear, and satisfaction fluctuates (Arriaga, 2001; Le & Agnew, 2001; VanderDrift, Lewandowski, & Agnew, 2011). An individual would not be expected to experience a severe, relationship-altering dip in commitment when cons momentarily outweigh the pros. Instead, commitment places individuals in a causal system that stably supports continuing membership (Kelley, 1983). In other words, although it is useful to consider what causal factors promote the development of commitment (i.e., the pros and cons), after that commitment is established, individuals allow it to drive their behavior in the service of maintaining the commitment (Kelley, 1983).

The causal system that commitment generates has numerous consequences for the involved individuals – what are collectively referred to as the processes of commitment (Kelley, 1983). The processes of commitment are, simply, what involved partners do to maintain their relationship in the face of changing situations (Rusbult & Buunk, 1993). Each of these processes serves to promote persistence and can serve to additionally increase commitment. Insofar as individuals experience these processes – which they do because they are committed – they will see their level of commitment rise. In that way, commitment has the potential to operate as a sort of closed process, in which the elements to sustain are generated by sustaining. There are numerous examples of such processes. In the following, we elaborate on a few.

Sunken costs and future plans. As couple members develop commitment to their relationship, invariably, they increase the amount they invest in their relationship. Investments, broadly speaking, are the resources that partners "put into" their relationship to enable it to deepen – time, money, effort, etc. (Goodfriend & Agnew, 2008). These resources become tied to the relationship and would decline in value or be lost should the relationship end (Rusbult et al., 1998). Investments can be tangible in nature, in that they physically exist and are tied, directly or indirectly, to the relationship (e.g., jointly made purchases, pets, or shared debt). They can also be intangible in nature, in that they do not have physical boundaries, but are nevertheless tied to the relationship in some way (e.g., memories, self-disclosures, or time). Both tangible and intangible resources drive commitment but also are fueled by commitment, such that committed individuals are comfortable with sinking more costs into the relationship. Additionally, because they are valuable only insofar as the relationship persists, they serve an important relationship maintenance function.

However, past investments pale in comparison to future plans in terms of their relationship-maintaining potential. Future plans, similar to the notion of "assurances" from other theoretical traditions (Canary & Stafford, 1992; Stafford, Chapter 7), are a form of investment that the involved individuals count on making in the future, including their goals and hopes for their selves and relationship (Goodfriend & Agnew, 2008). Future plans not only provide a maintaining force by being investments the participants do not want to risk losing; they also help maintenance by minimizing doubts. When individuals can easily call to mind the future plans they have for their relationship, they are more confident in their commitment and indeed, greater in commitment overall (Tan & Agnew, 2016). In this way, future plans enable individuals to maintain their relationship by preserving the confidence in the relationship needed to persist.

Derogation of alternative quality. As elaborated upon by Young and Simpson in Chapter 3, one of the most important external threats to an ongoing relationship is the existence of a high-quality, desirable alternative (Le & Agnew, 2003; Rusbult et al., 1998). Believing there is a course of action that would be preferable to the current one reduces individuals' interest in continuing with the course of action they are on. However, commitment plays two distinct roles in minimizing the threat posed by high-quality alternatives. First, commitment produces a perceptual bias against alternatives (Johnson & Rusbult, 1989; Miller, 1997). Committed relationships change partners' expectations about the ratio of good to bad outcomes they should receive in relationships. Insofar as the relationship reliably provides high-quality outcomes, the partners' expectations for outcomes become greater. For these individuals with high expectations, few alternative courses of action appear appealing, especially compared with those whose expectations have not been bolstered by a high-quality relationship (Vanderdrift et al., 2011). Furthermore, commitment produces a motivated bias against alternatives (Johnson & Rusbult, 1989). This bias works on the social psychological principle of dissonance: individuals in a committed relationship feel psychological tension when they recognize an attractive alternative to their relationship, and to alleviate the tension, they devalue, or derogate, the alternative. Together, the biases against alternatives facilitate the reduction of the potential negative impact of attractive alternatives to an ongoing relationship. Going one step further, lacking high-quality alternative courses of action serves to bolster commitment and create dependence, as not having a better option than the current one makes leaving the current one undesirable (Rusbult et al., 1998).

Inclusion of other in self. Relationship commitment is also associated with a cognitive restructuring of how one views the self, such that individuals perceive themselves less as individuals and more as part of a pluralistic self-and-other collective (Agnew, Van Lange, Rusbult, & Langston, 1998). In other words, committed individuals have a sense that their partner and their relationship are extensions of their sense of self (Kelley, 1983). This is sometimes termed *cognitive interdependence*, and individuals high in cognitive interdependence more often use plural pronouns when spontaneously describing their relationship (e.g., "we"), are more likely to confuse their partner's traits and preferences with their own when under pressure, and feel subjectively closer to their partners (e.g., Agnew et al., 1998). Importantly, experiencing high levels of cognitive interdependence makes all the necessary maintenance that goes into a relationship easier: insofar as a partner's preferences are cognitively mingled with one's own preferences, sacrificing some self-relevant outcomes so that the partner receives optimal outcomes is more natural and less costly. In other words, because of cognitive interdependence, pursuing pro-relationship or pro-partner outcomes has pro-self benefits. Going one step further, insofar as there is great pro-self benefit to maintaining a relationship, commitment to the relationship will grow, as the reward–cost ratio is a key factor promoting commitment.

Transformation of motivation. Perhaps the most influential of the processes that commitment generates is transformation of motivation (Kelley & Thibaut, 1978). This process entails movement from the given situation (e.g., the objective situation about which everyone would agree) to the effective situation (e.g., the situation as perceived by the involved actor). To illustrate, one can imagine that an individual, perhaps John again, would prefer to go out to eat Mexican food for dinner, but his partner, let's just call her Mary, prefers to eat leftovers at home. The given situation is just that information. However, John knows that Mary is typically very easy-going and often does what he wants, but today she is trying to be more responsible with money. John can consider all of this information and realize that this is an opportunity to support his partner and instead of insisting on his own self-interest, act on the effective, transformed situation and eat leftovers instead. Individuals do not simply react to the objective situation, but rather, weigh their long-term interests and goals, think about their past experiences in the relationship, and make a decision that takes all of this into account (Rusbult & Van Lange, 2003). If this sounds like an effortful process, it is. Luckily, the commitment individuals feel for their partners causes this process to occur more automatically, and over time, having sufficiently practiced the necessary transformation of motivation, individuals can come to be quite efficient at it (Wieselquist, Rusbult, & Foster, 1999).

The importance of transformation of motivation can hardly be overstated. It is the basis for the most important behavioral maintenance mechanisms that exist to support ongoing relationships. For instance, consider *willingness to sacrifice*, in which individuals are willing to (and do) sacrifice their own self-interest for their partner's, or for the interest of the relationship (Van Lange et al., 1997). These sacrifices include a full range, from more short-term and transitory actions (e.g., seeing an undesirable movie on date night) to more long-term and lasting actions (e.g., moving to a different country for

your partner's job). They also include doing something the individual otherwise would not have done because the partner wants them to (e.g., spending
a holiday with their family) or foregoing an activity they otherwise would have
done because the partner does not want them to (e.g., turning down an
attractive alternative partner). Each of these types of sacrifice occurs via
transforming motivation from self-focus to relationship-focus, and both are
important because they enable two interdependent, unique people to coordinate their lives so that each receives desirable outcomes.

Another behavioral maintenance mechanism that is a product of transformed motivation and vital for relationship longevity is *accommodation.*
Accommodation occurs when one's partner has behaved badly and one
suppresses the urge to retaliate in kind and instead responds in a pro-
relationship manner (Rusbult, Verette, Whitney, Slovik, & Lipkus, 1991).
According to models of accommodation, there are two dimensions underlying potential responses: valence and arousal. Partners can engage in the
ideal positive-valence, high-arousal response (i.e., voice), in which they
express why their partner's bad behavior is unacceptable in an attempt to
move past it, or the (woefully bad for the relationship) negative-valence, high-
arousal option (i.e., exit), in which the individual escalates the conflict or ends
the relationship without resolving the issue. The two low-arousal options (i.e.,
loyalty, which is positively valenced, and neglect, which is negatively so) both
involve ignoring the problem at hand and waiting for conditions to either
improve or deteriorate. Research suggests that both of these options are
equally bad for relationships, as neither resolves the underlying issue, and
the partner is unable to tell which the other is using in a given moment. As
such, the problem is likely to reoccur or to have negative effects on other
domains (Drigotas, Whitney, & Rusbult, 1995). Importantly, when individuals
transform motivation, suppress potential negative responses, and supplant
them with an active positive response, conflict is then not detrimental to the
relationship, and commitment can be strengthened as a result (Rusbult et al.,
1991).

MAINTENANCE AS THE DEFAULT CHOICE

Interdependence necessarily involves problems, in which the actors' needs
and goals are, at times, incompatible. Solving these problems, by either
cooperating or defecting, leaving or staying, has the potential to cumulate
into stable response patterns that change the way relationships are maintained. In offering and testing the construct of commitment, contemporary IT
theorists have laid out a process by which relationships can become self-
sustaining: committed partners engage in a predictable series of processes
(e.g., transformation of motivation, sinking costs, derogating alternatives) to
adapt to changing situations, all of which serve to increase commitment. In

other words, IT, concerned with specifying causal processes in relationship persistence, has identified what is essentially an ironic persistence effect: the more committed an individual is, the more commitment-enhancing processes occur (Wieselquist et al., 1999).

It may be tempting to assume that relationships are fragile and challenging to maintain. The main question of interest in a chapter on relationship maintenance might be: "How can we maintain relationships in the face of all the forces working to pull them apart?" However, an IT perspective suggests that the question to pose is an opposite one: "What forces could actually pull apart an ongoing, maintained relationship?" A relationship's inert state is one of persistence; the default choice in interdependence problems is "stay." Even if an individual finds the rewards from their relationship too few, and identifies an alternative course of action that they want to pursue, the action of leaving a relationship is significantly more challenging than simply staying. To leave requires an almost certainly emotionally distressing dissolution event of some sort, an uncoupling of physical and intangible investments and plans, and a separation of the self from the relationship. In sum, from the perspective of IT, relationship maintenance is the default.

This notion of relationship persistence being the default option might seem controversial, if not downright untenable, given the fact that humans have a drive to maximize rewards and reduce personal costs. Surely, threats enter all the time and derail the commitment processes that promote persistence! What comes of the relationship when commitment itself decreases? A model derived from IT – the Equilibrium Model of Relationship Maintenance – is perfectly suited to explaining how the threat of flagging commitment is mitigated (Murray, Holmes, Griffin, & Derrick, 2015). The theoretical work behind this model suggests that there are myriad events within relationships that can lead to commitment ebbing, ranging from "the mundane to the disheartening to the profound" (Murray et al., 2015, p. 93). When such threats arise, and commitment ebbs, individuals rely on threat-mitigation rules, that is, expedient and routine ways of managing the threat that do not rely on commitment processes. The three threat-mitigation rules are: 1) try to accommodate when a partner is hurtful, 2) ensure mutual dependence, and 3) resist devaluing a partner who impedes one's personal goals. The theorists use a basic need metaphor, and suggest that the rules come into play when the need is present (i.e., just as the behavior of drinking water comes into play when one is thirsty, the behavior of mitigating threat comes into play when commitment slips). Over time, the effectiveness of the threat-mitigation system acts as a reward, meaning that when commitment ebbs, the activation of the threat-mitigating system will be more instantaneous the more it has been activated in the past (see Stafford, Chapter 7, for additional information on the equilibrium model of relationship maintenance). Thus, even when commitment itself is threatened, the inherently rewarding nature of relationships provides individuals with the motivation to find a different, automatic process to sustain the relationship.

CONCLUSION

How do we keep our relationships intact? There are myriad ways to answer this question, but in this chapter we reviewed the way an IT theorist would do so. From this perspective, relationships are a fundamental aspect of the human experience that provide abundant positive contributions to well-being but introduce steep opportunity costs. To maintain them, commitment is vital. It is commitment that gives rise to numerous causal processes that serve to keep relationships stable in the face of changing and challenging situations, such as transformation of motivation, derogation of alternatives, making future plans, and inclusion of the other in the self. Once commitment is established and these processes are operating, maintaining a relationship becomes an automatic, default option under ordinary circumstances. In that way, IT is profoundly able to explain why, despite their costs, our relationships with others provide some of the most meaningful positive outcomes we experience.

REFERENCES

Agnew, C. R., Van Lange, P. A. M., Rusbult, C. E., & Langston, C. A. (1998). Cognitive interdependence: Commitment and the mental representation of close relationships. *Journal of Personality and Social Psychology*, *74*(4), 939–954. https://psycnet.apa.org/doi/10.1037/0022-3514.74.4.939

Arriaga, X. B. (2001). The ups and downs of dating: Fluctuations in satisfaction in newly formed romantic relationships. *Journal of Personality and Social Psychology*, *80*(5), 754–765. https://psycnet.apa.org/doi/10.1037/0022-3514.80.5.754

Arriaga, X. B., & Agnew, C. R. (2001). Being committed: Affective, cognitive, and conative components of relationship commitment. *Personality and Social Psychology Bulletin*, *27*(9), 1190–1203. https://doi.org/10.1177/0146167201279011

Baumeister, R. F., & Leary, M. R. (1995). The need to belong: Desire for interpersonal attachments as a fundamental human motivation. *Psychological Bulletin*, *117*(3), 497–529. https://hec.unil.ch/docs/files/56/618/b_and_m_need_to_belong_pb.pdf

Becker, H. S. (1960). Notes on the concept of commitment. *The American Journal of Sociology*, *66*(1), 32–40. https://psycnet.apa.org/doi/10.1086/222820

Canary, D. J., & Stafford, L. (1992). Relational maintenance strategies and equity in marriage. *Communication Monographs*, *59*(3), 243–267. https://doi.org/10.1080/03637759209376268

Clark, M. S., & Mills, J. (1979). Interpersonal attraction in exchange and communal relationships. *Journal of Personality and Social Psychology*, *37*(1), 12–24. https://psycnet.apa.org/doi/10.1037/0022-3514.37.1.12

Clark, M. S., Mills, J., & Powell, M. C. (1986). Keeping track of needs in communal and exchange relationships. *Journal of Personality and Social Psychology*, *51*(2), 333–338. http://dx.doi.org/10.1037/0022-3514.51.2.333

Drigotas, S. M., Whitney, G., & Rusbult, C. E. (1995). On the peculiarities of loyalty: A diary study of responses to dissatisfaction in everyday life. *Personality and Social Psychology Bulletin, 21*(6), 596–609. https://doi.org/10.1177/0146167295216006

Goodfriend, W., & Agnew, C. R. (2008). Sunken costs and desired plans: Examining different types of investments in close relationships. *Personality and Social Psychology Bulletin, 34*(12), 1639–1652. https://doi.org/10.1177/0146167208323743

Holt-Lunstad, J., Robles, T. F., & Sbarra, D. A. (2017). Advancing social connection as a public health priority in the United States. *American Psychologist, 72*(6), 517–530. https://doi.org/10.1037/amp0000103

Johnson, D. J., & Rusbult, C. E. (1989). Resisting temptation: Devaluation of alternative partners as a means of maintaining commitment in close relationships. *Journal of Personality and Social Psychology, 57*(6), 967–980. http://dx.doi.org/10.1037/0022-3514.57.6.967

Kelley, H. H. (1983). Love and commitment. In H. H. Kelley, E. Berscheid, A. Christensen, J. H. Harvey, T. L. Huston, G. Levinger, ... D. R. Peterson (Eds.), *Close relationships* (pp. 265–314). New York, NY: WH Freeman and Company.

Kelley, H. H. (1984). The theoretical description of interdependence by means of transition lists. *Journal of Personality and Social Psychology, 47*(5), 956–982. http://psycnet.apa.org/journals/psp/47/5/956/

Kelley, H. H., Holmes, J. G., Kerr, N. L., Reis, H. T., Rusbult, C. E., & Van Lange, P. A. M. (2003). Interpersonal situations: The context of social behavior. In *An atlas of interpersonal situations* (pp. 3–16). Cambridge University Press. http://dx.doi.org/10.1017/CBO9780511499845

Kelley, H. H., & Thibaut, J. W. (1978). *Interpersonal relations: A theory of interdependence.* New York, NY: Wiley.

Le, B., & Agnew, C. R. (2001). Need fulfillment and emotional experience in interdependent romantic relationships. *Journal of Social and Personal Relationships, 18*(3), 423–440. https://doi.org/10.1177/0265407501183007

Le, B., & Agnew, C. R. (2003). Commitment and its theorized determinants: A meta-analysis of the Investment Model. *Personal Relationships, 10*(1), 37–57. https://doi.org/10.1111/1475-6811.00035

Miller, R. S. (1997). Inattentive and contented: Relationship commitment and attention to alternatives. *Journal of Personality and Social Psychology, 73*(4), 758–766. http://psycnet.apa.org/journals/psp/73/4/758/

Murray, S. L., Holmes, J. G., Griffin, D. W., & Derrick, J. L. (2015). The equilibrium model of relationship maintenance. *Journal of Personality and Social Psychology, 108*(1), 93–113. https://doi.org/10.1037/pspi0000004

Rusbult, C. E., & Buunk, B. P. (1993). Commitment processes in close relationships: An interdependence analysis. *Journal of Social and Personal Relationships, 10*(2), 175–204. https://doi.org/10.1177/026540759301000202

Rusbult, C. E., Martz, J. M., & Agnew, C. R. (1998). The Investment Model Scale: Measuring commitment level, satisfaction level, quality of alternatives, and investment size. *Personal Relationships, 5*, 357–391. https://psycnet.apa.org/doi/10.1111/j.1475-6811.1998.tb00177.x

Rusbult, C. E., & Van Lange, P. A. M. (2003). Interdependence, interaction, and relationships. *Annual Review of Psychology, 54*(1), 351–375. https://doi.org/10.1146/annurev.psych.54.101601.145059

Rusbult, C. E., Verette, J., Whitney, G., Slovik, L. F., & Lipkus, I. (1991). Accommodation processes in close relationships: Theory and preliminary empirical evidence. *Journal of Personality*, 60(1), 53–78. http://psycnet.apa.org/jour nals/psp/60/1/53/

Tan, K., & Agnew, C. R. (2016). Ease of retrieval effects on relationship commitment. *Personality and Social Psychology Bulletin*, 42(2), 161–171. https://doi.org/10.1177 /0146167215617201

Thibaut, J. W., & Kelley, H. H. (1959). *The social psychology of groups*. New York, NY: Wiley.

Van Lange, P. A. M., Balliet, D. P., Parks, C. D., & Van Vugt, M. (2014). *Social dilemmas: Understanding human cooperation*. New York, NY: Oxford University Press.

Van Lange, P. A. M., Ouwerkerk, J. W., & Tazelaar, M. J. A. (2002). How to overcome the detrimental effects of noise in social interaction: The benefits of generosity. *Journal of Personality and Social Psychology*, 82(5), 768–780. https://doi.org/10.1037 /0022-3514.82.5.768

Van Lange, P. A. M., Rusbult, C. E., Drigotas, S. M., Arriaga, X. B., Witcher, B. S., & Cox, C. L. (1997). Willingness to sacrifice in close relationships. *Journal of Personality and Social Psychology*, 72(6), 1373–1395. https://psycnet.apa.org/doi/10 .1037/0022-3514.72.6.1373

VanderDrift, L. E., & Agnew, C. R. (2012). Need fulfillment and stay-leave behavior: On the diagnosticity of personal and relational needs. *Journal of Social and Personal Relationships*, 29(2), 228–245. https://doi.org/10.1177/0265407511431057

VanderDrift, L. E., Lewandowski, G. W., & Agnew, C. R. (2011). Reduced self-expansion in current romance and interest in relationship alternatives. *Journal of Social and Personal Relationships*, 28(3), 356–373. https://doi.org/10.1177 /0265407510382321

Walster, E., Walster, G., & Berscheid, E. (1978). *Equity theory and research*. Boston: Allyn and Bacon.

White, C. N., VanderDrift, L. E., & Heffernan, K. S. (2015). Social isolation, cognitive decline, and cardiovascular disease risk. *Current Opinion in Psychology*, 5, 18–23. https://doi.org/10.1016/j.copsyc.2015.03.005

Wieselquist, J., Rusbult, C. E., & Foster, C. A. (1999). Commitment, pro-relationship behavior, and trust in close relationships. *Journal of Personality and Social Psychology*, 77(5), 942–966. http://psycnet.apa.org/journals/psp/77/5/942/

3

An Evolutionary, Life History Theory Perspective on Relationship Maintenance

ETHAN S. YOUNG[1] AND JEFFRY A. SIMPSON[2]

Relationship maintenance is a central topic within relationship science. It is addressed in numerous theories (e.g., Levinger, 1983; Rusbult, 1980; Thibaut & Kelley, 1959), in several literature reviews (e.g., Agnew & VanderDrift, 2015; Lydon & Quinn, 2013), and in all contemporary relationship textbooks. The reason is straightforward: individuals often invest a great deal of time, effort, and resources in their closest relationships, so they should be motivated to protect and sustain them when threats emerge. To date, most research on relationship maintenance has been inspired by theories (e.g., Interdependence Theory; Kelley & Thibaut, 1978; Thibaut & Kelley, 1959) or models (e.g., the Investment Model; Rusbult, 1980) that focus on proximate causation – how and why current partner or relationship variables, such as commitment and satisfaction, influence the enactment of certain relationship maintenance tendencies or behaviors (see Chapter 2). Far less attention has been granted to distal factors, such as each partner's developmental history (i.e., ontogeny) or the possible evolutionary origins of relationship mainte-nance tendencies (i.e., ultimate causation). The primary goal of this chapter is to shed clarifying light on these understudied levels of analysis by viewing relationship maintenance processes from an evolutionary-developmental perspective couched within Life History Theory (LHT).

The chapter is organized around five sections. In the first section, we define relationship maintenance and discuss how it has been studied by prior scholars, most of whom have examined proximate-level variables (such as immediate threats to a relationship or an individual's degree of commitment to his/her partner or relationship) that typically elicit the motivation to maintain one's current romantic relationship. While doing so, we review four common threats to romantic relationships, along with research that has documented some of the key relationship maintenance processes and

[1] Department of Psychology, University of Minnesota, youn0737@umn.edu
[2] Department of Psychology, University of Minnesota, simps108@umn.edu

the cognitive, emotional, and behavioral responses associated with each type of threat. In the second section, we discuss the central tenets of LHT. After doing so, we describe two major models of human mating – the Evolutionary Model of Social Development, which highlights the events and pathways through which socialization unfolds in children raised in different environments (Belsky, 1997; Belsky, Steinberg, & Draper, 1991), and the Strategic Pluralism Model (Gangestad & Simpson, 2000), which identifies some of the factors in adulthood that should shape an individual's motivation to maintain or dissolve romantic relationships. In the third section, we blend these ideas and introduce the Developmental Strategic Pluralism Model, which articulates why certain developmental events presumed to shape whether an individual adopts a faster or a slower mating strategy should statistically interact with an individual's current environmental conditions. As such, the model explains how one's developmental history and current situational circumstances (e.g., whether threatening or nonthreatening) should work together to determine whether one is more versus less motivated to enact relationship maintenance tactics. The fourth section lays out a series of testable predictions derived from this model, including the conditions under which sex differences might emerge. The final section summarizes the key points in the chapter and offers some takeaway conclusions.

RELATIONSHIP MAINTENANCE PROCESSES: AN OVERVIEW

Partners in practically all close romantic relationships – even very happy and stable ones – occasionally encounter events that could threaten and destabilize their bond. Thus, the manner in which partners manage and react to these events is critical to the sustained longevity and well-being of virtually all intimate relationships (Rusbult & Buunk, 1993). Relationship maintenance processes reflect the specific perceptions, feelings, thoughts, and/or behaviors that allow romantic partners to avoid, reduce, or eliminate events that could or do threaten their existing relationship (Lydon & Quinn, 2013).

The vast majority of prior research has investigated how relationship partners deal with four broad types of relationship threat: the presence of attractive alternatives to the current partner/relationship, the enactment of partner transgressions, the occurrence of goal conflict between relationship partners, and how an individual's often ordinary (average) attributes are perceived by their partners. Each type of threat tends to be associated with a basic relationship maintenance process along with specific relationship maintenance responses or reactions. For example, individuals involved in happy, well-functioning, and committed relationships frequently fail to notice (Miller, 1997), pay less visual attention to (Maner, Rouby, & Gonzaga, 2008), consciously devalue (Johnson & Rusbult, 1989), or more effectively suppress (Gonzaga, Haselton, Smurda, Davies, & Poore, 2008) attraction to alternatives.

These effects usually operate via attentional processes that involve inattention to, or derogation of, potentially alluring alternatives to the current partner/relationship.

Other research has explored threats posed by partner transgressions (e.g., inconsiderate behavior or minor betrayals), which also can destabilize and undercut relationships (Holmes & Rempel, 1989). Individuals in happy, well-functioning, and committed relationships, for instance, frequently fail to notice minor partner transgressions (Fletcher & Fincham, 1991), do not make negative "responsibility attributions" for their partner's transgressions (Bradbury & Fincham, 1990), are more likely to accommodate when their partners transgress (Rusbult, Verette, Whitney, Slovik, & Lipkus, 1991), or tend to forgive their partners for most transgressions over time (Karremans & Van Lange, 2008). These effects are often driven by the benevolent attributions that individuals in stable, committed relationships usually make in the aftermath of minor – and sometimes more severe – partner transgressions.

Additional research has addressed how dealing with goal conflicts with one's romantic partner is related to relationship maintenance processes and outcomes. For example, individuals in happy, well-functioning, and committed relationships are more willing to – and actually do – sacrifice their own personal goals for what is best for their partner or relationship in the long run, which promotes more stable relationships characterized by higher levels of commitment (Van Lange et al., 1997). These effects are more pronounced when individuals make personal sacrifices based on positively framed approach motives rather than negatively framed avoidance motives (Impett, Gable, & Peplau, 2005). Most goal conflict effects, therefore, occur in response to enacted behaviors, such as when one partner gladly moves to a new city so that his/her partner can pursue a "dream job."

A fourth common threat to relationships centers on the "ordinariness" of one's partner relative to other available (or possible) romantic partners and relationships. To guard against such threats, individuals in happy, well-functioning, and committed relationships typically idealize their current partner's attributes and display relationship illusions, perceiving their partners and relationships as slightly better than other people do, including the partner. These perceptual biases sustain relationship satisfaction and stability at higher levels than is true of individuals who do not harbor these biases (Murray, Holmes, & Griffin, 1996). These effects, which operate primarily through partner and relationship evaluations, keep most established relationships from falling below partner or relationship "nonacceptability" thresholds.

All four of these threats and relationship maintenance processes typically operate in synchrony in individuals who are involved in happy, well-functioning, and committed relationships. For example, greater partner/relationship idealization often motivates individuals to ignore or downplay attractive alternatives, experience fewer goal conflicts with their partners (and behave in a more accommodating manner when they arise), and arrive at more benign attributions when their partners transgress. Each of these variables, however, is proximal in nature, focusing almost exclusively on proximate causation processes. Little if any attention has been paid to whether or how an individual's early developmental experiences might have shaped his/her motivation and inclination to enact relationship maintenance behaviors in adulthood, especially from an evolutionary perspective. We now turn to this significant, unaddressed topic in the relationship maintenance literature.

EVOLUTIONARY PERSPECTIVES ON RELATIONSHIP MAINTENANCE PROCESSES

Despite the fact that relationship maintenance processes have been widely studied within relationship science, three fundamental questions remain largely answered: (1) from the standpoint of ultimate causation, *why* do people engage in relationship maintenance?; (2) why is there so much variation between people in the motivation and extent to which they enact relationship maintenance strategies and tactics?; and (3) when (under which circumstances) do certain people engage in – or not engage in – relationship maintenance strategies/tactics?

From an evolutionary perspective, the motivation and tendency to maintain relationships should have been shaped by the costs and benefits associated with doing so, which would have been tied to the survival and reproductive success – the *reproductive fitness* – of our ancestors. It is well documented that, on average, relationship partners involved in happier, better-functioning, and more committed relationships tend to provide higher-quality parental care (Belsky & Jaffee, 2006), which should have conferred better reproductive fitness to both parents and their offspring (Geary, 2005). Regularly engaging in relationship maintenance behaviors, therefore, is likely to have served an important evolutionary function – keeping mates together long enough to ensure sufficiently high levels of parental investment in current (or future) offspring. However, there is a trade-off between investing time and effort in parenting and in mating. Engaging in high levels of parenting effort (i.e., devoting time, effort, and resources to current or future children) limits the amount of mating effort (i.e., devoting time, effort, and resources to finding, attracting, and retaining mates) in which an individual can engage. Indeed, in certain instances, allotting greater effort to mating than to parenting could have increased reproductive fitness, such as when the local environment was harsh or uncertain, which would have rendered additional investments of time, effort, and/or resources less valuable (Ellis, Figueredo, Brumbach, & Schlomer, 2009).

To understand how costs and benefits may have been traded off by our ancestors, we turn to two evolutionary models relevant to mating and parenting: the Evolutionary Model of Social Development (Belsky, 1997; Belsky, Steinberg, & Draper, 1991) and the Strategic Pluralism Model (Gangestad & Simpson, 2000). These models, both of which exist within the broader meta-theory known as Life History Theory (Kaplan & Gangestad, 2005; Del Giudice, Gangestad, & Kaplan, 2016), explain how an individual's general reproductive strategy, which entails his or her orientation toward both mating and parenting, should be influenced by certain types of environmental conditions.

The Evolutionary Model of Social Development addresses why and how relationship maintenance tendencies witnessed in adult romantic relationships could have been shaped by exposure to specific early childhood environments. The Strategic Pluralism Model, on the other hand, suggests how these tendencies might also be impacted by current environmental conditions. After reviewing each model, we blend them to propose a new Developmental Strategic Pluralism Model and then derive novel predictions regarding how an individual's early developmental history, in combination with his/her current environment, ought to interact to influence the extent to which s/he is motivated to engage in relationship maintenance behaviors in adult romantic relationships.

LIFE HISTORY THEORY AND SOCIAL DEVELOPMENT

Broadly speaking, LHT focuses on why certain clusters of traits and behaviors, which typically characterize specific reproductive strategies, develop across the lifespan. LHT is organized around the notion that time, effort, and resources are inherently limited, so individuals cannot simultaneously maximize all of the components that could contribute to their reproductive fitness. Individuals, for example, cannot devote the same amount of time, effort, or resources to survival, reproduction, and caring for offspring, at least at the same point in time during their development. As a result, they must make trade-offs in how they allocate their limited time, effort, and resources to certain components rather than others throughout their lives.

Three primary trade-off decisions, which often are made unconsciously (outside awareness), influence how individuals partition their limited time, energy, and resources (Kaplan & Gangestad, 2005). The first is whether to invest more in current (immediate) reproduction or in future (delayed) reproduction. The second is whether to invest more in a higher quantity of offspring or in higher-quality offspring. The third is whether to invest more in mating effort or in parenting effort. Greater investment in either side of each trade-off precludes an equally high investment in the other side. For example, investing more in current reproduction (i.e., by reproducing now) means that a person cannot invest as much in future reproduction. Indeed, in most Western societies, individuals who have children when they are very young (as teenagers) usually do not have the capacity to provide their children with higher levels of education than those who wait to have children later in life, when their lives and careers are better established.

During development, these trade-off decisions affect the traits and behaviors known to facilitate the enactment of specific reproductive strategies. At the most global level, reproductive strategies exist on a fast–slow continuum (Griskevicius et al., 2013). At one end of this continuum, a *faster strategy* is characterized by more investment in current (immediate) reproduction, having more offspring, and engaging in greater mating effort. Individuals who adopt a faster strategy should remain more open to alternative partners and relationships and, in general, should be less inclined to maintain most of their current romantic relationships. This strategy is akin to bet hedging (Promislow & Harvey, 1990), which allows individuals to diversify their reproductive portfolio. At the other end of this continuum, a *slower strategy* is defined by greater investment in future (delayed) reproduction, having fewer but higher-quality offspring, and engaging in greater parenting effort. Individuals pursuing a slower strategy tend to be less open to alternative partners/relationships and, on average, should be more motivated to maintain most of their current relationships. Supporting these claims, faster strategists often view their romantic relationships as short-term opportunities, which results in less stable pair-bonds and unstable relationships characterized by lower parental investment (Simpson & Belsky, 2016; Szepsenwol, Simpson, Griskevicius, & Raby, 2015). Conversely, slower strategists usually form more enduring, committed long-term relationships characterized by higher levels of parental investment (Simpson & Belsky, 2016; Szepsenwol et al., 2015). Table 3.1 shows how faster and slower individuals ought to differ in their general motivation and inclination to engage in relationship maintenance in response to the four major types of relationship threats discussed earlier.

The extent to which an individual adopts a faster versus slower strategy should depend on the type of environment to which s/he was exposed early in life. The two most important ecological conditions believed to affect the adaptive value of faster versus slower reproductive strategies are environmental harshness (i.e., the overall level of morbidity and mortality in the local environment) and unpredictability (i.e., the size of fluctuations in mortality rates across space and time in the local environment; Ellis et al., 2009). Harsh and/or unpredictable environments should shift individuals toward a faster reproductive strategy in adulthood, because future investments are less likely to pay off in highly dangerous, unstable, and unpredictable environments. Harsh and/or unpredictable environments may contain high levels of parental conflict, harsh parenting, lack of resources, violence in the neighborhood, and/or erratic daily routines in the home, whereas less harsh and/or more predictable environments tend to have the opposite features. In such rearing environments, it is more adaptive for individuals who have a fast reproductive strategy to hedge their bets against early death by diversifying reproductively, such as by investing (not

TABLE 3.1 *Major types of relationship maintenance and destabilizing processes*

Type of threat	Psychological process	Maintenance: slow response	Destabilizing: fast response
Attractive alternatives	Attention	Inattention to or devaluation of alternatives	Attention to or valuation of alternatives
Partner transgressions	Attributions	Benign attributions or accommodation	Hostile or threatening attributions and lack of accommodation
Partner goal conflicts	Behavior	Sacrifice	Manipulation, coercion, or engagement in conflict
Partner ordinariness	Evaluation	Idealization and affirmation	Heightened judgment, resentment, or disinterest

Adapted from Lydon & Quinn (2013).
Note: Highly committed individuals tend to engage in most or perhaps all of these relationship-maintenance processes/responses across time in different relationship-threatening contexts. Some individuals, however, react to relationship threats by engaging in destabilizing processes/responses. The extent to which individuals enact maintenance or destabilizing responses should depend on their reproductive strategy. Slow strategists should be more motivated to maintain their relationships, whereas fast strategists should be more likely to display destabilizing responses.

necessarily consciously) in multiple relationships in the hope that some will result in children who survive and eventually reproduce. On the other hand, safe, stable, and predictable environments should shunt individuals toward a slower adult reproductive strategy. Although harshness and unpredictability can at times impact children directly, very young children are not fully aware of the environmental conditions surrounding them. Thus, the behavior of their parents tends to be the conduit through which young children assess the conditions in their early life environments, which gradually shapes the reproductive strategy they adopt. On the basis of this logic, a central prediction follows: harsh and/or unpredictable environments should reduce the quality of care that children receive, leading them to enact a faster reproductive strategy in adulthood characterized by greater mating effort, less parenting effort, and lower likelihood of engaging in relationship maintenance behaviors in their adult romantic relationships.

STRATEGIC PLURALISM

Whereas the Evolutionary Model of Social Development focuses on the developmental context in which faster and slower reproductive strategies emerge, the Strategic Pluralism Model highlights how current environmental circumstances can influence this process. Gangestad and Simpson (2000) suggest that humans evolved to enact *conditional reproductive strategies* that are affected by features in their immediate local environment. According to the model, ancestral women may have evolved to make trade-offs between a potential mate's willingness to invest in her and her offspring and evidence of a mate's genetic viability (e.g., the quality of his health, attractiveness, and social dominance). The Strategic Pluralism Model further proposes that women evolved to prefer men who displayed greater ability and willingness to invest in them and their children when biparental care was required in the local environment – that is, when higher levels of parental investment had a positive effect on the reproductive fitness of parents and their offspring. Conversely, women may have evolved to prefer evidence of higher genetic quality in mates when the local environment contained many pathogens or was highly unpredictable, environments in which biparental care would have been less necessary and less effective in increasing reproductive fitness.

The Strategic Pluralism Model also claims that the reproductive strategies of women might have been more sensitive to the local environment (e.g., pathogen levels and the degree of environmental harshness), whereas the reproductive strategies of men may have been sensitive to what most women wanted in a mate in the local environment. If, for example, most women desired higher levels of investment in long-term relationships, most (but not all) men should have invested more heavily in longer-term mateships. When pathogens were prevalent, however, women should have placed greater emphasis on mates who displayed evidence of higher genetic quality, enabling such men to pursue short-term relationships or extra-pair matings more successfully.

With respect to relationship maintenance motives and behaviors, the Strategic Pluralism Model can be extrapolated to hypothesize that certain environmental conditions should modulate (shift) an individual's motivation and tendency to engage in – or not engage in – relationship maintenance. For example, in environments where biparental care can improve a child's long-term socialization and development, both sexes should engage in relationship maintenance behaviors to sustain their pair-bonds, which should facilitate better coparenting. However, in environments that nullify the importance of biparental care but elevate the importance of acquiring high-viability mates, relationship maintenance behaviors should decrease in both sexes. We now describe how these two evolutionary models can be integrated, yielding a new model that leads to the derivation of several novel predictions regarding relationship-maintenance tendencies.

DEVELOPMENTAL STRATEGIC PLURALISM

From an evolutionary developmental perspective, reproductive strategies should be shaped by the early environment to the extent that early environments are representative of what future environments will generally be like during one's lifetime (Simpson & Belsky, 2016). Several recent studies involving animals and humans, however, have discovered that behaviors associated with the enactment of faster and slower reproductive strategies are more strongly elicited when the environment in adulthood is similar to the childhood environment (Ellis, Bianchi, Griskevicius, & Frankenhuis, 2017). If, for example, an individual's early environment was harsh and/or unpredictable, s/he should engage in behaviors indicative of a faster reproductive strategy (e.g., by pursuing short-term mating, being less committed to the current partner, or attending to alternative mates), but primarily when the *current* environment is harsh and/or unpredictable. This concept, termed "sensitization," represents the intersection of the Evolutionary Model of Social Development and the Strategic Pluralism Model, forming what we call the *Developmental Strategic Pluralism Model*.

This model and its various stages are described in Figure 3.1. At its core, the model proposes that mating-relevant behaviors, including relationship maintenance tendencies, cannot be fully understood unless one has information on *both* an individual's early life environment (i.e., the degree to which it was harsh and/or unpredictable versus benign and predictable) and the current environment (i.e., the degree to which it is harsh and/or unpredictable versus benign and predictable). Humans are a moderately sexually dimorphic, K-selected species (Stearns, 1992). Thus, we typically enact slower reproductive strategies unless environments (1) reduce the value of biparental care or (2) increase the value of obtaining genetically fit mates. Most individuals, therefore, should enact a slower reproductive strategy in better environments but should shift toward a faster reproductive strategy when environments are harsh and/or unpredictable due to unforeseeable dangers, food shortages, predators, aggressive people, and so on. Framed another way, when environments become difficult and unpredictable, individuals should revert to a "secondary" reproductive strategy as a backup plan to promote their reproductive fitness as best they can under difficult circumstances.

One novel prediction of the Developmental Strategic Pluralism Model is that exposure to harsh and/or unpredictable environments in childhood may affect the flexibility and variability of the reproductive strategies an individual enacts across his or her lifetime. Exposure to highly harsh and/or unpredictable environments early in life, for example, should motivate most individuals to enact a faster reproductive strategy, improving the odds that they will reproduce before dying in such arduous environments.

According to the Developmental Strategic Pluralism Model, however, the behaviors that are the hallmark of a faster strategy – being opportunistic, seeking immediate rewards, having poorer emotion regulation, and keeping mating options open – should be most strongly evoked when the current environment is harsh and/or unpredictable. When it is predictable and

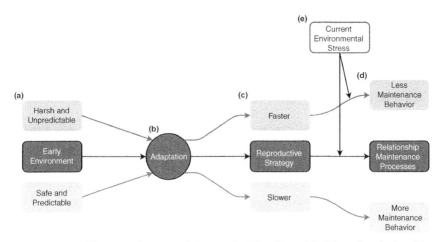

FIGURE 3.1 **The Developmental Strategic Pluralism Model and relationship maintenance processes.** (a) Early environmental circumstances, which can range from safe and predictable to harsh and unpredictable, influence which developmental trajectory is most adaptive. (b) The developing person detects signals in the early environment directly and/or indirectly (via parenting quality), which initiates the development of an appropriate reproductive strategy. (c) In adulthood, individuals express their reproductive strategy, which can range from fast to slow. Faster strategies allocate more effort toward current reproduction, quantity of offspring, and mating effort. Slower strategies allocate more effort toward future reproduction, quality of offspring, and parenting effort. (d) The particular reproductive strategy an individual adopts influences his/her general relationship maintenance behaviors. Fast strategists should engage in lower levels of maintenance behavior on average, whereas slow strategists should engage in higher levels of maintenance behavior on average. (e) Although an individual's reproductive strategy should influence his/her maintenance behavior directly, the current environment should elicit destabilizing behaviors associated with faster reproductive strategies. When the current environment is safe and predictable, most individuals should remain motivated to maintain their relationships. When the current environment becomes unpredictable, however, fast strategists should enact more relationship-destabilizing behaviors, whereas slow strategists should continue to enact more relationship maintenance behaviors.

resources are plentiful, faster strategists should be less motivated to engage in fast mating–relevant behaviors. This explains why individuals who adopt faster reproductive strategies are likely to display a wider range of different mating strategies during their lives; their specific strategy at a given point in time depends to a greater extent on what their current environment is like (i.e., whether it is unpredictable or predictable). In contrast, individuals raised in safe, predictable childhood environments with abundant resources should enact less variable reproductive strategies across their lives. For these individuals, their early life environment was less challenging, more predictable, and most likely more controllable (Mittal & Griskevicius, 2014). As a result, even when unpredictable events arise in adulthood, returns on their long-term investments (including children) are less likely to be viewed as threatened or outside their control. This is one of the main reasons why individuals who adopt a slower reproductive strategy also engage in greater parenting effort independently of current environmental circumstances (at least until they become too harsh and/or unpredictable).

DEVELOPMENTAL STRATEGIC PLURALISM AND RELATIONSHIP MAINTENANCE PROCESSES

According to the Developmental Strategic Pluralism Model, specific conditions should facilitate or impede relationship maintenance motives and behaviors. The most basic prediction is that prolonged exposure to harsh and/or unpredictable environments in childhood should lead individuals to adopt a faster reproductive strategy and be less motivated and willing to engage in relationship maintenance behaviors in other relationships later in life. This tendency, however, should be moderated by the degree of predictability versus unpredictability in the current environment, which should elicit (turn on) the characteristic behavioral tendencies of the individual's developmentally calibrated reproductive strategy.

One important question that flows from this model is "What are the environmental cues that activate and regulate an individual's reproductive strategy?" One approach might be to examine whether and how harsh, unpredictable stressors (e.g., unexpectedly losing a job or having to move, suddenly losing income, having unfamiliar people move in and out of one's house) impact relationship maintenance outcomes in different types of couples. These types of stressors may signal that one's investments in long-term relationships (including children), accrued resources, and other valued commodities could be at risk of being diminished or lost. By assessing the extent to which each romantic partner in a given relationship experienced a harsh and/or unpredictable childhood environment, one can test several novel predictions from the Developmental Strategic Pluralism Model. For instance, partners who are developmentally calibrated to enact a faster reproductive strategy should, on average, react to current unpredictable events – especially more severe and chronic ones – by disengaging from relationship maintenance and looking for better options, which should destabilize their current relationships. If, for example, an individual's income unexpectedly declines a great deal, his or her partner may start paying more attention to attractive alternatives (thereby destabilizing the relationship), particularly if the partner is pursuing a faster reproductive strategy. In contrast, those who grew up in predictable, plentiful conditions should double down and engage in more relationship-maintenance behaviors in order to protect their long-term investments (at least until their current environments become too difficult and unpredictable). In this scenario, a partner who has a slower strategy should respond to the sudden loss of income by *devaluing* attractive alternatives in order to bolster commitment and maintain the relationship.

PARTNERS AS CURRENT ENVIRONMENTAL CUES

According to the Developmental Strategic Pluralism Model, each relationship partner's reproductive strategy may also affect his/her *partner's* reproductive strategy and relationship maintenance tendencies. For instance, if both partners are enacting faster reproductive strategies, relationship maintenance motivations and behavior should be lower in both partners unless their levels of commitment are, for some reason, very high. Conversely, if both partners are enacting a slower reproductive strategy, the relationship maintenance motivations and behaviors of both partners should typically be higher, generating greater relationship stability.

More nuanced patterns might emerge when one partner adopts a faster strategy and the other partner adopts a slower one. For example, the reproductive strategy of individuals who grew up in harsh and/or unpredictable environments may be more environmentally contingent – and, thus, more changeable – in adulthood. When living in predictable current environments, for instance, such individuals should engage in more relationship mainte-nance behaviors, though not to the same extent as individuals who grew up in predictable childhood environments. Under harsh and/or unpredictable cur-rent conditions, however, individuals raised in harsh and/or unpredictable childhood environments should shift toward an even faster reproductive strategy, including even more reduced relationship maintenance tendencies and potentially more destabilizing behaviors. When partners have different reproductive strategies and the current environment is *not* harsh and/or unpredictable, both partners should remain relatively motivated to maintain their relationship. But if the current environment suddenly becomes unpre-dictable, the partner with the faster strategy may start to behave in a more "short-term" manner and become less inclined to enact relationship main-tenance behaviors. The partner who adopts the slower strategy, on the other hand, should continue to engage in relationship maintenance behaviors (up to a point), partly in an attempt to salvage long-term investments.

Current environmental threats can also be signaled directly by partners themselves. Consider the "partner transgression" relationship threat in Table 3.1. Such transgressions might signal to "fast" partners that the current environment is harsh (e.g., people in the environment are not trustworthy or supportive). Instead of responding by becoming more accommodating or making benign attributions for their partner's behavior, partners enacting a faster strategy may make hostile attributions, which ought to destabilize the relationship. Moreover, if a couple's goals become misaligned, partners who adopt a faster reproductive strategy are likely to sacrifice less, especially if making sacrifices is viewed as futile given current uncertainties. For example, if a partner wishes to pursue a dream job in another city, the partner adopting a fast strategy may view the situation as uncertain or unlikely to work out and, thus, may respond by making fewer sacrifices. In sum, people who adopt a faster reproductive strategy are likely to respond to potential threats in relationships with destabilizing thoughts, feelings, and behaviors, which should facilitate the enactment of a mating strategy designed to hedge one's bets against an uncertain future.

SEX DIFFERENCES

The Developmental Strategic Pluralism Model anticipates that both sexes should behave fairly similarly in reaction to the same early life experiences. That is, men and women who grow up in predictable environments should typically adopt slower reproductive strategies. However, parental investment theory (Trivers, 1972) predicts that males and females should adopt somewhat different reproductive strategies. Specifically, the sex that has the highest obligatory initial investment in offspring (such as the time and energy associated with gestation and lactation in mammals) should invest more in parenting effort. In humans, females have a higher initial obligatory investment in reproduction and, therefore, they typically adopt somewhat slower reproductive strategies than most males. In contrast, because initial obligatory investment is somewhat lower for males, men tend to pursue somewhat faster reproductive strategies than women in general. A considerable body of research has documented these sex differences (see Buss & Schmitt, 1993), even though there is much more variability in reproductive strategies within each sex than between them, on average (Gangestad & Simpson, 2000).

The Developmental Strategic Pluralism Model proposes that the early environment, perhaps in combination with biological sex (including sex differences in initial obligatory investment in reproduction), should shape the adoption of faster versus slower reproductive strategies. For example, men who grew up in harsh and/or unpredictable environments should pursue the fastest reproductive strategies, given both the nature of their early environment and their lower obligatory investment in reproduction. In contrast, women who grew up in plentiful, predictable environments should adopt the slowest reproductive strategies. For these women, future investments are more likely to pay off, and the cost of raising offspring without a partner is likely to be high (which may be true of many women).

In summary, an individual's developmental history should influence his or her perceptions of the degree to which long-term investments are likely to "pay off" over time. Moreover, an individual's biological sex also affects mating effort, given that males have no limit on the number of children they can conceive, whereas females are limited by both time and the finite number of children they can bear during their lives. Despite the implications of parental investment theory, however, both men and women should (and do) engage in the full gamut of reproductive behaviors, ranging from those that reflect high mating effort to those that reflect high parenting effort (Gangestad & Simpson, 2000). As a result, the early environment should play an important role in calibrating faster and slower reproductive strategies, not only within each sex, but also between them.

SUMMARY AND CONCLUSION

Relationship maintenance processes have been studied mostly from a proximate causation perspective, shedding light on how different kinds of relationship threats tend to elicit relationship maintenance behaviors. There are good reasons to believe, however, that more distal evolutionary perspectives can add to our understanding of relationship maintenance processes and outcomes. In this chapter, we have proposed that the tendency to engage in maintenance behaviors should depend on the adoption of specific reproductive strategies defined by LHT and Belsky and colleagues' (1991) Evolutionary Model of Social Development.

The central claim of these evolutionary models is that exposure to specific kinds of environments in childhood should shape which type of reproductive strategy an individual adopts. The childhood environment can directly or indirectly (via parenting) signal to young children what kinds of threats and opportunities they might expect in adulthood and, therefore, which reproductive strategy might be most adaptive. Early environments characterized by unpredictability in particular should lead to the adoption of faster reproductive strategies with an associated decrease in motivation to maintain relationships in adulthood. In contrast, safe, predictable environments should typically result in slower strategies characterized by higher levels of maintenance behaviors in adulthood.

The Strategic Pluralism Model, on the other hand, specifies which features of the *current* environment are likely to impact relationship maintenance processes. In environments where biparental care can significantly increase the reproductive fitness of parents and their children, individuals should invest more heavily in their romantic relationships. However, when the current environment renders biparental care less effective at improving fitness, individuals should invest relatively more in short-term mating opportunities.

In this chapter, we have suggested that the Developmental Strategic Pluralism model, which merges key features of these models, generates more precise predictions regarding who should be motivated to engage in more versus fewer relationship maintenance behaviors in adulthood. Our argument centers on the idea that the early environment often calibrates the specific reproductive strategy that an individual adopts. Because humans are a K-selected species, we tend to adopt slower reproductive strategies focused on investing higher amounts of time, effort, and resources in close relationships and parenting effort. However, exposure to dangerous and/or unpredictable early life environments should generate greater *flexibility* in reproductive strategies. This is because such environments encourage individuals to pursue a secondary (faster) reproductive strategy when environments become unpredictable or unsafe. The Developmental Strategic Pluralism Model, therefore, anticipates that behaviors associated with faster strategies – such as being opportunistic, seeking immediate rewards, having poor impulse control, and keeping mating opportunities open – should be witnessed primarily when the current environment is harsh and/or unpredictable. When it is safe and predictable, however, faster strategists may be somewhat more inclined to maintain their romantic relationships. Conversely, individuals raised in safe, predictable childhood environments might exhibit somewhat less flexibility in their reproductive strategies throughout their lives, because, even when unpredictable events arise, returns on their long-term investments (including children) are less likely to be perceived as threatened or beyond their control.

In terms of relationship maintenance processes, the Developmental Strategic Pluralism Model identifies both the developmental antecedents and the current environmental circumstances that should trigger relationship maintenance and destabilizing behaviors. Couples who are currently in safe, predictable environments should be motivated to engage in maintenance behaviors in most circumstances. However, when environments become harsh and/or unpredictable, partners who are developmentally calibrated to enact faster reproductive strategies should experience more destabilizing thoughts, feelings, and behaviors to hedge their bets against looming uncertainty. Partners raised in safe, predictable childhood environments, on the other hand, should engage in stronger or more relationship maintenance behaviors until such efforts prove futile.

In addition, sex differences might play a role in these processes. For example, men who grew up in highly unpredictable environments should exhibit the fastest reproductive strategies and display the most relationship-destabilizing behaviors, on average. Conversely, women who grew up in safe, predictable environments are likely to develop the slowest reproductive strategies and enact the most relationship maintenance behaviors, on average.

To test the key predictions of this model, relationship researchers should include measures of childhood experiences, current life stressors, and relationship maintenance behaviors in their studies. Ideally, childhood measures would be collected using prospective longitudinal research designs through childhood into adulthood to measure environmental stressors in real time.

Such designs, however, are both expensive and time-consuming. A more feasible approach is to employ retrospective reports of childhood experiences and environments using interview or questionnaire measures. Current life stressors could also be acquired with interviews or questionnaires. Another possibility is to induce stress in the laboratory by using a stressful paradigm (e.g., discussing a major relationship conflict) or an experimental manipulation in which participants are randomly assigned to either a "stress" or a "no stress" condition. After inducing stress, researchers could then measure the typical relationship maintenance responses of interest. The critical idea is that one's developmental history (assessed by retrospective reports) should modulate how either a laboratory stressor or self-reported currently stressful circumstances affect relationship maintenance outcomes.

In conclusion, the Developmental Strategic Pluralism Model recasts relationship-maintenance processes as an important set of behaviors tied to global reproductive strategies. In doing so, it addresses not only when individuals are more likely to maintain their relationships, but also when they should be motivated to perhaps destabilize them. The model also highlights the importance of considering trade-offs that shape different reproductive strategies and how these strategies may affect relationship maintenance behaviors in turn. We propose that the adaptive value of maintenance behaviors should depend on both a person's developmental history *and* his/her current environment. Our ultimate hope is that the Developmental Strategic Pluralism framework will allow researchers to think more deeply and clearly about both relationship maintenance and destabilizing behaviors at different levels of analysis, ranging from proximate causation, to ontogeny, to ultimate causation.

REFERENCES

Agnew, C. R., & VanderDrift, L. W. (2015). Relationship maintenance and dissolution. In M. Mikulincer, P. R. Shaver, J. A. Simpson, & J. F. Dovidio (Eds.), *APA handbook of personality and social psychology: Interpersonal relations* (Vol. 3, pp. 581–604). Washington, DC: American Psychological Association.

Belsky, J. (1997). Attachment, mating, and parenting: An evolutionary interpretation. *Human Nature, 8,* 361–381.

Belsky, J., & Jaffee, S. (2006). The multiple determinants of parenting. In D. Cicchetti & D. Cohen (Eds.), *Developmental psychopathology: Vol. 3. Risk, disorder, and adaptation* (2nd ed., pp. 38–85). Hoboken, NJ: Wiley.

Belsky, J., Steinberg, L., & Draper, P. (1991). Childhood experience, interpersonal development, and reproductive strategy: An evolutionary theory of socialization. *Child Development, 62,* 647–670.

Bradbury, T. N., & Fincham, F. D. (1990). Attributions in marriage: Review and critique. *Psychological Bulletin, 107,* 3–33.

Buss, D. M., & Schmitt, D. P. (1993). Sexual strategies theory: A contextual evolutionary analysis of human mating. *Psychological Review, 100,* 204–232.

Del Giudice, M., Gangestad, S. W., & Kaplan, H. S. (2016). Life history theory and evolutionary psychology. In D. M. Buss (Ed.), *The handbook of evolutionary psychology* (2nd ed., pp. 88–114). New York: Wiley.

Ellis, B. J., Bianchi, J., Griskevicius, V., & Frankenhuis, W. E. (2017). Beyond risk and protective factors: An adaptation-based approach to resilience. *Perspectives on Psychological Science, 12*, 561–587.

Ellis, B. J., Figueredo, A. J., Brumbach, B. H., & Schlomer, G. L. (2009). Fundamental dimensions of environmental risk: The impact of harsh versus unpredictable environments on the evolution and development of life history strategies. *Human Nature, 20*, 204–268.

Fletcher, G. J. O., & Fincham, F. D. (1991). Attribution processes in close relationships. In G. J. O. Fletcher & F. D. Fincham (Eds.), *Cognition in close relationships* (pp. 7–35). Hillsdale, NJ: Erlbaum.

Gangestad, S. W., & Simpson, J. A. (2000). The evolution of human mating: Trade-offs and strategic pluralism. *Behavioral and Brain Sciences, 23*, 573–587.

Geary, D. C. (2005). Evolution of paternal investment. In D. M. Buss (Ed.), *The handbook of evolutionary psychology* (pp. 483–505). New York: Wiley.

Gonzaga, G. C., Haselton, M. G., Smurda, J., Davies, M. S., & Poore, J. C. (2008). Love, desire, and the suppression of thoughts of romantic alternatives. *Evolution and Human Behavior, 29*, 119–126.

Griskevicius, V., Ackerman, J. M., Cantú, S. M., Delton, A. W., Robertson, T. E., Simpson, J. A., . . . Tybur, J. M. (2013). When the economy falters do people spend or save? Responses to resource scarcity depend on childhood environments. *Psychological Science, 24*, 197–205. doi:10.1177/0956797612451471

Holmes, J. G., & Rempel, J. K. (1989). Trust in close relationships. In C. Hendrick (Ed.), *Close relationships* (pp. 187–220). Newbury Park: Sage.

Impett, E. A., Gable, S. L., & Peplau, L. A. (2005). Giving up and giving in: The costs and benefits of daily sacrifice in intimate relationships. *Journal of Personality and Social Psychology, 89*, 327–344.

Johnson, D. J., & Rusbult, C. E. (1989). Resisting temptation: Devaluation of alternative partners as a means of maintaining commitment in close relationships. *Journal of Personality and Social Psychology, 57*, 967–980.

Kaplan, H. S., & Gangestad, S. W. (2005). Life history theory and evolutionary psychology. In D. M. Buss (Ed.), *The handbook of evolutionary psychology* (pp. 68–95). New York: Wiley.

Karremans, J. C., & Van Lange, P. A. M. (2008). Forgiveness in personal relationships: Its malleability and powerful consequences. *European Review of Social Psychology, 19*, 202–241.

Kelley, H. H., & Thibaut, J. W. (1978). *Interpersonal relations: A theory of interdependence.* New York: Wiley.

Levinger, G. (1983). Development and change. In H. H. Kelley, E. Berscheid, A. Christensen, J. H. Harvey, T. L. Huston, G. Levinger, E. McClintock, L. A. Peplau, & D. R. Peterson (Eds.), *Close relationships* (pp. 315–359). San Francisco: Freeman.

Lydon, J. E., & Quinn, S. K. (2013). Relationship maintenance processes. In J. A. Simpson & L. Campbell (Eds.), *The Oxford handbook of close relationships* (pp. 573–588). New York: Oxford University Press.

Maner, J. K., Rouby, D. A., & Gonzaga, G. C. (2008). Automatic inattention to attractive alternatives: The evolved psychology of relationship maintenance. *Evolution and Human Behavior, 29*, 343–349.

Miller, R. J. (1997). Inattentive and contented: Relationship commitment and attention to alternatives. *Journal of Personality and Social Psychology, 73,* 758–766.

Mittal, C., & Griskevicius, V. (2014). Sense of control under uncertainty depends on people's childhood environment: A life history theory approach. *Journal of Personality and Social Psychology, 107,* 621–637.

Murray, S. L., Holmes, J. G., & Griffin. D. W. (1996). The benefits of positive illusions: Idealization and the construction of satisfaction in close relationships. *Journal of Personality and Social Psychology, 70,* 79–98.

Promislow, D., & Harvey, P. (1990). Living fast and dying young: A comparative analysis of life-history variation among mammals. *Journal of the Zoological Society of London, 220,* 417–437.

Rusbult, C. E. (1980). Commitment and satisfaction in romantic associations: A test of the investment model. *Journal of Experimental Social Psychology, 16,* 172–186.

Rusbult, C. E., & Buunk, B. P. (1993). Commitment processes in close relationships: An interdependence analysis. *Journal of Social and Personal Relationships, 10,* 175–204.

Rusbult, C. E., Verette, J., Whitney, G. A., Slovik, L. F., & Lipkus, I. (1991). Accommodation processes in close relationships: Theory and preliminary empirical evidence. *Journal of Personality and Social Psychology, 60,* 53–78.

Simpson, J. A., & Belsky, J. (2016). Attachment theory within a modern evolutionary framework. In J. Cassidy & P. R. Shaver (Eds.), *Handbook of attachment: Theory, research, and clinical applications* (3rd ed., pp. 91–116). New York: Guilford.

Stearns, S. (1992). *The evolution of life histories.* New York: Oxford University Press.

Szepsenwol, O., Simpson, J. A., Griskevicius, V., & Raby, K. L. (2015). The effect of unpredictable early childhood environments on parenting in adulthood. *Journal of Personality and Social Psychology, 109,* 1045–1067.

Thibaut, J. W., & Kelley, H. H. (1959). *The social psychology of groups.* New York: Wiley.

Trivers, R. L. (1972). Parental investment and sexual selection. In B. Campbell (Ed.), *Sexual selection and the descent of man, 1871–1971* (pp. 136–179). Chicago: Aldine-Atherton.

Van Lange, P. A. M., Rusbult, C. E., Drigotas, S. M., Arriaga, X. B., Witcher, B. S., & Cox, C. L. (1997). Willingness to sacrifice in close relationships. *Journal of Personality and Social Psychology, 72,* 1373–1395.

4

Relationship Maintenance from an Attachment Perspective

JUWON LEE[1], GERY C. KARANTZAS[2], OMRI GILLATH[3],
AND R. CHRIS FRALEY[4]

The maintenance of romantic relationships can be defined as engaging in a set of behaviors (*maintenance strategies*; Ogolsky, Monk, Rice, Theisen, & Maniotes, 2017) that promote the healthy continuance of a romantic relationship. These behaviors can include active efforts to enhance relationship quality (e.g., positive and open communication), but can also involve efforts to mitigate threats to the relationship (e.g., derogation of attractive alternatives; Ogolsky et al., 2017). In the current chapter, we take an *attachment theoretical* (Bowlby, 1969/1982) perspective on relationship maintenance. We describe the associations between normative attachment processes and relationship maintenance, as well as the way individual differences in attachment are associated with relationship maintenance. We focus here on three maintenance behaviors that have been widely studied in relation to attachment: *support, communication,* and *commitment-enhancing behaviors.* Support behaviors are considered to enhance relationship quality, communication (including conflict management) is theorized to be related to both enhancing relationship quality and mitigating relationship threat, and commitment-enhancing behaviors, such as devaluating the attractiveness or dismissing the positive behaviors of an alternative mate (Cole, Trope, & Balcetis, 2016; Visserman & Karremans, 2014), are related to the mitigation of relationship threat.

Some people may stay together – and thus maintain the relationship – but report little relationship happiness or satisfaction (Davila & Bradbury, 2001; Heaton & Albrecht, 1991). According to Ogolsky et al. (2017), relationship maintenance processes are not only about mitigating dissolution (keeping couples together) but also about ensuring that couples maintain positive and satisfying relationships. We therefore end the chapter with a discussion of

[1] Department of Psychology, Carnegie Mellon University, juwonlee@andrew.cmu.edu
[2] School of Psychology, Deakin University, gery.karantzas@deakin.edu.au
[3] Department of Psychology, University of Kansas, ogillath@ku.edu
[4] Department of Psychology, University of Illinois at Urbana-Champaign, rcfraley@illinois.edu

individual differences in attachment and *relationship satisfaction*, which is considered an important outcome of relationship maintenance processes.

NORMATIVE ATTACHMENT PROCESSES AND ROMANTIC RELATIONSHIP MAINTENANCE

Attachment theory is one of the major theories in the study of close relationships (Gillath, Karantzas, & Fraley, 2016). According to Bowlby (1969/1982), all human beings are born with an *attachment behavioral system*. A behavioral system is a species-universal biological mechanism that regulates behavior in goal-driven ways. In the case of the attachment system, the proximate goal is to attain *felt security* (Bowlby, 1969/1982; Gillath et al., 2016). Felt security represents a physical and psychological state of safety. When this state of felt security is compromised, the person is motivated to seek proximity to someone who can provide support and protection when needed (termed an *attachment figure*), ultimately promoting survival in times of danger.

The attachment relationship serves three main functions. The first is termed *proximity seeking/maintenance* and involves the child remaining in close contact with the attachment figure during times of threat. Any form of separation from the attachment figure is met with distress. The second is termed *safe haven* and refers to the child using the attachment figure as a source of safety, comfort, support, and protection. The third function is termed *secure base* and pertains to the child's reliance on the attachment figure as a base from which to engage in nonattachment behaviors that enhance autonomy and personal growth, such as exploration. Although the functions of attachment were first documented in childhood (Bowlby, 1969/1982), according to Bowlby, attachment continues to play a role in human experience from the "cradle to the grave" (Bowlby, 1979, p.129).

Although early theoretical and empirical work on attachment was focused on infant–caregiver relationships (Ainsworth, Blehar, Waters, & Wall, 1978; Bowlby, 1969/1982), scholars have extended the theory to the study of adult relationships, with an emphasis on romantic relationships in particular (e.g., Collins & Read, 1990; Hazan & Shaver, 1987; Simpson, 1990). The attachment system is assumed to operate in adult relationships in ways that are similar to the way it operates in childhood (Gillath et al., 2016; Hazan & Shaver, 1994; Mikulincer & Shaver, 2016). That is, adults often use a romantic partner as a safe haven during times of distress and a secure base from which to explore the world (see Fraley & Shaver, 2000; Hazan, Gur-Yaish, & Campa, 2004).

Although scholars agree that the development of attachments in infancy and early childhood has clear biological functions (e.g., protection from predators, thermoregulation, and reliable nutrition; see Bowlby, 1969/1982), it is less clear whether there are apparent biological functions of attachment in adult romantic relationships (see Hazan & Zeifman, 1994; Kirkpatrick, 1998). Some theorists have argued that romantic attachment can benefit survival and reproduction by facilitating paternal investment, which increases the protection and care for offspring (Fletcher, Simpson, Campbell, & Overall, 2015; Fraley, Brumbaugh, & Marks, 2005).

For example, in times of challenge and threat, people turn to their romantic partners for both physical and psychological closeness. Importantly, such behaviors are likely to serve relationship maintenance functions. By endeavoring to stay near to and resist separation from one's romantic partner, the person is expected to spend more time with their romantic partner, which can facilitate greater couple interaction and engagement in joint activities (Aron, Norman, & Aron, 2001; Lewandowski & Ackerman, 2006). In turn, spending time with one another and having fun together are associated with lower susceptibility to romantic alternatives (Lewandowski & Ackerman, 2006), ultimately promoting the continuance of the relationship.

By becoming a safe haven, the partner provides feelings of safety and comfort, and thus helps foster felt security (Hazan & Shaver, 1994). As a result, the person repeatedly associates the partner with the positive feeling of security, which facilitates maintenance, as the romantic partner is deemed to play a central role in helping the person achieve the primary goal of the attachment system, which in turn makes the person more likely to want to stay with the partner. In addition, using the partner as a source of support in times of need promotes the maintenance of romantic relationships by providing an opportunity for the partner to give effective and responsive support, which increases relationship quality and thus promotes maintenance (Feeney & Collins, 2015; Ogolsky et al., 2017).

Last, using the partner as a secure base for engaging in nonattachment behaviors strengthens the relationship by enabling the partner to promote the person's personal growth and maturity (Collins & Feeney, 2000; Mikulincer & Shaver, 2009). The secure base function is realized through the partner's responsive support for the person's personal goals. Consequentially, being able to engage in personal growth in the absence of adversity is linked to feeling valued by the partner and greater happiness and self-esteem in the person (Feeney, 2004; Feeney & Collins, 2015). This in turn increases the importance of the partner to the person, which heightens motivation to prolong the relationship (Rusbult, Olsen, Davis, & Hannon, 2001). Moreover, the degree to which a partner provides comfort and support has been demonstrated to become more important in sustaining the relationship as it progresses (e.g., Kotler, 1985).

To further explain the psychological benefits of support from an attachment figure, Mikulincer and Shaver (2009) proposed a *broaden-and-build cycle of attachment security*. The cycle emphasizes how a reliable and dependable partner augments the person's capacity to effectively manage distress and restore emotional balance. In addition to maximizing personal adjustment, this increases interdependence in the relationship and strengthens the attachment bond between the person and the partner, which together enable the person to provide the partner with effective support in return (*coregulation* of attachment distress; Sbarra & Hazan, 2008). Relatedly, viewing each other as a secure base enables romantic partners to engage together in novel, fun activities, which in turn, expands their sense of the self (Aron et al., 2001) and heightens positive affect, ultimately benefitting relationship quality and increasing maintenance. In addition, Rusbult and colleagues (Rusbult, Arriaga, & Agnew, 2001) propose that adult attachment bonds facilitate the "transformation of motivation" in which self-serving motives of individuals are relinquished in favor of relationship-serving motivations, thereby enhancing relationship maintenance (Etcheverry, Le, Wu, & Wei, 2013).

Safe haven and secure base dynamics tend to function simultaneously in romantic couples. For example, one person can serve as a safe haven for the other partner while, at other times, the partner is serving as a safe haven for the person (Gillath et al., 2016; Sbarra & Hazan, 2008). This concurrency in attachment functions from both partners in the dyad contributes to the overall maintenance of the relationship (see Selcuk, Zayas, & Hazan, 2010 for a review of the attachment bond and marital functioning).

INDIVIDUAL DIFFERENCES IN ATTACHMENT ORGANIZATION AND ROMANTIC RELATIONSHIP MAINTENANCE

In addition to normative processes, which are common in all attachments, Bowlby (1969/1982) argued that individual differences develop in the organization of the attachment system based on early experiences with attachment figures. These individual differences are theorized to have their origins in early experiences with the availability and responsiveness of attachment figures. If the attachment figures are consistently responsive and available in times of need, the child attains *felt security* and constructs positive mental representations (or *internal working models*) of self and others (Bowlby, 1969/1982). The *model of self* represents perceptions regarding the degree to which one is worthy of love and support, while the *model of others* represents the degree to which attachment figures (and others more generally) are perceived as trustworthy and dependable (Bartholomew & Horowitz, 1991). Continued confidence in the availability and responsiveness of attachment figures leads to the development of positive mental representations of the self and other and supports the development of *security-based strategies of affect regulation* (Shaver & Mikulincer, 2002). These strategies focus on reducing distress by enacting problem-solving strategies and relying on supportive close relationships.

However, if attachment figures are inconsistently responsive in times of need, or consistently unresponsive, the child is theorized to experience insecurity, and as a consequence, begins to use either hyperactivating or deactivating strategies to regulate attachment distress. The extent to which the child engages in hyperactivation or deactivation of the attachment system depends on the viability of proximity seeking to an attachment figure. Those who appraise proximity as viable hyperactivate the attachment system, resulting in persistent attempts to attain proximity. These *hyperactivating strategies* (Dozier & Kobak, 1992) not only involve continuous, intense effort, but are also theorized to increase vigilance to threats and reduce the threshold for perceiving the unavailability of attachment figures. This results in increased emotional dependence, seeking excessive contact, and intense negative emotional responses to separation from the attachment figure (Sroufe, 1985; Stroufe, Fox, & Pancake, 1983). As such, when used continuously, hyperactivating strategies tend to result in overdependence on close others and clinging efforts to attain reassurance.

On the other hand, those who appraise their attachment figures as being inaccessible, such that further proximity seeking would be futile or undesirable, are theorized to engage in *deactivating strategies* (Dozier & Kobak, 1992) to reduce further frustration and distress. These manifest as the denial of proximity-seeking needs, distancing from closeness, and avoiding dependence. Deactivating strategies also involve heightened monitoring and dismissal or suppression of cues that signal threat and distress (Borelli, West, Weekes, & Crowley, 2014). When used habitually, deactivating strategies are assumed to lead to compulsive self-reliance and cognitive, behavioral, and emotional distancing from attachment figures (Bowlby, 1980).

These individual differences in the functioning of the attachment system are theorized to manifest in adult attachment relationships too, where they are often referred to as *attachment styles* (Hazan & Shaver, 1987; Mikulincer, Shaver, Bar-On, & Ein-Dor, 2010; Mikulincer, Shaver, & Pereg, 2003). Contemporary models of attachment styles in adulthood suggest that individual differences can be organized with respect to two dimensions: attachment anxiety and attachment avoidance (Brennan, Clark, & Shaver, 1998). People high on attachment anxiety are characterized by a fear of abandonment, a need for approval, and a preoccupation with relationships. Moreover, they tend to use hyperactivating strategies of affect and distress regulation (e.g., Brennan, Clark, & Shaver, 1998; Shaver & Mikulincer, 2006). People high on attachment avoidance are characterized by low trust in others, are uncomfortable with closeness, are highly independent, and engage in deactivating strategies of affect and distress regulation (e.g., Brennan et al., 1998; Shaver & Mikulincer, 2006). People who are low on both attachment anxiety and avoidance are considered to be securely attached. They tend to be comfortable with closeness, are trusting of others, and are comfortable with having others rely upon them for support. Moreover, they engage in security-based strate-gies of affect and distress regulation (e.g., Brennan et al., 1998; Shaver & Mikulincer, 2006) (see Gillath et al., 2016 and Mikulincer & Shaver, 2016 for reviews on correlates of adult attachment styles).

Because of these differences, people's attachment styles can play an important role in relationship processes in general and relationship maintenance specifically. If perceptions and beliefs about the partner and the relationship are negatively biased due to an insecure attachment style, this may impair the use of strategies that are crucial for relationship maintenance, such as support provision/seeking, communication and constructive management of conflict, and commitment-enhancing behaviors.

ATTACHMENT STYLE AND SUPPORT

Effective support is pertinent to maintaining healthy relationships (Cutrona, 2012); ineffective support can lead to relationship decline or dissolution (Jayamaha, Girme, & Overall, 2017). Many studies have found attachment styles to be associated with how support is provided, sought, and received in the relationship. For example, securely attached people tend to not only provide more comfort and reassurance, but also render support in a more sensitive and responsive manner, compared with insecurely attached people (Collins & Feeney, 2000; Feeney & Hohaus, 2001; Simpson, Rholes, & Phillips, 1996). In other words, secure people sense when the partner needs support or is seeking support, and render support with a sense of care and empathy, but also respect their partner's autonomy and sense of agency. As such, secure people provide support in a noninterfering manner that does not undermine that partner's competency and independence.

Anxiously attached people's hyperactivating strategies are associated with becoming overinvolved in partners' problems and in providing support that is intrusive, compulsive, and smothering (Feeney & Collins, 2001; Julal & Carnelley, 2012; Kunce & Shaver, 1994). To investigate how attachment anxiety can impede effective support provision, Jayamaha and colleagues (2017) conducted two studies in which romantic couples engaged in video-taped discussions about each other's most important personal goal. After each discussion, the person whose goal was discussed (i.e., the support recipient) reported how distressed he/she had felt, and the partner (i.e., the support provider) reported how valued and appreciated he/she had felt. Support providers high in attachment anxiety reported feeling less valued and appre-ciated when their partner reported greater distress, which was associated with exhibiting more negative support behaviors such as criticizing and blaming, insisting that the partner adopt the provider's approach, and invalidating the partner's point of view.

Avoidantly attached people's deactivating strategies are associated with distancing from a needy partner, which results in the provision of support in a manner that lacks empathy as well as being cold and controlling (Feeney & Collins, 2001; Kunce & Shaver, 1994; Simpson et al., 2011). In addition, Millings and Walsh (2009) surveyed romantic couples and found that those high in attachment avoidance scored lower on a measure of sensitive and responsive support.

Attachment styles have also been related to differences in seeking and receiving support. Securely attached people feel comfortable with relying on relationship partners, seek support when needed, and perceive their partners to be sensitive and responsive (Ognibene & Collins, 1998; Simpson, Collins, Tran, & Haydon, 2007). As a result, they tend to be satisfied with their partner's support, which results in subsequent maintenance behaviors such as a greater willingness to care for the partner (Feeney & Hohaus, 2001).

Anxiously attached people display an ambivalent pattern of support seeking. At times, consistent with hyperactivating strategies, they engage in excessive reassurance seeking from the partner, which is often viewed by the partner as intrusive and demanding (Feeney, 2008; Shaver, Schachner, & Mikulincer, 2005). However, in situations when their neediness is expected to be met with partner rejection, anxious people refrain from expressing their need for support (Feeney, 2008).

Avoidantly attached people, in line with their deactivating strategies, perceive their partners as rejecting and incapable of providing resources, protection, and encouragement (Mikulincer et al., 2003). As such, they are generally reluctant to seek proximity to, obtain comfort from, or depend on their partners in times of need (Collins & Feeney, 2000; Feeney, 2004; Simpson, Rholes, & Nelligan, 1992). When they do seek support, albeit rarely, it tends to be instrumental support rather than emotional support that is sought (Karantzas & Cole, 2011; Simpson et al., 1992). These individual differences in cognition, affect, and behaviors regarding support provision, seeking, and receiving, and the strong connection between support and relationship maintenance, suggest that attachment security facilitates constructive support-related processes. In turn, these functional support processes serve to increase the perception that the person is valued in the relationship (Feeney & Karantzas, 2017; Mikulincer & Shaver, 2003), which induces the person to feel more secure in the relationship and ultimately prolongs it (Kane, McCall, Collins, & Blascovich, 2012; Ogolsky et al., 2017).

ATTACHMENT STYLE AND COMMUNICATION

In addition to support processes, another variable that is largely behavioral and related to relationship-enhancing and threat-mitigation processes is communication (Ogolsky et al., 2017). For a relationship to function smoothly, people must convey their needs to each other in order for those needs to be met (Guerrero, Andersen, & Afifi, 2017). Researchers have shown that effective communication fosters relationship maintenance by providing the opportunity for the partner to respond in such a way that the discloser feels valued (Reis, Clark, & Holmes, 2004). This increases the perception that one is appreciated in the relationship (Pietromonaco, Greenwood, & Barrett, 2004), which boosts the frequency of other relationship maintenance behaviors such as engaging in joint activities (Stafford & Canary, 1991). When done ineffectively, however, (mis)communication can hinder maintenance and lead to deterioration or dissolution of the relationship (Reis et al., 2004).

Research on communication in relationships has focused on the role of individual differences (Dindia & Dainton, 2003; Guerrero et al., 2017), and over the last two decades, attachment styles have been found to be consistently linked to differences in communication patterns (Domingue & Mollen, 2009). Studies have found attachment security to be positively associated with a greater openness to communicate, manifesting in more self-disclosure (Dainton, 2007; Mikulincer & Nachshon, 1991). When communicating, secure people engage in more constructive, responsive, and sensitive patterns of communication; express feelings more accurately (Feeney, 1994); and use more messages that emphasize dedication to the partner and relationship (such as telling how much he/she means to them or discussing mutual plans for the future; Dainton, 2007). Insecure people were found to use more destructive communication patterns (Feeney, 1994; Feeney & Karantzas, 2017). For example, Jayamaha, Antonellis, and Overall (2016) found that people higher on attachment anxiety engaged in more negative guilt-inducing communication compared with those lower in anxiety. In addition, Dainton (2007) found attachment avoidance to be associated with a lower degree of openness with the partner and less use of messages emphasizing commitment to the partner. Related to nonverbal communication, those who were more secure displayed greater expressiveness, pleasantness, and atten-tiveness to their partners compared with those who were less secure (Guerrero, Farinelli, & McEwan, 2009; Tucker & Anders, 1998).

A study by Collins and Gillath (2012) found that differences in commu-nication by attachment style also manifested in the context of breaking up with a romantic partner. Secure people tended to use more open, direct, and compassionate termination strategies such as honestly explaining the reasons for desiring to break up. Anxious people reported using more strategies that enabled the option of reuniting in the future, such as blaming oneself instead of the partner. Avoidant people were found to use less direct breakup strate-gies, such as avoiding contact with the partner.

Individual differences in attachment have also been found to be asso-ciated with how people respond to their partner more generally – whether this be positive or negative in nature. Secure people have been found to show greater admiration, respect, and gratitude toward their partners compared with insecure people (Frei & Shaver, 2002; Mikulincer & Shaver, 2003). Secure people tend to respond with controlled expressions of anger and frustration during conflicts, without reflecting hatred, hostility, or vengeance toward the partner (Collins, 1996; Kachadourian, Fincham, & Davila, 2004; Mikulincer & Shaver, 2008). Secure people are also more likely to facilitate an apology after a partner's transgressions by openly accepting and acknowledging the partner's remorse (Burnette, Taylor, Worthington, & Forsyth, 2007; Feeney & Fitzgerald, 2012; Kachadourian et al., 2004; Van Monsjou et al., 2015). These responses make the partner feel valued and appreciated in the relationship, which facilitates relationship maintenance (Pietromonaco et al., 2004).

People high on attachment anxiety respond to their partner with gratitude and affection, but unlike in the case of secure people, this response tends to be accompanied by concerns about the partner or relationship, or expressions of inferiority about themselves (Mikulincer & Shaver, 2003). They also often express neediness, possessiveness, and jealousy (Feeney & Noller, 1990; Fricker & Moore, 2002). When reacting to a partner's negative behavior, anxious people exhibit uncontrolled emotional responses that tend to be characterized by anger, resentment, and/or hatred toward the partner (Burnette et al., 2007; Jang, Smith, & Levine, 2002; Van Monsjou et al., 2015) or oneself (Collins, 1996; Mikulincer, 1998; Rholes, Simpson, & Blakely, 1995). The latter reflects both a hyperactivating strategy of emotional regulation and a negative model of the self (Shaver & Mikulincer, 2006). In other words, the need for excessive reassurance and fear of abandonment by the partner results in negative behaviors. These behaviors might be meant to get more attention and support from the partner, but may ironically push the partner away (and hence reduce maintenance).

People high on attachment avoidance tend to express less gratitude and appreciation, even in response to positive and thoughtful behavior by the partner (Mikulincer, Shaver, & Horesh, 2006). This response is thought to reflect deactivating strategies of affect regulation. As these deactivating strategies also involve the suppression of emotion, when reacting to a partner's negative behavior, avoidant people tend to express anger in unintended ways, or engage in nonspecific hostility (Burnette et al., 2007; Collins, 1996; Rholes, Simpson, & Orina, 1999). In addition, avoidants perceive their partners to be less open and assuring of the relationship in their communication (Dainton, 2007). These tendencies frequently increase conflict and hinder repair of the relationship, thus compromising the positivity and maintenance of the relationship.

Conflict management can be viewed as an interactive process of threat mitigation in the relationship (Ogolsky et al., 2017). The strategies that people use to handle conflict have received much attention in adult attachment and relationship research (Noller, 2012; Rholes, Kohn, & Simpson, 2014). In particular, Feeney and Karantzas (2017) propose that severe or persistent couple conflict activates the attachment system. Those high on attachment security tend to use highly constructive and effective ways of dealing with conflict, such as attending to – and openly listening to – their partner's perspective, providing and soliciting disclosure, endeavoring to compromise and integrate both positions, accommodating anger or criticism from the partner, and attempting to deal with problems in a solution-focused manner (Feeney, Noller, & Hanrahan, 1994; Perunovic & Holmes, 2008; Simpson et al., 1992). A longitudinal study on couples experiencing the transition to parenthood found that secure people are both more skillful at handling conflict to begin with and improve in their use of effective conflict-resolution tactics over time compared with insecure individuals (Rholes et al., 2014). These constructive conflict patterns of secure people have been found to encourage useful problem-solving of relationship issues and buffer against the breakdown of relationships (Feeney et al., 1994; Simpson et al., 1992).

Studies have also shown that insecure people rely less on effective conflict-resolution strategies. For example, people high on attachment anxiety have been shown to destructively engage in conflict with behaviors that intensify conflict, such as blaming, coercing, and manipulating the partner, reflecting hyperactivating strategies (Feeney & Karantzas, 2017). People high on avoidance report responding to conflict by engaging in more withdrawing, distancing, avoidance of conflict interactions, and less negotiation, all indicative of deactivating strategies (Feeney, 1994; 1998; Rholes et al., 2014; Shaver & Mikulincer, 2006). These conflict strategies tend to leave conflicts unresolved and may perpetuate worse conflict in the future. Indeed, longitudinal studies show that behavioral patterns that reflect insecure attachment, such as manipulation and demand-withdrawal, have been found to increase the risk of relationship dissolution (Feeney, 1994; 1998; Saavedra, Chapman, & Rogge, 2010). These findings suggest that effective communication in relationships can serve to facilitate relationship maintenance, and, importantly, people with different attachment styles use different communication strategies (which can facilitate or hinder maintenance).

ATTACHMENT STYLE AND COMMITMENT-ENHANCING BEHAVIORS

Commitment refers to the extent to which a person has a long-term orientation toward his or her relationship. It is also regarded as a subjective manifestation of dependence between two partners (Le & Agnew, 2003). Commitment is a strong predictor of whether a relationship is sustained or dissolves (Rusbult, 1983) and has been shown to predict relationship-maintenance behaviors such as responding positively to negative partner behavior and a willingness to sacrifice time as well as resources to maintain the romantic relationship (Etcheverry et al., 2013). In addition, studies suggest that commitment sustains relationships by assuaging factors that threaten the relationship, such as decreasing aggression toward a partner (Slotter et al., 2012) or reducing interest in attractive alternative partners (Le, Korn, Crockett, & Loving, 2011; Lydon, Fitzsimons, & Naidoo, 2003; Miller, 2008). As such, the behaviors that people use that enhance commitment can be construed as serving relationship maintenance functions.

Studies show that people with different attachment styles vary in how committed they are to their relationships and the behaviors they enact to maintain their relationships. For example, those who are securely attached report higher levels of commitment (Shaver & Brennan, 1992; Simpson, 1990; Dandurand, Bouaziz, & Lafontaine, 2013) and engage in cognitive processes that enhance commitment, such as perceiving their partner to be more responsive (Segal & Fraley, 2016). This is probably because secure people harbor positive attachment working models, which facilitate endorsing relational goals that promote closeness and optimistic beliefs about the relationship (Bartz & Lydon, 2006; Hazan & Shaver, 1987; Simpson, 1990; Whiffen, 2005). These goals, in turn, might explain why secure people are less likely to get divorced (Hazan & Shaver, 1987).

Compared with secure people, insecure people report lower commitment to their romantic relationships and engage in behaviors that are detrimental to commitment. Specifically, anxious people tend to focus on the threats to commitment (Campbell, Simpson, Boldry, & Kashy, 2005; Meyer, Olivier, & Roth, 2005), activating their hypervigilance toward possible rejection (Shaver & Mikulincer, 2006). Avoidant people manifest their deactivating strategies by harboring relational goals that emphasize emotional distance and holding relational beliefs that downplay the importance of relationship maintenance (Gillath et al., 2006; Locke, 2008). These goals and beliefs are theorized to impede avoidant people from committing to their relationships (Feeney, 2008). Indeed, studies have found that avoidant people tend to invest less in relationships (Tempelhof & Allen, 2008) and, presumably as a result, report lower commitment and are more likely to experience relationship dissolution (Etcheverry et al., 2013).

One threat to an ongoing romantic relationship is the allure of alternative partners. High-quality romantic alternatives are theorized to endanger the relationship by perceiving it to have more costs because one is giving up spending time with an alternative partner to be with the current partner (Rusbult, 1983). This consequently lowers satisfaction and commitment to the current partner (Kenrick, Neuberg, Zierk, & Krones, 1994; Rusbult, 1983), endangering the maintenance of the current relationship. Despite this risk, attraction to alternative partners, infidelity, and break up due to viable potential partners frequently occurs (Baucom, Pentel, Gordon, & Snyder, 2017; Shackelford, Buss, & Bennett, 2002). Relatedly, attachment styles have been shown to predict individual differences in cognition, emotion, and behaviors regarding attraction to alternatives, such as experiencing more or less attraction to alternative partners and engagement in infidelity (e.g., DeWall et al., 2011; Overall & Sibley, 2008). This is because attachment orientations govern the approach toward, and the importance and value placed on, the current romantic relationship. For example, people high on attachment anxiety place a great amount of value on their current romantic relationship and thus engage in self-monitoring to derogate or ignore alternative partners to protect the current relationship and sustain the existing attachment bond (Overall & Sibley, 2008).

In contrast, people high on attachment avoidance are more self-reliant, exhibit discomfort with closeness and value independence, and therefore engage in tactics to maintain psychological distance from their romantic partners (Overall & Sibley, 2008). This is theorized to result in avoidant people being less committed to the relationship (Simpson, 1990), making them less likely to put effort into maintaining it. Thus, avoidant people would be less resistant to temptations from attractive alternatives and may even proactively pursue them (DeWall et al., 2011). Securely attached people tend to be comfortable with closeness and cherish their current romantic partner (Gillath et al., 2016). As such, secure people may display cognitions and behaviors similar to those of anxious people by actively engaging in efforts to maintain the existing relationship, as the alternative may heighten threat and distress regarding the future longevity of the current relationship.

The current literature corroborates these predictions. Compared with anxious and secure people, avoidant people display greater attention to alternatives (DeWall et al., 2011; Miller, 2008), perceive them more positively (DeWall et al., 2011), and report experiencing more romantic attraction to alternatives (Overall & Sibley, 2008). Avoidant people also report more positive attitudes toward infidelity (Brennan & Shaver, 1995; DeWall et al., 2011; Schachner & Shaver, 2002), express greater interest in meeting (DeWall et al., 2011) or being seduced by (Schachner & Shaver, 2002) alternatives, and engage in more infidelity (DeWall et al., 2011) compared with those low on avoidance. Moreover, studies have found these associations between attachment avoidance and cognitions/behaviors regarding alternatives to be mediated by lower levels of commitment to their partner (DeWall et al., 2011). This implies that those high on avoidance have less of a long-term orientation toward their partner, which makes them more susceptible to attending to alternatives and infidelity, which lowers relationship quality and increases the risk of relationship dissolution (Ogolsky et al., 2017).

ATTACHMENT STYLE AND RELATIONSHIP SATISFACTION

From an attachment perspective, romantic relationship satisfaction reflects the degree to which the relationship meets the basic needs for comfort and care (Hazan & Shaver, 1994; Hendrick, 1988). As such, satisfaction can be seen as an outcome of successful maintenance strategies (Dainton, 2007; Weigel & Ballard-Reisch, 2008). In turn, failure to engage in behaviors that heighten relationship satisfaction increases the risk of relationship dissolution (Hazan & Shaver, 1994). There is a wealth of studies, both cross-sectional (Collins & Read, 1990; Saavedra, Chapman, & Rogge, 2010) and longitudinal (Holland, Fraley, & Roisman, 2012; Sadikaj, Moskowitz, & Zuroff, 2015; Simpson, 1990), demonstrating that securely attached people have more satisfying relationships compared with insecure people. For example, one longitudinal study of married couples found that attachment security was associated with greater marital satisfaction after 15 years (Hirschberger, Srivastava, Marsh, Cowan, & Cowan, 2009). In addition, those high in attachment security tend to have more stable relationships, such as marriages that are less likely to end in divorce (for a review see Mikulincer, Florian, Cowan, & Cowan, 2002).

In addition to the degree to which a relationship meets one's basic needs (Hazan & Shaver, 1994), it is theorized that satisfaction in relationships is determined by the extent to which outcomes exceed one's expectations (and are therefore rewarding) and that the ratio of rewarding outcomes is greater than relationship costs (as long as this ratio exceeds a person's expectations for the relationship; Le & Agnew, 2003; Rusbult, 1983; Thibaut & Kelley, 1959). From this perspective, attachment styles (which are associated with distinct needs and expectations) determine the estimates of rewards and costs associated with a relationship (Hazan & Shaver, 1994). Insecure people are likely to perceive lower rewards and higher costs compared with secure people (Etcheverry et al., 2013), resulting in lower relationship satisfaction. Furthermore, a study by MacDonald and colleagues (MacDonald, Locke, Spielmann, & Joel, 2013) suggests that the lower satisfaction experienced by insecure people is qualitatively different depending on whether the person is high on attachment anxiety or avoidance. The researchers investigated the similarity and intensity of perceptions of social threat, such as concerns over rejection, and of social reward, such as opportunities for closeness, in romantic relationships. Both anxious and avoidant people reported the simultaneous presence of strong positive and negative perceptions of relationships, reflected by similarity in threat and reward perceptions. However, people high in anxiety reported highly intense threat and reward perceptions, whereas people high in avoidance reported low intensity threat and reward perceptions. These results suggest that although both highly anxious and highly avoidant people exhibit concurrent perceptions of relationship reward and threat, the processes underlying these perceptions are qualitatively different for highly anxious and avoidant people. For highly anxious people, the similarity in levels of threat and reward reflects intensified threat perceptions, whereas for avoidant people, the concurrence reflects a dampening of perceived rewards and a resulting indifference.

Attachment styles may determine how relationship satisfaction changes when couples are going through major life transitions. One example of a major life transition is becoming a parent. A study by Kohn and colleagues (Kohn et al., 2012) collected data from married couples once before, and four times after, the birth of their first child. They found that highly anxious people declined in satisfaction when they perceived their partner to be less supportive and more negative toward them. In contrast, highly avoidant people declined in satisfaction when they perceived greater work–family conflict and family demands. These findings suggest that when stressors deter the attainment of important attachment goals for insecure people (closeness for anxious and autonomy for avoidant people), satisfaction in the romantic relationship is negatively affected.

SUMMARY

In this chapter, we provided an overview of the theoretical and empirical associations linking the normative functioning of the attachment system and relationship-maintenance behaviors. We also reviewed evidence regarding individual differences in adult attachment and relationship maintenance behaviors, with specific emphasis on social support, communication and conflict patterns, and commitment-enhancing behaviors. We concluded our review by focusing on the association between attachment style and relationship satisfaction, which is often regarded as an important indicator of the successful maintenance of romantic relationships (e.g., Dainton, 2007; Aron et al., 2001). Overall, the normative functions of the attachment system are well aligned with the maintenance of an attachment relationship, and attachment security tends to be positively associated with the enactment of maintenance behaviors.

We emphasized the idea that attachment predicts commitment, but we should be clear that commitment may also predict attachment security. Longitudinal studies may help understand causal or reciprocal associations between attachment and commitment. It is plausible that across the course of a relationship, heightened perceptions of commitment and explicit evidence of commitment behaviors by a partner may enhance a person's sense of attachment security over time, to the point of even shifting those with an insecure attachment style to a more secure attachment.

Longitudinal studies can also reveal how the association between attachment style and commitment changes over time. A study by Arriaga and colleagues (Arriaga, Kumashiro, Finkel, VanderDrift, & Luchies, 2014) that assessed attachment style, trust toward the partner, and perceived goal valida- tion by the partner serves as an example. The researchers found in the cross- sectional analyses that trust predicted lower attachment anxiety and goal validation predicted lower attachment avoidance, but this pattern was reversed in the longitudinal analyses: trust predicted lower attachment avoid- ance and goal validation predicted lower attachment anxiety. In addition, dyadic studies would be important (both cross-sectional and longitudinal) to determine the role that partners can play in enhancing commitment, and whether their commitment behaviors help with attachment security.

Finally, much of what is discussed in this chapter reflects (to a large extent) theoretical assumptions regarding the linkages between the function- ing of the attachment system, individual differences in adult attachment, and perceptions of commitment and commitment-enhancing behaviors. To this end, a concerted effort needs to be made to provide empirical evidence for a number of the theoretical assumptions proposed in the chapter. For instance, what role does the normative operation of the attachment system and attachment functions play in enhancing interdependence, and in turn, fostering commitment within adult romantic pair-bonds? We believe that future research should integrate normative as well as individual difference aspects of attachment when discussing relationship maintenance.

REFERENCES

Ainsworth, M. D. S., Blehar, M. C., Waters, E., & Wall, S. N. (1978). *Patterns of attachment: Assessed in the strange situation and at home.* Hillsdale, NJ: Erlbaum.

Arriaga, X. B., Kumashiro, M., Finkel, E. J., VanderDrift, L. E., & Luchies, L. B. (2014). Filling the void: Bolstering attachment security in committed relationships. *Social Psychological and Personality Science, 5,* 398–406.

Aron, A., Norman, C. C., & Aron, E. N. (2001). Shared self-expanding activities as a means of maintaining and enhancing close romantic relationships. In J. H. Harvey & A. E. Wenzel (Eds.), *Close romantic relationships: Maintenance and enhancement* (pp. 47–66). Mahwah, NJ: Lawrence Erlbaum.

Bartholomew, K., & Horowitz, L. M. (1991). Attachment styles among young adults: A test of a four-category model. *Journal of Personality and Social Psychology, 61*(2), 226–244.

Bartz, J. A., & Lydon, J. E. (2006). Navigating the interdependence dilemma: Attachment goals and the use of communal norms with potential close others. *Journal of Personality and Social Psychology, 91,* 77–96.

Baucom, D. H., Pentel, K. Z., Gordon, K. C., & Snyder, D. K. (2017). An integrative approach to treating infidelity in couples. In J. Fitzgerald (Ed.), *Foundations for couples' therapy: Research for the real world* (pp. 206–215). New York, NY: Routledge.

Borelli, J. L., West, J. L., Weekes, N. Y., & Crowley, M. J. (2014). Dismissing child attachment and discordance for subjective and neuroendocrine responses to vulnerability. *Developmental Psychobiology, 56,* 584–591.

Bowlby, J. (1969/1982). *Attachment and loss: Vol. 1. Attachment* (2nd ed.). New York: Basic Books. (2nd ed., 1982; 1st ed., 1969).

Bowlby, J. (1979). On knowing what you are not supposed to know and feeling what you are not supposed to feel. *The Canadian Journal of Psychiatry, 24,* 403–408.

Bowlby, J. (1980). *Attachment and loss: Vol. 3. Sadness and depression.* New York: Basic Books.

Brennan, K. A., Clark, C. L., & Shaver, P. R. (1998). Self-report measurement of adult attachment: An integrative overview. In J. A. Simpson & W. S. Rholes (Eds.), *Attachment theory and close relationships* (pp. 46–76). New York: Guilford.

Brennan, K. A., & Shaver, P. R. (1995). Dimensions of adult attachment, affect regulation, and romantic relationship functioning. *Personality and Social Psychology Bulletin, 21,* 267–283.

Burnette, J. L., Taylor, K. W., Worthington, E. L., & Forsyth, D. R. (2007). Attachment and trait forgivingness: The mediating role of angry rumination. *Personality and Individual Differences, 42,* 1585–1596.

Campbell, L., Simpson, J. A., Boldry, J., & Kashy, D. A. (2005). Perceptions of conflict and support in romantic relationships: The role of attachment anxiety. *Journal of Personality and Social Psychology, 88,* 510–531.

Cole, S., Trope, Y., & Balcetis, E. (2016). In the eye of the betrothed: Perceptual downgrading of attractive alternative romantic partners. *Personality and Social Psychology Bulletin, 42,* 879–892.

Collins, N. L. (1996). Working models of attachment: Implications for explanation, emotion, and behavior. *Journal of Personality and Social Psychology, 71,* 810–832.

Collins, N. L., & Feeney, B. C. (2000). A safe haven: An attachment theory perspective on support seeking and caregiving in intimate relationships. *Journal of Personality and Social Psychology, 78,* 1053–1073.

Collins, N. L., & Read, S. J. (1990). Adult attachment, working models, and relationship quality in dating couples. *Journal of Personality and Social Psychology, 58,* 644–663.

Collins, T. J., & Gillath, O. (2012). Attachment, breakup strategies, and associated outcomes: The effects of security enhancement on the selection of breakup strategies. *Journal of Research in Personality, 46,* 210–222.

Cutrona, C. E. (2012). Recent advances in research on social support in couples. In P. Noller & G. C. Karantzas (Eds.), *The Wiley-Blackwell handbook of couples and family relationships* (pp. 392–405). New York: Wiley-Blackwell.

Dainton, M. (2007). Attachment and marital maintenance. *Communication Quarterly, 55,* 283–298.

Dandurand, C., Bouaziz, A. R., & Lafontaine, M. F. (2013). Attachment and couple satisfaction: The mediating effect of approach and avoidance commitment. *Journal of Relationships Research, 4,* e3.

Davila, J., & Bradbury, T. N. (2001). Attachment insecurity and the distinction between unhappy spouses who do and do not divorce. *Journal of Family Psychology, 15,* 371–393.

DeWall, C. N., Lambert, N. M., Slotter, E. B., Pond Jr, R. S., Deckman, T., Finkel, E. J., . . . & Fincham, F. D. (2011). So far away from one's partner, yet so close to romantic alternatives: Avoidant attachment, interest in alternatives, and infidelity. *Journal of Personality and Social Psychology, 101,* 1302–1316.

Dindia, K., & Dainton, M. (2003). *Maintaining relationships through communication: Relational, contextual, and cultural variations.* Mahwah, NJ: Lawrence Erlbaum.

Domingue, R., & Mollen, D. (2009). Attachment and conflict communication in adult romantic relationships. *Journal of Social and Personal Relationships, 26,* 678–696.

Dozier, M., & Kobak, R. R. (1992). Psychophysiology in attachment interviews: Converging evidence for deactivating strategies. *Child Development, 63,* 1473–1480.

Etcheverry, P. E., Le, B., Wu, T. F., & Wei, M. (2013). Attachment and the investment model: Predictors of relationship commitment, maintenance, and persistence. *Personal Relationships, 20,* 546–567.

Feeney, B. C. (2004). A secure base: Responsive support of goal strivings and exploration in adult intimate relationships. *Journal of Personality and Social Psychology, 87,* 631–648.

Feeney, B. C., & Collins, N. L. (2001). Predictors of caregiving in adult intimate relationships: An attachment theoretical perspective. *Journal of Personality and Social Psychology, 80,* 972–994.

Feeney, B. C., & Collins, N. L. (2015). A new look at social support: A theoretical perspective on thriving through relationships. *Personality and Social Psychology Review, 19,* 113–147.

Feeney, J. A. (1994). Attachment style, communication patterns, and satisfaction across the life cycle of marriage. *Personal Relationships, 1,* 333–348.

Feeney, J. A. (1998). Adult attachment and relationship-centered anxiety: Responses to physical and emotional distancing. In J. A. Simpson, & W. S. Rholes (Eds.), *Attachment theory and close relationships* (pp. 189–219). New York: Guilford Press.

Feeney, J. A. (2008). Adult romantic attachment: Developments in the study of couple relationships. In J. Cassidy & P. R. Shaver (Eds.), *Handbook of attachment: Theory, research, and clinical applications* (2nd ed., pp. 456–581). New York: Guilford Press.

Feeney, J. A., & Fitzgerald, J. (2012). Facilitating apology, forgiveness, and relationship security following hurtful events. In P. Noller & G. C. Karantzas (Eds.), *The Wiley-Blackwell handbook of couples and family relationships* (pp. 289–304). New York: Wiley-Blackwell.

Feeney, J. A., & Hohaus, L. (2001). Attachment and spousal caregiving. *Personal Relationships, 8,* 21–39.

Feeney, J. A., & Karantzas, G. C. (2017). Couple conflict: Insights from an attachment perspective. *Current Opinion in Psychology, 13,* 60–64.

Feeney, J. A., & Noller, P. (1990). Attachment style as a predictor of adult romantic relationships. *Journal of Personality and Social Psychology, 58,* 281–291.

Feeney, J. A., Noller, P., & Hanrahan, M. (1994). Assessing adult attachment: Developments in the conceptualization of security and insecurity. In M. B. Sperling & W. H. Berman (Eds.), *Attachment in adults: Clinical and developmental perspectives* (pp. 128–152). New York, NY: Guilford Press.

Fletcher, G. J., Simpson, J. A., Campbell, L., & Overall, N. C. (2015). Pair-bonding, romantic love, and evolution: The curious case of Homo sapiens. *Perspectives on Psychological Science, 10,* 20–36.

Fraley, R. C., Brumbaugh, C. C., & Marks, M. J. (2005). The evolution and function of adult attachment: a comparative and phylogenetic analysis. *Journal of Personality and Social Psychology, 89,* 731–746.

Fraley, R. C., & Shaver, P. R. (2000). Adult romantic attachment: Theoretical developments, emerging controversies, and unanswered questions. *Review of General Psychology, 4,* 132–154.

Frei, J. R., & Shaver, P. R. (2002). Respect in close relationships: Prototype definition, self-report assessment, and initial correlates. *Personal Relationships, 9,* 121–139.

Fricker, J., & Moore, S. (2002). Relationship satisfaction: The role of love styles and attachment styles. *Current Research in Social Psychology*, *7*, 182–204.

Gillath, O., Karantzas, G., & Fraley, R. C. (2016). *Adult attachment: A concise introduction to theory and research*. USA: Academic Press.

Gillath, O., Mikulincer, M., Fitzsimons, G. M., Shaver, P. R., Schachner, D. A., & Baragh, J. A. (2006). Automatic activation of attachment-related goals. *Personality and Social Psychology Bulletin*, *32*, 1375–1388.

Guerrero, L. K., Andersen, P. A., & Afifi, W. A. (2017). *Close encounters: Communication in relationships* (5th ed.) Thousand Oaks, CA: Sage.

Guerrero, L. K., Farinelli, L., & McEwan, B. (2009). Attachment and relational satisfaction: The mediating effect of emotional communication. *Communication Monographs*, *76*, 487–514.

Hazan, C., Gur-Yaish, N., & Campa, M. (2004). What does it mean to be attached? In W. S. Rholes & J. A. Simpson (Eds.), *Adult attachment: New directions and emerging issues* (pp. 55–85). New York: Guilford.

Hazan, C., & Shaver, P. (1987). Romantic love conceptualized as an attachment process. *Journal of Personality and Social Psychology*, *52*, 511–524.

Hazan, C., & Shaver, P. R. (1994). Attachment as an organizational framework for research on close relationships. *Psychological Inquiry*, *5*, 1–22.

Hazan, C., & Zeifman, D. (1994). Sex and the psychological tether. In K. Bartholomew & D. Perlman (Eds.), *Advances in personal relationships: Attachment processes in adulthood* (Vol. 5, pp. 151–177). London: Jessica Kingsley.

Heaton, T. B., & Albrecht, S. L. (1991). Stable unhappy marriages. *Journal of Marriage and Family*, *53*, 747–758.

Hendrick, S. S. (1988). A generic measure of relationship satisfaction. *Journal of Marriage and the Family*, *50*, 93–98.

Hirschberger, G., Srivastava, S., Marsh, P., Cowan, C. P., & Cowan, P. A. (2009). Attachment, marital satisfaction, and divorce during the first fifteen years of parenthood. *Personal Relationships*, *16*, 401–420.

Holland, A. S., Fraley, R. C., & Roisman, G. I. (2012). Attachment styles in dating couples: Predicting relationship functioning over time. *Personal Relationships*, *19*, 234–246.

Jang, S. A., Smith, S., & Levine, T. (2002). To stay or to leave? The role of attachment styles in communication patterns and potential termination of romantic relationships following discovery of deception. *Communication Monographs*, *69*, 236–252.

Jayamaha, S. D., Antonellis, C., & Overall, N. C. (2016). Attachment insecurity and inducing guilt to produce desired change in romantic partners. *Personal Relationships*, *23*, 311–338.

Jayamaha, S. D., Girme, Y. U., & Overall, N. C. (2017). When attachment anxiety impedes support provision: The role of feeling unvalued and unappreciated. *Journal of Family Psychology*, *31*, 181–191.

Julal, F. S., & Carnelley, K. B. (2012). Attachment, perceptions of care and caregiving to romantic partners and friends. *European Journal of Social Psychology*, *42*, 832–843.

Kachadourian, L. K., Fincham, F., & Davila, J. (2004). The tendency to forgive in dating and married couples: The role of attachment and relationship satisfaction. *Personal Relationships*, *11*, 373–393.

Kane, H. S., McCall, C., Collins, N. L., & Blascovich, J. (2012). Mere presence is not enough: Responsive support in a virtual world. *Journal of Experimental Social Psychology*, *48*, 37–44.

Karantzas, G. C., & Cole, S. F. (2011). Arthritis and support seeking tendencies: The role of attachment. *Journal of Social and Clinical Psychology, 30,* 404–440.

Kenrick, D. T., Neuberg, S. L., Zierk, K. L., & Krones, J. M. (1994). Evolution and social cognition: Contrast effects as a function of sex, dominance, and physical attractiveness. *Personality and Social Psychology Bulletin, 20,* 210–217.

Kirkpatrick, L. A. (1998). Evolution, pair-bonding, and reproductive strategies: A reconceptualization of adult attachment. In J. A. Simpson & W. S. Rholes (Eds.), *Attachment theory and close relationships* (pp. 353–393). New York, NY: Guilford Press.

Kohn, J. L., Rholes, S. W., Simpson, J. A., Martin III, A. M., Tran, S., & Wilson, C. L. (2012). Changes in marital satisfaction across the transition to parenthood: The role of adult attachment orientations. *Personality and Social Psychology Bulletin, 38,* 1506–1522.

Kotler, T. (1985). Security and autonomy within marriage. *Human Relations, 38,* 299–321.

Kunce, L. J., & Shaver, P. R. (1994). An attachment-theoretical approach to caregiving in romantic relationships. In K. Bartholomew & D. Perlman (Eds.), *Attachment processes in adulthood. Advances in personal relationships* (pp. 205–237). London, UK: Jessica Kingsley.

Le, B., & Agnew, C. R. (2003). Commitment and its theorized determinants: A meta-analysis of the Investment Model. *Personal Relationships, 10,* 37–57.

Le, B., Korn, M. S., Crockett, E. E., & Loving, T. J. (2011). Missing you maintains us: Missing a romantic partner, commitment, relationship maintenance, and physical infidelity. *Journal of Social and Personal Relationships, 28,* 653–667.

Lewandowski, G. W., & Ackerman, R. A. (2006). Something's missing: Need fulfillment and self-expansion as predictors of susceptibility to infidelity. *The Journal of Social Psychology, 146,* 389–403.

Locke, K. D. (2008). Attachment styles and interpersonal approach and avoidance goals in everyday couple interactions. *Personal Relationships, 15,* 359–374.

Lydon, J. E., Fitzsimons, G. M., & Naidoo, L. (2003). Devaluation versus enhancement of attractive alternatives: A critical test using the calibration paradigm. *Personality and Social Psychology Bulletin, 29,* 349–359.

MacDonald, G., Locke, K. D., Spielmann, S. S., & Joel, S. (2013). Insecure attachment predicts ambivalent social threat and reward perceptions in romantic relationships. *Journal of Social and Personal Relationships, 30,* 647–661.

Meyer, B., Olivier, L., & Roth, D. A. (2005). Please don't leave me! BIS/BAS, attachment styles, and responses to a relationship threat. *Personality and Individual Differences, 38,* 151–162.

Mikulincer, M. (1998). Attachment working models and the sense of trust: An exploration of interaction goals and affect regulation. *Journal of Personality and Social Psychology, 74,* 1209–1224.

Mikulincer, M., Florian, V., Cowan, P. A., & Cowan, C. P. (2002). Attachment security in couple relationships: A systemic model and its implications for family dynamics. *Family Process, 41,* 405–434.

Mikulincer, M., & Nachshon, O. (1991). Attachment styles and patterns of self-disclosure. *Journal of Personality and Social Psychology, 61,* 321–331.

Mikulincer, M., & Shaver, P. R. (2003). The attachment behavioral system in adulthood: Activation, psychodynamics, and interpersonal processes. In M. P. Zanna (Ed.), *Advances in experimental social psychology* (pp. 53–152). New York, NY: Academic Press.

Mikulincer, M., & Shaver, P. R. (2008). Adult attachment and affect regulation. In J. Cassidy & P. R. Shaver (Eds.), *Handbook of attachment: Theory, research, and clinical applications* (2nd ed., pp. 503–531). New York: Guilford Press.

Mikulincer, M., & Shaver, P. R. (2009). An attachment and behavioral systems perspective on social support. *Journal of Social and Personal Relationships, 26,* 7–19.

Mikulincer, M., & Shaver, P. R. (2016). *Attachment in adulthood: Structure, dynamics, and change* (2nd ed.). New York, NY: Guilford Press.

Mikulincer, M., Shaver, P. R., Bar-On, N., & Ein-Dor, T. (2010). The pushes and pulls of close relationships: Attachment insecurities and relational ambivalence. *Journal of Personality and Social Psychology, 98,* 450–468.

Mikulincer, M., Shaver, P. R., & Horesh, N. (2006). Attachment bases of emotion regulation and posttraumatic adjustment. In D. K. Snyder, J. A. Simpson, & J. N. Hughes (Eds.), *Emotion regulation in families: Pathways to dysfunction and health* (pp. 77–99). Washington, DC: American Psychological Association.

Mikulincer, M., Shaver, P. R., & Pereg, D. (2003). Attachment theory and affect regulation: The dynamics, development, and cognitive consequences of attachment-related strategies. *Motivation and Emotion, 27,* 77–102.

Miller, R. S. (2008). Attending to temptation: The operation (and perils) of attention to alternatives in close relationships. In J. P. Forgas & J. Fitness (Eds.), *Social relationships: Cognitive, affective and motivational processes* (pp. 321–337). New York: Psychology Press.

Millings, A., & Walsh, J. (2009). A dyadic exploration of attachment and caregiving in long-term couples. *Personal Relationships, 16,* 437–453.

Noller, P. (2012). Conflict in family relationships. In P. Noller & G. C. Karantzas (Eds.), *The Wiley-Blackwell handbook of couples and family relationships* (pp. 129–143). New York: Wiley-Blackwell.

Ognibene, T. C., & Collins, N. L. (1998). Adult attachment styles, perceived social support and coping strategies. *Journal of Social and Personal Relationships, 15,* 323–345.

Ogolsky, B. G., Monk, J. K., Rice, T. M., Theisen, J. C., & Maniotes, C. R. (2017). Relationship maintenance: A review of research on romantic relationships. *Journal of Family Theory & Review, 9,* 275–306.

Overall, N. C., & Sibley, C. G. (2008). Attachment and attraction toward romantic partners versus relevant alternatives within daily interactions. *Personality and Individual Differences, 44,* 1126–1137.

Perunovic, M., & Holmes, J. G. (2008). Automatic accommodation: The role of personality. *Personal Relationships, 15,* 57–70.

Pietromonaco, P. R., Greenwood, D., & Barrett, L. F. (2004). Conflict in adult close relationships: An attachment perspective. In W. S. Rholes and J. A. Simpson (Eds.), *Adult attachment: Theory, research, and clinical implications* (pp. 267–299). New York: Guilford Press.

Reis, H. T., Clark, M. S., & Holmes, J. G. (2004). Perceived partner responsiveness as an organizing construct in the study of closeness and intimacy. In D. J. Mashek & A. Aron (Eds.), *Handbook of closeness and intimacy* (pp. 201–225). Mahwah, NJ: Erlbaum.

Rholes, W. S., Kohn, J. L., & Simpson, J. A. (2014). A longitudinal study of conflict in new parents: The role of attachment. *Personal Relationships, 21,* 1–21.

Rholes, W. S., Simpson, J. A., & Blakely, B. S. (1995). Adult attachment styles and mothers' relationships with their young children. *Personal Relationships, 2,* 35–54.

Rholes, W. S., Simpson, J. A., & Orina, M. M. (1999). Attachment and anger in an anxiety-provoking situation. *Journal of Personality and Social Psychology, 76,* 940–957.

Rusbult, C. E. (1983). A longitudinal test of the investment model: The development (and deterioration) of satisfaction and commitment in heterosexual involvements. *Journal of Personality and Social Psychology, 45,* 101–117.

Rusbult, C. E., Arriaga, X. B., & Agnew, C. R. (2001). Interdependence in close relationships. In G. J. O. Fletcher & M. S. Clark (Eds.), *Blackwell handbook of social psychology, vol.2: Interpersonal processes* (pp. 359–387). Oxford: Blackwell.

Rusbult, C. E., Olsen, N., Davis, J. L., & Hannon, P. A. (2001). Commitment and relationship maintenance mechanisms. In J. Harvey & A. Wenzel (Eds.), *Close romantic relationships: Maintenance and enhancement* (pp. 87–113). Mahwah, NJ: Erlbaum.

Saavedra, M. C., Chapman, K. E., & Rogge, R. D. (2010). Clarifying links between attachment and relationship quality: Hostile conflict and mindfulness as moderators. *Journal of Family Psychology, 24,* 380–390.

Sadikaj, G., Moskowitz, D. S., & Zuroff, D. C. (2015). Felt security in daily interactions as a mediator of the effect of attachment on relationship satisfaction. *European Journal of Personality, 29,* 187–200.

Schachner, D. A., & Shaver, P. R. (2002). Attachment style and human mate poaching. *New Review of Social Psychology, 1,* 122–129.

Sbarra, D. A., & Hazan, C. (2008). Coregulation, dysregulation, self-regulation: An integrative analysis and empirical agenda for understanding adult attachment, separation, loss, and recovery. *Personality and Social Psychology Review, 12,* 141–167.

Segal, N., & Fraley, R. C. (2016). Broadening the investment model: An intensive longitudinal study on attachment and perceived partner responsiveness in commitment dynamics. *Journal of Social and Personal Relationships, 33,* 581–599.

Selcuk, E., Zayas, V., & Hazan, C. (2010). Beyond satisfaction: The role of attachment in marital functioning. *Journal of Family Theory & Review, 2,* 258–279.

Shackelford, T. K., Buss, D. M., & Bennett, K. (2002). Forgiveness or breakup: Sex differences in responses to a partner's infidelity. *Cognition & Emotion, 16,* 299–307.

Shaver, P. R., & Brennan, K. A. (1992). Attachment styles and the "Big Five" personality traits: Their connections with each other and with romantic relationship outcomes. *Personality and Social Psychology Bulletin, 18,* 536–545.

Shaver, P. R., & Mikulincer, M. (2002). Attachment-related psychodynamics. *Attachment & Human Development, 4,* 133–161.

Shaver, P. R., & Mikulincer, M. (2006). Attachment theory, individual psychodynamics, and relationship functioning. In D. Perlman & A. Vangelisti (Eds.), *The Cambridge handbook of personal relationships* (pp. 251–271). New York: Cambridge University Press.

Shaver, P. R., Schachner, D. A., & Mikulincer, M. (2005). Attachment style, excessive reassurance seeking, relationship processes, and depression. *Personality and Social Psychology Bulletin, 31,* 343–359.

Simpson, J. A. (1990). Influence of attachment styles on romantic relationships. *Journal of Personality and Social Psychology, 59,* 971–980.

Simpson, J. A., Collins, W. A., Tran, S., & Haydon, K. C. (2007). Attachment and the experience and expression of emotions in romantic relationships: A developmental perspective. *Journal of Personality and Social Psychology, 92,* 355–367.

Simpson, J. A., Kim, J. S., Fillo, J., Ickes, W., Rholes, W. S., Oriña, M. M., & Winterheld, H. A. (2011). Attachment and the management of empathic accuracy in relationship-threatening situations. *Personality and Social Psychology Bulletin, 37,* 242–254.

Simpson, J. A., Rholes, W. S., & Nelligan, J. S. (1992). Support seeking and support giving within couples in an anxiety-provoking situation: The role of attachment styles. *Journal of Personality and Social Psychology, 62,* 434–446.

Simpson, J. A., Rholes, W. S., & Phillips, D. (1996). Conflict in close relationships: An attachment perspective. *Journal of Personality and Social Psychology, 71,* 899–914.

Slotter, E. B., Finkel, E. J., DeWall, C. N., Pond Jr, R. S., Lambert, N. M., Bodenhausen, G. V., & Fincham, F. D. (2012). Putting the brakes on aggression toward a romantic partner: The inhibitory influence of relationship commitment. *Journal of Personality and Social Psychology, 102,* 291–305.

Sroufe, L. A. (1985). Attachment classification from the perspective of infant-caregiver relationships and infant temperament. *Child Development, 56,* 1–14.

Sroufe, L. A., Fox, N. E., & Pancake, V. R. (1983). Attachment and dependency in developmental perspective. *Child Development, 54,* 1615–1627.

Stafford, L., & Canary, D. J. (1991). Maintenance strategies and romantic relationship type, gender and relational characteristics. *Journal of Social and Personal Relationships, 8,* 217–242.

Tempelhof, T. C., & Allen, J. S. (2008). Partner-specific investment strategies: Similarities and differences in couples and associations with sociosexual orientation and attachment dimensions. *Personality and Individual Differences, 45,* 41–48.

Thibaut, J. W., & Kelley, H. H. (1959). *The social psychology of groups.* New York: Wiley.

Tucker, J. S., & Anders, S. L. (1998). Adult attachment style and nonverbal closeness in dating couples. *Journal of Nonverbal Behavior, 22,* 109–124.

Van Monsjou, E., Struthers, C. W., Khoury, C., Guilfoyle, J. R., Young, R., Hodara, O., & Muller, R. T. (2015). The effects of adult attachment style on post-transgression response. *Personal Relationships, 22,* 762–780.

Visserman, M. L., & Karremans, J. C. (2014). Romantic relationship status biases the processing of an attractive alternative's behavior. *Personal Relationships, 21,* 324–334.

Weigel, D. J., & Ballard-Reisch, D. S. (2008). Relational maintenance, satisfaction, and commitment in marriages: An actor-partner analysis. *Journal of Family Communication, 8,* 212–229.

Whiffen, V. E. (2005). The role of partner characteristics in attachment insecurity and depressive symptoms. *Personal Relationships, 12,* 407–423.

Zeifman, D. M., & Hazan, C. (2016). Pair bonds as attachments: Mounting evidence in support of Bowlby's hypothesis. In J. Cassidy & P. R. Shaver (Eds.), *Handbook of attachment: Theory, research, and clinical applications* (3rd ed.) (pp. 416–434). New York, NY: Guilford Press.

5

Uncertainty Perspectives on Relationship Maintenance

JENNIFER A. THEISS[1]

Close relationships constitute a vital cornerstone of people's lives and serve as an important resource for comfort, support, advice, affection, and connection. Despite the many benefits that are derived from close relationships, they are not without their fair share of challenges. In particular, coordinating expectations for behavior and establishing a shared understanding of interpersonal events can be fraught with difficulty and confusion for relationship partners. These challenges manifest as *relational uncertainty*, which reflects questions that individuals have about the nature and degree of involvement in a close relationship (Berger & Bradac, 1982; Knobloch & Solomon, 1999). When people experience uncertainty about a partner or a relationship, they struggle to create interpersonal understanding and cultivate shared meaning in the relationship. Moreover, relational uncertainty constrains people's behavioral options in relationships because it hampers the ability to identify appropriate interpersonal actions or judge the probability of particular outcomes (e.g., Berger & Gudykunst, 1991). In other words, under conditions of relational uncertainty, individuals lack a sufficient framework to guide their own behavior and correctly interpret the actions of their partner.

Relationship maintenance involves strategic efforts to enhance relationship quality, as well as routine behaviors that support day-to-day relationship functioning (Dainton & Stafford, 1993). The experience of relational uncertainty can both shape and reflect the relationship maintenance behaviors that partners enact. On the one hand, relational uncertainty can make it difficult for people to effectively process interpersonal information and produce interpersonal messages (Knobloch & Satterlee, 2009), which could make it difficult to enact and interpret relationship maintenance. On the other hand, when partners fail to enact behaviors that will maintain relationship quality and satisfaction, the interpersonal climate is likely to raise questions about relationship involvement. Core relationship maintenance strategies, such as

[1] School of Communication and Information, Rutgers University, jtheiss@comminfo.rutgers.edu

positivity, openness, assurances, giving advice, managing conflicts, sharing tasks, and enjoying social networks (e.g., Stafford & Canary, 1991; Stafford, Dainton, & Haas, 2000), are strong predictors of relationship characteristics such as commitment, love, and satisfaction (e.g., Dainton & Aylor, 2002; Stafford, 2003; Stafford & Canary, 1991). When these relationship maintenance behaviors are absent, this contributes to interpersonal conditions that are ripe for relational uncertainty. Thus, relational uncertainty can be an antecedent for relationship maintenance behaviors as well as an outcome of insufficient relationship maintenance.

Understanding how relational uncertainty and relationship maintenance are interrelated is important for anticipating the conditions in which romantic relationships are likely to decline or thrive. Although relationship maintenance behaviors tend to be associated with a variety of positive relationship outcomes (Ogolsky & Bowers, 2013), some interpersonal circumstances can undermine people's motivation to engage in the relational labor that is necessary to maintain a relationship. Ambivalence and uncertainty about a relationship may contribute to conditions in which relationship-maintenance efforts are perceived as too costly (e.g., Young, Curran, & Totenhagen, 2012). Thus, it is important to understand how relational uncertainty might shape or reflect relationship maintenance behaviors. This chapter begins with an overview of the theoretical perspectives that have explicated the sources of uncertainty in close relationships, followed by an examination of relational uncertainty as an antecedent and an outcome of relationship maintenance, and concludes with a discussion of opportunities for future research.

SOURCES OF UNCERTAINTY IN CLOSE RELATIONSHIPS

There are a variety of theoretical perspectives that focus on the experience and impact of uncertainty in close relationships. Uncertainty reduction theory was the first perspective to explore the ways in which initial interactions with a new partner are rife with questions about what to think, how to behave, and how to interpret a partner's actions (Berger & Calabrese, 1975). This theory introduced two broad forms of uncertainty in interpersonal contexts that reflect ambiguity about the cognitions or behaviors of one's self or one's partner. *Cognitive uncertainty* involves questions about how to interpret the content or meaning of interpersonal encounters (Berger, 1979). People tend to experience cognitive uncertainty when they lack sufficient knowledge, experience, or information to make sense of interpersonal events or to correctly assess a partner's attitudes, beliefs, or state of mind. Thus, cognitive uncertainty is manifest in questions about the definition, goals, or value of a close relationship (Baxter & Wilmot, 1985; Knobloch & Solomon, 1999; Sunnafrank, 1990). *Behavioral uncertainty* involves questions about what actions are expected and appropriate for an interaction or a relationship (Berger, 1979). This can involve questions about how an individual should personally behave as well as expectations of how the partner is likely to behave. In other words, behavioral uncertainty reflects ambiguity about the rules and norms for behavior in a close relationship. Taken together, cognitive uncertainty and behavioral uncertainty reflect ambiguity about the most fundamental aspects of relating; therefore, they comprise the foundation upon which broader questions about relational involvement are built.

Although cognitive and behavioral uncertainty are expected to peak during the early stages of relationship development and decline as partners increase their knowledge about each other and coordinate norms for behavior, established relationships are by no means free of ambiguity. Developing a long-term, intimate relationship simply invites new questions and different forms of uncertainty. A variety of transition points in close relationships, such as the birth of a child (e.g., Theiss, Estlein, & Weber, 2013), the diagnosis of illness (e.g., Solomon, Weber, & Steuber, 2010), and the shift to an empty nest (e.g., Nagy & Theiss, 2013), create changes to people's roles and routines that can elicit doubts about relational involvement. *Relational uncertainty* refers to the degree of confidence that people have in their perceptions of relationship involvement (Knobloch & Solomon, 1999). Rather than focusing on the cognitive or behavioral content of the uncertainty, relational sources of uncertainty focus on the locus of doubt. In particular, relational uncertainty points to self-focused, partner-focused, and relationship-focused sources of ambiguity (Berger & Bradac, 1982; Knobloch & Solomon, 1999). *Self-uncertainty* refers to a lack of confidence in one's own perceptions of relational involvement (e.g., "Am I satisfied in this relationship?"; "Is this a relationship that I want to pursue?"). Under conditions of self-uncertainty, individuals struggle to identify their own goals for the relationship as well as the attitudes and behaviors that are required to accomplish their relational goals (Berger, 1975; Berger & Bradac, 1982). *Partner uncertainty* involves a lack of confidence in one's perceptions of a partner's involvement in the relationship (e.g., "Is my partner attracted to me?"; "Is my partner committed to this relationship?"). Thus, partner uncertainty reflects other-focused sources of ambiguity in a relationship and tends to emerge when individuals have insufficient information about a partner's unique attitudes, values, expectations, and norms for behavior (Berger, 1979; Berger & Gudykunst, 1991). *Relationship uncertainty* involves a lack of confidence in people's perceptions of the relationship itself (e.g., "How do we define this relationship?"; "Where is this relationship headed?"). This type of uncertainty can include questions about norms for behavior in the relationship, mutuality of feelings between partners, the definition of the relationship, and the future of the relationship (Berger, 1988; Berger & Bradac, 1982). Relationship uncertainty exists at a broader level of abstraction and can encompass questions related to self- and partner uncertainty.

There are two schools of thought with regard to the relationship conditions that are most likely to prompt appraisals of relational uncertainty. The uncertainty reduction theory perspective suggests that uncertainty is heightened during the early stages of relationship development when partners have limited information about each other and intimacy levels are low (e.g., Berger & Calabrese, 1975). From this perspective, individuals are likely to experience increased uncertainty at the beginning of a relationship because they lack sufficient information to be able to interpret meaning in their partner's actions or to plan their own interpersonal behaviors. This perspective suggests that uncertainty should subside during later stages of relationship development as individuals gain knowledge and experience to guide their perceptions and actions. Notably, the enactment of relationship maintenance strategies during the early stages of relationship development can help to reduce uncertainty about a partner in ways that build trust and increase commitment to the relationship (Rusbult, Olsen, Davis, & Hannon, 2001).

An alternative perspective based on relational turbulence theory suggests that whereas self- and partner-focused sources of uncertainty may follow a negative linear trajectory over the course of relationship development, relationship-focused sources of uncertainty tend to follow a curvilinear trajectory, such that they peak at moderate levels of intimacy as partners transition from casual involvement to serious commitment in a relationship (e.g., Solomon & Knobloch, 2004). From this perspective, the very beginning of a relationship should correspond to limited ambiguity about the status of the relationship itself, as there is little question that the relationship is noninti-mate. Similarly, individuals in long-term, established relationships should enjoy limited amounts of relational uncertainty because the status of the relationship and feelings of commitment have been confirmed. The middle stages of relationship development, however, present countless opportunities for uncertainty as partners attempt to make sense of interpersonal involvement and anticipate their relational future. During these moments of ambiguity, proactive and constructive relationship-maintenance behaviors can promote stability in an otherwise tumultuous and chaotic relational climate (Guerrero, Eloy, & Wabnik, 1993).

Although relational uncertainty is often viewed as a global assessment of relationship functioning that fluctuates at different stages of relationship development (Afifi & Burgoon, 1998; Solomon & Knobloch, 2001), it can also emerge in response to specific events or circumstances (Afifi & Metts, 1998; Turner, 1990). *Episodic relational uncertainty* refers to the questions that are elicited in response to specific interpersonal episodes in close relationships (Knobloch & Solomon, 2002). Any number of critical turning points (Bullis, Clark, & Sline, 1993) or problematic events (Samp & Solomon, 1998) can elicit relational uncertainty that is specifically tied to that particular experience. Although the doubts that arise in these contexts still index self, partner, and relationship sources of uncertainty, they reflect concerns about the relationship in response to a specific event rather than concerns about the relationship as a whole. In addition, some scholars have argued that relational uncertainty is heightened during periods of transition in close relationships (e.g., Solomon, Knobloch, Theiss, & McLaren, 2016; Solomon & Theiss, 2011). External factors can create transitions in close relationships, such as the diagnosis of illness, the start of a new job, or the transition to parenthood, that can bring about changes to interpersonal roles and routines and invite questions about how individual partners and the relationship should evolve or adapt to new circumstances. Relationship maintenance can be especially difficult in the context of highly uncertain relationship transitions, because partners struggle to know what actions might be most appropriate for their new relational roles or most effective for promoting new interpersonal routines during these tumultuous times (e.g., Theiss & Weber, 2016).

As this review demonstrates, uncertainty can manifest in different forms and is prompted by a variety of circumstances in close relationships. Uncertainty can reflect broad forms of ambiguity about what to think or how to act, as well as specific questions about the nature, quality, or desirability of relational involvement. In addition, uncertainty can be experienced as a global, diffuse appraisal of relationship conditions, or it can arise in response to specific events, episodes, or transitions. The literature on relational uncertainty demonstrates that it is associated with a variety of deleterious cognitive, emotional, and behavioral outcomes in close relationships. Relationship maintenance involves behavioral action to sustain the relationship as well as cognitive appraisals of a partner's efforts to bolster relationship functioning; thus, it is likely to share unique associations with relational uncertainty as both an antecedent and an outcome of ambiguous relational circumstances.

RELATIONAL UNCERTAINTY AS AN ANTECEDENT OF RELATIONSHIP MAINTENANCE

Relational uncertainty is assumed to be most strongly implicated in people's subjective experiences of their close relationships (Solomon et al., 2016). Individuals experiencing relational uncertainty lack insight about the nature of their relationship, which makes it difficult to process and comprehend the relational meaning of interpersonal events (e.g., Berger & Calabrese, 1975; Knobloch & Satterlee, 2009). Without clear parameters for making sense of relational information, individuals turn to heuristic cues to understand interpersonal situations (Pronin, Gilovich, & Ross, 2004) and tend to make more biased attributions to explain their own and their partner's behaviors and motivations (Kruger & Gilovich, 2004). Under these conditions, individuals may struggle to identify and enact relationship maintenance strategies that would be most effective for enhancing their relationship, and they are less likely to recognize the efforts their partner is making to maintain or improve the relationship. This logic is formalized within the relational turbulence theory, which positions relational uncertainty as a mechanism that can foster turmoil and upheaval in relationships. In this section, I describe the role of relational uncertainty in the relational turbulence theory and I summarize empirical evidence pointing to diminished relationship maintenance behaviors as a marker of relational turbulence.

RELATIONAL UNCERTAINTY AS A MECHANISM OF RELATIONAL TURBULENCE

The relational turbulence theory offers a framework for understanding the impacts of relational uncertainty in close relationships (Solomon et al., 2016). Relational turbulence theory argues that people are more reactive to otherwise mundane events during relationship transitions due to emerging questions about relationship involvement and disrupted patterns of interdependence (Solomon & Knobloch, 2004; Solomon et al., 2016). Thus, the theory points to relational uncertainty and interdependence processes as two relationship characteristics that are particularly salient during times of transition and increase reactivity to relationship events. Drawing on Knobloch and Satterlee's (2009) analysis, relational turbulence theory argues that relational uncertainty compromises relationship functioning because individuals lack a clear conceptual framework to make sense of relationship events under these conditions (Solomon et al., 2016). Relational uncertainty compromises interpersonal communication due to a shortage of information and contextual cues that are necessary to accurately interpret a partner's behavior or correctly derive meaning from their messages. Consequently, making sense of a partner's behavior and relationship events is compromised under conditions of relational uncertainty because cognitive appraisals tend to be more biased when information is limited.

The second relationship parameter that is implicated in experiences of relational turbulence is interdependence. Drawing on Berscheid's (1983) logic, the theory argues that people allow different levels of influence from a romantic partner as they navigate relationship transitions (Solomon & Knobloch, 2001; 2004; Solomon et al., 2016). As partners exercise greater influence in each other's daily routines, opportunities exist for a partner to disrupt personal goals (Knobloch & Solomon, 2004). *Interference from a partner* refers to the extent to which a partner prevents desired outcomes or makes activities more difficult. Whereas relational uncertainty undermines cognitive appraisals, the theory argues that a partner's interference predicts the intensity of emotional responses to relationship events (Berscheid, 1983; Solomon & Knobloch, 2004; Solomon et al., 2016). Taken together, relational uncertainty and interference from partners are expected to intensify partners' cognitive and emotional reactivity to interpersonal events, which results in polarized communication behaviors (Solomon et al., 2016).

As relationship partners accumulate interpersonal episodes that are characterized by biased cognitions, intensified emotions, and polarized communication behaviors, these experiences coalesce into perceptions that the relationship is turbulent (Solomon et al., 2016). The theory defines *relational turbulence* as a global, diffuse, and persistent appraisal of the relationship as tumultuous, chaotic, and unstable that reflects the cumulative effect of specific interpersonal episodes over time. As relationship partners navigate repeated encounters that are marked by amplified emotions, cognitions, and communication, they reach a breaking point where the stress and exhaustion associated with these dynamics contribute to a more fragile relational system. Relational turbulence can also shape the ways in which partners relate to one another and engage with their social environment; thus, the theory asserts that relational turbulence has a pervasive impact on individual and relational social functioning. Accordingly, the theory highlights a variety of dyadic processes that are undermined under conditions of relational turbulence, including collaborative planning, communicating support, drawing relational inferences, and engaging with social networks (Solomon et al., 2016). Relationship maintenance behaviors represent another dyadic process in close relationships that are affected by the conditions of relational turbulence.

RELATIONSHIP MAINTENANCE AS A FORM OF RELATIONAL TURBULENCE

Drawing on the logic of relational turbulence theory, the absence of relationship-maintenance behaviors is a potential marker of relational turbulence that is shaped by experiences of relational uncertainty. When individuals are unsure about their own desire for the relationship, they are unlikely to expend much effort to maintain a relationship toward which they feel ambivalent. Similarly, when individuals question their partner's involvement in the relationship, engaging in behaviors designed to maintain or bolster the relationship could be perceived as face-threatening because they present opportunities for rejection, embarrassment, and inequity. In addition, when the long-term viability of a relationship is in question, engaging in relationship-maintenance behaviors could be a wasted investment in a partnership that has no longevity. Thus, self-, partner, and relationship uncertainty can be barriers to effective relationship maintenance.

A variety of studies have documented negative associations between relational uncertainty and relationship maintenance in romantic relationships and friendships. A pair of studies on cross-sex friendships in which partners had differing levels of romantic interest revealed negative associations between relational uncertainty and a variety of common relationship maintenance behaviors, such as relationship talk, conversations about outside romance, routine contact and activity, social networking, instrumental support, and humor or gossip (Guerrero & Chavez, 2005; Weger & Emmett, 2009). Research on romantic relationships has also indicated that relationship-maintenance behaviors decline under conditions of relational uncertainty. Multiple studies of dating relationships have found negative associations between relational uncertainty and the five core relationship maintenance strategies identified by Stafford and Canary (1991), including assurances, positivity, openness, sharing tasks, and social networks (Dainton, 2003; Dainton & Aylor, 2001). In addition, a study of relational turbulence among military couples following deployment found that relational uncertainty was negatively associated with assurances, openness, and conflict management (Theiss & Knobloch, 2014). Thus, there is considerable empirical evidence suggesting that relational uncertainty corresponds with a decline in relationship-maintenance behaviors.

A handful of studies have further probed these associations to explore the complexity of the relationship between uncertainty and maintenance. For example, the study of military couples by Theiss and Knobloch (2014) examined the potential mediated and moderated effects among relationship satisfaction, relational uncertainty, and relationship maintenance behaviors. The results of the mediation analysis revealed that self-uncertainty fully mediated associations between relationship satisfaction and relationship maintenance behaviors. In addition, relationship satisfaction moderated associations between the sources of relational uncertainty and relationship maintenance, such that the negative association between relational uncertainty and maintenance behaviors was strongest at high levels of relationship satisfaction. This finding suggests that highly satisfied couples might be particularly troubled by the experience of relational uncertainty. Whereas dissatisfied individuals may be less bothered by relational uncertainty because it is a normative and familiar aspect of dyadic functioning, highly satisfied individuals are unaccustomed to coping with tumultuous conditions in their relationship, which might intensify their reactions to atypical interpersonal circumstances. Similarly, a longitudinal, dyadic study of romantic relationships examined the moderating effect of relational uncertainty on the association between working to improve the relationship and relational quality (Young et al., 2012). The results of this study indicated that relational uncertainty mitigated the positive effects of relationship maintenance on relational quality, such that the positive association was stronger on days when individuals reported low relational uncertainty and weaker on days when they reported high relational uncertainty. Taken together, these studies reveal a complex web of associations between relational uncertainty, efforts to improve or maintain a relationship, and perceptions of relational quality.

Research has also examined interdependence between partners' experiences of relational uncertainty and relationship maintenance. For example, a dyadic study of couples during the transition to parenthood revealed actor and partner effects, such that the actor's relational uncertainty was negatively associated with assurances, openness, conflict management, and shared activity, whereas the partner's relational uncertainty was negatively associated with assurances and openness (Theiss & Weber, 2016). In other words, not only do individuals engage in less relationship maintenance when encountering their own ambiguity about the relationship, but they also do less to maintain the relationship when their partner is experiencing relational uncertainty. Notably, the direction of these partner effects is unclear. Is it the case that individuals grow uncertain about the relationship when their partner fails to enact maintenance behaviors, or do people do less to maintain their relationship when they sense that a partner is unsure about relational involvement? Additional research is needed to tease out the nature of this interdependence between partners.

An interesting body of work has also considered the associations between relational uncertainty and *negative relationship maintenance*, which refers to the undesirable, inappropriate, or invasive strategies that people might use in an effort to maintain a desired relationship (Dainton & Gross, 2008). Negative relationship-maintenance strategies can include attempts to induce jealousy, avoidance of undesirable or sensitive topics, spying or monitoring a partner's activities, engaging in infidelity to prevent boredom, instigating arguments or destructive conflicts, and allowing a partner to have control over individual decisions and activities. Relational uncertainty tends to increase the likelihood that individuals will engage in negative relationship maintenance behaviors. Prior research has revealed positive associations between relational uncertainty and jealousy induction (Pytlak, Zerega, & Houser, 2015), partner surveillance (Stewart, Dainton, & Goodboy, 2014), and topic avoidance (Knobloch & Theiss, 2011). A dyadic study of negative relationship maintenance found that relationship uncertainty, specifically, was positively associated with all of the negative maintenance strategies (Dainton, Goodboy, Borzea, & Goldman, 2017). In addition, there was an interaction between actors' and partners' relationship uncertainty, such that when both partners had low levels of uncertainty they were less likely to use negative relationship maintenance strategies; however, when actors had high levels of uncertainty they were more likely to use negative relationship-maintenance strategies regardless of the partner's level of uncertainty (Dainton et al., 2017). Thus, relational uncertainty is positively associated with negative maintenance behaviors and negatively associated with positive maintenance behaviors. Questions remain about the causal direction of these effects, but the most likely explanation is that relational uncertainty and relationship maintenance share a reciprocal influence over time.

RELATIONAL UNCERTAINTY AS AN OUTCOME OF RELATIONSHIP MAINTENANCE

Although negative associations between relational uncertainty and relationship maintenance are well documented in the literature on personal relationships, the predominantly cross-sectional nature of this research makes it difficult to discern the direction of those effects. On the one hand, theory and research from a relational uncertainty perspective would argue that ambiguity and ambivalence about relationship involvement diminish people's motivation and desire to invest in the relationship (e.g., Guerrero & Chavez, 2005; Theiss & Knobloch, 2014; Theiss & Weber, 2016). On the other hand, theory and research from a relationship maintenance perspective suggest that relationship maintenance behaviors can improve relationship quality and resolve questions about involvement (e.g., Dainton & Aylor, 2001; Stafford et al., 2000). Although discerning the direction of effects between relationship maintenance and relational quality can be complex, considerable evidence suggests that they share a reciprocal influence that is complicated by factors such as relationship length, stage of relationship development, and levels of commitment and investment (e.g., Monk, Vennum, Ogolsky, & Fincham, 2014; Ogolsky, 2009). Thus, relationship-maintenance behaviors can both reflect the condition of the relationship and shape the relational climate (e.g., Canary & Zelley, 2000).

Research on the positive effects of maintenance behaviors points to improved relational quality when partners enact behaviors to sustain, enhance, or repair the relationship. Strategic relationship maintenance behaviors, or the actions that are performed intentionally to improve a relationship (Dainton & Stafford, 1993; Dindia, 1994), can be especially important for relationship repair following interpersonal conflict or transgressions (e.g., Canary & Dainton, 2006; Emmers & Canary, 1996). In contrast, some scholars have argued that the mundane interpersonal behaviors of everyday life between partners are where the true sustenance of relationships happens (e.g., Dainton & Stafford, 1993; Duck, 1994; Stafford et al., 2000). Multiple studies have linked both strategic and routine relationship maintenance with positive relational outcomes, including increased relationship satisfaction (e.g., Dindia & Canary, 1993; Stafford, 2016; Stafford & Canary, 1991) and commitment (e.g., Canary & Stafford, 1992; Dainton & Aylor, 2002; Ogolsky, 2009), although there is some evidence that routine maintenance has a stronger effect on these global relationship qualities (e.g., Dainton & Aylor, 2002). Ogolsky and Bowers (2013) conducted a meta-analysis of the correlates of relationship maintenance and found positive associations with satisfaction, commitment, love, liking, and the mutuality of control between partners. Thus, the literature is fairly robust in documenting the positive relational outcomes of relationship maintenance.

When individuals engage in relationship maintenance, they enact pro-social interpersonal behaviors that signal to one's self and to one's partner an interest and investment in the future of the relationship (Dindia & Canary, 1993), which can help to resolve uncertainty about relationship involvement. Just as relationship maintenance increases feelings of satisfaction, commitment, and love in the relationship, it can also reduce questions and ambiguity that individuals might have about their own or their partner's investment in the relationship. In addition, engaging in relationship maintenance can help to clarify the rules and norms for behavior in a relationship, which often contribute to misunderstanding, confusion, and uncertainty between partners. On the other hand, failing to engage in behaviors that sustain the relationship can increase uncertainty or ambivalence about the relationship, particularly when one's partner neglects relationship maintenance. Engaging in relationship maintenance can be interpreted as a sign of investment in the quality and longevity of the relationship. Along these lines, Canary and Stafford (1992) found that both husbands' and wives' definitions of relational equity were associated with perceptions of their partner's maintenance behaviors, and that individuals who felt underbenefitted in their relationship were less likely to enact relationship maintenance behaviors than those who felt equal or overbenefitted. In other words, failure to maintain the relationship can result in perceptions of inequity, dissatisfaction, and reduced commitment, which are likely to raise renewed questions about relationship involvement.

Notably, the assumptions of relational turbulence theory also account for the reciprocal effects that turbulent interpersonal episodes can have on the broader relationship conditions that originally gave rise to tumult (Solomon et al., 2016). Interpersonal encounters marked by volatility, reactivity, and turbulence can increase doubts about relational involvement and norms for behavior. In addition, negative relationship maintenance behaviors that are enacted under these conditions are likely to exacerbate relationship tensions (Dainton & Gross, 2008). On the other hand, partners who take action to address and resolve relational turbulence tend to enjoy decreased relational uncertainty and increased efficacy in their ability to maintain the relationship through tumultuous circumstances. Longitudinal research employing the relational turbulence framework has found that engaging in open communication about relational uncertainty (Theiss & Solomon, 2008) and jealousy (Theiss & Solomon, 2006) can decrease subsequent uncertainty and increase relational intimacy. In addition, engaging in relationship talk, which involves open communication about the nature and status of a relationship, can also decrease subsequent relational uncertainty, whereas avoiding relationship talk increases subsequent relational uncertainty (Knobloch & Theiss, 2011). Thus, positive relationship maintenance behaviors such as openness and assurances are likely to reduce relational uncertainty, whereas negative relational maintenance strategies such as avoidance may result in increased relational uncertainty.

OPPORTUNITIES FOR FUTURE RESEARCH

As research on relational uncertainty and relationship maintenance continues to evolve, scholars have the potential to move this literature forward on a few fronts. One question that requires further exploration involves the direction of the associations between relational uncertainty and relationship maintenance. Although some research has started to document the causal direction of these effects (e.g., Monk et al., 2014; Ogolsky, 2009), additional longitudinal research is needed to confirm how maintenance behaviors can both shape and reflect relationship characteristics. Beyond addressing the simple question of causality, longitudinal studies would also enable researchers to examine how patterns of relational uncertainty and relationship maintenance unfold over time. As argued by relational turbulence theory, periods of transition in close relationships are prone to polarized reactions to interpersonal events, which give rise to a climate of relational turbulence that undermines dyadic functioning (Solomon et al., 2016). Some studies have documented a decline in relationship maintenance behaviors as a marker of turbulent transitions (e.g., Theiss & Knobloch, 2014; Theiss & Weber, 2016), but additional research is needed to explore the ways that routine maintenance behaviors might be compromised under conditions of relational turbulence.

A second avenue for future research involves exploration of the interdependence that exists between partners' relational uncertainty and relationship maintenance behaviors. Along these lines, one important question that deserves scrutiny is the degree of equity in partners' relationship maintenance efforts and how relational uncertainty might be associated with disruptions in the equanimity of maintenance behaviors. Do both partners enact similar levels of relationship maintenance? How might relational uncertainty be an antecedent condition or a relational consequence of unbalanced relationship maintenance efforts? Another interesting question related to dyadic interdependence in this context might focus on the degree of accuracy in people's perceptions of and attributions for a partner's maintenance behaviors. Do individuals recognize all their partner's actions that serve to maintain the relationship, particularly those actions and behaviors that are performed as part of routine relationship maintenance? When relationship maintenance behaviors are perceived, what motives do individuals ascribe to their partner's actions? And how might relational uncertainty both shape and reflect the attributions that people make for their partner's relationship maintenance behaviors? Future research should employ dyadic data analysis to document the accuracy of people's perceptions and the equity in partners' actions with regard to relationship maintenance behaviors.

CONCLUSION

As this chapter illustrates, relational uncertainty can be both an antecedent and an outcome of relationship maintenance behaviors. On the one hand, experiencing ambiguity or uncertainty about a relationship can dampen people's motivation or desire to invest the effort that may be required to effectively sustain the relationship. On the other hand, enacting relationship maintenance behaviors can have a positive effect on a relationship, resulting in increased satisfaction and commitment and decreased relational uncertainty. This creates a bit of a paradox for relationship partners: when individuals are experiencing relational uncertainty they lack the motivation and ability to enact effective relationship maintenance behaviors, yet active relationship maintenance is needed to reduce relational uncertainty and improve relationship quality. These circumstances create the potential for a downward spiral in close relationships, where people who are unsure about relational involvement do less to invest in the relationship, thereby making them less satisfied and even more uncertain about the desirability or viability of the relationship over time. In contrast, individuals who make a concerted effort to enact behaviors that sustain and enhance their relationship may enjoy an upward spiral, such that relationship maintenance increases confidence in relational involvement and encourages more prosocial actions. Thus, managing the complex dynamics between relational uncertainty and relationship maintenance may require partners to make investments in their relationship, even if they are unsure about the eventual outcome of those efforts.

REFERENCES

Afifi, W. A., & Burgoon, J. K. (1998). "We never talk about that": A comparison of cross-sex friendships and dating relationships on uncertainty and topic avoidance. *Personal Relationships, 5*, 255–272. doi:10.1111/j.1475-6811.1998.tb00171.x

Afifi, W. A., & Metts, S. (1998). Characteristics and consequences of expectation violations in close relationships. *Journal of Social and Personal Relationships, 15*, 365–393. doi:10.1177/0265407598153004

Baxter, L. A., & Wilmot, W. W. (1985). Taboo topics in close relationships. *Journal of Social and Personal Relationships, 2*, 253–269. doi:10.1177/0265407585023002

Berger, C. R. (1975). Proactive and retroactive attribution processes in interpersonal communications. *Human Communication Research, 2*, 33–50. doi:10.1111/j.1468-2958.1975.tb00467.x

Berger, C. R. (1979). Beyond initial interaction: Uncertainty, understanding, and the development of interpersonal relationships. In H. Giles & R. St. Clair (Eds.), *Language and social psychology* (pp. 122–144). Baltimore, MD: University Park Press.

Berger, C. R. (1988). Uncertainty and information exchange in developing relationships. In S. Duck (Ed.), *Handbook of personal relationships* (pp. 239–256). Chichester, UK: Wiley.

Berger, C. R., & Bradac, J. J. (1982). *Language and social knowledge: Uncertainty in interpersonal relationships*. London: Edward Arnold.

Berger, C. R., & Calabrese, R. J. (1975). Some exploration in initial interaction and beyond: Toward a developmental theory of communication. *Human Communication Research*, *1*, 99–112. doi:10.1111/j.1468-2958.1975.tb00258.x

Berger, C. R., & Gudykunst, W. B. (1991). Uncertainty and communication. In B. Dervin and M. J. Voight (Eds.), *Progress in communication sciences, volume 10* (pp. 21–66). Norwood, NJ: Ablex.

Berscheid, E. (1983). Emotion. In H. H. Kelley, E. Berscheid, A. Christensen, J. H. Harvey, T. L. Huston, G. Levinger, . . . D. R. Peterson (Eds.), *Close relationships* (pp. 110–168). New York, NY: Freeman.

Bullis, C., Clark, C., & Sline, R. (1993). From passion to commitment: Turning points in romantic relationships. In P. Kalbfleisch (Ed.), *Interpersonal communication: Evolving interpersonal relationships* (pp. 213–236). Hillsdale, NJ: Erlbaum.

Canary, D. J., & Dainton, M. A. (2006). Maintaining and repairing personal relationships. In A. L. Vangelisti & D. Perlman (Eds.), *The Cambridge handbook of personal relationships* (pp. 727–745). Cambridge, UK: Cambridge University Press.

Canary, D., & Stafford, L. (1992). Relationship maintenance strategies and equity in marriage. *Communication Monographs*, *59*, 243–267. doi:10.1080/03637759209376268

Canary, D. J., & Zelley, E. D. (2000). Current research programs on relational maintenance behaviors. *Communication Yearbook*, *23*, 305–339. doi:10.1080/23808985.2000.11678976

Dainton, M. (2003). Equity and uncertainty in relational maintenance. *Western Journal of Communication*, *67*, 164–186. doi:10.1080/10570310309374765

Dainton, M., & Aylor, B. (2001). A relational uncertainty analysis of jealousy, trust, and the maintenance of long-distance versus geographically-close relationships. *Communication Quarterly*, *49*, 172–188. doi:10.1080/01463370109385624

Dainton, M., & Aylor, B. A. (2002). Routine and strategic maintenance efforts: Behavioral patterns, variations associated with relational length, and the prediction of relational characteristics. *Communication Monographs*, *69*, 52–66. doi:10.1080/03637750216533

Dainton, M., Goodboy, A. K., Borzea, D., & Goldman, Z. W. (2017). The dyadic effects of relationship uncertainty on negative relational maintenance. *Communication Reports*, *30*, 170–181. doi:10.1080/08934215.2017.1282529

Dainton, M., & Gross, J. (2008). The use of negative behaviors to maintain relationships. *Communication Research Reports*, *25*, 179–191. doi:10.1080/08824090802237600

Dainton, M., & Stafford, L. (1993). Routine maintenance behaviors: A comparison of relationship type, partner similarity and sex differences. *Journal of Social and Personal Relationships*, *10*, 255–271. doi:10.1177/026540759301000206

Dindia, K. (1994). A multiphasic view of relationship maintenance strategies. In D. J. Canary & L. Stafford (Eds.), *Communication and relational maintenance* (pp. 91–114). New York: Academic Press.

Dindia, K., & Canary, D. J. (1993). Definitions and theoretical perspectives on maintaining relationships. *Journal of Social and Personal Relationships*, *10*, 163–173. doi:10.1177/026540759301000201

Duck, S. W. (1994). Steady as (s)he goes: Relational maintenance as a shared meaning system. In D. J. Canary & L. Stafford (Eds.), *Communication and relational maintenance* (pp. 45–60). New York: Academic Press.

Emmers, T., & Canary, D. J. (1996). The effect of uncertainty reducing strategies on young couples' relational repair and intimacy. *Communication Quarterly, 44,* 166–182. doi:10.1080/01463379609370008

Guerrero, L. K., & Chavez, A. M. (2005). Relational maintenance in cross-sex friendships characterized by different types of romantic intent: An exploratory study. *Western Journal of Communication, 69,* 339–358. doi:10.1080/10570310500305471

Guerrero, L. K., Eloy, S. V., & Wabnik, A. I. (1993). Linking maintenance strategies to relationship development and disengagement: A reconceptualization. *Journal of Social and Personal Relationships, 10,* 273–283. doi:10.1177/026540759301000207

Knobloch, L. K., & Satterlee, K. L. (2009). Relational uncertainty: Theory and application. In T. D. Afifi & W. A. Afifi (Eds.), *Uncertainty, information management, and disclosure decisions: Theories and applications* (pp. 106–127). New York, NY: Routledge.

Knobloch, L. K., & Solomon, D. H. (1999). Measuring the sources and content of relational uncertainty. *Communication Studies, 50,* 261–278. doi:10.1080/10510979909388499

Knobloch, L. K., & Solomon, D. H. (2002). Intimacy and the magnitude and experience of episodic relational uncertainty within romantic relationships. *Personal Relationships, 9,* 457–478. doi:10.1111/1475-6811.09406

Knobloch, L. K., & Solomon, D. H. (2004). Interference and facilitation from partners in the development of interdependence within romantic relationships. *Personal Relationships, 11,* 115–130. doi:10.1111/j.1475-6811.2004.00074.x

Knobloch, L. K., & Theiss, J. A. (2011). Relational uncertainty and relationship talk within courtship: A longitudinal actor-partner interdependence model. *Communication Monographs, 78,* 3–26. doi:10.1080/03637751.2010.542471

Kruger, J., & Gilovich, T. (2004). Actions, intentions, and self-assessment: The road to self-assessment is paved with good intentions. *Personality and Social Psychology Bulletin, 30,* 328–339. doi:10.1177/0146167203259932

Monk, J. K., Vennum, A. V., Ogolsky, B. G., & Fincham, F. D. (2014). Commitment and sacrifice in emerging adult romantic relationships. *Marriage and Family Review, 50,* 416–434. doi:10.1080/01494929.2014.896304

Nagy, M. E., & Theiss, J. A. (2013). Applying the relational turbulence model to the empty nest transition: Sources of relationship change, relational uncertainty, and interference from partners. *Journal of Family Communication, 13,* 280–300. doi:10.1080/15267431.2013.823430

Ogolsky, B. (2009). Deconstructing the association between relationship maintenance and commitment: Testing two competing models. *Personal Relationships, 16,* 99–115. doi:10.1111/j.1475-6811.2009.01212.x

Ogolsky, B. G., & Bowers, J. R. (2013). A meta-analytic review of relationship maintenance and its correlates. *Journal of Social and Personal Relationships, 30,* 343–367. doi:10.1177/0265407512463338

Pronin, E., Gilovich, T., & Ross, L. (2004). Objectivity in the eye of the beholder: Divergent perceptions of bias in self versus others. *Psychological Review, 111,* 781–799. doi:10.1037/0033-295X.111.3.781

Pytlak, M. A., Zerega, L. M., & Houser, M. L. (2015). Jealousy evocation: Understanding commitment, satisfaction, and uncertainty as predictors of jealousy-evoking behaviors. *Communication Quarterly, 63,* 310–328. doi:10.1080/01463373.2015.1039716

Rusbult, C. E., Olsen, N., Davis, J. L., & Hannon, P. A. (2001). Commitment and relationship maintenance mechanisms. In J. Harvey & A. Wenzel (Eds.), *Close relationships: Maintenance and enhancement* (pp. 87–114). Mahwah, NJ: Erlbaum.

Samp, J. A., & Solomon, D. H. (1998). Communicative responses to problematic events in close relationships I: The variety and facets of goals. *Communication Research*, 25, 66–95. doi:10.1177/009365098025001003

Solomon, D. H., & Knobloch, L. K. (2001). Relationship uncertainty, partner interference, and intimacy within dating relationships. *Journal of Social and Personal Relationships*, 18, 804–820. doi:10.1177/0265407501186004

Solomon, D. H., & Knobloch, L. K. (2004). A model of relational turbulence: The role of intimacy, relational uncertainty, and interference from partners in appraisals of irritations. *Journal of Social and Personal Relationships*, 21, 795–816. doi:10.1177/0265407504047838

Solomon, D. H., Knobloch, L. K., Theiss, J. A., & McLaren, R.M. (2016). Relational turbulence theory: Explaining variation in subjective experiences and communication within romantic relationships. *Human Communication Research*, 42, 507–532. doi:10.1111/hcre.12091

Solomon, D. H., & Theiss, J. A. (2011). Relational turbulence: What doesn't kill us makes us stronger. In W. R. Cupach & B. H. Spitzberg (Eds.), *The dark side of close relationships II* (pp. 197–216). New York, NY: Routledge.

Solomon, D. H., Weber, K. M., & Steuber, K. R. (2010). Turbulence in relationship transitions. In S. W. Smith & S. R. Wilson (Eds.), *New directions in interpersonal communication research* (pp. 115–134). Thousand Oaks, CA: Sage. doi:10.4135/9781483349619.n6

Stafford, L. (2003). Maintaining romantic relationships: Summary and analysis of one research program. In D. J. Canary & M. Dainton (Eds.), *Maintaining relationships through communication: Relational, contextual, and cultural variations* (pp. 51–78). Hillsdale, NJ: Lawrence Erlbaum.

Stafford, L. (2016). Marital sanctity, relationship maintenance, and marital quality. *Journal of Family Issues*, 37, 119–131. doi:10.1177/0192513X13515884

Stafford L., & Canary, D. J. (1991). Maintenance strategies and romantic relationship type, gender, and relational characteristics. *Journal of Social and Personal Relationships*, 8, 217–242. doi:10.1177/0265407591082004

Stafford, L., Dainton, M., & Haas, S. (2000). Measuring routine and strategic relational maintenance: Scale development, sex versus gender roles, and the prediction of relational characteristics. *Communication Monographs*, 67, 306–323. doi:10.1080/03637750009376512

Stewart, M. C., Dainton, M., & Goodboy, A. K. (2014). Maintaining relationships on Facebook: Associations with uncertainty, jealousy, and satisfaction. *Communication Reports*, 27, 13–26. doi:10.1080/08934215.2013.845675

Sunnafrank, M. (1990). Predicted outcome value and uncertainty reduction theories: A test of competing perspectives. *Human Communication Research*, 17, 76–103. doi:10.1111/j.1468-2958.1990.tb00227.x

Theiss, J. A., Estlein, R., & Weber, K. M. (2013). A longitudinal assessment of relationship characteristics that predict new parents' relationship satisfaction. *Personal Relationships*, 20, 216–235. doi:10.1111/j.1475-6811.2012.01406.x

Theiss, J. A., & Knobloch, L. K. (2014). Relational turbulence during the post-deployment transition: Self, partner, and relationship focused turbulence. *Communication Research*, 41, 27–51. doi:10.1177/0093650211429285

Theiss, J. A., & Solomon, D. H. (2006). Coupling longitudinal data and hierarchical linear modeling to examine the antecedents and consequences of jealousy experiences in romantic relationships: A test of the relational turbulence model. *Human Communication Research*, 32, 469–503. doi:10.1111/j.1468-2958.2006.00284.x

Theiss, J. A., & Solomon, D. H. (2008). Parsing the mechanisms that increase relational intimacy: The effects of uncertainty amount, open communication about uncertainty, and the reduction of uncertainty. *Human Communication Research, 34*, 625–654. doi:10.1111/j.1468-2958.2008.00335.x

Theiss, J. A., & Weber, K. M. (2016, November). *Antecedents and outcomes of relationship maintenance behaviors during the transition to parenthood.* A paper presented at the meeting of the National Communication Association, Philadelphia, PA.

Turner, L. H. (1990). The relationship between communication and marital uncertainty: Is "her" marriage different from "his" marriage? *Women's Studies in Communication, 13*, 57–83. doi:10.1080/07491409.1990.11089746

Weger, H., & Emmett, M. C. (2009). Romantic intent, relationship uncertainty, and relationship maintenance in young adults' cross-sex friendships. *Journal of Social and Personal Relationships, 26*, 964–988. doi:10.1177/0265407509347937

Young, V., Curran, M., & Totenhagen, C. (2012). A daily diary study: Working to change the relationship and relational uncertainty in understanding positive relationship quality. *Journal of Social and Personal Relationships, 30*, 132–148. doi:10.1177/0265407512453826

6

The Self-Expansion Model and Relationship Maintenance

XIAOMENG XU[1], GARY LEWANDOWSKI JR.[2], AND ARTHUR ARON[3]

This chapter focuses on the self-expansion model and relationship maintenance. There are many ways to conceptualize maintenance, but for the purposes of this chapter, we define maintenance broadly as keeping relationships in good repair and/or in a satisfactory state. This broad conceptualization of maintenance includes enhancement strategies (e.g., trying to maximize satisfaction) as well as more preventative strategies (e.g., trying to reduce boredom or stop the relationship from getting into a rut).

This chapter begins with a brief overview of the self-expansion model, including a review of some foundational research as well as newer developments in the field. Following this introduction, we review research findings that self-expansion positively influences relationship maintenance and discuss how this effect occurs. Next, we delve into individual self-expansion and its implications for relationship maintenance. Finally, we end with a summary and discussion of potential future directions for better understanding self-expansion and relationship maintenance.

THE SELF-EXPANSION MODEL

Researchers have used the term "self-expansion" in various ways, referring to the theoretical model, to the motivational principle of the model (the motivation to expand one's sense of self or to grow as a person), and the act of engaging in activities that are self-expanding (novel, exciting, interesting, and/or challenging, which increases one's self-concept). For this chapter, we note when we are referring to the model itself, the motivational principle, and/or self-expanding experiences. In this section, we elucidate the basic model of self-expansion, the foundation of the applications we will be discussing,

[1] Department of Psychology, Idaho State University, xuxiao@isu.edu
[2] Department of Psychology, Monmouth University, glewando@monmouth.edu
[3] Department of Psychology, Stony Brook University, Arthur.aron@stonybrook.edu

including briefly reviewing some of the basic research support and noting emerging directions, all emphasizing the aspects most relevant to relationship maintenance.

The Model

The self-expansion model (Aron & Aron, 1986; for reviews, see Aron, Aron, & Norman, 2001 and Aron, Lewandowski, Mashek, & Aron, 2013) was developed to address theoretical and applied questions about basic processes underlying experiences and behaviors in the context of close relationships (and since, extended to other contexts). The model has two key principles:

1. **Motivational principle:** People seek to expand their potential efficacy to increase their ability to accomplish goals. That is, a fundamental human motive is posited to be what other scholars have previously described as exploration, effectance, self-improvement, curiosity, competence, or a broadening of one's perspective. Further, given the importance of this motivation, experiencing novelty, interest, and/or challenge (or even experiences typically associated with rapid expansion, such as exciting experiences involving novelty) should be particularly rewarding.

2. **Inclusion-of-other-in-the-self principle:** One way in which people seek to expand the self is through close relationships, because in a close relationship the other's resources, perspectives, and identities are experienced, to some extent, as one's own.

Each of these basic principles has had considerable research support; a thorough review of this evidence can be found in Aron et al. (2013). As the focus of the present chapter is on application to relationship maintenance, we will only briefly review a few example studies that provide support for each of these principles in the context of relationships.

Evidence of Self-Expansion

Implications of the self-expansion model have been tested in a wide variety of relationship contexts. In terms of initial interpersonal attraction (see Aron & Lewandowski, 2002), almost any relationship is likely to provide some degree of self-expansion. When relationship formation is uncertain, consistent with the standard similarity-attraction effect, the self-expansion model suggests that perceived similarity is most desirable (because similarity serves as an indication that a relationship – and thus expansion of the self by including the other in the self – is likely to develop). However, the self-expansion model also suggests that when relationship development is more certain, differences can be particularly desirable. For example, a relationship with a person who has different interests offers even greater opportunities for expansion through including that person in the self. Aron, Steele, Kashdan, and Perez (2006) tested this possibility in the context of same-sex friendships and perceived similarities/differences in interests. As predicted, when the likelihood of forming a relationship was unknown, participants preferred similarity. However, when participants were led to believe a relationship was likely, participants (especially men) preferred dissimilarity.

Wright, McLaughlin-Volpe, and Brody (2004) tested the idea that differences would be especially important in directing attraction when the desire for self-expansion was high. Researchers manipulated the intensity of participants' self-expansion motive by providing bogus feedback from a supposed personality measure (either your current life is overstimulating or your life is dull and boring). Then, in what participants thought was an unrelated part of the study, the participants selected whom they would most like to work with on a joint task from a list of other students. As predicted, participants in the high self-expansion motive condition selected more potential partners who were dissimilar (in this study, with names that indicated a different ethnicity than their own) than did participants in the low self-expansion motive condition.

Another line of research investigated expansion of the self when falling in love (Aron, Paris, & Aron, 1995). Participants across two studies completed standard measures of self-esteem, self-efficacy, and spontaneous self-concept (open-ended response to "Who are you today?") every 2 weeks over a 10-week period. In one study, participants indicated every 2 weeks whether they had fallen in love and completed a love scale. In the other study, researchers used a less obvious procedure, such that at each testing they completed a checklist of "significant life events" that had occurred in the past 2 weeks; buried in this list was an item asking whether they had "fallen in love." In both studies, and on each self-measure, those who fell in love showed significantly greater self-concept increases (including increased number of responses to the "Who are you today?" question) from before to after falling in love, both when compared with other time periods when they did not fall in love and when compared with other participants who did not report the experience of falling in love. That is, falling in love appears to literally expand the self.

Yet another major line of research relevant to the self-expansion model's notion that falling in love is associated with self-expansion, and especially the greatly anticipated (and highly rewarding) self-expansion from a relationship with this person, has focused on the neural correlates of early-stage romantic love. This self-expansion (and especially the substantial perceived opportunity for self-expansion as a relationship is created) in early-stage, intense romantic love is hypothesized to be a powerful motivational state represented in the brain by activation of the dopamine reward system. Several functional magnetic resonance imaging (fMRI) studies have demonstrated greater activation in this brain system when viewing a facial photo of (or being subliminally shown the name of) a person with whom one has recently fallen in love versus various familiar others (see Acevedo & Aron, 2014, for review).

These findings have been replicated cross-culturally (e.g., Xu et al., 2011) for people still intensely in love with someone who has rejected them (Fisher, Brown, Aron, Strong, & Mashek, 2010), those claiming to be intensely in love with someone to whom they have been married for more than 20 years (Acevedo, Aron, Fisher, & Brown, 2012), and across genders and sexual orientation (Zeki & Romaya, 2010). Further, recent research suggests that this activation resulting from intense romantic love is sufficient to offset pain response to aversive stimuli (Younger, Aron, Parke, Chatterjee, & Mackey, 2010) and to undermine craving for tobacco (e.g., Xu et al., 2012; Xu, Aron, Westmaas, Wang, & Sweet, 2014; Xu, Floyd, Westmaas, & Aron, 2010). In sum, the consistent patterns of brain systems activated across these studies of intense love support the self-expansion model's implication that passionate love is a motivational state involving high levels of expected reward (in contrast to other unsupported models suggesting that passionate love is a unique emotional state, or that it is primarily rooted in sexual desire).

Most research to date on self-expansion has focused on shared self-expanding activities. When a relationship is initially developing, experienced high levels of self-expansion through rapidly including the partner in the self seem almost inevitable. Yet over time, as the partner becomes familiar, the rate of self-expansion typically slows. At this point, the model hypothesizes that engaging together in highly interesting activities that generate the kind of excited engagement typically experienced with high levels of self-expansion (so that the relationship is associated with the experience) can reinvigorate a sense of self-expansion. Such activities can be anything new and engaging (e.g., a new activity such as sailing or skiing that the couple has never done before, attending a class together on something they would both like to learn about, or going out to a new event such as a county fair or comedy show). There are now quite a few studies providing consistent support for this hypothesis, as described in the Self-Expansion and Relationship Maintenance section later in this chapter.

A direct indication of the role of self-expansion in relationships is the research showing that greater relationship quality is associated with higher scores on a measure of relationship self-expansion, the Self-Expansion Questionnaire (SEQ; Lewandowski & Aron, 2002). Example items include "How much does your partner help to expand your sense of the kind of person you are?" "How much does your partner increase your ability to accomplish new things?" and "How much do you see your partner as a way to expand your own capabilities?"

The key idea underlying the inclusion-of-other-in-the-self aspect of the self-expansion model is that, in a close relationship, the cognitive structure and content of the self literally overlaps and shares elements with the cognitive structure and content of one's close other's self (Aron, Aron, Tudor, & Nelson, 1991; see also VanderDrift & Agnew, Chapter 2, for a review of cognitive interdependence). This has been shown directly with the "me-not-me response-time procedure" in which individuals rate themselves and a close other on various traits (e.g., Aron et al. 1991, Study 3). Later, participants view each trait and indicate whether or not it is true of themselves. The greater self-reported closeness between self and other, the slower one is in responding to traits on which self and other differ, because it is difficult to disentangle which trait is truly one's own versus the partner's. Other studies have determined, for example, that closeness predicts difficulty in distinguishing between memories relevant to the self and to a close other (Mashek, Aron, & Boncimino, 2003), greater spontaneous sharing of resources with close others (e.g., Aron et al., 1991, Study 1), and more overlapping neural areas when hearing the names of the self and a close other (Aron, Whitfield, & Lichty, 2007). Indeed, a pictorial self-report measure of perceived overlap of self and other, the Inclusion of Other in the Self Scale (IOS Scale; Aron, Aron, & Smollan, 1992), has been used in hundreds of studies to date.

Recent Developments in Self-Expansion

In addition to the main relevant lines of work over the last 30 years or so, there are many extensions, including five that are particularly relevant to the current chapter. First, as described in more detail in the section on Non-Relational Self-Expansion's Implications for Relationships, several experiments have demonstrated personal benefits of individual self-expansion (e.g., Mattingly & Lewandowski, 2013a; 2014a), personal benefits that are likely to improve any relationship that person is in. Second, an experiment (Fivecoat, Tomlinson, Aron, & Caprariello, 2014) has shown that, after the early relationship stage (i.e., in this study, after 13 months together), receiving active support from one's partner for an individual self-expansion opportunity caused significant increases in relationship satisfaction. Third, some other studies (e.g., Lewandowski & Ackerman, 2006; VanderDrift, Lewandowski, & Agnew, 2011) have found effects of relationship-associated self-expansion minimizing interest in potential alternative partners, something that is particularly likely in the context of acute stress (e.g., Lewandowski, Mattingly, & Pedreiro, 2014). Finally, there has recently been a significant extension of core principles, the two-dimensional model (Mattingly, Lewandowski, & McIntyre, 2014), which proposes and demonstrates that relationships can produce self-change along two dimensions: direction (increase vs. decrease in content) and valence (positivity vs. negativity of content).

There are also some recent developments regarding the inclusion principle with important potential practical implications. First, studies have indicated that it is possible to have too much inclusion (e.g., Mashek, Le, Israel, & Aron, 2011). Another line of work, using a version of the "me-not-me response time approach," has shown that to some extent people include aspirant partners (i.e., those to whom they are attracted but with whom they have not yet formed a relationship) in the self (Slotter & Gardner, 2009). Finally, perceiving one's partner as being satisfied leads to perceiving one's partner as including the person into the partner's self, which in turn leads to the person including the partner in the self (Tomlinson & Aron, 2013). Although the applied implications of these recent findings have only been minimally explored, and we will not further elaborate on them in this chapter, we believe they each suggest important potential applications for relationship maintenance.

SELF-EXPANSION AND RELATIONSHIP MAINTENANCE

Much of the foundational self-expansion literature has focused on shared self-expanding experiences, where both members of the romantic couple engage in novel, interesting, exciting, and/or challenging activities together. Sharing in self-expanding experiences with a partner has many benefits, including helping to keep the relationship exciting/less boring and contributing to feelings of reward and relationship satisfaction (see also the subsection *Mechanisms for How Self-Expansion Contributes to Relationship Maintenance* later in this chapter). Of particular note is Reissman, Aron, and Bergen's (1993) randomized controlled trial. This 10-week couples' intervention focused on relationship satisfaction and randomized 53 married couples to one of three interventions: exciting activities (experimental group), pleasant activities (control activity group), or no special activities (no activity control group). Relationship satisfaction was measured at the beginning and end of the 10 weeks. Each week, for 1.5 hours, couples in the experimental group and control activity group completed their assigned activity, which (depending on randomization) they both had separately rated as highly exciting (but only moderately pleasant) or highly pleasant (but only moderately exciting). Couples in the no activity control group received no instructions to engage in specific activities together. The results of the study showed that individuals in the experimental group, who had engaged in highly exciting activities, exhibited significantly greater post-intervention relationship satisfaction than those in either control groups. These results provide evidence that engaging in self-expanding activities together (rather than just spending time together) enhances relationship satisfaction. Notably, both members of the couples rated the self-expanding activities assigned in the experimental condition as highly exciting. Because excitement is subjective, there is no one list of activities that will be self-expanding for all couples, and recommendations for self-expanding activities need to be tailored for optimal effect. However, there are some general tips for optimizing self-expansion. Partners should engage in joint activities that both are passionate about (Philippe, Vallerand, Houlfort, Lavigne, & Donahue, 2010) and seek a high ratio of positive to negative emotions, as this is associated with increased complex understanding of the other and self-other overlap (Waugh & Fredrickson, 2006). Additionally, partners should engage in self-expanding activities that encourage flow (a mental state characterized by full immersion, energized focus, and enjoyment of an activity where there is a high level of challenge that matches the individual's skill, but not so much challenge as to make the activity overwhelming or impossible), as this increases the chances of lasting positive effects (Graham, 2008).

Although excitement may bring to mind physiological arousal, self-expansion does not require participation in roller coaster rides, bungee jumping, or other adrenaline rush activities. Research has indicated that self-expansion is distinct from physiological arousal and can occur even without arousal, such as when couples take a class together where they learn something new (Mattingly & Lewandowski, 2013a; Tomlinson, Lewandowski, & Aron, 2017).

Other studies have also shown that self-expansion provides positive effects on relationships. For example, Coulter and Malouff (2013) conducted a study with 100 couples randomized to a 1.5 hour per week self-expansion intervention or a wait-list control. They found that the intervention group showed significantly higher levels of positive affect, relationship excitement, and relationship satisfaction both at the end of the 4-week intervention and 4 months after the intervention was over (suggesting that shared self-expanding activities may have lasting impacts).

Whereas longitudinal randomized controlled trial studies provide the strongest evidence of the effects of self-expansion, cross-sectional studies and laboratory experiments demonstrate that even very brief (e.g., 7 minutes) shared novel, challenging, and exciting activities increase relationship quality (e.g., Aron, Norman, Aron, McKenna, & Heyman, 2000). One mechanism through which self-expansion enhances relationships is that when we engage in exciting activities with our partners, we tend to view both our partners and our relationships as exciting. For example, increased relationship satisfaction via mindfulness interventions can be attributable to the couples' subjective sense that the intervention was exciting (Carson, Carson, Gil, & Baucom, 2007). Because engaging in self-expansion with partners increases feelings of passionate love and closeness, it can also facilitate affiliation and maintenance behaviors (Leary, 2007). Note that while couples can self-expand with each other and experience increased closeness, self-expansion can also occur beyond just the couple context, for example with other couples during double date–like situations (Slatcher, 2010). Additionally, engaging in exciting activities that are physiologically arousing with a new partner or potential partner may also lead to greater attraction to the partner via a spillover effect and/or misattribution of arousal (e.g., Dutton & Aron's classic 1974 bridge study).

Engaging in self-expansion with our partners not only helps to enhance our relationships but also mitigates potential negative outcomes. For example, insufficient self-expansion (e.g., insufficient novelty, interest, challenge, or excitement) is related to feeling that the relationship is boring, which is associated with negative affect (Harasymchuk & Fehr, 2010). Relationship boredom and insufficient self-expansion can be detrimental to relationship maintenance, as boredom is not only related to long-term (nine-year) decreased marital satisfaction (Tsapelas, Aron, & Orbuch, 2009) but is also associated with susceptibility to infidelity, as it becomes more motivating to find another relationship that can provide sufficient self-expansion (Lewandowski & Ackerman, 2006; VanderDrift et al., 2011). Thus, ensuring that we engage in sufficient self-expansion with our partners not only provides us with direct benefits but also helps to attenuate boredom, which has negative implications for relationship maintenance.

Although self-expansion provides many benefits, it is important to note that there are a number of factors that influence engagement in self-expansion and the impact of self-expansion. For example, individuals are more likely to seek relationship self-expansion with their partners if those partners are instrumental to highly motivating goals (Fitzsimons & Fishbach, 2010). That is, if a person very strongly would like to become a better cook, taking a cooking class with their partner would be an especially appealing self-expansion opportunity (provided their partner also genuinely wants to take the class). Similarly, a person may be especially motivated to go on a trip with their partner to a part of the world he/she always wanted to visit (even if it is not something they would ever seek to do on their own), because they understand that this trip would allow them to move toward an ideal self that is well traveled. The Michelangelo Phenomenon (Rusbult, Finkel, & Kumashiro, 2009), wherein couples help to "sculpt" each other into the partner's own ideal self, is a great illustration of this process of engaging in joint self-expansion, where at least one member of the couple gets to meet important goals. Keeping the partner's goals and motivations in mind also helps to avoid overwhelming the partner by engaging in continuous self-expansion at an uncomfortable pace. Ideal relationship self-expansion, therefore, benefits all relationship members rather than disproportionately or selfishly providing new resources, perspectives, and identities to one partner at the expense of the other (Burris, Rempel, Munteanu, & Therrien, 2013).

People differ on their desire for and engagement with self-expansion. At least two individual factors positively affect motivation for self-expansion. One is approach motivation, with research finding that people high in approach motivation (who are more likely to take action and move toward desired endpoints) are especially attracted to those who offer many expansion opportunities (Mattingly, McIntyre, & Lewandowski, 2012). Another is attachment anxiety, with research showing that those high in attachment anxiety have particularly malleable self-concepts and are especially motivated to engage in self-expansion (Slotter & Gardner, 2012). This research suggests that shared self-expansion may be particularly impactful for those high on attachment anxiety and/or approach motivation, and that those whose partners have these qualities may need to be especially supportive by providing self-expansion opportunities (see Lee, Karantzas, Gillath, & Fraley, Chapter 4, for more on attachment and relationship maintenance).

Finally, it is important to note that although shared self-expansion confers many benefits, it may not be feasible (or desired) for partners to always engage in self-expansion together. Each person can also pursue self-expansion individually, with some common methods including hobbies, socializing, and spiritual experiences. In cases of nonshared self-expansion, the partner may still be involved via support and responsiveness, with active (rather than passive) support for these individual self-expansion activities contributing to relationship satisfaction (Fivecoat et al., 2014).

Mechanisms by Which Self-Expansion Contributes to Relationship Maintenance

So far, we have covered a number of studies that showcase the maintenance benefits (whether enhancing satisfaction or attenuating boredom) of self-expansion. In this section we discuss some of the mechanisms by which self-expansion can have such positive effects. One of the tenets of the self-expansion model is that self-expansion is a fundamental human motivation. It is not surprising, then, that neuroimaging studies of intense passionate love (a very intense and often rapid form of self-expansion) find activation in dopamine-rich regions of the brain strongly associated with reward, motivation, and learning (e.g., Acevedo et al., 2012; Aron et al., 2005; Xu et al., 2011), and the partner acts as a source of reward (Cacioppo, Grafton, & Bianchi-Demicheli, 2012). Additionally, self-expansion involves neural networks important for interpersonal awareness and representations of the self and partner (Decety & Sommerville, 2003), as well as the mirror neuron system, which may have an impact on understanding the intentions and actions of others (Ortigue & Bianchi-Demicheli, 2008) as well as greater empathy (Chen, Chen, Lin, Chou, & Decety, 2010).

The motivational principle of the self-expansion model also suggests that people seek to enhance the self. Research indicates that self-expansion is associated with increased feelings of self-efficacy and growth in the self-concept (e.g., Mattingly & Lewandowski, 2013a). This growth may occur in the context of a romantic relationship (e.g., falling in love, engaging in shared self-expansion) but may also occur at the individual level when a person engages in novel and challenging tasks (Mattingly & Lewandowski, 2013b). Self-expansion (whether shared or engaged in individually) functions as an approach motivation (Mattingly et al., 2012), and approach goals (e.g., focusing on the pursuit of positive experiences) are associated with increased short-term and long-term relationship satisfaction. This increase is due in part to approach goals facilitating partners' responsiveness to each other's needs (Impett et al., 2010). Because self-expansion leads to increases in self-efficacy and increased effort and persistence (Mattingly & Lewandowski, 2013a; 2013b; Mattingly, Lewandowski, & Carson, 2011), it may facilitate willingness to engage in relationship maintenance behaviors such as helping one another, being physically affectionate, and sharing problems (Ledbetter, 2013; also see Leo, Leifker, Baucom, & Baucom, Chapter 11, for more information on conflict management and problem solving). Increased maintenance behaviors may also reflect the link between self-expansion and growth beliefs. That is, the belief that relationships are not predestined but rather, that partners can work to make the relationship stronger is beneficial (Knee & Canevello, 2006).

Self-expansion likely also contributes to relationship maintenance because it is associated with admiration and adoration of the partner (Schindler, Paech, & Löwenbrück, 2014) as well as long-term feelings of intense romantic love (O'Leary, Acevedo, Aron, Huddy, & Mashek, 2012). These positive feelings facilitate an approach motivation toward the partner (and relationship), which can facilitate sexual desire and help buffer against declines in sexual desire over time (Impett, Strachman, Finkel, & Gable, 2008; also see Impett, Muise, & Rosen, Chapter 12, for more on sex and relationship maintenance).

Finally, as self-expansion involves inclusion-of-other-in-the self, we can incorporate our partners' self-expansion and successes as part of our own selves. This allows us to feel positively about our partner's accomplishments and to celebrate their successes without suffering decreases to our self-esteem via social comparison (Gable & Reis, 2010; Gardner, Gabriel, & Hochschild, 2002).

IMPLICATIONS OF NONRELATIONAL SELF-EXPANSION FOR RELATIONSHIPS

As discussed, individuals experience self-expansion in their close relationships largely through inclusion of others in the self (Aron & Aron, 1986; Aron et al., 2013) and through engaging in self-expanding activities with their partner (Aron et al., 2000).

Although the research on the model emphasizes how individuals self-expand through close relationships (Aron & Aron, 1986; Aron et al., 2013), the basic model focuses on self-expansion as a fundamental motivation for individuals to increase their knowledge and abilities. Thus, individuals should seek appropriate experiences and activities that would be expected to broaden an individual's sense of self not just through relationships but in all kinds of contexts, including nonrelational self-expansion (Mattingly & Lewandowski, 2014a). Recent research supports this by demonstrating that self-expansion also occurs within individuals (e.g., Mattingly & Lewandowski, 2013a). Parallel to relational self-expansion, nonrelational expansion arises from an individual's need to "broaden her/his horizons" or add to their sense of self by adding new perspectives, developing new skills, acquiring new identities, and enhancing capabilities (e.g., Aron & Aron, 1986; Aron & Aron, 1997; Aron et al., 2013).

In the first test of nonrelational self-expansion, researchers conducted a series of six experimental studies to determine whether the types of self-expanding activities that benefit relationships would also benefit individuals in a nonrelational context (Mattingly & Lewandowski, 2013a). As the self-expansion model would predict, those who engaged in a novel, interesting, and challenging task (i.e., carrying items with chopsticks) reported greater expansion than those who carried items by hand. A potential complication with most research on shared or relational self-expansion is that the activities couples engaged in were physical and potentially arousing in addition to being novel, interesting, exciting, and challenging (e.g., Aron et al., 2000). However, research subsequently showed that excitement and arousal are distinct experiences that influence relationships differently, with excitement being the important beneficial aspect of shared activities in established relationships (Tomlinson et al., 2017).

To similarly address the possibility that physical arousal was responsible for creating a sense of self-expansion in individuals, Mattingly and Lewandowski (2013a, Study 2) created an expanding activity (reading new and interesting facts) that is almost completely devoid of arousal. Again, consistent with the self-expansion model's predictions in relationships, reading new and interesting facts led to greater awareness, perspectives, knowledge, and learning and increased sense of the ability to accomplish new things, compared with those who read mundane facts.

Like relational self-expansion, the model suggests that nonrelational self-expansion should also result in an enhanced self-concept, increased self-efficacy and greater effort (Aron et al., 2013). Across three studies, research has confirmed that nonrelational self-expansion increases the size of the individual's self-concept (Mattingly & Lewandowski, 2014b). According to the self-expansion model, these increases in the self-concept provide benefits to the individual, such as greater self-efficacy. To test this, researchers examined the association between increased self-concept size and greater self-efficacy in a series of four studies (Mattingly & Lewandowski, 2013b) using a variety of manipulations and measures and found that a fuller self-concept was associated with greater self-efficacy. If an individual feels more capable and more likely to experience success, it should increase the amount of effort expended. Again, across several studies, researchers confirmed that those who had engaged in novel, interesting, and challenging (i.e., self-expanding) tasks exerted more effort on physical and cognitive tasks (Mattingly & Lewandowski, 2013a).

Nonrelational Self-Expansion's Potential Benefits for Relationships

Importantly, the research on nonrelational self-expansion establishes that new, challenging, and interesting activities can result in self-expansion, which produces a series of benefits (increased self-concept, efficacy, and effort). Although nonrelational self-expansion occurs outside the relationship and is not directly associated with the romantic partner, it is likely that it can provide benefits for the individual's relationship. This is especially true if partners support each other's individual self-expansion (Fivecoat et al., 2014).

Understanding nonrelational self-expansion is important, because many couples spend at least some time apart each day. During time apart, each individual has the opportunity to experience self-expansion in a variety of ways, such as via business travel to a new city, taking a class at the gym, or tackling a challenging and interesting project at work. In each case, though not physically present for those experiences, the other partner still garners the benefits of self-expansion. This is particularly true if the partners are highly included in the self (Aron et al., 1992). In highly included relationships where each partner's sense of self overlaps with each other, the partner's experiences and newly acquired perspectives and skills are likely felt to a considerable extent as one's own. As a result, both partners get to experience the feeling of self-growth that ultimately facilitates relationship maintenance. Thus, a person who continually improves his or her own self-concept also has more positive qualities to provide to their partner.

An individual's self-expansion experiences should also directly benefit the relationship by leading an individual to put forth more effort (Mattingly & Lewandowski, 2013a) and feel more confident in their ability to succeed in future tasks (Mattingly & Lewandowski, 2013b). The increased effort that an individual is willing to put forth following self-expansion can be put directly into the relationship. For example, after experiencing self-expansion from finishing reading a new book, an individual may feel a greater willingness to work through and discuss a problem in order to maintain relationship quality.

A greater willingness to put forth effort is beneficial, because research shows that individuals who put more effort into their relationships report more satisfaction and higher levels of relationship stability (Shafer, Jensen, & Larson, 2014). Similarly, individual self-expansion leads to greater self-efficacy, a construct that positively correlates with relationship satisfaction

(Roggero, Vacirca, Mauri, & Ciairano, 2012). Further, greater self-efficacy also attenuated the negative effects of stress on the relationship (Roggero et al., 2012), perhaps because the individual felt more capable of dealing with relationship difficulties. Some may argue that putting more effort into individual or nonrelational self-expanding activities may mean that the person has less time and interest for the relationship. Although this is possible, it is likely to be largely a matter of degree. It is certainly possible for a person to experience self-expansion both within and outside the relationship (e.g., engaging in self-expanding activities with the partner and also working on a self-expanding project at work), and people report experiencing self-expansion in multiple ways (e.g., Xu et al., 2010). Some recent research has shown, for example, that jobs can be expanding in similar ways to relationships (McIntyre, Mattingly, Lewandowski, & Simpson, 2014). Provided that nonrelational self-expansion does not occur at the expense of relational self-expansion, it is unlikely to harm the relationship.

Although not yet empirically tested, it is likely that the two-dimensional model of self-change from relationships could also operate at the individual level (Mattingly et al., 2014). That is, through their own independent actions, individuals could gain or lose either positive or negative traits. In particular, gaining positive (self-expansion) and losing negative (self-pruning) traits should enhance an individual's value as a relationship partner. For example, a person who learns yoga and begins to practice meditation to help reduce stress and quit smoking may become a better partner within the relationship, thus allowing the relationship to function at a higher level and sustaining it over time. Interestingly, self-expansion may facilitate these behaviors; for example, some research identified a link between self-expansion and smoking abstinence/cessation (Xu et al., 2010) and, as noted briefly earlier, neural attenuation of cigarette cue-reactivity (Xu et al., 2012; 2014).

In each of these cases, for an individual's nonrelational self-expansion experiences to optimally benefit the relationship, a high degree of inclusion of other in the self should be present in the relationship. In this way, if a person's highly included partner learns to play the guitar and recently went on a business trip to Italy, the person can benefit from their partner's self-expansion by gaining new knowledge and perspectives about Italy and enjoying the partner's new guitar skills. A high degree of inclusion also minimizes the risk that either individual's nonrelational self-expansion will come at the expense of the relationship. Additionally, knowing about a partner's interests and self-expansion experiences can also help the person become a better partner (and strengthen the relationship). In this example, the person could provide support and encouragement to their partner as they learn to play the guitar, show interest in hearing about their trip to Italy, and offer to help with travel logistics. In contemporary industrial cultures (as well as in traditional agricultural societies), a large portion of at least one member of a couple's time apart is spent at work. Daily job satisfaction is positively correlated with daily relationship satisfaction, and this association is especially strong for those with greater integration of their work and family roles (Ilies, Wilson, & Wagner, 2009). Increased job satisfaction is also important because negative experiences and work-related stress may "spill over" into a relationship, undermining relationship quality (Neff & Karney, 2004). In fact, on days when couples experienced greater stress at work than usual, they were less likely to view the relationship positively and were more likely to engage in negative behaviors toward their partner (Buck & Neff, 2012).

Spillover can also happen when the employee's partner perceives conflicts between work and family life or when the partner expresses negative attitudes toward the employee's work (Green, Bull Schaefer, MacDermid, & Weiss, 2011). In fact, employees who had partners with negative perceptions were more likely to look for another job and had lower levels of career resilience, or the ability to grow or "bounce back" from negative experiences or setbacks.

Much as self-expansion helps improve relationship satisfaction (Aron et al., 2000), it also benefits individuals in the workplace (McIntyre et al., 2014). Employees who reported greater self-expansion from their job also felt a greater sense of satisfaction and commitment toward their job. Given the negative implications of "spillover" on relationships, although indirect, self-expansion's ability to improve job satisfaction can also be an important way to promote relationship maintenance.

CONCLUSION

Since the conceptualization of the self-expansion model over 30 years ago, work built on it has grown to include vast amounts of research across multiple disciplines and perspectives. However, there is still much work to be done in terms of exploring the many ways in which self-expansion operates at the individual, dyadic, and group levels, and the impact this has on relationship maintenance. As noted at the outset, most work building on the self-expansion model has focused on theoretical questions about basic relationship processes (and more recently also basic processes in other domains, such as individual self-expansion and intergroup relations). In this chapter, we have tried to pull together self-expansion's main practical, real-world implications for optimizing close relationships, notably including a consideration of the implications for relationships of the relatively recent lines of work emphasizing individual self-expansion. However, in this process of examining the various applied relationship implications of the model, we are reminded of the many other unexplored opportunities to "expand" the model's applied side in this context.

Some future directions include testing some of the findings from experiments and short-term interventions using a more clinical-trial approach, with longer-term follow-up, and with samples that are more diverse in order to examine potential moderators. Some of the implications of basic research that we considered here could also be tested for their real-world applications in terms of helping or hindering relationship maintenance processes and behaviors. These could include the two-dimensional model, effects of individual and relationship-based self-expansion on health, mental health, and addictions, how individual and couple-level self-expansion experiences may reciprocally interact over time, more attention to considering and testing applied implications of the model's inclusion principle, and considering potential costs and limitations of expanding processes.

Another valuable future direction might be studies examining the extent to which self-expansion processes partially mediate the effects of existing couple interventions and activities, such as marital enrichment programs (or even marital counseling) or joint attendance at religious services. These programs may be helpful to couples, as they focus on relationship maintenance through improving communication, solving conflicts, and strengthening closeness and bonding, which can include encouraging self-expansion (e.g., rediscovering passion and promoting self-disclosure and inclusion-of-other-in-the-self). To the extent that self-expansion partially mediates the effects of any such programs, strengthening self-expanding aspects of the intervention would be beneficial.

Finally, it would be valuable to consider self-expansion-related benefits that have been studied only in the context of romantic/marital relationships for their generalization to other relationship contexts. Self-expansion in the context of other relationships can not only strengthen those relationships (offering additional sources of life satisfaction and meaning) but also provide the couple with further domains for self-expanding. That is, when a person's friendships and work relationships are especially exciting, novel, interesting, and so on, they have new things to share with their partner, new people they can introduce their partner to, and new contexts through which they can learn about themselves, their partner, and the perspectives that they and their partner hold.

Although the self-expansion model has come a long way since it was first proposed, there is still much to learn and many more advances to be made to better understand self-expansion's role in relationship maintenance. The next few decades will be an exciting time for both basic and applied self-expansion researchers, as well as for all the people we are hoping will benefit from everything this work will uncover.

REFERENCES

Acevedo, B., & Aron A. (2014). Romantic love, pair-bonding, and the dopaminergic reward system. In M. Mikulincer & P. R. Shaver (Eds.), *Nature and development of social connections: From brain to group* (pp. 55–69). Washington, DC: American Psychological Association.

Acevedo, B. P., Aron, A., Fisher, H. E., & Brown, L. L. (2012). Neural correlates of long-term intense romantic love. *Social Cognitive and Affective Neuroscience, 7*, 145–159. doi:10.1093/scan/nsq092

Aron, A., & Aron, E. (1986). *Love and the expansion of self: Understanding attraction and satisfaction*. New York: Hemisphere.

Aron, A., & Aron, E. N. (1997). Self-expansion motivation and including other in the self. In S. Duck (Ed.), *Handbook of personal relationships: Theory, research and interventions* (pp. 251–270). Hoboken, NJ: John Wiley & Sons.

Aron, A., Aron, E. N., & Norman, C. (2001). The self-expansion model of motivation and cognition in close relationships and beyond. In M. Clark & G. Fletcher (Eds.), *Blackwell handbook in social psychology, Vol. 2: Interpersonal processes* (pp. 478–501). Oxford, UK: Blackwell.

Aron, A., Aron E. N., & Smollan, D. (1992). Inclusion of other in the self scale and the structure of interpersonal closeness. *Journal of Personality and Social Psychology, 63*, 596–612. doi:10.1037/0022-3514.63.4.596

Aron, A., Aron, E. N., Tudor, M., & Nelson, G. (1991). Close relationships as including other in the self. *Journal of Personality and Social Psychology, 60*, 241–253. doi:10.1037/0022-3514.60.2.241

Aron, A., Fisher, H., Mashek, D. J., Strong, G., Li, H., & Brown, L. L. (2005). Reward, motivation, and emotion systems associated with early stage intense romantic love. *Journal of Neurophysiology, 94*, 327–337. doi:10.1152/jn.00838.2004

Aron, A., & Lewandowski, G. W. Jr. (2002). Interpersonal attraction, psychology of. In N. J. Smelser & P. B. Baltes (Eds.), *International encyclopedia of the social and behavioral sciences* (pp. 7860–7862). Oxford: Pergamon.

Aron, A., Lewandowski, G. W. Jr., Mashek, D., & Aron, E. N. (2013). The self-expansion model of motivation and cognition in close relationships. In J. A. Simpson & L. Campbell (Eds.), *The Oxford handbook of close relationships* (pp. 90–115). New York: Oxford University Press.

Aron, A., Norman, C., Aron, E., McKenna, C., & Heyman, R. (2000). Couples' shared participation in novel and arousing activities and experienced relationship quality. *Journal of Personality and Social Psychology, 78*, 273–284. doi:10.1037//0022-3514.78.2.273

Aron, A., Paris, M., & Aron, E. N. (1995). Falling in love: Prospective studies of self-concept change. *Journal of Personality and Social Psychology, 69*, 1102–1112. doi:10.1037/0022-3514.69.6.1102

Aron, A., Steele, J. L., Kashdan, T. B., & Perez, M. (2006). When similars do not attract: Tests of a prediction from the self-expansion model. *Personal Relationships, 13*, 387–396. doi:10.1111/j.1475–6811.2006.00125.x

Aron, A., Whitfield, S., & Lichty, W. (2007). Whole brain correlations: Examining similarity across conditions of overall patterns of neural activation in fMRI. In S. Sawilowsky (Ed.), *Real data analysis* (pp. 365–369). Charlotte, NC: American Educational Research Association / Information Age Publishing.

Buck, A. A., & Neff, L. A. (2012). Stress spillover in early marriage: The role of self-regulatory depletion. *Journal of Family Psychology, 26*(5), 698–708. doi:10.1037/a0029260

Burris, C. T., Rempel, J. K., Munteanu, A. R., & Therrien, P. A. (2013). More, more, more: The dark side of self-expansion motivation. *Personality and Social Psychology Bulletin, 39*, 578–595. doi:10.1177/0146167213479134

Cacioppo, S., Grafton, S. T., & Bianchi-Demicheli, F. (2012). The speed of passionate love, as a subliminal prime: A high-density electrical neuroimaging study. *NeuroQuantology*, *10*, 715–724.

Carson, J. W., Carson, K. M., Gil, K. M., & Baucom, D. H. (2007). Self-expansion as a mediator of relationship improvements in a mindfulness intervention. *Journal of Marital and Family Therapy*, *33*, 517–528. doi:10.1111/j.1752-0606.2007.00035.x

Chen, Y., Chen, C., Lin, C., Chou, K., & Decety, J. (2010). Love hurts: An fMRI study. *NeuroImage*, *51*, 923–929. doi:10.1016/j.neuroimage.2010.02.047

Coulter, K., & Malouff, J. M. (2013). Effects of an intervention designed to enhance romantic relationship excitement: A randomized-control trial. *Couple and Family Psychology: Research and Practice*, *2*, 34–44. doi:10.1037/a0031719

Decety, J., & Sommerville, J. A. (2003). Shared representations between self and other: A social cognitive neuroscience view. *TRENDS in Cognitive Science*, *7*, 527–533. doi:10.1016/j.tics.2003.10.004

Dutton, D. G., & Aron, A. P. (1974). Some evidence for heightened sexual attraction under conditions of high anxiety. *Journal of Personality and Social Psychology*, *30* (4), 510–517. doi:10.1037/h0037031

Fisher, H. E., Brown, L. L., Aron, A., Strong, G., & Mashek, D. (2010). Reward, addiction, and emotion regulation systems associated with rejection in love. *Journal of Neurophysiology*, *104*, 51–60. doi:10.1152/jn.00784.2009

Fitzsimons, G. M., & Fishbach, A. (2010). Shifting closeness: Interpersonal effects of personal goal progress. *Journal of Personality and Social Psychology*, *98*, 535–549. doi:10.1037/a0018581

Fivecoat, H. C., Tomlinson, J. M., Aron, A., & Caprariello, P. A. (2014). Partner support for individual self-expansion opportunities: Effects on relationship satisfaction in long-term couples. *Journal of Social and Personal Relationships*, *32*, 1–18. doi:10.1177/0265407514533767

Gable, S. L., & Reis, H. T. (2010).Good news! Capitalizing on positive events in an interpersonal context. In M. P. Zanna (Ed.), *Advances in experimental social psychology* (vol. 42, pp. 195–257). San Diego, CA: Elsevier Academic Press.

Gardner, W. L., Gabriel, S., & Hochschild, L. (2002). When you and I are "we," you are not threatening: The role of self-expansion in social comparison. *Journal of Personality and Social Psychology*, *82*, 239–251. doi:10.1037/0022-3514.82.2.239

Graham, J. M. (2008). Self-expansion and flow in couples' momentary experiences: An experience sampling study. *Journal of Personality and Social Psychology*, *95*, 679–694. doi:10.1037/0022-3514.95.3.679

Green, S. G., Bull Schaefer, R. A., MacDermid, S. M., & Weiss, H. M. (2011). Partner reactions to work-to-family conflict: Cognitive appraisal and indirect crossover in couples. *Journal of Management*, *37*(3), 744–769. doi:10.1177/0149206309349307

Harasymchuk, C., & Fehr, B. (2010). A script analysis of relationship boredom: Causes, feelings, and coping strategies. *Journal of Social and Clinical Psychology*, *29*, 988–1019. doi:10.1521/jscp.2010.29.9.988

Ilies, R., Wilson, K. S., & Wagner, D. T. (2009). The spillover of daily job satisfaction onto employees' family lives: The facilitating role of work-family integration. *Academy of Management Journal*, *52*(1), 87–102. doi:10.5465/AMJ.2009.36461938

Impett, E. A., Gordon, A. M., Kogan, A., Oveis, C., Gable, S. L., & Keltner, D. (2010). Moving toward more perfect unions: Daily and long-term consequences of approach and avoidance goals in romantic relationships. *Journal of Personality and Social Psychology*, *99*, 948–963. doi:10.1037/a0020271

Impett, E. A., Strachman, A., Finkel, E. J., & Gable, S. L. (2008). Maintaining sexual desire in intimate relationships: The importance of approach goals. *Journal of Personality and Social Psychology, 94*, 808–823. doi:10.1037/0022-3514.94.5.808

Knee, C. R., & Canevello, A. (2006). Implicit theories of relationships and coping in romantic relationships. In K. D. Vohs & E. J. Finkel (Eds.), *Self and relationships: Connecting intrapersonal and interpersonal processes* (pp. 160–176). New York, NY: Guilford Press.

Leary, M. R. (2007). Motivational and emotional aspects of the self. *Annual Review of Psychology, 58*, 317–344. doi:10.1146/annurev.psych.58.110405.085658

Ledbetter, A. M. (2013). Relational maintenance and inclusion of other in the self: Measure development and dyadic test of a self-expansion theory approach. *Southern Communication Journal, 78*, 289–310. doi:10.1080/1041794X.2013.815265

Lewandowski, G. W. Jr., & Ackerman, R. A. (2006). Something's missing: Need fulfillment and self-expansion as predictors of susceptibility to infidelity. *The Journal of Social Psychology, 146*, 389–403. doi:10.3200/SOCP.146.4.389-403

Lewandowski, G. W., Jr., & Aron, A. (2002, February). *The Self-expansion Scale: Construction and validation.* Paper presented at the Third Annual Meeting of the Society of Personality and Social Psychology, Savannah, GA.

Lewandowski, G. W., Jr., Mattingly, B. A., & Pedreiro, A. (2014). Under pressure: The effects of stress on positive and negative relationship behaviors. *Journal of Social Psychology, 154*, 463–473. doi:10.1080/00224545.2014.933162

Mashek, D., Aron, A., & Boncimino, M. (2003). Confusions of self with close others. *Personality and Social Psychology Bulletin, 29*, 382–392. doi:10.1177/0146167202250220

Mashek, D., Le, B., Israel, K., & Aron, A. (2011). Wanting less closeness in romantic relationships. *Basic and Applied Social Psychology, 33*, 333–345. doi:10.1080/01973533.2011.614164

Mattingly, B. A., & Lewandowski, G. W. Jr. (2013a). An expanded self is a more capable self: The association between self-concept size and self-efficacy. *Self and Identity, 12*, 621–634. doi:10.1080/15298868.2012.718863

Mattingly, B. A., & Lewandowski, G. W., Jr. (2013b). The power of one: Benefits of individual self-expansion. *The Journal of Positive Psychology, 8*, 12–22. doi:10.1080/17439760.2012.746999

Mattingly, B. A., & Lewandowski, G. W. Jr. (2014a). Broadening horizons: Self-expansion in relational and nonrelational contexts. *Social and Personality Psychology Compass, 8*, 30–40. doi:10.1111/spc3.12080

Mattingly, B. A., & Lewandowski, G. W. Jr. (2014b). Expanding the self brick by brick: Non-relational self-expansion and self-concept size. *Social Psychological and Personality Science, 5*, 483–489. doi:10.1177/1948550613503886

Mattingly, B. A, Lewandowski, G. W. Jr., & Carson, R. E. A. (2011). Solving the unsolvable: The effects of self-expansion on generating solutions to impossible problems. Poster presented at the 12th Annual Society for Personality and Social Psychology Conference, San Antonio, TX.

Mattingly, B. A., Lewandowski, G. W. Jr., & McIntyre, K. P. (2014). You make me a better/worse person: A two-dimensional model of relationship self-change. *Personal Relationships, 21*, 176–190. doi:10.1111/pere.12025

Mattingly, B. A., McIntyre, K. P., & Lewandowski, G. W. Jr. (2012). Approach motivation and the expansion of self in close relationships. *Personal Relationships, 19*, 113–127. doi:10.1111/j.1475-6811.2010.01343.x

McIntyre, K. P., Mattingly, B. A., Lewandowski, G. W., Jr., & Simpson, A. (2014). Workplace self-expansion: Implications for job satisfaction, commitment, self-concept clarity and self-esteem among the employed and unemployed. *Basic and Applied Social Psychology, 36,* 59–69. doi:10.1080/01973533.2013.856788

Neff, L. A., & Karney, B. R. (2004). How does context affect intimate relationships? Linking external stress and cognitive processes within marriage. *Personality and Social Psychology Bulletin, 30,* 134–148. doi:10.1177/0146167203255984

O'Leary, K. D., Acevedo, B. P., Aron, A., Huddy, L., & Mashek, D. (2012). Is long-term love more than a rare phenomenon? If so, what are its correlates? *Social Psychological and Personality Science, 3,* 241–249. doi:10.1177/1948550611417015

Ortigue, S., & Bianchi-Demicheli, F. (2008). Why is your spouse so predictable? Connecting mirror neuron system and self-expansion model of love. *Medical Hypotheses, 71,* 941–944. doi:10.1016/j.mehy.2008.07.016

Philippe, F. L., Vallerand, R. J., Houlfort, N., Lavigne, G. L., & Donahue, E. G. (2010). Passion for an activity and quality of interpersonal relationships: The mediating role of emotions. *Journal of Personality and Social Psychology, 98,* 917–932. doi:10.1037/a0018017

Reissman, C., Aron, A., & Bergen, M. R. (1993). Shared activities and marital satisfaction: Causal direction and self-expansion versus boredom. *Journal of Social and Personal Relationships, 10,* 243–254. doi:10.1177/026540759301000205

Roggero, A., Vacirca, M., Mauri, A., & Ciairano, S. (2012). The transition to cohabitation: The mediating role of self-efficacy between stress management and couple satisfaction. In M. Vassar (Ed.), *Psychology of life satisfaction* (pp. 147–171). Hauppauge, NY: Nova Science Publishers.

Rusbult, C. E., Finkel, E. J., & Kumashiro, M. (2009). The Michelangelo Phenomenon. *Current Directions in Psychological Science, 18,* 305–309.

Schindler, I., Paech, J., & Löwenbrück, F. (2014). Linking admiration and adoration to self-expansion: Different ways to enhance one's potential. *Cognition and Emotion, 29*(2), 292–310. doi:10.1080/02699931.2014.903230

Shafer, K., Jensen, T. M., & Larson, J. H. (2014). Relationship effort, satisfaction, and stability: Differences across union type. *Journal of Marital and Family Therapy, 40*(2), 212–232. doi:10.1111/jmft.12007

Slatcher, R. B. (2010). When Harry and Sally met Dick and Jane: Creating closeness between couples. *Personal Relationships, 17,* 279–297. doi:10.1111/j.1475-6811.2010.01276.x

Slotter, E. B., & Gardner, W. L. (2009). Where do you end and I begin? Evidence for anticipatory, motivated self–other integration between relationship partners. *Journal of Personality and Social Psychology, 96,* 1137–1151. doi:10.1037/a0013882

Slotter, E. B., & Gardner, W. L. (2012). How needing you changes me: The influence of attachment anxiety on self-concept malleability in romantic relationships. *Self and Identity, 11,* 386–408. doi:10.1080/15298868.2011.591538

Tomlinson, J. M., & Aron, A. (2013). The path to closeness: A mediational model for overcoming the risks of increasing closeness. *Journal of Social and Personal Relationships, 30*(6), 805–812.

Tomlinson, J. M., Lewandowski, G. W., & Aron, A. (2017, June). Perceived excitement drives benefits of self-expanding activities. In A. Aron (Chair), Advances in self-expansion research, Symposium presented at International Association of Relationship Research Mini-Conference, Syracuse, NY.

Tsapelas, I., Aron, A., & Orbuch, T. (2009). Marital boredom now predicts less satisfaction 9 years later. *Psychological Science, 20,* 543–545. doi:10.1111/j.1467-9280.2009.02332.x

VanderDrift, L. E., Lewandowski, G. W., Jr., & Agnew, C. R. (2011). Reduced self-expansion in current romance and interest in relationship alternatives.

Journal of Social and Personal Relationships, 28, 356–373. doi:10.1177/0265407510382321

Waugh, C. E., & Fredrickson, B. L. (2006). Nice to know you: Positive emotions, self-other overlap, and complex understanding in the formation of a new relationship. *Journal of Positive Psychology, 1*, 93–106. doi:10.1080/17439760500510569

Wright, S. C., McLaughlin-Volpe, T., & Brody, S. M. (2004, January). Seeking and finding an expanded "me" outside my ingroup: Outgroup friends and self change, Presentation at the Society for Personality and Social Psychology conference, Austin, TX.

Xu, X., Aron, A., Brown, L., Cao, G., Feng, T., & Weng, X. (2011). Reward and motivation systems: A brain mapping study of early-stage intense romantic love in Chinese participants. *Human Brain Mapping, 32*, 249–257. doi:10.1002/hbm.21017

Xu, X., Aron, A., Westmaas, J. L., Wang, J., & Sweet, L. H. (2014). An fMRI study of nicotine-deprived smokers' reactivity to smoking cues during novel/exciting activity. *PLoS ONE, 9*(4), e94598. doi:10.1371/journal.pone.0094598

Xu, X., Floyd, A. H. L., Westmaas, J. L., & Aron, A. (2010). Self-expansion and smoking abstinence. *Addictive Behaviors, 35*, 295–301. doi:10.1016/j.addbeh.2009.10.019

Xu, X., Wang, J., Lei, W., Aron, A., Westmaas, L., & Weng, X (2012). Intense passionate love attenuates cigarette cue-reactivity in nicotine-deprived smokers: An fMRI study. *PLoS ONE, 7*(7), e42235. doi:10.1371/journal.pone.0042235

Younger, J., Aron, A., Parke, S., Chatterjee, N., & Mackey, S. (2010). Viewing pictures of a romantic partner reduces experimental pain: Involvement of neural reward systems. *PLoS ONE, 5*, 1–7. doi:10.1371/journal.pone.0013309

Zeki, S., & Romaya, J. P. (2010). The brain reaction to viewing faces of opposite- and same sex romantic partners. *PLoS ONE, 5*(12): e15802. doi:10.1371/journal.pone.0015802

PART III

PROCESSES OF RELATIONSHIP MAINTENANCE

7

Communication and Relationship Maintenance

LAURA STAFFORD[1]

Communication is the fundamental means of relational maintenance. This is not to say that all communication functions to maintain relationships, that communication and relationships are isomorphic, or that communication alone maintains relationships. Maintenance mechanisms beyond communication are abundant. Some maintenance mechanisms can be accomplished through communicative or noncommunicative means. Other means of maintenance are solely noninteractive. Yet, communication has a unique role to play in the maintenance of relationships, as it serves both as a maintenance mechanism and as the means through which other maintenance mechanisms are made manifest.

In order to limit the scope of this chapter, I focus on romantic relationships. I briefly review the four most often invoked definitions of maintenance and propose a fifth definition, maintenance as growth. I then provide a succinct synopsis of the history of the study of communication and relational maintenance by reviewing typologies, motivations, antecedents, and the complex connections among maintenance behaviors and relational features. Finally, I consider how we communicate maintenance in accordance with definitions of relational maintenance and offer some directions for future investigation.

DEFINING RELATIONAL MAINTENANCE AS GROWTH

As noted elsewhere in this text (e.g., Ogolsky & Monk, Chapter 1), Dindia's (2003) four definitions of relational maintenance are commonly offered, widely accepted definitions of relational maintenance. These are as follows: to keep a relationship in existence; to keep a relationship in a specified state or condition; to keep a relationship in a satisfactory condition; and to keep a relationship in repair (Dindia, 2003, pp. 3–4). A fifth definition is offered herein, not to supplant prior ones but to extend them: to keep a relationship growing, that is, in a state and process of growth. To elaborate, this fifth

[1] School of Media and Communication, Bowling Green State University, llstaff@bgsu.edu

heretofore unarticulated (at least explicitly) view of maintenance is one wherein maintenance is seen as the process of keeping a relationship growing: maintenance *is* growth.

As early as 1926, Burgess pointed out that intimate relationships, including marriage, were ever evolving and forever fluctuating. Early-stage models of relationships recognized that relationships that have bonded still experience change, and change never leads to the same place (Knapp, 1984). Wilmot (1994) regarded the ebbs and flows around a given point as a characteristic of maintenance. Stafford (1994) observed that "change is recognized by most writers invoking maintenance" (p. 302). Of course, not all change is positive. Growth, however, is positive change.

Continued positive change within the bonded "stage" is maintenance as growth. Strengthening of relational characteristics such as commitment and love is maintenance as growth. Continued expansion of self in other is growth. Increased (healthy) interdependence is growth. Deepening comfort in security and experiencing novelty is growth. In ongoing, satisfied bonded relationships, maintenance is intrinsically positive change, that is, growth.

This view is consistent with previous articulations of maintenance. Several scholars have contended that it is obvious that *healthy* ongoing relationships do and must change (Baxter, 1994). Similarly, Wilmot (1994) asked not only how we keep relationships from dissolving but also how we *improve* relationships. In his discussion of relational maintenance, channeling the Woody Allen character Alvy Singer, Wilmot concluded: like sharks, "relationships move forward, or they die" (p. 76). Yet, prior definitions of relationship maintenance do not capture this fundamental truth. To my knowledge, growth has not been overtly stated as a definition of maintenance. Perhaps it is precisely because both scholars and lay folks alike recognize that relationship growth is so fundamentally and inherently embedded in relational maintenance that it has not been previously articulated as such. Maintenance as growth stands beside prior definitions such as maintenance as existence, a given state, a satisfactory state, or repair.

A BRIEF REVIEW

The study of communication and maintenance of romantic relationships is predated by decades of research on marital stability and marital satisfaction (Perlman, 2001). The bulk of early investigations did not focus on communication; rather, demographic or static factors such as age at time of marriage and income were the foci in delineating predictors of marital stability.

The notion that communication played a large role in the stability of marital relationships gathered prominence in the 1960s. In an early foray into the link between maintenance and communication, Davis (1973) purported that "Once intimates manage to attain their communion, they struggle to sustain it" (1973, p. 200). Intimate relations "have a tendency to become loose [and] can be tightened by *preventative maintenance* before they become loose, or by *corrective maintenance* afterward" (p. 210, emphasis in original). He offered several communicative means through which this maintenance occurred, such as metacommunication, relational talk, and rituals.

The idea that communication is strongly tied to not only marital stability but also marital satisfaction took hold in the 1970s (see Spanier & Lewis, 1980). Invoking a social exchange perspective, Braiker and Kelley (1979) termed talk with one's partners about the relationship in order to reduce costs and maximize rewards as maintenance. Gottman's (1979) pioneering and continuing scholarship (Gottman & Gottman, 2017) revealed strong associations between communication and marital satisfaction and stability. Into the 1980s, this association was widely accepted and became a primary focal point of communication and relational scholars (see Fitzpatrick & Badzinski, 1985, for a review). Underscoring the essential role of communication in relationships, Duck's (1988) observation that we spend more time in relationships than in developing or terminating them called for increased investigation into the, at that time, understudied stage of relational maintenance. The quest to discover communication behaviors contributing to relationship maintenance became a central area of study (Perlman, 2001).

TYPOLOGIES OF COMMUNICATIVE MAINTENANCE BEHAVIORS

Some approaches to communication and maintenance have focused on a particular domain of communication, such as daily conversation (Alberts, Yoshimura, Rabby, & Loschiavo, 2005) or forgiveness (Waldron & Kelley, 2008). Specific modalities such as Facebook (Stewart, Dainton, & Goodboy, 2014) or activities such as watching TV together (Yoshimura & Alberts, 2008) have also been considered. However, the vast majority of research on communication and the maintenance of romantic relationships has focused on factors or typologies of maintenance behaviors. This work is briefly reviewed.

It appears that the first compiled list of actions or activities intended to maintain relationships was put forward by Davis (1973) in his seminal text *Intimate Relations*. Dindia and Baxter (1987) built directly on this. Other early maintenance typologies were developed by Ayres (1983) and Bell, Daly, and Gonzalez (1987).

The first typology to take root was the five factor model of Stafford and Canary (1991; Canary & Stafford, 1992). Akin to the definition of maintenance as keeping a relationship in a satisfactory state or condition, they defined relational maintenance behaviors as "actions and activities used to sustain desired relational definitions" (Canary & Stafford, 1994, p. 5). They developed a measure of maintenance behaviors and labeled the factors "strategies"

(Stafford & Canary, 1991). The initial five factors were positivity, openness, assurances, social networks, and sharing tasks.

Positivity involves interacting with the partner in a cheerful, optimistic and uncritical manner. Openness refers to directly discussing the nature of the relationship and disclosing one's desires for the relationship. Assurances include messages that stress one's continuation in the relationship. Use of social networks includes interaction with or relying on common affiliations and relatives. Finally, shared tasks are attempts to maintain the relationship by performing one's responsibilities, such as household chores. (Canary & Stafford, 1992, pp. 243–244)

Dainton and Stafford (1993) differentiated between routine and strategic behaviors, a distinction that Canary and Stafford adopted. Strategic behaviors are those performed with the intent of maintaining the relationship, whereas routine behaviors are not performed with that goal in mind. Rather, routine maintenance behaviors are those wherein relational maintenance occurs as a "by-product" (Dainton & Stafford, 1993). In direct extensions, Stafford, Dainton, and Haas (2000) added two categories: conflict management and advice. A seven-factor measure dividing the factor of openness into two factors (self-disclosure and relationship talks) and adding the factor of understanding was developed by Stafford (2011). The measure was labeled the Relational Maintenance *Behavior* Measure (RMBM), rather than strategies, in order to indicate that these behaviors were not necessarily either strategic or routine. These seven factors were positivity, assurances, shared networks, tasks, self-disclosure, relationship talk, and understanding.

It should be noted that although the focus herein is upon the strategies or factors, Canary and Stafford (1994) also put forward basic propositions about the nature of relational maintenance. Some of these include the notion that all relationships require maintenance or they will deteriorate; people are motived by (in)equity; maintenance varies by type of relationship; maintenance behaviors may be used in combinations; they are interactive and noninteractive; and they can be strategic or routine. Stafford (2005) offered additional propositions, including that forces act both to keep a relationship together and to tear it apart; that maintenance varies among active, latent, and commemorative relationships, between voluntary and obligatory ones, and between long-distance and geographically close ones; and that maintenance mechanisms "simultaneously sustain desired relational definitions and are manifestations" of those definitions (p. 113). Although seldom explicitly acknowledged, these premises are often evident in maintenance scholarship.

Other scholarship in this tradition built upon those factors in multiple relationship types and contexts. Some of the additions and variations included a focus on self, joint/shared activities, avoidance/antisocial behavior, humor, support, affection, small talk, the use of mediated communication technologies, and being in supportive environments (see Stafford, 2003 for a review). Dainton and Gross (2008) expounded on antisocial strategies to identify negative main-tenance. Such maintenance behaviors are those that are typically considered adverse or antisocial, such as deception, lying, avoidance, inducing jealousy, spying on one's partner, or even infidelity. These are considered maintenance behaviors when enacted in efforts to maintain the relationship.

At about the same time, but taking a different approach, Sigman (1991) presented a typology of relational continuity constructional units (RCCUs). He sought to understand the "persistence" of relationships beyond face-to-face encounters. He proposed three categories of RCCUs: prospective units, intro-spective units, and retrospective units. Prospective units occur prior to separa-tion. They "signal an impending interaction separation" and "establish the relational definition during separation" (p. 115). Introspective units function when relational partners are separated and "identify the existence of prior relationships and obligations" (p. 118). Retrospective units occur upon reunion and act to "confirm the participants as members of some conjointly experienced history" (p. 118). Sigman contended that these units occurred across all relation-ship types and settings.

Gilbertson, Dindia, and Allen (1998) explored Sigman's (1991) RCCUs in the context of the maintenance and satisfaction of romantic relationships. They found that the use of RCCUs was related to satisfaction and played a role in "constructing the continuity of a relationship across periods of absence" (p. 789). Merolla (2010) extended this area of inquiry to propose three "supraca-tegories" of maintenance (intrapersonal, dyadic, and network) that inter-sected with Sigman's to yield "nine factors of maintenance performed over time, in and out of partners' physical copresence" (p. 174).

Other investigations have also sought to provide overarching cate-gories or underlying dimensions. Based in self-expansion theory or "inclu-sion of other in the self," Ledbetter, Stassen, Muhammad, and Kotey (2010) asserted that "relational maintenance behaviors are communicative acts that foster perception of shared resources, identities, and perspec-tives" (p. 22). Attempting to develop a "lower inference measure" of maintenance than prior typologies, Ledbetter (2013) grouped maintenance factors into four overarching types: shared resources, shared perspectives, shared networks, and physical affection. These categories largely corre-spond with "dimensions of self-other inclusion identified by self-expansion theory" (p. 305). See Xu, Lewandowski, and Aron (Chapter 6) on the self-expansion model.

MOTIVATIONS

Typologies have been one focus. An additional, compatible approach has focused on motivations driving maintenance behaviors, communicative or otherwise. A motivation orientation was offered by Davis (1973), who surmised that (in)equity, equilibrium, threat mitigation, and appetitive drives all serve as motivations for relational maintenance.

The desire for equity has frequently been put forward as a motivator. One premise of an equity theory approach to maintenance is that we are motivated to maintain relationships that we perceive as equitable. Although the typology of maintenance factors proposed by Canary and Stafford is not derived from equity theory, consistent with equity theory, Canary and Stafford (1994; Stafford & Canary, 2006) argued that individuals are more motivated to maintain relationships perceived as equitable than those that are perceived as inequitable. Thus, individuals in equitable relationships engage in a greater use of maintenance behaviors (Stafford & Canary, 2006).

Equity theory is not the only exchange theory that has been considered. Dainton (2017) invoked three social exchange theories: equity, equality, and self-interest. All social exchange theories are concerned with rewards and costs. Equity theories concern perceptions of the fair distribution of these rewards and costs. Individuals desire the ratio of their rewards to costs to be fair. An equality approach to relational maintenance concerns reciprocity. It is argued that individuals prefer both partners to give, and receive, equal rewards and costs. Both partners should contribute equally to the relationship, and both partners should be rewarded equally. Social exchange theories also share a presumption that individuals act in their own best interest (Roloff, 1981). A self-interest approach to social exchange is that engaging in maintenance behaviors "may not operate via either equity or reciprocal exchange mechanisms alone; it may be that self-interest, in the terms of the partner's use of maintenance without consideration of one's own use of maintenance" that is important (Dainton, 2017, p. 252). That is, per this position, individuals are most concerned with the amount of their own rewards, regardless. Dainton (2017) found that reciprocal exchange, self-interest, and equity all contributed to the prediction of maintenance behaviors.

Another maintenance motivation is equilibrium. The proposal that relationship maintenance sustains *dynamic equilibrium* was put forth by Davis (1973). Similarly, Baxter and Dindia (1990) posed that maintenance refers to partners' "efforts to sustain a dynamic equilibrium in their relationship definition and satisfaction levels as they cope with the ebb and flow of everyday relating" (p. 188). Baxter and Dindia (1990) sought to isolate the dimensions underlying perceptions of maintenance strategies and reported them to be constructive/destructive communication styles, ambivalence-based versus situation-based conditional use, and proactivity/passivity. This "three dimensional space consisted of six neighborhoods of basic strategy types: *Constructive Strategies* and *Destructive Strategies* which represent the extremes of dimension one; *Last Report Strategies* and *Satiation Strategies* which are represented by the second dimension; and *Inward Withdrawal*

Strategies and *Problem Avoidance Strategies*, both of which represent passive responses along dimension three" (p. 204, italics in original).

Murray, Holmes, Griffin, and Derrick (2015) also proposed an equilibrium model of relationship maintenance. They postulated that, similarly to homeostatic models, relationships have regular cycles of maintenance wherein relationships oscillate between state threat mitigation and state relationship well-being. Invoking interdependence theory, also a social exchange orientation, and apparently operating from a repair orientation, "the equilibrium model assumes that experiencing declines in satisfaction and commitment relative to one's usual sentiment or referent point motivates threat-mitigating thoughts and behaviors aimed at replenishing or bolstering these desired sentiments" (Murray et al., 2015, p. 94). They advocated the protection of relationships by following threat-mitigating rules of "(a) justifying costs, (b) ensuring mutual dependence, and (c) accommodating rather than retaliation in response to hurt" (p. 94). Accommodation is "one of the most widely researched maintenance strategies to manage relationship threat" (Girme, Overall, & Faingataa, 2014, p. 134). Rusbult, Drigotas, and Verette (1994) referred to "biting the bullet and responding constructively" (p. 126) to a partner's negative behaviors as accommodation. (For other research based in interdependence theory, see Dainton, 2000; Ragsdale & Brandau-Brown, 2005; Rusbult et al., 1994; Vanderdrift & Agnew, Chapter 2.)

Relationship-enhancement strategies are born of appetitive motivations. An appetitive motive "pertains to psychological processes and behavior associated with desired, positive outcomes" (Gable & Reis, 2001, p. 170), whereas threat-mitigation strategies seem to be oriented toward repair, as they are "reactionary and situationally specific . . . relationship enhancement strategies keep relationships moving forward" (Ogolsky, Monk, Rice, Theisen, & Maniotes, 2017, p. 276). The challenge to maintenance "lies not in the growth of negativity but rather in the decline of positivity . . . intervention [should be] aimed at regenerating the appetitive qualities" (Gable & Reis, 2001, p. 189).

Combining scholarship on typologies and motives, Ogolsky and colleagues (2017) developed an expansive model wherein all maintenance mechanisms can be considered under two overarching motives, those of mitigation and enhancement. Threat-mitigation motives are aimed at "regulating forces that threaten satisfaction and stability," and enhancement "occurs when partners engage in activities to promote positive relational processes and outcomes independent of outside threat" (p. 276). Each of these motives can be manifested in interactive (communicative) and individual ways. For example, interactive threat mitigation includes conflict management, whereas individual threat mitigation includes idealization. Interactive enhancement might involve social support, humor, and joint leisure activities, whereas individual enhancement might occur through generosity, gratitude, or prayer.

ANTECEDENTS

"Antecedents are theorized to influence the frequency and type of maintenance behaviors invoked" (Stafford, 2003, p. 62). In addition to the motives
outlined earlier, other antecedents include, but are not limited to, one's
perception of the relationship; one's perceptions of one's partner's perceptions of the relationship; one's perceptions of one's partner's use of maintenance behaviors; individual traits, states, or characteristics, such as gender,
depression, hope predisposition, and attachment style; relational uncertainty;
worldviews regarding relationships; and relationship type, such as stage and
duration. The most frequently examined outcomes of such antecedents are
Stafford and Canary's (1991) five factors.

Overall, one's commitment, satisfaction, trust, love, liking, perceptions of
(in)equity, and perceptions of one's partner's use of maintenance behaviors
have been found to be correlated with one's own use of maintenance behaviors (Canary & Stafford, 1992; 2001; Stafford & Canary, 2006; Dainton &
Stafford, 2000; Ogolsky, 2009). In addition, Pytlak, Zerega, and Houser (2015)
considered jealousy-invoking behaviors as "intentionally or strategically
behaving in a way that induces feelings of jealousy in one's partner" (p. 312).
They found that perceptions of one's partner's commitment and satisfaction
were negatively associated with the use of jealousy-evoking maintenance
behaviors such as flirting with a potential rival.

Relational uncertainty has been found to be predictive of both positive
maintenance behaviors (Dailey, Hampel, & Roberts, 2010) and negative maintenance behaviors (Dainton, Goodboy, Borzea, & Goldman, 2017). Dainton
and colleagues found that partners with high relationship uncertainty were
more likely to use negative maintenance behaviors than those with low
uncertainty. Negative maintenance behaviors may be a "response to relational
uncertainty" (p. 9). When uncertain about a relationship, one might attempt
to evoke jealousy, for example, in hopes that one's partner will then be
motivated to express their commitment to the relationship, thus reducing
uncertainty.

Turning to individual characteristics, women appear to "perform and
perceive more maintenance behaviors than men, although the effect size is
small" (Ogolsky & Bowers, 2013, p. 363). Depressive symptoms have been
associated with a lower propensity to engage in relationship maintenance
behaviors (Fowler & Gasiorek, 2017). Buttressing the idea that one's state of
mind may be associated with relational maintenance behaviors, Merolla
(2014) found that hope may prompt individuals toward greater enhancement
maintenance efforts. "Maintenance behaviors, then, are the very types of
enhancement activities high hope individuals are likely to enact in their
romantic relationships" (Merolla, 2014, p. 369). Also considering individual

differences, trait affection is predictive of the use of assurances (Pauley, Hesse, & Mikkelson, 2014), and excessive reassurance-seeking tendencies have been positively associated with self-reported use of maintenance behaviors (Fowler & Gasiorek, 2017). Guerrero and Bachman (2006) found that individuals with secure attachment were more likely to report the use of assurances, romantic affection, and openness. Level of avoidance was predictive of less expression of affection and openness.

Beliefs about relationships have been called "implicit relationship theories" (Knee, Patrick, & Lonsbary, 2003). These individually held naïve or lay theories of relationships reflect orientations toward responding to relationship challenges in different ways. Such beliefs about relationships likely influence our engagement in relationship maintenance behaviors. According to Knee and colleagues, there are two basic implicit theories of relationships. Individuals tend to believe in relationships as destiny (a relationship is meant to be or not) or as growth (relationships take work and communication). It is also possible for individuals to hold both beliefs. Knee and colleagues provide the example of believing that destiny plays a role in bringing people together, whereas that same person might believe that it takes work for a relationship to last.

Weigel, Lalasz, and Weiser (2016) found that individuals with a growth belief engaged in more positivity, assurances, and tasks than those with a destiny belief. In a similar vein, Weigel, Weiser, and Lalasz (2017) found that approach goal orientations were positively associated with the use of the Canary and Stafford factors, but avoidance goals were not. Individuals motivated by "pleasurable, rewarding, and satisfying elements of their relationships" are motivated to sustain those through the use of maintenance behaviors. However, some individuals "focus more on avoiding the costly, unpleasant side of relationships and are less inclined to engage in relationship maintenance" (Weigel et al., 2017, p. 358).

Exploring the often found correlation between religious beliefs and marital satisfaction, Stafford (2016) considered the belief in the sanctification or sacred nature of marriage. Collapsing the relational behaviors into one index, she found that those who held this belief engaged in more maintenance behaviors than the individuals who did not hold this belief. Maintenance behaviors mediated the correlation between sanctification and marital satisfaction.

Some of the research presented earlier seeks to understand predictors of certain types of maintenance behaviors, for example, positivity versus openness. Other work attempts to understand the propensity to engage in maintenance behaviors, or the extent to which they might be offered at all. Regardless, whether deemed motives or antecedents, and whether predicting a particular type of maintenance or maintenance in general, there is no one predictor of engagement in relationship maintenance behaviors. Multiple combinations of motives or antecedents, many beyond those discussed here, predict maintenance.

EFFICACY AND CAUSALITY

Intrinsically, the driving question in the study of relational maintenance and communication is "What communication behaviors function to maintain our relationships?" This is *the* question regardless of any particular definition of relational maintenance. Based on a comprehensive meta-analysis, Ogolsky and Bowers (2013) concluded that a wide range of studies have found that all the five original Canary and Stafford factors impact numerous outcomes, including commitment, love, liking, and satisfaction. Their findings revealed that assurances and positivity seem to be the most predictive of satisfaction, and assurances the most closely tied to commitment. Emphasizing the communicative nature of relational maintenance, they concluded: "Relationship maintenance serves a number of rewarding functions in the context of relationships. Maintenance can communicate commitment to one's partner, and it can promote satisfaction, love, and liking through the exchange of pro-relationship behaviors and control mutuality through the establishment of clear expectations" (Ogolsky & Bowers, 2013, p. 363). However, they also pointed out that they were unable to make definitive casual inferences, as most studies consider maintenance behaviors and relational characteristics concurrently. Very little research has been devoted to predicting the long-term efficacy of maintenance behaviors.

Although not using the term "maintenance," Gottman's body of research provides the strongest empirically substantiated insight into the efficacy of some maintenance mechanisms. He has offered the Sound Relationship House Theory, built, with numerous colleagues, over 40 years (Gottman & Gottman, 2017). This theory focuses on the role of cognition (e.g., positive and negative sentiment override), constructive conflict management, creation of shared meaning, and building commitment and trust. Many elements, such as demonstrating positive affect, assuming continued enactment, have been found to be predictive of marital stability and satisfaction several years into the future of that relationship.

To enact a maintenance function, maintenance behaviors must be performed on an ongoing basis. Considering causal directionality and examining maintenance and relational characteristics across several months, Canary, Stafford, and Semic (2002) found that maintenance and relational characteristics are "substantially and concurrently associated" (p. 404), whereas neither maintenance behaviors nor relational characteristics had much predictive ability on each other. That is, associations between maintenance and relational characteristics "decline after a short time, which suggests that spouses need to engage continually in maintenance activities" (p. 403).

Directly exploring the cyclical causality of relationship features and communication, Weigel and Ballard-Reisch (2014) found that an "individual's level of commitment is associated with her or his own expressions of commitment, those expressions of commitment are noticed by their partners, and the partner's level of commitment is associated with those perceptions of the other's expressions of commitment" (p. 329). Similarly, Ogolsky (2009) found that not only did maintenance influence commitment, but commitment also influenced maintenance behaviors.

In brief, to be efficacious, maintenance behaviors must be ongoing. Further, "maintenance is both cause and consequence of other relationship processes" (Ogolsky, 2009, p. 294). The duration, directionality, and pathways among antecedents, motives, maintenance behaviors, and the maintenance of relationships and relational features are minimally circular and reflexive; it is likely to be significantly more complex with numerous mediators and moderators at play.

COMMUNICATING MAINTENANCE

Given that definitions of maintenance overlap (Dindia, 2003) and that maintenance mechanisms are multiphasic (Dindia, 1994), it follows that the ways we communicate maintenance are relevant to more than one definition. Communicating existence, a given state, a satisfactory state, repair, and growth share communicative behaviors. Nonetheless, each definition is considered in turn.

Communicating Existence

Dindia's (2003) first definition of maintenance is one of keeping the relationship in existence. This "simply means that a relationship continues without termination." This definition "does not specify whether relationships change or remain stable" (Dindia & Canary, 1993, p. 164). Prior to consideration of how one communicates the existence of a relationship, the question must be asked: is it possible for a relationship to cease to exist? Dating partners break up. Married couples become divorced. But, does a relationship ever stop being? Many have argued that relationships change, but continue to exist (e.g., Wilmot, 1995). For example, Agnew and VanderDrift (2015) have proposed that divorced partners with children maintain a relationship with each other, albeit a different one.

Rather than ceasing, relationships might become dormant (Rawlins, 1994). Primarily referring to long-lost friends, Ramirez, Sumner, and Spinda (2017) considered relational reconnection as an extension of relational maintenance. Relational reconnection is "a process that encompasses both the re-initiation of a relationship as well as its continued maintenance after initial contact" (Ramirez & Bryant, 2014, p. 2). The process of reconnection implies that the relationship is continued in some sort of latent form. As "long as the option of a future reconnection continues to exist, dormant ties are not dead" (Levin, Walter, & Murnighan, 2011, p. 923).

Relational reconnection occurs in romantic relationships as well. Individuals in dating relationships may terminate their relationship and then experience a renewal (Dailey, Jin, Pfiester, & Beck, 2011). Romantic reconnections can also be rekindled, sometimes decades later (Kalish, 2005). Although not common, it is not unheard of for divorced individuals to remarry each other.

Even death, some would argue, does not end a relationship. Much of the grieving process and the rituals of grief serves the purpose of "assisting people to maintain an appropriate connection to the deceased" (Romanoff, 1998, p. 698). Romanoff commented on Western culture's general lack of grief rituals as a "failure to acknowledge the need to maintain" this relationship (p. 703).

Given the all-encompassing nature of this definition, as well as the question of whether a relationship can cease to exist, individuals might communicate the existence of a relationship in a myriad of ways: ways that are, at least in part, contingent on the nature of the relationship that is continued, as well as the nature of the relationship that is no longer. Communicating the existence of a relationship that has changed in its funda-mental nature might occur through a social media status change to "single" or "it's complicated." Some relationships, commemorative ones, only exist in memories (Rawlins, 1994). Yet, such commemorative relationships might also be communicated to others through introspective RCCUs (Sigman, 1991), such as a widow continuing to wear her wedding band, displaying pictures, or reliving events through storytelling.

Communicating a Specified State or Condition

This definition "implies not only that the relationship is maintained but also the fundamental nature of the relationship is maintained, as it currently exists" (Dindia, 2003, p. 3). Dindia is, in part, referring to a relational stage or type such as marriage as well as the continuation of the "fundamental nature" of that relationship. Maintaining a specified state or condition also refers to keeping a relationship not only from terminating but also from escalating (Dindia, 2003).

Dindia (2003) observed that the definitions of relational maintenance are not mutually exclusive. This is clearly the case, as maintaining a specified state or condition is "to maintain the stage of the relationship and the characteristics of the relationship associated with the stage of the relationship," such as "maintaining the closeness, the trust, the commitment, the liking, and so on" (p. 3). The next definition, of keeping a relationship in a satisfactory state, likewise involves relational characteristics. Thus, communicating a satisfactory state, and the relational features that accompany that state, is considered in the next section. Here, I discuss the communication of a specific stage.

Knapp's (1984) stage model of relationships is based on the premise that communication is different at various relational stages. Although this model has been given limited empirical research attention (for exceptions, see Avtgis, West, & Anderson, 1998; Dunleavy & Booth-Butterfield, 2009), the primary premise that the stage of a relationship evidences differing types of communication is widely accepted. To look at this from another perspective, people communicate the stage of their relationships.

Considering Knapp's stages, Avtgis and colleagues (1998) asked individuals to report how they communicated in the different stages. One of his findings is that during bonding, couples talk about future plans, and couples who are in the throes of decline "only discuss general matters [with] no talk about the relationship" (p. 285). During terminating, talk may be about staying in touch. The use of idioms among partners is greater during escalation than decline, and talking about plans for the future is indicative of relational growth rather than decline (Dunleavy & Booth-Butterfield, 2009). Dindia (2003) explains that, in this view, a relationship might be maintained at a higher or lower level, and "thus the relationship is maintained, but the level of the relationship is not" (p. 3).

Communicating a Satisfactory State

This definition shares some conceptual similarity to that of maintaining a specific state or condition. The maintenance of desired relational features is present in both. Communicating a satisfactory state is best understood through the consideration of communicating desired relational features including satisfaction, commitment, and love.

There are countless ways of communicating the unsatisfactory state of relationships. Gottman's findings have clearly indicated how we communicate our dissatisfaction (see Gottman & Gottman, 2017, for a review). Partners criticize, show contempt, act defensively, and stonewall (emotionally withdraw from interaction). Individuals make "bids for connection" in their relationships. That is, they directly or implicitly request or attempt to elicit a positive response such as affection, attention, or affirmation. Dissatisfied partners either do not notice these bids or choose not to respond to them; that is, they "turn away." However, satisfied partners notice these bids and "turn toward" their partners; they acknowledge and respond. Satisfied couples communicate with more positivity, affection, and respect. They not only "nurture fondness and admiration"; they demonstrate it (Gottman & Gottman, 2017). Turning toward communicates a satisfactory state.

Commitment is expressed continuously through day-to-day behaviors (Weigel, 2008). These behaviors include being supportive, showing respect, reassuring partners of feelings, offering tangible reminders (gifts and surprises), creating a relationship future (doing things together), behaving with integrity (being honest, remaining faithful, doing one's fair share), and working on the relationship (Weigel & Ballard-Reisch, 2014). Yamaguchi, Smith, and Ohtsubo (2015) also found that romantic partners reported that they "signaled" commitment in multiple ways, including providing social support, listening to problems, doing activities together, and engaging in costly positive behaviors on special occasions. Interestingly, they also found that failure to engage in behaviors such as gift giving on special occasions or failure to maintain secrets indicated a lack of commitment. Furthermore, behaviors that were costly signaled greater commitment than those less costly. Failure to engage in costly positive behaviors such as gift giving on appropriate occasions signaled less commitment. This comports with observations that gift giving is a ritual sign of involvement (Goffman, 1967).

Sacrifice may be another mechanism for communicating commitment. Although it is likely that both commitment and sacrifice influence the other (Monk, Vennum, Ogolsky, & Fincham, 2014), "sacrifice may be one of the more tangible ways that partners can demonstrate genuine commitment in the relationship in the day-to-day of life together" (Stanley, Whitton, Sadberry, Clements, & Markman, 2006, p. 291).

Although scholars have considered many features of long-term marriages and resilience, little work has examined how love is communicated in these resilient relationships. Gottman and Gottman (2017) emphasized that long-term love involves cherishing the other, nurturing gratitude, and showing those to one's partner. In one of the few studies to consider the expression of love in long-term marriages, Schoenfeld, Bredow, and Huston (2012) found that married couples expressed love in their daily lives through affection and pointed out that affection also promotes love.

Saying "I love you" is a well-known turning point in developing relationships (Baxter & Pittman, 2001). The importance of this phrase in long-term relationships has received much less attention. Just as the absence of gift giving may communicate decreased commitment, conceivably not saying "I love you" says more about long-term love than saying it.

Communicating Repair

Dindia's (2003) final definition is that of keeping a relationship in repair. The need to communicate repair implies that something has gone awry. Dindia and Baxter (1987) envisaged repair as remedial efforts once relational health has started to deteriorate. Davis (1973) outlined means for "making up" that he termed "work-it-outs" and "have-it-outs." Davis also identified "state of the relationship talks" and recommitment rituals to communicate repair.

Two familiar means of communicating repair are offering apologies and granting forgiveness. Apologies and forgiveness are related. Both are offered and accepted, and "apologies seem to facilitate forgiveness" (Lewis, Parra, & Cohen, 2015, p. 58). Lewis and colleagues identified five common components of apologies: acknowledging wrongdoing, accepting responsibility, expressing remorse, offering compensation, and promising not to engage in the offense again.

Forgiveness in marriage has been studied extensively by Fincham and colleagues (see Fincham, 2010; Fincham, Hall, & Beach, 2006, for reviews). Waldron and Kelley's (2008) work on communicating or granting forgiveness directly exemplifies communicating repair. They outlined numerous forgiveness-granting tactics and noted that sometimes forgiveness is explicit, wherein individuals say "I forgive you." "It is a kind of speech act that conveys an unconditional pardon" and "communicates a sense of finality" (p. 120). Forgiveness is also communicated nonverbally at times. Waldron and Kelley reported that depending on the nature and severity of the transgressions, sometimes partners renegotiate or reaffirm their relationships. Of course, not all repair is communicated explicitly; gifts can be expressions of apology, and forgiveness may be communicated by a return to normalcy. Importantly, poorly communicating forgiveness can be problematic. It can be offered in a disingenuous, one-upping abusive or retaliatory or humiliating manner (Fincham et al., 2006). For a review on forgiveness as relational maintenance, see McNulty and Dugas (Chapter 8).

Communicating Growth

Earlier in this chapter, I proposed that a fifth definition of maintenance be added to prior definitions. I argued that maintenance as growth involves continued positive change after a couple has bonded. According to Knapp (1984), in relationships that continue until the death of one partner, bonding is the "final stage." As has been often pointed out, most of us spend more time in this stage than any other (Duck, 1988). Indeed, the prior absence of attention to how this stage is sustained is the reason for the advent of research on relational maintenance. Repair orientations are born of the idea that relationships innately have problems, stagnate, or otherwise decline. This is undoubtedly the case. However, to be maintained, relationships must not only rebound from things gone awry; they also must grow. Growth is largely a preemptive strategy. Growth staves off repairs necessitated by boredom and stagnation, which often ravage relationships over time. Furthermore, a growth orientation also means that relationships do not stop at a bonding stage; they continue to evolve.

Various motivational approaches to maintenance involve growth. However, the question of how one communicates growth has not been considered. Communicating growth may be especially complicated. As soon as one communicates the desire for growth, perhaps through novelty (e.g., "let's do something different"), one has almost inherently communicated a feeling or belief that perhaps the relationship is no longer growing or is perhaps even stagnating. Requests for change stereotypically reference requests for changes in a negative behavior, not a positive one. Growth can likely be communicated in expressions such as "I love you more than I did when we first got married" or "I love you more every day."

Growth in intimacy or commitment is often considered the hallmark of *developing* relationships. In most stage views, these relationships have finished developing and are in the normatively desirable long haul of stability or "bonding." Although it has been often reported that satisfaction is at its highest in the early years of marriage, the "honeymoon-as-ceiling effect" (Proulx, Ermer, & Kanter, 2017), the possibility that other relational features might deepen has received limited attention. Continued movement toward greater intimacy, commitment, security, and love likely continues throughout a healthy marriage or other long-term romantic relationship. Once achieved, "bonding" is not the endpoint of an enduring, healthy relationship. Presumably, the partners in the relationship are aware of this growth, so there must be a mechanism through which to display it. That is, just as communication changes in development, communication likely changes with growth during maintenance. Studies of long-lasting marriages and characteristics that contribute to that resilience provide some insight. However, the communication of growth per se remains an enigma.

CONCLUSION

As several chapters in this volume evidence, communication is not the only mechanism that serves a relational maintenance function. However, it is the most fundamental one, as it intersects with, or acts as a part of, other means of maintenance. Arguably, some relationships exist without communication. Some "relationships" exist only biologically or structurally, or perhaps in one's mind (Stafford, 2005). Legally, a biological parent who has never met a child might be the next of kin. That is, society says there is a relationship, whether that "parent" wants it or not. A grandparent who has never met or interacted with a grandchild may feel there is a relationship. And again, legally there may well be one, as in the case of a legal heir. Imagined interactions (see Honeycutt, 2010) notwithstanding, felt connections with the deceased are devoid of communication. Dormant relationships may be on a communicative hiatus. Commemorative relationships live on through memories. During long periods of separation, some committed, satisfactory relationships may be maintained primarily or solely via intrapersonal, intro-spective RCCUs. Such relational instantiations typically are not the types of connections individuals in ongoing committed romantic relationships desire, at least not indefinitely. Communication is necessary for the maintenance of active relationships.

Relational maintenance is no longer understudied. There is little debate as to the important role communication plays in relational maintenance. However, it has not been sufficiently studied. The quest to comprehend the role of communication is far from complete. As previously noted, neither maintenance as growth nor how growth is communicated has been the subject of study. Nor has the question of what exactly constitutes growth been explored. In addition, numerous factors such as multiplexity, valence, timing, context, absences, and extremes have received little study. No parti-cular behavior necessarily communicates or serves as maintenance. Behaviors must be considered as part of a larger multiplex of factors.

Maintenance is a Multiplex of Behaviors

The engagement in one particular maintenance behavior in the absence of a larger set of maintenance behaviors is likely to be meaningless. For example, *only* engaging in positivity devoid of relational reassurances is not likely to serve a relational maintenance function. Further, it is unlikely that any one behavior is always meant to be, indicative of, or interpreted as maintenance. Engaging in positivity is a basic customer service skill and orientation. Being positive does not mean that the store clerks believes, or is indicating, that there is an ongoing relationship to be maintained. Similarly, tasks may be shared without a relational maintenance intent or function.

Further, behaviors do and must act in concert. Offering verbal reassurances but not acting in accordance with those reassurances (e.g., having an affair) undoubtedly undermines the value of those reassurances. Incongruence in maintenance behaviors may be problematic. Offering reassurances about the future of the relationship in a negative and contemptuous way would be an implausible maintenance message.

The absence of certain behaviors may be more problematic than others. Perhaps the absence of positivity is more damaging than the absence of interacting with shared networks, or vice versa. In addition, current measures do not allow the exploration of the extremes. Measures are based in Likert scales, wherein one might strongly disagree that one's partner is positive or reassuring. However, these measures do not assess the extent to which one's partner might express negativity or relational doubts. On the other end of the continuum, current assessments do not consider the overengagement in behaviors. Can one offer too many assurances? Do too much with shared networks? Be overly, annoyingly, positive? Nor do current measures consider mixed or conflicting messages, or messages in context. Additional research on the relative importance of behaviors, the absence of those behaviors, consideration of individual behaviors as part of a larger holistic pattern of interaction, and the possibility of overengagement in maintenance behaviors, or even the potential harm inflicted by the logical antithesis of maintenance behaviors, could further our understanding of relational maintenance.

Consider Valence

Positivity is, arguably, always positive. Overtly negative maintenance behaviors aside, virtually all other purported maintenance behaviors could be enacted in positive or negative ways. Engaging in shared activities or sharing social networks is presumed to be enjoyed by both parties. Small talk is thought to be pleasant. Yet, one person might not enjoy the activity or might dislike some members of the network. Advice or support may be unwanted. Humor can be at the partner's expense. Tasks can be undertaken begrudgingly, assurances offered condescendingly, joint activities engaged in unwillingly, and so forth. As another example, sharing the tasks of housework, although generally positive, might be undertaken at a time, or with the intent, of avoiding another activity desired by one's partner, such as spending time with relatives.

Perceptions of intent surely come into play in the interpretation of valence as well. Was unwanted advice perceived to be offered with good intentions or as an opportunity to belittle and berate? Valence is in the eye of the beholder.

Even though positivity is, by definition, positive, there may well be times when positivity is received negatively. Perhaps even positivity is unwanted at times when a companion with whom to commiserate, at least momentarily, is preferred to a sunny partner offering optimism and cheer. Clearly, additional research on the valence of the behaviors offered is needed, as well as consideration of the context in which these behaviors are offered.

Context, Timing, and Intent

Small talk when watching television together appears to serve a maintenance function (Ledbetter, 2017; Yoshimura & Alberts, 2008). The same small talk when watching a movie in a theater or when in the midst of a sacred ritual (e.g., mass) probably does not. In one of the few studies on timing and context, Denes, Dhillon, and Speer (2017) found that following sexual activity, positivity and assurances are most likely to be used, and used successfully. Talking about shared networks following sex was negatively related to liking, commitment, and satisfaction. Postcoital openness was also negatively related to satisfaction. Denes and colleagues posed that the content of post-sex openness was not always positive. Indeed, several studies have indicated either little variance accounted for by openness, or even a negative association between openness and relational features, once positivity has been taken into account (Stafford, 2003).

Openness is not the relational panacea that is often advocated. At certain times, or in certain contexts, or depending on the content, openness is not always desired or helpful. Although interpersonal communication scholars have long known that not all openness is equally helpful, or even helpful at all (Parks, 1982), little work has carried forward that basic truth in the context of the openness factor in maintenance research.

In sum, the first work to receive significant continued research attention in the study of relational maintenance was the typology offered by Stafford and Canary (1991; Canary & Stafford, 1992). Their typology has been expanded and elaborated. Canary and Stafford (1994) at the outset and in subsequent work (e.g., Canary, 2011; Stafford, 2011) agreed that there is no one finite set of maintenance strategies. They urged extension and expansion of these factors. Canary (2011), referencing the scale assessments of maintenance behaviors, noted that "items should and have been adopted and expanded to different relational types and maintenance forms" (p. 310). He concluded that the items used to assess maintenance should be those that best fit the research question at hand. This same logic extends to typologies.

These typologies appear to have served the study of maintenance well. Despite the expansions and extensions, Stafford and Canary's "original five factor model remains the most prominently used" (Ledbetter, Stassen-Ferrara, & Dowd, 2013, p. 39). Motivational approaches complement and extend this work. Yet, no particular behavior necessarily maintains relationships. The efficacy of and associations among maintenance behaviors, motivations, and relational characteristics warrant continued study, as do numerous factors that might mitigate those associations.

I began this chapter with definitions of maintenance. The definitions offered by Dindia (2003) were reviewed and an additional definition, maintenance as keeping a relationship growing was introduced. Unless one is satisfied with a tautological definition of maintenance (Stafford, 1994), it is unlikely that any one definition or one approach can suffice. Multiple definitions of maintenance provide multiple facets from which to continue to examine communication and the central, critical role it plays in the maintenance of relationships.

REFERENCES

Agnew, C. R., & VanderDrift, L. E. (2015). Relationship maintenance and dissolution. In M. Mikulincer, P. R. Shaver, J. A. Simpson, & J. F. Dovidio (Eds.), *APA handbooks in psychology. APA handbook of personality and social psychology, Vol. 3. Interpersonal relations* (pp. 581–604). Washington, DC: American Psychological Association.

Alberts, J. K., Yoshimura, C. G., Rabby, M., & Loschiavo, R. (2005). Mapping the topography of couples' daily conversation. *Journal of Social and Personal Relationships*, 22, 299–322. doi:10.1177/0265407505050941

Avtgis, T. A., West, D. V., & Anderson, T. L. (1998). Relationship stages: An inductive analysis identifying cognitive, affective, and behavioral dimensions of Knapp's relational stages model. *Communication Research Reports*, 15, 280–287. doi:10.1080/08824099809362124

Ayres, J. (1983). Strategies to maintain relationships: Their identification and perceived usage. *Communication Quarterly*, 31, 62–67.

Baxter, L. A. (1994). A dialogic approach to relational maintenance. In D. J. Canary & L. Stafford (Eds.), *Communication and relational maintenance* (pp. 233–254). New York: Academic Press.

Baxter, L. A., & Dindia, K. (1990). Marital partners' perceptions of marital maintenance strategies. *Journal of Social and Personal Relationships*, 7, 187–208. doi:10.1177/0265407590072003

Baxter, L. A., & Pittman, G. (2001). Communicatively remembering turning points of relational development in heterosexual romantic relationships. *Communication Reports*, 14, 1–17. doi:10.1080/08934210109367732

Bell, R. A., Daly, J. A., & Gonzalez, M. C. (1987). Affinity-maintenance in marriage and its relationship to women's marital satisfaction. *Journal of Marriage and the Family*, 49, 445–454.

Braiker, H. B., & Kelley, H. H. (1979). Conflict in the development of close relationships. In R. L. Burgess & T. L. Huston (Eds.), *Social exchange in developing relationships* (pp. 135–168). New York: Academic Press.

Burgess, E. W. (1926). The family as a unity of interacting personalities. *The Family*, 7, 3–9.

Canary, D. J. (2011). On babies, bathwater, and absolute claims: Reply to Stafford. *Journal of Social and Personal Relationships*, 28, 304–311. doi:10.1177/0265407510397523

Canary, D. J., & Stafford, L. (1992). Relational maintenance strategies and equity in marriage. *Communication Monographs*, 59, 243–267. doi:10.1080/03637759209376268

Canary, D. J., & Stafford, L. (1994). Maintaining relationships through strategic and routine interaction. In D. J. Canary & L. Stafford (Eds.), *Communication and relational maintenance* (pp. 3–22). San Diego, CA: Academic Press.

Canary, D. J., & Stafford, L. (2001). Equity in the preservation of personal relationships. In J. Harvey & A. Wenzel (Eds.), *Close romantic relationships: Maintenance and enhancement* (pp. 133–151). Mahwah, NJ: Lawrence Erlbaum.

Canary, D. J., Stafford, L., & Semic, B. A. (2002). A panel study of the associations between maintenance strategies and relational characteristics. *Journal of Marriage and Family*, 64, 395–406.

Dailey, R. M., Hampel, A. D., & Roberts, J. B. (2010). Relational maintenance in on-again/off-again relationships: An assessment of how relational maintenance, uncertainty, and commitment vary by relationship type and status. *Communication Monographs*, 77(1), 75–101. doi:10.1080/03637750903514292

Dailey, R. M., Jin, B., Pfiester, A., & Beck, G. (2011). On-again/off-again dating relationships: What keeps partners coming back? *The Journal of Social Psychology*, 151, 417–440.

Dainton, M. (2000). Maintenance behaviors, expectations for maintenance, and satisfaction: Linking comparison levels to relational maintenance strategies. *Journal of Social and Personal Relationships*, 17, 827–842. doi:10.1177/0265407500176007

Dainton, M. (2017). Equity, equality, and self-interest in marital maintenance. *Communication Quarterly, 65*, 247–221. doi:10.1080/01463373.2016.1227346

Dainton, M., Goodboy, A. K., Borzea, D., & Goldman, Z. W. (2017). The dyadic effects of relationship uncertainty on negative relational maintenance. *Communication Reports, 30*, 170–181. doi:10.1080/08934215.2017.1282529

Dainton, M., & Gross, J. (2008). The use of negative behaviors to maintain relationships. *Communication Research Reports, 25*, 179–191. doi:10.1080/08824090802237600

Dainton, M., & Stafford, L. (1993). Routine maintenance behaviors: A comparison of relationship type, partner similarity and sex differences. *Journal of Social and Personal Relationships, 10*, 255–271. doi:10.1177/026540759301000206

Dainton, M., & Stafford, L. (2000). Predicting maintenance enactment from relational schemata, spousal behavior, and relational characteristics. *Communication Research Reports, 17*, 171–180. doi:10.1080/08824090009388763

Davis, M. S. (1973). *Intimate relations*. New York: Free Press.

Denes, A., Dhillon, A., & Speer, A. C. (2017). Relational maintenance strategies during the post sex time interval. *Communication Quarterly, 65*, 307–332. doi:10.1080/01463373.2016.1245206

Dindia, K. (1994). A multiphasic view of relationship maintenance strategies. In D. J. Canary & L. Stafford (Eds.), *Communication and relational maintenance* (pp. 91–112). New York: Academic Press.

Dindia, K. (2003). Definitions and perspectives on relational maintenance communication. In D. J. Canary & M. Dainton (Eds.), *Maintaining relationships through communication: Relational, contextual and cultural variations* (pp. 1–28). Mahwah, NJ: Lawrence Erlbaum.

Dindia, K., & Baxter, L. A. (1987). Strategies for maintaining and repairing marital relationships. *Journal of Social and Personal Relationships, 4*, 143–158. doi:10.1177/0265407587042003

Dindia, K., & Canary, D. J. (1993). Definitions and theoretical perspectives on maintaining relationships. *Journal of Social and Personal Relationships, 10*, 163–173.

Duck, S. W. (1988). *Relating to others*. Chicago: Dorsey.

Dunleavy, K. N., & Booth-Butterfield, M. (2009). Idiomatic communication in the stages of coming together and falling apart. *Communication Quarterly, 57*, 416–432. doi:10.1080/01463370903320906

Fincham, F. D. (2010). Forgiveness: Integral to a science of close relationships? In M. Mikulincer & P. Shaver (Eds.), *Prosocial motives, emotions, and behavior: The better angels of our nature* (pp. 347–365). Washington, DC: American Psychological Association.

Fincham, F., Hall, J., & Beach, S. (2006). Forgiveness in marriage: Current status and future directions. *Family Relations, 55*, 415–427.

Fitzpatrick, M. A., & Badzinski, D. M. (1985). All in the family: Interpersonal communication in kin relationships. In M. L. Knapp & G. R. Miller (Eds.), *Handbook of interpersonal communication* (pp. 687–736). Thousand Oaks, CA: Sage.

Fowler, C., & Gasiorek, J. (2017). Depressive symptoms, excessive reassurance seeking, and relationship maintenance. *Journal of Social and Personal Relationships, 34*, 91–113. doi:10.1177/0265407515624265

Gable, S. L., & Reis, H. T. (2001). Appetitive and aversive social interaction. In J. Harvey & A. Wenzel (Eds.), *Close romantic relationships: Maintenance and enhancement* (pp. 169–194). Mahwah, NJ: Lawrence Erlbaum.

Gilbertson, J., Dindia, K., & Allen, M. (1998). Relational continuity constructional units and the maintenance of relationships. *Journal of Social and Personal Relationships, 15*(6), 774–790. doi:10.1177/0265407598156004

Girme, Y. U., Overall, N. C., & Faingataa, S. (2014). "Date nights" take two: The maintenance function of shared relationship activities. *Personal Relationships, 21,* 125–149. doi:10.1111/pere.12020

Goffman, E. (1967). *Interaction ritual; essays on face-to-face behavior* (1st ed.). Garden City, NY: Doubleday.

Gottman, J. M. (1979). *Marital interaction: Experimental investigations.* New York: Academic Press.

Gottman, J., & Gottman, J. (2017). The natural principles of love. *Journal of Family Theory & Review, 9,* 7–26. doi:10.1111/jftr.12182

Guerrero, L. K., & Bachman, G. F. (2006). Associations among relational maintenance behaviors, attachment-style categories, and attachment dimensions. *Communication Studies, 57,* 341–361.

Honeycutt, J. M. (2010). *Imagine that: Studies in imagined interactions.* Cresskill, NJ: Hampton Press.

Kalish, N. (2005). *Lost & found lovers: Facts and fantasies of rekindled romances.* Lincoln: iUniverse.

Knapp, M. L. (1984). *Interpersonal communication and human relationships.* Boston: Allyn & Bacon.

Knee, C., Patrick, H., & Lonsbary, C. (2003). Implicit theories of relationships: Orientations toward evaluation and cultivation. *Personality and Social Psychology Review, 7,* 41–55. doi:10.1207/S15327957PSPR0701_3

Ledbetter, A. M. (2013). Relational maintenance and inclusion of the other in the self: Measure development and dyadic test of a self-expansion theory approach. *The Southern Communication Journal, 78,* 289–310. doi:10.1080/1041794X.2013.815265

Ledbetter, A. M. (2017). Relational maintenance behavior and shared TV viewing as mediators of the association between romanticism and romantic relationship quality. *Communication Studies, 68,* 95–20. doi:10.1080/10510974.2016.1263804

Ledbetter, A. M., Stassen, H., Muhammad, A., & Kotey, E. N. (2010). Relational maintenance as including the other in the self. *Qualitative Research Reports in Communication, 11,* 21–28. doi:10.1080/17459430903413457

Ledbetter, A. M., Stassen-Ferrara, H. M., & Dowd, M. M. (2013). Comparing equity and self-expansion theory approaches to relational maintenance. *Personal Relationships, 20,* 38–51.

Levin, D. Z., Walter, J., & Murnighan, J. K. (2011). Dormant ties: The value of reconnecting. *Organization Science, 22,* 923–939. doi:10.1287/orsc.1100.0576

Lewis, J. T., Parra, G. R., & Cohen, R. (2015). Apologies in close relationships: A review of theory and research. *Journal of Family Theory & Review, 7,* 47–61. doi:10.1111/jftr.12060

Merolla, A. (2010). Relational maintenance and noncopresence reconsidered: Conceptualizing geographic separation in close relationships. *Communication Theory, 20,* 169–193. doi:10.1111/j.1468-2885.2010.01359.x

Merolla, A. J. (2014). The role of hope in conflict management and relational maintenance. *Personal Relationships, 21,* 365–386. doi:10.1111/pere.12037

Monk, J. K., Vennum, A. V., Ogolsky, B. G., & Fincham, F. D. (2014). Commitment and sacrifice in emerging adult romantic relationships. *Marriage & Family Review, 50,* 416–434. doi:10.1080/01494929.2014.896304

Murray, S., Holmes, J., Griffin, D., & Derrick, J. (2015). The equilibrium model of relationship maintenance. *Journal of Personality and Social Psychology, 108,* 93–113. doi:10.1037/pspi0000004

Ogolsky, B. (2009). Deconstructing the association between relationship maintenance and commitment: Testing two competing models. *Personal Relationships, 16,* 99–115. doi:10.1111/j.1475-6811.2009.01212.x

Ogolsky, B. G., & Bowers, J. R. (2013). A meta-analytic review of relationship maintenance and its correlates. *Journal of Social and Personal Relationships, 30,* 343–367. doi:10.1177/0265407512463338

Ogolsky, B. G., Monk, J. K., Rice, T. M., Theisen, J. C., & Maniotes, C. R. (2017). Relationship maintenance: A review of research on romantic relationships. *Journal of Family Theory & Review, 9,* 275–306. doi:10.1111/jftr.12205

Parks, M. (1982). Ideology in interpersonal communication: Off the couch and into the world. In M. Burgoon (Ed.), *Communication yearbook 5* (pp. 79–107). New Brunswick, NJ: Transaction.

Pauley, P. M., Hesse, C., & Mikkelson, A. C. (2014). Trait affection predicts married couples' use of relational maintenance behaviors. *Journal of Family Communication, 14,* 167–187.

Perlman, D. (2001). Maintaining and enhancing relationships: Concluding commentary. In J. Harvey & A. Wenzel (Eds.), *Close romantic relationships: Maintenance and enhancement* (pp. 357–378). Mahwah, NJ: Lawrence Erlbaum.

Proulx, C. M., Ermer, A. E., & Kanter, J. B. (2017). Group-based trajectory modeling of marital quality: A critical review. *Journal of Family Theory & Review, 9*(3), 307–327.

Pytlak, M. A., Zerega, L. M., & Houser, M. L. (2015). Jealousy evocation: Understanding commitment, satisfaction, and uncertainty as predictors of jealousy-evoking behaviors. *Communication Quarterly, 63,* 310–328. doi:10.1080/01463373.2015.1039716

Ragsdale, J. D., & Brandau-Brown, F. E. (2005). Individual differences in the use of relational maintenance strategies in marriage. *Journal of Family Communication, 5,* 61–75. doi:10.1207/s15327698jfc0501_4

Ramirez, A., & Bryant, E. M. (2014). Relational reconnection on social network sites: An examination of relationship persistence and modality switching. *Communication Reports, 27,* 1–12. doi:10.1080/08934215.2013.851725

Ramirez, A., Sumner, E. M., & Spinda, J. (2017). The relational reconnection function of social network sites. *New Media & Society, 19,* 807–825. doi:10.1177/1461444815614199

Rawlins, W. K. (1994). Being there and growing apart: Sustaining friendships during adulthood. In D. J. Canary & L. Stafford (Eds.), *Communication and relational maintenance* (pp. 275–294). New York: Academic Press.

Roloff, M. E. (1981). *Interpersonal communication: The social exchange approach.* Beverly Hills, CA: Sage.

Romanoff, B. D. (1998). Rituals and the grieving process. *Death Studies, 22,* 697–711. doi:10.1080/074811898201227

Rusbult, C. E., Drigotas, S. M., & Verette, J. (1994). The investment model: An interdependence analysis of commitment processes and relationship maintenance phenomena. In D. J. Canary & L. Stafford (Eds.), *Communication and relational maintenance* (pp. 114–140). New York: Academic Press.

Schoenfeld, E. A., Bredow, C. A., & Huston, T. L. (2012). Do men and women show love differently in marriage? *Personality and Social Psychology Bulletin, 38,* 1396–1409. doi:10.1177/0146167212450739

Sigman, S. J. (1991). Handling the discontinuous aspects of continuous social relation-ships: Toward research on the persistence of social forms. *Communication Theory*, *1*, 106–127. doi:10.1111/j.1468-2885.1991.tb00008.x

Spanier, G. B., & Lewis, R. A. (1980). Marital quality: A review of the seventies. *Journal of Marriage and Family*, *42*, 825–839.

Stafford, L. (1994). Tracing the threads of spider webs. In D. J. Canary & L. Stafford (Eds.), *Communication and relational maintenance* (pp. 297–306). New York: Academic Press.

Stafford, L. (2003). Definitions and perspectives on relational maintenance commu-nication. In D. J. Canary & M. Dainton (Eds.), *Maintaining relationships through communication: Relational, contextual and cultural variations* (pp. 1–30). Mahwah, NJ: Lawrence Erlbaum.

Stafford, L. (2005). *Maintaining long-distance and cross-residential relationships*. Mahwah, NJ: Lawrence Erlbaum.

Stafford, L. (2011). Measuring relationship maintenance behaviors: Critique and development of the revised relationship maintenance behavior scale. *Journal of Social and Personal Relationships*, *28*, 278–303. doi:10.1177/0265407510378125

Stafford, L. (2016). Marital sanctity, relationship maintenance, and marital quality. *Journal of Family Issues*, *37*, 119–131.

Stafford, L., & Canary, D. J. (1991). Maintenance strategies and romantic relationship type, gender and relational characteristics. *Journal of Social and Personal Relationships*, *8*, 217–242. doi:10.1177/0265407591082004

Stafford, L., & Canary, D. J. (2006). Equity and interdependence as predictors of relational maintenance strategies. *Journal of Family Communication*, *6*, 227–254. doi:10.1207/s15327698jfc0604_1

Stafford, L., Dainton, M., & Haas, S. (2000). Measuring routine and strategic relational maintenance: Scale revision, sex versus gender roles, and the prediction of rela-tional characteristics. *Communication Monographs*, *67*, 306–323. doi:10.1080/03637750009376512

Stanley, S. M., Whitton, S. W., Sadberry, S. L., Clements, M. L., & Markman, H. J. (2006). Sacrifice as a predictor of marital outcomes. *Family Process*, *45*, 289–303.

Stewart, M. C., Dainton, M., & Goodboy, A. K. (2014). Maintaining relationships on Facebook: Associations with uncertainty, jealousy, and satisfaction. *Communication Reports*, *27*, 13–26. doi:10.1080/08934215.2013.845675

Waldron, V. R., & Kelley, D. L. (2008). *Communicating forgiveness*. Los Angeles: Sage Publications.

Weigel, D. J. (2008). A dyadic assessment of how couples indicate their commitment to each other. *Personal Relationships*, *15*, 17–39. doi:10.1111/j.1475-6811.2007.00182.x

Weigel, D. J., & Ballard-Reisch, D. S. (2014). Constructing commitment in intimate relationships: Mapping interdependence in the everyday expressions of commitment. *Communication Research*, *41*, 311–332. doi:10.1177/0093650212440445

Weigel, D. J., Lalasz, C. B., & Weiser, D. A. (2016). Maintaining relationships: The role of implicit relationship theories and partner fit. *Communication Reports*, *29*, 23–34. doi:10.1080/08934215.2015.1017653

Weigel, D. J., Weiser, D. A., & Lalasz, C. B. (2017). Testing a motivational model of relationship maintenance: The role of approach and avoidance relationship goals. *Western Journal of Communication*, *81*, 341–361. doi:10.1080/10570314.2016.1240372

Wilmot, W. W. (1994). Relationship rejuvenation. In D. J. Canary & L. Stafford (Eds.), *Communication and relational maintenance* (pp. 255–273). New York: Academic Press.

Wilmot, W. W. (1995). *Relational communication* (1st ed.). New York: McGraw-Hill.

Yamaguchi, M., Smith, A., & Ohtsubo, Y. (2015). Commitment signals in friendship and romantic relationships. *Evolution and Human Behavior, 36,* 467–474.

Yoshimura, C. G., & Alberts, J. K. (2008). Television viewing and relational maintenance. In T. Moyrly (Ed.), *Studies in applied interpersonal communication* (pp. 287–307). Thousand Oaks, CA: Sage.

8

Attributions, Forgiveness, and Gratitude as Relationship Maintenance Processes

JAMES K. MCNULTY[1] AND ALEXANDER DUGAS[2]

This chapter focuses on relationship maintenance defined not merely as avoiding relationship dissolution but as remaining satisfied with a relationship over time. To some extent, successfully maintaining satisfaction with a relationship begins and ends in one's head. Indeed, over the past several decades, researchers across a variety of disciplines have identified numerous cognitive strategies by which people can maintain higher levels of relationship satisfaction over time. The goal of this chapter is to briefly outline the critical findings regarding three such processes: benevolent attributions, forgiveness, and gratitude. What will become obvious through this review is that, with respect to each process, the benefits are not straightforward; rather, whether benevolent attributions, forgiveness, and gratitude are beneficial depends on various contextual factors (see McNulty, 2016; McNulty & Fincham, 2012). Thus, each section will explore not only how these processes can help benefit relationships but also how they can incur costs. We end each by outlining aspects of the dyad members, their relationship, and the situation that determine whether each process is mostly associated with benefits or costs.

ATTRIBUTIONS

Attributions are causal explanations for an observed event (see Heider, 1958; Kelley, 1971), which is frequently one's own or another's behavior. According to the vast literature on attribution processes (Bradbury & Fincham, 1990; Kelley, 1967; Weiner, 1985), attributions can vary along several dimensions, including locus (is the source of the behavior an aspect of the target or the situation?), stability (how likely is it that the source of the behavior will change?), globality (will the source of the behavior cause other behaviors?), intentionality (was the behavior enacted on purpose?), and blameworthiness

[1] Department of Psychology, Florida State University, mcnulty@psy.fsu.edu
[2] Department of Psychology, Florida State University, dugas@fsu.edu

(is the person ultimately responsible for the behavior?). In the context of relationships, people can make attributions for various events, but much of the research has focused on the attributions people make for their partners' undesirable behaviors (see Bradbury & Fincham, 1990). Faced with a partner who returns home late from work, for example, Sally might attribute the behavior to the weather (external/unstable/unintentional), her partner's care-lessness (internal/stable/unintentional), or his thoughtlessness (internal/stable/intentional). We refer to more benevolent attributions as those that explain the partner's behavior in a more positive light – i.e., explaining a partner's qualities or behaviors in terms of causes that are more external, specific, unstable, and outside the partner's control.

There are several reasons to expect that benevolent attributions should be associated with the maintenance of higher levels of relationship satisfaction. First, viewing one's partner positively in the present moment should cause one to view one's partner more positively generally, which is associated with higher levels of relationship satisfaction, at least on average (Fletcher & Kerr, 2010; Murray, Holmes, & Griffin, 1996; Murray et al., 2011). Second, down-playing the implications of a partner's negative behavior should avoid conflict that would otherwise be costly or painful for the relationship, which is also associated with enhanced relationship satisfaction on average (Heyman, 2001). In other words, benevolent attributions may allow partners to acknowl-edge specific negative experiences from their partner while reducing the impact of these experiences on their overall relationship satisfaction (see McNulty & Karney, 2001). Indeed, a large body of research indicates that more satisfied intimates make more benevolent attributions (Bradbury & Fincham, 1990). Given this promising research, marital therapists began to look into the idea of supplementing behavioral marital therapies with cogni-tive interventions aimed at also targeting attributional processes (e.g., Christensen, Atkins, Yi, Baucom, & George, 2006; Jacobson, Christensen, Prince, Cordova, & Eldridge, 2000).

Of course, such cross-sectional research should be interpreted with cau-tion for several reasons. First, any cross-sectional association may reflect the fact that satisfaction predicts benevolent attributions rather than vice versa, and longitudinal research indicates that the association between the two variables is indeed bidirectional (see Fincham, Harold, & Gano-Phillips, 2000). Second, even when benevolent attributions do lead to changes in satisfaction, the effects may be temporary. That is, attributing a partner's behavior to external causes may lead a person to feel satisfied in the moment, and perhaps even the next day, but a key question regarding relationship maintenance concerns whether the benefits last over a substantial period of time.

And, to this point, there is reason to question whether any long-term benefits of benevolent attributions are unconditional. Scholars outside the domain of close relationships research have pointed out the potential costs associated with overly positive interpretations (Baumeister, 1989; Colvin, Block, & Funder, 1995; Crocker, Major, & Steele, 1998; Dillard, McCaul, & Klein, 2006; Robins & Beer, 2001). In particular, cognitions that minimize perceived failure in a specific domain can reduce the motivation to seek improvement in that domain (e.g., Crocker et al., 1998; Major & Schmader, 1998; Steele, Spencer, & Aronson, 2002). Given their interdependent nature (Kelley & Thibaut, 1978; Fitzsimons, Finkel, & VanDellen, 2015), relationships frequently require that partners regulate not only their own behavior but also their partners' behavior (Overall, Fletcher, & Simpson, 2006; Overall, Fletcher, Simpson, & Sibley, 2009; Overall & McNulty, 2017), and it is thus possible that minimizing a partner's role in a problem may minimize regulation efforts and thereby allow that problem to fester or even worsen over time.

Far fewer studies have addressed the implications of benevolent attributions over a substantial period of time, and a close examination of that research reveals that evidence of their benefits is rather mixed. Several initial studies revealed long-term benefits of benevolent attributions (Fincham & Bradbury, 1987; 1993; Fincham et al., 2000). For example, Fincham and Bradbury (1993) demonstrated that more benevolent attributions for a spouse's behavior at baseline were associated with higher levels of marital satisfaction than were less benign attributions one year later. But other research suggests that there are important limits to such benefits. In an extreme example, women in abusive relationships who excuse their partner's violence through external, benevolent attributions are less likely to terminate the relationship compared with women who perceive partner violence as the abusive partner's fault (Katz, Arias, Beach, Brody, & Roman, 1995; Pape & Arias, 2000; Truman-Schram, Cann, Calhoun, & Vanwallendael, 2000), possibly risking further abuse. Further, there seem to be some cases in which benefits do not emerge even on average within samples, such as for husbands in the longitudinal study described by Fincham and Bradbury (1987).

Considering the fact that benevolent attributions may have both benefits *and* costs offers a way to reconcile these and other seemingly inconsistent findings. Given that they may be adaptive by minimizing unnecessary conflict but maladaptive by minimizing necessary conflict, it may be that benevolent attributions are adaptive when regulating a partner is unnecessary, such as when the partner's behavior is unlikely to affect the relationship in undesirable ways, but maladaptive when regulating a partner is necessary to prevent future conflict. McNulty, O'Mara, & Karney (2008) provided direct evidence consistent with this possibility by demonstrating that whether benevolent cognitions are beneficial or costly depends on the severity of the problems the couples tend to face in the relationship. In particular, they used two separate longitudinal studies of newly married couples to show that the nature of spouses' attributions interacted with the severity of couples' relationship problems to predict the trajectory of their marital satisfaction over the first four years of marriage. At the onset of marriage, benevolent attributions, such as seeing the partner as the cause of and responsible for undesirable behaviors, were associated with higher levels of initial satisfaction only for couples facing frequent negative behavior and more severe problems. Controlling for these cross-sectional associations, however, a different pattern emerged over time. For spouses who experienced relatively minor problems in their relationship, engaging in benevolent attributions (e.g., tending to perceive that the partner was not responsible for a negative behavior) was associated with less decline in relationship satisfaction over time. For spouses who experienced relatively major problems, in contrast, engaging in less positive attributions (e.g., tending to perceive that the partner was responsible for negative behavior) was associated with less decline in relationship satisfaction. These effects were mediated by changes in the severity of the problems themselves. In other words, although benevolent attributions were associated with somewhat stable problem severity over time among couples with minor problems, benevolent attributions were associated with growing problems over time among couples with major problems.

This contextual analysis suggests a different way of considering adaptive relationship cognition. A long trend in social-cognitive research has been to focus on the possible merits of positive illusions (see Taylor & Brown, 1988; Murray et al., 1996), arguing that a modicum of positive bias may be beneficial to mental and relationship health (see Baumeister, 1989). There may indeed be such merits, as others have focused on the reciprocal tendency for less happy and mentally healthy people to perceive the world more accurately (Alloy & Abramson, 1979; though see Ackermann & DeRubeis, 1991; Lemay & Teneva, Chapter 13). But recent research addressing this question directly demonstrates that even the effects of positive bias are contextually determined. O'Mara, McNulty, and Karney (2011) conducted interviews of 502 members of 251 marriages regarding their stressful experiences across numerous life domains (health, finances, and career), made objective ratings of those experiences, and asked the participants themselves to rate those experiences. They then used bias scores (participants' ratings compared with the researchers' ratings) to predict mental health over the subsequent four years. The implications of bias for changes in mental health depended on the mean of the researchers' objective ratings of the participants' experiences. For participants whose experiences were rated relatively positively by the experimenters, positively biased perceptions were associated with better mental health. But, in stark contrast, positively biased perceptions were associated with worse mental health for participants whose experiences were rated relatively more negatively by the experimenters. Further, in one of the studies, these interactive effects were mediated by changes in interviewers' ratings of the objective qualities of participants' lives – positively biased perceptions by people facing particularly negative circumstances were associated with worsening problems, even as judged by the interviewers. It appears, then, that dealing with severe challenges appears to require an approach that acknowledges and confronts these problems in a way that motivates a behavioral change – even though this approach may sometimes be more painful and distressing in the moment.

In sum, benevolent attributions (e.g., explaining the partner's behavior in terms of external and unstable causes, giving the partner the benefit of the doubt, etc.) can be quite beneficial when the behavior in question is infrequent or unlikely to have long-term repercussions. Such attributions may be more costly, however, when applied to undesirable behaviors that are more frequent or the cause of serious problems; in such cases, more accurate perceptions may help people better maintain relationship satisfaction.

Given that this more contextual approach to the implications of cognition is still in its infancy, there are several further avenues of future research that may allow us to fully understand how benevolent attributions can both help and hurt relationships. For example, future research might expand on the dimensions of attributes described at the beginning of this section and how different types of benevolent attributions can produce different effects. It is possible that a locus-related attribution (e.g., "my partner is irritable because his job is stressful") serves different functions than a stability-related attribution (e.g., "my partner is irritable, but only temporarily"). Further research could also aim to more fully understand the contexts in which benevolent cognitions are helpful and harmful (see McNulty, 2016). For example, because nonbenevolent attributions may sometimes provide benefits because they motivate people to address their problems, any benefits may further depend on whether the problems are solvable and whether partners are already motivated to resolve them. Likewise, given that one function of less benevolent attributions presumably is to help motivate people to address and correct their problems, the benefits of such attributions may also depend on the controllability of the partner behavior in question; whereas it may be beneficial to make less benevolent attributions about severe or frequent undesirable partner behaviors that are controllable, it may be beneficial to make more benevolent attributions about partner behaviors that are relatively uncontrollable, regardless of their frequency and severity (see Jacobson et al., 2000).

FORGIVENESS

Whereas benevolent attributions can free a partner from responsibility and blame, forgiveness refers to a process by which people cope with undesirable behavior for which they perceive the partner is blameworthy. Although forgiveness is a concept that has appeared throughout the history of philosophy and religion, it received little attention in the field of psychology until the 1990s. As defined by McCullough, Worthington, & Rachal (1997, pp. 321–322), forgiveness is "a set of motivational changes whereby one becomes (a) decreasingly motivated to retaliate against an offending relationship partner, (b) decreasingly motivated to maintain estrangement from the offender, and (c) increasingly motivated by conciliation and goodwill for the offender, despite the offender's hurtful actions." Forgiveness is not a motivation per se but instead refers to the overall transformation that occurs when one's motivation to seek revenge and separation decreases, and the motivation to pursue compromise increases.

There are several reasons to believe that forgiving a close relationship partner should help people maintain satisfying relationships. First, forgiveness is associated with reductions in negative affect toward the partner (see McCullough et al., 1998), negative affect that may otherwise become automatically associated with the partner (even in the absence of deliberative and propositional reasoning processes; McNulty, Olson, Jones, & Acosta, 2017), potentially to the eventual detriment of the relationship (McNulty, Olson, Meltzer & Shaffer, 2013). Second, forgiveness involves thinking more benevolently about the partner (e.g., Fincham & Beach, 2002; Paleari, Regalia, & Fincham, 2005), and such benevolent cognitions are associated with immediate benefits to relationship satisfaction (see Bradbury & Fincham, 1990). Third, forgiveness is associated with immediately behaving more benevolently toward the partner (see Karremans & Van Lange, 2004), and such positive behaviors are also associated with immediate benefits on average (Heyman, 2001; though see McNulty & Russell, 2010; Overall et al., 2009). Finally, forgiveness may lead transgressors to behave more benevolently in the future (see Fincham & Beach, 2002).

Several cross-sectional studies have provided evidence suggesting the potential benefits of forgiveness (see Fincham, Hall, & Beach, 2006, for a review). For example, Fincham, Beach, and Davila (2004) found that forgiveness is associated with the tendency to engage in more positive behaviors in marriage. In particular, wives who were more benevolent and husbands who engaged in less retaliation and avoidance were associated with partners' reports of effective conflict resolution. Fincham and Beach (2002) also showed that those with forgiving partners reported perpetrating less psychological aggression in the relationship compared with those with less forgiving partners.

Of course, as was the case with attributions, it is possible that such associations emerge because satisfaction predicts forgiveness rather than vice versa, and evidence of more long-term benefits has been more limited (Fincham & Beach, 2007; Fincham, Beach, & Davila, 2007; McNulty, 2008; Paleari et al., 2005; Tsang, McCullough, & Fincham, 2006). In one study, Paleari and colleagues (2005) demonstrated that spouses who were initially more forgiving reported greater relationship satisfaction six months later, but these effects only emerged indirectly through concurrent forgiveness. In another study, Fincham and Beach (2007) reported that wives', but not husbands', initial forgiveness predicted their marital quality one year after their initial assessment, controlling for their initial reports of marital quality.

One reason why evidence for the long-term benefits of forgiveness is limited may be that forgiveness can actually fail to minimize the likelihood that some transgressors reoffend, which may erode or even reverse any immediate benefits of forgiveness for well-being. Specifically, transgressors' perceptions that they have been forgiven may protect them from negative consequences of their transgressions, such as the victims' anger and withdrawal. Given that people are less likely to repeat behaviors that are followed by undesirable consequences (e.g., Skinner, 1969), perceiving forgiveness, rather than anger and/or withdrawal, may leave transgressors feeling free to transgress again. Indeed, although forgivers may not intend to signal that the transgressor's behavior was tolerable, some people assume that forgiveness signals accepting, tolerating, condoning, and/or excusing the transgression (Kearns & Fincham, 2004; Younger, Piferi, Jobe, & Lawler, 2004).

Consistent with these potential long-term costs, several recent studies indicate that intimates' forgiveness is associated with a greater likelihood that their partners will continue transgressing (McNulty, 2010; 2011). First, a diary study of newlywed couples indicated that spouses who reported forgiving their partner for a transgression on one day were more likely to report that the partner behaved in a hurtful manner again the next day (McNulty, 2010). Second, a longitudinal study demonstrated that more forgiving spouses experienced continued physical and psychological aggression from their partners over the first four years of marriage, whereas less forgiving spouses experienced declines in aggression (McNulty, 2011).

As was the case with benevolent attributions, more recent research helps reconcile these apparent costs and benefits by indicating that whether forgiveness has benefits or costs depends on various contextual factors. In one study, for example, McNulty (2008) showed that whether forgiveness was beneficial or costly to marital satisfaction depended on the frequency of the partner's negative behavior. This two-year longitudinal study of 72 couples demonstrated that more forgiving people remained more satisfied over time when their partners rarely behaved negatively, but experienced steeper declines in satisfaction when their partners engaged in frequent negative behaviors. Similarly, forgiving husbands with wives who engaged in frequent negative behavior reported an increase in problem severity over time, whereas less forgiving husbands reported more stable problem severity. In other research, Luchies, Finkel, McNulty, and Kumashiro (2010) used two experiments and two longitudinal studies to demonstrate that the link between forgiveness and self-respect depends on whether the offender has apologized.

In one of the longitudinal studies, self-respect over the first five years of marriage was positively associated with one's tendency to forgive, but only among people with agreeable partners; among people with disagreeable partners, in contrast, forgiveness was associated with less self-respect. Finally, McNulty and Russell (2016) used four studies, including a cross-sectional survey, an experimental study, a four-year longitudinal study, and a two-week diary, to demonstrate that the link between forgiveness and likelihood of partner offending also depends on partner agreeableness. Forgiveness was associated with less subsequent offending if one's partner was highly agreeable, and increased subsequent offending if one's partner was low in agreeableness. Further, the diary study provided evidence of the specific mechanisms of this effect; agreeable people were less likely to transgress against forgiving partners because they felt obligated to reciprocate their partner's kindness, whereas those low in agreeableness were more likely to offend a forgiving partner because they perceived their partners to be less likely to show anger.

Other research offers ways intimates may capitalize on the potential benefits of forgiveness and avoid these costs. Specifically, Russell, Baker, McNulty, and Overall (2018) used two studies to demonstrate that supplementing forgiveness with direct oppositional behaviors can minimize the likelihood that offenders will repeat their transgressions. In an experimental study of emerging adult couples, participants were asked to report their partners' tendencies to engage in partner-regulation behaviors, led to believe their partners were either forgiving or unforgiving, and given the opportunity to transgress against their partners. In a longitudinal study of newlywed couples, participants were asked to report their tendencies to forgive their partners, observed during problem-solving discussions, and then asked to report their satisfaction with their partners' considerateness every six months for four years. In both studies, forgiveness was associated with more offending/less benevolence among intimates who did not also demand changes from their partners. In stark contrast, forgiveness was associated with less offending/more benevolence among intimates who also demanded changes from their partners. These findings suggest that supplementing forgiveness with direct partner-regulation behaviors can help couples avoid the undesirable outcomes and maximize desirable outcomes associated with forgiveness.

In sum, forgiveness may be most adaptive for relationships when it is granted for behaviors that are infrequent or relatively minor. In such cases, forgiveness may allow both partners to move past an offense. Granting forgiveness for behaviors that are more frequent or severe, in contrast may sometimes come with costs. For example, forgiving partners who are not already motivated to refrain from transgressing may allow those transgressions to continue, unless the forgiveness is accompanied by other behaviors that motivate the partner to refrain from future transgressions.

As was also the case with attributions, there are numerous needs and opportunities regarding future research. For example, the effect of forgiving a partner for a transgression might have different outcomes depending on how controllable the offense was (due to either the offender's levels of self-control or the nature of the offense) and whether the offense was accidental or motivated by malicious intent. Additionally, there may be partner qualities other than agreeableness that help determine the implications of forgiveness. For example, other factors associated with existing levels of transgressors' motivation to reoffend, such as their automatic evaluations of their partners (McNulty et al., 2013), may determine whether forgiveness is associated with less or more reoffending. Finally, the timing of forgiveness may help determine whether forgiveness is associated with more or less reoffending. Specifically, given that delayed forgiveness may create enough distress in the transgressor to motivate him or her to refrain from reoffending, delayed forgiveness may allow people to capitalize on the benefits of forgiveness and avoid some of the potential costs.

GRATITUDE

Whereas gratitude and forgiveness describe cognitive responses to a partner's undesirable behavior, gratitude is a cognitive response to a partner's desirable behavior. Early conceptions of gratitude (e.g., Trivers, 1971) defined it as an evolved mechanism for reciprocal altruism – an economic accounting method that keeps track of the costs and benefits of an altruistic act, informing individuals on whether or how they should reciprocate. Several scholars (e.g., McCullough, Kimeldorf, & Cohen, 2008) have argued that gratitude primarily serves to facilitate new relationships between acquaintances by increasing trust and encouraging prosocial behavior. Building upon this work, Algoe (2012) posits that gratitude serves not just to enhance and develop relationships with strangers or acquaintances, but also to help maintain close romantic relationships. Drawing on the idea that perceived partner responsiveness (the perception that a partner is understanding, caring, and responsive to one's needs) is a critical component of close communal relationships (Reis, Clark, & Holmes, 2004), Algoe (2012) theorized that gratitude functions to promote communal relationships over time by helping individuals (a) identify responsive partners and (b) form communal bonds with those partners by fostering responsive exchanges with those partners over time.

Recent evidence supports these ideas. In one study, for example, Algoe, Haidt, and Gable (2008) examined naturally occurring gratitude during a week of gift-giving between members of college sororities and demonstrated that the extent to which participants perceived that their benefactors had been responsive predicted feelings of gratitude beyond the mere cost of the gift. These feelings of gratitude, in turn, predicted more positive ratings of relationship quality both at the time of the gift and at a one-month follow-up. In other research, Lambert and Fincham (2011) used both longitudinal and experimental designs to demonstrate that expressing gratitude to a close friend or partner led to increased positive perceptions of that partner, which led participants to feel more comfortable with voicing their concerns with that partner (another key component of relationship maintenance; Stafford & Canary, 1991). Likewise, Joel, Gordon, Impett, MacDonald, and Keltner (2013) provided direct evidence for the idea that gratitude functions to bind partners together by showing that one partner's relationship investments increased the other partner's investments through the latter partner's gratitude. Finally, several studies provide evidence that one person's gratitude can influence both members of the relationship (Algoe, Gable, & Maisel, 2010; Gordon, Arnette, & Smith, 2011). For instance, a two-week diary study (Algoe et al., 2010) demonstrated that the gratitude participants felt toward their romantic partner on one day predicted their own and their partner's feelings of relationship satisfaction the following day. These studies suggest that feelings of gratitude come not just from a mere cost/benefit analysis, but also from a sense that the benefactor is responsive to one's needs. This is precisely why we feel much more grateful upon receiving a personalized gift from a friend that's worth $20 compared with simply receiving a $20 bill.

Despite these benefits, there is reason to believe that there may also be some costs to gratitude, at least in some circumstances. Gratitude is theorized to function as a relationship maintenance strategy by fostering communal feelings in a partner. However, as noted throughout this chapter, similar processes associated with communal orientation, such as forgiveness, only provide long-term benefits in contexts that are reciprocally communal (Luchies et al., 2010; McNulty & Russell, 2016; Nowak & Sigmund, 1993; Van Kleef, Homan, Beersma, & van Knippenberg, 2010). If they are not, there is the potential for one to exploit a partner who is engaging in communal behaviors, ultimately hurting the relationship.

There is evidence that gratitude functions in a similar way. In one study by Algoe and Zhaoyang (2016), participants were randomly assigned to express gratitude over the course of a month or assigned to a control condition. Among those with high partner responsiveness, those in the expressed gratitude condition reported more daily positive emotions. Among those with low partner responsiveness, however, those in the expressed gratitude condition actually reported more frequent negative emotions. McNulty and Dugas (2019) provided more direct evidence that the benefits of gratitude depend on the communal nature of the relationship context by showing that own gratitude interacted with partner gratitude to predict the trajectory of marital satisfaction over the first three years of marriage. Although husbands' and wives' gratitude was associated with some benefits to satisfaction when their partners were also relatively high in gratitude, their own gratitude was associated with significant costs to satisfaction when their partners were relatively low in gratitude.

Given that gratitude has only recently been studied as an important relationship-maintenance process, there is still much to learn about how exactly gratitude functions. Because it seems that the benefits of gratitude are only apparent when both partners are high in gratitude, clinical practitioners who use gratitude interventions (see Bolier et al., 2013, for a review) might look to design interventions that take care to improve both partners' gratitude. Further research can also examine how exactly partner responsiveness can influence the effectiveness of gratitude.

CONCLUSION AND FUTURE DIRECTIONS

As we hope this chapter makes clear, relationship maintenance is not easy or straightforward; the same cognitive process that maintains satisfaction for some people or in some circumstances (e.g., benevolent attributions, forgiveness, or gratitude) may not help maintain satisfaction for other people or in other circumstances. So, where do we go from here? An analysis of the three relationship maintenance processes described in this chapter seems to suggest that future research could benefit from using a contextual framework to study relationship maintenance processes. Even processes that are often considered to be universally benevolent – such as positive attributions, forgiveness, and gratitude – can be deleterious in certain contexts.

Given that the research mentioned here has demonstrated the usefulness of considering contextual factors with regard to these processes, it seems relevant to briefly discuss a systematic, theoretical framework for analyzing these contextual factors. How can we classify these contextual qualities that determine whether a particular process or trait is good or bad?

McNulty (2016) describes three broad categories of contextual factors. The first category describes qualities associated with the two members of the couple. Each individual will have a variety of qualities that affect his or her motivation and ability to engage in relationship maintenance processes. For example, individuals low in conscientiousness – the personality quality most associated with motivation – tend to benefit more from self-directed opposition, such as self-criticism (Baker & McNulty, 2011). With respect to the partner, as mentioned in the section on forgiveness, the effectiveness of forgiveness as a relationship maintenance process depends on the agreeableness of one's partner; likewise in the section on gratitude, we reviewed evidence that the effectiveness of gratitude on relationship outcomes depends on the partner's level of gratitude.

Given the important role of motivation in many of the effects described throughout this chapter, it is worth considering other qualities of the two partners that may determine each partner's communal motivations. One factor that may be particularly important in this regard is people's automatic evaluations of their partners. McNulty et al. (2013) demonstrated that people's ability to categorize positive and negative words after being exposed to photos of their partners, a measure of one's automatic attitude to the partner (see Fazio, Jackson, Dunton, & Williams, 1995), predicted the trajectory of their marital satisfaction over the first four years of marriage, whereas self-reported marital satisfaction did not. Dual process models of social cognition (e.g., Fazio & Olson, 2014) posit that such automatic attitudes drive attention, construal, and behavior, particularly when people lack sufficient cognitive resources, such as when they are faced with stress (see Buck & Neff, 2012). Accordingly, people with more positive automatic partner attitudes may have a default response to behave communally toward their partners and thus, may not require the additional motivation to behave communally that can be offered by withholding forgiveness, making accurate attributions, and withholding gratitude. In other words, intimates with partners who possess more positive attitudes toward them may be freer to think in benevolent ways without negative repercussions. It may be the partners with more negative automatic partner attitudes that need to be held in check.

The second broad category of contextual factors encompasses the qualities of the relationship itself. Specific qualities of a relationship can determine whether a particular relationship process is beneficial or detrimental. As described in the section on attributions, benevolent attributions are only beneficial if the relationship itself only involves relatively minor problems, suggesting that the severity of problems is a critical factor that determines the costs and benefits of these maintenance processes. Of course, given that less benevolent cognitions are presumed to provide benefits in the context of severe problems because they motivate people to take appropriate steps to resolve the problem, the controllability of those problems may play an additional role. That is, less benevolent cognitions may only be beneficial in the face of severe problems that are controllable.

Finally, the third class of contextual factors involves those related to the external environment (see Karney & Bradbury, 1995). The most notable factor in this regard is stress. As noted earlier, stress depletes cognitive resources (Buck & Neff, 2012) that are necessary for enacting self-control (Baumeister, Heatherton, & Tice, 1994). Accordingly, the most notable effect of stress may be minimizing the extent to which people are able to enact various relationship maintenance strategies (see Neff & Karney, 2009). But, in line with the ideas discussed here, stress might also moderate the implications of various relationship maintenance strategies by leading people to be guided more by their automatic inclinations, whatever they may be. Accordingly, completely understanding the implications of relationship maintenance requires knowing not only the extent of each partner's communal motivations but also their automatic tendencies and levels of stress. Indeed, stress has been shown to limit self-regulation, a process that has been shown to be important for romantic relationships (e.g., Balliet, Li, & Joireman, 2011; Finkel & Campbell, 2001), which may sometimes benefit the relationship. For example, Righetti, Finkenauer, and Finkel (2013) demonstrated that people with low self-control were *more* willing to sacrifice for a partner.

Finally, it is also important to point out methodological tools that can help illustrate how and why these processes seem to be beneficial to relationship maintenance in some contexts but not others. Given that the benefit or cost of a particular process can depend on the qualities of the partner, we recommend a dyadic analysis that is able to capture both partners' qualities, as illustrated by the work of McNulty and Russell (2016) and McNulty and Dugas (2019). Assessing only one partner's traits might only tell half the story. We also advocate for the use of within-subject longitudinal studies over a substantial period of time that allow researchers to examine how various processes are associated not only with initial levels of satisfaction but with changes in satisfaction over time. A crucial limitation of cross-sectional research is that relationship maintenance processes are incredibly dynamic and can change over time. Processes that seem beneficial in the short term may actually end up incurring more costs in the long term (e.g., a partner making positive attributions to avoid conflict in the short term but causing long-term problems by refusing to address these problems). Relationship maintenance is, after all, a long-term process.

CONCLUSION

Relationship maintenance processes are complicated. Research on these processes can benefit greatly by examining the specific contexts where they benefit relationships as well as the contexts where they incur costs. We hope our review of the processes described in this chapter illustrates the point that it is unlikely that relationship maintenance processes are universally positive or universally negative. Embracing the complicated, contextual nature of these processes can help us reconcile seemingly contradictory findings. Looking at how qualities of the two partners, the relationship, and the surrounding environment affect these processes allows us to begin to paint a fuller picture of how individuals use these processes in their romantic relationships.

REFERENCES

Ackermann, R., & DeRubeis, R. J. (1991). Is depressive realism real? *Clinical Psychology Review, 11*, 565–584.

Algoe, S. B. (2012). Find, remind, and bind: The functions of gratitude in everyday relationships. *Social and Personality Psychology Compass, 6*(6), 455–469.

Algoe, S. B., & Zhaoyang, R. (2016). Positive psychology in context: Effects of expressing gratitude in ongoing relationships depend on perceptions of enactor responsiveness. *The Journal of Positive Psychology, 11*(4), 399–415.

Algoe, S. B., Gable, S. L., & Maisel, N. C. (2010). It's the little things: Everyday gratitude as a booster shot for romantic relationships. *Personal Relationships, 17*(2), 217–233.

Algoe, S. B., Haidt, J., & Gable, S. L. (2008). Beyond reciprocity: Gratitude and relationships in everyday life. *Emotion, 8*(3), 425.

Alloy, L. B., & Abramson, L. Y. (1979). Judgment of contingency in depressed and nondepressed students: Sadder but wiser? *Journal of Experimental Psychology: General, 108*, 441–485.

Baker, L. R., & McNulty, J. K. (2011). Self-compassion and relationship maintenance: The moderating roles of conscientiousness and gender. *Journal of Personality and Social Psychology, 100*(5), 853.

Balliet, D., Li, N. P., & Joireman, J. (2011). Relating trait self-control and forgiveness within prosocials and proselfs: Compensatory versus synergistic models. *Journal of Personality and Social Psychology, 101*(5), 1090.

Baumeister, R. F. (1989). The optimal margin of illusion. *Journal of Social and Clinical Psychology, 8*, 176–189.

Baumeister, R. F., Heatherton, T. F., & Tice, D. M. (1994). *Losing control: How and why people fail at self-regulation.* Cambridge, MA: Academic Press.

Bolier, L., Haverman, M., Westerhof, G. J., Riper, H., Smit, F., & Bohlmeijer, E. (2013). Positive psychology interventions: A meta-analysis of randomized controlled studies. *BMC Public Health, 13*(1), 119.

Bradbury, T. N., & Fincham, F. D. (1990). Attributions in marriage: Review and critique. *Psychological Bulletin, 107*(1), 3.

Buck, A. A., & Neff, L. A. (2012). Stress spillover in early marriage: The role of self-regulatory depletion. *Journal of Family Psychology, 26*(5), 698.

Christensen, A., Atkins, D. C., Yi, J., Baucom, D. H., & George, W. H. (2006). Couple and individual adjustment for 2 years following a randomized clinical trial comparing traditional versus integrative behavioral couple therapy. *Journal of Consulting and Clinical Psychology, 74*(6), 1180.

Colvin, C. R., Block, J., & Funder, D. C. (1995). Overly positive self-evaluations and personality: Negative implications for mental health. *Journal of Personality and Social Psychology, 68*(6), 1152.

Crocker, J., Major, B., & Steele, C. (1998). Social stigma. In D. T. Gilbert & S. T. Fiske (Eds.), *The handbook of social psychology* (Vol. 2, 4th ed., pp. 504–533). Boston: McGraw-Hill.

Dillard, A. J., McCaul, K. D., & Klein, W. M. (2006). Unrealistic optimism in smokers: Implications for smoking myth endorsement and self-protective motivation. *Journal of Health Communication, 11*(S1), 93–102.

Fazio, R. H., & Olson, M. A. (2014). The MODE model: Attitude–behavior processes as a function of motivation and opportunity. In J. W. Sherman, B. Gawronski, & Y. Trope (Eds.), *Dual-process theories of the social mind* (pp. 155–171). New York, NY: Guilford Press.

Fazio, R. H., Jackson, J. R., Dunton, B. C., & Williams, C. J. (1995). Variability in automatic activation as an unobtrusive measure of racial attitudes: A bona fide pipeline? *Journal of Personality and Social Psychology, 69*, 1013–1027.

Fincham, F. D., & Beach, S. R. (2002). Forgiveness in marriage: Implications for psychological aggression and constructive communication. *Personal Relationships, 9*(3), 239–251.

Fincham, F., & Beach, S. R. (2007). Forgiveness and marital quality: Precursor or consequence in well-established relationships? *The Journal of Positive Psychology, 2*(4), 260–268.

Fincham, F. D., Beach, S. R. H., & Davila, J. (2004). Forgiveness and conflict resolution in marriage. *Journal of Family Psychology, 18*, 72–81.

Fincham, F. D., Beach, S. R. H., & Davila, J. (2007). Longitudinal relations between forgiveness and conflict resolution in marriage. *Journal of Family Psychology, 21*(3), 542–545.

Fincham, F. D., & Bradbury, T. N. (1987). The assessment of marital quality: A reevaluation. *Journal of Marriage and the Family, 49*, 797–809.

Fincham, F. D., & Bradbury, T. N. (1993). Marital satisfaction, depression, and attributions: A longitudinal analysis. *Journal of Personality and Social Psychology, 64*(3), 442.

Fincham, F. D., Hall, J., & Beach, S. R. (2006). Forgiveness in marriage: Current status and future directions. *Family Relations, 55*(4), 415–427.

Fincham, F. D., Harold, G. T., & Gano-Phillips, S. (2000). The longitudinal association between attributions and marital satisfaction: Direction of effects and role of efficacy expectations. *Journal of Family Psychology, 14*(2), 267–285.

Finkel, E. J., & Campbell, W. K. (2001). Self-control and accommodation in close relationships: An interdependence analysis. *Journal of Personality and Social Psychology, 81*(2), 263.

Fitzsimons, G. M., Finkel, E. J., & vanDellen, M. R. (2015). Transactive goal dynamics. *Psychological Review, 122*, 648–673.

Fletcher, G. J. O., & Kerr, P. S. G. (2010). Through the eyes of love: Reality and illusion in intimate relationships. *Psychological Bulletin, 136*(4), 627–658.

Gordon, C. L., Arnette, R. A., & Smith, R. E. (2011). Have you thanked your spouse today? Felt and expressed gratitude among married couples. *Personality and Individual Differences, 50*(3), 339–343.

Heider, F. (1958). *The psychology of interpersonal relations*. New York: John Wiley.

Heyman, R. E. (2001). Observation of couple conflicts: Clinical assessment applications, stubborn truths, and shaky foundations. *Psychological Assessment, 13*(1), 5–35.

Jacobson, N. S., Christensen, A., Prince, S. E., Cordova, J., & Eldridge, K. (2000). Integrative behavioral couple therapy: An acceptance-based, promising new treatment for couple discord. *Journal of Consulting and Clinical Psychology, 68*(2), 351.

Joel, S., Gordon, A. M., Impett, E. A., MacDonald, G., & Keltner, D. (2013). The things you do for me: Perceptions of a romantic partner's investments promote gratitude and commitment. *Personality and Social Psychology Bulletin, 39*(10), 1333–1345.

Karney, B. R., & Bradbury, T. N. (1995). The longitudinal course of marital quality and stability: A review of theory, methods, and research. *Psychological Bulletin, 118*(1), 3.

Karremans, J. C., & Van Lange, P. A. (2004). Back to caring after being hurt: The role of forgiveness. *European Journal of Social Psychology, 34*(2), 207–227.

Katz, J., Arias, I., Beach, S. R., Brody, G., & Roman, P. (1995). Excuses, excuses: Accounting for the effects of partner violence on marital satisfaction and stability. *Violence and Victims, 10*(4), 315.

Kearns, J. N., & Fincham, F. D. (2004). A prototype analysis of forgiveness. *Personality and Social Psychology Bulletin, 30*(7), 838–855.

Kelley, H. H. (1967). Attribution theory in social psychology. In D. Levine (Ed.), *Nebraska Symposium on Motivation* (Volume 15, pp. 192–238). Lincoln: University of Nebraska Press.

Kelley, H. H. (1971). *Attributions in social interactions.* Morristown, NJ: General Learning Press.

Kelley, H. H., & Thibaut, J. W. (1978). *Interpersonal relations: A theory of independence.* New York: Wiley.

Lambert, N. M., & Fincham, F. D. (2011). Expressing gratitude to a partner leads to more relationship maintenance behavior. *Emotion, 11*(1), 52.

Luchies, L. B., Finkel, E. J., McNulty, J. K., & Kumashiro, M. (2010). The doormat effect: When forgiving erodes self-respect and self-concept clarity. *Journal of Personality and Social Psychology, 98*(5), 734.

Major, B., & Schmader, T. (1998). Coping with stigma through psychological disengagement. In J. K. Swim & C. Stangor (Eds.), *Prejudice: The target's perspective* (pp. 219–241). San Diego, CA: Academic Press.

McCullough, M. E., Kimeldorf, M. B., & Cohen, A. D. (2008). An adaptation for altruism: The social causes, social effects, and social evolution of gratitude. *Current Directions in Psychological Science, 17*(4), 281–285.

McCullough, M. E., Rachal, K. C., Sandage, S. J., Worthington Jr, E. L., Brown, S. W., & Hight, T. L. (1998). Interpersonal forgiving in close relationships: II. Theoretical elaboration and measurement. *Journal of Personality and Social Psychology, 75*(6), 1586.

McCullough, M. E., Worthington, E. L., & Rachal, K. C. (1997). Interpersonal forgiving in close relationships. *Journal of Personality and Social Psychology, 73*, 321–336.

McNulty, J. K. (2008). Forgiveness in marriage: Putting the benefits into context. *Journal of Family Psychology, 22*, 171–175.

McNulty, J. K. (2010). Forgiveness increases the likelihood of subsequent partner transgressions in marriage. *Journal of Family Psychology, 24*, 787–790.

McNulty, J. K. (2011). The dark side of forgiveness: The tendency to forgive predicts continued psychological and physical aggression in marriage. *Personality and Social Psychology Bulletin, 37*, 770–783.

McNulty, J. K. (2016). Highlighting the contextual nature of interpersonal relationships. In J. M. Olson & M. P. Zanna (Eds.), *Advances in experimental social psychology* (Vol. 54, pp. 247–315). San Diego, CA: Academic Press.

McNulty, J. K., & Dugas, A. (2019). A dyadic perspective on gratitude sheds light on both its benefits and its costs: Evidence that low gratitude acts as a "weak link." *Journal of Family Psychology.* doi:10.1037/fam0000533.

McNulty, J. K., & Fincham, F. D. (2012). Beyond positive psychology? Toward a contextual view of psychological processes and well-being. *American Psychologist, 67*, 101–110.

McNulty, J. K., & Karney, B. R. (2001). Attributions in marriage: Integrating specific and global evaluations of a relationship. *Personality and Social Psychology Bulletin, 27*(8), 943–955.

McNulty, J. K., Olson, M. A., Jones, R. E., & Acosta, L. (2017). Automatic associations between one's partner and one's affect as the proximal mechanism of change in relationship satisfaction: Evidence from evaluative conditioning. *Psychological Science, 28,* 1031–1040.

McNulty, J. K., Olson, M. A., Meltzer, A. L., & Shaffer, M. J. (2013). Though they may be unaware, newlyweds implicitly know whether their marriage will be satisfying. *Science, 342,* 1119–1120.

McNulty, J. K., O'Mara, E. M., & Karney, B. R. (2008). Benevolent cognitions as a strategy of relationship maintenance: "Don't sweat the small stuff" . . .. But it is not all small stuff. *Journal of Personality and Social Psychology, 94*(4), 631.

McNulty, J. K., & Russell, V. M. (2010). When "negative" behaviors are positive: A contextual analysis of the long-term effects of problem-solving behaviors on changes in relationship satisfaction. *Journal of Personality and Social Psychology, 98*(4), 587.

McNulty, J. K., & Russell, V. M. (2016). Forgive and forget, or forgive and regret? Whether forgiveness leads to less or more offending depends on offender agreeableness. *Personality and Social Psychology Bulletin, 42*(5), 616–631.

Murray, S. L., Griffin, D. W., Derrick, J. L., Harris, B., Aloni, M., & Leder, S. (2011). Tempting fate or inviting happiness? Unrealistic idealization prevents the decline of marital satisfaction. *Psychological Science, 22,* 619–626.

Murray, S. L., Holmes, J. G., & Griffin, D. W. (1996). The self-fulfilling nature of positive illusions in romantic relationships: Love is not blind, but prescient. *Journal of Personality and Social Psychology, 71*(6), 1155.

Neff, L. A., & Karney, B. R. (2009). Stress and reactivity to daily relationship experiences: How stress hinders adaptive processes in marriage. *Journal of Personality and Social Psychology, 97*(3), 435–450.

Nowak, M., & Sigmund, K. (1993). A strategy of win-stay, lose-shift that outperforms tit-for-tat in the Prisoner's Dilemma game. *Nature, 364*(6432), 56–58.

O'Mara, E. M., McNulty, J. K., & Karney B. R. (2011). Positively biased appraisals in everyday life: When do they benefit mental health and when do they harm it? *Journal of Personality and Social Psychology, 101,* 415–432.

Overall, N. C., Fletcher, G. J. O., & Simpson, J. A. (2006). Regulation processes in intimate relationships: The role of ideal standards. *Journal of Personality and Social Psychology, 91*(4), 662–685.

Overall, N. C., Fletcher, G. J. O., Simpson, J. A., & Sibley, C. G. (2009). Regulating partners in intimate relationships: The costs and benefits of different communication strategies. *Journal of Personality and Social Psychology, 96,* 620–639.

Overall, N. C., & McNulty, J. K. (2017). What type of communication during conflict is beneficial for intimate relationships? *Current Opinion in Psychology, 13,* 1–5.

Paleari, F. G., Regalia, C., & Fincham, F. (2005). Marital quality, forgiveness, empathy, and rumination: A longitudinal analysis. *Personality and Social Psychology Bulletin, 31,* 368–378.

Pape, K. T., & Arias, I. (2000). The role of perceptions and attributions in battered women's intentions to permanently end their violent relationships. *Cognitive Therapy and Research, 24*(2), 201–214.

Reis, H. T., Clark, M. S., & Holmes, J. G. (2004). Perceived partner responsiveness as an organizing construct in the study of intimacy and closeness. In D. Mashek & A. Aron (Eds.), *The handbook of closeness and intimacy* (pp. 201–225). Mahwah, NJ: Lawrence Erlbaum Associates.

Righetti, F., Finkenauer, C., & Finkel, E. J. (2013). Low self-control promotes the willingness to sacrifice in close relationships. *Psychological Science, 24*(8), 1533–1540.

Robins, R. W., & Beer, J. S. (2001). Positive illusions about the self: Short-term benefits and long-term costs. *Journal of Personality and Social Psychology, 80*(2), 340.

Russell, V. M., Baker, L. R., McNulty, J. K., & Overall, N. C. (2018). "You're forgiven, but don't do it again!" Direct partner regulation buffers the costs of forgiveness. *Journal of Family Psychology, 32*(4), 435–444.

Skinner, B. F. (1969). *Contingencies of reinforcement.* East Norwalk, CT: Appleton-Century-Crofts.

Stafford, L., & Canary, D. J. (1991). Maintenance strategies and romantic relationship type, gender and relational characteristics. *Journal of Social and Personal Relationships, 8*(2), 217–242.

Steele, C. M., Spencer, S. J., & Aronson, J. (2002). Contending with group image: The psychology of stereotype and social identity threat. In M. Zanna (Ed.), *Advances in experimental social psychology* (pp. 379–440). San Diego, CA: Academic Press.

Taylor, S. E., & Brown, J. D. (1988). Illusion and well-being: A social psychological perspective on mental health. *Psychological Bulletin, 103*(2), 193–210.

Trivers, R. L. (1971). The evolution of reciprocal altruism. *The Quarterly Review of Biology, 46*(1), 35–57.

Truman-Schram, D. M., Cann, A., Calhoun, L., & Vanwallendael, L. (2000). Leaving an abusive dating relationship: An investment model comparison of women who stay versus women who leave. *Journal of Social and Clinical Psychology, 19*, 161–183.

Tsang, J. A., McCullough, M. E., & Fincham, F. D. (2006). The longitudinal association between forgiveness and relationship closeness and commitment. *Journal of Social and Clinical Psychology, 25*(4), 448–472.

Van Kleef, G. A., Homan, A. C., Beersma, B., & van Knippenberg, D. (2010). On angry leaders and agreeable followers: How leaders' emotions and followers' personalities shape motivation and team performance. *Psychological Science, 21*(12), 1827–1834.

Weiner, B. (1985). An attributional theory of achievement motivation and emotion. *Psychological Review, 92*(4), 548–573.

Younger, J. W., Piferi, R. L., Jobe, R. L., & Lawler, K. A. (2004). Dimensions of forgiveness: The views of laypersons. *Journal of Social and Personal Relationships, 21*(6), 837–855.

9

Social Networks and Relationship Maintenance

SUSAN SPRECHER[1], DIANE FELMLEE[2], JEFFREY E. STOKES[3],
AND BRANDON MCDANIEL[4]

Relationships are embedded in social networks consisting of each dyad member's family, friends, and acquaintances. Whether a relationship is developed, how it is maintained, and the likelihood that it dissolves are influenced by factors associated with social networks, in addition to factors internal to the relationship. However, social network characteristics, such as network approval for the relationship and network overlap between relational partners, have been relatively neglected in relationship research, and particularly in regard to the maintenance of close ties. In this chapter, we focus specifically on the influence of social networks on relationship maintenance. We define relationship maintenance as the processes by which partners keep their relationship intact and sustain it at a high quality with regard to relationship attributes such as satisfaction and commitment.

In the first section following, we discuss how integrating one's relationship with social networks (particularly doing activities with mutual friends) represents one of several strategies people do to keep their relationships maintained, and one that is represented in the Relational Maintenance Strategies Measure (RMSM) (Canary & Stafford, 1992). In the second section, we discuss the literature from the Investment model perspective (Rusbult, Drigotas, & Verette, 1994) on how social networks affect dyad members' motivation and ability to engage in various maintenance mechanisms as processes that follow from commitment. We end the second section by considering how provisions from the social network toward maintaining relationships may vary across the life course and relationship stage. In the third section, we discuss the literature on the role of advice from the social network in helping couples maintain and repair their relationships, especially

[1] Department of Sociology & Anthropology, Illinois State University, sprecher@ilstu.edu
[2] Department of Sociology & Criminology, Pennsylvania State University, dhf@psu.edu
[3] Department of Gerontology, University of Massachusetts Boston, jeffrey.stokes@umb.edu
[4] Health Services and Informatics Research, Parkview Research Center, BTMcDaniel.PhD@gmail.com

when there has been damage to the relationships. In the fourth section, we turn to macro-level issues regarding how structural dimensions of social networks (network overlap and composition of the network) can affect dyad members' ability to maintain their relationship.

In today's world of hyperconnectivity, social networks influence couples' relationship maintenance not only in face-to-face settings but also through social media and computer-mediated communication; our fifth section discusses how social networks can influence relationship maintenance through communication technology. We end the chapter with suggestions for further research in the intersection of networks and relationship maintenance.

SOCIAL NETWORKS AS A MAINTENANCE STRATEGY: RESULTS FROM RESEARCH WITH THE RELATIONAL MAINTENANCE STRATEGIES MEASURE

One of the most commonly used instruments for assessing the prevalence and efficacy of various maintenance strategies is the RMSM. The original RMSM distinguished among five domains of maintenance strategies: positivity, assurances, openness, sharing tasks, and – the focus of this chapter – social networks (Canary & Stafford, 1992; Stafford & Canary, 1991). The RMSM has changed over time, including the addition of new questions on social networks (Canary & Stafford, 1992), and it remains widely used for studying maintenance strategies (Canary, 2011; Stafford, Chapter 7).

Although the domains of maintenance strategies are distinct from one another, they are not mutually exclusive. In general, partners who engage in any relationship maintenance tend to use strategies across the five domains. A meta-analysis of research using the RMSM found correlations among the five maintenance strategy domains ranging from 0.37 to 0.65, all of which were significant, with correlations involving social networks in particular ranging from 0.37 (with openness) to 0.45 (with positivity; see Ogolsky & Bowers, 2013). In other words, engaging with mutual friends and family members to help sustain a healthy relationship goes hand-in-hand with other maintenance strategies, albeit less so than some of the intra-dyadic behaviors (e.g., openness and assurances, which correlate at $r = 0.65$, or assurances and positivity, where $r = 0.64$). Moreover, a partner's maintenance behaviors matter as well: the strongest predictor of whether an individual uses social networks as a maintenance strategy is the perception that his or her partner does so (Dainton & Stafford, 2000; Weigel & Ballard-Reisch, 1999a).

Research using the RMSM suggests that social network maintenance behaviors – i.e., the use of one's social network as a resource for maintaining an intimate relationship – can play an important role in promoting successful relationships. For instance, social network maintenance behaviors have been linked with greater commitment, liking, and satisfaction, as well as with reduced jealousy and relational uncertainty (e.g., Dainton & Aylor, 2001; Stafford, Dainton, & Haas, 2000). Even when accounting for the fact that individuals simultaneously use various maintenance strategies, research indicates that social networks in particular can help foster positive relationship outcomes (e.g., commitment), although not all results are consistent across studies (e.g., Canary & Stafford, 1992; Dainton, Stafford, & Canary, 1994; Stafford, 2011; Stafford et al., 2000; Weigel & Ballard-Reisch, 1999a). Social network maintenance is also critical for relationship stability. For example, individuals in on-again/off-again relationships report less social network maintenance – as well as more negative and fewer positive relationship experiences – than their noncyclical counterparts, suggesting that social network maintenance may reduce the number or likelihood of relationship transitions (i.e., breakups and renewals; Dailey, Hampel, & Roberts, 2010; Dailey, Pfiester, Jin, Beck, & Clark, 2009).

When assessing maintenance behaviors via the RMSM, it is crucial to take into account who reports and about whom. For instance, women report engaging in significantly more social network maintenance behaviors than men do, yet women also believe their partners engage in more social network maintenance than men believe *their* partners do, although these differences are relatively small (Ogolsky & Bowers, 2013). There is also some evidence that wives' maintenance behaviors are more consequential than husbands' maintenance behaviors for both spouses' satisfaction, commitment, and love (Weigel & Ballard-Reisch, 1999b). As pertains to social network maintenance behaviors specifically, a meta-analysis underscores that the characteristics and context of the reporter matter for effects on relationship outcomes as well. Links between social network maintenance and certain relationship outcomes (e.g., satisfaction and liking) were stronger (1) when participants reported on perceptions of a partner's maintenance behaviors rather than their own and (2) when participants were women. However, no such sex differences arose concerning links between social network maintenance and the relationship outcomes of commitment, love, or duration (Ogolsky & Bowers, 2013).

Social networks can serve as a resource for either strategic or routine relationship maintenance (e.g., Dainton & Stafford, 1993). Whereas certain behaviors can be considered routine because they are a "by-product" of typically enacted behaviors, strategic maintenance behaviors are those done with the intent of maintaining or enhancing the relationship. These two forms of social network maintenance behaviors are related to one another, as those who engage in strategic maintenance tend also to engage in routine maintenance. Indeed, the same behaviors may be used at certain times routinely and at other times strategically (Dindia, 2000; Stafford et al., 2000). However, only routine social network maintenance increases with relationship duration; strategic social network maintenance does not (Dainton & Aylor, 2002).

Researchers have used the RMSM scale to assess relationship maintenance behaviors for over 25 years. As the RMSM continues to adapt with time
(Canary, 2011), its further use presents researchers with opportunities for new
insights into social network maintenance behaviors, including application of
the RMSM to social networks that are increasingly mediated by internet-
based social media platforms (e.g., Dainton, 2013; Ledbetter, 2010).

EFFECTS OF PROVISIONS FROM THE SOCIAL NETWORK ON MAINTENANCE MECHANISMS

As described in the prior section, relational partners report that they use their
social network (e.g., spending time with mutual friends) to help maintain
a high-quality relationship (Stafford & Canary, 1991). People also have many
other strategies to maintain their relationships, and the use of these strategies
can be influenced by social networks. To discuss these issues, we refer to the
Investment model, which originated from Interdependence theory (Kelley &
Thibaut, 1978) and has been extended to understand how maintenance cognitions and behaviors follow from commitment (see also VanderDrift & Agnew,
Chapter 2).

According to the Investment model (Rusbult, 1983), commitment is
increased based on high satisfaction (ratio of rewards to costs), low perceived
quality of alternatives, and greater investments. Extensions of the theory
argue that commitment leads relational partners to be motivated to engage
in relational maintenance mechanisms to enhance the likelihood that their
relationship continues (e.g., Rusbult, Agnew, & Arriaga, 2012; Rusbult &
Buunk, 1993; Rusbult et al., 1994). In particular, Rusbult and other
Investment model theorists (e.g., Agnew & VanderDrift, 2015; Rusbult et al.,
1994) have identified cognitive and behavioral mechanisms that follow from
commitment and are used to maintain or increase interdependence in the
relationship. Cognitive maintenance mechanisms include developing
a feeling of mutuality or cognitive interdependence, perceiving one's relationship to be superior to others, engaging in other positive illusions (idealizing
the partner), and ignoring or even derogating alternatives to the relationship.
Behavioral maintenance mechanisms include forgiving one's partner for
a transgression, accommodating to a partner's irritating behavior, engaging
in leisure time together, and sacrificing for one's partner.

Using the extension of the Investment model to maintenance mechanisms (Rusbult et al., 1994), we argue that approval from the social network for
relationships can indirectly influence whether relational partners are motivated to engage in maintenance mechanisms. More specifically, social network reactions can influence relational partners' satisfaction and
commitment, which then influence the likelihood that they engage in cognitions and behaviors to maintain the relationship. Indeed, considerable

research has indicated that social network approval is a distinct constraint variable that contributes to commitment (above and beyond other Investment model predictors) and can be considered a reward that leads to satisfaction and commitment (Blair & Holmberg, 2008; Cox, Wexler, Rusbult, & Gaines, 1997; Lehmiller & Agnew, 2007; Rodrigues, Lopes, Monteiro, & Prada, 2017; Sinclair, Felmlee, Sprecher, & Wright, 2015). In addition to the indirect influence of social networks on maintenance strategies (through their effects on satisfaction and commitment), reactions and provisions from social networks are more directly involved in certain maintenance strategies identified as following from commitment (Rusbult et al., 1994), as we discuss next.

SOCIAL NETWORKS AND COGNITIVE MAINTENANCE STRATEGIES

People come to think of themselves and their partners as a unit or a "we," which is a cognition that helps maintain the relationship. Investment model theorists have referred to this process in various ways, including cognitive interdependence, mutuality, and self–other overlap (Agnew, Van Lange, Rusbult, & Langston, 1998). Network researchers have invoked a similar concept to explain the positive effect of social network support on the quality of relationships. Drawing from the social interactionist perspective (Waller & Hill, 1951), network researchers argue that couples develop a dyadic identity based on positive reactions from others (Felmlee & Sprecher, 2000; Lewis, 1973; Sprecher & Felmlee, 1992). Thus, the more that network members react positively to a couple – such as saying that the two make a good pair, inviting them as a couple to an event, and buying them a joint present (e.g., Sprecher, 2011) – the more likely it is that the couple will develop a dyadic identity or cognitive interdependence (Agnew et al., 1998).

Another cognitive maintenance mechanism that is fostered by commitment and involves the social network is perceived superiority (Rusbult & Buunk, 1993; Van Lange & Rusbult, 1995), which is believing that one's relationship is superior to and likely to have more positive outcomes than the relationships of others. People compare their relationship with those of network members, and if committed, come to see their own relationship as better than the relationships of others (Rusbult, Van Lange, Wildschut, Yovetich, & Verette, 2000; Van Lange & Rusbult, 1995). This may occur for a variety of reasons, including the greater salience of negative information than of positive information learned about others' relationships. It may also occur due to a motivation to seek downward social comparisons (versus upward social comparisons) in order to protect one's relationship (Buunk, 2001). However, the perceived superiority effect has been found to be weaker when the comparison is with the relationship of a specific close friend (Reis, Caprariello, & Velickovic, 2011).

SOCIAL NETWORKS AND BEHAVIORAL MAINTENANCE MECHANISMS

One behavioral maintenance technique is for partners to spend time together, which is associated with relationship satisfaction and commitment (Reissman, Aron, & Bergen, 1993; see Xu, Lewandowski, & Aron, Chapter 6). Not all time with one's partner is likely to be equal in terms of maintaining and enhancing the relationship, however. Engaging in novel, stimulating activities, in particular, has been found to be associated with enhanced satisfaction (Girme, Overall, & Faingataa, 2013). For example, experimental research shows that couples randomly assigned to a novel stimulating activity, as opposed to a more mundane, typical activity, reported greater satisfaction (Aron, Norman, Aron, McKenna, & Heyman, 2000; Reissman et al., 1993). Furthermore, the degree to which couples spend time together and have the resources to engage in fun, novel, and stimulating activities can be affected by supportive social networks. For example, friends and family members babysit small children so that young parents can go on dates or even vacations. Parents who have the financial means may also offer a vacation home or money to help couples engage in enjoyable, stimulating activities that can enhance their relationship (Fingerman, Miller, Birditt, & Zarit, 2009).

One specific novel activity that can aid in maintaining a relationship is to engage in fun activities with other couples. Spending time with other couples, particularly new couple friends, can provide couples with an opportunity to strengthen their bond. Experience sampling studies (in which participants answer survey questions at random times across many days) have demonstrated that people report more positive moods when they are with both their spouse and friends than when being with any other possible others or combination of others, including only the spouse (Larson, Mannell, & Zuzanek, 1986). As noted by Slatcher (2010), the positive affect that is generated by spending time with other couples can extend to positive feelings for one's partner through positive reinforcement. Slatcher conducted a creative experiment in which two couples arrived at a laboratory session at the same time (60 couples in total) and were randomly assigned to engage in either intimate self-disclosure or small talk. Relational partners in the intimate condition with another couple reported feeling closer to each other (and to the other couple) than relational partners assigned to the small talk condition. At a one-month follow-up, partners in the experimental group continued to feel closer to each other (although marginally so). In addition, couples in the high-disclosure condition at the follow-up reported being more committed to the relationship success of the other couple.

Although social networks can help happy couples do more of what they are already doing (experiencing cognitive interdependence, perceiving their relationship to be superior, and finding time to play together), there may be times when a threat is encountered in the relationship, and special maintenance mechanisms are needed to prevent the relationship from dissolving (Agnew & VanderDrift, 2015; Lydon & Quinn, 2013). For example, if one partner commits a transgression (e.g., betrayal or infidelity), partners may engage in mainte-nance cognitions and behaviors to respond to the threat. These maintenance/repair strategies include particular attribution patterns (e.g., making external, unstable attributions for the partner's negative behavior), accommodation (e.g., engaging in voice and loyalty), and forgiveness (Lydon & Quinn, 2013).

Although social networks may affect, at least indirectly, any of these maintenance mechanisms, recent research has focused on how networks can influence the likelihood that individuals forgive their partner for a transgression. As noted by Green, Davis, and Reid (2014), when indivi-duals experience a transgression by their partner, they are likely to disclose to third parties, who are close to them, were not involved in the transgres-sion, and may also know the transgressor. The third parties may express their own opinions about the transgression and in addition, often decide themselves whether to forgive the transgressor. Through their actions and words, third parties can affect whether the victim forgives the transgressing partner; this is referred to as the *third party forgiveness effect*. Green, Burnette, and Davis (2008) hypothesized that third parties are generally less likely than the victim to forgive the transgressing partner, and found support for this prediction in two vignette experiments. However, as noted by Green et al. (2014), there may be times when a third party facilitates forgiveness in the relationship, especially if the third party is committed to both partners. Therefore, social network members can be involved in help-ing individuals engage in forgiveness, a maintenance strategy (see McNulty & Dugas, Chapter 8).

SOCIAL NETWORK PROVISIONS SPECIFIC TO LIFE-STAGE AND RELATIONSHIP-STAGE ISSUES

The type of network support that helps couples maintain their relationships is likely to vary across relationship stages and also the life stages of the relational partners (Rauer & Proulx, Chapter 17). What may be especially important to young adults who are in newly developing relationships is approval from friends and family for their relationship, particularly during times of uncer-tainty, which are common during transitional periods of a relationship (Keneski & Loving, 2014; Solomon & Knobloch, 2001). In addition, in order to develop a strong identity as a couple, young couples early in their relation-ship may realign their social networks. For instance, they may withdraw from their social ties to focus on each other, referred to as *dyadic withdrawal* (Huston & Burgess, 1979). Developing couples may also withdraw from only certain friends and spend more time with kin and mutual friends in a process identified as *dyadic realignment* (Johnson & Leslie, 1982; Milardo, Johnson, & Huston, 1983). Thus, social networks can help new romantic pairs maintain their developing relationships by responding to their attempts to refocus their social connections to better suit their current needs as a couple.

After relational partners become fully committed to each other, they may no longer need social network members to help them reduce uncertainty about the partner or aid them in developing a couple identity. However, committed relational partners may rely on the social network for other provisions to assist them in maintaining their relationship. For example, couples who move through stages of parenthood may want assistance in caring for their children in order to have time for each other, as noted earlier. In addition, couples may face stressors over the life course, such as unemployment and illness, which place them at risk for dissatisfaction and dissolution. Supportive networks can help couples cope with such stressors and maintain their relationships (Karney & Bradbury, 1995). Furthermore, marriage has been described as "greedy" in terms of taking time away from family and friends (Sarkisian & Gerstel, 2016), but despite this "greediness," relationships with parents and in-laws can influence marital satisfaction throughout adulthood, and become particularly important during periods of need or transition, such as bereavement (Bryant, Conger, & Meehan, 2001; Reczek, Liu, & Umberson, 2010; Stokes, 2016).

After years of marriage, older couples may still need assistance from their network to maintain their relationships. For example, with increased health issues faced by one or both partners in a relationship, social network members (such as adult children) may be instrumental in helping a couple still live together in their home – although support provision may also strain those relationships (e.g., Kim et al., 2017). Furthermore, because of divorce and widowhood, many individuals enter new relationships in middle age and later life. Social networks (including children) are likely to be instrumental in affecting whether a particular relationship (after divorce or widowhood) is developed and maintained (Gray, Franco, Garcia, Gesselman, & Fisher, 2016).

Throughout adulthood, there are many other close connections that need to be nurtured beyond the romantic/marital relationship. In fact, other close relationships can become more important over the life course (Wrzus, Hänel, Wagner, & Neyer, 2013). Parents want to maintain ties with their adult children who no longer live with them, and adult children share this same sentiment. Sibling relationships can be influential throughout the life course and need maintenance (Vogl-Bauer, 2003). Furthermore, some people enter into a new type of familial relationship, with grandchildren, and these intergenerational connections also require attention and are often mediated by the middle generation (Mansson, 2016; Monserud, 2008).

Socioemotional selectivity theory (Carstensen, Isaacowitz, & Charles, 1999) suggests that as people age or become closer to death, they prefer to maintain fewer relationships but at a higher level of intimacy. Thus, older adults may focus their maintenance efforts on a few close others rather than spending time broadening their social connectivity (Waldinger, Cohen, Schulz, & Crowell, 2015). Yet, not all social network reductions in later life are intentional, and older adults may lack the social resources needed to initiate new relationships or successfully rekindle those that have lapsed (Rook, 2009). Adults in later life can encounter difficulty in "compensating" for intimate relationship losses, for instance, underscoring the importance of developing extended network ties that are maintained throughout earlier life stages.

SPECIAL ASSISTANCE DURING RELATIONSHIP DAMAGE: ADVICE FROM THE NETWORK

Couples also use their social connections to gather advice regarding the maintenance of their relationship during the initial stages of a romance as well as during times when an established pair faces challenges to their bond. Such advice gathering is quite common. According to a national survey, a large majority (73%) of US adults reported acting as a confidant in a situation in which a friend, sibling, or acquaintance discussed with them relationship problems regarding minor disagreements or more serious issues, such as emotional abuse and infidelity (Seal, Doherty, & Harris, 2016). A study of young adults found that friends remain the most important source for romantic partners to garner support and guidance as they progress through various relationship stages (Baxter, Dun, & Sahistein, 2001). In spite of the commonality of network-offered relationship advice, studies of the processes through which networks provide advice are relatively limited (MacGeorge & Hall, 2014).

Social network members can offer many types of guidance for those in relationships. According to Baxter et al. (2001), unsolicited advice in the form of relaying "relationship rules" was one of the most frequent ways in which friends, especially those of the same sex, provided relationship assistance. Common rules emerged regarding relationship maintenance, for example, including those enforcing relationship fidelity, openness and honesty, and informational discretion. Individuals reported high levels of compliance with such relationship rules and the presence of negative sanctions from network members if they violated the rules.

Romantic couples also engage their friends in "marriage [or relationship] work" (Oliker, 1989), wherein they involve network members in conversations regarding relationship concerns (Jensen & Rauer, 2015). Wives are more likely than husbands to discuss such problems with friends, and wives' feelings about their marriage tend to improve following such interactions (Oliker, 1989; Rubin, 1985). On the other hand, discussing relationship problems frequently with friends, but seldom with one's partner, results in poorer relationship outcomes, including lower happiness, commitment, and love (Jensen & Rauer, 2014), and compromised marital quality (Helms, Crouter, & McHale, 2003). Similarly, conflict arises when wives discuss sensitive marital matters with friends more than with their husbands (Proulx, Helms, & Payne, 2004). Engaging in relationship work with one's network may be beneficial, in other words, but not when it comes at the cost of ignoring this type of relationship-maintenance labor directly with one's partner. At the same time, these patterns of handling marriage work may be more germane to young couples as compared with those who are older. According to Jensen and Rauer (2015), many older couples may prefer to avoid openly discussing dyadic conflict in an attempt to focus primarily on emotional, marital rewards.

EFFECTS OF STRUCTURAL ASPECTS OF THE NETWORK ON RELATIONSHIP MAINTENANCE

In this section, we turn to more macro-level issues regarding the compositional or structural dimensions of social networks and the ways in which they play a role in the maintenance of couples' relationships. One of the features of composition that have received research focus is network overlap, the degree to which the partners' networks converge. Research demonstrates that the social ties of a romantic dyad increase in shared friends as the relationship develops (Milardo, 1982) and over the life course for married and cohabiting couples (Kalmijn, 2003). Individuals also tend to befriend their partner's friends (exhibiting friendship transitivity) and reach out to new couple friends as well.

There are several conceptual mechanisms by which network overlap might contribute to keeping relationships intact. One of the main arguments is that the more entwined are the social connections of relational partners, the more difficult it becomes to dissolve the bond, suggesting that network overlap represents a form of structural commitment (Johnson, Caughlin, & Huston 1999), or "social capital," at the couple level. Joint network members tend to share values and norms, which they convey to a couple and which may strengthen the relationship; in addition, network members may coordinate attempts to influence couples in positive ways (Milardo & Helms-Erikson, 2000). Moreover, trying to break up in the face of an interlinked set of friends and family ties involves informing mutual network members, who may be invested heavily in the relationship (Milardo, 1982), be upset about a breakup, and even actively work to oppose such an ending. Common friends also may help mend strained relationship bonds by employing some of the mechanisms discussed earlier – offering support, sharing advice, identifying the two people as a couple, and involving the pair in enjoyable activities and events.

Empirical studies find support for the argument that network overlap enhances intimate relationships. For example, according to a study of older married adults (Cornwell, 2012), contact with a spouse's network members was linked to positive relationship outcomes, including considering one's spouse as a source of support. In one study, network overlap of family relationships related negatively to the likelihood of the breakup of unmarried relationships, although it was not significantly related to the breakup of marriages (Hogerbrugge, Komter, & Scheepers, 2013). Disclosing to other couples also improves feelings of closeness and commitment among couples (Slatcher, 2010; see earlier), and therefore, having shared couple friends probably contributes to relationship maintenance. Several studies find, too, that social network approval often mediates the effect of network overlap on relationship stability and/or quality (Felmlee, 2001; Sprecher & Felmlee, 1992; 2000). That is, one of the reasons why network overlap contributes positively to relationships is that conjoint networks tend to be more supportive and approving of a couple's relationship than those that are disjoint.

At the same time, social network overlap tends to unravel when couples begin to disengage and break up (Milardo, 1982). Such a pattern is likely to be particularly true with respect to network members who provide emotional support during a breakup, in which case people may prefer to divulge confidences solely to friends who are *not* shared with their mate. For example, individuals do not view their primary relationship supporters as emanating from their overlapping network, according to Klein and Milardo (2000), but instead see their supporters as located among their separate, same-sex friends. Moreover, husbands and wives in chronically strained marriages have crisis support networks that only rarely overlap, consisting instead of almost completely disjoint sets of confidants (Veiel, Crisand, Stroszeck-Somschor, & Herrie, 1991).

Couples also differ in the composition of their conjoint, or duocentric, networks, with differences in the degree to which they share family and friends (Stein, Bush, Ross, & Ward, 1992) and variance in the extent to which the male's versus the female's network dominates (Widmer, Kellerhals, & Levy, 2004). Network composition also can differ by race and ethnicity. For example, in one study, Mexican American couples were found to be more likely to live with or near other family members than were Euro Americans, a pattern primarily accounted for by differences in social class associated with ethnicity (Sarkisian, Gerena, & Gerstel, 2007). In addition, research finds that the composition of Black couples' networks exhibits disadvantages as compared with those of Whites. Blacks have fewer than half of the joint network ties of White couples, and a higher proportion of Black couples' mutual contacts have a positive relationship with only one member of the pair (Jackson, Kennedy, Bradbury, & Karney, 2014).

Network size also can matter for ongoing relationship maintenance, and specifically the degree to which there are network members available who can act as alternative sources of resources. According to Finkel, Hui, Carswell, and Larson (2014), today's romantic relationships suffer from what is termed "suffocation," in that couples end up depending on each other for an increasingly wide and demanding range of behaviors. However, in a large and extensive network, there may be constituents who exhibit "substitutability" for a romantic partner, in that they provide some of the same types of rewards, such as companionship, economic resources, and emotional and/or even physical intimacy (Marsiglio & Scanzoni, 1995). One maintenance strategy individuals have is to enlist the assistance of their "exchangeable" network members in addressing individual and relationship needs, instead of relying solely on their partner. Such an approach might alleviate the burden placed on partners to provide for all of each other's needs.

Nevertheless, it is possible that high levels of substitutability could undermine relationship stability in some circumstances. Felmlee (2001), for example, found that participants who reported being extremely close to a best friend experienced relatively high rates of breakup in their intimate relationship over time as compared with those without such a strongly connected friend. Having a very close friend probably allowed detachment from an unsatisfying or dysfunctional relationship. Note that not all relationships should be sustained at all costs; some are deleterious to one or both partners. Therefore, network substitutability could either operate as a strategy used to counter couple "suffocation," or, alternatively, it could be a mechanism to aid in extricating oneself from a truly problematic involvement.

Finally, the relationship status of social network members also can influence eventual couple outcomes. Using longitudinal data from the Framingham Heart Study, McDermott, Fowler, and Christakis (2013) found that divorce occurs in clusters within a larger social network, and that divorce can spread through the network up to a distance of two connections away (i.e., friend of a friend). Attending to the sustainability of one's friends' marriages, therefore, may help to improve the stability of one's own marital relationship. In addition, the divorce rate among couples in a sample from the Netherlands was higher when individuals had experienced a parental divorce, had divorced siblings, and lived in a municipality with a high divorce rate (Hogerbrugge et al., 2013). It appears that marriages that fail to endure, in other words, often do so within the context of communities of people who cannot easily encourage or model lasting relationships.

In sum, research regarding network composition (i.e., overlap, size, and relationship status) receives much less attention in the relationships literature than other aspects of networks, such as support and encouragement. Yet, we see here that the structure and construction of the joint social network also play a substantial part in shaping relationship processes and stability.

ROLE OF SOCIAL NETWORKS IN RELATIONSHIP MAINTENANCE VIA TECHNOLOGY

Living in an ever-present and always connected environment presents individuals in relationships with both advantages and disadvantages in regard to the influence of social networks on relationship maintenance. In this section, we focus on how social networks can affect relationship maintenance via technology. Although the research on this topic is limited and has had a negative undertone, we attempt to highlight some of the positives for relationship maintenance of couples being connected with their social networks through technology.

Social media sites, such as Facebook, are often used for relationship maintenance (Ellison, Steinfield, & Lampe, 2007). Although there is not space for an exhaustive review, we provide a few examples (for more detail, see Caughlin & Wang, Chapter 16). Being positive about one's partner (e.g., sending messages the partner will enjoy) and giving relationship assurances (e.g., posting "I love you" on a partner's wall) via Facebook are positively associated with relationship satisfaction (Dainton, 2013). Social media sites can also allow those who are insecure or uncertain about their relationship to monitor their partner (Darvell, Walsh, & White, 2011; Fox & Warber, 2014; Stewart, Dainton, & Goodboy, 2014). Those with more anxious attachment styles are more likely to desire that their relationship status be visible on social media to help to convey the centrality of their relationship to others (Emery, Muise, Dix, & Le, 2014).

One of the most common uses of social networking sites is to connect and maintain ties with others (Ellison, Vitak, Gray, & Lampe, 2014b; Ellison et al., 2007). This can help to build social capital, giving individuals access to a variety of informational, psychological, and other resources from others. In general, social capital and feeling supported have been linked with psychological well-being, such as life satisfaction (Bargh & McKenna, 2004). Furthermore, some research has shown that feeling more connected to the social network (specifically family and friends) via the internet may indirectly influence perceptions of other aspects of life, such as greater satisfaction with one's current romantic relationship (e.g., McDaniel, Coyne, & Holmes, 2012). Individuals may also use posts and updates on social media sites to seek information or other assistance (Ellison, Gray, Lampe, & Fiore, 2014a), and it is likely that some of these requests relate to ways to strengthen one's current romantic relationship. These questions and requests can be linked with higher social capital (Ellison et al., 2014a); however, no research appears to have examined whether requests that are relationship-oriented improve the current relationship.

Network overlap has been shown to be an important predictor of relationship-maintenance processes, as discussed earlier in this chapter. Network overlap has also been considered with regard to social networking sites, and research suggests that individuals with greater overlap in their Facebook networks show greater commitment and investment in their current relationship (Castañeda, Wendel, & Crockett, 2015). Yet, Toma and Choi (2015) found a negative association between the number of mutual friends on Facebook and relationship commitment (contrary to what they expected). They suggested that this negative effect may be due to larger social networks resulting in more relationship alternatives.

It is also now easier to form and maintain long-distance relationships, and individuals in such relationships are more likely to perform relationship maintenance via social media sites than those in geographically close relationships (Billedo, Kerkhof, & Finkenauer, 2015). However, their social network members may still express expectations that the relationships should be maintained face-to-face, and these network expectations may cause strain for long-distance couples who utilize technology as their primary way of staying connected (e.g., Billedo et al., 2015; Fox, Osborn, & Warber, 2014). Additionally, the ability of one's network to post information to social media that one may not have wished a partner to see could cause relationship conflict (Fox et al., 2014).

Due to the widespread use of social networking sites, one's network of friends, family, and acquaintances can now "like" or comment on a wide variety of relationship information shared by partners. Social network members may band together for or against a particular relationship and therefore, could be influential in affecting the potential future of that relationship (e.g., Fox, Warber, & Makstaller, 2013). Additionally, millennials, more than any other generation, appear to seek external praise and validation (Daly, 2015). Therefore, current young adults may, throughout their life, place value on what their social networks say online in terms of likes, hearts, and comments on their relationship posts. For example, if negative comments are made about one's relationship posts, others in the network may begin to feel more negatively about the relationship as well (Ballantine, Lin, & Veer, 2015). At the same time, these processes also could work in a positive direction, with fully supportive comments validating commitment to an intimate relationship.

Furthermore, individuals can learn about their relationship identity through the process of becoming "Facebook official" (FBO; i.e., declaring they are in a relationship) and receiving feedback from their social network (see also Weick, 1995). In general, individuals (especially women) believe that becoming FBO is an indication of greater commitment to the relationship (Fox & Warber, 2013; Fox et al., 2013; Lane, Piercy, & Carr, 2016). Individuals generally expect their network to see their relationship status change and make comments. Even the decision to become "Facebook official" may be affected by anticipated reactions of friends and family (Lane & Piercy, 2017). Becoming FBO could help to increase the stability of the relationship if the network perceives the individual as off-limits (Lane & Piercy, 2017).

Technology may influence how social networks affect the maintenance of relationships in another way. It is becoming common for individuals to begin their relationships online, in part because of the reduced stigma of online dating (Rosenfeld & Thomas, 2012; Smith & Duggan, 2013). Based on a national sample of partnered individuals, Rosenfeld and Thomas (2012) found that among those who met online, 74% had no knowledge of each other or prior social connections before meeting. In other words, their social networks did not overlap. Some emerging work suggests that those who meet online and do not share social networks perceive less support for their relationship from their social network (Sassler & Miller, 2015). Furthermore, a study of online relationship partners found that those who perceived more disapproval from their offline networks were less satisfied with their online relationship (Wildermuth, 2004). It is as yet unclear whether relationships that begin online are more difficult to maintain due to less network overlap and potential greater network disapproval or whether they are eventually integrated into their networks, meaning that relationships that begin online might lack only initial social network support. Indeed, some researchers have found that marriages that began online were less likely to break up as compared with those that met via offline in more traditional settings (Cacioppo, Cacioppo, Gonzaga, Ogburn, & VanderWeele, 2013).

Finally, no discussion of the role of social networks via technology in relationship maintenance could be complete without referring to how individuals are now tethered to their devices and often expected to be continuously available to others (e.g., Hall & Baym, 2012). This hyperconnectivity can be a double-edged sword, depending on how the technology is used by romantic partners. Constant connection could make planning relationship-building experiences and activities easier with friends and family; however, some individuals develop problematic habits with their devices or social media, such as using them too much, using them to manage their emotions, and allowing the device to interrupt face-to-face interactions (e.g., "techno-ference"; Bianchi & Phillips, 2005; Elphinston & Noller, 2011; McDaniel & Coyne, 2016). Still others use technology to connect with prior romantic partners or to monitor their partner online (Drouin, Miller, & Dibble, 2014; McDaniel, Drouin, & Cravens, 2017; Muise, Christofides, & Desmarais, 2009; 2014). Also, having one's social network constantly at one's fingertips can lead to social comparisons on social media sites. Some emerging research has shown that these comparisons often have a negative effect on one's psychological well-being and sometimes, on one's perceptions of the current romantic relationship (e.g., Coyne, McDaniel, & Stockdale, 2017). This negative effect can occur due to the positive bias that exists in most social media posts by others (i.e., individuals often present their best moments), leading some to question why their relationship is not filled with the positive activities they see in others' relationships.

FUTURE DIRECTIONS

We have noted in several places in this chapter that more research is needed to thoroughly examine how social networks affect the ability and motivation of relational partners to engage in mechanisms that maintain and even enhance their relationship. In this section, we speculate more specifically about research directions in this area.

We first encourage a greater variety of research designs to investigate how social networks affect relationship maintenance, as each method has strengths. Survey research, especially when conducted with large and diverse samples, can demonstrate how associations between network attributes and relationship maintenance may differ as a function of many other factors, including relationship stage, relationship duration, relationship type (e.g., same-sex vs. different-sex), and partner characteristics. We encourage such research, especially to explore differences in the influence of social networks in different contexts.

We encourage longitudinal designs and experience sampling designs (in which relationship partners are surveyed on a daily basis) in order to untangle causal directions. Although many of the studies referred to in this chapter follow from a Social Network perspective as an elaboration of the Investment model framework (i.e., network approval and provisions contribute to commitment, which in turn leads to relationship maintenance), there can also be an argument for reverse causal directions. When relational partners engage in strategies to maintain their relationship, and especially those that are visible to network members, network support to facilitate the maintenance of the relationship likely follows. The causal associations also could be investigated with experimental designs, for example, by priming network support or the lack thereof and then examining the effects of the priming on participants' reports of the likelihood of engaging in various maintenance strategies in their relationship.

Obtaining data directly from network members to supplement data from the partners on network approval and support is another important avenue for future research. Only a few studies in the extant literature on social networks have collected data from one or both members of the couples *and* also asked members of their social network about their perceptions of the relationship (e.g., Agnew, Loving, & Drigotas, 2001; Etcheverry, Le, & Charania, 2008). Research with data collected from multiple informants can lead to new and interesting research questions, including the effects of invisible support from the network – support provisions identified by the network to help the targeted couple maintain their relationship but that are outside the awareness of the couple. Invisible network support may even have more positive effects on the relationship than more obvious, visible support, similarly to how invisible dyadic support for individuals can be particularly effective (Bolger, Zuckerman, & Kessler, 2000).

Although the focus of this chapter has been on how positive reactions and helpful provisions from social networks increase the likelihood that partners will engage in maintenance behaviors and cognitions, network members may sometimes try to impair partners' ability to maintain their relationship. Whether such network interference attempts have their intended effects and lead to the couple's dissolution – or whether they have the opposite effects and lead to relationship maintenance – would be another important topic to examine with (longitudinal) data collected from multiple informants. A classic study (Driscoll, Davis, & Lipetz, 1972) demonstrated that perceived increases in parental interference in a romantic relationship over a six-month period were associated with an increase in love experienced by the couple; this "Romeo and Juliet" effect was attributed to the effect of reactance. Because many studies have shown just the opposite (network approval, not disapproval, leads to more positive outcomes; e.g., Sinclair, Hood, & Wright, 2014), the Driscoll et al. findings have remained an anomaly in the network literature.

We suggest that the original "Romeo and Juliet" finding can be interpreted within the concept of negative relationship maintenance. Dainton and Gross (2008) defined negative maintenance behavior as antisocial things that people do to keep their relationship maintained or in a desired state. They identified several negative behaviors, including deception, jealousy induction, spying, and avoidance. The process of resisting a threat to one's relationship, in the form of interference from the network (such as by parents), could be a type of negative maintenance mechanism used by some couples. That is, the process of the partners sharing the experience of resisting the threat may lead to intensification of the relationship.

The research conducted with the RMSM has distinguished between maintenance as a strategic action and maintenance as a by-product of routine, everyday interactions (Stafford et al., 2000). Similarly, the social network literature has distinguished between exogenous and endogenous effects of the social network (Sprecher, Felmlee, Orbuch, & Willetts, 2002), with exogenous effects referring to social networks' deliberate intentions to influence the dyads and endogenous effects referring to dyad members' attempts to influence networks to obtain the support or provisions they need to maintain their relationship (e.g., saying positive things about one's partner in order to obtain network support). Combining these two distinctions emerging from different literatures suggests that there may be three ways that social network reactions and provisions influence relational partners' enactment of maintenance: (1) social network driven; (2) couple or partner driven; and (3) happenstance from routine interactions. Future research might further examine the potential unique effects of each type of network support for partners' maintenance behaviors and cognition.

Although research has found that face-to-face interactions within dyads can be negatively affected by being hyperconnected with others (e.g., McDaniel & Coyne, 2016), the positive effects on the current romantic relationship of being connected with others through communication devices and social media need to be more thoroughly investigated. Furthermore, because more and more couples are meeting through internet dating sites without any assistance from their social network, we need additional research to study when and how dyad members begin to involve the social network in helping them to maintain their internet-initiated relationship. In general, there also needs to be more research on how networks through social media sites may influence relationship maintenance behaviors and cognition, especially because studies often examine only the direct behaviors and feelings of the relationship partners on social media.

We end our chapter by stating that there are many other avenues of research at the intersection of social networks and relationship maintenance. Although our chapter focused on how social networks influence the maintenance of dyadic relationships (with a focus on romantic relationships), there are many other relationships that individuals maintain. In fact, people may engage in strategic actions to sustain entire sectors of their network, such as in-laws, high school friends, colleagues, neighbors, and activity friends (e.g., one's card club). Sometimes the maintenance of entire network sectors is compatible with the maintenance of a romantic relationship, and at other times it can be incompatible because of competing demands, a topic worthy of future investigation.

REFERENCES

Agnew, C. R., Loving, T. J., & Drigotas, S. M. (2001). Substituting the forest for the trees: Social networks and the prediction of romantic relationship state and fate. *Journal of Personality and Social Psychology, 81,* 1042–1057.

Agnew, C. R., Van Lange, P. A. M., Rusbult, C. E., & Langston, C. A. (1998). Cognitive interdependence: Commitment and the mental representation of close relationships. *Journal of Personality and Social Psychology, 74,* 939–954.

Agnew, C. R., & VanderDrift, L. E. (2015). Relationship maintenance and dissolution. In M. Mikulincer, P. R. Shaver, J. A. Simpson, & J. F. Dovidio (Eds.), *APA handbook of personality and social psychology, Volume 3: Interpersonal relations* (pp. 581–604). Washington, DC: American Psychological Association.

Aron, A., Norman, C. C., Aron, E. N., McKenna, C., & Heyman, R. E. (2000). Shared participation in self-expanding activities: Positive effects on experienced marital quality. In P. Noller & J. A. Feeney (Eds.), *Understanding marriage: Developments in the study of couple interaction* (pp. 177–200). Cambridge, UK: Cambridge University Press.

Ballantine, P. W., Lin, Y., & Veer, E. (2015). The influence of user comments on perceptions of Facebook relationship status updates. *Computers in Human Behavior, 49,* 50–55.

Bargh, J. A., & McKenna, K. Y. (2004). The Internet and social life. *Annual Review of Psychology, 55,* 573–590.

Baxter, L. A., Dun, T., & Sahlstein, E. (2001). Rules for relating communicated among social network members. *Journal of Social and Personal Relationships, 18,* 173–199.

Bianchi, A., & Phillips, J. (2005). Psychological predictors of problem mobile phone use. *CyberPsychology & Behavior, 8,* 39–51.

Billedo, C. J., Kerkhof, P., & Finkenauer, C. (2015). The use of social networking sites for relationship maintenance in long-distance and geographically close romantic relationships. *Cyberpsychology, Behavior, and Social Networking, 18,* 152–157.

Blair, K. L., & Holmberg, D. (2008). Perceived social network support and well-being in same-sex versus mixed-sex romantic relationships. *Journal of Social and Personal Relationships, 25,* 769–791.

Bolger, N., Zuckerman, A., & Kessler, R. C. (2000). Invisible support and adjustment to stress. *Journal of Personality and Social Psychology, 79,* 953–961.

Bryant, C. M., Conger, R. D., & Meehan, J. M. (2001). The influence of in-laws on change in marital success. *Journal of Marriage and Family, 63,* 614–626.

Buunk, B. P. (2001). Perceived superiority of one's own relationship and perceived prevalence of happy and unhappy relationships. *British Journal of Social Psychology, 40,* 565–574.

Cacioppo, J. T., Cacioppo, S., Gonzaga, G. C., Ogburn, E. L., & VanderWeele, T. J. (2013). Marital satisfaction and break-ups differ across on-line and off-line meeting venues. *Proceedings of the National Academy of Sciences, 110,* 10135–10140.

Canary, D. J. (2011). On babies, bathwater, and absolute claims: Reply to Stafford. *Journal of Social and Personal Relationships, 28,* 304–311.

Canary, D. J., & Stafford, L. (1992). Relational maintenance strategies and equity in marriage. *Communications Monographs, 59,* 243–267.

Carstensen, L. L., Isaacowitz, D. M., & Charles, S. T. (1999). Taking time seriously: A theory of socioemotional selectivity. *American Psychologist, 54,* 165–181.

Castañeda, A. M., Wendel, M. L., & Crockett, E. E. (2015). Overlap in Facebook profiles reflects relationship closeness. *The Journal of Social Psychology, 155,* 395–401.

Cornwell, B. (2012). Spousal network overlap as a basis for spousal support. *Journal of Marriage and Family, 74,* 229–238.

Cox, C. L., Wexler, M. O., Rusbult, C. E., & Gaines Jr, S. O. (1997). Prescriptive support and commitment processes in close relationships. *Social Psychology Quarterly, 60,* 79–90.

Coyne, S. M., McDaniel, B. T., & Stockdale, L. A. (2017). "Do you dare to compare?" Associations between maternal social comparisons on social networking sites and parenting, mental health, and romantic relationship outcomes. *Computers in Human Behavior, 70,* 335–340.

Dailey, R. M., Hampel, A. D., & Roberts, J. B. (2010). Relational maintenance in on-again/off-again relationships: An assessment of how relational maintenance, uncertainty, and commitment vary by relationship type and status. *Communication Monographs, 77,* 75–101.

Dailey, R. M., Pfiester, A., Jin, B., Beck, G., & Clark, G. (2009). On-again/off-again dating relationships: How are they different from other dating relationships? *Personal Relationships, 16,* 23–47.

Dainton, M. (2013). Relationship maintenance on Facebook: Development of a measure, relationship to general maintenance, and relationship satisfaction. *College Student Journal, 47,* 113–121.

Dainton, M., & Aylor, B. (2001). A relational uncertainty analysis of jealousy, trust, and maintenance in long-distance versus geographically close relationships. *Communication Quarterly, 49,* 172–188.

Dainton, M., & Aylor, B. (2002). Routine and strategic maintenance efforts: Behavioral patterns, variations associated with relational length, and the prediction of relational characteristics. *Communication Monographs, 69,* 52–66.

Dainton, M., & Gross, J. (2008). The use of negative behaviors to maintain relationships. *Communication Research Reports, 25,* 179–191.

Dainton, M., & Stafford, L. (1993). Routine maintenance behaviors: A comparison of relationship type, partner similarity and sex differences. *Journal of Social and Personal Relationships, 10,* 255–271.

Dainton, M., & Stafford, L. (2000). Predicting maintenance enactment from relational schemata, spousal behavior, and relational characteristics. *Communication Research Reports, 17,* 171–180.

Dainton, M., Stafford, L., & Canary, D. J. (1994). Maintenance strategies and physical affection as predictors of love, liking, and satisfaction in marriage. *Communication Reports, 7,* 88–98.

Daly, A. (2015). Generation validation: Why everyone just wants to be liked. Elle.com. Retrieved from www.elle.com/life-love/a14618/generation-validation/

Darvell, M. J., Walsh, S. P., & White, K. M. (2011). Facebook tells me so: Applying the theory of planned behavior to understand partner-monitoring behavior on Facebook. *Cyberpsychology, Behavior, and Social Networking, 14,* 717–722.

Dindia, K. (2000). Relational maintenance. In C. Hendrick & S. S. Hendrick (Eds.), *Close relationships: A sourcebook* (pp. 286–299). Thousand Oaks, CA: Sage.

Driscoll, R., Davis, K. E., & Lipetz, M.E. (1972). Parental interference and romantic love: The Romeo & Juliet effect. *Journal of Personality and Social Psychology, 24,* 1–10.

Drouin, M., Miller, D. A., & Dibble, J. L. (2014). Ignore your partners' current Facebook friends; beware the ones they add! *Computers in Human Behavior, 35,* 483–488.

Ellison, N. B., Gray, R., Lampe, C., & Fiore, A. T. (2014a). Social capital and resource requests on Facebook. *New Media & Society, 16,* 1104–1121.

Ellison, N. B., Steinfield, C., & Lampe, C. (2007). The benefits of Facebook "friends:" Social capital and college students' use of online social network sites. *Journal of Computer-Mediated Communication, 12,* 1143–1168.

Ellison, N. B., Vitak, J., Gray, R., & Lampe, C. (2014b). Cultivating social resources on social network sites: Facebook relationship maintenance behaviors and their role in social capital processes. *Journal of Computer-Mediated Communication, 19,* 855–870.

Elphinston, R. A., & Noller, P. (2011). Time to face it! Facebook intrusion and the implications for romantic jealousy and relationship satisfaction. *Cyberpsychology, Behavior, and Social Networking, 14,* 631–635.

Emery, L. F., Muise, A., Dix, E. L., & Le, B. (2014). Can you tell that I'm in a relationship? Attachment and relationship visibility on Facebook. *Personality and Social Psychology Bulletin, 40*, 1466–1479.

Etcheverry, P., Le, B., & Charania, M. (2008). Perceived versus reported social referent approval and romantic relationship commitment and persistence. *Personal Relationships, 15*, 281–295.

Felmlee, D. H. (2001). No couple is an island: A social network perspective on dyadic stability. *Social Forces, 4*, 1259–1287.

Felmlee, D. H., & Sprecher, S. (2000). Close relationships and social psychology: Intersections and future paths. *Social Psychology Quarterly, 63*, 365–376.

Fingerman, K., Miller, L., Birditt, K., & Zarit, S. (2009). Giving to the good and the needy: Parental support of grown children. *Journal of Marriage and Family, 71*, 1220–1233.

Finkel, E. J., Hui, C. M., Carswell, K. L., & Larson, G. M. (2014). The suffocation of marriage: Climbing Mount Maslow without enough oxygen. *Psychological Inquiry, 25*, 1–41.

Fox, J., Osborn, J. L., & Warber, K. M. (2014). Relational dialectics and social networking sites: The role of Facebook in romantic relationship escalation, maintenance, conflict, and dissolution. *Computers in Human Behavior, 35*, 527–534.

Fox, J., & Warber, K. M. (2013). Romantic relationship development in the age of Facebook: An exploratory study of emerging adults' perceptions, motives, and behaviors. *Cyberpsychology, Behavior, and Social Networking, 16*, 3–7.

Fox, J., & Warber, K. M. (2014). Social networking sites in romantic relationships: Attachment, uncertainty, and partner surveillance on Facebook. *Cyberpsychology, Behavior, and Social Networking, 17*, 3–7.

Fox, J., Warber, K. M., & Makstaller, D. C. (2013). The role of Facebook in romantic relationship development: An exploration of Knapp's relational stage model. *Journal of Social and Personal Relationships, 30*, 771–794.

Girme, Y. U., Overall, N. C., & Faingataa, S. (2013). "Date nights" take two: The maintenance function of shared relationship activities. *Personal Relationships, 21*, 125–149.

Gray, P. B., Franco, C. Y., Garcia, J. R., Gesselman, A. N., & Fisher, H. E. (2016). Romantic and dating behaviors among single parents in the United States. *Personal Relationships, 23*, 491–504.

Green, J. D., Burnette, J. L., & Davis, J. L. (2008). Third-party forgiveness: (Not) forgiving your close others' betrayer. *Personality and Social Psychology Bulletin, 34*, 407–418.

Green, J. D., Davis, J. L., & Reid, C. A. (2014). Third-party forgiveness: Social influences on intimate dyads. In C. R. Agnew (Ed.), *Social influences on romantic relationships: Beyond the dyad* (pp. 171–187). Cambridge: Cambridge University Press.

Hall, J. A., & Baym, N. K. (2012). Calling and texting (too much): Mobile maintenance expectations, (over) dependence, entrapment, and friendship satisfaction. *New Media & Society, 14*, 316–331.

Helms, H. M., Crouter, A. C., & McHale, S. M. (2003). Marital quality and spouses' marriage work with close friends and each other. *Journal of Marriage and Family, 65*, 963–977.

Hogerbrugge, M. J. A., Komter, A. E., & Scheepers, P. (2013). Dissolving long-term romantic relationships: Assessing the role of the social context. *Journal of Social and Personal Relationships, 30*, 320–342.

Huston, T. L., & Burgess, R. L. (1979). Social exchange in developing relationships: An overview. In R. L. Burgess & T. L. Huston (Eds.), *Social exchange in developing relationships* (pp. 3–28). San Diego, CA: Academic Press.

Jackson, G. L., Kennedy, D., Bradbury, T. N., & Karney, B. R. (2014). A social network comparison of low-income black and white newlywed couples. *Journal of Marriage and Family, 76,* 967–982.

Jensen, J. F., & Rauer, A. J. (2014). Turning inward versus outward: Relationship work in young adults and romantic functioning. *Personal Relationships, 21,* 451–467.

Jensen, J. F., & Rauer, A. J. (2015). Marriage work in older couples: Disclosure of marital problems to spouses and friends over time. *Journal of Family Psychology, 29,* 732–743.

Johnson, M. P., Caughlin, J. P., & Huston, T. L. (1999). The tripartite nature of marital commitment: Personal, moral, and structural reasons to stay married. *Journal of Marriage and Family, 61,* 160–177.

Johnson, M. P., & Leslie, L. (1982). Couple involvement and network structure: A test of the dyadic withdrawal hypothesis. *Social Psychology Quarterly, 45,* 34–43.

Kalmijn, M. (2003). Shared friendship networks and the life course: An analysis of survey data on married and cohabiting couples. *Social Networks, 25,* 231–249.

Karney, B. R., & Bradbury, T. N. (1995). The longitudinal course of marital quality and stability: A review of theory, method, and research. *Psychological Bulletin, 118,* 3–34.

Kelley, H. H., & Thibaut, J. W. (1978). *Interpersonal relations: A theory of interdependence.* New York: John Wiley & Sons.

Keneski, E., & Loving, T. J. (2014). Network perceptions of daters' romances. In C. R. Agnew (Ed.), *Social influences on romantic relationships: Beyond the dyad* (pp. 126–147). Cambridge, UK: Cambridge University Press.

Kim, K., Bangerter, L. R., Liu, Y., Polenick, C. A., Zarit, S. H., & Fingerman, K. L. (2017). Middle-aged offspring's support to aging parents with emerging disability. *The Gerontologist, 57,* 441–450.

Klein, R. C. A., & Milardo, R. M. (2000). The social context of couple conflict: Support and criticism from informal third parties. *Journal of Social and Personal Relationships, 17,* 618–637.

Lane, B. L., & Piercy, C. W. (2017). Making sense of becoming Facebook official: Implications for identity and time. In N. Punyanunt-Carter & J. S. Wrench (Eds.), *The impact of social media in modern romantic relationships* (pp. 31–46). Lanham, MD: Lexington Books.

Lane, B. L., Piercy, C. W., & Carr, C. T. (2016). Making it Facebook official: The warranting value of online relationship status disclosures on relational characteristics. *Computers in Human Behavior, 56,* 1–8.

Larson, R., Mannell, R., & Zuzanek, J. (1986). Daily well-being of older adults with friends and family. *Psychology and Aging, 1,* 117–126.

Ledbetter, A. M. (2010). Assessing the measurement invariance of relational maintenance behavior when face-to-face and online. *Communication Research Reports, 27,* 30–37.

Lehmiller, J. J., & Agnew, C. R. (2007). Perceived marginalization and the prediction of romantic relationship stability. *Journal of Marriage and Family, 69,* 1036–1049.

Lewis, R. (1973). Social reactions and the formation of dyads: An interactionist approach to mate selection. *Sociometry, 36,* 409–418.

Lydon, J. E., & Quinn, S. K. (2013). Relationship maintenance processes. In J. Simpson & L. Campbell (Eds.), *The Oxford handbook of close relationships* (pp. 573–588). New York, NY: Oxford University Press.

MacGeorge, E. L., & Hall, E. D. (2014). Relationship advice. In C. R. Agnew (Ed.), *Social influences on romantic relationships: Beyond the dyad* (pp. 188–208). Cambridge, UK: Cambridge University Press.

Mansson, D. H. (2016). American grandchildren's use of relational maintenance behaviors with their grandparents. *Journal of Intergenerational Relationships, 14,* 338–352.

Marsiglio, W., & Scanzoni, J. (1995). *Families and friendships.* New York, NY: HarperCollins.

McDaniel, B. T., & Coyne, S. M. (2016). "Technoference": The interference of technology in couple relationships and implications for women's personal and relational well being. *Psychology of Popular Media Culture, 5,* 85–98.

McDaniel, B. T., Coyne, S. M., & Holmes, E. K. (2012). New mothers and media use: Associations between blogging, social networking, and maternal well-being. *Maternal and Child Health Journal, 16,* 1509–1517.

McDaniel, B. T., Drouin, M., & Cravens, J. D. (2017). Do you have anything to hide? Infidelity-related behaviors on social media sites and marital satisfaction. *Computers in Human Behavior, 66,* 88–95.

McDermott, R., Fowler, J., & Christakis, N. (2013). Breaking up is hard to do, unless everyone else is doing it too: Social network effects on divorce in a longitudinal sample. *Social Forces, 92,* 491–519.

Milardo, R. M. (1982). Friendship networks in developing relationships: Converging and diverging social environments. *Social Psychology Quarterly, 45,* 162–172.

Milardo, R. M., & Helms-Erikson, H. (2000). Network overlap and third-party influence in close relationships. In C. Hendrick & S. S. Hendrick (Eds.), *Close relationships: A sourcebook* (pp. 33–45). Thousand Oaks, CA: Sage.

Milardo, R. M., Johnson, M. P., & Huston, T. L. (1983). Developing close relationships: Changing patterns of interaction between pair members and social networks. *Journal of Personality and Social Psychology, 44,* 964–976.

Monserud, M. A. (2008). Intergenerational relationships and affectual solidarity between grandparents and young adults. *Journal of Marriage and Family, 70,* 182–195.

Muise, A., Christofides, E., & Desmarais, S. (2009). More information than you ever wanted: Does Facebook bring out the green-eyed monster of jealousy? *CyberPsychology & Behavior, 12,* 441–444.

Muise, A., Christofides, E., & Desmarais, S. (2014). "Creeping" or just information seeking? Gender differences in partner monitoring in response to jealousy on Facebook. *Personal Relationships, 21,* 35–50.

Ogolsky, B. G., & Bowers, J. R. (2013). A meta-analytic review of relationship maintenance and its correlates. *Journal of Social and Personal Relationships, 30,* 343–367.

Oliker, S. J. (1989). *Best friends and marriage: Exchange among women.* Berkeley: University of California Press.

Proulx, C. M., Helms, H. M., & Payne, C. C. (2004). Wives' domain-specific "marriage work" with friends and spouses: Links to marital quality. *Family Relations, 53,* 393–404.

Reczek, C., Liu, H., & Umberson, D. (2010). Just the two of us? How parents influence adult children's marital quality. *Journal of Marriage and Family, 72,* 1205–1219.

Reis, H. T., Caprariello, P. A., & Velickovic, M. (2011). The relationship superiority effect is moderated by the relationship context. *Journal of Experimental Social Psychology, 47,* 481–484.

Reissman, C., Aron, A., & Bergen, M. R. (1993). Shared activities and marital satisfaction: Causal direction and self-expansion versus boredom. *Journal of Social and Personal Relationships, 10,* 243–254.

Rodrigues, D., Lopes, D., Monteiro, L., & Prada, M. (2017). Perceived parent and friend support for romantic relationships in emerging adults. *Personal Relationships, 24,* 4–16.

Rook, K. S. (2009). Gaps in social support resources in later life: An adaptational challenge in need of further research. *Journal of Social and Personal Relationships, 26,* 103–112.

Rosenfeld, M. J., & Thomas, R. J. (2012). Searching for a mate: The rise of the Internet as a social intermediary. *American Sociological Review, 77,* 523–547.

Rubin, L. B. (1985). *Just friends: The role of friendship in our lives.* New York: Harper & Row.

Rusbult, C. E. (1983). A longitudinal test of the investment model: The development (and deterioration) of satisfaction and commitment in heterosexual involvements. *Journal of Personality and Social Psychology, 45,* 101–117.

Rusbult, C. E., Agnew, C. R., & Arriaga, X. B. (2012). The Investment model of commitment processes. In P. A. M. Van Lange, A. W. Kruglanski, & E. T. Higgins (Eds.), *Handbook of theories of social psychology,* volume 2 (pp. 218–231). Los Angeles, CA: Sage.

Rusbult, C. E., & Buunk, B. P. (1993). Commitment processes in close relationships: An interdependence analysis. *Journal of Social and Personal Relationships, 10,* 175–204.

Rusbult, C. E., Drigotas, S. M., & Verette, J. (1994). The investment model: An interdependence analysis of commitment processes and relationship maintenance phenomena. In D. Canary & L. Stafford (Eds.), *Communication and relational maintenance* (pp. 115–139). New York: Academic Press.

Rusbult, C. E., Van Lange, P. A., Wildschut, T., Yovetich, N. A., & Verette, J. (2000). Perceived superiority in close relationships: Why it exists and persists. *Journal of Personality and Social Psychology, 79,* 521–545.

Sarkisian, N., Gerena, M., & Gerstel, N. (2007) Extended family integration among Euro and Mexican Americans: Ethnicity, gender, and class. *Journal of Marriage and Family, 69,* 40–54.

Sarkisian, N., & Gerstel, N. (2016). Does singlehood isolate or integrate? Examining the link between marital status and ties to kin, friends, and neighbors. *Journal of Social and Personal Relationships, 33,* 361–384.

Sassler, S., & Miller, A. J. (2015). The ecology of relationships: Meeting locations and cohabitors' relationship perceptions. *Journal of Social and Personal Relationships, 32,* 141–160.

Seal, K. L., Doherty, W. J., & Harris, S. M. (2016). Confiding about problems in marriage and long-term committed relationships: A national study. *Journal of Marital and Family Therapy, 42,* 438–450.

Sinclair, H. C., Felmlee, D., Sprecher, S., & Wright, B. L. (2015). Don't tell me who I can't love: A multimethod investigation of social network and reactance effects on romantic relationships. *Social Psychology Quarterly, 78,* 7–99.

Sinclair, H. C., Hood, K. B., & Wright, B. L. (2014). Revisiting the Romeo and Juliet effect (Driscoll, Davis, & Lipetz, 1972): Reexamining the links between social network opinions and romantic relationship outcomes. *Social Psychology, 45,* 170–178.

Slatcher, R. B. (2010). When Harry and Sally met Dick and Jane: Creating closeness between couples. *Personal Relationships, 17,* 279–297.

Smith, A., & Duggan, M. (2013). Online dating & relationships. *Pew Research Center.* Retrieved from www.pewinternet.org/2013/10/21/online-dating-relationships/

Solomon, D. H., & Knobloch, L. K. (2001). Relationship uncertainty, partner interference, and intimacy within dating relationships. *Journal of Social and Personal Relationships, 18,* 804–820.

Sprecher, S. (2011). The influence of social networks on romantic relationships: Through the lens of the social network. *Personal Relationships, 18,* 630–644.

Sprecher, S., & Felmlee, D. H. (1992). The influence of parents and friends on the quality and stability of romantic relationships: A three-wave longitudinal investigation. *Journal of Marriage and Family, 54,* 888–900.

Sprecher, S., & Felmlee, D. H. (2000). Romantic partners' perceptions of social network attributes with the passage of time and relationship transitions. *Personal Relationships, 7,* 325–340.

Sprecher, S., Felmlee, D. H., Orbuch, D. L., & Willetts, M. C. (2002). Social networks and change in personal relationships. In A. Vangelisti, H. Reis, & M. A. Fitzpatrick (Eds.), *Stability and change in relationships* (pp. 257–284). Cambridge: Cambridge University Press.

Stafford, L. (2011). Measuring relationship maintenance behaviors: Critique and development of the revised relationship maintenance behavior scale. *Journal of Social and Personal Relationships, 28,* 278–303.

Stafford, L., & Canary, D. J. (1991). Maintenance strategies and romantic relationship type, gender and relational characteristics. *Journal of Social and Personal Relationships, 8,* 217–242.

Stafford, L., Dainton, M., & Haas, S. (2000). Measuring routine and strategic relational maintenance: Scale revision, sex versus gender roles, and the prediction of relational characteristics. *Communications Monographs, 67,* 306–323.

Stein, C. H., Bush, E. G., Ross, R. R., & Ward, M. (1992). Mine, yours and ours: A configural analysis of the networks of married couples in relation to marital satisfaction and individual well-being. *Journal of Social and Personal Relationships, 9,* 365–383.

Stewart, M. C., Dainton, M., & Goodboy, A. K. (2014). Maintaining relationships on Facebook: Associations with uncertainty, jealousy, and satisfaction. *Communication Reports, 27,* 13–26.

Stokes, J. E. (2016). The influence of intergenerational relationships on marital quality following the death of a parent in adulthood. *Journal of Social and Personal Relationships, 33,* 3–22.

Toma, C. L., & Choi, M. (2015). The couple who Facebooks together, stays together: Facebook self-presentation and relationship longevity among college-aged dating couples. *Cyberpsychology, Behavior, and Social Networking, 18,* 367–372.

Van Lange, P. A., & Rusbult, C. E. (1995). My relationship is better than – and not as bad as – yours is: The perception of superiority in close relationships. *Personality and Social Psychology Bulletin, 21,* 32–44.

Veiel, H. O. F., Crisand, M., Stroszeck-Somschor, H., & Herrie, J. (1991). Social support networks of chronically strained couples: Similarity and overlap. *Journal of Social and Personal Relationships, 8,* 279–292.

Vogl-Bauer, S. (2003). Maintaining family relationships. In D. J. Canary & M. Dainton (Eds.), *Maintaining relationships through communication: Relational, contextual, and cultural variations* (pp. 31–49). Mahwah, NJ: Erlbaum.

Waldinger, R. J., Cohen, S., Schulz, M. S., & Crowell, J. A. (2015). Security of attachment to spouses in late life: Concurrent and prospective links with cognitive and emotional well-being. *Clinical Psychological Science, 3,* 516–529.

Waller, W., & Hill, R. (1951). *The family: A dynamic interpretation.* New York: Dryden Press.

Weick, K. E. (1995). *Sensemaking in organizations.* Thousand Oaks: Sage Publications.

Weigel, D. J., & Ballard-Reisch, D. S. (1999a). How couples maintain marriages: A closer look at self and spouse influences upon the use of maintenance behaviors in marriages. *Family Relations, 48,* 263–269.

Weigel, D. J., & Ballard-Reisch, D. S. (1999b). Using paired data to test models of relational maintenance and marital quality. *Journal of Social and Personal Relationships, 16,* 175–191.

Widmer, E. D., Kellerhals, J., & Levy R. (2004) Types of conjugal networks, conjugal conflict and conjugal quality. *European Sociological Review, 20,* 63–77.

Wildermuth, S. M. (2004). The effects of stigmatizing discourse on the quality of on-line relationships. *CyberPsychology & Behavior, 7,* 73–84.

Wrzus, C., Hänel, M., Wagner, J., & Neyer, F. J. (2013). Social network changes and life events across the life span: A meta-analysis. *Psychological Bulletin, 139,* 53–80.

10

Dyadic Coping as Relationship Maintenance

ASHLEY K. RANDALL[1] AND SHELBY MESSERSCHMITT-COEN[2]

Not surprisingly, finances, work-related stress, and the overall economy are significant sources of stress for people around the world (see Falconier, Randall, & Bodenmann, 2016). In addition, due to the current political climate, Americans are reporting threats to personal safety and terrorism as a significant source of stress (American Psychological Association, 2016), which is probably an experience felt by many throughout the world. Importantly, sources of stress can also be due to an individual's underrepresented status (Rostosky & Riggle, 2017), illness (Badr & Acitelli, 2017), and, perhaps most importantly, their interpersonal relationships (e.g., couple conflict or infidelity; Feeney & Karantzas, 2017; Fincham & May, 2017).

According to the American Psychological Association (2015), approximately 78% of adults report experiencing at least one symptom of stress within the past year. As social beings (Baumeister & Leary, 1995; Coan & Sbarra, 2015), much of this stress is likely to be experienced in the presence of close others, such as one's romantic partner. Given partners' interdependence (see VanderDrift & Agnew, Chapter 2), the experience of an individual's stress is likely to impact their partner's experience as well, which, if not properly dealt with, can result in the demise of the relationship (e.g., Falconier, Nussbeck, Bodenmann, Schneider, & Bradbury, 2015b). Thus, understanding ways in which partners can adjust their behaviors in their relationship to cope with the stress is of paramount importance for relationship scholars and mental health professionals working with couples (Dindia, 2000). Here, we propose that *dyadic coping* – partners' interdependent coping efforts in response to stress (Bodenmann, 1995) – can be considered a relationship maintenance strategy (see Ogolsky, Monk, Rice, Theisen, & Maniotes, 2017, for a review), which can be utilized by couples to combat the deleterious effects of stress on well-being. Specifically, we propose that engaging in positive dyadic coping

[1] Counseling and Counseling Psychology, Arizona State University, Ashley.K.Randall@asu.edu
[2] Counselor Education and Supervision, The Ohio State University, coen.49@osu.edu

(and refraining from negative dyadic coping) can be considered a relationship maintenance strategy that helps to preserve the relationship and increase partners' resilience during times of distress, which is positively associated with relationship satisfaction and length (Ogolsky & Bowers, 2013). In the text that follows, both theoretical and empirical research is presented to support dyadic coping as a relationship maintenance strategy (Falconier, Jackson, Hilpert, & Bodenmann, 2015a).

ROLE OF STRESS IN CLOSE RELATIONSHIPS

Before understanding how dyadic coping can be considered a relationship maintenance strategy, one must first identify different types of stressors and acknowledge their role in relational functioning. According to their seminal article, Randall and Bodenmann (2009) conceptualized stress on three different dimensions: *origin, intensity, and duration.* For example, stress can originate either outside the relationship (external stress), as in experiencing stress from work, or inside the relationship (internal stress), as in navigating differing relational goals with one's partner. Regardless of the origin, the stress can be considered a crucial life event (major stressor), such as an illness (Badr & Acitelli, 2017) or dealing with stressful situations/environments (e.g., lower income; Neff & Karney, 2017), or something that may occur daily (minor stressor), such as daily hassles (Falconier et al., 2015b; Totenhagen, Serido, Curran, & Butler, 2012). Lastly, stress can occur over the course of time (chronic stress) or be short-lived, lasting momentarily or across a few days (acute stress).

Stress can have deleterious effects on relational well-being (Randall & Bodenmann, 2009; 2017). For example, relationship satisfaction is thought to be negatively affected by hassles and problems experienced within the relationship, which may arise due to the experience of external stress (Bodenmann, Ledermann, & Bradbury, 2007). Building upon traditional stress theories (e.g., Lazarus & Folkman, 1984), relational scholars have examined ways in which one partner's stressful experiences can also affect the other partner's experience of stress (i.e., stress spillover and cross-over; Neff & Karney, 2017; Totenhagen, Randall, Cooper, Tao, & Walsh, 2017). Bodenmann's (2005) stress-divorce model postulates the ways in which stress can have harmful effects on couples' relational well-being (see Figure 10.1).

Bodenmann's (2005) stress-divorce model focuses on the chronic minor stressors couples may face, which are associated with negative relational outcomes (Randall & Bodenmann, 2009; 2017). Consider, for example, a couple wherein one partner may be experiencing stress due to school or work. The experience of this (external) stress may lead to decreased communication between partners, as the nonstressed partner may not want to talk about their day after hearing about their partner's stressful day. As such, the

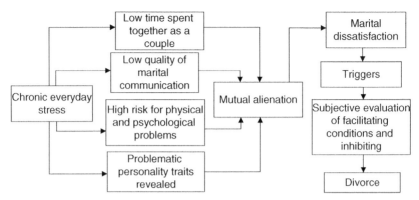

FIGURE 10.1　Bodenmann's (2005) stress-divorce model.

experience of one partner's stress could lead to less quality time spent between partners (Milek, Randall, Nussbeck, Breitenstein, & Bodenmann, 2017). If not properly dealt with, over time these interactions (or lack thereof) can lead to mutual dissatisfaction and ultimately, relationship dissolution. However, partners are able to help each other cope effectively with such stressors by engaging in positive dyadic coping.

COPING WITH STRESS: THE SYSTEMIC TRANSACTIONAL MODEL

Dyadic coping is conceptualized in a number of ways (see Revenson, Kayser, & Bodenmann, 2005), which are based on the premise that "dyadic coping is more than the sum of two individuals' coping responses" (Folkman, 2009, p. 73). One way dyadic coping has been conceptualized is by the systemic transactional model (STM; Bodenmann, 1995), which theorizes dyadic coping based on the interdependence of partners' stress experiences, such that one partner's experience of stress affects the other (stress spillover; Neff & Karney, 2004). As such, "your stress" or "my stress" is considered "we-stress;" thus, the well-being of each partner is dependent on both partners' joint stress regulation and coping efforts. According to the STM (Bodenmann, 1995), engaging in dyadic coping serves two important functions as a relationship maintenance strategy: it helps to reduce the level of stress each partner experiences, and it helps to fosters feelings of mutuality (we-ness), trust, and intimacy within the relationship (Bodenmann, 2005) as partners learn that they can rely on one another during times of distress.

Conceptualizing dyadic coping. Although conceptually similar, dyadic coping is distinct from social support (Cutrona, Bodenmann, Randall, Clavel, &

Johnson, 2018). As noted by Bodenmann, Pihet, and Kayser (2006), there are a distinct differences between these two constructs. First, support that occurs as part of dyadic coping comes from a romantic partner, which differs from support from family and friends; romantic support carries a different meaning and importance to partners and their relationship compared with social support from others. Second, unlike social support, dyadic coping includes a commitment of both partners to promote each other's well-being. Finally, the conceptualization of dyadic coping not only includes the notion of stress-management behaviors, in which both partners engage when confronted with shared stressors, but also theorizes how partners communicate their stress (i.e., stress communication). Taken together, these factors highlight how dyadic coping, a construct distinct from social support, can be considered a relationship maintenance strategy; dyadic coping is reliant on the sense of commitment and behavioral engagement in order to preserve the relationship and increase its functionality (see Cutrona et al., 2018, for more information).

Forms of dyadic coping. Dyadic coping, specifically engaging in positive dyadic coping, can be considered a relationship maintenance strategy, as it helps to preserve the relationship during times of distress (Dindia, 2000). Various forms of dyadic coping exist, which are described in detail below.

Positive dyadic coping. Positive forms of dyadic coping can be categorized as supportive dyadic coping (*emotion-* and *problem-*focused) or *delegated* dyadic coping. *Emotion-focused dyadic coping* consists of efforts to manage the negative emotions characteristic in a stressful situation, which can be experienced as an empathetic understanding of the partner's stress (see Baker & Berenbaum, 2011). *Problem-focused dyadic coping* consists of a partner offering specific problem-solving advice to help mitigate the feelings of stress, which could include joint problem solving and concrete help with daily tasks (Bodenmann, 1997; 2005). Supportive dyadic coping (either emotion- or problem-focused) can be expressed by providing practical advice or empathic understanding, helping one's partner reframe the situation, or helping with daily tasks (Bodenmann, 1997). Importantly, supportive dyadic coping is not considered an altruistic behavior, because it involves efforts to support the partner with the added goal of reducing one's own stress, given partners' interdependence (Bodenmann, 1995).

Delegated dyadic coping occurs when one partner takes over the responsibilities of the other in order to reduce the other partner's stress (Bodenmann, 2005). Unlike supportive dyadic coping, in delegated dyadic coping the partner is asked directly to work on tasks that one would typically do oneself in order to ease stress; this form of dyadic coping is most commonly used in response to problem-oriented stressors. For example, married undergraduate students may experience stress due to their underrepresented status in addition to experiencing stress due to managing their schoolwork. The buildup of this stress may be mitigated if the partner offers to take on some of their stress partner's tasks (Messerschmitt, 2017).

Common dyadic coping. *Common dyadic coping* can occur when both partners are experiencing stress and try to manage the situation by coping together, as in the case of a partner diagnosed with diabetes trying to adhere to dietary and exercise regimens (Johnson et al., 2013). Similarly to supportive dyadic coping, forms of common dyadic coping include *emotion-focused* and *problem-focused coping* (Bodenmann, 2005). Emotion-focused common dyadic coping occurs when partners engage in relaxing activities together in order to reduce stress (e.g., talking a walk or watching a movie together). Problem-focused common dyadic coping occurs when partners work together to analyze the situation and search for a solution in an attempt to reduce the stress.

Negative dyadic coping. Unfortunately, partners can also engage in negative forms of dyadic coping in the face of stress. *Negative dyadic coping* includes various forms, such as hostile, ambivalent, or superficial coping (Bodenmann, 2005). *Hostile dyadic coping* is accompanied by belittling, distancing, mocking or using sarcasm, expressing open disinterest, or minimizing the seriousness of the partner's stress. Using the prior example, Partner B may tell Partner A that his or her stress accrued from additional work tasks is not something to be concerned about (e.g., "Don't stress over that"), or they may mock Partner A for being stressed (e.g., "Ohh, you have *so* much going on!"). *Ambivalent dyadic coping* occurs when one partner supports the other unwillingly. For example, Partner B may hold the belief that Partner A should figure out the problem on their own and, as such, not offer a solution or support (Falconier et al., 2015b). *Superficial dyadic coping* consists of support that is insincere, for example, asking questions about the partner's feelings without listening or supporting the partner without empathy (Bodenmann, 2005). Partner B may ask questions regarding Partner A's additional tasks, but may clearly not be paying attention to Partner A's responses. When negative dyadic coping strategies are utilized, over time, the partner seeking help may not be as willing to share stressful experiences with the other partner, which could lead to relationship dissatisfaction (Bodenmann, 2005).

Process of dyadic coping. During a couple's interaction, partners' emotions are communicated both verbally and nonverbally (see Randall & Schoebi, 2018). As such, the process of dyadic coping starts with the partner's *stress communication*, either by discussing the cause of the stress (verbal) or by "shutting down" in an attempt to cope with the stress on their own (nonverbal). A partner's stress responses (both verbal and nonverbal) are appraised by the nonstressed partner, who then determines how to respond (Bodenmann, 1995). For example, Partner B (nonstressed) may identify that their partner is experiencing stress (Partner A) and in response, may give Partner A advice about how to move forward and get tasks accomplished (i.e., problem-focused supportive dyadic coping), or they could complete the chores at the request of Partner A (i.e., delegated dyadic coping). Partner B's response – engagement in dyadic coping – may help the stressed partner feel better (as a result of engaging in positive dyadic coping) or worse (as a result of engaging in negative dyadic coping), which then would dictate the course of the interaction (Bodenmann, 2000).

Dyadic coping can be driven by a number of factors. First, when looking at the type of stress that one is experiencing (e.g., external vs. internal, minor vs. major, or chronic vs. acute), a partner's awareness and ability to recognize the source of the stressor may assist in his or her ability to identify and offer the appropriate type of coping to their stressed partner. Second, the type of stressor that one partner or both partners experience may dictate the form of coping utilized. As an example, Baker and Berenbaum (2007) were interested in understanding the effectiveness of dyadic coping approaches as determined by two different forms of stress: interpersonal stress (e.g., having a relative with cancer) and achievement stress (e.g., exam scores, grades, and work tasks). Participants engaged in more emotional coping (vs. problem-focused) when the stress was interpersonal. Although Baker and Berenbaum's (2007) research was not grounded in the STM (Bodenmann, 1995; 2005), understanding the types of coping that would be most appropriate in specific contexts would be an important direction for future examination. Partners' abilities to recognize their partner's stress can play a large role in the maintenance of the relationship. In addition, motivational factors, such as relationship satisfaction or the longevity of the relationship (i.e., relationship length), are considered to influence partners' dyadic coping behaviors (Bodenmann, 2005). As such, when partners are invested in the satisfaction and longevity of their relationship, they may use more positive dyadic coping and/or fewer negative dyadic coping strategies in order to maintain or increase their level of satisfaction.

DYADIC COPING AS RELATIONSHIP MAINTENANCE

Research on dyadic coping has grown exponentially over the past 20 years. Scholars interested in the intersection between stress and coping research have examined the associations between dyadic coping and well-being in a variety of contexts, ranging from the experience of common everyday stressors (e.g., work stress; Schaer, Bodenmann, & Klink, 2008) to the experience of stress as a result of underrepresented status (e.g., Messerschmitt, 2017; Randall, Totenhagen, Walsh, Adams, & Tao, 2017) to psychological distress (e. g., depression; Johnson, Galambos, Finn, Neyer, & Home, 2017) and severe illness (e.g., cancer; Regan et al., 2015). Most commonly, researchers have examined how dyadic coping is associated with reports of relationship quality (Bodenmann, Meuwly, & Kayser, 2011), as measured by relationship satisfaction (Falconier et al., 2015a). As exemplified by the chapters in this volume, numerous definitions of relationship maintenance exist. Here, we consider (positive) dyadic coping as a relationship maintenance strategy in the face of stress, which is positively associated with relationship satisfaction and length (Ogolsky & Bowers, 2013).

Relationship satisfaction. Relationship satisfaction is strongly associated with psychological and physical well-being (e.g., Beach, Katz, Kim, & Brody, 2003; Proulx, Helms, & Buehler, 2007) and lower levels of relationship instability and dissolution (Gottman & Levenson, 1992). Furthermore, numerous studies have shown stress to be negatively associated with relationship satisfaction (see Randall & Bodenmann, 2009; 2017). These results have been supported in couples experiencing a number of stressors, including but not limited to daily hassles (e.g., Falconier et al., 2015b), infertility (Drosdzol & Skrzypulec, 2009), symptoms of psychological distress (e.g., PTSD; Klaric et al., 2011), and stress related to sexuality identity and expression (e.g., Gamarel, Reisner, Laurenceau, Nemoto, & Operario, 2014; Otis, Riggle, & Rostosky, 2006).

Relationship satisfaction is a common outcome examined in dyadic coping research (Falconier et al., 2015a). Despite the strong negative association between stress and relationship satisfaction, positive dyadic coping has consistently been found to moderate the association between these two variables. According to Bodenmann (2005), this moderation occurs through two mechanisms: it lessens the negative impact of stress on the relationship and reinforces the feeling of shared trust and intimacy (i.e., "we-ness"). A couple's sense of "we-ness" has been found to be associated with positive relationship outcomes (see VanderDrift & Agnew, Chapter 2; see also Seider, Hirschberger, Nelson, & Levenson, 2009; Vedes, Bodenmann, Nussbeck, Randall, & Lind, 2013). Positive dyadic coping is thought to reestablish a sense of stability for the partner and for the couple in the face of trials, whereas negative dyadic coping is presumed to weaken the partners' adjustment to stressors and, over time, partners' assessment of the other partner and their relationship (Falconier et al., 2015a). Indeed, in their meta-analysis of dyadic coping and relationship satisfaction, Falconier et al. (2015a) found that positive dyadic coping was a stronger predictor of relationship satisfaction than negative dyadic coping, in that higher reports of positive dyadic coping specified a stronger association with higher relationship satisfaction as compared with reports of negative dyadic coping.

Positive dyadic coping. Individuals' perceptions of stress communication and positive dyadic coping were all significant positive predictors of relationship satisfaction (Falconier et al., 2015a). Positive associations between positive dyadic coping and relationship satisfaction have been found across the globe (Hilpert et al., 2016), including, but not limited to, Canada (Levesque, Lafontaine, Caron, Flesch, & Bjornson, 2014), China (Xu & Hiew, 2016), Germany (Herzberg, 2013), Italy (Donato et al., 2015), Spain (García-López, Sarriá, Pozo, & Recio, 2016), Switzerland (Bodenmann, Bradbury, & Pihet, 2009), and the United States (Papp & Witt, 2010; Randall, Hilpert, Jimenez-Arista, Walsh, & Bodenmann, 2016). A majority of these studies used community samples of nonclinical couples, and results have also been found in reports of prospective relationship satisfaction (Merz, Meuwly, Randall, & Bodenmann, 2014).

Associations between positive dyadic coping and relationship satisfaction have also been examined in a number of unique samples. For example, Falconier, Nussbeck, and Bodenmann (2013) examined the associations between positive dyadic coping and relationship satisfaction using a sample of Latino immigrants living in the United States. They found that positive dyadic coping strategies, specifically supportive dyadic coping provided by the male partner and common dyadic coping in both partners, weakened the negative association of various aspects of Latinas' immigration stress, mostly with their relationship satisfaction and to some extent, their male partner's as well. García-López et al. (2016) examined associations between positive dyadic coping and relationship satisfaction for parents with a child diagnosed with Autism Spectrum Disorder. They found that supportive dyadic coping was associated with higher relationship satisfaction for both parents; mothers' and fathers' supportive dyadic coping predicted their own relationship satisfaction as well as their partner's relationship satisfaction. Using a sample of 215 Christian Orthodox couples, Rusu, Hilpert, Beach, Turliuc, and Bodenmann (2015) found that supportive dyadic coping moderated the association between marital sanctity (i.e., seeing the relationship as sacred or holy) and relationship satisfaction. More specifically, positive dyadic coping strengthened the positive association between marital sanctity and relationship satisfaction. Last, although many studies examining associations between positive dyadic coping and relationship satisfaction have utilized samples of heterosexual couples (see Falconier et al., 2015a), researchers have begun to examine associations between positive dyadic coping and relational well-being in same-sex couples. For example, in a nonclinical sample of both different and same-sex partners, both lesbian and gay individuals reported higher levels of positive dyadic coping as compared with heterosexual individuals (Weaver, 2014), which has been associated with relationship satisfaction. Further understanding of dyadic coping as a relationship maintenance strategy for underrepresented couples (e.g., immigrants and same-sex couples) and couples facing specific stressors (e.g., due to a child's chronic condition or the experience of specific minority stressors) are important areas for future research.

Negative dyadic coping. Not surprisingly, partners' engagement in negative dyadic coping has been associated with lower reports of relationship satisfaction (e.g., Bodenmann et al., 2009). In Falconier et al.'s (2015a) meta-analysis, hostile and ambivalent coping were significant negative predictors of relationship satisfaction; higher use of these strategies was linked with lower relationship satisfaction. As an example, in a sample of 42 heterosexual couples wherein one partner was diagnosed with prostate cancer, Regan et al. (2014) found that use of negative dyadic coping by both patient and partner was significantly associated with decreased relationship satisfaction. In addition, using a sample of 109 nonclinical couples, Bodenmann et al. (2009) found in a pre- and post-test study that higher relationship satisfaction was associated with a decrease in negative dyadic coping over the course of a dyadic coping skills training intervention. This suggests that relationship satisfaction can improve as long as partners minimize the use of superficial support that they provide and offer less criticism while supporting their partner (Bodenmann et al., 2009).

Perception of partner's dyadic coping. Importantly, the perception of a partner's (positive and negative) dyadic coping, as measured by the Dyadic Coping Inventory (for an overview, see Nussbeck & Jackson, 2016), has been more strongly linked to reports of relationship satisfaction than a partner's actual reports of their own dyadic coping behaviors (Falconier et al., 2015b; Landis, Peter-Wight, Martin, & Bodenmann, 2013). Based on the meta-analysis by Falconier et al. (2015a), one's own perception of one's partner's engagement in dyadic coping is an equally strong predictor of relationship satisfaction in comparison with one's own reported engagement in dyadic coping; a result that has been found for both men and women, young and older couples, in newer and established relationships, and within individuals from different nationalities, which is similar to research on relationship maintenance and its associations (Ogolsky et al., 2017). As such, the perception of a partner's engagement in dyadic coping behaviors has been shown to be a strong predictor of one's own relationship satisfaction and in predicting other indices of well-being (e.g., symptoms of depression; Randall, Tao, Totenhagen, Walsh, & Cooper, in press).

Additional considerations. Interestingly, gender differences in dyadic coping (positive and negative) and relationship satisfaction have not been found (Falconier et al., 2015a; for exceptions see Bodenmann et al., 2006; Papp & Witt, 2010; Ruffieux, Nussbeck, & Bodenmann, 2014), despite differing levels of reported stress (American Psychological Association, 2016) and stress communication (Randall et al., 2016) between men and women. Notably, in heterosexual relationships, dyadic coping is thought to be equally important for women's and men's relationship quality (e.g., Bodenmann et al., 2011). Thus, understanding the potential gender differences for men and women in same-sex relationships is a promising area for future research (e.g., Meuwly, Feinstein, Davila, Nuñez, & Bodenmann, 2013). Additionally, it is important to note that a majority of research that has examined associations between dyadic coping and relationship satisfaction has been done with cross-sectional samples. Accordingly, causality cannot be inferred. Falconier et al. (2015a) reported that data from longitudinal studies have yielded smaller effect sizes as compared with cross-sectional studies. However, in a two-year longitudinal study by Bodenmann et al. (2006), dyadic coping was found to be a significant positive of relationship satisfaction. Therefore, another fruitful area for future research is examining the long-term effects of dyadic coping as a relationship maintenance strategy in diverse samples.

Relationship duration. Although limited in nature, research has examined the importance of engaging in (positive) dyadic coping as a relationship maintenance strategy for the longevity of the relationship. Couples who experience an overwhelming amount of chronic stress have a higher probability of dissolution (Bodenmann, 2000). Engaging in positive dyadic coping may serve as an important relationship maintenance strategy to combat these deleterious effects (e.g., Bodenmann & Shantinath, 2004).

There have been a handful of longitudinal studies that have identified the positive associations between dyadic coping and relationship duration Bodenmann et al., 2006; 2009; Wunderer & Schneewind, 2008). For example, Bodenmann and Cina (2006) reported that couples in "stable" relationships (i.e., still in a married relationship) demonstrated more effective positive dyadic coping compared with couples classified as "distressed" or separated over the same time period (Ruffieux et al., 2014). In a longitudinal study using 90 nonclinical heterosexual couples, Bodenmann et al. (2006) found that over a two-year period, wives reported their marital quality, tenderness, and togetherness to be significantly lower than those who were not in long-term relationships. Dyadic coping moderated this association, such that those who reported more positive dyadic coping and less negative dyadic coping also reported significantly higher marital quality, tenderness, and togetherness; for women, both their own dyadic coping and that of their partner was significant, whereas for men, only their own dyadic coping was predictive of these outcomes.

Grounded in the STM, Bodenmann and colleagues (2009) examined the effectiveness of the Couples Coping Enhancement Training (CCET), a skill-based intervention for couples based on the systemic transactional model (Bodenmann, 1995) that helps couples develop dyadic coping skills and educates them on the nature of stress and coping. Compared with a control group, couples who participated in CCET showed increases in positive pro-blem-solving and positive dyadic coping behaviors, and decreases in negative problem-solving and negative dyadic coping behaviors. Therefore, it can be inferred that partners who utilize positive dyadic coping as a relationship maintenance strategy are able to combat the deleterious effects of stress while increasing their relationship satisfaction (and ultimately, longevity).

Taken together, engaging in positive dyadic coping can be considered an effective relationship maintenance strategy that assists partners in preserving their relationship, particularly as it applies to relationship satisfaction. Although longitudinal research regarding dyadic coping and relationship longevity is fairly new, existing research suggests that engaging in positive dyadic coping during times of distress can help couples cope with the momentary experience of stress, ultimately fostering partners' connection and trust over time. There is a need, however, for more longitudinal data that examines associations between dyadic coping and relationship duration in order to better understand its function.

CONCLUSION

Stress and relationships are two concepts that go hand-in-hand; however, partners' relationship maintenance strategies that buffer stress' deleterious effects may not be as intuitive (see Ogolsky & Bowers, 2013). Couples and relational scholars alike are encouraged to acknowledge stress and coping as interdependent processes, which functions at the level of the individual (e.g., experience and stress communication) and at the dyadic level (e.g., coping processes). Greater understanding is needed with respect to how the experience of coping with specific stressors may impact a couple's functioning and engage-ment in specific relationship-maintenance behaviors, particularly as it applies to minority stressors and minority couples. The available research, however, suggests that engaging in positive dyadic coping can be considered a relation-ship maintenance strategy that fosters the upkeep of the relationship, main-taining partners' relationship satisfaction over time.

REFERENCES

American Psychological Association. (2015). Stress in America [Data file]. Retrieved from www.apa.org/news/press/releases/stress/2015/snapshot.aspx

American Psychological Association (2016). Stress in America [Data file]. Retrieved from www.apa.org/news/press/releases/stress/2016/coping-with-change.pdf

Badr, H., & Acitelli, L. K. (2017). Re-thinking dyadic coping in the context of chronic illness. *Current Opinion in Psychology, 13*, 44–48. doi:10.1016/j.copsyc.2016.03.001

Baker, J. P., & Berenbaum, H. (2007). Emotional approach and problem-focused coping: A comparison of potentially adaptive strategies. *Cognition and Emotion, 21*(1), 95–118. doi:10.1080/02699930600562276

Baker, J. P., & Berenbaum, H. (2011). Dyadic moderators of the effectiveness of problem-focused and emotional-approach coping interventions. *Cognitive Therapy and Research, 35*, 550–559. doi:10.1007/s10608-011-9386-7

Baumeister, R. F., & Leary, M. R. (1995). The need to belong: Desire for interpersonal attachments as a fundamental human motivation. *Psychological Bulletin, 117*(3), 497–529. doi:10.1037/0033-2909.117.3.497

Beach, S. R. H., Katz, J., Kim, S., & Brody, G. H. (2003). Prospective effects of marital satisfaction on depressive symptoms in established marriages: A dyadic model. *Journal of Social and Personal Relationships, 20*, 355–371. doi:10.1177/0265407503020003005

Bodenmann, G. (1995). A systemic-transactional conceptualization of stress and coping in couples. *Swiss Journal of Psychology, 54*, 34–49.

Bodenmann, G. (1997). Dyadic coping – a systemic-transactional view of stress and coping among couples: Theory and empirical findings. *European Review of Applied Psychology, 47*, 137–140.

Bodenmann, G. (2000). *Stress und Coping bei Paaren* [Stress and coping in couples]. Gottingen, Germany: Hogrefe.

Bodenmann, G. (2005). Dyadic coping and its significance for marital functioning. In T. A. Revenson, K. Kayser, & G. Bodenmann (2005) *Couples coping with stress: Emerging perspectives on dyadic coping*. Washington, DC: American Psychological Association.

Bodenmann, G., Bradbury, T. N., & Pihet, S. (2009). Relative contributions of treatment-related changes in communication skills and dyadic coping skills to the longitudinal course of marriage in the framework of marital distress prevention. *Journal of Divorce & Remarriage, 50*, 1–21. doi:10.1080/10502550802365391

Bodenmann, G., & Cina, A. (2006). Stress and coping among stable-satisfied, stable-distressed, and separated/divorced Swiss couples: A 5-year prospective longitudinal study. *Journal of Divorce & Remarriage, 44*, 71–89. doi:10.1300/J087v44n01_04

Bodenmann, G., Ledermann, T., & Bradbury, T. N. (2007). Stress, sex, and satisfaction in marriage. *Personal Relationships, 14*, 551–569.

Bodenmann, G., Meuwly, N., & Kayser, K. (2011). Two conceptualizations of dyadic coping and their potential for predicting relationship quality and individual well-being: A comparison. *European Psychologist, 16*(4), 255–266. doi:10.1027/1016-9040/a000068

Bodenmann, G., Pihet, S., & Kayser, K. (2006). The relationship between dyadic coping and marital quality: A 2-year longitudinal study. *Journal of Family Psychology, 20*, 485–493. doi:10.1037/0893-3200.20.3.485

Bodenmann, G., & Shantinath, S. D. (2004). The Couples Coping Enhancement Training (CCET): A new approach to prevention of marital distress based upon stress and coping. *Family Relations, 53*, 477–484.

Coan, J. A., & Sbarra, D. A. (2015). Social baseline theory: The social regulation of risk and effort. *Current Opinion in Psychology, 1,* 87–91. doi:10.1016/j.copsyc.2014.12.021

Cutrona, C., Bodenmann, G., Randall, A. K., Clavel, F., & Johnson, M. (in press). Stress, dyadic coping, and social support: Moving toward integration. In A. Vangelisti & D. Perlman (Eds.), *The Cambridge handbook of personal relationships* (pp. 341–352). Cambridge: Cambridge University Press.

Dindia, K. (2000). Relational maintenance. In C. Hendrick & S. S. Hendrick (Eds.), *Close relationships: A sourcebook* (pp. 287–299). Thousand Oaks, CA: Sage.

Donato, S., Parise, M., Iafrate, R., Bertoni, A., Finkenauer, C., & Bodenmann, G. (2015). Dyadic coping responses and partners' perceptions for couple satisfaction: An actor-partner interdependence analysis. *Journal of Social and Personal Relationships, 32*(5), 580–600. doi:10.1177/0265407514541071

Drosdzol, A., & Skrzypulec, V. (2009). Evaluation of marital and sexual interactions of Polish infertile couples. *Journal of Sexual Medicine, 6,* 3335–3346. doi:10.1111/j.1743-6109.2009.01355.x

Falconier, M. K., Jackson, J. B., Hilpert, P., & Bodenmann, G. (2015a). Dyadic coping and relationship satisfaction: A meta-analysis. *Clinical Psychology Review, 42,* 28–46. doi:10.1016/j.cpr.2015.07.002

Falconier, M. K., Nussbeck, F., & Bodenmann, G. (2013). Immigration stress and relationship satisfaction in Latino couples: The role of dyadic coping. *Journal of Social and Clinical Psychology, 320*(8), 813–843. doi:10.1521/jscp.2013.32.8.813

Falconier, M. K., Nussbeck, F., Bodenmann, G., Schneider, H., & Bradbury, T. (2015b). Stress from daily hassles in couples: Its effects on intradyadic stress, relationship satisfaction, and physical and psychological well-being. *Journal of Marital and Family Therapy, 41*(2), 221–235. doi:10.111/jmft.12073

Falconier, M. K., Randall, A. K., & Bodenmann, G. (Eds.). (2016). *Couples coping with stress: A cross-cultural perspective.* New York, NY: Routledge.

Feeney, J. A., & Karantzas, G. C. (2017) Couple conflict: Insights from an attachment perspective. *Current Opinion in Psychology, 13,* 60–64. doi:10.1016/j.copsyc.2016.04.017

Fincham, F. D., & May, R. W. (2017). Infidelity in romantic relationships. *Current Opinion in Psychology, 13,* 70–74. doi:10.1016/j.copsyc.2016.03.008

Folkman, S. (2009). Commentary on the special section "Theory-based approaches to stress and coping": Questions, answers, issues, and next steps in stress and coping research. *European Psychologist, 14*(1), 72–77.

Gamarel, K. E., Reisner, S. L., Laurenceau, J. P., Nemoto, T., & Operario, D. (2014). Gender minority stress, mental health, and relationship quality: A dyadic investigation of transgender women and their cisgender male partners. *Journal of Family Psychology, 28*(4), 437–447. doi:10.1037/a0037171

García-López, C., Sarriá, E., Pozo, P., & Recio, P. (2016). Supportive dyadic coping and psychological adaptation in couples parenting children with autism spectrum disorder: The role of relationship satisfaction. *Journal of Autism and Developmental Disorders, 46*(11), 3434–3477. doi:10.1007/s10803-016-2883-5

Gottman, J. M., & Levenson, R. W. (1992). Marital processes predictive of later dissolution: Behavior, physiology, and health. *Journal of Personality and Social Psychology, 63,* 221–233. doi:10.1037/0022-3514.63.2.221

Herzberg, P. Y. (2013). Coping in relationships: The interplay between individual and dyadic coping and their effects on relationship satisfaction. *Anxiety, Stress, & Coping, 26*(2), 136–153. doi:10.1080/10615806.2012.655726

Hilpert, P., Randall, A. K., Sorokowski, P., Atkins, D. C., Sorokowska, A., Ahmadi, K., … Yoo, G. (2016). The associations of dyadic coping and relationship satisfaction vary between and within nations: A 35-nation study. *Frontiers in Psychology, 7,* article 1106, 1–16. doi:10.3389/fpsyg.2016.01106

Johnson, M. D., Anderson, J. R., Walker, A., Wilcox, A., Lewis, V. L., & Robbins, D. C. (2013). Common dyadic coping is indirectly related to dietary and exercise adherence via patient and partner diabetes efficacy. *Journal of Family Psychology, 27,* 722–730. http://dx.doi.org/10.1037/a0034006

Johnson, M. D., Galambos, N. L., Finn, C., Neyer, F. J., & Home, R. M. (2017). Pathways between self-esteem and depression in couples. *Developmental Psychology, 53*(4), 787–799. doi:10.1037/dev0000276

Klaric, M., Franciskovic, T., Stevanovic, A., Petrov, B., Jonovska, S., & Nemcic Moro, I. (2011). Marital quality and relationship satisfaction in war veterans and their wives in Bosnia and Herzegovina. *European Journal of Psychotraumatology, 2,* 8077. doi:10.3402/ejpt.v2i0.8077

Landis, M., Peter-Wight, M., Martin, M., & Bodenmann, G. (2013). Dyadic coping and marital satisfaction of older spouses in long-term marriage. *GeroPsych, 26*(1), 39–47. doi:10.1024/1662–9647/a000077

Lavner, J. A., & Bradbury, T. N. (2010). Patterns of change in marital satisfaction over the newlywed years. *Journal of Marriage and Family, 72,* 1171–1187. doi:10.1111/j.1741-3737.2010.00757.x

Lavner, J. A., & Bradbury, T. N. (2012). Why do even satisfied newlyweds eventually go on to divorce? *Journal of Family Psychology, 26,* 1–10. doi:10.1037/a0025966

Lazarus, R. S., & Folkman, S. (1984). *Stress, appraisal, and coping.* New York, NY: Springer.

Levesque, C., Lafontaine, M., Caron, A., Flesch, J. L., & Bjornson, S. (2014). Dyadic empathy, dyadic coping, and relationship satisfaction: A dyadic model. *Europe's Journal of Psychology, 10*(1), 118–134. doi:10.5964/ejop.v10i1.697

Merz, C. A., Meuwly, N., Randall, A. K., & Bodenmann, G. (2014). Engaging in dyadic coping: Buffering the impact of everyday stress on prospective relationship satisfaction. *Family Science, 5,* 30–37. doi:10.1080/19424620.2014.927385

Messerschmitt, S. (2017). Coping with stress association with anticipated stigma: The role of dyadic coping in married, undergraduate students (Unpublished master thesis). Arizona State University, Tempe, AZ.

Meuwly, N., Feinstein, B. A., Davila, J., Nuñez, D. G., & Bodenmann, G. (2013). Relationship quality among Swiss women in opposite-sex versus same-sex romantic relationships. *Swiss Journal of Psychology, 72,* 229–233.

Milek, A., Randall, A. K., Nussbeck, F. W., Breitenstein, C. J., & Bodenmann, G. (2017). Deleterious effects of stress on time spent with one's partner and relationship satisfaction. *Journal of Couple and Relationship Therapy, 16,* 210–231.

Neff, L. A., & Karney, B. R. (2004). How does context affect intimate relationships? Linking external stress and cognitive processes within marriage. *Personality and Social Psychology Bulletin, 30,* 134–148. doi:10.1177/0146167203255984

Neff, L. A., & Karney, B. R. (2017). Acknowledging the elephant in the room: How stressful environmental contexts shape relationship dynamics. *Current Opinion in Psychology, 13,* 107–110. http://dx.doi.org/10.1016/j.copsyc.2016.05.013

Nussbeck, F. W., & Jackson, J. B. (2016). Measuring dyadic coping across cultures. In M. K. Falconier, A. K. Randall, & G. Bodenmann (Eds.), *Couples coping with stress: A cross-cultural perspective* (pp. 36–53). New York, London: Routledge.

Ogolsky, B. G., & Bowers, J. R. (2013). A meta-analytic review of relationship maintenance and its correlates. *Journal of Social and Personal Relationships, 30*(3), 343–367. doi:10.1177/0265407512463338

Ogolsky, B. G., Monk, J. K., Rice, T. M., Theisen, J. C., & Maniotes, C. R. (2017). Relationship maintenance: A review of research on romantic relationships. *Journal of Family Theory and Review*, 9, 275–306. doi:10.1111/jftr.12205

Otis, M. D., Riggle, E. D. B., & Rostosky, S. S. (2006). Impact of mental health on perceptions of relationship satisfaction and quality among female same-sex couples. *Journal of Lesbian Studies*, 10(1–2), 267–283. doi:10.1300/J155v10n01_14

Papp, L. M., & Witt, N. L. (2010). Romantic partners' individual coping strategies and dyadic coping: Implications for relationship functioning. *Journal of Family Psychology*, 24(5), 551–559. doi:10.1037/a0020836

Proulx, C. M., Helms, H. M., & Buehler, C. (2007). Marital quality and personal well-being: A meta-analysis. *Journal of Marriage and Family*, 69(3), 576–593. doi:10.1111/j.1741-3737.2007.00393.x

Randall, A. K., & Bodenmann, G. (2009). The role of stress on close relationships and marital satisfaction. *Clinical Psychology Review*, 29, 105–115. doi:10.1016/j.cpr.2008.10.004

Randall, A. K., & Bodenmann, G. (2017). Stress and its associations with relationship satisfaction. *Current Opinion in Psychology*, 13, 96–106. doi:10.1016/j.copsyc.2016.05.010

Randall, A. K., Hilpert, P., Jimenez-Arista, L. E., Walsh, K. J., & Bodenmann, G. (2016). Dyadic coping in the U.S.: Psychometric properties and validity for use of the English version of the Dyadic Coping Inventory. *Current Psychology*, 35, 570–582. doi:10.1007/s12144-015-9323-0

Randall, A. K., & Schoebi, D. (Eds.). (2018). *Interpersonal emotion dynamics in personal relationships*. Cambridge, UK: Cambridge Press.

Randall, A. K., Tao, C., Totenhagen, C. J., Walsh, K. J., & Cooper, A. (2017). Associations between sexual orientation discrimination and depression among same-sex couples: Moderating effects of dyadic coping. *Journal of Couple and Relationship Therapy*, 4, 325–345.

Randall, A. K., Totenhagen, C. J., Walsh, K. J., Adams, C., & Tao, C. (2017). Coping with workplace minority stress: Associations between dyadic coping and anxiety among women in same-sex relationships. *Journal of Lesbian Studies*, 21(1), 70–87. doi:10.1080/10894160.2016.1142353

Regan, T. W., Lambert, S. D., Kelly, B., Falconier, M., Kissane, D., & Levesque, J. V. (2015). Couples coping with cancer: Exploration of theoretical frameworks from dyadic studies. *Psycho-Oncology*, 24(12), 1605–1617. doi:10.1002/pon.3854

Regan, T. W., Lambert, S. D., Kelly, B., McElduff, P., Girgis, A., Kayser, K., & Turner, J. (2014). Cross-sectional relationships between dyadic coping and anxiety, depression, and relationship satisfaction for patients with prostate cancer and their spouses. *Patient Education and Counseling*, 96, 120–127. doi:10.1016/j.pec.2014.04.010

Revenson, T. A., Kayser, K., & Bodenmann, G. (Eds.) (2005). *Couples coping with stress: Emerging perspectives on dyadic coping*. Washington, DC: American Psychological Association.

Ruffieux, M., Nussbeck, F. W., & Bodenmann, G. (2014). Long-term prediction of relationship satisfaction and stability by stress, coping, communication, and well-being. *Journal of Divorce & Remarriage*, 55, 485–501. doi:10.1080/10502556.2014.931767

Rusu, P. P., Hilpert, P., Beach, S. R., Turliuc, M. N., & Bodenmann, G. (2015). Dyadic coping mediates the association of sanctification with marital satisfaction and well-being. *Journal of Family Psychology*, 29(6), 843. doi:10.1037/fam0000108

Schaer, M., Bodenmann, G., & Klink, T. (2008). Balancing work and relationship: Couples coping enhancement training (CCET) in the workplace. *Applied Psychology: An International Review*, 57, 71–89. doi:10.1111/j.1464-0597.2008.00355.x

Seider, B. H., Hirschberger, G., Nelson, K. L., & Levenson, R. W. (2009). We can work it out: Age differences in relational pronouns, physiology, and behavior in marital conflict. *Psychology and Aging, 24*, 604–613. doi:10.1037/a0016950

Totenhagen, C. J., Randall, A. K., Cooper, A., Tao, C., & Walsh, K. J. (2017). Stress spill-over in same-sex couples: Concurrent and lagged daily effects. *Journal of GLBT Family Studies, 31*, 236–256.

Totenhagen, C. J., Serido, J., Curran, M. A., & Butler, E. A. (2012). Daily hassles and uplifts: A diary study on understanding relationship quality. *Journal of Family Psychology, 26*, 719–728. doi:10.1037/a0029628

Vedes, A., Bodenmann, G., Nussbeck, F., Randall, A. K., & Lind, W. (2013, June). *The role of we-ness in mediating the associations between dyadic coping and relationship satisfaction.* Poster presented at the Sixth International Meeting of Stress and Dyadic Coping – Couples coping with Cancer-Related Stress: Translating Research into Practice. University of Louisville, KY.

Weaver, K. M. (2014). *An investigation of gay male, lesbian, and transgender dyadic coping in romantic relationships* (Doctoral dissertation, available from ProQuest Dissertations and Theses database. UMI No. 3632070).

Wunderer, E., & Schneewind, K. A. (2008). The relationship between marital standards, dyadic coping, and marital satisfaction. *European Journal of Social Psychology, 38*, 462–476. doi:10.1002/ejsp.405

Xu, F., & Hiew, D. N. (2016). Dyadic coping in Chinese couples. In M. K. Falconier, A. K. Randall, & G. Bodenmann (Eds.), *Couples coping with stress: A cross-cultural perspective* (pp. 218–235). New York, London: Routledge.

11

Conflict Management and Problem Solving as Relationship Maintenance

KARENA LEO[1], FEEA R. LEIFKER[2], DONALD H. BAUCOM[3], AND BRIAN R. W. BAUCOM[4]

Maintaining and enhancing a committed relationship over a long period of time is a challenging task for couples for a variety of reasons. The two partners need to be responsive to each partner's preferences and needs, make certain that they are functioning well as a unit, and be attentive to their physical and social environment. Maintaining a balance among these factors can be difficult, particularly given that all of these domains are likely to change over time. As a result, partners almost inevitably experience conflict as they engage in this ongoing process, often differing in their approaches to the myriad factors they must address. Therefore, conflict can be seen as a normative process that has the potential to help a couple move forward adaptively by restoring balance within the relationship when the differences between partners are addressed.

If conflict is normative and perhaps even adaptive, why are some couples able to work through conflict in a manner that ultimately seems to be facilitative, whereas for other couples, conflict appears to be destructive, perhaps even contributing to relationship dissolution? Rather than the occurrence or nonoccurrence of conflict being an indicator of relationship distress or health, numerous theoretical models (e.g., Hooley & Gotlib, 2000; Karney & Bradbury, 1995) and significant empirical evidence (e.g., Cohan & Bradbury, 1997) suggest that the way a couple *handles* conflict is much more important for short- and long-term relationship maintenance. In other words, how an individual within a partnership behaves and expresses emotions during conflict, and experiences the behaviors and expressions of the other partner, determines whether the occurrence of conflict contributes to relationship maintenance, defined here as relationship satisfaction and relationship stability. Built on this foundational assumption about the nature of

[1] Department of Psychology, University of Utah, karena.leo@utah.edu
[2] Department of Psychology, University of Utah, feea.leifker@utah.edu
[3] Department of Psychology and Neuroscience, University of North Carolina, don_baucom@unc.edu
[4] Department of Psychology, University of Utah, brian.baucom@utah.edu

conflict, this chapter presents a conceptual model of conflict management, which suggests that (a) relationship conflict can be associated with relationship maintenance or decline; (b) the behaviors of each partner and the patterns of behaviors between partners during conflict determine whether conflict is associated with positive or negative relationship outcomes; (c) conflict behavior primarily varies along two dimensions, valence and togetherness, that are central to relationship well-being; (d) the function of conflict behavior is best understood within the context of cognitions, emotions, and physiological responses of each partner and the co-occurrence of these between partners; (e) conflict behavior and emotional expressions can have different associations with relational versus individual outcomes; and (f) the short-term versus long-term consequences of conflict behavior might differ considerably. We begin with an overview of our conceptual model, turn to a review of empirical evidence, and close with suggestions for future research and continued theoretical refinement.

THE MULTIFINALITY OF RELATIONSHIP CONFLICT

The manner in which couples behave during conflict moderates[5] the association between relationship stressors and relationship functioning, resulting in either positive or negative outcomes (Cohan & Bradbury, 1997). Just as there are a variety of stressors that may impact relationship outcomes, behaviors and affective expressions displayed during conflict vary greatly within and between couples (Cohan & Bradbury, 1997). Maladaptive behaviors may exacerbate the negative effects of stressors on the relationship, leading to an

---

[5] Communication behaviors and affective expressions have been conceptualized, tested, and empirically supported as both moderators and mediators of the associations between relationship conflict and relationship functioning (e.g., Bradbury & Karney, 2004; Cohan & Bradbury, 1997; Conger, Rueter, & Elder, 1999). Although these results may appear inconsistent with one another, methodological differences between studies examining communication and affective expression as moderators and as mediators suggest that the two lines of research are complementary rather than contradictory. Studies examining communication behavior as a moderator of relationship conflict to relationship functioning measure relationship conflict as a construct that has gradations from low to high levels and that varies between couples (i.e., some couples experience more and/or more intense conflict; e.g., Cohan & Bradbury, 1997; Woodin, 2011). This approach to measuring conflict is the one we adopt in our model. Studies examining communication as a mediator generally, though not always, measure communication and affective expression presuming equivalent levels or intensity of conflict between couples (see Heyman, 2001 for a review). Laboratory-based observational assessment paradigms where couples are asked to discuss their most distressing area of conflict are a primary example of this type of methodology. In this design, the conflict to which couples are exposed is experimentally controlled to be as equivalent as possible. In other words, studies examining communication behavior and affective expression as a moderator ask the question "If couples have experienced high levels of conflict, is it more strongly/weakly related to relationship outcomes depending on behavior?" while studies examining communication behavior and affective expression as a mediator ask the question "When couples experience equivalently intense conflict, does the type of behavior/affective expression that occurs during the conflict predict relationship outcomes?"

increase in future conflicts, whereas adaptive behaviors may attenuate the negative effects of stressors, resulting in relationship maintenance or growth (Cohan & Bradbury, 1997).

Conger et al. (1999) found that conflict results in relationship distress only in couples with ineffective problem-solving skills. However, if couples with poor problem-solving skills express positive affect during conflict, these couples often fare as well as couples with high problem-solving skills (Bradbury & Karney, 2004). These findings are further corroborated by a recent study examining how the stress of moving to wealthier neighborhoods impacted relationship quality in low-income couples (Nguyen, Williamson, Karney, & Bradbury, 2017). Moving to a wealthier neighborhood was strongly associated with reduced relationship quality when wives showed low positivity and less effective problem-solving skills. However, relationship quality remained unchanged when wives exhibited high positivity and effective problem-solving skills (Nguyen et al., 2017). It is important to note, though, that it is not only positive communication behaviors and affective expression that may reduce the negative effect of stressors on relationship functioning. For example, Cohan and Bradbury (1997) found that wives' anger reduced the negative effect of high numbers of stressful life events on relationship satisfaction. In this case, anger was adaptive, as it promoted engagement and led to conflict resolution (Cohan & Bradbury, 1997).

THE VALENCE-AFFECTIVE-CONNECTION (VAC) COMMUNICATIVE SPACE MODEL

Although it is clear that communication behaviors and affective expression during conflict moderate the association between the intensity of relationship conflict/stressors and relationship outcomes, there is much less agreement about which behaviors and affective expressions are most important for well-functioning relationships. Part of this debate stems from the wide range of lines of research on relationship conflict, communication behavior, and the well-being of romantic partners. These constructs were initially studied primarily by behaviorally and cognitive behaviorally oriented researchers, whose primary focus was on understanding how couples who seek couple therapy interacted differently around conflict relative to satisfied couples (Weiss & Heyman, 1997; Wills, Weiss, & Patterson, 1974). Guided by social exchange theory, these researchers largely focused on positive and negative behaviors.

More recently, these same behavioral and affective constructs have been examined by researchers interested in mental and physical health outcomes (e.g., Guyll, Cutrona, Burzette, & Russell, 2010; Uebelacker, Courtnage, & Whisman, 2003). These lines of research grew out of different theoretical traditions (e.g., diathesis-stress [e.g., Hooley & Gotlib, 2000] and personality/individual differences [e.g., Horowitz et al., 2006], respectively). As a result, these lines of research conceptualize and measure communication behaviors and affective expressions as differentially distinct from one another and as varying along different dimensions. More specifically, researchers focused on mental health outcomes have historically drawn strong distinctions between behavior and affective expression, and researchers focused on physical health outcomes have traditionally suggested that behaviors and affective expressions can be distinguished in terms of being positive versus negative and communal versus independent.

We propose that communication behaviors and affective expressions are best understood as they impact the totality of partners' well-being, including their relationship health, mental health, and physical health, in both the short and the long term. This supposition is supported by a large body of evidence linking communication behaviors and affective expressions during conflict to outcomes in each of these three domains (e.g., Brown & Smith, 1992; Knobloch-Fedders et al., 2014; Uebelacker et al., 2003) and by a large body of evidence linking outcomes in each domain to one another (Robles, Slatcher, Trombello, & McGinn, 2014; Whisman & Uebelacker, 2009). Taking this perspective suggests that a conceptual model of communication behavior and affective expression would need to incorporate each of the dimensions identified in the different lines of research (i.e., positive vs. negative and communal vs. independent) in order to measure communication behaviors and affective expressions in a way that is likely to have relevance across all three outcome domains.

We propose the valence-affective-connection (VAC) communicative space model as one such integrative conceptual and measurement model (see Figure 11.1). Drawing on all three research traditions, the model integrates three dimensions: positive versus negative behaviors, hard versus soft affective expressions, and communal versus individualistic orientation. In the following, we briefly define each of the axes and describe the theoretical underpinnings of the dimension.

Positive and negative communication behaviors. A recent meta-analysis of behaviorally and cognitive behaviorally oriented relationship research suggests that most communication behaviors can be categorized as being either positive or negative (Woodin, 2011). Positive behaviors are constructive and amiable in nature, whereas negative behaviors are aversive, aggressive, and hostile (Heyman, 2001; Woodin, 2011). Examples of positive behaviors include, but are not limited to, affection, interest, empathy, disclosure, and acceptance, whereas examples of negative behaviors include, but are not limited to, criticism, blame, contempt, and belligerence (Coan & Gottman, 2007; Sanford, 2007). Positive conflict behaviors are associated with higher levels of trust and responsiveness between partners as well as increased conflict resolution, resulting in higher relationship stability and satisfaction

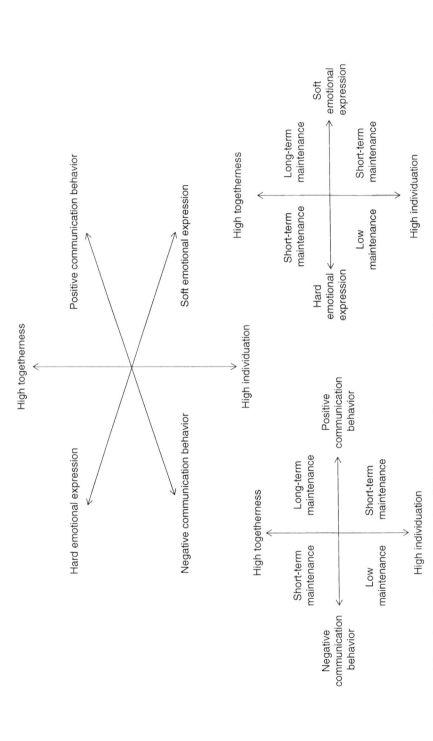

FIGURE 11.1 The valence-affective-connection (VAC) communicative space model.

(Baucom & Atkins, 2013). In contrast, negative conflict behaviors are associated with exacerbation of existing conflicts as well as an increased likelihood of future conflict, resulting in higher levels of distress and polarization (i.e., a cycle of coercive behaviors that results in partners becoming increasingly distant from one another; Jacobson & Christensen, 1996) between partners (Baucom & Atkins, 2013; Cohan & Bradbury, 1997).

Classifying behaviors as either positive or negative has a long and storied tradition in relationship science dating back to social exchange theory (Thibaut & Kelley, 1959). Social exchange theory suggests that behaviors exchanged between two individuals are reinforced by rewards and costs, which, in part, determine relationship satisfaction (Emerson, 1976; Thibaut & Kelley, 1959; Vanderdrift & Agnew, Chapter 2). The centrality of the ratio of positive to negative reinforcers in this theoretical account of relationship functioning led to an emphasis on examining positive and negative behaviors in early behavioral research on couples.

Hard and soft emotional expressions. Emotions can be differentiated into hard and soft emotions (Jacobson & Christensen, 1996). Hard emotions, such as anger and contempt, convey power and control (Sanford, 2007). Soft emotions convey vulnerability and include emotions such as loneliness and sadness (Jacobson & Christensen, 1996; Johnson & Greenberg, 1987; Sanford, 2007). Hard negative emotions are associated with higher levels of negative communication behavior, whereas soft emotions are associated with increased positive communication behavior. Expressions of sadness or loneliness communicate distress and increase the likelihood of positive communication behaviors from the other partner, which facilitates constructive communication and increased intimacy in the relationship (Sanford, 2007).

The use of soft and hard emotions as well as positive and negative communication behaviors can result in various relational and individual outcomes. For example, similarly to the idea that the way a couple handles conflict determines how it impacts relationship maintenance, the way that other members of a family react to one family member's psychopathology is strongly related to treatment outcomes (Miklowitz, 2004). Much research in this area has focused on the role of expressed emotions (EE). High EE is characterized by hard emotional processes such as criticism and hostility as well as emotional overinvolvement, which may be expressed as anxiety and worry that are directed toward an individual with psychopathology (Hooley & Gotlib, 2000; Miklowitz, 2004). Low EE is often thought of as the opposite and is characterized by acceptance, warmth, and other soft affective expression (Hooley & Gotlib, 2000). Interactions between a high-EE family member and the individual with psychopathology are often characterized by high negative reciprocity and hostile nonverbal behaviors, and may result in conflict escalation (Miklowitz, 2004). Low-EE interactions are often calming for the individual with psychopathology, are neutral in nature, and have the ability to stop conflict escalation (Miklowitz, 2004). As such, high levels of EE have been found to predict poorer treatment outcomes and increased relapse rates for various psychopathologies (Butzlaff & Hooley, 1998); additionally, this line of research adds further, convergent evidence that expressions of hard negative emotions are detrimental for family members and their relationships with one another because they are linked to poor well-being and low relationship functioning. On the other hand, soft emotions are constructive and beneficial for individuals and their relationships.

Communality and individualistic behaviors and affective expressions. Viewing a relationship problem as a shared issue that members of the couple need to address together results in a collaborative set. Numerous theoretical models of relationship functioning (e.g., Jacobson & Christensen, 1996) suggest that this perception is vital for short- and long-term relationship maintenance. One particular theoretical model where communality is prominent is the interpersonal circumplex model, which suggests that partners' behaviors and affective expressions are motivated by either communal goals or agentic goals (Horowitz et al., 2006). A communal goal is the motivation to connect with others, whereas an agentic goal is motivation related to the self (Horowitz et al., 2006). Therefore, the goal of each partner determines their own behavior and affective expression as well as how they respond to their partner's behavior and expression during conflict. An individual's response may either help to achieve the goals of the partner or may interfere with the goals of the other person because it conflicts with his/her own goals (Horowitz et al., 2006). Conflicting goals and subsequent behavior and affect may result in misunderstanding and higher levels of negative and hostile exchanges between partners (Horowitz et al., 2006). For example, couples who attempt to exert control and influence over one another are more direct, less friendly, more hostile, and display higher levels of anger during interactions (Brown & Smith, 1992).

Context-dependent prioritization of competing and complementary goals during conflict. Finally, this conceptual model distinguishes the impact of communication behaviors as they relate to relationship maintenance in both the short and the long term. Short-term relationship maintenance refers to increasing harmony between partners and reducing distress that either or both partners are feeling in the immediate moment during the conflict. In contrast, long-term relationship maintenance refers to addressing and reconciling conflict in a manner that is sustainable and that achieves an enduring solution that both partners find acceptable.

Guided by multiple goals models of communication (e.g., Caughlin, 2010), we propose that partners have to balance and prioritize numerous competing and complementary needs during any conflict. A primary distinction between these needs is whether they serve the self, the partner, or the relationship, and whether they do so in the short term and/or the long term. We propose that partners in distressed relationships often prioritize their own short-term needs over those of the partner and the relationship, whereas partners in satisfied relationships flexibly vacillate between short- and long-term needs of the self, partner, and relationship, provided that the conflict is not so intense as to overwhelm their regulatory capacity for distress. In instances where satisfied partners experience higher levels of subjective distress than they can tolerate and/or have a stronger physiological stress response than they can regulate, they will prioritize meeting their own short-term regulatory needs before being able to attend to the short- or long-term needs of the partner or the relationship (e.g., Gottman, 1993).

Bringing in other areas of our model, we propose that long-term relationship maintenance can be achieved through positive behaviors that foster intimacy and unite couples in approaching problems as a team. These positive behaviors function to achieve shared goals that the couple might have and prioritize the needs of the relationship over the needs of either individual partner. Positive behaviors that foster long-term relationship maintenance include "we" requests that are specific in nature (Mitnick, Heyman, Malik, & Slep, 2009), disclosures, and acceptance.

Positive behaviors that prioritize the needs of either partner often result in short-term relationship maintenance. For example, protective buffering (i. e., behaviors that function to avoid conflict, such as submitting or failing to disclose concerns; Coyne & Smith, 1991) and accommodation (i.e., behaviors that an individual engages in to alleviate distress in his or her partner; Fischer & Baucom, in press) are positive in that they temporarily increase harmony and decrease distress. However, these behaviors often prioritize one partner's short-term needs at the expense of the other and the relationship. Though the relationship is maintained in the short term, prolonged use may lead to conflict becoming worse over time because the root cause of the conflict is unaddressed.

As with conflict, not all negative behaviors are detrimental to relationship maintenance. Although negative behaviors such as demanding (e.g., blame and criticism) are linked to concurrent relationship dissatisfaction (e.g., Schrodt, Witt, & Shimkowski, 2013), other studies have classified demanding behaviors as direct negative behaviors and shown that they are associated with higher relationship satisfaction over time (e.g., Overall, Fletcher, Simpson, & Sibley, 2009). The VAC model suggests that negative behaviors lead to short-term relationship maintenance when enacted in the pursuit of shared goals and to low maintenance when driven by individual needs (e.g., Schrodt et al., 2013). For example, soft negative affective expression and negative communication behaviors can function to communicate distress to the other partner, and, if the couple has a collaborative set and shared goal, both partners can engage to resolve the present conflict, bringing about adaptive change in the relationship (McNulty & Russell, 2010). In contrast, negative communication behaviors and hard affective expressions that humiliate, vilify, or invalidate the other partner prioritize individual goals (e.g., exerting power over the partner) and those that communicate lack of investment or willingness to work toward a solution (e.g., withdrawing) are associated with distress during the conversation as well as concurrent and long-term relationship dissatisfaction. These behaviors and expressions also increase the likelihood of polarization between partners resulting in relationship dissolution.

SPECIFIC LONG- AND SHORT-TERM MAINTENANCE STRATEGIES

In the following, we discuss the specific conflict-management behaviors and emotional expressions engaged in by couples that lead to long-term relationship maintenance, short-term relationship maintenance, or low relationship maintenance. We then review how the strategies impact broader relational processes such as unexpected life circumstances (e.g., diagnosis of a health problem) and critical relationship transitions (e.g., transition to parenthood).

Long-Term Relationship Maintenance

Long-term relationship maintenance occurs when couples engage in positive, communally oriented problem-solving behaviors that prioritize the shared goals of the relationship. Couples will continually have needs and requests that must be addressed throughout their relationship, and expressing these needs and requests is associated with higher levels of relationship satisfaction that are sustained over time (Mitnick et al., 2009). When these needs are expressed as specific "we" requests, disclosures and expressions of vulnerability, and acceptance, it helps bring partners closer to one another and helps to resolve both new and longstanding issues (Mitnick et al., 2009).

Change requests. Requesting change is a necessary and normative component in a relationship, but it is how the requests are made that determines whether conflict is resolved and the relationship is maintained. "We" requests are requests for change that frame the issue as a shared or couple-level issue rather than the issue of one of the partners alone (i.e., "you" requests; Mitnick et al., 2009). In a study by Mitnick and colleagues (2009), wives' "we" requests were associated with less resistance from their husbands and increased relationship satisfaction (Mitnick et al., 2009). However, when either partner used "you" requests, those requests were met with increased resistance and reactance (Mitnick et al., 2009). "We" requests help the couple to view and approach the problem as a team, preventing the message that the change requested can only be achieved if the other partner changes his/her behaviors (Mitnick et al., 2009).

One of the main mechanisms by which conflict and problem solving are linked to long-term relationship maintenance is the promotion of intimacy and emotional connection. Behaviors that increase intimacy are associated with higher relationship satisfaction (Mirgain & Cordova, 2007; Woodin, 2011), perhaps due to increased engagement between partners. Increased engagement facilitates conflict resolution by letting partners progress together to find a solution (Sanford, 2014). Further, the promotion of intimacy and emotional connection is likely to have direct benefit for the relationships in and of themselves (e.g., Christensen & Heavey, 1990).

"We" requests promote intimacy by reducing blame and the attribution of fault to one partner. These behaviors are likely to reduce resistance, increase engagement, and encourage effective problem solving. Because "we" requests lead to less disengagement, this results in fewer requests, as it becomes unnecessary to repeat demands (Mitnick et al., 2009), reducing the likelihood of using and intensifying aversive behaviors in order to obtain change. Specific change requests are another form of positive, communal behavior that promotes long-term relationship maintenance. Specific change requests made by either partner are associated with less resistance from the other partner, and specific requests made by wives to husbands are associated with higher relationship satisfaction for wives (Mitnick et al., 2009). Specific requests promote long-term relationship maintenance by reducing ambiguity and helping partners to identify the problems in the relationship, what each expects of the other, and what needs to be changed (Mitnick et al., 2009). These conditions help partners strategize and better problem solve to reach a solution that is beneficial for both partners and the relationship (Mitnick et al., 2009). Furthermore, specificity allows opportunities for partners to provide support to one another (Manne et al., 2007), increasing intimacy between partners.

Soft emotional expression. Long-term relationship maintenance is also enhanced when partners share and disclose emotional vulnerabilities to one another during conflict. Sharing emotional vulnerabilities helps promote closeness between partners, increases positive, communally oriented communication, and decreases negative, individualistically oriented communication (Sanford, 2007). Partners may share their vulnerabilities verbally and/or through affective expressions such as using soft emotions. Soft emotions include expressions of hurt and sadness and are considered "prosocial emotions" (Sanford, 2007). Sanford (2007) found that the use of soft emotions and perception of a partner's use of soft emotions were associated with increased conflict resolution and positive, communally oriented communication. Further, the use of soft emotions during a conflict was related to a stronger perception that the problem being discussed is harder to solve but is of increased importance (Sanford, 2007).

Many emotion-focused couple-based interventions teach couples to share soft emotions (e.g., sadness) rather than hard emotions (e.g., contempt) because partners are more likely to respond to soft emotional expressions with empathy, which facilitates increased understanding and closeness between partners (Fischer & Baucom, in press). This mechanism is also at work when couples engage in acceptance by listening and understanding their partner's perspective, even though they may disagree. These are constructive behaviors, because they lead to better conflict resolution and increased relationship satisfaction (Woodin, 2011).

Acceptance. Lastly, couples do not have to agree every time they face a conflict. Third-wave cognitive behavioral couple therapies, such as Integrative Behavior Couple Therapy (IBCT[6]; Jacobson & Christensen, 1996), emphasize acceptance strategies. Acceptance strategies include validating, listening, and understanding the other partner's emotions and perspectives even if the individual does not agree (Fischer & Baucom, in press). Acceptance is a positive communication behavior, because when partners accept each other's behaviors and perspectives during conflict, they put the goals of the relationship first and their own goals second, which subsequently promotes changes that enhance long-term maintenance (Jacobson et al., 2000).

Short-Term Relationship Maintenance

Short-term relationship maintenance occurs when couples engage in negative, communal communication behaviors that function to promote awareness between partners or through positive communication behaviors that are individualistic in nature. Though these strategies often work to ameliorate the immediate situation, they frequently impair effective problem solving in the long term. Furthermore, many maladaptive behaviors are focused on solving the short-term issue rather than focusing on the long-term outcome, which results in escalation of problem severity in the long term.

Accommodation and protective buffering.
Behaviors such as protective buffering and accommodation are well-intentioned behaviors that are individualistic in nature and prioritize the needs of the other partner over the self. Both types of behavior function to lessen the other partner's distress during conflict or when one individual is requesting assistance (Fischer & Baucom, in press). Although accommodation behaviors

---

[6] Results of a large-scale, randomized clinical trial demonstrate that IBCT is efficacious in promoting increased relationship functioning and does so at levels comparable to Behavioral Marital Therapy (e.g., Jacobson, Christensen, Prince, Cordova, & Eldridge, 2000).

are more common in relationships where one or both partners are experiencing psychological distress (e.g., Fischer & Baucom, in press), and protective buffering is most commonly observed in conversations related to physical health problems (e.g., Hinnen, Hagedoorn, Ranchor, & Sanderman, 2008; Manne et al., 2007), they occur in relationships generally and impact relationship maintenance in the same way across contexts. For example, partners may inhibit their desires in the relationship, minimize the importance of the change, overlook differences in the relationship, and hide worries or concerns so as to avoid conflict or not burden the other partner (Hinnen et al., 2008; Jacobson & Christensen, 1996; Manne et al., 2007). Though this may temporarily lessen the distress that one or both partners experience during conflict, these behaviors cannot be sustained for long periods of time, because they prevent conflict resolution and exacerbate the severity of the problem in the long term.

Strategies that result in short-term relationship maintenance often function to bring about temporary engagement and/or help couples to down-regulate the intensity of conflict in the present moment. Though these behaviors may be effective in achieving individuals' short-term goals, over time they impede conflict resolution and escalate existing conflict. This pattern of relationship outcomes occurs because avoidance of bringing up worries and concerns about the other partner's behavior or about the relationship results in reduced awareness of the problems a partner is experiencing. Consequently, this leads to missing an opportunity to engage in constructive problem-solving behaviors (e.g., support; Manne et al., 2007). Additionally, by minimizing the importance of change or inhibiting their own desires for change so as not to burden the other partner, partners fail to realize that not providing each other with the opportunity to disclose vulnerabilities impedes the facilitation of intimacy (Manne et al., 2007).

Direct individualistic behaviors and affective expressions. Hard, communal affect and negative, individualistic behaviors may also foster short-term relationship maintenance, as they function to reflect and communicate distress in the relationship, bringing about awareness of and engagement with the existing relationship problem. Hard, communal affective expressions may lead to short-term relationship maintenance because they provide concrete information about partners' needs and elicit temporary change through conflict engagement. For example, husbands' expressions of hard, communal emotions are associated with better couple conflict communication (Sanford, 2007). It is theorized that the use of hard emotions communicates care and investment in the relationship, leading to better communication (Sanford, 2007). Behaviors such as demanding change and expressions of negative affectivity are also considered "direct" negative behaviors (McNulty & Russell, 2010). Direct negative behaviors clearly highlight the importance and magnitude of the problem for the relationship (McNulty & Russell, 2010). For example, McNulty & Russell (2010) found that for couples with severe problems, direct negative behaviors reduce the severity of problems

Low Relationship Maintenance

Withdrawal. One way an individual can respond to the demands of his or her partner is by withdrawing from the conflict, which results in an asymmetrical pattern of behavior known as the demand-withdraw interaction pattern. The demand-withdraw interaction pattern occurs when one partner blames and criticizes to obtain change while the other partner responds by withdrawing or avoiding the conversation (Baucom & Atkins, 2013). This interaction pattern is associated with intimate partner violence, negative health outcomes, and increased relationship distress (Eldridge, Sevier, Jones, Atkins, & Christensen, 2007; Schrodt et al., 2013). When an individual withdraws from a conflict, the individual is disengaging from the problem at hand, resulting in conflict escalation rather than resolution. Over time, demanders increase the frequency and intensity of their behavior, while the withdrawers do the same, resulting in increased disengagement from the conflict and polarization within the couple, further exacerbating relationship distress (Baucom & Atkins, 2013; Fischer & Baucom, in press). Partners may also respond to demands with an extreme form of withdrawal whereby they acquiesce to whatever is being requested in order to end the conversation. High levels of demanding and submission are associated with lower relationship quality (Knobloch-Fedders et al., 2014), perhaps because the couple is engaging in nonauthentic resolution.

Negative reciprocity. Partners in the relationship may also respond to one another's requests and demands using increasingly negative behaviors during conflict, resulting in a hostile behavioral exchange known as negative reciprocity (Baucom & Atkins, 2013). Though negative reciprocity may serve to increase awareness of the problems within the relationship through engagement, negative reciprocity is detrimental to the relationship in both the short and the long term and has been shown to distinguish distressed couples from nondistressed couples (Baucom & Eldridge, 2013). When couples engage in this extremely negative cycle, they are unable to effectively resolve their conflict and may gradually drift apart over time (Jacobson & Christensen, 1996).

Individualistic negative behaviors are frequently unsuccessful in bringing about change in the relationship, and, in the limited instances in which they do engender change, it often comes at the expense of the other partner's wants and needs. Further, the aversive nature of these behaviors often leads to increased resistance from the other partner, preventing authentic and promoting nonauthentic resolution. When partners respond to demanding behavior by withdrawing, this prevents further exploration of potential solutions to the problem and often changes the topic of conversation to focus on the withdrawal itself rather than on the problem being discussed. Likewise, when partners respond to negative behaviors with negative behaviors of their own, this pattern often escalates conflict and momentary distress rather than focusing on the problematic aspect of the relationship. As this process unfolds over time, the intensity and frequency of both partners' negative behaviors increase, which in turn leads to less intimacy, increased distance between partners (i.e., polarization), and increased likelihood of eventual relationship dissolution (Jacobson & Christensen, 1996).

IMPACT OF CONFLICT-MANAGEMENT STRATEGIES ON BROADER RELATIONAL PROCESSES

The strategies and mechanisms mentioned previously can facilitate adaptability or decrease relationship maintenance for couples when they are faced with unexpected life circumstances (e.g., physical illness, onset of psychopathology, or change in socioeconomic status) as well as critical transitional periods in their relationship (e.g., transition to parenthood). Both these types of events call for change and can increase the level of stress that partners experience as well as the level of burden placed on the relationship. Although couples face many critical transitional periods in their relationship, we focus on the transition to parenthood and diagnosis with a life-threatening illness as examples of how conflict-management and problem-solving strategies help or hinder couples' adaptations to critical transitions.

Transition to Parenthood

The transition to parenthood is a major event in couples' lives and requires adjustment to the many challenges and changes (e.g., having less time together) that come with this period (Kluwer & Johnson, 2007). During this time, couples are more vulnerable to relationship deterioration and to poorer individual well-being (e.g., Doss, Rhoades, Stanley, & Markman, 2009; Figueiredo & Conde, 2011; Gawlik et al., 2014). Couples typically experience a sharp decline in satisfaction coupled with an increase in negative communication, decrease in conflict management, and increase in the perceived intensity of relationship problems (Doss et al., 2009). Though the transition to parenthood does not necessarily bring about new conflict, it does intensify preexisting relationship problems (Kluwer & Johnson, 2007). Reducing conflict management coupled with increasing demands on the couple may escalate the frequency of conflict during this time, and higher instances of conflict during pregnancy are associated with lower relationship quality

(Kluwer & Johnson, 2007). Individuals in the relationship are also more at risk for anxiety and depression, especially during the perinatal period (Figueiredo & Conde, 2011).

Although many partners experience anxiety while adjusting to their new circumstances, partners better maintain their relationship when they share their worries and anxiety concerning the new baby with one another (e.g., Halford, Petch, & Creedy, 2010). By disclosing their vulnerabilities and worries, partners create opportunities for each other to engage in positive behaviors, such as providing support and validation, thus fostering greater intimacy (e.g., Doss, Cicila, Hsueh, Morrison, & Carhart, 2014). Couples may also be tempted to engage in accommodation and protective buffering behaviors during this period (e.g., Crohan, 1996). For example, John may have noticed that he and his wife have not been making time to enjoy their normal leisure activities. However, he is hesitant to bring up his concern, as he does not want to add stress or end up fighting with his wife, who is pregnant with their first child. In this instance, John successfully avoids any complicated discussions but fails to bring awareness of his concerns and impedes progress toward resolving them. He is also denying himself and his partner the opportunity to build intimacy together as a couple by participating in shared activities, which could help to increase relationship functioning over time.

Consistently with this example, partners who handle perinatal conflict using positive, collaborative behaviors engender less resistance and withdrawal in one another, maintain higher levels of intimacy, and report higher levels of long-term relationship maintenance (e.g., Cox, Paley, Burchinal, & Payne, 1999; Trillingsgaard, Baucom, & Heyman, 2014). Conversely, couples who engage in hostile, individualistic communication behaviors such as character assassinations experience lower levels of relationship satisfaction following the birth of their first child. Couples who handle perinatal conflict using more positive, communal behaviors are also at lower risk for depressive and anxiety symptoms (e.g., Milgrom, Schembri, Ericksen, Ross, & Gemmill, 2011). Depression, relationship distress, and anxiety are known to be bidirectionally associated with one another (Whisman & Uebelacker, 2009). Relationship distress is associated with higher levels of depressive symptoms, and depressive and anxiety symptoms further exacerbate relationship distress and are associated with low relationship satisfaction (Whisman & Uebelacker, 2009). Therefore, higher levels of depression and anxiety symptoms following the birth of a child may lead to increased engagement in accommodation and protective buffering behaviors, resulting in a cycle that erodes relationship stability.

Life-Threatening Illness

Many couples face unexpected life circumstances, such as one or both partners being diagnosed with a life-threatening illness (e.g., cancer). Partners respond to these circumstances with a range of reactions, including the tendency to engage in protective buffering to help alleviate the diagnosed partner's distress and to prevent an increase in perceived burden. Though intended to be helpful to the ill partner, higher levels of protective buffering are associated with declines in lower levels of relationship satisfaction, for example, among couples who reported high relationship satisfaction prior to one partner receiving a breast cancer diagnosis. In contrast, there is no association between relationship satisfaction post diagnosis and protective buffering in couples who were low in relationship satisfaction prior to diagnosis (Manne et al., 2007). One possible explanation for these findings is that partners who experience high relationship satisfaction prior to learning about the diagnosis may experience a breakdown in intimacy when they fail to disclose their vulnerabilities and worries about the situation. Partners who experienced low relationship satisfaction prior to learning about the diagnosis may already have been engaging in little disclosure with one another and experiencing low levels of intimacy. Thus, there may be little change from what these partners are used to relative to what they experience when engaging in protective buffering.

CONCLUSION

Conflict is a normative experience for couples and can be beneficial for a relationship, because it allows the relationship to change, progress, and grow. This chapter presented the VAC model as an integrative conceptual model comprised of three axes along which conflict-management and problem-solving tactics vary (behavioral valence, hard vs. soft emotional expression, and communal vs. individualistic orientation) and two timeframes of relationship maintenance (short- and long-term). This conceptual model integrates core ideas from numerous existing models of relationship functioning and presents a framework for future research on conflict management, problem solving, relationship maintenance, and individual mental and physical well-being.

The review of existing data supporting the VAC model reveals several areas that would be valuable to explore in future research. First, it would be valuable for future research to distinguish communication behavior from affective expression, both conceptually and in operationalization, and to examine variability in relationship and individual outcomes across combinations of behavioral enactment and affective expression. The field presently knows considerably more about congruent behavioral enactments and affective expressions (e.g., angry demanding, anxious withdrawal; Heavey, Layne, & Christensen, 1993) than about incongruent behavioral enactments and affective expressions (e.g., anxious demanding, angry withdrawal). Existing work on incongruent conflict-management and problem-solving tactics suggests that such strategies are a valuable area for future research. For example, the Interpersonal Model of Depression suggests that incongruent responses (e.g., "I love you, but I don't want to be around you") of nonde-pressed partners to depressed partners results in increased symptom display and excessive reassurance seeking (e.g., Coyne, Thompson, & Palmer, 2002). This cycle of behavior is similar to the polarization process described earlier and is likely to occur in couples where one or both partners are diagnosed with a wide range of psychopathology.

Second, it would be valuable for future research to test moderators of the associations between behavior, affective expression, and relationship maintenance outcomes. Relationship maintenance is related to numerous other factors, such as enduring individual differences between partners (e. g., personality), commitment to the relationship, and willingness and ability to change (Jacobson & Christensen, 1996). These factors influence both the level of conflict the couple experiences and the nature of the associations between behavior, affective expression, and relationship-maintenance outcomes. Additionally, the nature of the associations between behavior, affective expression, and relationship maintenance out-comes may vary as a function of other variables not directly related to relationship maintenance itself, such as gender (e.g., Robles et al., 2014). For example, though more intense conflict during the perinatal period is associated with lower relationship quality for women and men, changes in relationship quality occur more slowly for husbands than for wives (Kluwer & Johnson, 2007).

Increased understanding of the use of conflict-management and pro-blem-solving strategies has the potential not only to improve the field's understanding of why and how they are related to relationship maintenance but also to inform future adaptations of couple-based interventions to prevent, ameliorate, and improve maladaptive responses to couple conflict and life stress. Such information would contribute to a broader appreciation of the role of relational processes in individual well-being and dysfunction, particularly for researchers who do not identify as relationship scientists (e. g., Beach et al., 2007). It is our hope that the VAC model can contribute to this continuing evolution by providing a framework for deriving testable hypotheses that build on well-established relational theories and incorpo-rate key principles from individual models of psychopathology and physical health.

REFERENCES

Baucom, B. R., & Atkins, D. C. (2013). Understanding marital distress: Polarization processes. In M. A. Fine & F. D. Fincham (Eds.), *Handbook of family theories: A content-based approach* (pp. 145–166). New York, NY: Routledge.

Baucom, B. R., & Eldridge, K. (2013). Marital communication. In A. Vangelisti (Ed.), *Handbook of family communication, second edition* (pp. 65–79). New York, NY: Routledge.

Beach, S. R., Wamboldt, M. Z., Kaslow, N. J., Heyman, R. E., First, M. B., Underwood, L. G., & Reiss, D. (Eds.). (2007). *Relational processes and DSM-V: Neuroscience, assessment, prevention, and treatment*. Washington, DC: American Psychiatric Publishers.

Bradbury, T. N., & Karney, B. R. (2004). Understanding and altering the longitudinal course of marriage. *Journal of Marriage and Family, 66*, 862–879. doi:10.1111/j.0022-2445.2004.00059.x

Brown, P. C., & Smith, T. W. (1992). Social influence, marriage, and the heart: Cardiovascular consequences of interpersonal control in husbands and wives. *Health Psychology, 11*, 88–96. doi:10.1037/0278-6133.11.2.88

Butzlaff, R. L., & Hooley, J. M. (1998). Expressed emotion and psychiatric relapse: A meta-analysis. *Archives of General Psychiatry, 55*, 547–552. doi:10.1001/archpsyc.55.6.547

Caughlin, J. P. (2010). Invited Review Article: A multiple goals theory of personal relationships: Conceptual integration and program overview. *Journal of Social and Personal Relationships, 27*, 824–848. doi:10.1177/0265407510373262

Christensen, A., & Heavey, C. L. (1990). Gender and social structure in the demand/withdraw pattern of marital conflict. *Journal of Personality and Social Psychology, 59*, 73–81. doi:10.1037/0022-3514.59.1.73

Coan, J. A., & Gottman, J. M. (2007). The specific affect coding system (SPAFF). In J. A. Coan & J. J. B. Allen (Eds.), *Series in affective science. Handbook of emotion elicitation and assessment* (pp. 267–285). New York: Oxford University Press.

Cohan, C. L., & Bradbury, T. N. (1997). Negative life events, marital interaction, and the longitudinal course of newlywed marriage. *Journal of Personality and Social Psychology, 73*, 114–128. doi:10.1037/0022-3514.73.1.114

Conger, R. D., Rueter, M. A., & Elder, G. H. (1999). Couple resilience to economic pressure. *Journal of Personality and Social Psychology, 76*, 54–71. doi:10.1037/0022-3514.76.1.54

Coyne, J. C., & Smith, D. A. F. (1991). Couples coping with a myocardial infarction: A contextual perspective on wives' distress. *Journal of Personality and Social Psychology, 61*, 404–412. doi:10.1037/0022-3514.61.3.404

Coyne, J. C., Thomson, R., & Palmer, S. C. (2002). Marital quality, coping with conflict, marital complaints, and affection in couples with a depressed wife. *Journal of Family Psychology, 16*, 26–37. doi:10.1037/0893-3200.16.1.26

Cox, M. J., Paley, B., Burchinal, M., & Payne, C. C. (1999). Marital perceptions and interactions across the transition to parenthood. *Journal of Marriage and Family, 61*, 611–625. doi:10.2307/353564

Crohan, S. E. (1996). Marital quality and conflict across the transition to parenthood in African American and White couples. *Journal of Marriage and Family, 58*, 933–944. doi:10.2307/353981

Doss, B. D., Cicila, L. N., Hsueh, A. C., Morrison, K. R., & Carhart, K. (2014). A randomized controlled trial of brief coparenting and relationship interventions during the transition to parenthood. *Journal of Family Psychology, 28*, 483–494. doi:10.1037/a0037311

Doss, B. D., Rhoades, G. K., Stanley, S. M., & Markman, H. J. (2009). The effect of the transition to parenthood on relationship quality: An 8-year prospective study. *Journal of Personality and Social Psychology, 96*, 601–619. doi:10.1037/a0013969

Eldridge, K. A., Sevier, M., Jones, J., Atkins, D. C., & Christensen, A. (2007). Demand-withdraw communication in severely distressed, moderately distressed, and nondistressed couples: Rigidity and polarity during relationship and personal problem discussions. *Journal of Family Psychology, 21,* 218–226. doi:10.1037/0893-3200.21.2.218

Emerson, R. M. (1976). Social exchange theory. *Annual Review of Sociology, 2,* 335–362. doi:10.1146/annurev.so.02.080176.002003

Figueiredo, B., & Conde, A. (2011). Anxiety and depression in women and men from early pregnancy to 3-months postpartum. *Archives of Women's Mental Health, 14,* 247–255. doi:10.1007/s00737-011-0217-3

Fischer, M. S., & Baucom, D. H. (in press). Cognitive-behavioral couple-based interventions for relationship distress and psychopathology. In B. Fiese, M. Whisman, M. Celano, K. Deater-Deckard, & E. Jouriles (Eds.), *APA handbook of contemporary family psychology.* Washington, DC: American Psychological Association.

Gawlik, S., Müller, M., Hoffmann, L., Dienes, A., Wallwiener, M., Sohn, C., ... Reck, C. (2014). Prevalence of paternal perinatal depressiveness and its link to partnership satisfaction and birth concerns. *Archives of Women's Mental Health, 17,* 49–56. doi:10.1007/s00737-013-0377-4

Gottman, J. M. (1993). A theory of marital dissolution and stability. *Journal of Family Psychology, 7,* 57–75. doi:10.1037/0893-3200.7.1.57

Guyll, M., Cutrona, C., Burzette, R., & Russell, D. (2010). Hostility, relationship quality, and health among African American couples. *Journal of Consulting and Clinical Psychology, 78,* 646–654. doi:10.1037/a0020436

Halford, W. K., Petch, J., & Creedy, D. K. (2010). Promoting a positive transition to parenthood: A randomized clinical trial of couple relationship education. *Prevention Science, 11,* 89–100. doi:10.1007/s11121-009-0152-y

Heavey, C. L., Layne, C., & Christensen, A. (1993). Gender and conflict structure in marital interaction: A replication and extension. *Journal of Consulting and Clinical Psychology, 61,* 16–27. doi:10.1037//0022-006X.61.1.16

Heyman, R. E. (2001). Observation of couple conflicts: Clinical assessment applications, stubborn truths, and shaky foundations. *Psychological Assessment, 13,* 5–35. doi:10.1037/1040-3590.13.1.5

Hinnen, C., Hagedoorn, M., Ranchor, A. V., & Sanderman, R. (2008). Relationship satisfaction in women: A longitudinal case-control study about the role of breast cancer, personal assertiveness, and partners' relationship focused coping. *British Journal of Health Psychology, 13,* 737–754. doi:10.1348/135910707X252431

Hooley, J. M., & Gotlib, I. H. (2000). A diathesis-stress conceptualization of expressed emotion and clinical outcome. *Applied and Preventive Psychology, 9,* 135–151. doi:10.1016/S0962-1849(05)80001-0

Horowitz, L. M., Wilson, K. R., Turan, B., Zolotsev, P., Constantino, M. J., & Henderson, L. (2006). How interpersonal motives clarify the meaning of interpersonal behavior: A revised circumplex model. *Personality and Social Psychology Review, 10,* 67–86. doi:10.1207/s15327957pspr1001_4

Jacobson, N. S., & Christensen, A. (1996). *Integrative couple therapy: Promoting acceptance and change.* New York, NY: W. W. Norton & Company.

Jacobson, N. S., Christensen, A., Prince, S. E., Cordova, J., & Eldridge, K. (2000). Integrative Behavioral Couple Therapy: An acceptance-based, promising new treatment for couple discord. *Journal of Consulting and Clinical Psychology, 68,* 351–355. doi:10.1037/0022-006X.68.2.351

Johnson, S. M., & Greenberg, L. S. (1987). Emotionally focused marital therapy: An overview. *Psychotherapy: Theory, Research, Practice, Training, 24,* 552–560. doi:10.1037/h0085753

Karney, B. R., & Bradbury, T. N. (1995). The longitudinal course of marital quality and stability: A review of theory, methods, and research. *Psychological Bulletin, 118*, 3–34. doi:10.1037/0033-2909.118.1.3

Kluwer, E. S., & Johnson, M. D. (2007). Conflict frequency and relationship quality across the transition to parenthood. *Journal of Marriage and Family, 69*, 1089–1106. doi:10.1111/j.1741-3737.2007.00434.x

Knobloch-Fedders, L. M., Critchfield, K. L., Boisson, T., Woods, N., Bitman, R., & Durbin, C. E. (2014). Depression, relationship quality, and couples' demand/withdraw and demand/submit sequential interactions. *Journal of Counseling Psychology, 61*, 264–279. doi:10.1037/a0035241

Krokoff, L. J., Gottman, J. M., & Roy, A. K. (1988). Blue-collar and white-collar marital interaction and communication orientation. *Journal of Social and Personal Relationships, 5*, 201–221. doi:10.1177/026540758800500205

Manne, S. L., Norton, T. R., Ostroff, J. S., Winkel, G., Fox, K., & Grana, G. (2007). Protective buffering and psychological distress among couples coping with breast cancer: The moderating role of relationship satisfaction. *Journal of Family Psychology, 21*, 380–388. doi:10.1037/0893-3200.21.3.380

McNulty, J. K., & Russell, V. M. (2010). When "negative" behaviors are positive: A contextual analysis of the long-term effects of problem-solving behaviors on changes in relationship satisfaction. *Journal of Personality and Social Psychology, 98*, 587–604. doi:10.1037/a0017479

Miklowitz, D. J. (2004). The role of family systems in severe and recurrent psychiatric disorders: A developmental psychopathology view. *Development and Psychopathology, 16*, 667–688. doi:10.1017/S0954579404004729

Milgrom, J., Schembri, C., Ericksen, J., Ross, J., & Gemmill, A. W. (2011). Towards parenthood: An antenatal intervention to reduce depression, anxiety and parenting difficulties. *Journal of Affective Disorders, 130*, 385–394. doi:10.1016/j.jad.2010.10.045

Mitnick, D. M., Heyman, R. E., Malik, J., & Slep, A. M. S. (2009). The differential association between change request qualities and resistance, problem resolution, and relationship satisfaction. *Journal of Family Psychology, 23*, 464–473. doi:10.1037/a0015982

Mirgain, S. A., & Cordova, J. V. (2007). Emotion skills and marital health: The association between observed and self-reported emotion skills, intimacy, and marital satisfaction. *Journal of Social and Clinical Psychology, 26*, 983–1009. doi:10.1521/jscp.2007.26.9.983

Nguyen, T. P., Williamson, H. C., Karney, B. R., & Bradbury, T. N. (2017). Communication moderates effects of residential mobility on relationship quality among ethnically diverse couples. *Journal of Family Psychology, 31*, 753–764. doi:10.1037/fam0000324

Overall, N. C., Fletcher, G. J. O., Simpson, J. A., & Sibley, C. G. (2009). Regulating partners in intimate relationships: The costs and benefits of different communication strategies. *Journal of Personality and Social Psychology, 96*, 620–639. doi:10.1037/a0012961

Robles, T. F., Slatcher, R. B., Trombello, J. M., & McGinn, M. M. (2014). Marital quality and health: A meta-analytic review. *Psychological Bulletin, 140*, 140–187. doi:10.1037/a0031859

Sanford, K. (2007). Hard and soft emotion during conflict: Investigating married couples and other relationships. *Personal Relationships, 14*, 65–90. doi:10.1111/j.1475-6811.2006.00142.x

Sanford, K. (2014). A latent change score model of conflict resolution in couples: Are negative behaviors bad, benign, or beneficial? *Journal of Social and Personal Relationships, 31*, 1068–1088. doi:10.1177/0265407513518156

Schrodt, P., Witt, P. L., & Shimkowski, J. R. (2013). A meta-analytical review of the demand/withdraw pattern of interaction and its associations with individual, relational, and communicative outcomes. *Communication Monographs, 81*, 28–58. doi:10.1080/03637751.2013.813632

Thibaut, J. W., & Kelley, H. H. (1959). *The social psychology of groups.* New York; Wiley.

Trillingsgaard, T., Baucom, K. J. W., & Heyman, R. E. (2014). Predictors of change in relationship satisfaction during the transition to parenthood. *Family Relations, 63*, 667–679. doi:10.1111/fare.12089

Uebelacker, L. A., Courtnage, E. S., & Whisman, M. A. (2003). Correlates of depression and marital dissatisfaction: Perceptions of marital communication style. *Journal of Social and Personal Relationships, 20*, 757–769. doi:10.1177/ 0265407503206003

Weiss, R. L., & Heyman, R. E. (1997). A clinical-research overview of couples interactions. In W. K. Halford & H. J. Markman (Eds.), *Clinical handbook of marriage and couples interventions* (pp. 13–41). Hoboken, NJ: John Wiley.

Whisman, M. A., & Uebelacker, L. A. (2009). Prospective associations between marital discord and depressive symptoms in middle-aged and older adults. *Psychology and Aging, 24*, 184–189. doi:10.1037/a0014759

Wills, T. A., Weiss, R. L., & Patterson, G. R. (1974). A behavioral analysis of the determinants of marital satisfaction. *Journal of Consulting and Clinical Psychology, 42*, 802–811. doi:10.1037/h0037524

Woodin, E. M. (2011). A two-dimensional approach to relationship conflict: Meta-analytic findings. *Journal of Family Psychology, 25*, 325–335. doi:10.1037/a0023791

12

Sex as Relationship Maintenance

EMILY A. IMPETT[1], AMY MUISE[2], AND NATALIE O. ROSEN[3]

When people are asked to consider what makes their lives meaningful, no factor is listed more consistently and prominently than having close, satisfying relationships (Berscheid & Reis, 1998). Meta-analyses have documented that having high-quality, supportive relationships is an equal or stronger predictor of mortality than other known health risk factors such as smoking, physical activity, and body mass index (Holt-Lunstad, Smith, & Layton, 2010). Key reasons why supportive, close relationships promote health and well-being are that they help people cope with stress and enable them to fulfill basic needs for social connection, intimacy, and companionship (see Pietromonaco & Collins, 2017, for a review). One factor that has been surprisingly absent from the literature on relationship maintenance and well-being is the role of sexuality, a striking omission given that sexuality is a key factor that distinguishes romantic relationships from other types of close relationships, and sexual satisfaction is strongly linked to the maintenance of relationships and overall well-being (see Impett, Muise, & Peragine, 2014, for a review). For example, in North America, more people see a happy sexual relationship as very important for a successful relationship (70%) than having an adequate income (53%) or having shared interests (46%; Taylor, Funk, & Clark, 2007). Further, in a multinational study conducted in 29 countries, the people who were the most sexually satisfied were the most satisfied with their lives in general (Laumann et al., 2006).

Despite the importance of sex for relationships, couples face numerous challenges to maintaining desire and satisfying sexual relationships. For example, sexual desire tends to peak in the beginning stages of romantic

[1] Department of Psychology, University of Toronto Mississauga, emily.impett@utoronto.ca

[2] Department of Psychology, York University, muiseamy@yorku.ca

[3] Departments of Psychology & Neuroscience and Obstetrics & Gynaecology, Dalhousie University, natalie.rosen@dal.ca

This chapter was supported by an Insight Grant from the Social Sciences and Humanities Research Council awarded to Emily A. Impett and Amy Muise, and a grant from the Canadian Institute of Health Research awarded to Natalie O. Rosen and Emily A. Impett.

relationships as intimacy is rapidly developing (Baumeister & Bratslavsky, 1999) and often declines over time as partners become more secure and comfortable in the relationship (Impett, Muise, & Peragine, 2014). Similarly, although couples begin their relationships quite satisfied with their sex lives, sexual satisfaction steadily declines, in one study beginning at about a year into the relationship (Schmiedeberg & Schröder, 2016). As a result of these changes, romantic partners will inevitably encounter situations in which their sexual interests differ (see Impett & Peplau, 2003, for a review), and many long-term couples find themselves in situations in which they have discrepant levels of sexual desire (Davies, Katz, & Jackson, 1999; Mark, 2012). Couples may disagree about when and how frequently to engage in sex, or the specific activities in which they wish to engage, and these sexual conflicts of interest are not inconsequential. In a national study of couples married fewer than five years, disagreements about sexual frequency were among the top three most cited arguments between partners (Risch, Riley, & Lawler, 2003). Further, conflicts of interest about sex are among the most common reasons why couples seek marital therapy (Rosen, 2000), and this is one of the most difficult types of conflict to successfully resolve (Sanford, 2003).

Yet, the positive side to this connection between sexual quality and relationship quality is that, when negotiated with care and responsiveness, sex can be a powerful mechanism for maintaining and enhancing relationships. That is, when couples can successfully navigate sexual issues, feelings of closeness and intimacy in the relationship can be maintained and strengthened (Rehman et al., 2011). This chapter focuses on the role of sexuality in relationship maintenance, and in particular, how couples can maintain sexual desire, sexual satisfaction, as well as relationship satisfaction and feelings of commitment to their relationship over time, or remain satisfied in spite of changes to their sexual relationship. We use the term *relationship maintenance* to refer to couples' abilities to maintain stable relationships (i.e., commitment and relationship longevity), sustain the high levels of relationship quality with which they began their relationships (e.g., satisfaction and passion), and overcome challenges to their relationships during periods when relationship and sexual satisfaction are known to decline, such as in the transition to parenthood. However, given that sexual desire – defined as the need, drive, or motivation to engage in sexual activities (Diamond, 2004) – involves the rewards and positive emotional experiences associated with the approach motivational system (Impett, Strachman, Finkel, & Gable, 2008), in this chapter, we also focus on couples' abilities to experience increases in both relationship and sexual satisfaction – that is, to grow and thrive in their relationships – as another key component of relationship maintenance.

We begin the chapter by discussing the ways that sex can benefit relationships, focusing on links between sexual frequency, physical affection, sexual satisfaction, and the quality and maintenance of relationships. Then, we discuss the factors that enable couples to stave off declines in sexual desire and satisfaction, including sexual goals, sexual communal motivation, sexual communication, and sexual expectations. Throughout the chapter, we integrate available evidence on the role of sexuality in relationship maintenance during a period of great life transition for couples (e.g., the transition to parenthood) and in situations where couples are faced with significant sexual dysfunction, such as pain during intercourse. We conclude the chapter by discussing five promising directions for future research on sexuality and relationship maintenance.

THE BENEFITS OF SEX FOR RELATIONSHIPS

Although navigating sexual issues in long-term, romantic relationships can be challenging, we also know that regular, satisfying sex has the power to connect people, create affection, and sustain relationships. In this section, we consider how the maintenance of relationships is impacted by three factors: (1) sexual frequency (i.e., the frequency with which couples engage in sexual activity, broadly defined, in their relationship), (2) affection frequency (i.e., the frequency with which couples engage in physically affectionate activities in either sexual or nonsexual contexts), and (3) sexual satisfaction (i.e., the affective response arising from the subjective evaluation of the positive and negative aspects of one's sexual relationship).

SEXUAL FREQUENCY AND RELATIONSHIP MAINTENANCE

Numerous studies indicate that people who engage in sex more frequently in their relationships enjoy greater sexual as well as relationship satisfaction. Beginning with sexual satisfaction, research has shown that people's sexual satisfaction in their romantic relationships is positively correlated with their sexual frequency (e.g., Cheung et al., 2008; McNulty, Wenner, & Fisher, 2015; Rahmani, Khoei, & Gholi, 2009). Multi-wave, longitudinal research with couples indicates that the link between sexual frequency and sexual satisfaction is bidirectional, such that sexually satisfied couples pursue sex more frequently, and frequent sex leads to increases in sexual satisfaction (McNulty et al., 2015). Further, this link is consistent for men and women (McNulty et al., 2015), for people living in Western and non-Western countries (e.g., Cheung et al., 2008; Rahmani et al., 2009), and for same-sex and mixed-sex couples (Blair & Pukall, 2014). Recent research demonstrates that sex does not just increase satisfaction in the moment, but that married couples experience a sexual *afterglow* – where sexual satisfaction remains elevated for about 48 hours following a sexual experience – and this is particularly true for highly satisfying sexual experiences (Meltzer et al., 2017). In this work, couples who reported higher levels of sexual afterglow also remained more satisfied in their marriage over a four-month period of time.

Sexual frequency is also associated with people's satisfaction with their relationships and lives more generally. In one early study, low sexual frequency was the second strongest predictor of marital dissatisfaction, ranking only behind age and controlling for other important predictors of sexual frequency, such as relationship duration and whether or not couples had children living at home (Call, Sprecher, & Schwartz, 1995). Further, in a study using data from the National Survey of Families and Households, a nationally representative survey conducted in the USA, Yabiku and Gager (2009) found that lower sexual frequency was associated with higher rates of relationship dissolution among both cohabiting and married couples, although the link was stronger for cohabiting couples. Sexual frequency is also associated with greater life satisfaction. In three studies including more than 30,000 participants, Muise, Schimmack, and Impett (2016) showed that couples who reported engaging in more frequent sex also reported greater satisfaction with their lives overall, yet the benefits of sex for well-being were maximized when couples engaged in sex once per week. Demonstrating the practical utility of these findings, the increase in well-being in this study that was gained from having sex once a week rather than having sex once a month was equivalent to the increase in well-being gained from making $75,000 per year compared with $25,000 (Muise et al., 2016). Finally, in a longitudinal study, increases in sexual frequency were associated with increases in sexual satisfaction and life satisfaction over time (Schmiedeberg, Huyer-May, Castiglioni, & Johnson, 2017).

Sex also facilitates relationship maintenance by buffering romantic couples against negative relationship outcomes. Both attachment insecurity (see Cassidy & Shaver, 1999, for a review) and neuroticism (e.g., Karney & Bradbury, 1997) have been consistently associated with relationship dissatisfaction. However, research has shown that the negative effects of both factors are attenuated for people who engage in more frequent sex. Russell and McNulty (2011) demonstrated that the lower relationship satisfaction typically experienced by people high in neuroticism was not present among spouses who engaged in relatively frequent sex; that is, neuroticism was not associated with less satisfaction for couples engaging in more frequent sex. Likewise, Little, McNulty, and Russell (2010) demonstrated that attachment avoidance was unassociated with marital satisfaction among spouses who engaged in more frequent sex. This effect was mediated by expectations of partner availability, suggesting that more frequent sex may alleviate avoidant individuals' automatic concerns over abandonment.

THE IMPORTANCE OF PHYSICAL AFFECTION

One reason why sexual frequency is associated with greater well-being is that couples who engage in more frequent sex also tend to be more affectionate with each other. Across four studies, the association between sexual frequency and personal well-being (i.e., satisfaction with life and positive emotions) was partially accounted for by the frequency with which couples engaged in affectionate behaviors (e.g., cuddling, kissing, and caressing) in their relationship (Debrot, Meuwly, Muise, Impett, & Schoebi, 2017). In fact, when romantic couples reported on their sexual and affectionate experiences four times a day for a two-week period, engaging in sex at one time point during the day was associated with increases in affectionate behavior at the next time point, and affection at one time point was also associated with a greater likelihood of engaging in sex at the next time point (Debrot et al., 2017). In addition, Muise, Giang, and Impett (2014) found that sex has positive implications for sexual and relationship satisfaction because of affectionate experiences *after* sex. In particular, couples who spent longer engaging in affection after sex (i.e., kissing, cuddling, and caressing) felt more satisfied with the sexual experience and with their relationship. Notably, the duration of after-sex affection was a stronger predictor of sexual and relationship satisfaction than the amount of time spent engaging in foreplay or sex itself, and this was true for both men and women.

Given that sexual frequency is important for the maintenance of relationships, it seems as if the fact that sexual frequency tends to decline with age (Waite, Laumann, Das, & Schumm, 2009) could pose a problem for the maintenance of relationship satisfaction over time (see Rauer & Proulx, Chapter 17). Nevertheless, physically affectionate behaviors, such as kissing, cuddling, and caressing, do not seem to decline with age (Waite et al., 2009). Couples who are able to move beyond the notion that penetrative sex is the primary or only mode of sexual expression and incorporate a broader repertoire of sexual and affectionate behaviors seem better able to maintain – or experience heightened – sexual satisfaction in older adulthood (Hinchliff & Gott, 2008). In a study of mixed-sex couples in midlife and older adulthood conducted in five countries, affectionate behaviors such as kissing, cuddling, and caressing were associated with increased sexual satisfaction for both men and women, and this effect held above and beyond the association between sexual frequency and satisfaction (Heiman, Long, Smith, Fisher, & Sand, 2010). Interestingly, despite women's tendency to focus more on relational aspects of sexuality relative to men (see Diamond, 2004, for a review), the association between affection and sexual satisfaction was stronger for men than for women, and physical affection was a significant predictor of men's, but not women's, relationship satisfaction. Finally, research with clinical populations has also shown that when penetrative sex is painful, more daily physical affection – in both sexual and nonsexual contexts – was linked to greater relationship satisfaction for both partners compared with when daily affection was lower (Vannier, Rosen, Mackinnon, & Bergeron, 2017).

SEXUAL SATISFACTION AND RELATIONSHIP MAINTENANCE

People's affective responses arising from their subjective evaluations of the quality of their sex lives – that is, how satisfied people *feel* about their sex lives – may be an even better predictor of how they feel about their relationships than how frequently they engage in sex. McNulty and colleagues (2015) demonstrated that the effects of sexual frequency on relationship satisfaction were indirect, such that they emerged through sexual satisfaction. In other words, having a satisfying sexual relationship appears to be most important to relationship quality, regardless of how one gets there. In a multinational study of people from 29 countries, Laumann et al. (2006) demonstrated that people who were the most sexually satisfied were also the happiest with their romantic relationships and with their lives in general. In one of the strongest demonstrations of the association between sexual and relationship satisfaction, in two eight-wave longitudinal studies of married couples, McNulty et al. (2015) found that sexual satisfaction at one time point positively predicted changes in marital satisfaction from that time point to the next (see also Fallis, Rehman, Woody, & Purdon, 2016). Marital satisfaction at one time point also positively predicted changes in sexual satisfaction from that time point to the next, suggesting that the link between sexual and relationship satisfaction flows in both directions. Extensive research has also shown that couples who enjoy positive, satisfying sexual relationships have more stable relationships than couples who are less sexually satisfied or who report experiencing sexual problems (e.g., Sprecher, 2002). In fact, sexual dissatisfaction and incompatibility are key reasons why couples ultimately break up and dissolve their relationships (Sprecher, 1994).

The importance of sexual satisfaction for the maintenance of satisfying relationships is also highlighted by research demonstrating that, like sexual frequency, sexual satisfaction explains and attenuates the effects of critical individual difference factors on relationship quality. For example, Fisher and McNulty (2008) demonstrated that sexual satisfaction mediated the effects of neuroticism on marital satisfaction – that is, the low marital satisfaction of people high in neuroticism was accounted for by their low sexual satisfaction. Likewise, Little et al. (2010) found that sexual satisfaction moderated the effects of attachment anxiety on global relationship satisfaction, such that attachment anxiety was unrelated to marital satisfaction among those who were satisfied with their sex lives. This finding is important because it demonstrates that even those who are high in attachment anxiety – who tend to report lower relationship quality – can benefit from engaging in satisfying sex with a close partner.

Although the association between sexual satisfaction and relationship satisfaction tends to be fairly robust, some couples successfully maintain satisfaction with their relationship even when their sexual satisfaction is low. For example, women who suffer from pain during sex report significantly lower sexual satisfaction than women without this problem, but report their relationship satisfaction to be similar to women without this pain (Smith & Pukall, 2011). Similar patterns have been observed among people coping with other sexual dysfunctions (e.g., erectile dysfunction or low sexual interest), whereby the link between sexual functioning and sexual satisfaction is stronger than the link between sexual functioning and overall satisfaction with the relationship (Rosen, Heiman, Long, Fisher, & Sand, 2016). Couples who have adapted their sexual scripts to account for difficulties in sexual functioning (e.g., focusing on nonpenetrative sexual activities when intercourse is painful or there are erectile problems), or who continue to engage in behaviors that benefit the overall relationship but are typically associated with sex (e.g., expressing affection, cuddling, and responsiveness), may experience less interference with their feelings about their relationship more generally (Burri, Giuliano, McMahon, & Porst, 2014; Vannier et al., 2017).

PREVENTING DECLINES IN SEXUAL DESIRE AND SATISFACTION OVER TIME

Given that keeping up a regular sex life and feeling satisfied with one's sex life can help couples maintain their relationships over time, it is important to understand how some couples are able to stave off such declines or remain satisfied in the face of changes to their sexuality. Indeed, although sexual desire tends to decline or waver over the course of a relationship on average (Sims & Meana, 2010), romantic love, which is characterized by high sexual interest, engagement, and intensity, does not decline for everyone (Acevedo & Aron, 2009), and not everyone experiences accompanying declines in relationship satisfaction (Lavner & Bradbury, 2010; Sims & Meana, 2010). Indeed, although many couples in which one partner has a higher desire for sex than the other (i.e., "desire-discrepant couples") experience lower sexual and relationship satisfaction than couples in which partners have more matched levels of desire (Davies et al., 1999; Mark, 2012; Rosen, Bailey, & Muise, 2018), some of these couples successfully navigate these differences and maintain satisfaction (Bridges & Horne, 2007). Similarly, despite the stressors and demands associated with the transition to parenthood, about one-third to one-half of couples maintain or even report an increase in their sexual and relationship satisfaction during this period (Ahlborg, Rudeblad, Linnér, & Linton, 2008; Shapiro, Gottman, & Carrere, 2000). In this section, we review research on four factors that can help couples stave off declines in sexual desire and satisfaction or remain satisfied in the face of changes to their sexual relationship, including research on (1) sexual goals, (2) sexual communal motivation, (3) sexual communication, and (4) sexual expectations.

Sexual Goals

Although engaging in more frequent sex with a romantic partner is associated with greater sexual and relationship satisfaction, research on sexual motivation suggests that an important predictor of what differentiates satisfying sexual experiences and relationships from dissatisfying ones concerns people's reasons or goals for engaging in sex (see reviews by Impett, Muise, & Rosen, 2015; Muise & Impett, 2016). Links between sexual goals and sexual and relationship satisfaction have been most extensively researched through the lens of approach-avoidance motivational theory (see Gable & Impett, 2012). This work has shown that when people engage in sex for *approach goals*, such as to enhance intimacy or express love for their partner, they experience more positive emotions, and both partners report higher sexual and relationship satisfaction (Impett, Peplau, & Gable, 2005; Muise, Impett, & Desmarais, 2013). In contrast, when people engage in sex for *avoidance goals*, such as to avoid conflict or a partner's disappointment, they experience more negative emotions and relationship conflict, and both partners report lower sexual and relationship satisfaction. In a longitudinal study of long-term married and cohabiting couples, people who engaged in sex more frequently for avoidance goals over the course of a three-week daily experience study reported lower sexual satisfaction at a four-month follow-up and had partners who felt less sexually satisfied and committed to maintaining their relationship four months later (Muise, Impett, & Desmarais, 2013). In addition, these same patterns have also been observed among couples coping with significant sexual problems, such as pain during sex (Rosen, Muise, et al., 2018). These findings are consistent with research on sacrifice – a type of pro-relationship behavior in which partners give up their own self-interests for the sake of their partner or the relationship (see Righetti & Impett, 2017). This work on sacrifice has also shown that while making sacrifices for a romantic partner for approach goals increases the relationship satisfaction of both the giver and the recipient over time, making sacrifices for a romantic partner in pursuit of avoidance goals is particularly destructive to the maintenance of relationships over time (Impett, Gable, & Peplau, 2005; Impett, Gere, Kogan, Gordon, & Keltner, 2014).

Other research guided by self-determination theory (e.g., Deci & Ryan, 2000) has found that people experience greater psychological well-being and relationship quality when they engage in sex for goals that are more *self-determined* in nature – such as for the enjoyment of being sexual or the pleasure of sharing an intimate experience with a partner – as compared with when they engage in sex for goals that are more *controlled* in nature –

such as out of feelings of pressure by a partner or concerns about withholding sex in their relationship (Brunell & Webster, 2013). Similarly, sexual interactions characterized by higher levels of autonomy, competence, and relatedness are associated with more positive sexual experiences (Smith, 2007) and greater need fulfillment in monogamous and consensually nonmonogamous relationships (Wood, Desmarais, Burleigh, & Milhausen, 2018). Taken together, this work suggests that engaging in sex in pursuit of approach or self-determined goals can enable couples to maintain satisfying sex lives and relationships over time, whereas engaging in sex for controlled or avoidance goals can present challenges to the maintenance of relationships.

Although we are gaining a greater understanding of how sexual goals shape the quality of sexual relationships, we know much less about how goals might be changed to the ultimate benefit of relationships. The lack of research on this topic likely reflects the challenges in conducting experimental work in the area of sexuality. For example, in one experimental study, participants who were asked to double their sexual frequency unexpectedly experienced *lower* satisfaction than participants not given this manipulation, possibly due to reduced feelings of autonomy around sexual decision-making (Loewenstein, Krishnamurti, Kopsic, & McDonald, 2015). Recent experimental work on approach and avoidance sexual goals suggests that it is possible to enhance people's approach goals for sex and ultimately, their satisfaction. In a sample of people currently involved in a romantic relationship, half of the participants were told about the benefits of approach sexual goals and were asked to try to focus on approach reasons for sex over the next week, and the other half were given no instructions about sexual goals. When participants completed a follow-up survey one week later, those in the approach condition reported higher sexual and relationship satisfaction compared with those in the control group (Muise, Boudreau, & Rosen, 2017). Therefore, incorporating information on the benefits of approach-motivated (or self-determined) sex in relationships might enhance the efficacy of interventions for couples with low sexual desire or sexual dissatisfaction.

Sexual Communal Motivation

Another motivational factor that is linked with increased sexual desire and satisfaction in couples is *sexual communal motivation* (see Impett et al., 2015; Muise & Impett, 2016), defined as the extent to which people are motivated to be noncontingently responsive to their partner's sexual needs (Muise, Impett, Kogan, & Desmarais, 2013). People high in sexual communal motivation report being more likely to have sex with their partner when they are not entirely in the mood, being open-minded about their partner's preferences, communicating with their partner about their sexual likes and dislikes, and ensuring that the sexual relationship is mutually satisfying (Muise & Impett,

2016). In a sample of long-term couples who had been together for an average of 11 years, people who were higher in sexual communal motivation felt more sexual desire for their partner and had more enjoyable sexual experiences than those lower in sexual communal motivation (Muise, Impett, Kogan, et al., 2013). More specifically, whereas people lower in sexual communal motivation declined in desire over a four-month period of time, more communal people began the study with slightly higher desire and were able to maintain high levels of sexual desire over time (Muise, Impett. Kogan, et al., 2013). The partners of people high in sexual communal motivation also reaped benefits, as they reported that their partners were highly responsive to their needs during sex and in turn, they felt more satisfied with and committed to their relationship (Muise & Impett, 2015). Related research suggests that, at times, changing sexual habits – or making *sexual transformations* – for a partner can benefit the relationship (Burke & Young, 2012). In one study, people who made more (compared with less) frequent sexual changes for the sake of their romantic partner had partners who reported being more satisfied in their relationship. In addition, people who felt more positive about changing their sexual habits for their partner felt more satisfied with their relationships and had partners who reported feeling more satisfied as well (Burke & Young, 2012). These findings are consistent with the literature on sacrifice, which has shown that on days when people report giving up their own needs to benefit their partner or their relationship, they report increased relationship satisfaction (Ruppel & Curran, 2012), as well as findings from a recent meta-analysis linking broad individual differences in communal orientation with increased personal well-being and relationship quality (Le, Impett, Lemay, Muise, & Tskhay, 2018).

Communally motivated people are even motivated to meet their partner's needs in situations when it is not particularly easy – for example, in situations in which their partner is interested in sex but their own desire for sex is low. In these situations, people higher in sexual communal motivation remain motivated to make their partner feel loved and desired, and focus less on what they personally have to lose from engaging in sex, such as feeling tired or giving up time spent on personal activities (Day, Muise, Joel, & Impett, 2015). As a result of their increased motivation to pursue benefits for their partner and decreased motivation to avoid costs to themselves, individuals high in sexual communal motivation are more likely to engage in sex in these desire-discrepant situations, and both partners report greater sexual and relationship satisfaction as a result. Similarly, being higher in sexual communal motivation also helps couples maintain sexual and relationship satisfaction in the face of sexual dysfunction, such as pain during sex (Muise, Bergeron, et al., 2017).

Our review of the research showing the benefits of sexual communal motivation in relationships is not meant to suggest that people should *always* be willing to meet each other's sexual needs. While the willingness to sacrifice or incur costs to benefit a partner – both inside and outside the bedroom – is inevitable and necessary to sustain relationships (see reviews by Impett et al., 2015; Righetti & Impett, 2017), incurring personal costs to meet a partner's needs is not always beneficial (e.g., Impett, Gable, et al., 2005).

Indeed, research on unmitigated communion (Fritz & Helgeson, 1998) – the tendency to give to others in a manner that is devoid of agency and concern for one's own needs – has shown that individuals high in unmitigated communion experience more negative affect and less positive affect in situations of interpersonal conflict (Nagurney, 2007). In essence, people higher in unmitigated communion take the value of interpersonal connectedness to an unhealthy extreme, prioritizing the needs of others while neglecting their own psychological and physical well-being (Fritz & Helgeson, 1998).

Recently, theories of unmitigated communion have been extended to the domain of sexuality. In a 21-day dyadic daily experience study, on days when people (or their romantic partner) reported higher sexual communal strength, they felt more connected to their partner during sex, and in turn, both partners experienced greater daily sexual and relationship satisfaction. In contrast, on days when people reported higher unmitigated sexual communion, they felt more disconnected from their partner during sex, and in turn, experienced lower relationship and sexual satisfaction (Impett, Muise, & Harasymchuk, 2019). Similarly, in a clinical sample of couples in which the woman experiences pain during sex, on days when people reported higher sexual communal motivation, both they and their partners reported better sexual function and sexual and relationship satisfaction. In contrast, on days when people reported higher *unmitigated sexual communion* (i.e., they focused on their partner's sexual needs to the exclusion of their own needs), both partners reported poorer sexual function as well as lower sexual and relationship satisfaction (Muise, Bergeron, et al., 2017). These findings suggest that even though people higher in unmitigated sexual communion report being solely focused on meeting their partner's sexual needs, their partners are not benefiting from their hypervigilance to their sexual needs and may, in fact, be even less satisfied with their sex lives and relationships.

Sexual Communication

Another factor that influences both sexual and relationship satisfaction is sexual communication. Sexual self-disclosure may be an important way for couples to maintain sexual desire and satisfaction over the course of long-term relationships (MacNeil & Byers, 2009). Indeed, couples who report more open and effective communication about their sex lives also report higher sexual and relationship satisfaction (Byers & Demmons, 1999), including in situations in which one person suffers from a sexual dysfunction such as pain during sex (Rancourt, Flynn, Bergeron, & Rosen, 2017). In fact, general self-disclosure as well as disclosure about specific sexual likes and dislikes contributes to sexual satisfaction (Byers & Demmons, 1999). It is not just communication about sex outside the bedroom that has implications for sexual satisfaction; communication during sex matters too. One study found that nonverbal sexual communication (i.e., participants' own reports of their touch, gestures, and eye gaze during sex), but not verbal communication (i.e., participants' own reports of how much they communicate their pleasure or satisfaction with their partner during sex), was associated with increased sexual satisfaction (Babin, 2012). Still other research that has examined more specific types of verbal sexual communication suggests that it matters. For example, Hess and Coffelt (2012) found that using more sexual terms during sexual discussions with a partner (especially slang terms, such as *give head*, as opposed to clinical terms, such as *fellatio*) was associated with greater relationship quality and closeness. One reason for this association is that the use of more sexual terms might indicate that couples are talking about sex more frequently and have greater comfort with sexual communication. Further, in research by Jonason, Betteridge, and Kneebone (2016), more relationship-oriented talk during sex was associated with greater sexual and relationship satisfaction compared with more self-focused types of erotic talk.

Individual differences in romantic attachment also influence comfort with sexual communication as well as sexual and relationship satisfaction. Securely attached people (i.e., those who are comfortable with intimacy and closeness) generally have committed, stable, and satisfying romantic relationships and enjoy sex in the context of relationships, more so than more insecurely attached people (i.e., those high in attachment anxiety and/or avoidance; Birnbaum, Reis, Mikulincer, Gillath, & Orpaz, 2006). One key reason why secure people have more satisfying sex lives and relationships than less securely attached people stems from their increased comfort with communicating about sexuality with a romantic partner (Shaver & Mikulincer, 2005). In one study, secure individuals reported less inhibited sexual communication compared with anxious and avoidant individuals, and this was found to mediate the relationship between attachment and sexual satisfaction (Davis et al., 2006). Similarly, in a more recent study of partnered gay men, securely attached individuals reported the highest levels of sexual communication and experienced greater relationship quality, and men with securely attached partners were the most likely to report having sex with their partners at least once per week (Starks & Parsons, 2014).

Sexual communication may be particularly important as couples navigate changes to their lives or to their relationships. For example, during the transition to parenthood, parents juggle a host of novel sexual stressors that may strain their emotional and physical resources and interfere with their ability to connect as a couple (Schlagintweit, Bailey, & Rosen, 2016). Therefore, how partners communicate with each other about their sex lives during this transition is likely to shape relationship and sexual satisfaction. Indeed, in one study, new mothers reported that communication with their partner about discrepancies in sexual desire was central to negotiating different sexual needs between partners and enhancing their sexual satisfaction during the transition to parenthood (Olsson, Lundqvist, Faxelid, & Nissen, 2005).

Sexual Expectations

In addition to being shaped by the way couples communicate about sex and their motivations for engaging in sex, sexual and relationship satisfaction are also likely shaped by people's expectations about sex – for example, their expectations about how sexual desire will change over time in their relationship and their expectations for what it takes to maintain sexual desire and satisfaction. Generally speaking, people are motivated to view their relationships positively, and these cognitive processes help to maintain romantic relationships over time (Murray et al., 2011), at least for those in healthy relationships at the outset (McNulty, O'Mara, & Karney, 2008). Recent research has shown the same to be true in the sexual domain of relationships. de Jong and Reis (2015) showed that partners higher in commitment tend to view their current partner as their ideal sexual partner and feel optimistic about their future sex lives, motivational processes that bolster people's resolve to persist in their relationships. Assuming that such processes are occurring in healthy, well-functioning relationships, they may predict better sexual outcomes over time, and additional research is needed to test this possibility.

People also have expectations about how satisfied they expect to feel with their sex lives in the future, and through a process of perceptual confirmation, it is possible that they eventually evaluate their sex lives in a way that is consistent with their initial expectations. In one study, both romantic partners reported their sexual satisfaction and sexual frequency at one time point, and in a seven-day diary study, made predictions about how sexually satisfied they expected to feel the next day (McNulty & Fisher, 2008). Women with more positive sexual expectations were more sexually satisfied six months later. For men, in contrast, over a six-month period, changes in sexual frequency, rather than expectations, predicted changes in their sexual satisfaction: engaging in less frequent sex at the six-month follow-up compared with the beginning of the study was associated with lower sexual satisfaction. Because women's sexual experiences are more influenced by contextual factors such as acculturation, education, and religion (e.g., Peplau, 2003), women's expectations about a sexual relationship may more strongly influence their sexual satisfaction, whereas men's sexual satisfaction may be more strongly influenced by objective aspects such as sexual frequency.

Research also suggests that people's implicit beliefs about how sexual satisfaction and attraction are maintained over time in a relationship have implications for their sexual and relationship quality (Bohns, Scholer, & Rehman, 2015; Maxwell et al., 2017). A robust body of research demonstrates that people's implicit theories regarding whether particular behaviors are innate or take effort to cultivate can shape the ways people approach and ultimately engage in such behaviors (Dweck, 2008). In the domain of sexuality, Maxwell and colleagues (2017) distinguished between two types of beliefs about sexual satisfaction. Whereas *sexual growth* believers think that sexual satisfaction is maintained by work and effort, *sexual destiny* believers think that sexual satisfaction results from finding a highly compatible partner, their sexual "soulmate." The results of six studies showed that sexual growth believers were more responsive sexual partners and reported higher sexual and relationship satisfaction as a result. In contrast, sexual destiny believers used their sexual compatibility with their partner as a barometer for relationship quality, and as such, were more sensitive to sexual disagreements and experienced lower relationship satisfaction (Maxwell et al., 2017).

Sexual expectations may be especially important when people face entirely new experiences, such as when parents welcome their first baby into the family. New parents generally have positive expectations of their ability to navigate this transition (Belsky, 1985), which likely leads to expectations that their sex lives will "return to normal" soon after the baby is born. Unfortunately, given the prevalence and wide range of sexual concerns experienced by new parents (Schlagentweit et al., 2016), they are unlikely to have these expectations met. Unmet expectations may lead to feelings of disappointment and increased relationship conflict (Rusbult & Arriaga, 1997), with repercussions for the sexual and relationship satisfaction of both parents. However, people with a stronger set of cognitive and behavioral resources, such as those who make more adaptive attributions for changes to their sexual relationship, have better sexual communication, or are more responsive to a partner's needs, should be better equipped to cope when their expectations are not met, and experience fewer negative consequences as a result (Harwood, McLean, & Durkin, 2007). Indeed, when new mothers reported less stable and fewer partner attributions for postpartum sexual concerns, they were more sexually satisfied, and when they attributed less responsibility for sexual concerns to their partners, they were more satisfied with their overall relationship (Vannier, Adare, & Rosen, 2018). Further, Maxwell et al. (2017) found that holding stronger sexual growth beliefs and having a partner who is higher in sexual growth beliefs were both associated with greater sexual and relationship satisfaction during the transition to parenthood.

FUTURE DIRECTIONS FOR RESEARCH ON SEX
AND RELATIONSHIP MAINTENANCE

In recent years, sexuality research and relationship science have become more integrated (Impett & Muise, 2018; Muise, Maxwell, & Impett, 2018). As such, we have learned a great deal about how healthy and satisfying sexual relationships can strengthen relationships and boost well-being. Yet, since the integration of these fields is still relatively new, many unanswered questions remain. In this section, we highlight five promising directions for future research on sex and relationship maintenance, including (1) research on how people decline (or reject) their partners' sexual advances as well as respond to sexual rejection; (2) research on accuracy and bias in perceptions of a partner's sexual motives, feelings, and behaviors; (3) research using diverse methodological approaches, such as modeling trajectories (including nonlinear trajectories) of sexual outcomes over time in relationships; (4) research that moves beyond the use of self-report measures; and (5) additional research on sexuality during important relationship and life transitions.

One promising direction for future research on sex and relationship maintenance involves moving beyond the almost exclusive focus on understanding what happens when couples *do* have sex to understand what happens when couples *do not* have sex, including how people decline a partners' request for sex and deal with sexual rejection. Given that it is normative for desire to ebb and flow over time in relationships and partners cannot always be in sync with their sexual interests (Impett, Muise, et al., 2014), people will inevitably need to decline or reject their partner's sexual advances. Sexual rejection is common in romantic relationships: in a study of dating relationships, most people reported either declining their partner's sexual advances or having their advances declined at least once per week, and relationship satisfaction was lower when people had their sexual advances declined as opposed to accepted (Byers & Heinlein, 1989). There are likely some situations and life stages when rejection is more relevant to and frequent in relationships, such as the transition to parenthood. We currently know very little about the *ways* in which people reject their partner for sex, or if there are particular ways of doing so that protect couples against experiencing declines in relationship and sexual satisfaction. Findings from a recent study suggest that, in the context of long-term romantic relationships, there might be times when it is better for people to decline their partner's sexual advances in reassuring ways, such as by telling their partner they are still loved and desired, than to engage in sex reluctantly to avoid conflict or hurting a partner's feelings (Kim, Muise, & Impett, 2018). Much more research is needed, however, to determine which particular sexual rejection behaviors more effectively buffer couples against the sting of sexual rejection, both in the moment when couples experience rejection and when particular types of rejection are used more chronically over time.

The flip side to delivering sexual rejection is understanding how people respond to or cope with *being rejected*. Although it is sometimes important to be responsive to a partner's needs to engage in sex (Muise & Impett, 2016), at other times it is important to be understanding about a partner's need to *not* engage in sex. In a study of couples who had recently had their first child – a time when romantic partners experience many novel sexual concerns, including a dip in sexual desire (Schlagentweit et al., 2016) – showing understanding about a partner's need not to have sex was just as important for relationship and sexual satisfaction as being responsive to a partner's need to engage in sex. In particular, when new mothers and fathers were more motivated to be responsive to their partner's need not to engage in sex, they felt more satisfied with their sex lives and relationships (Muise, Rosen, et al., 2017). In addition, having a partner who was more understanding about the need not to have sex was associated with greater sexual and relationship satisfaction for new mothers. Understanding how both partners can be buffered against the negative consequences of a partner's lack of interest in sex and possible sexual rejection are crucial to our understanding of the role of sex in relationship maintenance.

A second area of inquiry that has the potential to lead to important insights about sexuality and relationship maintenance is accuracy and bias in perceptions of a partner's motives, feelings, and behaviors. We know from dyadic research on sexuality that partners influence each other's experiences and outcomes in relationships, but we know far less about how accurate or biased people are in their perceptions of their partner's intentions. For example, although research has shown that a person's sexual goals are associated with their partner's desire and satisfaction (Muise, Impett, & Desmarais, 2013), there is only a weak correlation between one person's sexual goals and the partner's perceptions of their sexual goals (Impett, Peplau, et al., 2005). In fact, recent work has demonstrated that although people are reasonably accurate at detecting daily changes in their partner's sexual desire, men on average tend to underestimate their partner's sexual desire (Muise, Stanton, Kim, & Impett, 2016). Although underestimating a partner's desire could mean that couples are missing out on opportunities for sex, this work has also shown that on days when men underperceive their partner's sexual desire, their partner feels more satisfied with the relationship. While we do not yet know why women feel more satisfied when their partners underperceive their desire, it may be because their partners work harder to entice their interest, although future research is needed to test this possibility. New modeling techniques – such as the Truth and Bias Model (West & Kenny, 2011) and response surface analyses (Barranti, Carlson, & Côté, 2017) – provide novel opportunities for researchers to test how accurate and biased people are in detecting their partner's sexual motives, feelings, and behaviors and the consequences of these perceptions for sexual and relationship outcomes.

A third direction for future research is the use of novel methodological approaches, including mapping, longitudinally, how sexual outcomes such as desire and satisfaction ebb and flow over time in relationships. With advanced statistical methods, including growth curve analyses, researchers have begun to examine trajectories of sexual and relationship satisfaction over time (e.g., Fallis et al., 2016; McNulty et al., 2015). Still, the majority of longitudinal research examining how sexuality-related factors shape the satisfaction and maintenance of relationships has focused on predicting relationship outcomes (e.g., three or six months later) rather than trajectories, and has included only two time points, precluding any examination of nonlinear patterns. Research on support in relationships more broadly suggests that a curvilinear association, whereby the benefits of responsive support toward a partner do not increase with increasing support but – at least for avoidantly attached people – are negative at low and extremely high levels of support but positive at moderate levels of support, demonstrates the importance of modeling nonlinear outcomes (Girme, Overall, Simpson, & Fletcher, 2015). In research on sexual frequency and well-being, Muise et al. (2016) found that the associations between sexual frequency and both relationship and life satisfaction were best represented by a curvilinear association, whereby the benefits of engaging in sex for well-being did not increase after a frequency of about once a week. Although many people in committed romantic relationships experience declines in sexual desire and satisfaction over time, this is not true for everyone, yet the possibility of nonlinear trends has been largely ignored in research to date. Given that sexual desire, preferences, and behaviors are known to ebb and flow in relationships and to be especially responsive to novel stressors or life transitions (e.g., Jawed-Wessel & Sevick, 2017), longitudinal studies focusing on trajectories will enhance our understanding of how sex can help maintain or interfere with the maintenance of relationships for different couples over time.

A fourth direction for future research is to move beyond the use of self-report measures. Given the challenges of studying sexuality in relationships using experimental methods, the vast majority of the research in this area is based on self-report measures. An important direction for future research is to combine self-reports with other approaches, such as behavioral observation and psychophysiological assessments. In one study in which couples had in-laboratory conversations about a sexual and a nonsexual conflict and researchers coded their communication behaviors, the results showed that *how* couples communicated about difficult issues – such as the amount of negative emotional expressions (i.e., defensiveness, contempt) and positive emotional expressions (i.e., responsiveness, caring) they displayed – was associated with marital satisfaction, and that discussions of sexual conflicts were particularly impactful for satisfaction (compared with nonsexual conflict discussions; Rehman et al., 2011). Further, among couples coping with pain during sex, when women demonstrated greater empathic responses during a discussion about how the pain impacted their lives, they and their partners reported higher sexual and relationship satisfaction (Bois et al., 2015; Rosen, Bois, Mayrand, Vannier, & Bergeron, 2016). Coding couple interactions, as well as assessing physiological responses (such as stress responses), could provide important insights into the factors that are associated with the successful navigation of sexual conflicts in relationships. Sexuality researchers have assessed physiological responses to sexual stimuli in terms of genital arousal, which has garnered important insights into gender differences in sexual responses and the correspondence between genital and self-reported arousal (see Chivers, Seto, Lalumiere, Laan, & Grimbos, 2010, for a review). However, this work is not often positioned in the context of romantic relationships, nor has it focused on how couples can more successfully navigate sexual challenges in their relationships.

A fifth direction for future research is the need for more work on changes to sexuality over important life and relationship transitions. Much of the research examining how sex contributes to relationship maintenance has focused on couples in dating or committed relationships, but who are still relatively young and healthy. Much can be learned about the role of sex in relationship maintenance when couples are faced with challenging life transitions or situations that can interfere with their relationship. In this chapter, we highlighted recent work on the transition to parenthood, a key period in which couples are known to experience many new sexual concerns (Schlagintweit et al., 2016), and which is typically accompanied by significant declines in sexual and relationship satisfaction (Maas, McDaniel, Feinberg, & Jones, 2018; Serati et al., 2010). We believe that the transition to parenthood is an ideal time to examine the role of sex in relationship maintenance, because there is a clearly identifiable "transition" – the birth of the child – that can trigger changes to the sexual relationship. The transition to parenthood is only one example of a life transition that presents novel sexual and relationship challenges. The transition to older adulthood is another period when many couples experience declines in their sexual functioning, commonly as a result of other physical health problems or life stressors (Laumann et al., 2006). Interestingly, older adults experience less sexual distress than younger individuals with similar sexual function problems, and many remain sexually active and satisfied well into late adulthood (Mitchell et al., 2013). Further, individuals who maintain their sexual connection into older adulthood not only report greater well-being but show lower mortality rates (see Diamond & Huebner, 2012, for a review). There is a lot to learn from how older adults navigate and maintain the quality of their sexual and intimate relationships, and these insights might be fruitfully applied to understand the role of sex in relationship maintenance in other samples.

CONCLUSION

Successfully navigating sexual challenges and maintaining sexual fulfillment have great potential to enhance the quality and stability of romantic relationships, and some of the lines of research described in this chapter have begun to shed light on how couples may best do this. We hope that our review of the growing literature on the role of sex in relationship maintenance highlights how much we have learned and sparks increased interest in a topic that is integral to strengthening the quality and longevity of romantic relationships.

REFERENCES

Acevedo, B. P., & Aron, A. (2009). Does a long-term relationship kill romantic love? *Review of General Psychology, 13*, 59–65.

Ahlborg, T., Rudeblad, K., Linnér, S., & Linton, S. (2008). Sensual and sexual marital contentment in parents of small children – A follow-up study when the first child is four years old. *Journal of Sex Research, 45*, 295–304.

Babin, E. (2012). An examination of predictors of nonverbal and verbal communication of pleasure during sex and sexual satisfaction. *Journal of Social and Personal Relationships, 30*, 270–292.

Barranti, M., Carlson, E., & Côté, S. (2017). How to test questions about similarity in personality and social psychology research: Description and empirical demonstration of response surface analysis. *Social Psychological and Personality Science, 8*(4). Retrieved from https://doi.org/10.1177/1948550617698204

Baumeister, R. F., & Bratslavsky, E. (1999). Passion, intimacy, and time: Passionate love as a function of change in intimacy. *Personality and Social Psychology Review, 3*, 49–67.

Belsky, J. (1985). Exploring individual differences in marital change across the transition to parenthood: The role of violated expectations. *Journal of Marriage and the Family, 47*, 1037–1044.

Berscheid, E., & Reis, H. T. (1998). Attraction and close relationships. In D. T. Gilbert, S. T. Fiske, & G. Lindzey (Eds.), *The handbook of social psychology*. New York, NY: McGraw-Hill.

Birnbaum, G. E., Reis, H. T., Mikulincer, M., Gillath, O., & Orpaz, A. (2006). When sex is more than just sex: Attachment orientations, sexual experience, and relationship quality. *Journal of Personality and Social Psychology, 91*, 929–943.

Blair, K. L., & Pukall, C. F. (2014). Can less be more? Comparing duration vs. frequency of sexual encounters in same-sex and mixed-sex relationships. *The Canadian Journal of Human Sexuality, 23*, 123–136.

Bohns, V. K., Scholer, A. A., & Rehman, U. (2015). Implicit theories of attraction. *Social Cognition, 33*, 284–307.

Bois, K., Bergeron, S., Rosen, N., Mayrand, M. H., Brassard, A., & Sadikaj, G. (2016). Intimacy, sexual satisfaction, and sexual distress in vulvodynia couples: An observational study. *Health Psychology, 35*, 531–540.

Bridges, S. K., & Horne, S. G. (2007). Sexual satisfaction and desire discrepancy in same sex women's relationships. *Journal of Sex & Marital Therapy, 33*, 41–53.

Brunell, A. B., & Webster, G. D. (2013). Self-determination and sexual experience in dating relationships. *Personality and Social Psychology Bulletin, 39*, 970–987.

Burke, T. J., & Young, V. J. (2012). Sexual transformations and intimate behaviors in romantic relationships. *Journal of Sex Research, 49*, 454–463.

Burri, A., Giuliano, F., McMahon, C., & Porst, H. (2014). Female partner's perception of premature ejaculation and its impact on relationship breakups, relationship quality, and sexual satisfaction. *The Journal of Sexual Medicine, 11*, 2243–2255.

Byers, E. S., & Demmons, S. (1999). Sexual satisfaction and sexual self-disclosure within dating relationships. *Journal of Sex Research, 36*, 180–189.

Byers, E. S., & Heinlein, L. (1989). Predicting initiations and refusals of sexual activities in married and cohabiting heterosexual couples. *Journal of Sex Research, 26*, 210–231.

Call, V., Sprecher, S., & Schwartz, P. (1995). The incidence and frequency of marital sex in a national sample. *Journal of Marriage and Family, 57*, 639–652.

Cassidy, J., & Shaver, P. R. (Eds.). (1999). *Handbook of attachment: Theory, research, and clinical applications.* New York: Guilford Press.

Cheung, M. W. L., Wong, P. W. C., Liu, K. Y., Yip, P. S. F., Fan, S. Y., & Lam, T. (2008). A study of sexual satisfaction and frequency among Hong Kong Chinese couples. *Journal of Sex Research, 45*, 129–139.

Chivers, M. L., Seto, M. C., Lalumiere, M. L., Laan, E., & Grimbos, T. (2010). Agreement of self-reported and genital measures of sexual arousal in men and women: A meta-analysis. *Archives of Sexual Behavior, 39*, 5–56.

Davies, S., Katz, J., & Jackson, J. L. (1999). Sexual desire discrepancies: Effects on sexual and relationship satisfaction in heterosexual dating couples. *Archives of Sexual Behavior, 28*, 553–567.

Davis, D., Shaver, P. R., Widaman, K. F., Vernon, M. L., Follette, W. C., & Beitz, K. (2006). "I can't get no satisfaction": Insecure attachment, inhibited sexual communication, and sexual dissatisfaction. *Personal Relationships, 13*, 465–483.

Day, L. C., Muise, A., Joel, S., & Impett, E. A. (2015). To do it or not to do it? How communally motivated people navigate sexual interdependence dilemmas. *Personality and Social Psychology Bulletin, 41*, 791–804.

Debrot, A., Meuwly, N., Muise, A., Impett, E. A., & Schoebi, D. (2017). More than just sex: Affection mediates the association between sexual activity and well-being. *Personality and Social Psychology Bulletin, 43*, 287–299.

Deci, E. L., & Ryan, R. M. (2000). The "what" and "why" of goal pursuits: Human needs and the self-determination of behavior. *Psychological Inquiry, 11*, 227–268.

de Jong, D. C., & Reis, H. T. (2015). We do it best: Commitment and positive construals of sex. *Journal of Social and Clinical Psychology, 34*, 181–202.

Diamond, L. M. (2004). Emerging perspectives on distinctions between romantic love and sexual desire. *Current Directions in Psychological Science, 13*, 116–119.

Diamond, L. M., & Huebner, D. M. (2012). Is good sex good for you? Rethinking sexuality and health. *Social and Personality Psychology Compass, 6*, 54–69.

Dweck, C. S. (2008). Can personality be changed? The role of beliefs in personality and change. *Current Directions in Psychological Science, 17*, 391–394.

Fallis, E. E., Rehman, U. S., Woody, E. Z., & Purdon, C. (2016). The longitudinal association of relationship satisfaction and sexual satisfaction in long-term relationships. *Journal of Family Psychology, 30*, 822–831.

Fisher, T. D., & McNulty, J. K. (2008). Neuroticism and marital satisfaction: The mediating role played by the sexual relationship. *Journal of Family Psychology, 22*, 112–122.

Fritz, H. L., & Helgeson, V. S. (1998). Distinctions of unmitigated communion from communion: Self-neglect and overinvolvement with others. *Journal of Personality and Social Psychology, 75*, 121–140.

Gable, S. L., & Impett, E. A. (2012). Approach and avoidance motives and close relationships. *Social and Personality Psychology Compass, 6*, 95–108.

Girme, Y. U., Overall, N. C., Simpson, J. A., & Fletcher, G. J. (2015). "All or nothing": Attachment avoidance and the curvilinear effects of partner support. *Journal of Personality and Social Psychology, 108*, 450–475.

Harwood, K., McLean, N., & Durkin, K. (2007). First-time mothers' expectations of parenthood: What happens when optimistic expectations are not matched by later experiences? *Developmental Psychology, 43*, 1–12.

Heiman, J. R., Long, S. J., Smith, S. N., Fisher, W. A., & Sand, M. S. (2010). Sexual satisfaction and relationship happiness in midlife and older couples in five countries. *Archives of Sexual Behavior, 40*, 741–753.

Hess, J. A., & Coffelt, T. A. (2012). Verbal communication about sex in marriage: Patterns of language use and its connection with relational outcomes. *Journal of Sex Research, 49*, 603–612.

Hinchliff, S., & Gott, M. (2008). Challenging social myths and stereotypes of women and aging: Heterosexual women talk about sex. *Journal of Women & Aging, 20*, 65–81.

Holt-Lunstad, J., Smith, T. B., & Layton, J. B. (2010). Social relationships and mortality risk: A meta-analytic review. *PLOS Medicine, 7*, e1000316.

Impett, E. A., Gable, S. L., & Peplau, L. A. (2005). Giving up and giving in: The costs and benefits of daily sacrifice in intimate relationships. *Journal of Personality and Social Psychology, 89*, 327–344.

Impett, E. A., Gere, J., Kogan, A., Gordon, A. M., & Keltner, D. (2014). How sacrifice impacts the giver and the recipient: Insights from approach-avoidance motivational theory. *Journal of Personality, 82*, 390–401.

Impett, E. A., & Muise, A. (2018). The sexing of relationship science: Impetus for the special issue. *Journal of Social and Personal Relationships, 35*, 433–439.

Impett, E. A., Muise, A., & Harasymchuk, C. (2019). Giving in the bedroom: The costs and benefits of responding to a partner's sexual needs in daily life. *Journal of Social and Personal Relationships, 36*, 2455–2473.

Impett, E. A., Muise, A., & Peragine, D. (2014). Sexuality in the context of relationships. In D. L. Tolman, L. M. Diamond, J. A. Bauermeister, W. H. George, J. G. Pfaus, & L. M. Ward (Eds.), *APA handbook of sexuality and psychology* (Vol. 1, pp. 269–315). Washington, DC: American Psychological Association.

Impett, E. A., Muise, A., & Rosen, N. O. (2015). Is it good to be giving in the bedroom? A prosocial perspective on sexual health and well-being in romantic relationships. *Current Sexual Health Reports, 7*, 180–190.

Impett, E. A., & Peplau, L. A. (2003). Sexual compliance: Gender, motivational, and relationship perspectives. *Journal of Sex Research, 40*, 87–100.

Impett, E. A., Peplau, L. A., & Gable, S. L. (2005). Approach and avoidance sexual motives: Implications for personal and interpersonal well-being. *Personal Relationships, 12*, 465–482.

Impett, E. A., Strachman, A., Finkel, E. J., & Gable, S. L. (2008). Maintaining sexual desire in intimate relationships: The importance of approach goals. *Journal of Personality and Social Psychology, 94*, 808–823.

Jawed-Wessel, S., & Sevick, E. (2017, February). The impact of pregnancy and child-birth on sexual behaviors: A systematic review. *The Journal of Sex Research, 54*(4–5), 411–423.

Jonason, P. K., Betteridge, G. L., & Kneebone, I. I. (2016). An examination of the nature of erotic talk. *Archives of Sexual Behavior, 45,* 21–31.

Karney, B. R., & Bradbury, T. N. (1997). Neuroticism, marital interaction, and the trajectory of marital satisfaction. *Journal of Personality and Social Psychology, 72,* 1075–1092.

Kim, J. J., Muise, A., & Impett, E. A. (2018). The relationship implications of rejecting a partner for sex kindly versus having sex reluctantly. *Journal of Social and Personal Relationships, 35,* 485–508.

Laumann, E. O., Paik, A., Glasser, D. B., Kang, J. H., Wang, T., Levinson, B., Moreira, E. D., Nicolosi, A., & Gingell, C. (2006). A cross-national study of subjective sexual well-being among older women and men: Findings from the Global Study of Sexual Attitudes and Behaviors. *Archives of Sexual Behavior, 35,* 143–159.

Lavner, J. A., & Bradbury, T. N. (2010). Patterns of change in marital satisfaction over the newlywed years. *Journal of Marriage and Family, 72,* 1171–1187.

Le, B. M., Impett, E. A., Lemay, E. P., Muise, A., & Tskhay, K. O. (2018). Communal motivation and subjective well-being in interpersonal relationships: An integrative review and meta-analysis. *Psychological Bulletin, 144,* 1–25.

Little, K. C., McNulty, J. K., & Russell, V. M. (2010). Sex buffers intimates against the negative implications of attachment insecurity. *Personality and Social Psychology Bulletin, 36,* 484–498.

Loewenstein, G., Krishnamurti, T., Kopsic, J., & McDonald, D. (2015). Does increased sexual frequency enhance happiness? *Journal of Economic Behavior & Organization, 116,* 206–218.

Maas, M. K., McDaniel, B. T., Feinberg, M. E., & Jones, D. E. (2018). Division of labor and multiple domains of sexual satisfaction among first-time parents. *Journal of Family Issues, 39,* 104–127.

MacNeil, S., & Byers, E. S. (2009). Role of sexual self-disclosure in the sexual satisfaction of long-term heterosexual couples. *Journal of Sex Research, 46,* 3–14.

Mark, K. P. (2012). The relative impact of individual sexual desire and couple desire discrepancy on satisfaction in heterosexual couples. *Sexual and Relationship Therapy, 27,* 133–146.

Maxwell, J. A., Muise, A., MacDonald, G., Day, L. C., Rosen, N. O., & Impett, E. A. (2017). How implicit theories of sexuality shape sexual and relationship well-being. *Journal of Personality and Social Psychology, 112,* 238–279.

McNulty, J. K., & Fisher, T. D. (2008). Gender differences in response to sexual expectancies and changes in sexual frequency: A short-term longitudinal study of sexual satisfaction in newly married couples. *Archives of Sexual Behavior, 37,* 229–240.

McNulty, J. K., O'Mara, E. M., & Karney, B. R. (2008). Benevolent cognitions as a strategy of relationship maintenance: "Don't sweat the small stuff" …. But it is not all small stuff. *Journal of Personality and Social Psychology, 94,* 631–646.

McNulty, J. K., Wenner, C. A., & Fisher, T. D. (2015). Longitudinal associations among marital satisfaction, sexual satisfaction, and frequency of sex in early marriage. *Archives of Sexual Behavior, 45,* 85–97.

Meltzer, A. L., Makhanova, A., Hicks, L. L., French, J. E., McNulty, J. K., & Bradbury, T. N. (2017). Quantifying the sexual afterglow: The lingering benefits of sex and their implications for pair-bonded relationships. *Psychological Science, 28,* 587–598.

Mitchell, K. R., Mercer, C. H., Ploubidis, G. B., Jones, K. G., Datta, J., Field, N., … Wellings, K. (2013). Sexual function in Britain: Findings from the Third National Survey of Sexual Attitudes and Lifestyles (Natsal-3). *Lancet, 382*, 1817–1829.

Muise, A., Bergeron, S., Impett, E. A., & Rosen, N. O. (2017). The costs and benefits of sexual communal motivation for couples coping with vulvodynia. *Health Psychology, 36*(8), 819–827.

Muise, A., Boudreau, G. K., & Rosen, N. O. (2017). Seeking connection versus avoiding disappointment: An experimental manipulation of approach and avoidance sexual goals and the implications for desire and satisfaction. *The Journal of Sex Research, 54*, 296–307.

Muise, A., Giang, E., & Impett, E. A. (2014). Post sex affectionate exchanges promote sexual and relationship satisfaction. *Archives of Sexual Behavior, 43*, 1391–1402.

Muise, A., & Impett, E. A. (2015). Good, giving, and game. The relationship benefits of communal sexual motivation. *Social Psychological and Personality Science, 6*, 164–172.

Muise, A., & Impett, E. A. (2016). Applying theories of communal motivation to sexuality. *Social and Personality Psychology Compass, 10*, 455–467.

Muise, A., Impett, E. A., & Desmarais, S. (2013). Getting it on versus getting it over with: Sexual motivation, desire, and satisfaction in intimate bonds. *Personality and Social Psychology Bulletin, 39*, 1320–1332.

Muise, A., Impett, E. A., Kogan, A., & Desmarais, S. (2013). Keeping the spark alive: Being motivated to meet a partner's sexual needs sustains sexual desire in long-term romantic relationships. *Social Psychological and Personality Science, 4*, 267–273.

Muise, A., Maxwell, J., & Impett, E. A. (2018). What theories and methods from relationship science can offer sex research. *Annual Review of Sex Research, 55*(4–5), 540–562.

Muise, A., Rosen, N. O., Kim, J. J., & Impett, E. A. (2017). Understanding when a partner is not in the mood: Sexual communal strength in couples transitioning to parenthood. *Archives of Sexual Behavior, 46*(7), 1993–2006.

Muise, A., Schimmack, U., & Impett, E. A. (2016). Sexual frequency predicts greater well-being, but more is not always better. *Social Psychological and Personality Science, 7*, 295–302.

Muise, A., Stanton, S. C. E., Kim, J. J., & Impett, E. A. (2016). Not in the mood? Men under (not over) perceive their romantic partner's sexual desire in established intimate relationships. *Journal of Personality and Social Psychology, 110*, 725–742.

Murray, S. L., Griffin, D. W., Derrick, J. L., Harris, B., Aloni, M., & Leder, S. (2011). Tempting fate or inviting happiness? Unrealistic idealization prevents the decline of marital satisfaction. *Psychological Science, 22*, 619–626.

Nagurney, A. J. (2007). The effects of relationship stress and unmitigated communion on physical and mental health outcomes. *Stress and Health, 23*, 267–273.

Olsson, A., Lundqvist, M., Faxelid, E., & Nissen, E. (2005). Women's thoughts about sexual life after childbirth: Focus group discussions with women after childbirth. *Scandinavian Journal of Caring Sciences, 19*, 381–387.

Peplau, L. A. (2003). Human sexuality: How do men and women differ? *Current Directions in Psychological Science, 12*, 37–40.

Pietromonaco, P. R., & Collins, N. C. (2017). Interpersonal mechanisms linking close relationships to health. *American Psychologist, 72*, 531–542.

Rahmani, A., Khoei, E. M., & Gholi, L. A. (2009). Sexual satisfaction and its relation to marital happiness in Iranians. *Iranian Journal of Public Health, 38*, 77–82.

Rancourt, K., Flynn, M., Bergeron, S., & Rosen, N. O. It takes two: Sexual communication patterns and the sexual and relational adjustment of couples coping with provoked vestibulodynia. *Journal of Sexual Medicine, 14*, 434–443.

Rehman, U. S., Janssen, E., Newhouse, S., Heiman, J., Holtzworth-Munroe, A., Fallis, E., & Rafaeli, E. (2011). Marital satisfaction and communication behaviors during sexual and nonsexual conflict discussions in newlywed couples: A pilot study. *Journal of Sex & Marital Therapy, 37,* 94–103.

Righetti, F., & Impett, E. A. (2017). Sacrifice in close relationships: Motives, emotions, and relationship outcomes. *Social and Personality Psychology Compass, 11,* e12342.

Risch, G. S., Riley, L. A., & Lawler, M. G. (2003). Problematic issues in the early years of marriage: Content for premarital education. *Journal of Psychology & Theology, 31,* 253–269.

Rosen, R. C. (2000). Prevalence and risk factors of sexual dysfunction in men and women. *Current Psychiatry Reports, 2,* 189–195.

Rosen, R. C., Heiman, J. R., Long, J. S., Fisher, W. A., & Sand, M. S. (2016). Men with sexual problems and their partners: Findings from the International Survey of Relationships. *Archives of Sexual Behavior, 45,* 159–173.

Rosen, N. O., Bailey, K., & Muise, A. (2018). Degree and direction of sexual desire discrepancy are linked to sexual and relationship satisfaction in couples transitioning to parenthood. *Journal of Sex Research, 55,* 214–225.

Rosen, N. O., Bois, K., Mayrand, M. H., Vannier, S., & Bergeron, S. (2016). Observed and perceived disclosure and empathy are associated with better relationship adjustment and quality of life in couples coping with vulvodynia. *Archives of Sexual Behavior, 45,* 1945–1956.

Rosen, N. O., Muise, A., Impett, E. A., Delisle, I., Baxter, M. L., & Bergeron, S. (2018). Sexual cues mediate the daily relations between interpersonal goals, pain, and well-being in couples coping with vulvodynia. *Annals of Behavioral Medicine, 52(3),* 216–227.

Ruppel, E. K., & Curran, M. A. (2012). Relational sacrifices in romantic relationship: Satisfaction and the moderating role of attachment. *Journal of Social and Personal Relationships, 29,* 508–529.

Rusbult, C. E., & Arriaga, X. B. (1997). Interdependence processes in close relationships. In S. Duck (Ed.), *Handbook of personal relationships* (2nd ed.) (pp. 221–250). Chichester: Wiley.

Russell, V. M., & McNulty, J. K. (2011). Frequent sex protects intimates from the negative implications of their neuroticism. *Social Psychological and Personality Science, 2,* 220–227.

Sanford, K. (2003). Problem-solving conversations in marriage: Does it matter what topics couples discuss? *Personal Relationships, 10,* 97–112. http://doi.org/10.1111/1475-6811.00038

Schlagintweit, H., Bailey, K. & Rosen, N. O. (2016). A new baby in the bedroom: Frequency and severity of postpartum sexual concerns and their associations with relationship satisfaction in new parent couples. *The Journal of Sexual Medicine, 13,* 1455–1465.

Schmiedeberg, C., Huyer-May, B., Castiglioni, L., & Johnson, M. D. (2017). The more or the better? How sex contributes to life satisfaction. *Archives of Sexual Behavior, 46,* 1–9.

Schmiedeberg, C., & Schröder, J. (2016). Does sexual satisfaction change with relationship duration? *Archives of Sexual Behavior, 45,* 99–107.

Serati, M., Salvatore, S., Siesto, G., Cattoni, E., Zanirato, M., Khullar, V., … Bolis, P. (2010). Female sexual function during pregnancy and after childbirth. *The Journal of Sexual Medicine, 7,* 2782–2790.

Shapiro, A. F., Gottman, J. M., & Carrere, S. (2000). The baby and the marriage: Identifying factors that buffer against decline in marital satisfaction after the first baby arrives. *Journal of Family Psychology, 14,* 59–70.

Shaver, P. R., & Mikulincer, M. (2005). Attachment theory and research: Resurrection of the psychodynamic approach to personality. *Journal of Research in Personality, 39*, 22–45.

Sims, K. E., & Meana, M. (2010). Why did passion wane? A qualitative study of married women's attributions for declines in sexual desire. *Journal of Sex & Marital Therapy, 36*, 360–380.

Smith, C. V. (2007). In pursuit of "good" sex: Self-determination and the sexual experience. *Journal of Social and Personal Relationships, 24*, 69–85.

Smith, K. B., & Pukall, C. F. (2011). A systematic review of relationship adjustment and sexual satisfaction among women with provoked vestibulodynia. *Journal of Sex Research, 48*, 166–191.

Sprecher, S. (1994). Two sides to the breakup of dating relationships. *Personal Relationships, 1*, 199–222.

Sprecher, S. (2002). Sexual satisfaction in premarital relationships: Associations with satisfaction, love, commitment, and stability. *Journal of Sex Research, 39*, 190–196.

Starks, T. J., & Parsons, J. T. (2014). Adult attachment among partnered gay men: Patterns and associations with sexual relationship quality. *Archives of Sexual Behavior, 43*, 107–117.

Taylor, P., Funk, C., & Clark, A. (2007). Generation gap in values, behaviours: As marriage and parenthood drift apart, public is concerned about social impact. Pew Research Center. Retrieved from www.pewresearch.org/wp-content/uploads/sites/3/2010/10/Marriage.pdf

Vannier, S. A., Adare, K. E., & Rosen, N. O. (2018). Is it me or you? First-time mothers' attributions for postpartum sexual concerns are associated with sexual and relationship satisfaction in the transition to parenthood. *Journal of Social and Personal Relationships, 35*, 577–599.

Vannier, S. A., Rosen, N. O., Mackinnon, S. P., & Bergeron, S. (2017). Maintaining affection despite pain: Daily associations between physical affection and sexual and relationship well-being in women with genito-pelvic pain. *Archives of Sexual Behavior, 46*, 2021–2031.

Waite, L. J., Laumann, E. O., Das, A., & Schumm, L. P. (2009). Sexuality: Measures of partnerships, practices, attitudes, and problems in the National Social Life, Health, and Aging Study. *The Journals of Gerontology Series B: Psychological Sciences and Social Sciences, 64B*, i56–i66.

West, T. V., & Kenny, D. A. (2011). The truth and bias model of judgment. *Psychological Review, 118*, 357–378.

Wood, J. Desmarais, S., Burleigh, T., & Milhausen, R.R. (2018). Reasons for sex and relational outcomes in consensually non-monogamous and monogamous relationships: A self-determination theory approach. *Journal of Social and Personal Relationships, 35*, 632–654.

Yabiku, S. T., & Gager, C. T. (2009). Sexual frequency and the stability of marital and cohabiting unions. *Journal of Marriage and Family, 71*, 983–1000.

13

Accuracy and Bias in Relationship Maintenance

EDWARD P. LEMAY, JR.[1] AND NADYA TENEVA[2]

Nearly all the topics covered in this volume have connections to the topic of interpersonal perception. People perceive their relationships as rewarding or costly (VanderDrift & Agnew, Chapter 2), detect environmental and social influences on relationships (Sprecher, Felmlee, Stokes, & McDaniel, Chapter 9; Young & Simpson, Chapter 3), and perceive their partner's relationship maintenance efforts (Stafford, Chapter 7), all of which may make them feel (in)secure in their partner's care and commitment (Lee, Karantzas, Gillath, & Fraley, Chapter 4) and (un)certain about the relationship (Theiss, Chapter 5). They perceive characteristics of their partners and relationships, which motivates many of the relationship maintenance processes and behaviors described in this book, such as incorporating partner characteristics into their own self-concepts (Xu, Lewandowski, & Aron, Chapter 6), forgiving and appreciating their partner (McNulty & Dugas, Chapter 8), having sex with their partner (Impett, Muise, & Rosen, Chapter 12), and enacting constructive conflict behaviors (Leo, Leifker, Baucom, & Baucom, Chapter 11). Hence, it seems clear that the way people perceive their partners and relationships is critical for understanding relationship maintenance. The current chapter emphasizes some of the social-cognitive processes that contribute to relationship perceptions and influence many of the relationship maintenance processes examined in these other chapters.

Several studies have revealed that relationship perceptions are partly veridical and partly biased. For example, Murray, Holmes, and Griffin (1996) demonstrated that people had perceptions of their romantic partner's interpersonal qualities that converged with their partner's self-perceptions. Such convergence is typically viewed as an indicator of accuracy. At the same time, perceptions of the partner's qualities appeared to be biased. Those who perceived themselves as possessing desirable qualities tended to believe that

[1] Department of Psychology, University of Maryland, College Park, elemay@umd.edu
[2] Department of Psychology, University of Maryland, College Park, nteneva@terpmail.umd.edu

their partners were desirable, too, suggesting a projection or assumed similarity bias in which people assume that their partners are similar to themselves (Kenny & Acitelli, 2001; Krueger, 2008). In addition, people's perceptions of their partner's qualities were predicted by their relationship ideals (i.e., the qualities that they hope to have in a romantic partner), suggesting an idealization bias. In other words, people tended to exaggerate the extent to which their partner was similar to their images of the ideal partner. Other investigations provide additional demonstrations that accuracy and bias can coexist across many domains of judgment (Gagne & Lydon, 2004; Kenny & Acitelli, 2001). A meta-analysis of accuracy and bias in romantic relationship perceptions across a variety of judgment domains found evidence for both accuracy and *mean-level bias,* a tendency to perceive partners more positively than would be suggested by benchmarks of the partner's true qualities (Fletcher & Kerr, 2010).

The current chapter reviews research on the effects of accuracy and bias on relationship maintenance. A key conclusion emerging from this literature is that people's perceptions of their relationships, including both accurate and biased perceptions, shape behaviors and motivations involved in relationship maintenance. Before embarking on this review, it is important to clarify what we mean by relationship maintenance. Some definitions of relationship maintenance emphasize behavioral processes. For example, relationship maintenance has been described as the behaviors that assist in maintaining desired relational characteristics (Stafford & Canary, 1991) and includes behaviors such as positivity (e.g., expressing positive regard), openness (e.g., self-disclosure), providing assurances (e.g., expressing love), sharing social networks (e.g., the existence of shared friends), sharing tasks (e.g., performing household chores), and conflict management (e.g., apologizing; Stafford, 2011; Stafford & Canary, 1991). These behavioral strategies seem to be important for relationship quality. For example, many of them are associated with greater relationship satisfaction (Ogolsky & Bowers, 2013). However, psychological variables are also important indicators that people are motivated to maintain their relationships. For instance, relationship commitment involves a strong motivation to maintain the relationship (Rusbult & Buunk, 1993), and love involves approach-oriented states, such as high desire (Gonzaga, Keltner, Londahl, & Smith, 2001). These motivational variables may be critical for relationship maintenance because they motivate people to enact the relationship maintenance behaviors described earlier and perhaps others that are not included in typologies of relationship maintenance behavior. Indeed, commitment and love are associated with many relationship maintenance behaviors (Ogolsky & Bowers, 2013; Rusbult, Verette, Whitney, Slovik, & Lipkus, 1991). Similarly, communal motivation (i.e., care for a partner's welfare) is a critical aspect of most close relationships and appears to promote a variety of prosocial behaviors (Mills, Clark, Ford, & Johnson, 2004). We also consider

relationship persistence as a rather crude indicator of relationship maintenance, given that it suggests some degree of motivation and ability to remain
in the relationship

ACCURACY AND BIAS IN PERCEPTIONS OF PARTNER'S BENEVOLENCE

This chapter focuses on research examining accuracy and bias with regard to
perceiving partners' benevolence toward the self and the implications of this
accuracy and bias for the enactment of relationship maintenance behaviors
and adoption of relationship-maintenance motivation. Perceptions of
a partner's benevolence refer to beliefs that a partner values one's welfare
and is motivated to promote that welfare. We focus on these perceptions
because of their central position in many theoretical perspectives on relationships. The perception of a partner's benevolence is central to trust (Holmes &
Rempel, 1989) and perceived partner responsiveness, which is the perception
that partners respond to the self in ways that communicate understanding,
validation, and care (Reis, Clark, & Holmes, 2004). Related constructs, such as
perceptions of the partner's regard for the self, perceptions of the partner's
commitment to the relationship, and perceptions of the partner's willingness
to provide support, also reflect one's confidence that a partner has benevolent
motivations toward the self now and in the future (Arriaga, Reed, Goodfriend,
& Agnew, 2006; Murray, Holmes, & Collins, 2006). These perceptions are
strong predictors of relationship satisfaction, relationship persistence, willingness to depend on partners, and motivation to enact maintenance behaviors (Arriaga et al., 2006; Gable, Gonzaga, & Strachman, 2006; Holmes &
Rempel, 1989; Murray et al., 2006; Reis et al., 2004; Wieselquist, Rusbult,
Foster, & Agnew, 1999). Hence, perceptions of the partner's benevolence
seem critical to maintaining high-quality relationships.

   Given the significance of these perceptions, it is important to understand
how they are formed. Extant research suggests a complex coexistence of
accuracy with a variety of biases. Two of the most frequently studied biases
involve a) perceiving the partner's benevolence as consistent with one's
preexisting beliefs or expectancies and b) perceiving the partner's benevolence as consistent with one's goals. In addition, some findings suggest that
accurate detection of a partner's benevolence is important for relationship
maintenance. These processes are depicted in Figure 13.1. This model assumes
that perceptions of a partner's benevolent motivations and behaviors are
determined by the partner's actual motivations and behaviors (accuracy) as
well as the perceiver's preexisting beliefs and goals (biases). In turn, these
perceptions of the partner's benevolent motivations and behaviors, both
accurate and biased, are thought to guide relationship maintenance motivation and behavior. The model paths are reviewed in turn in the following.

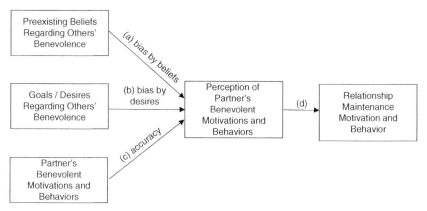

FIGURE 13.1 Guiding model of accuracy and bias in relationship maintenance.

PERCEPTIONS OF A SPECIFIC PARTNER'S BENEVOLENCE ARE BIASED BY PREEXISTING BELIEFS (PATH A IN FIGURE 13.1)

Confirmation bias is the ubiquitous tendency to process information in ways that support existing beliefs, expectations, or hypotheses (Nickerson, 1998). In other words, once a belief is formed, people seem to process new information in ways that produce conclusions that are consistent with that belief. Several lines of research suggest that this kind of bias can distort people's perceptions of their close relationship partners.

Research on attachment anxiety provides evidence for this sort of process. Attachment anxiety involves chronic fears of rejection and abandonment by close relationship partners (Brennan, Clark, & Shaver, 1998; Hazan & Shaver, 1987). In turn, when anxious individuals enter romantic relationships, these chronic doubts appear to contaminate their perceptions of their romantic partners. Relative to nonanxious individuals, anxious individuals report less trust in their romantic partner (Mikulincer, 1998) and believe that their partner's negative behaviors are due to their partner's lack of responsiveness and trustworthiness (Collins, 1996; Collins, Ford, Guichard, & Allard, 2006; Lemay & Spongberg, 2015). They perceive their romantic partner's behavior as less supportive and more upsetting, even when that behavior is experimentally or statistically controlled (Collins & Feeney, 2004). Lemay and Spongberg (2015) examined this bias with regard to everyday relationship experiences in a daily diary study. Participants who were high in attachment anxiety perceived their partners as less accepting, admiring, committed, and motivated to care for their needs on a daily basis, and this effect was independent of their partner's self-reported acceptance, admiration, commitment, and care. These findings suggest that anxiously attached individuals perceive their partner's benevolence as being consistent with their negative expectations (Path A in Figure 13.1). In turn, these negative biases have implications for relationship maintenance (Path D in Figure 13.1). For example, anxiously attached individuals report intentions to engage in antagonistic behaviors toward their partners (Collins, 1996; Collins et al., 2006) and are less satisfied with their relationships (Kimmes, Durtschi, Clifford, Knapp, & Fincham, 2015; Murray, Holmes, Griffin, Bellavia, & Rose, 2001; Sümer & Cozzarelli, 2004), and these effects are partly explained by negative interpretations of the partner's behavior. Doubts about being loved and appreciated by their partners also explain why anxiously attached individuals are less supportive of their partners (Jayamaha, Girme, & Overall, 2017). These findings suggest that chronic negative beliefs regarding others' benevolence toward oneself shape people's perceptions of their partners, with implications for relationship maintenance.

Similarly to attachment anxiety, rejection sensitivity involves expectations that one will be rejected by others (Downey & Feldman, 1996), and these negative expectations appear to contaminate perceptions of specific relationship partners (Path A in Figure 13.1). For example, rejection-sensitive individuals attribute hypothetical negative behaviors enacted by their romantic partner to their partner's intentions to be hurtful (Downey & Feldman, 1996). They also underestimate their romantic partner's satisfaction and commitment (Downey & Feldman, 1996). These negative biases seem to interfere with relationship maintenance. Rejection-sensitive individuals are perceived as jealous or hostile by their partners, which appears to undermine their partner's relationship satisfaction (Downey & Feldman, 1996; Downey, Freitas, Michaelis, & Khouri, 1998). Rejection sensitivity is also associated with an increased likelihood of relationship dissolution (Downey et al., 1998), suggesting that this negative bias reduces people's tendencies to engage in behaviors that maintain relationships.

Self-esteem is also associated with people's interpersonal expectations. People with low self-esteem have doubts about being accepted by others (Leary & Baumeister, 2000), which appear to infiltrate their relationship perceptions (Path A in Figure 13.1). Individuals with low self-esteem underestimate their romantic partner's regard and love for them (Murray, Holmes, & Griffin, 2000), and these doubts are exacerbated when they encounter acute threats to their self-esteem (e.g., poor intellectual performance) or to their relationship (e.g., a partner's bad mood; Bellavia & Murray, 2003; Murray, Holmes, MacDonald, & Ellsworth, 1998; Murray, Rose, Bellavia, Holmes, & Kusche, 2002). In turn, these pessimistic perceptions of being valued by their partner appear to interfere with relationship maintenance. For instance, individuals with low self-esteem respond to doubts about their partner's regard and love by derogating their partner, feeling hostile to their partner, and perceiving their relationships as less close or important (Bellavia & Murray, 2003; Murray et al., 1998; 2000; 2002).

Some theoretical perspectives may be interpreted as suggesting that individuals with low self-esteem benefit from receiving negative evaluations from their partners. For example, self-verification theory (Swann, 1983) posits that people rely on their self-views to predict and control their social environment, and so they should seek feedback from others that confirms their self-views and feel more satisfied in relationships when they receive confirmatory feedback. However, risk of rejection appears to constrain self-verification strivings. When risk of rejection is high, people abandon self-verification goals and prefer to be viewed in a positive manner, which is conducive to acceptance (Kwang & Swann, 2010). Individuals with low self-esteem tend to chronically perceive high risk of rejection (Leary & Baumeister, 2000), and so they may chronically prefer positive feedback from their partners relative to negative feedback that may be more self-confirmatory (Bernichon, Cook, & Brown, 2003). Furthermore, people prefer to be viewed positively in domains that are central to the functioning of relationships, even when they have negative self-views in those domains (Swann, Bosson, & Pelham, 2002). Given that global regard and acceptance are central to maintaining the partner's commitment, even people with negative self-views should typically desire to be viewed positively in a global sense.

These research programs suggest that negative beliefs regarding others' motivations toward oneself, reflected in attachment anxiety, rejection sensitivity, and low self-esteem, often bias people's perceptions within specific romantic relationships. However, it is important to keep in mind that attachment anxiety, rejection sensitivity, and low self-esteem are not direct and "pure" measures of negative beliefs regarding other people's benevolence. Rejection sensitivity involves not just the anticipation of rejection but also a tendency to think that interpersonal acceptance is important. The measure of rejection sensitivity used in most research on this construct combines negative expectations with high concern about acceptance (Downey & Feldman, 1996). Similarly, attachment anxiety involves not just expectations of rejection and abandonment but also a high desire for closeness (Brennan et al., 1998). Lastly, self-esteem is a global evaluation of the self, rather than a belief regarding how others feel about the self. Indeed, self-esteem is predicted by factors that are largely unrelated to others' benevolence toward the self, such as dominance and efficacious action (Blackhart, Nelson, Knowles, & Baumeister, 2009; Franks & Marolla, 1976; Leary, Cottrell, & Phillips, 2001). Hence, these constructs are not ideal operationalizations of chronic beliefs or expectations regarding others' benevolence toward the self.

These considerations suggest the importance of directly and exclusively measuring generalized perceptions of others' benevolence. Lemay and Spongberg (2015) developed a multiple-item measure of perceived interpersonal value, which assesses global perceptions of being valued by others (e.g., "People value their relationships with me"; "Most of the time, other people seem to like and accept me"). In an extended replication of prior attachment research

(Collins, 1996; Collins et al., 2006), they found that those with low perceived interpersonal value made relationship-threatening interpretations of hypothetical negative behaviors enacted by their partner, such as attributing the behavior to the partner's rejection or waning commitment. They also reported intentions to respond to this behavior in hostile and punishing ways. Subsequent studies (Lemay & Spongberg, 2015) demonstrated similar patterns with regard to actual relationship events, demonstrating that people with low perceived interpersonal value had unfounded doubts about their partner's care and commitment and perceived their partners to enact less responsive and more negative behavior. Perceived interpersonal value predicted these outcomes more strongly than attachment anxiety or self-esteem and explained most of the effects of anxiety and self-esteem. These results underscore the importance of isolating the "active ingredient" in these constructs (i.e., global perceptions of being valued by others) that shape interpersonal perception and behavior.

Rather than examining individual differences, other studies have emphasized the biasing effects of preexisting beliefs regarding a particular partner's benevolence when encountering novel situations with that partner. For example, Murray and colleagues (Murray, Bellavia, Rose, & Griffin, 2003) found that participants who had chronic doubts about their spouse's positive regard at the outset of the study perceived more rejection and less acceptance, and felt more anxious about acceptance, during daily interactions with their spouse, and this effect was exacerbated following relationship threats (i.e., conflict, their spouse's negative behavior, or their spouse's negative mood). In turn, these negative perceptions were associated with more negative reactions to their spouse the following day, such as negative behavior, anger, and reduced closeness. Suggesting a similar effect, Shallcross and Simpson (2012) found that participants who reported a high level of trust in their romantic partners at the outset of the study tended to exaggerate their partner's helpfulness and cooperation during a laboratory discussion of relationship sacrifices (relative to objective observers' ratings of the partner's behavior). In turn, highly trusting participants were more accommodating in response to their partner's requests. Both studies suggest that perceptions of a partner's benevolence in specific situations are biased by preexisting beliefs regarding that partner, and that this bias has implications for the enactment of relationship-maintenance behaviors.

PERCEPTIONS OF A SPECIFIC PARTNER'S BENEVOLENCE ARE BIASED BY PERCEIVERS' GOALS AND DESIRES (PATH B IN FIGURE 13.1)

Research on motivated cognition suggests that goals tend to bias cognitive functioning in ways that produce desired conclusions (Kunda, 1990). In other words, people seem to engage in "wishful thinking" and reach conclusions that are more consistent with their desires than what an objective assessment of the evidence would suggest. This bias appears to operate on people's perceptions of their romantic relationships (Murray, 1999; Rusbult, Lange, Wildschut, Yovetich, & Verette, 2000). For example, Murray and colleagues (Murray et al., 1996) demonstrated that people tend to see their partners' traits as being more consistent with what they ideally wanted for their romantic relationships, and that these positive illusions predicted greater relationship satisfaction. Furthermore, in a meta-analysis of predictors of relationship persistence, positive illusions emerged as one of the strongest predictors of persistence (Le, Dove, Agnew, Korn, & Mutso, 2010).

More relevant to the current chapter, desires appear to bias perceptions of partners' benevolence (Path B in Figure 13.1). For example, people who strongly desire to develop or maintain a close, caring bond with a romantic partner appear motivated to see the partner as being caring and supportive toward them. In two dyadic studies of romantic relationships, participants' own motivation to care for their partner's welfare or provide support to their partner predicted perceptions of the partner's reciprocation of care or supportiveness (Lemay, Clark, & Feeney, 2007). This "projection" effect was observed even after controlling for the partner's self-reports of their care or supportiveness, suggesting that people's motivations biased their perceptions. Priem, Solomon, and Steuber (2009) found evidence for a similar projection process with regard to perceptions of spouses' emotional support. That is, those who provided emotional support to their spouse also tended to believe that they were supported by their spouse. Furthermore, this projection effect has been extended to other relationship types, including friendships (Lemay & Clark, 2008) and roommates (Canevello & Crocker, 2010). Similarly, Campbell and colleagues (Campbell, Overall, Rubin, & Lackenbauer, 2013) found evidence that people who view their partner as ideal (i.e., their partner meets their ideal standards) tend to assume that their partner views them as ideal in return. In other words, those who are most satisfied with their partners, in terms of perceiving that partners live up to their ideals, tend to believe that their partners are similarly satisfied with them.

Daily diary studies demonstrate similar patterns. Lemay et al. (2007) found that participants who provided a large number of benefits to their spouses on a particular day reported receiving a large number of benefits in return on that day, independently of their spouses' reports of providing benefits. Likewise, participants who reported a high degree of care for their partner's welfare as the motivation for providing benefits to their spouse tended to assume that their spouse had a similar motivation toward them, independently of their spouse's self-reported motivation. By including the partner's reports of the benefits they provided and their motivation for providing those benefits as covariates, these analyses controlled for accuracy and suggest that participants projected their own benevolence onto their partners. Projection of daily care and support have been replicated in two other investigations (Bar-Kalifa, Rafaeli, & Sened, 2016; Debrot, Cook, Perrez, & Horn, 2012). These results suggest that day-to-day vacillation in participants' own motivations to be benevolent toward their partners is associated with corresponding vacillation in perceptions of the partner's benevolence. These findings are particularly important in light of the strong links between perceptions of partners' relationship maintenance behaviors and important relationship outcomes, such as commitment to the relationship (Ogolsky & Bowers, 2013). These perceptions of partners' relationship maintenance behaviors may often be biased by perceivers' motivations.

A limitation of using the partner's self-reports to index the partner's true thoughts and feelings in studies of accuracy and bias is that these self-reports may be contaminated by response tendencies, impression-management concerns, or lack of self-knowledge (Podsakoff, MacKenzie, Lee, & Podsakoff, 2003). To address these issues, some studies controlled for other indicators of the partner's actual care and supportiveness. For example, evidence suggesting projection bias has been found after controlling for not just the partner's self-reported care for the perceiver but also an external informant's (friend's or acquaintance's) perceptions of the partner's care for the perceiver (Lemay & Clark, 2008). Priem and colleagues (2009) found evidence for projection of emotional supportiveness during a recorded laboratory discussion about stressors while controlling for four objective observers' assessments of the target spouse's supportive behavior during that interaction. Using a similar approach, Lemay and Neal (2014) also found evidence for biased perceptions of a partner's support during a laboratory conversation while controlling for objective observers' perceptions. Menzies-Toman and Lydon (2005) used objective ratings to demonstrate that relationship commitment biases perceptions of a partner's relationship transgressions. Committed participants saw their partner's transgressions as less severe relative to the judgments made by objective observers who read descriptions of those transgressions. Hence, people who most want to cultivate close relationships (e.g., those who are most caring, supportive, or committed toward a partner) tend to view their partner's behavior as more benevolent, and this effect is independent of more objective indicators of the partner's behavior.

Projection effects may be strong because they are inflated by shared method variance (Podsakoff et al., 2003). For example, a study examining projection of care may operationalize projection as an association between self-reported care for a partner and self-reported perception of the partner's care, usually using highly similar measures to assess the two constructs. Similarity in participants' interpretation of items across the two measures, as well as similarity in response style, could artificially inflate this association. For example, someone with a very liberal definition of "care" might be more likely to agree to items such as "I care for my partner" and "My partner cares for me" relative to someone with a stricter definition of "care," magnifying the association between reports of own motivation to care for the partner and the partner's motivation to care for the self. To address this issue, Lemay and Clark (2008) examined the projection of care while controlling for participants' care toward a third person. Reports of care toward a third person should be equally contaminated by shared method variance, and so including this as a statistical control should partial out shared method variance from the projection effect. After making this statistical adjustment, they continued to find a robust projection effect, suggesting that shared method variance cannot account for the effect.

Experimental manipulations provide another way to address shared method variance. They can also provide a strong control for accuracy. For example, exposing participants to a randomly assigned manipulation that elevates their care for a relationship partner may reveal effects on perceptions of the partner's reciprocated care, consistent with projection. Such a study reduces concerns over shared method variance, given that the projection effect is operationalized as an effect of the manipulation rather than an association between two variables measured in a similar way. It also provides strong controls for accuracy, given that it is unlikely that participants randomly assigned to one condition had partners who were truly more or less caring relative to participants randomly assigned to the other condition. Of course, experimental studies are also useful for demonstrating causal effects.

Several studies have found evidence for biased perceptions while using an experimental approach. In one study (Lemay et al., 2007), participants were assigned to experience ease or difficulty while recalling instances in which they provided help to their partner. This was accomplished by asking participants to recall two instances in which they provided help to their partner, which should be easy to do, or eight instances of providing help, which should be more difficult. Experiencing and reflecting on ease during recall of their own helpful acts should encourage participants to perceive themselves as caring for their partner (see Schwarz et al., 1991), which should bolster their motivation to have partners reciprocate support. In contrast, those who experience and reflect on difficulty during recall of their own helpful acts should think they are less caring, which may reduce motivation for the partner to reciprocate support. This process occurs because, consistent with the availability heuristic, judgments are biased by the ease with which instances come to mind (Schwarz et al., 1991; Tversky & Kahneman, 1973). That is, if it is easy to think of examples supporting a particular conclusion, people tend to assume that the conclusion must be true. Hence, those who experience ease while recalling their own helpful behavior should feel more caring than those who experience difficulty. In turn, according to the projection hypothesis, these individuals should also perceive their partner as helpful and caring in return. Results supported this prediction; those who recalled two instances of providing help perceived their partner as more caring relative to those who recalled eight instances of providing help. Other studies manipulated participants' experience of caring for their partners by asking them to vividly recall prior events involving their own unresponsive behavior (Lemay & Clark, 2008) or asking them to behave in a warm or neutral manner (Lemay & Clark, 2008). These manipulations had downstream effects on perceptions of the partner's responsiveness. Those who recalled their own unresponsive behavior perceived their partner as less responsive to them relative to participants in a control condition, despite the fact that, given random assignment to conditions, actual partner responsiveness was likely equivalent across conditions (Lemay & Clark, 2008). Likewise, those instructed to engage in warm behavior toward a new interaction partner saw that partner as more responsive relative to those instructed to engage in neutral behavior, even after statistically controlling for the partner's self-reported responsiveness.

These findings suggest that people's motivations toward their partners bias their perceptions of partners' benevolence. Several cognitive processes may conspire to create this belief. Lemay and Neal (2013) provided evidence for the role of biased memories. In a daily report study, participants were asked to report on their partner's care, regard, and commitment at the end of every day for a week. On each day, they also reported their memories of their partner's care, regard, and commitment that had occurred yesterday. Those who were motivated to maintain a close relationship with their partner (i.e., they had high levels of care and commitment toward their partner) had more positive memories of their partner's care, regard, and commitment. A subsequent study demonstrated biased memory of support interactions involving romantic partners (Lemay & Neal, 2013). Participants who were strongly motivated to maintain a relationship with their partner had more positive memories of their partner's supportive behavior during laboratory interactions two weeks and six months following the interaction. These effects were independent of initial perceptions of the partner's behavior, suggesting that the biased memory process was distinct from biases that operate on more immediate perceptions, consistent with distinctions between encoding and retrieval in memory research.

People may also interpret situations in ways that maintain the perception that their partner cares for them. Lemay and Melville (2014) examined this possibility with regard to perceptions of self-disclosure. Disclosure of one's needs and desires to a partner provides an opportunity for the partner to respond supportively, and, therefore, people should view situations involving their own disclosure as diagnostic of the partner's motives. Lemay and Melville (2014) tested the prediction that people who are motivated to maintain a bond with their partner downplay their own self-disclosure (i.e., believe they disclosed less than they actually did) if their partner behaved in an unresponsive manner, such as being hostile, selfish, or neglectful, because doing so allows them to attribute the partner's negative behavior to their own lack of disclosure of needs and desires rather than their partner's lack of care. In other words, downplaying the extent of one's self-disclosure may effectively reduce concern that the hurtful behavior is diagnostic of the partner's true sentiments. Consistent with this prediction, people who strongly valued their relationship with a partner reported especially low levels of disclosure of needs and desires in situations characterized by the partner's unresponsive behavior. A behavioral observation study suggested that these low perceptions of self-disclosure following their partner's unresponsive behavior were underestimations of actual self-disclosure. In turn, perceiving lack of self-disclosure in situations characterized by the partner's lack of responsiveness was associated with greater trust.

Experimental studies also provided support for this model (Lemay & Melville, 2014). For example, the tendency to downplay self-disclosure was reduced when participants were provided with another method to justify their partner's unresponsive behavior. This pattern suggests that downplaying self-disclosure is a motivated process; a hallmark of motivated processes is that they discontinue once the goals driving them are satisfied (Bargh, Gollwitzer, Lee-Chai, Barndollar, & Trötschel, 2001). All of these findings suggest that motivated perceivers may diffuse the negative impact of a partner's unresponsive behavior by convincing themselves that they did not adequately communicate their needs, which may protect trust that the partner cares for those needs.

Several studies have demonstrated that these biases have implications for relationship maintenance (Path D in Figure 13.1). People who care for their partner feel more satisfied in their relationship, maintain their care over time, engage in self-disclosure, have more positive evaluations of their partner, and express more warmth partly because they assume that their partner reciprocates their care (Lemay & Clark, 2008; Lemay et al., 2007). People who report being responsive to their partners on a particular day reported feeling more intimacy, in part because they assumed that their partner was responsive in return (Debrot et al., 2012). People who have positively biased memories of their partner's responsiveness exhibit less emotional reactivity and feel more trust (Lemay & Neal, 2013). People who downplay their own self-disclosure when their partner is unresponsive feel less upset and continue to evaluate their relationship positively in spite of that unresponsive behavior (Lemay & Melville, 2014). Biased perceptions of responsiveness in observed support interactions predicted perceivers' relationship satisfaction just after the interaction, two weeks later, and six months later (Lemay & Neal, 2014). Similar findings have been found in other types of relationships. For example, people who care for their roommate's welfare tend to maintain that care over time partly because they assume that their roommate is responsive to them (Canevello & Crocker, 2010). These findings suggest that interpersonal goals or desires distort perceptions of partners' benevolence, and this process has important consequences for relationship maintenance.

ACCURATE DETECTION OF PARTNER BENEVOLENCE
(PATH C IN FIGURE 13.1)

Although it seems intuitive that relationship quality should depend on having accurate perception, effects of accuracy on relationship quality are modest at best. Some findings do suggest benefits of accuracy. For example, Neff and Karney (2005) demonstrated that wives' accurate perceptions of their husbands on specific attributes (e.g., intellectual ability, physical attractiveness, and personality traits) were associated with more positive support provision, more feelings of control, and less likelihood of divorce. In this research, accuracy was operationalized as the association between wives' perceptions of husbands and husbands' self-reports. Luo and Snider (2009) found similar effects of accuracy on marital satisfaction. Swann and colleagues (Swann, De La Ronde, & Hixon, 1994) found that accurate perceptions of the partner in specific domains (e.g., intellectual capability, physical attractiveness, and athletic ability) were positively associated with the partner's feelings of intimacy in marital relationships, but not in dating relationships. However, other findings suggest that accuracy is not a robust predictor. In a study examining accuracy in perceiving a partner's love, trust, and commitment, men's relationship satisfaction was associated with their greater accuracy in perceiving their partner's feelings of love, but not with their accuracy in perceiving their partner's commitment or trust (Tucker & Anders, 1999). Surprisingly, for women, no positive effects of accuracy emerged, and accuracy in perceiving their partner's trust was associated with women's reduced satisfaction. That is, women were more satisfied when they were less accurate about their partner's trust. Furthermore, a meta-analysis revealed a small and nonsignificant association between relationship quality and tracking accuracy, which is the association between perceptions and some reality benchmark (Fletcher & Kerr, 2010).

It is important to consider why accuracy does not have a more robust effect on relationship outcomes. One issue may be that indices of accuracy used in most research involve accurate detection of both relationship-enhancing and relationship-threatening qualities of a partner or relationship. Although accuracy may often enhance relationship quality by helping people select relationship maintenance behaviors tailored to the reality at hand (McNulty, O'Mara, & Karney, 2008; Reis, Lemay, & Finkenauer, 2017), accurate detection of negative qualities often involves detection of relationship costs or threats that detract from satisfaction (Rusbult & Buunk, 1993). Perhaps these two effects compete with each other in terms of predicting relationship outcomes. Studies using signal-detection techniques to disentangle accurate detection of positive qualities from accurate detection of negative qualities support this reasoning. Accurately detecting that a partner engaged in compassionate or caring acts (a "hit") was associated with greater satisfaction relative to accurately detecting that a partner did not engage in such acts (a "correct rejection"). Furthermore, those who accurately detected that partners did not enact compassionate behaviors were less satisfied with the relationship than those who had inaccurately believed that their partners did enact these behaviors (a "false alarm"), despite, and perhaps because of, their greater accuracy.

A related issue is that, after accurately detecting a threatening relationship problem, partners may not know how to solve it. In such cases, accuracy may bring awareness of relationship threats that do not have clear solutions, which may be a rather negative experience. For instance, what does one do to improve a relationship after accurately detecting that a partner does not care for one's welfare? When problems cannot easily be corrected, accuracy may hurt more than it helps. This prediction is central to Ickes and Simpson's (2003) empathic accuracy model. Empirical tests of this model with married couples suggest that accurately detecting a partner's relationship-threatening thoughts and feelings was associated with declines in the perceiver's feelings of closeness, whereas accurate detection of nonthreatening thoughts and feelings was associated with greater closeness (Simpson, Orina, & Ickes, 2003).

Accuracy need not be conceptualized as a predictor variable in order to be important for relationship maintenance. Indeed, when conceptualized as a pathway linking reality to perceptions (Path C in Figure 13.1), rather than a predictor variable, accuracy seems to be quite important for relationship maintenance. For example, Lemay et al. (2007) found that people were more satisfied with their romantic relationships when they had caring or supportive partners, and this effect was largely explained by accurate detection of that care or support. A similar process occurs at the daily level. People appear to feel more intimate with their partners (Debrot et al., 2012) and experience more positive affect (Reis, Maniaci, & Rogge, 2017) on days when their partners enact more prosocial behaviors, but only to the extent that this behavior is detected. Canevello and Crocker (2010) similarly demonstrated that people detect their roommate's responsive behavior, which predicts the maintenance of care over time. These results suggest that accurate detection of a partner's benevolent motivations can be beneficial for relationship quality. These results are consistent with some meta-analytic findings suggesting that perceiving partners' enactment of relationship maintenance behavior is a more proximal predictor of relationship outcomes, such as commitment, relative to partners' self-reported enactment of that behavior (Ogolsky & Bowers, 2013). When predicting relationship quality, perceptions of partners' behavior often appear to be critical mediators of many relationship maintenance behaviors enacted by partners.

SUGGESTIONS FOR FUTURE RESEARCH

The current chapter emphasized perceptions that primarily reflect warmth, one of the fundamental dimensions of person perception, with competence being the other (Cuddy, Fiske, & Glick, 2008). Some preliminary findings suggest that competence-related perceptions and biases are also important. For example, Barelds and Dijkstra (2011) found that people who perceived themselves as highly conscientious, emotionally stable, and intelligent tended to have overly positive perceptions of their romantic partners on these traits, relative to their partner's self-views, and these perceptions were associated with relationship quality. In other words, people appeared to project their competence-related traits onto their partners. More research is needed to understand the impact of accurate and biased perceptions of partners' competence on relationship maintenance, and whether those effects are distinct from, or interact with, the warmth-related perceptions reviewed in the current chapter.

Most research on interpersonal perception examines perceptions of the present. However, perceptions of the future may be particularly important, because they guide people's relationship decisions (Lemay & Venaglia, 2016). For example, independently of other key predictors of relationship commitment, expectations of future satisfaction strongly predict relationship commitment and the enactment of pro-relationship behaviors (Lemay, 2016). Similarly, Baker and colleagues (Baker, McNulty, & VanderDrift, 2017) demonstrated strong effects of expected future satisfaction on relationship commitment. Also suggesting the importance of relationship forecasts, Murray and Holmes (1997) found that optimism about the future of the relationship was associated with a variety of positive sentiments and behaviors (e.g., trust, love, less conflict, and less destructiveness). Related research on relational uncertainty suggests that uncertainty about the self, partner, and relationship can shape emotional experience and maintenance strategies in relationships (Solomon, Knobloch, Theiss, & McLaren, 2016; Theiss, Chapter 5). Some research suggests that perceptions of the future are biased by existing goals and beliefs (Gagne & Lydon, 2001; Lemay, Lin, & Muir, 2015). However, more research is needed to understand the factors that shape expectations of relationship futures, and the mechanisms through which these expectations impact relationship maintenance.

The biases reviewed in this chapter may be somewhat controllable, and more research is needed on how people monitor and modify them to best serve their interests. For example, Ayduk and colleagues (Ayduk et al., 2000) have found that high self-control (i.e., delay of gratification) attenuated the link between rejection sensitivity and interpersonal problems, suggesting that self-control can confer an ability to resist some of the biases reviewed in this chapter.

Biases may be controlled through a variety of specific strategies. Insecure individuals can feel secure in their romantic relationships if they try to view their partner's compliments as meaningful and significant (Marigold, Holmes, & Ross, 2007). In addition, they can insulate themselves from relationship threats by affirming themselves in other domains (Jaremka, Bunyan, Collins, & Sherman, 2011) or by distracting themselves from threatening information (Ayduk, Mischel, & Downey, 2002). Projection biases may be controlled by reminding oneself that other people are different (to decrease projection) or that other people are similar (to increase projection) (Gollwitzer, Schwörer, Stern, Gollwitzer, & Bargh, 2017). Relationship partners may also help insecure individuals dispel their negative biases by enacting behaviors that communicate a high level of positive regard and care (Lemay & Dudley, 2011).

More attention is also needed to the interplay between interpersonal expectations and desires. Prior research examining this issue has suggested a few opposing patterns. One study found that highly rejection-sensitive men were more likely to commit dating violence when they were highly invested in romantic relationships, but more likely to withdraw from relationships when their investment was low (Downey, Feldman, & Ayduk, 2000). Such a pattern could suggest that the expectancies for rejection are particularly painful when people have a stronger desire to affiliate. However, other findings indicate that individuals with low self-esteem become more motivated to maintain closeness when interpersonal relationships are highly important to self-definition, suggesting that desire to affiliate can compensate for negative expectancies when predicting relationship maintenance behaviors (Baker & McNulty, 2013). Strong motivation to be valued by others could create more negative emotions, and therefore stronger behavioral reactions, when people feel devalued, but could also create a motivation to regulate emotion and engage in relationship-maintenance behaviors despite feeling devalued.

CONCLUSION

The current chapter suggests that there is strong evidence for two important biases that shape people's perceptions of their partner's motivations and behaviors toward the self. First, people seem to use their current beliefs about themselves, people in general, and their specific partner to make inferences regarding their partner's current motivations and behaviors toward them. Second, people seem to perceive their partner's motivations and behaviors in a manner that is consistent with their goals and desires, such as the desire to have caring, stable, and mutually supportive relationships. These biases appear important for relationship maintenance, shaping important outcomes such as evaluation of the partner and relationship, care for the partner over time, self-disclosure, support provision, and relationship persistence. In addition, the current chapter suggests that accuracy can serve as an important mechanism that shapes interpersonal perceptions and, in turn, relationship maintenance. Overall, this chapter suggests that perceptions of being loved and cared for by partners, both accurate and biased, have a critical influence on how and whether relationships are maintained.

REFERENCES

Arriaga, X. B., Reed, J. T., Goodfriend, W., & Agnew, C. R. (2006). Relationship perceptions and persistence: Do fluctuations in perceived partner commitment undermine dating relationships? *Journal of Personality and Social Psychology*, *91*(6), 1045–1065.

Ayduk, O., Mendoza-Denton, R., Mischel, W., Downey, G., Peake, P. K., & Rodriguez, M. (2000). Regulating the interpersonal self: Strategic self-regulation for coping with rejection sensitivity. *Journal of Personality and Social Psychology*, *79*(5), 776–792.

Ayduk, O., Mischel, W., & Downey, G. (2002). Attentional mechanisms linking rejection to hostile reactivity: The role of "hot" versus "cool" focus. *Psychological Science*, *13*(5), 443–448.

Baker, L. R., & McNulty, J. K. (2013). When low self-esteem encourages behaviors that risk rejection to increase interdependence: The role of relational self-construal. *Journal of Personality and Social Psychology*, *104*(6), 995–1018.

Baker, L. R., McNulty, J. K., & VanderDrift, L. E. (2017). Expectations for future relationship satisfaction: Unique sources and critical implications for commitment. *Journal of Experimental Psychology, General*, *146*(5), 700–721.

Barelds, D. P., & Dijkstra, P. (2011). Positive illusions about a partner's personality and relationship quality. *Journal of Research in Personality*, *45*(1), 37–43.

Bargh, J. A., Gollwitzer, P. M., Lee-Chai, A., Barndollar, K., & Trötschel, R. (2001). The automated will: Nonconscious activation and pursuit of behavioral goals. *Journal of Personality and Social Psychology*, *81*(6), 1014–1027. doi:10.1037/0022-3514.81.6.1014

Bar-Kalifa, E., Rafaeli, E., & Sened, H. (2016). Truth and bias in daily judgments of support receipt between romantic partners. *Personal Relationships*, *23*(1), 42–61.

Bellavia, G., & Murray, S. (2003). Did I do that? Self esteem-related differences in reactions to romantic partner's mood. *Personal Relationships*, *10*(1), 77–95.

Bernichon, T., Cook, K. E., & Brown, J. D. (2003). Seeking self-evaluative feedback: The interactive role of global self-esteem and specific self-views. *Journal of Personality and Social Psychology*, *84*(1), 194–204.

Blackhart, G. C., Nelson, B. C., Knowles, M. L., & Baumeister, R. F. (2009). Rejection elicits emotional reactions but neither causes immediate distress nor lowers self-esteem: A meta-analytic review of 192 studies on social exclusion. *Personality and Social Psychology Review*, *13*(4), 269–309.

Brennan, K. A., Clark, C. L., & Shaver, P. R. (1998). Self-report measurement of adult attachment: An integrative overview. In J. A. Simpson & W. S. Rholes (Eds.), *Attachment Theory and Close Relationships* (pp. 46–76). New York, NY: Guilford Press.

Campbell, L., Overall, N. C., Rubin, H., & Lackenbauer, S. D. (2013). Inferring a partner's ideal discrepancies: Accuracy, projection, and the communicative role of interpersonal behavior. *Journal of Personality and Social Psychology*, *105*(2), 217–233.

Canevello, A., & Crocker, J. (2010). Creating good relationships: Responsiveness, relationship quality, and interpersonal goals. *Journal of Personality and Social Psychology, 99*(1), 78–106.

Collins, N. L. (1996). Working models of attachment: Implications for explanation, emotion, and behavior. *Journal of Personality and Social Psychology, 71*(4), 810–832.

Collins, N. L., & Feeney, B. C. (2004). Working models of attachment shape perceptions of social support: Evidence from experimental and observational studies. *Journal of Personality and Social Psychology, 87*(3), 363–383.

Collins, N. L., Ford, M. B., Guichard, A. C., & Allard, L. M. (2006). Working models of attachment and attribution processes in intimate relationships. *Personality and Social Psychology Bulletin, 32*(2), 201–219.

Cuddy, A. J., Fiske, S. T., & Glick, P. (2008). Warmth and competence as universal dimensions of social perception: The stereotype content model and the BIAS map. *Advances in Experimental Social Psychology, 40*, 61–149.

Debrot, A., Cook, W. L., Perrez, M., & Horn, A. B. (2012). Deeds matter: Daily enacted responsiveness and intimacy in couples' daily lives. *Journal of Family Psychology, 26*(4), 617–627.

Downey, G., & Feldman, S. I. (1996). Implications of rejection sensitivity for intimate relationships. *Journal of Personality and Social Psychology, 70*(6), 1327–1343.

Downey, G., Feldman, S., & Ayduk, O. (2000). Rejection sensitivity and male violence in romantic relationships. *Personal Relationships, 7*(1), 45–61.

Downey, G., Freitas, A. L., Michaelis, B., & Khouri, H. (1998). The self-fulfilling prophecy in close relationships: Rejection sensitivity and rejection by romantic partners. *Journal of Personality and Social Psychology, 75*(2), 545–560.

Fletcher, G. J. O., & Kerr, P. S. G. (2010). Through the eyes of love: Reality and illusion in intimate relationships. *Psychological Bulletin, 136*(4), 627–658. doi:10.1037/a0019792

Franks, D. D., & Marolla, J. (1976). Efficacious action and social approval as interacting dimensions of self-esteem: A tentative formulation through construct validation. *Sociometry, 39*(4), 324–341.

Gable, S. L., Gonzaga, G. C., & Strachman, A. (2006). Will you be there for me when things go right? Supportive responses to positive event disclosures. *Journal of Personality and Social Psychology, 91*(5), 904–917.

Gagne, F. M., & Lydon, J. E. (2001). Mind-set and close relationships: When bias leads to (in)accurate predictions. *Journal of Personality and Social Psychology, 81*(1), 85–96.

Gagne, F. M., & Lydon, J. E. (2004). Bias and accuracy in close relationships: An integrative review. *Personality and Social Psychology Review, 8*(4), 322–338.

Gollwitzer, A., Schwörer, B., Stern, C., Gollwitzer, P. M., & Bargh, J. A. (2017). Up and down regulation of a highly automatic process: Implementation intentions can both increase and decrease social projection. *Journal of Experimental Social Psychology, 70*, 19–26.

Gonzaga, G. C., Keltner, D., Londahl, E. A., & Smith, M. D. (2001). Love and the commitment problem in romantic relations and friendship. *Journal of Personality and Social Psychology, 81*(2), 247–262.

Hazan, C., & Shaver, P. (1987). Romantic love conceptualized as an attachment process. *Journal of Personality and Social Psychology, 52*(3), 511–524.

Holmes, J. G., & Rempel, J. K. (1989). Trust in close relationships. In C. Hendrick (Ed.), *Close relationships* (pp. 187–220). Thousand Oaks, CA: Sage.

Ickes, W., & Simpson, J. A. (2003). Motivational aspects of empathic accuracy. In G. J. O. Fletcher & M. S. Clark (Eds.), *Blackwell handbook of social psychology: Interpersonal processes* (pp. 229–249). Malden, MA: Blackwell.

Jaremka, L. M., Bunyan, D. P., Collins, N. L., & Sherman, D. K. (2011). Reducing defensive distancing: Self-affirmation and risk regulation in response to relationship threats. *Journal of Experimental Social Psychology, 47*(1), 264–268.

Jayamaha, S. D., Girme, Y. U., & Overall, N. C. (2017). When attachment anxiety impedes support provision: The role of feeling unvalued and unappreciated. *Journal of Family Psychology, 31*(2), 181–191.

Kenny, D. A., & Acitelli, L. K. (2001). Accuracy and bias in the perception of the partner in a close relationship. *Journal of Personality and Social Psychology, 80*(3), 439–448.

Kimmes, J. G., Durtschi, J. A., Clifford, C. E., Knapp, D. J., & Fincham, F. D. (2015). The role of pessimistic attributions in the association between anxious attachment and relationship satisfaction. *Family Relations, 64*(4), 547–562.

Krueger, J. I. (2008). From social projection to social behaviour. *European Review of Social Psychology, 18*(1), 1–35.

Kunda, Z. (1990). The case for motivated reasoning. *Psychological Bulletin, 108*(3), 480–498.

Kwang, T., & Swann, W. B., Jr. (2010). Do people embrace praise even when they feel unworthy? A review of critical tests of self-enhancement versus self-verification. *Personality and Social Psychology Review, 14*(3), 263–280. http://dx.doi.org/10.1177/1088868310365876

Le, B., Dove, N. L., Agnew, C. R., Korn, M. S., & Mutso, A. A. (2010). Predicting nonmarital romantic relationship dissolution: A meta-analytic synthesis. *Personal Relationships, 17*(3), 377–390.

Leary, M. R., & Baumeister, R. F. (2000). The nature and function of self-esteem: Sociometer theory. In M. P. Zanna (Ed.), *Advances in experimental social psychology* (Vol. 32, pp. 1–62). San Diego, CA: Academic Press.

Leary, M. R., Cottrell, C. A., & Phillips, M. (2001). Deconfounding the effects of dominance and social acceptance on self-esteem. *Journal of Personality and Social Psychology, 81*(5), 898–909.

Lemay, E. P., Jr. (2016). The forecast model of relationship commitment. *Journal of Personality and Social Psychology, 111*(1), 34–52.

Lemay, E. P., Jr., & Clark, M. S. (2008). How the head liberates the heart: Projection of communal responsiveness guides relationship promotion. *Journal of Personality and Social Psychology, 94*(4), 647–671.

Lemay, E. P., Jr., Clark, M. S., & Feeney, B. C. (2007). Projection of responsiveness to needs and the construction of satisfying communal relationships. *Journal of Personality and Social Psychology, 92*(5), 834–853.

Lemay, E. P., Jr., & Dudley, K. L. (2011). Caution: Fragile! Regulating the interpersonal security of chronically insecure partners. *Journal of Personality and Social Psychology, 100*(4), 681–702.

Lemay, E. P., Jr., Lin, J. L., & Muir, H. J. (2015). Daily affective and behavioral forecasts in romantic relationships: Seeing tomorrow through the lens of today. *Personality and Social Psychology Bulletin, 41*(7), 1005–1019.

Lemay, E. P., Jr., & Melville, M. C. (2014).Diminishing self-disclosure to maintain security in partners' care. *Journal of Personality and Social Psychology, 106*(1), 37–57.

Lemay, E. P., Jr., & Neal, A. M. (2013). The wishful memory of interpersonal responsiveness. *Journal of Personality and Social Psychology, 104,* 653–672.

Lemay, E. P., Jr., & Neal, A. M. (2014). Accurate and biased perceptions of responsive support predict well-being. *Motivation and Emotion, 38*(2), 270–286.

Lemay, E. P., & Spongberg, K. (2015). Perceiving and wanting to be valued by others: Implications for cognition, motivation, and behavior in romantic relationships. *Journal of Personality, 83*(4), 464–478.

Lemay Jr, E. P., & Venaglia, R. B. (2016). Relationship expectations and relationship quality. *Review of General Psychology, 20*(1), 57–70.

Luo, S., & Snider, A. G. (2009). Accuracy and biases in newlyweds' perceptions of each other: Not mutually exclusive but mutually beneficial. *Psychological Science, 20*(11), 1332–1339.

Marigold, D. C., Holmes, J. G., & Ross, M. (2007). More than words: Reframing compliments from romantic partners fosters security in low self-esteem individuals. *Journal of Personality and Social Psychology, 92*(2), 232–248.

McNulty, J. K., O'Mara, E. M., & Karney, B. R. (2008). Benevolent cognitions as a strategy of relationship maintenance: "Don't sweat the small stuff" . . .. But it is not all small stuff. *Journal of Personality and Social Psychology, 94*(4), 631–646.

Menzies-Toman, D. A., & Lydon, J. E. (2005). Commitment-motivated benign appraisals of partner transgressions: Do they facilitate accommodation? *Journal of Social and Personal Relationships, 22*(1), 111–128.

Mikulincer, M. (1998). Attachment working models and the sense of trust: An exploration of interaction goals and affect regulation. *Journal of Personality and Social Psychology, 74*(5), 1209–1224.

Mills, J., Clark, M. S., Ford, T. E., & Johnson, M. (2004). Measurement of communal strength. *Personal Relationships, 11*(2), 213–230.

Murray, S. L. (1999). The quest for conviction: Motivated cognition in romantic relationships. *Psychological Inquiry, 10*(1), 23–34.

Murray, S. L., Bellavia, G. M., Rose, P., & Griffin, D. W. (2003). Once hurt, twice hurtful: How perceived regard regulates daily marital interactions. *Journal of Personality and Social Psychology, 84*(1), 126–147.

Murray, S. L., & Holmes, J. G. (1997). A leap of faith? Positive illusions in romantic relationships. *Personality and Social Psychology Bulletin, 23*(6), 586–604. doi:10.1177/0146167297236003

Murray, S. L., Holmes, J. G., & Collins, N. L. (2006). Optimizing assurance: The risk regulation system in relationships. *Psychological Bulletin, 132*(5), 641–666.

Murray, S. L., Holmes, J. G., & Griffin, D. W. (1996). The benefits of positive illusions: Idealization and the construction of satisfaction in close relationships. *Journal of Personality and Social Psychology, 70*(1), 79–98.

Murray, S. L., Holmes, J. G., & Griffin, D. W. (2000). Self-esteem and the quest for felt security: How perceived regard regulates attachment processes. *Journal of Personality and Social Psychology, 78*(3), 478–498.

Murray, S. L., Holmes, J. G., Griffin, D. W., Bellavia, G., & Rose, P. (2001). The mismeasure of love: How self-doubt contaminates relationship beliefs. *Personality and Social Psychology Bulletin, 27*(4), 423–436.

Murray, S. L., Holmes, J. G., MacDonald, G., & Ellsworth, P. C. (1998). Through the looking glass darkly? When self-doubts turn into relationship insecurities. *Journal of Personality and Social Psychology, 75*(6), 1459–1480.

Murray, S. L., Rose, P., Bellavia, G. M., Holmes, J. G., & Kusche, A. G. (2002). When rejection stings: How self-esteem constrains relationship-enhancement processes. *Journal of Personality and Social Psychology, 83*(3), 556–573.

Neff, L. A., & Karney, B. R. (2005). To know you is to love you: The implications of global adoration and specific accuracy for marital relationships. *Journal of Personality and Social Psychology, 88*(3), 480–497.

Nickerson, R. S. (1998). Confirmation bias: A ubiquitous phenomenon in many guises. *Review of General Psychology, 2*(2), 175–220.

Ogolsky, B. G., & Bowers, J. R. (2013). A meta-analytic review of relationship maintenance and its correlates. *Journal of Social and Personal Relationships, 30*(3), 343–367.

Podsakoff, P. M., MacKenzie, S. B., Lee, J.-Y., & Podsakoff, N. P. (2003). Common method biases in behavioral research: A critical review of the literature and recommended remedies. *Journal of Applied Psychology, 88*(5), 879–903.

Priem, J. S., Solomon, D. H., & Steuber, K. R. (2009). Accuracy and bias in perceptions of emotionally supportive communication in marriage. *Personal Relationships, 16*(4), 531–552.

Reis, H. T., Clark, M. S., & Holmes, J. G. (2004). Perceived partner responsiveness as an organizing construct in the study of intimacy and closeness. In D. J. Mashek & A. P. Aron (Eds.), *Handbook of closeness and intimacy* (pp. 201–225). Mahwah, NJ: Lawrence Erlbaum Associates.

Reis, H. T., Lemay, E. P., & Finkenauer, C. (2017). Toward understanding understanding: The importance of feeling understood in relationships. *Social and Personality Psychology Compass, 11*(4).

Reis, H. T., Maniaci, M. R., & Rogge, R. D. (2017). Compassionate acts and everyday emotional well-being among newlyweds. *Emotion, 17*(4), 751–763.

Rusbult, C. E., & Buunk, B. P. (1993). Commitment processes in close relationships: An interdependence analysis. *Journal of Social and Personal Relationships, 10*(2), 175–204.

Rusbult, C. E., Lange, P. A. M. V., Wildschut, T., Yovetich, N. A., & Verette, J. (2000). Perceived superiority in close relationships: Why it exists and persists. *Journal of Personality and Social Psychology, 79*(4), 521–545.

Rusbult, C. E., Verette, J., Whitney, G. A., Slovik, L. F., & Lipkus, I. (1991). Accommodation processes in close relationships: Theory and preliminary empirical evidence. *Journal of Personality and Social Psychology, 60*(1), 53–78.

Schwarz, N., Bless, H., Strack, F., Klumpp, G., Rittenauer-Schatka, H., & Simons, A. (1991). Ease of retrieval as information: Another look at the availability heuristic. *Journal of Personality and Social Psychology, 61*(2), 195–202.

Shallcross, S. L., & Simpson, J. A. (2012). Trust and responsiveness in strain-test situations: A dyadic perspective. *Journal of Personality and Social Psychology, 102*(5), 1031–1044. doi:10.1037/a0026829

Simpson, J. A., Orina, M. M., & Ickes, W. (2003). When accuracy hurts, and when it helps: A test of the empathic accuracy model in marital interactions. *Journal of Personality and Social Psychology, 85*(5), 881–893.

Solomon, D. H., Knobloch, L. K., Theiss, J. A., & McLaren, R. M. (2016). Relational turbulence theory: Explaining variation in subjective experiences and communication within romantic relationships. *Human Communication Research, 42*(4), 507–532.

Stafford, L. (2011). Measuring relationship maintenance behaviors: Critique and development of the revised relationship maintenance behavior scale. *Journal of Social and Personal Relationships, 28*(2), 278–303.

Stafford, L., & Canary, D. J. (1991). Maintenance strategies and romantic relationship type, gender and relational characteristics. *Journal of Social and Personal Relationships, 8*(2), 217–242.

Sümer, N., & Cozzarelli, C. (2004). The impact of adult attachment on partner and self-attributions and relationship quality. *Personal Relationships, 11*(3), 355–371.

Swann, W. B., Jr. (1983). Self-verification: Bringing social reality into harmony with the self. In J. Suls & A. G. Greenwald (Eds.), *Social psychological perspectives on the self* (Vol. 2, pp. 33–66). Hillsdale, NJ: Erlbaum.

Swann, W. B., Jr., Bosson, J. K., & Pelham, B. W. (2002). Different partners, different selves: Strategic verification of circumscribed identities. *Personality and Social Psychology Bulletin, 28*(9), 1215–1228.

Swann, W. B., Jr., De La Ronde, C., & Hixon, J. G. (1994). Authenticity and positivity strivings in marriage and courtship. *Journal of Personality and Social Psychology, 66*(5), 857–869.

Tucker, J. S., & Anders, S. L. (1999). Attachment style, interpersonal perception accuracy, and relationship satisfaction in dating couples. *Personality and Social Psychology Bulletin, 25*(4), 403–412.

Tversky, A., & Kahneman, D. (1973). Availability: A heuristic for judging frequency and probability. *Cognitive Psychology, 5*, 207–232.

Wieselquist, J., Rusbult, C. E., Foster, C. A., & Agnew, C. R. (1999). Commitment, pro-relationship behavior, and trust in close relationships. *Journal of Personality and Social Psychology, 77*(5), 942–966.

PART IV

THE SOCIAL CONTEXT OF RELATIONSHIP
MAINTENANCE

14

Gender and Race Perspectives on Relationship Maintenance

KATHERINE FIORI[1] AND AMY RAUER[2]

Relationship maintenance has been used to refer to both relationship-enhancing behaviors and threat-mitigating strategies that serve to keep relationships either in existence, in a given state, in a satisfactory state, or in good repair (e.g., Dindia, 2003; Ogolsky, Monk, Rice, Theisen, & Maniotes, 2017). Although scholars differ in what they theorize that couples are trying to achieve with maintenance, an underlying assumption across these definitions appears to be that the said goals are uniform both within and across couples. However, couples or even partners within the same relationship may differ in how they define a satisfactory state based on their own characteristics and experiences. The goal of our chapter will be to consider this diversity, not only in how couples go about maintaining the relationship but also in how these maintenance behaviors influence the quality of the relationship. We focus here on the roles of gender and race, as both have been implicated as salient contexts for relationship maintenance (Canary & Stafford, 1992; Dainton, 2017; Ogolsky & Bowers, 2013). Drawing when possible upon a dyadic approach to understanding relationship maintenance, we will focus on the primary romantic relationship contexts in which gender and race are manifested (i.e., different-sex and same-sex couples; intraracial and interracial couples) and the key correlates of maintenance within these relationships (e.g., satisfaction and commitment).

THEORETICAL BACKGROUND

Prevailing theoretical perspectives in the literature on relationship maintenance provide some insight into the existence and nature of gender and race differences, though there is less theoretical guidance to suggest how race may shape the form and function of relationship maintenance. Interdependence

[1] The Gordon F. Derner School of Psychology, Adelphi University, fiori@adelphi.edu
[2] Department of Child and Family Studies, University of Tennessee, arauer@utk.edu

Theory (Thibaut & Kelley, 1959) and the related Equity Perspective (Stafford & Canary, 2006) posit that balance between partners is critical for relationship success and that equity (versus feeling underbenefitted) is an influential force in the implementation of maintenance behaviors. To the extent that equity is more valued by one gender, this theory might predict differences in maintenance behaviors. Some research indicates that equity is more important for wives' marital satisfaction than for husbands' (Van Yperen & Buunk, 1990), implying that they may have greater motivations to enact maintenance behaviors. Relatedly, the effects of equity on maintenance behaviors might differ by race. For example, *unity*, rather than equity, has been found to be more important in Black marriages (Dainton, 2017; Marks et al., 2008), implying that the relationship-maintenance behaviors of White couples may be more sensitive to equity.

In contrast, according to the Communal Perspective (Mills & Clark, 1982), maintenance behaviors are driven by the goal of optimizing the welfare of the partner. Thus, sex/gender differences (but not necessarily race differences) might be expected, because research and theory suggest that women may be likely to prioritize such a goal (Taylor et al., 2000). This perspective might also predict higher levels of relationship-maintenance behaviors within same-sex relationships, particularly lesbian couples, due to the sex/gender differences seen in communal behavior. Across these theoretical frameworks, the role of gender in shaping the effects of maintenance are mixed, with the equity perspective suggesting that it may be consequential in theory but the communal perspective giving it prime status.

Regardless of the framework employed, it is unclear whether biological sex or gender roles are driving differences in relationship maintenance. From an evolutionary perspective, females are thought to be better served by creating and maintaining social networks than they are by fighting or fleeing in times of stress (Taylor et al., 2000). This implies that women may be more biologically driven than men to engage in the types of nurturing behaviors that are inherent in relationship maintenance (e.g., assurances and positivity) and may be more motivated to maintain the relationship status quo. Social Role Theory (Eagly, 1987), on the other hand, holds that men and women specialize in different behaviors due to a traditional division of labor, such that some or many gender differences may simply be learned adaptation to contextual demands. For example, men in occupations that require sensitivity and the provision of emotional support, such as psychology, tend to be just as adept at decoding emotions as women (Marshall, 2009). Furthermore, stereotypically masculine traits (e.g., dominance; Bem, 1974) are associated with inhibited communication and disclosure, which are both critical aspects of relationship maintenance behaviors, whereas stereotypical femininity is associated with greater openness in both men *and* women (Marshall, 2009). This theory implies that gender role differences in relationship maintenance will be stronger than sex differences.

GENDER AND RELATIONSHIP MAINTENANCE

The vast majority of research on gender differences in relationship maintenance behaviors has focused on different-sex relationships. However, the past decade has seen numerous advances in this literature, from research addressing *biological sex* versus *gender roles* (Aylor & Dainton, 2004; Stafford, Dainton, & Haas, 2000) to more complex approaches to examining gender differences within couples (e.g., consideration of actor-partner effects and self- and cross-spouse perceptions; e.g., Weigel & Ballard-Reisch, 1999; 2008). In reviewing these advances, we address mean-level differences in strategy use as well as gender as a moderator in understanding the associations between strategy use and relationship processes and outcomes (e.g., satisfaction), first in different-sex couples and then in same-sex couples.

ARE THERE SEX AND/OR GENDER DIFFERENCES IN RELATIONSHIP MAINTENANCE?

Women tend to use maintenance behaviors more often than men (Canary & Stafford, 1992; Dainton & Stafford, 1993; Ottu, 2012; Ragsdale, 1996); in fact, women report using more of a number of relationship maintenance behaviors (positivity, openness, assurances, social networks, sharing tasks, and forgiveness; Miller, Worthington, & McDaniel, 2008; Ogolsky & Bowers, 2013). Generally, the strategies themselves are more strongly correlated with each other in women than in men (Ogolsky & Bowers, 2013). This implies that for men, the enactment or perception of a behavior in one domain is not necessarily related to whether or how they enact or perceive a behavior in another domain. However, there is some research to indicate that sex differences only emerge for everyday, "routine" maintenance behaviors (Marshall, 2009) as opposed to strategic behaviors that are consciously and intentionally invoked for maintaining a relationship (e.g., Canary & Stafford, 1992). For example, women are more likely to show routine openness (Aylor & Dainton, 2004). Although women engage in maintenance behaviors more frequently overall, the order of frequency of use between partners tends to be similar (e.g., tasks used most often, followed by positivity; Ragsdale, 1996). Furthermore, sex differences in maintenance behaviors may depend on a number of contextual factors, including marital status (Dainton & Stafford, 1993) and parental status (Malinen, Rönkä, & Sevón, 2010).

Consistent with Social Role Theory (Eagly, 1987), however, only weak evidence links biological sex to maintenance behaviors, whereas there are strong links between gender and maintenance (Aylor & Dainton, 2004;

Stafford et al., 2000). Interestingly, Aylor and Dainton (2004) found that although femininity was associated only with routine maintenance behaviors, masculinity was associated only with strategic behaviors. Androgyny best predicts relational maintenance activities and thus, relationship satisfaction, because androgynous individuals may be best at utilizing *both* expressive, routine maintenance behaviors (traditionally "feminine" behaviors) and more directive, instrumental communication (traditionally "masculine" behaviors). This is consistent with research showing that couples experiencing the poorest marital quality are those with extremely traditionally gender-typed wives and gender-typed husbands (Helms, Proulx, Klute, McHale, & Crouter, 2006). The possibility that *gaps* in levels of maintenance behaviors, rather than absolute levels, predict relationship quality highlights the complexity of considering the role of gender in relationship maintenance behaviors and motivations and the importance of taking a dyadic approach to understanding relationship maintenance.

ARE MEN AND WOMEN DIFFERENTIALLY MOTIVATED TO ENGAGE IN RELATIONSHIP MAINTENANCE?

Not only may men and women differ in their reported use of maintenance behaviors, but the underlying reasons for their use may be distinct as well. Men's use of relationship maintenance behaviors appears to be more dependent on their perceptions of the relationship (e.g., commitment or threat of attractive alternatives) and individual characteristics (e.g., personality; Baker & McNulty, 2011; Ragsdale & Brandau-Brown, 2005). Gagné and Lydon (2003) found that women use positive illusions regardless of their level of commitment to the relationship in question, whereas only men who are more committed to their partner report this type of routine threat-mitigation maintenance behavior. It may be that women's motivations are more tied to their feelings of equity (Stafford & Canary, 2006). For example, women's reports of equity are more highly associated with relational stability than are men's reports (i.e., greater likelihood of breakup; Sprecher, 2001), and wife-defined equity is more predictive of positive maintenance behaviors than is husband-defined equity (Canary & Stafford, 1992; Stafford & Canary, 2006). However, not all studies have found this interaction between equity and gender in predicting maintenance use (Dainton, 2016). Furthermore, research using dyadic analyses (Weigel & Ballard-Reisch, 2008) shows that perceptions of *both* partners are important in the use of maintenance behaviors in marriage, such that the spouse's perceptions of satisfaction and commitment are associated with both their own and their partner's use of maintenance behaviors.

Relatedly, perceptions of the spouse's maintenance behaviors may be more important than their actual behaviors (Ogolsky & Bowers, 2013;

Stafford & Canary, 1991). Canary and Stafford (1992) found that husbands perceived wives as using more openness and sharing tasks than wives perceived their husbands as using. However, women actually report perceiving that their partners engage in higher levels of a number of relationship maintenance behaviors (Ogolsky & Bowers, 2013). This discrepancy could be because women are simply more aware of maintenance efforts (Stafford & Canary, 1991). However, evidence from other fields of psychology suggests that these gender differences are not solely due to increased awareness in women, but rather, that women are actually expending more energy on relationship maintenance (Baker & McNulty, 2011; Canary & Wahba, 2006).

WHY MIGHT WOMEN ENGAGE IN MORE RELATIONSHIP MAINTENANCE AND DOES IT MATTER?

Women are more likely than men to report that developing and maintaining relationships is a primary goal of the relationship (Baker & McNulty, 2011; Canary & Wahba, 2006), implying that the "pro-relationship" thinking necessary for relationship maintenance may be more of a general disposition among women than among men. Acitelli (1992) found that not only did wives talk more about their relationships than their husbands, but their marital satisfaction was also positively associated with the degree to which their husbands engaged in relationship talk with them. Husbands' relationship satisfaction, in contrast, was not associated with either spouse's relationship talk. Women's greater use of openness may be related to their tendency to emotionally self-disclose more than men (Magai, Consedine, Fiori, & King, 2009). Women may also be less likely to use avoidance when confronting relationship problems, as they appear to prefer more direct discussion (Stafford & Canary, 2006). Furthermore, women's larger, denser, more supportive, and more diverse social networks (Antonucci, 1994; Liebler & Sandefur, 2002) may also drive their use of social networks as a relationship maintenance behavior. However, although the use of the "shared network" is considered a positive relationship maintenance strategy (i.e., relying on the support of mutual friends and family), not all relationships are shared, and women's "non-shared" relationships, in particular, can actually introduce problems into the relationship (Helms, Crouter, & McHale, 2003).

Dyadic research indicates that stronger associations exist between relationship strategies and relationship processes and outcomes (e.g., satisfaction and commitment) among women, perhaps because they are socialized to be more sensitive to these types of events (Canary & Wahba, 2006; Weigel & Ballard-Reisch, 1999). Weigel and Ballard-Reisch found that for wives, both self-perceptions of marital quality and cross-spouse perceptions were related to their use of maintenance behaviors. In contrast, husbands' use of maintenance behaviors had only a few associations with self or partner perceptions of marital quality. Similarly, Ogolsky and Bowers's (2013) meta-analysis showed larger effect sizes for women compared with men for the correlations between *most* relationship maintenance factors and satisfaction. However, they found that for "liking," the effect sizes were actually larger among men. It is important to note, though, that for certain interactive threat-mitigation strategies (Ogolsky et al., 2017), men's relationship maintenance contributions may be particularly consequential. Rauer and Volling (2013) found that couples in which men were actively and constructively engaged in conflict discussions reported better marital functioning, regardless of wives' use of this maintenance behavior (which was in fact greater on average than husbands'). Across these studies, however, it appears not only that women are more likely to engage in maintenance, but also that their efforts in this regard appear particularly important for both partners. Again, this work highlights the critical need to take a dyadic perspective and to consider the sex and gender role make-up of the dyad.

RELATIONSHIP MAINTENANCE IN SAME-SEX COUPLES

Differences in relationship maintenance may arise in same-sex couples compared with different-sex couples because of more flexibility in sex roles (Haas, 2002; 2003) and higher expectations of equality and reciprocity (Haas, 2003). Furthermore, same-sex couples may experience unique challenges related to (1) stigma and minority stress; (2) lack of social norms; and (3) until recently, the lack of legal recognition (Ogolsky & Gray, 2016). In general, however, there are more similarities than differences between same-sex couples and different-sex couples in their relationships (Holmberg, Blair, & Phillips, 2010; Kurdek, 2006). Unfortunately, there is little research explicitly addressing relationship *maintenance* among same-sex couples. Of the existing research, samples are small (e.g., Haas, 2002; Haas & Stafford, 1998), comparison groups of different-sex couples are not included (e.g., Haas, 2002; Haas & Stafford, 1998; Ogolsky, 2009; Ogolsky & Gray, 2016) and findings are difficult to interpret due to confounds such as the presence of chronic illness (Haas, 2002) or the lack of legal recognition (Haas & Stafford, 2005).

Existing research conducted without heterosexual comparison groups (e.g., Haas, 2002; 2003; Haas & Stafford, 1998) indicates that same-sex couples use very similar maintenance behaviors to those found in prior research on different-sex couples. However, some unique maintenance behaviors emerge, with the use of social network support being particularly salient for same-sex couples (Haas, 2002; Haas & Stafford, 1998). For example, being "out" as a couple and the use of gay/lesbian supportive environments in the face of stigma may be particularly important for same-sex couples (Haas & Stafford, 1998; Ogolsky et al., 2017). Additional research on same-sex couples shows that conflict is negatively associated with reports of a partner's relationship maintenance, and that the association is mediated by negative emotion (Ogolsky & Gray, 2016); however, it is unclear whether this would also apply to different-sex couples.

In studies directly comparing same-sex couples with different-sex couples, few differences have been found in the utilization of relationship maintenance behaviors (e.g., Metz, Rosser, & Strapko, 1994) or in the links between maintenance behaviors and relationship outcomes (Goldberg, Smith, & Kashy, 2010; Haas & Stafford, 2005). For example, idealization and positive illusion – both individual-level threat-mitigating strategies (Ogolsky et al., 2017) – have been related to greater relationship satisfaction for both same- and different-sex couples (Conley, Roesch, Peplau, & Gold, 2009). Thus, similarities in relationship maintenance and their associations with relationship satisfaction between same- and different-sex couples appear to be the norm rather than the exception. Furthermore, differences that do arise may be due more to social stigma and a historical lack of legal marital status among same-sex couples (Haas & Stafford, 2005), as well as social gender role factors (Metz et al., 1994), than to the sex make-up of the dyads per se. We turn now to research on relationship maintenance among other couples experiencing social stigma: namely, minority couples and interracial couples.

RACE AND RELATIONSHIP MAINTENANCE

Black couples are both less likely to get married and more likely to divorce than are White couples (Dainton, 2017; Dixon, 2009). Furthermore, comparative studies indicate that Black couples evaluate their marriages less positively than do White couples (Acitelli, Douvan, & Veroff, 1997). Although this work could imply that maintenance behaviors are used either less frequently and/or less effectively, it is more likely that external circumstances (e.g., racism, discrimination, and financial struggles) are stronger predictors of marital quality in these couples than are interpersonal interactions and relationship maintenance behaviors. Indeed, Veroff and colleagues (Veroff, Douvan, & Hatchett, 1995) write that Black couples "interpret their marital experiences in the context of their social worlds, their ... kin, [and] their economic situations – all within a backdrop of institutional racism" (p. xiii). Unfortunately, there is very little research examining race differences in factors related to sustaining positive and satisfying marriages (Goodwin, 2003), which is likely due in part to a focus in the literature on a "deficit" perspective of Black marriages (Dainton, 2017; Marks et al., 2008).

Not surprisingly, then, much of the research discussed earlier on gender differences in relationship maintenance does not address race differences; either the race of the sample was not mentioned at all (Canary & Stafford, 1992; Dainton & Stafford, 1993; Ragsdale, 1996) or samples were primarily White and race was not considered in the analyses (Aylor & Dainton, 2004;

Stafford & Canary, 2006; Weigel & Ballard-Reisch, 2008). Even in research using ethnically diverse samples (e.g., Dainton, 2016), race and ethnicity are often not considered as potential factors or mentioned as control variables. Also concerning is that one of the only studies that have explicitly focused on race differences in relationship maintenance was conducted only among wives (Goodwin, 2003). Furthermore, much of the research that is available has focused on *interracial* couples; and, because these couples face unique challenges similar to those faced by same-sex couples (i.e., social stigma), they may not offer insight into potential intraracial differences in relationship maintenance.

Although we use the terms "Black" and "White" Americans throughout this chapter for consistency, it should be noted that in spite of notable diversity within these groups (Bryant, Taylor, Lincoln, Chatters, & Jackson, 2008; Bryant et al., 2010), much of the limited research on race differences has focused almost exclusively on African Americans and nonimmigrant White Americans. However, both groups are diverse. Black Americans, for example, include both African Americans and Black Caribbean Americans, whose sociohistorical backgrounds are considerably different and whose marital relationships appear to differ as well (Bryant et al., 2008; 2010). Unless otherwise specified, the following research focuses on differences between African Americans and White European Americans, since the research is focused on these groups, and uses the terms "Black Americans" and "African Americans" interchangeably.

WHY MIGHT THERE BE RACE DIFFERENCES IN RELATIONSHIP MAINTENANCE?

Despite the limited research, there are reasons to suspect race differences in relationship maintenance. First, Black marriages are *perceived* as egalitarian, particularly in family roles (McAdoo, 1993), in part because Black husbands tend to perform more housework than White husbands (Dillaway & Broman, 2001). Indeed, stronger role sharing appears to be related to greater marital stability among Black couples but not White couples (Veroff et al., 1995), and it is believed that role sharing may be particularly important for Black couples (Marks et al., 2008). However, at the same time, Black husbands tend to be more dissatisfied than White husbands about taking on a greater share of household tasks (Dillaway & Broman, 2001). In fact, they may resist such involvement as a way to exert greater power in their marriage (Bryant et al., 2010; Orbuch & Eyster, 1997) and to counteract negative stereotypes about "strong Black women" (Dainton, 2017). Regardless, it could be that unity and collaboration, rather than equity, is more important in these marriages (Marks et al., 2008; Orbuch, Veroff, & Hunter, 1999). Goodwin (2003) further postulates that White women may place more importance on issues of equity than do Black women because balancing work and family roles is a more recent phenomenon among the former. Thus, the theoretical frame operating to explain the use of relational strategies that has been used primarily with White couples (i.e., equity theory) may not be as applicable to Black couples.

Second, Black individuals may be less inclined to self-disclose than White individuals (Magai et al., 2009), perhaps related in part to a cultural focus on stoicism (Dilworth-Anderson, 1998) and/or experiences of marginalization (Ogolsky et al., 2017). Black individuals also tend to report lower levels of a range of negative emotions (Consedine & Magai, 2002), and in terms of coping styles, are more likely to engage in positive reframing or positive reappraisal than are White individuals (Brantley, O'Hea, Jones, & Mehan, 2002; Plummer & Slane, 1996). It is difficult to know how these differences in self-disclosure and emotions intersect with gender in predicting relationship maintenance behaviors. Although this is speculative, Black individuals might use less openness and more positivity in their romantic relationships compared with White individuals.

Third, social networks play a particularly integral role in Black Americans' cultural traditions (Black, Cook, Murry, & Cutrona, 2005; Brown, Orbuch, & Maharaj, 2010; Sarkisian & Gerstel, 2004), perhaps due in part to a long history of adverse structural, economic, and social factors (i.e., racism and discrimination; Jackson, 2000; Murry, Brown, Brody, Cutrona, & Simons, 2001). Extended kin networks constructed from close, trusted family and friends ("fictive kin") are thought to provide vital support to Black Americans that may be unavailable from more traditional, formal sources (Sarkisian & Gerstel, 2004; Taylor et al., 2003). This support, however, may come with additional burdens for Black married couples (Marks et al., 2008; Sarkisian & Gerstel, 2004), including greater demands from network members compared with White married couples (McLoyd, Hill, & Dodge, 2005). As a result, Black couples may limit contact with network members as a coping strategy to prevent marital strain (Orbuch, Bauermeister, Brown, & McKinley, 2013); this suggests that the maintenance strategy of "networks" may be used less often. Furthermore, research shows that the links between social networks and marital quality are weaker for Black couples than for White couples (Fiori et al., 2017), implying that the use of "networks" as a maintenance strategy may also not be as effective for Black couples.

Finally, Black couples may experience unique strengths and challenges to their marriages that may be less relevant among White couples. Black couples tend to espouse stronger religious orientations than their White counterparts, which could act as an important resource for their marriages (Allen & Olson, 2001; Marks et al., 2008; Taylor & Chatters, 1988). Prayer has been identified as a critical form of relationship enhancement at the individual level (Ogolsky et al., 2017), and thus, Black couples may be able to draw on this form of maintenance to a greater extent than White couples. On the other hand, Black couples also face numerous socioeconomic barriers related to marginalization that may make their marriages particularly vulnerable, including financial strain, racial discrimination, and minority status (Bryant et al., 2010).

In one of the earliest comparative studies on relationship maintenance in Black and White married couples, Diggs and Stafford (1998) found that the 55 Black and 42 White couples in their sample were similar in terms of positivity, openness, and assurance strategies. However, Black couples reported *lower* levels of "sharing tasks" as a maintenance strategy. This finding is in line with the idea that equity and agreement on roles may not be as important in Black marriages as previously speculated (see Allen & Olson, 2001; Goodwin, 2003; Marks et al., 2008; Orbuch et al., 1999). White couples may be more likely to address equity in sharing tasks because of historic inequities in White male–female relationships. Networks were not mentioned by either group, suggesting that social networks may not be used more often for maintenance among Black couples. Again, this is consistent with the possibility that Black couples may actually limit contact with network members to prevent marital strain (Orbuch et al., 2013). Interestingly, religion was only mentioned by the Black individuals, consistent with expectations about the importance of religion/ spirituality as a resource for Black couples (Marks et al., 2008). Similarly, in a study of 260 Black and 232 White married couples, Dainton (2017) found that religion and spirituality were positively related to positive maintenance behaviors and negatively related to negative maintenance behaviors only among the Black couples. In contrast, White respondents reported using *more* assurances and social networks than did the Black respondents, and the Black respondents reported using more jealousy induction, although these differences were small and not predictive of marital outcomes. Broman (2005), on the other hand, found that race differences in negative maintenance behaviors *fully* explained race differences in marital quality.

As to whether race differences exist in how these strategies predict relationship processes/outcomes, studies suggest some key differences. Dainton (2017) found that although assurance strategies significantly pre-dicted marital satisfaction in both Black and White couples, sharing tasks and positivity were significant predictors only for Whites. Similarly to Diggs and Stafford (1998), Dainton reasoned that performing household tasks may be less important for Black marriages because of the egalitarian nature of these unions. She also suggests that authenticity is valued more than "being nice" in Black communities, such that positivity may be less impactful in Black marriages, despite earlier speculation that it may occur with greater fre-quency. Furthermore, in contrast to White couples (for whom avoidance was unrelated to marital satisfaction, and openness was counterintuitively *negatively* associated with marital satisfaction; Dainton, 2017; Stafford et al., 2000), openness was *positively* associated with marital satisfaction and avoidance was negatively associated with marital satisfaction among only the Black couples in the sample. According to Dainton (2017), a pattern emerges from these findings indicating "a cultural preference for engaging in direct communication among Black individuals" (p. 77). Similarly, although Goodwin (2003) found some similarities in the predictors of marital well-being between Black and White wives, in-law relations affected the marital well-being of Black wives only. The importance of positive relations with in-laws for marital well-being is consistent with the emphasis on strong family ties among Black Americans (Sarkisian & Gerstel, 2004; Taylor et al., 2003).

Qualitative studies of Black couples also reveal additional salient relationship-maintenance behaviors. Marks and colleagues (2008) uncovered several challenges of Black marriages among 30 Black couples, including balancing work and family life and providing needed support to family. To overcome these external challenges, the couples primarily reported relying on each other and using communication and understanding. Furthermore, in describing how they maintained the quality of their marriages, couples highlighted the importance of both conflict management, a dyadic threat-mitigating maintenance strategy (Ogolsky et al., 2017), and sharing time together (especially in religious activities), an interactive relationship-enhancement strategy. Finally, these couples emphasized the importance of "unity" in marriage, as a "synergy that was appreciated by two different but mutually committed individuals" (p. 180). Similarly, Dainton (2017), in her interviews of 10 Black couples, uncovered the following relationship maintenance themes: friendship/time together, prayer, active listening, a focus on nonverbal communication, and celebrating the past. Dainton suggests that these themes reflect the importance of Black couples celebrating their shared history together, coming together to cope with racism and discrimination, and being role models for other young Black individuals.

INTERRACIAL COUPLES

Dainton (2015) posits that "the differences between maintaining interracial marriage and intraracial marriage might not exist in the amount of effort necessary but in the nature of that effort" (p. 782). Consistent with this interpretation is research indicating that although individuals in marginalized relationships (e.g., interracial couples and same-sex couples) invest less than those in nonmarginalized relationships, marginalized partners appear to utilize compensatory strategies to maintain high levels of commitment despite this lower investment (Lehmiller & Agnew, 2006). In Dainton's (2015) sample of 53 men and 36 women in interracial marriages (primarily Black/White), she found that whereas infidelity and avoidance negatively predicted satisfaction in these individuals, conflict management and the use of social networks were positive predictors. This finding is in contrast to studies of primarily intra-racial couples showing the importance of assurances, in particular, for pre-dicting marital satisfaction (Dainton, 2017; Stafford, 2003).

According to Steinbugler (2012), interracial partners may engage in unique forms of relationship maintenance that revolve around "how and when to initiate discussions of race, interpret and translate their perspectives, critically evaluate their own racial positions, conceal their emotions, or introduce humor" (p. 101). In interviews with gay, lesbian, and heterosexual interracial couples, Steinbugler found that most interracial partners engaged in what she termed "emotional labor" as an attempt to understand differences in racial statuses and dispositions between the partners. Although most of this "racework" was routinized, it still involved quite a bit of emotional effort for both partners. Most of this talk was directly about race, although other couples also used humor, and still others engaged in strategic avoidance by purposely and consciously *not* engaging in racework. It was clear to most of the couples in this study that this type of work was necessary to maintain their relationships.

FUTURE DIRECTIONS AND CONCLUSIONS

In sum, gender and race appear to be important contexts that shape both how couples maintain satisfying relationships and the extent to which their efforts are successful. Women are generally more likely to engage in maintenance behaviors, especially routine openness, and these behaviors seem to have more of an impact on both partners' levels of satisfaction than do men's. However, gender roles may be more important than sex per se, with feminin-ity linked to routine maintenance and masculinity linked to strategic main-tenance. That being said, same-sex couples are largely similar to different-sex couples in terms of both the most commonly used maintenance strategies and their effects on relationship satisfaction. Some of the unique maintenance strategies utilized by both same-sex couples and interracial couples may arise from the social stigma surrounding these relationships (Lehmiller & Agnew, 2006). Similarly, Black couples, compared with White couples, appear to engage in some maintenance behaviors likely shaped by barriers associated with racism and discrimination, although they also show many similarities to White couples.

Despite numerous advances made in this area over the past decade, more research is needed to explore the intersection of sex/gender and race in both intraracial couples (e.g., Black wives vs. White wives in intraracial marriages) and interracial couples (e.g., White wife/Black husband vs. Black wife/White husband relationships). Furthermore, given that gender and sexual orientation also intersect, overlaying race onto these considerations seems an important next step for beginning to understand how sensitive maintenance may be to the various individual, relational, and cultural contexts in which it occurs. In the only known study to approach this intersectionality question, Dainton (2017) did not find any statistically significant interactions between race and gender predicting relationship maintenance behaviors or relationship satisfaction. However, she recognized that these null findings could be due in part to the fact that the central variables that seem to differentiate Black and White people are not included in traditional maintenance measures. Thus, it is critical that researchers move beyond the relationship maintenance measures originally developed from samples of heterosexual White couples to develop measures that tap into constructs relevant for a wider range of couples. Appropriately tailoring our measures might change the assumptions made about different groups engaging in "less maintenance."

Relationship maintenance across cultures will be addressed more explicitly by Gaines & Ferenczi (Chapter 15), but clearly, more research is needed on how relationship maintenance behaviors are enacted among different ethnic groups within the USA (e.g., Latino Americans, White European immigrants, and Asian Americans), including both intraethnic and interethnic marriages. For example, there may be unique marital challenges for couples who immigrate to the USA from other countries (Rodriguez, Helms, Supple, & Hengstebeck, 2016). More broadly, although there is some evidence that the gender differences in relationship maintenance outlined in this chapter are found outside the USA as well (e.g., among Nigerian married couples; Ottu, 2012), more research is needed to determine whether the gender differences we are seeing are universal or not.

Another important avenue for future research is considering maintenance as a *process*. The methodologies currently utilized to capture maintenance behaviors treat them more statically than they are probably occurring. Couples may begin to tailor their behaviors based on the responsivity of their partners (Dainton, 2017). On a broader level, and as discussed in more detail by Rauer & Proulx (Chapter 17), relationship maintenance may change across the lifespan as well. It is important to consider how the gender and race differences outlined in the present chapter (focused primarily on middle-aged adults) may play out across the lifespan. Even in adolescent romantic relationships, girls appear to have a greater influence on their partners in terms of autonomy processes than do boys (McIsaac, Connolly, McKenney, Pepler, & Craig, 2008). Later in life, particularly in the context of life-threatening illness, gendered tendencies to enact maintenance behaviors may become less salient due to the demands associated with caregiving (Badr & Taylor, 2008). Gendered tendencies may also decline with age more generally, given evidence of increases in androgyny among men into late life (Hyde, Krajnik, & Skuldt-Niederberger, 1991) as well as historical changes showing decreases in femininity among women over time (Twenge, 1997). Relatedly, more research is needed to understand changes in relationship maintenance for both same- and different-sex couples across important life transitions (e.g., parenthood; Goldberg et al., 2010).

Finally, as alluded to in our opening paragraph, it is possible that the perceptions and meanings of both maintenance behaviors and marital quality differ within and across couples. There is some evidence, for example, that "supportive wives" means different things to Black and White husbands (Orbuch et al., 1999). Researchers need to begin asking different questions about what it is that is being maintained and what those maintenance behaviors *mean* to individuals of differing genders, races, and sexual orientations. Simply put, understanding differences in *what* couples are trying to maintain may be just as important as exploring differences in who is doing so, how, and why.

REFERENCES

Acitelli, L. K. (1992). Gender differences in relationship awareness and marital satisfaction among young married couples. *Personality and Social Psychology Bulletin*, *18*, 102–110.

Acitelli, L. K., Douvan, E., & Veroff, J. (1997). The changing influence of interpersonal perceptions on marital well-being among black and white couples. *Journal of Social and Personal Relationships*, *14*(3), 291–304. doi:10.1177/0265407597143001

Allen, W. D., & Olson, D. H. (2001). Five types of African-American marriages. *Journal of Marital and Family Therapy*, *27*(3), 301–314. doi:10.1111/j.1752-0606.2001. tb00326.x

Antonucci, T. C. (1994). A life-span view of women's social relations. In B. F. Turner & L. E. Troll (Eds.), *Women growing older: Psychological perspectives* (pp. 239–269). Thousand Oaks, CA: Sage.

Aylor, B., & Dainton, M. (2004). Biological sex and psychological gender as predictors of routine and strategic relational maintenance. *Sex Roles*, *50*(9/10), 689–697. doi:10.1023/B:SERS.0000027570.80468.a0

Badr, H., & Taylor, C. L. C. (2008). Effects of relationship maintenance on psychological distress and dyadic adjustment among couples coping with lung cancer. *Health Psychology*, *27*(5), 616–627. doi:10.1037/0278-6133.27.5.616

Baker, L., & McNulty, J. K. (2011). Self-compassion and relationship maintenance: The moderating roles of conscientiousness and gender. *Journal of Personality and Social Psychology*, *100*(5), 853–873. doi:10.1037/a0021884

Bem, S. L. (1974). The measurement of psychological androgyny. *Journal of Consulting and Clinical Psychology*, *42*(2), 155–162.

Black, A. R., Cook, J. L., Murry, V. M., & Cutrona, C. E. (2005). Ties that bind: Implications of social support for rural, partnered African American women's health functioning. *Women's Health Issues*, *15*(5), 216–223. doi:10.1016/j.whi.2005.05.003

Brantley, P. J., O'Hea, E. L., Jones, G., & Mehan, D. J. (2002). The influence of income level and ethnicity on coping strategies. *Journal of Psychopathology and Behavioral Assessment*, *24*(1), 39–45. doi:10.1023/A:1014001208005

Broman, C. L. (2005). Race differences in marital well-being. *Journal of Marriage and Family*, *55*(3), 724–732. doi:10.2307/353352

Brown, E., Orbuch, T. L., & Maharaj, A. (2010). Social networks and marital stability among Black American and White American couples. In K. Sullivan & J. Davila (Eds.), *Support processes in intimate relationships* (pp. 318–334). New York, NY: Oxford University Press.

Bryant, C. M., Taylor, R. J., Lincoln, K. D., Chatters, L. M., & Jackson, J. S. (2008). Marital satisfaction among African Americans and Black Caribbeans: Findings from the national survey of American life. *Family Relations, 57*(2), 239–253. doi:10.1111/j.1741-3729.2008.00497.x

Bryant, C. M., Wickrama, K. A. S., Bolland, J., Bryant, B. M., Cutrona, C. E., & Stanik, C. E. (2010). Race matters, even in marriage: identifying factors linked to marital outcomes for African Americans. *Journal of Family Theory and Review, 2*(3), 157–174. doi:10.1111/j.1756-2589.2010.00051.x

Canary, D. J., & Stafford, L. (1992). Relational maintenance strategies and equity in marriage. *Communication Monographs, 59*(3), 243–267. doi:10.1080/03637759209376268

Canary, D. J., & Wahba, J. (2006). Do women work harder than men at maintaining relationships? In K. Dindia & D. J. Canary (Eds.), *Sex differences and similarities in communication* (2nd ed., pp. 359–377). Mahwah, NJ: Lawrence Erlbaum Associates.

Conley, T. D., Roesh, S. C., Peplau, L. A., & Gold, M. S. (2009). A test of positive illusions versus shared reality models of relationship satisfaction among gay, lesbian, and heterosexual couples. *Journal of Applied Social Psychology, 39*(6), 1417–1431.

Consedine, N. S., & Magai, C. (2002). The uncharted waters of emotion: Ethnicity, trait emotion and emotion expression in older adults. *Journal of Cross-Cultural Gerontology, 17*(1), 71–100. doi:10.1023/A:1014838920556

Dainton, M. (2015). An interdependence approach to relationship maintenance in interracial marriage. *Journal of Social Issues, 71*(4), 772–787. doi:10.1111/josi.12148

Dainton, M. (2016). Equity, equality, and self-interest in marital maintenance. *Communication Quarterly, 65*(3), 1–21. doi:10.1080/01463373.2016.1227346

Dainton, M. (2017). *Maintaining Black marriage: Individual, interpersonal, and contextual dynamics*. Lanham, MD: Lexington Books.

Dainton, M., & Stafford, L. (1993). Routine maintenance behaviors: A comparison of relationship type, partner similarity and sex differences. *Journal of Social and Personal Relationships, 10*(2), 255–271. doi:10.1177/02654075930100020

Diggs, R. C., & Stafford, L. (1998). Maintaining marital relationships: A comparison between African American and European American married individuals. In V. J. Duncan (Ed.), *Towards achieving MAAT: Communication patterns in African American, European, American, and interracial relationships* (pp. 191–202). Dubuque, IA: Kendall/Hunt.

Dillaway, H., & Broman, C. (2001). Race, class, and gender differences in marital satisfaction and divisions of household labor among dual-earner couples. *Journal of Family Issues, 22*(3), 309–327. doi:10.1177/019251301022003003

Dilworth-Anderson, P. (1998). Emotional well-being in adult and later life among African Americans: A cultural and sociocultural perspective. In K. W. Schaie & M. P. Lawton (Eds.), *Annual review of gerontology and geriatrics: Focus on emotion and adult development* (Vol. 17, pp. 282–302). New York, NY: Springer.

Dindia, K. (2003). Relationship maintenance communication. In D. J. Canary & M. Dainton (Eds.), *Maintaining relationships through communication: Relational, contextual, and cultural variations* (pp. 1–28). New York, NY: Psychology Press.

Dixon, P. (2009). Marriage among African Americans: What does the research reveal? *Journal of African American Studies, 13*(1), 29–46. doi:10.1007/s12111-008-9062-5

Eagly, A. H. (1987). Reporting sex differences. *American Psychologist, 42*(7), 756–757. doi:10.1037/0003-066X.42.7.755

Fiori, K., Rauer, A., Birditt, K., Brown, E., Jager, J., & Orbuch, T. (2017). Social network typologies of Black and White couples in midlife. *Journal of Marriage and Family, 79,* 571–589.

Gagné, F. M., & Lydon, J. E. (2003). Identification and the commitment shift: Accounting from gender differences in relationship illusions. *Personality and Social Psychology Bulletin, 29*(7), 907–919. doi:10.1177/0146167203029007009

Goldberg, A. E., Smith, J. Z., & Kashy, D. A. (2010). Preadoptive factors predicting lesbian, gay, and heterosexual couples' relationship quality across the transition to adoptive parenthood. *Journal of Family Psychology, 24*(3), 221–232. doi:10.1037/a0019615

Goodwin, P. Y. (2003). African American and European American women's marital well-being. *Journal of Marriage and Family, 65*(3), 550–560. doi:10.1111/j.1741-3737.2003.00550.x

Haas, S. M. (2002). Social support as relationship maintenance in gay male couples coping with HIV or AIDS. *Journal of Social and Personal Relationships, 19*(1), 87–111. doi:10.1177/0265407502191005

Haas, S. M. (2003). Relationship maintenance in same-sex couples. In D. J. Canary & M. Dainton (Eds.), *Maintaining relationships through communication: Relational, contextual, and cultural variations* (pp. 209–230). New York, NY: Psychology Press.

Haas, S. M., & Stafford, L. (1998). An initial examination of maintenance behaviors in gay and lesbian relationships. *Journal of Social and Personal Relationships, 15*(6), 846–855. doi:10.1177/0265407598156008

Haas, S. M., & Stafford, L. (2005). Maintenance behaviors in same-sex and marital relationships: A matched sample comparison. *The Journal of Family Communication, 5*(1), 43–60. doi:10.1207/s15327698jfc0501_3

Helms, H. M., Crouter, A. C., & McHale, S. M. (2003). Marital quality and spouses' marriage work with close friends and each other. *Journal of Marriage and Family, 65* (4), 963–977. doi:10.1111/j.1741-3737.2003.00963.x

Helms, H. M., Proulx, C. M., Klute, M. M., McHale, S. M., & Crouter, A. C. (2006). Spouses' gender-typed attributes and their links with marital quality: A pattern analytic approach. *Journal of Social and Personal Relationships, 23*(6), 843–864.

Holmberg, D., Blair, K. L., & Phillips, M. (2010). Women's sexual satisfaction as a predictor of well-being in same-sex versus mixed-sex relationships. *The Journal of Sex Research, 47*(1), 1–11. doi:10.1080/00224490902898710

Hyde, J. S., Krajnik, M., & Skuldt-Niederberger, K. (1991). Androgyny across the lifespan: A replication and longitudinal follow-up. *Developmental Psychology, 27* (3), 516–519. doi:10.1037/0012–1649.27.3.516

Jackson, R. (2000). *The global covenant: Human conduct in a world of states.* New York, NY: Oxford Press.

Kurdek, L. A. (2006). Differences between partners from heterosexual, gay, and lesbian cohabiting couples. *Journal of Marriage and Family, 68*(2), 509–528. doi:10.1111/j.1741-3737.2006.00268.x

Lehmiller, J. J., & Agnew, C. R. (2006). Marginalized relationships: The impact of social disapproval on romantic relationship commitment. *Personality and Social Psychology Bulletin, 32,* 40–51.

Liebler, C. A., & Sandefur, G. D. (2002). Gender differences in the exchange of social support with friends, neighbors, and co-workers at midlife. *Social Science Research, 31*(3), 364–391. doi:10.1016/S0049-089X(02)00006-6

Magai, C., Consedine, N. S., Fiori, K. L., & King, A. R. (2009). Sharing the good, sharing the bad: The benefits of emotional self-disclosure among middle-aged and older adults. *Journal of Aging and Health*, 21(2), 286–313. doi:10.1177/0898264308328980

Malinen, K., Rönkä, A., & Sevón, E. (2010). Good moments in parents' spousal relationships: A daily relational maintenance perspective. *Family Sciences*, 1(3–4), 230–241. doi:10.1080/19424620.2010.570968

Marks, L. D., Hopkins, K., Chaney, C., Monroe, P. A., Nesteruk, O., & Sasser, D. D. (2008). "Together, we are stronger": A qualitative study of happy, enduring African American marriages. *Family Relations*, 57(2), 172–185. doi:10.1111/j.1741-3729.2008.00492.x

Marshall, T. C. (2009). Gender, peer relations, and intimate romantic relationships. In J. C. Chrisler & D. R. McCreary (Eds.), *Gender research in social and applied psychology* (Vol. 2, pp. 281–310). New York, NY: Springer.

McAdoo, J. L. (1993). The roles of African American fathers: An ecological perspective. *Families in Society*, 74(1), 28–35.

McIsaac, C., Connolly, J., McKenney, K. S., Pepler, D., & Craig, W. (2008). Conflict negotiation and autonomy processes in adolescent romantic relationships: An observational study of interdependency in boyfriend and girlfriend effects. *Journal of Adolescence*, 31(6), 691–707. doi:10.1016/j.adolescence.2008.08.005

McLoyd, V. C., Hill, N. E., & Dodge, K. A. (2005). *African American family life: Ecological and cultural diversity*. New York, NY: Guilford.

Metz, M. E., Rosser, B. R. S., & Strapko, N. (1994). Differences in conflict-resolution styles among heterosexual, gay, and lesbian couples. *The Journal of Sex Research*, 31(4), 293–308.

Miller, A. J., Worthington, E. L., & McDaniel, M. A. (2008). Gender and forgiveness: A meta-analytic review and research agenda. *Journal of Social and Clinical Psychology*, 27(8), 843–876.

Mills, J., & Clark, M. S. (1982). Exchange and communal relationships. *Review of Personality and Social Psychology*, 3, 133–156.

Murry, V. M., Brown, P. A., Brody, G. H., Cutrona, C. E., & Simons, R. L. (2001). Racial discrimination as a moderator of the links among stress, maternal psychological functioning, and family relationships. *Journal of Marriage and Family*, 63(4), 915–926. doi:10.1111/j.1741-3737.2001.00915.x

Ogolsky, B. G. (2009). Deconstructing the association between relationship maintenance and commitment: Testing two competing models. *Personal Relationships*, 16(1), 99–115.

Ogolsky, B. G., & Bowers, J. R. (2013). A meta-analytic review of relationship maintenance and its correlates. *Journal of Social and Personal Relationships*, 30(3), 343–367. doi:10.1177/0265407512463338

Ogolsky, B. G., & Gray, C. R. (2016). Conflict, negative emotion, and reports of partners' relationship maintenance in same-sex couples. *Journal of Family Psychology*, 30(2), 171–180. doi:10.1037/fam0000148

Ogolsky, B. G., Monk, J. K., Rice, T. M., Theisen, J. C., & Maniotes, C. R. (2017). Relationship maintenance: A review of research on romantic relationships. *Journal of Family Theory & Review*, 9(3), 275–306.

Orbuch, T. L., Bauermeister, J. A., Brown, E., & McKinley, B. (2013). Early family ties and marital stability over 16 years: The context of race and gender. *Family Relations*, 62(2), 255–268. doi:10.1111/fare.12005

Orbuch, T. L., & Eyster, S. L. (1997). Division of household labor among black couples and white couples. *Social Forces*, 76(1), 301–332. doi:10.1093/sf/76.1.301

Orbuch, T. L., Veroff, J., & Hunter, A. G. (1999). Black couples, white couples: The early years of marriage. In E. M. Hetherington (Ed.), *Coping with divorce, single parenting, and remarriage: A risk and resiliency perspective* (pp. 23–43). Mahwah, NJ: Lawrence Erlbaum.

Ottu, I. F. (2012). Psychological health indexing in marriage: A pilot study of empathic-accuracy, personal-relational dialectics, and gender in relationship maintenance among Ibibio couples. *IFE PsychologIA*, *20*(1), 294–322.

Plummer, D. L., & Slane, S. (1996). Patterns of coping in racially stressful situations. *Journal of Black Psychology*, *22*(3), 302–315. doi:10.1177/00957984960223002

Ragsdale, J. D. (1996). Gender, satisfaction level, and the use of relational maintenance strategies in marriage. *Communication Monographs*, *63*(4), 354–369. doi:10.1080/03637759609376399

Ragsdale, J. D., & Brandau-Brown, F. E. (2005). Individual differences in the use of relational maintenance strategies in marriage. *Journal of Family Communication*, *5*(1), 61–75. doi:10.1207/s15327698jfc0501_4

Rauer, A. J., & Volling, B. L. (2013). More than one way to be happy: A typology of marital happiness. *Family Process*, *52*, 519–534.

Rodriguez, Y., Helms, H. M., Supple, J. A., & Hengstebeck, N. D. (2016). Mexican immigrant wives' acculturative stress and spouses' marital quality: The role of wives' marriage work with husbands and close friends. *Journal of Family Issues*, *37*(12), 1678–1702. doi:10.1177/0192513X14561519

Sarkisian, N., & Gerstel, N. (2004). Kin support among Blacks and Whites: Race and family organization. *American Sociological Review*, *69*(6), 812–837. doi:10.1177/000312240406900604

Sprecher, S. (2001). Equality and social exchange in dating couples: Associations with satisfaction, commitment, and stability. *Journal of Marriage and Family*, *63*(3), 599–613. doi:10.1111/j.1741-3737.2001.00599.x

Stafford, L. (2003). Maintaining romantic relationships. In D. J. Canary & M. Dainton (Eds.), *Maintaining relationships through communication: Relational, contextual, and cultural variations* (pp. 51–77). New York, NY: Psychology Press.

Stafford, L., & Canary, D. J. (1991). Maintenance strategies and romantic relationship type, gender and relational characteristics. *Journal of Social and Personal Relationships*, *8*(2), 217–242. doi:10.1177/0265407591082004

Stafford, L., & Canary, D. J. (2006). Equity and interdependence as predictors of relational maintenance strategies. *The Journal of Family Communication*, *6*(4), 227–254. doi:10.1207/s15327698jfc0604_1

Stafford, L., Dainton, M., & Haas, S. (2000). Measuring routine and strategic relational maintenance: Scale revision, sex versus gender roles, and the prediction of relational characteristics. *Communication Monographs*, *63*(3), 306–323. doi:10.1080/03637750009376512

Steinbugler, A. C. (2012). *Beyond loving: Intimate racework in lesbian, gay, and straight interracial relationships*. New York, NY: Oxford University Press.

Taylor, J. R., & Chatters, L. M. (1988). Church members as a source of informal social support. *Review of Religious Research*, *30*(2), 193–203. doi:10.2307/3511355

Taylor, R. J., Chatters, L. M., & Celious, A. (2003). Extended family households among Black Americans. *African American Research Perspectives*, *9*(1), 133–151.

Taylor, S. E., Klein, L. C., Lewis, B. P., Gruenewald, T. L., Gurung, R. A. R., & Updegraff, J. A. (2000). Biobehavioral responses to stress in females: Tend-and-befriend, not fight-or-flight. *Psychological Review*, *107*(3), 411–429. doi:10.1037/0033-295X.107.3.411

Thibaut, J. W., & Kelley, H. H. (1959). *The social psychology of groups*. New York, NY: Wiley.

Twenge, J. M. (1997). Changes in masculine and feminine traits over time: A meta-analysis. *Sex Roles, 36*(5–6), 305–325.

Van Yperen, N. W., & Buunk, B. P. (1990). A longitudinal study of equity and satisfaction in intimate relationships. *European Journal of Social Psychology, 20,* 287–309.

Veroff, J., Douvan, E., & Hatchett, S. (1995). *Marital instability.* Westport, CT: Praeger.

Weigel, D. J., & Ballard-Reisch, D. S. (1999). How couples maintain marriages: A closer look at self and spouse influences upon the use of maintenance behaviors in marriages. *Family Relations, 48*(3), 263–269. doi:10.2307/585635

Weigel, D. J., & Ballard-Reisch, D. S. (2008). Relational maintenance, satisfaction, and commitment in marriages: An actor-partner analysis. *Journal of Family Communications, 8*(3), 212–229. doi:10.1080/15267430802182522

Relationship Maintenance across Cultural Groups

STANLEY O. GAINES, JR.[1] AND NELLI FERENCZI[2]

Certainly the relationships between culture and personality are too profound and too complex to treat briefly. More for the sake of completeness than for any other reason[,] it must be pointed out that in general[,] the paths by which the main goals in life are achieved are often determined by the nature of the particular culture. The ways in which self-esteem may be expressed and achieved are in large part, although not completely, culturally determined. The same is true for the love relations. We win the love of other people and express our affections for them through culturally approved channels. The fact that[,] in a complex society, status roles are also in part culturally determined will often shift the expression of personality syndromes....

Abraham H. Maslow,
Motivation and Personality (1970, 2nd ed., p. 314)

In *Marriage, a History: How Love Conquered Marriage*, Stephanie Coontz (2005) credited humanistic psychologist Abraham Maslow (1954) with anticipating Americans' post–World War II shift from prioritizing fulfillment of their deficit-oriented or "lower" psychological needs to prioritizing fulfillment of their growth-oriented or "higher" needs. Furthermore, in a target article from *Psychological Inquiry* on "The Suffocation of Marriage: Climbing Mount Maslow without Enough Oxygen," subsequently, Eli Finkel and colleagues (Finkel, Hui, Carswell, & Larson, 2014) contended that Americans' post–Women's Rights Era shift from prioritizing fulfillment of their already-high love/belonging needs to prioritizing fulfillment of their still-higher esteem/respect and self-actualization needs could be understood as a logical consequence of Americans' long-term progression through Maslow's (1943; 1970) hierarchy of needs. Finally, in *Personality and Close Relationship Processes*, Stanley Gaines (2016) argued that Maslow's (1954) *self-actualization theory* (which emphasizes the positive aspects of human nature) deserves greater

[1] Centre for Culture and Evolution, Brunel University London, Stanley.Gaines@brunel.ac.uk
[2] Regent's University London, n.ferenczi@gold.ac.uk
The authors are grateful to Brian Ogolsky and Kale Monk for their insightful comments regarding previous versions of the present chapter.

attention than it has received within relationship science as a conceptual framework for hypothesizing and testing links between individuals' achieved self-actualization and interdependence processes (the latter of which may be interpreted as relationship maintenance processes; Lydon & Quinn, 2013) within and beyond the USA.

In a critique of Maslow's (1968) self-actualization theory, Robert Ewen (1998) noted that the results of Maslow's psychobiographical "study" of self-actualized persons (some of whom were alive, others of whom were deceased, at the time that Maslow wrote about them) omit many details regarding demographic characteristics of the persons in question. For example, Maslow did not disclose self-actualizers' socioeconomic status (SES) – a variable that, according to Cohen (2009; 2010), is an indicator of culture (although SES might be better conceptualized as a covariate of individuals' cultural group membership, rather than a cultural variable per se; e.g., Markus, 2008; Phinney, 1996). However, David McClelland (1985/1987) concluded that much of the appeal regarding Maslow's self-actualization theory can be attributed to the implicit sociopolitical message that persons from disadvantaged backgrounds (including low-SES and/or ethnic minority groups) were less likely to obtain opportunities to become self-actualized than were persons from advantaged backgrounds within a given (e.g., American) society. Furthermore, as the quote that we cited at the beginning of the present chapter indicates, Maslow (1970) overtly acknowledged that culture may be reflected in the ways that individuals fulfill (or, alternatively, fail to fulfill) their psychological needs.

The present chapter addresses relationship maintenance among members of various cultural groups, where *culture* is defined as "a system of solutions to unlearned problems, as well as of learned problems and their solutions, acquired by members of a recognizable group and shared by them" (Ullman, 1965, p. 5). Among several definitions of relationship maintenance that Dindia and Canary (1993) identified within the relationship science literature, we will emphasize the overlapping definitions of relationship maintenance as (a) keeping a relationship continued in a specified state and (b) keeping a relationship in a satisfactory condition (both of which are embedded within interdependence theory; Kelley, 1979; Kelley & Thibaut, 1978; Thibaut & Kelley, 1959). First, we examine (1) Maslow's self-actualization theory in general (e.g., Maslow, 1968; 1970; 1971) and (2) Finkel and colleagues' suffocation model of marriage in particular (e.g., Finkel, Cheung, Emery, Carswell, & Larson, 2015; Finkel, Hui, et al., 2014; Finkel, Larson, Carswell, & Hui, 2014) as the primary conceptual foundations of the present chapter. Second, we transition from our conceptual framework to our review of relevant empirical studies by introducing an East–West dichotomy (proposed by Cho & Gilgen, 1980; Gilgen & Cho, 1979a,b) that, in principle, can be applied to studies of culture and relationship maintenance.

Finally, we examine the extent to which results of studies concerning (1) mean differences and similarities in scores on a variety of relationship maintenance behaviors across two or more cultural groups, as well as (2) cultural group membership as a moderator of links between relationship maintenance behaviors and other relational variables, can be understood from the vantage point of the suffocation model (supplementing self-actualization theory and the suffocation model with the self-expansion model of Aron & Aron, 1986, in the process).

CONCEPTUAL BACKGROUND FOR THE PRESENT CHAPTER

Self-actualization theory. Maslow's self-actualization theory (e.g., Maslow, 1968; 1970; 1971) was derived partly from Kurt Goldstein's (1939; 1940) *organismic psychology*, which is based on the premise that a single motive (i.e., *self-actualization*, or the need to fulfill one's inner potential) is central to individuals' physical and psychological well-being (Hall & Lindzey, 1970). Notably, Maslow's hierarchy of needs (i.e., physiological, safety, love/belonging, esteem/respect, and self-actualization, listed from "lowest" to "highest") is by no means limited to self-actualization. However, Maslow believed that self-actualization is the most difficult need for individuals to fulfill, partly because individuals must fulfill all of the other needs to some extent – in sequence – before they can realistically hope to attain self-actualization (Ewen, 1998).

In an early synopsis of self-actualization theory, Maslow (1943) contended that most (if not all) persons are unaware of the needs that largely determine their own behavior. Thus, Maslow conceived of individuals' need fulfillment as a set of primarily unconscious processes. Nevertheless, from the perspective of some modern-day positive psychologists who have acknowledged the influence of Maslow's (1971) self-actualization theory (e.g., Oishi, Diener, Lucas, & Suh, 1999) on their research, individuals are aware of their own pursuit of happiness (e.g., achieving life satisfaction as part of their overall *subjective well-being*; Diener, Oishi, & Lucas, 2003) via their entry into particular social roles within a given society (e.g., wage earner, spouse). (In fact, the first edition of *Toward a Psychology of Being* contained a chapter that alluded to "positive psychology"; Maslow, 1962.) Therefore, even though individuals might not be able to explain how psychological needs are reflected in their own behavior, they realize that adopting versus forfeiting (or, perhaps, relinquishing) certain social roles over the short term can make them happier versus less happy over the long term (see also Ryan & Deci, 2001).

Maslow (1943) refrained from claiming in absolute terms that his hierarchy of needs was universal across all individuals, from all cultural groups. Nevertheless, Maslow (1970) believed that (a) culture is highly relevant to the behavior that is more versus less likely to help individuals fulfill their needs (e.

g., entry into specific social roles), whereas (b) culture is *not* especially relevant to individuals' possession of those needs in the first instance. One important implication of Maslow's self-actualization theory is that different societies (and, for that matter, different ethnic groups within a particular society) may offer different means by which individuals can fulfill the same psychological needs (see Gaines, 1997).

The suffocation model. As we noted earlier in the present chapter, Finkel and colleagues' (e.g., Finkel et al., 2015; Finkel, Hui, et al., 2014; Finkel, Larson, et al., 2014) suffocation model of marriage was inspired largely by Maslow's (e. g., Maslow, 1943; 1970) self-actualization theory. According to the suffocation model, Americans in the post–Women's Rights Era are more likely to seek fulfillment of their esteem/respect and self-actualization needs (and, conversely, are *less* likely to seek fulfilment of their physiological and safety needs) within the context of marriage than has been the case at any other time in US history (Gaines, 2016). Although Maslow's hierarchy of needs is faithfully reflected in Finkel and colleagues' suffocation model, it is clear that the suffocation model is more cognitive in its orientation than is self-actualization theory (possibly due to Finkel's conviction that a principle of *instrumentality* or individual-oriented, consciously experienced pattern of goal-directed behavior is fundamental to all interpersonal attraction processes in which individuals are involved; e.g., Finkel & Eastwick, 2015).

The unconscious versus conscious orientation is one of several distinctions that we can make between Maslow's (e.g., Maslow, 1943; 1970) self-actualization theory and Finkel and colleagues' (e.g., Finkel et al., 2015; Finkel, Hui, et al., 2014; Finkel, Larson, et al., 2014) suffocation model. For example, self-actualization theory is not limited in scope to any particular nation or institution, whereas the suffocation model focuses squarely on individuals and marriages within the USA. Also, self-actualization theory emphasizes individual *similarities* in psychological needs, whereas the suffocation model raises the possibility of individual *differences* in psychological needs. In addition, self-actualization theory assumes that human nature is essentially positive (although societies frequently prevent individuals from fulfilling their true potential), whereas the suffocation model makes no assumptions regarding human nature as positive versus negative. Finally, self-actualization theory ultimately emphasizes individual-level personality processes, whereas the suffocation model ultimately emphasizes dyad-level behavioral processes.

Like Maslow's (e.g., Maslow, 1943; 1970) self-actualization theory, Finkel and colleagues' (e.g., Finkel et al., 2015; Finkel, Hui, et al., 2014; Finkel, Larson, et al., 2014) suffocation model can be criticized for not attending sufficiently to SES and/or (other) bases for cultural group membership as influences on individuals' behavior (e.g., Pietromonaco & Perry-Jenkins, 2014). Moreover, both Maslow and Finkel and colleagues responded to their critics in ways that might invite further criticism. However, like Maslow, Finkel and colleagues were careful not to rule out the prospect of cultural group differences in the behavioral paths through which individuals end up fulfilling (or failing to fulfill) their psychological needs. In this connection, cultural differences can be conceptualized in a sociogeographic framework of an East–West dichotomy, and these predict differences in individual, relational, and group processes (e.g., Hofstede, 2001; Markus & Kitayama, 1991; 1994; 2010). Thus, this approach can provide one lens through which differences in relationship maintenance behaviors and further, the role of relationships in the fulfilment of psychological needs can be understood.

PROMISE AND PITFALLS: APPLYING AN EAST–WEST DICHOTOMY TO STUDIES OF RELATIONSHIP MAINTENANCE ACROSS CULTURAL GROUPS

Gilgen and Cho (1979b; Cho & Gilgen, 1980) contended that Eastern (i.e., nondualistic) and Western (i.e., dualistic) value systems differ along five dimensions: (1) *Man and the spiritual*; (2) *man and nature*; (3) *man and society*; (4) *man and himself*; and (5) *the rationality (and nonrationality) of man*. However, Gilgen and Cho's East-West Questionnaire (EWQ) operationalizes "Eastern (versus Western) thought" as a single, bipolar dimension (for a review, see Braithwaite & Scott, 1991). In any event, we are not aware of any research within relationship science in which the EWQ has been administered. Part of the problem may be that many researchers in relationship science and other fields within the social sciences use national group membership as a proxy for Eastern versus Western values rather than measuring those values directly. This is part of a broader issue concerning the use of nationality as a stand-in for cultural values, self-construals, and related constructs within much of cultural psychology (for a critique of this practice, see Matsumoto, 1999).

How useful is an East–West dichotomy for understanding relationship maintenance across cultural groups? On the one hand, Gaines and Hardin (2013) speculated that the construct of loyalty (i.e., individuals' passive, yet constructive, responses to partners' anger or criticism; Rusbult, Verette, Whitney, Slovik, & Lipkus, 1991) – which forms part of the higher-order relationship maintenance construct of accommodation (i.e., individuals' pattern of constructive, rather than destructive, responses to partners' anger or criticism; see also Rusbult & Buunk, 1993) – has not been consistently correlated with other relationship-relevant variables within Western nations (usually the USA; Drigotas, Whitney, & Rusbult, 1995) and warrants further consideration within Eastern nations. On the other hand, Gaines and Ketay (2013) concluded that the East–West dichotomy did not demonstrate sufficient promise as a conceptual tool for understanding cultural influences on inclusion of other in the self (i.e., individuals' cognitive blurring of boundaries between significant others and themselves; Aron, Aron, & Smollan, 1992) – which forms part of the higher-order relationship maintenance construct of cognitive interdependence (i.e., mutual influence of relationship partners upon each other's thoughts; see Agnew, van Lange, Rusbult, & Langston, 1998) – to warrant further consideration. At first glance, the utility of a simple East–West dichotomy seems to be debatable (see also Gaines, 1997).

Goodwin and Pillay (2006) concluded that cultural group membership was best conceived (1) as a direct influence on *levels* of relationship-related variables and (2) as a moderating influence on *covariance* among relationship-related variables. Exactly *which* cultural group memberships matter, however, is not entirely clear; Goodwin and Pillay mentioned Western versus non-Western groups, as well as Western versus Eastern groups, in their coverage of culture and relationship dynamics within a historical context of social change. If the East–West dichotomy is viewed as a panoramic, sociocultural lens through which one might profitably view relationship maintenance as a dynamic process that is subject to change across and within historical cohorts, then perhaps the East–West dichotomy demonstrates promise after all (see also Goodwin, 1999). Next, we turn to the role of cultural group membership (operationalized as Eastern relative to Western cultures within the global and particular sociopolitical and national contexts) both as a direct predictor of relationship-maintenance behaviors and as a moderator of their association with other relationship-relevant factors.

IMPACT OF CULTURAL GROUP MEMBERSHIP ON MEAN LEVELS OF RELATIONSHIP MAINTENANCE BEHAVIORS

National group membership as a predictor. Finkel and colleagues' suffocation model does not make explicit predictions concerning mean levels of relationship maintenance behaviors across national groups. However, in their target article, which introduced the suffocation model to the relationship science literature, Finkel and colleagues (Finkel, Hui, et al., 2014) hinted at an overall East–West difference, such that persons from Eastern nations were less likely to have ascended from a *companionate era* (during which individuals tend to prioritize fulfillment of their love/belongingness need) to a *self-expressive era* (during which individuals tend to prioritize fulfilment of their esteem/respect and self-actualization needs; Finkel et al., 2015) than were Americans or persons from other Western nations. Given the heightened demands on individuals' highest-order need fulfillment in romantic relationships (including nonmarital relationships, which frequently serve as the basis for marital relationships; see Le, Dove, Agnew, Korn, & Mutso, 2010) within the USA relative to romantic relationships within Eastern nations, we expect that Americans will need to work harder than persons within Eastern nations just to maintain their relationships. We hasten to add, however, that the central tenets of the suffocation model (elaborated by Finkel, Larson, et al., 2014) often refer solely to the USA.

In a study of five relationship maintenance behaviors (i.e., positivity, assurances, openness, sharing tasks, and social networks, as measured by the Relational Maintenance Strategies Measure, or RMSM; Stafford & Canary, 1991) among individuals in romantic (primarily nonmarital) relationships, Yum and Li (2007) compared scores from two large US samples (i.e., one sample from the continental USA and one sample from Hawaii) and one large South Korean sample. Yum and Li conducted their research prior to the development of Finkel and colleagues' (e.g., Finkel et al., 2015; Finkel, Hui, et al., 2014; Finkel, Larson, et al., 2014) suffocation model. Nevertheless, Yum and Li's results were in the direction that we would expect (i.e., on average, individuals in both the US samples scored significantly higher on all five of the relationship maintenance behaviors than did individuals in the South Korean sample).

In another study of the five relationship maintenance behaviors in question (measured by a slightly revised RMSM; Canary & Stafford, 1992) among individuals in romantic (mostly nonmarital) relationships, Yum and colleagues (Yum, Canary, & Baptist, 2015) compared scores from one large US sample, one large Malaysian sample, and one medium-to-large Singaporean sample. The result of the USA–Singapore comparison was in the direction that we would expect (i.e., on average, individuals in the US sample scored significantly higher on all five of the relationship maintenance behaviors than did individuals in the Singapore sample). However, results of comparisons involving Malaysia were inconsistent with our predictions. On average, individuals in Malaysia scored significantly higher on all five of the relationship-maintenance behaviors than did individuals in Singapore. Individuals in the US and Malaysian samples did not score significantly differently from each other on three of the five relationship maintenance behaviors, although US scores were significantly higher for assurances and social networks than were Malaysian scores.

Finally, in yet another study of the five relationship maintenance behaviors in question (measured by the slightly revised RMSM; Canary & Stafford, 1992) among individuals in romantic (mostly nonmarital) relationships, Yum and Canary (2009) compared scores from one large US sample, one large Spanish sample, one small-to-medium Czech sample, one large South Korean sample, one medium-to-large Chinese sample, and one medium-to-large Japanese sample. Yum and Canary's results generally were in the direction that we would expect. On average, individuals in the US and

Spanish samples scored significantly higher on all five of the relationship maintenance behaviors than did individuals in the South Korean, Chinese, and Japanese samples. Individuals in the US and Spanish samples did not score significantly differently from each other on any of the relationship maintenance behaviors. With some exceptions, individuals in the South Korean, Chinese, and Japanese samples did not score significantly differently from each other on the relationship maintenance behaviors. Although we did not make predictions concerning the Czech sample (given that the Czech Republic does not fit neatly within the East–West dichotomy), we note that individuals from that sample tended to fall between the Western and Eastern samples on relationship maintenance behaviors. It should also be noted that the Czech Republic experienced a transition in the 1990s from a socialist Eastern Bloc country (which reflected collectivist values) to a Western-style system. In this vein, the nation-level score for the Individualism–Collectivism dimension for the Czech Republic falls approximately in the middle of the spectrum, lower than other Western European and North American countries (58/100; Hofstede, 2001; Hofstede, Hofstede, & Minkov, 2010). Indeed, Czech participants reported greater individualism *and* collectivism compared with Vietnamese participants living in the Czech Republic. Taken together, these findings parallel the trends for Yum and Canary's study (2009).

Why did we not receive more support for our a posteriori hypotheses regarding Finkel and colleagues' (e.g., Finkel et al., 2015; Finkel, Hui, et al., 2014; Finkel, Larson, et al., 2014) suffocation model from the Malaysian sample in the Yum et al. (2015) study? As it turns out, Yum et al.'s results generally were consistent with Inglehart's (1997; Inglehart & Baker, 2000; Inglehart & Welzel, 2005) *cultural modernization theory* (which posits that nations differ in their emphasis on promoting individuals' survival versus self-expression values and in their emphasis on promoting individuals' secular/rational versus traditional/religious values; see Goodwin, 1999) – a theory which, in its current form, indirectly bears the influence of Maslow's (1968) self-actualization theory (for a review of Maslow's influence on an early version of Inglehart's cultural modernization theory, see Braithwaite & Scott, 1991). Specifically, the USA and Malaysia tend to emphasize self-expression values, whereas Singapore tends to emphasize survival values (see also Ogolsky, Monk, Rice, Theisen, & Maniotes, 2017). (Following Gaines, 2016, we define *values* as individuals' answer to the question "What do you believe in?", whereas we define *needs* or *motives* as individuals' answer to the question "What drives you to do what you do?", with the caveat that individuals do not necessarily know the answer to that latter question.) Finkel and colleagues did not cite Inglehart's cultural modernization theory. Perhaps the East–West dichotomy that is explicit in much of cultural psychology (e.g., Fiske, Kitayama, Markus, & Nisbett, 1998) – and implicit in Finkel and colleagues' suffocation model – is insufficient to account for cultural group differences in relationship-maintenance behaviors (see

Heine, 2010, for a perspective from cultural psychology that transcends the East–West dichotomy).

Notwithstanding the partial support for our predictions in the study by Yum et al. (2015), results of studies comparing Eastern versus Western nations generally support our hypothesis (based on our interpretation of Finkel and colleagues' suffocation model) that individuals in Western nations tend to report higher levels of relationship maintenance behaviors than do individuals in Eastern nations (see Yum & Canary, 2003, for summaries of additional studies that support our hypothesis, comparing scores for persons in the USA with scores for persons in South Korea). Given that most of the relevant studies compared samples from one Western nation (i.e., the USA) with samples from a handful of East Asian nations, we cannot be certain about the generality of the results (see Fiske et al., 1998, for a discussion of the prevalence of studies in cultural psychology that compare American and/or Western European samples with East Asian samples). Nevertheless, based on the pattern of results that has emerged to date, we believe that the suffocation model shows promise as a conceptual tool for developing culturally informed hypotheses concerning individuals' attempts to maintain their romantic relationships.

Ethnic group membership, within a given nation, as a predictor. So far, we have approached studies of cultural group membership and relationship maintenance from the standpoint of *cross-cultural psychology*, which tends to equate cultural group membership with nationality (e.g., Goodwin, 1999). However, the field of cultural psychology also includes *ethnic psychology*, which tends to equate cultural group membership with race (and, less often, religion) within a given nation (e.g., Gaines, 1997). In the remainder of the present section, we shall consider ethnic (and, specifically, racial) group membership as a predictor of individuals' relationship-maintenance behaviors.

Based on our understanding of Finkel and colleagues' (e.g., Finkel et al., 2015; Finkel, Hui, et al., 2014; Finkel, Larson, et al., 2014) suffocation model, we would not expect to find ethnic group differences in relationship maintenance within a particular nation unless the ethnic groups in question are (1) Asian-descent persons (who, presumably, are more likely to embrace Eastern culture) and (2) European-descent persons (who, presumably, are more likely to embrace Western culture; Fiske et al., 1998). In the aforementioned study by Yum and Li (2007), European-descent persons from the US mainland were compared with a diverse array of Hawaiians, approximately two-thirds of whom could be characterized as Asian-descent. Yum and Li found that their US mainland and Hawaii samples did not differ significantly on any of the relationship maintenance behaviors (as measured by the original RMSM; Stafford & Canary, 1991). Although we appreciate Yum and Li's stated rationale for including their entire Hawaiian sample in their analyses (i.e., the disparity in subsample sizes made it impractical for them to exclude members of any of the non-Asian-descent groups purely on statistical grounds; see Tabachnick & Fidell, 2007), we are not sure why non-European-descent persons apparently were excluded from their US mainland sample. In any event, we are not surprised at their lack of significant findings concerning ethnic group differences in relationship maintenance behaviors.

Another relevant study concerning ethnic group differences within a particular nation is Ballard-Reisch, Weigel, and Zaguidoulline's (1999) study of relationship-maintenance behaviors among married couples within Russia. Data were collected from a large sample of couples in Russian-only marriages, a large sample of couples in Tatar-only marriages, and a small-to-medium sample of couples in Russian–Tatar marriages regarding relationship maintenance behaviors (as measured by the slightly revised RMSM; Canary & Stafford, 1992). In the absence of clearly defined Eastern or Western samples, our reading of Finkel and colleagues' (e.g., Finkel et al., 2015; Finkel, Hui, et al., 2014; Finkel, Larson, et al., 2014) suffocation model would not lead us to predict differences among the couple pairings in question. Indeed, results indicated that couples in the three types of marriages did not differ significantly on any of the relationship-maintenance behaviors. These findings may reflect the still uncertain and changing cultural context of Tatarstan following its transition in 1994 from a former Soviet republic (with an overarching national, collectivist membership, which was argued to supersede ethnic group membership) to an independent republic with its own political system and an opportunity to reclaim religious and cultural traditions (Ballard-Reisch et al., 1999). Here again, the West–East dichotomy does not account for the particular historical context.

Of course, any results that essentially confirm the null hypothesis must be interpreted with caution, especially where one or two studies are involved (see Hayes, 2013). Nonetheless, Finkel and colleagues (Finkel et al., 2015; Finkel, Hui, et al., 2014) specifically advised relationship scientists against making ethnic group comparisons unless a substantive conceptual case underpins the comparisons. On the basis of the evidence that we have uncovered, we conclude that – when East–West comparisons are not feasible – within-nation ethnic group differences in relationship maintenance are nonexistent.

COVARIANCE BETWEEN RELATIONSHIP MAINTENANCE BEHAVIORS AND OTHER RELATIONSHIP-RELEVANT VARIABLES: THE MODERATING ROLE OF CULTURAL GROUP MEMBERSHIP

National group membership as a moderator. As far as we can tell, Finkel and colleagues' (e.g., Finkel et al., 2015; Finkel, Hui, et al., 2014; Finkel, Larson, et al., 2014) suffocation model does not anticipate an East–West difference in *covariance* between individuals' scores on relationship maintenance behaviors and individuals' scores on other relationship-relevant behaviors. However, Arthur Aron and Elaine Aron's (1986) *self-expansion model* (which posits that individuals are motivated to form close relationships in an effort to incorporate other persons into their selves) was built largely upon Maslow's (1971) self-actualization theory (although Aron and Aron have de-emphasized the self-actualization roots of their self-expansion model in recent years; e.g., Aron, Lewandowski, Mashek, & Aron, 2013) and, in turn, served as one of the conceptual building blocks for Finkel and colleagues' suffocation model (although Finkel expressed reservations about the reward-versus-cost emphasis of the self-expansion model; e.g., Finkel & Eastwick, 2015). Aron and Aron's self-expansion model offers testable hypotheses concerning national group membership as a moderating influence on relationship processes, highlighting the extent to which such processes do or do not generalize beyond the USA (see Aron, Norman, & Aron, 2001; see also Xu, Lewandowski, & Aron, Chapter 6).

With regard to the impact of perceived equity (as measured by the Hatfield Global Measure, or HGM; Hatfield, Walster, & Berscheid, 1978) on relationship-maintenance behaviors (as measured by the slightly modified RMSM by Canary & Stafford, 1992), according to Aron and Aron's (1986) self-expansion model, we would expect an equity norm (i.e., to the extent that individuals perceive themselves as neither underbenefitting nor overbenefitting in their close relationships, those individuals will tend to engage in the highest levels of relationship maintenance behaviors) to govern relationship processes within Western nations in general, and within the USA in particular. The results of the aforementioned study by Yum and Canary (2009) support such predictions. Within the USA, individuals who perceived their relationships as equitable scored significantly higher on all five relationship-maintenance behaviors than did persons who viewed themselves as underbenefitting or overbenefitting. Similar results were obtained within Spain, although the differences were marginal rather than significant. In contrast, Yum and Canary's results do not support the existence of such a norm within Eastern nations (or in nations that fall outside the East–West dichotomy). In fact, within the South Korean sample (but not within the Chinese or Japanese samples), individuals who viewed themselves as *overbenefitting* were significantly more likely to engage in positivity, openness, and assurances than were individuals who viewed their relationships as equitable or who viewed themselves as underbenefitting in their relationships. Aron and Aron's self-expansion model would explain the latter finding in terms of a greater emphasis on a higher, panhuman, capital-*S* Self that presumably encompasses all human, small-*s* selves in some Eastern nations (i.e., overbenefitting leads individuals to try to

reestablish harmony in their relationships in service of the panhuman Self;
Aron & Aron, 1996) compared with some Western nations.

The results of the aforementioned study by Yum et al. (2015) similarly
support an equity norm only for Western nations, such that the tendency for
individuals who viewed their relationships as equitable (measured by the
HGM; Hatfield et al., 1978) to engage in relationship maintenance behaviors
(measured by the slightly revised RMSM; Canary & Stafford, 1992) at significantly higher levels compared with underbenefitted or overbenefitted individuals held true only for the USA. However, the results of Yum et al. did not
support our prediction regarding an alternative, Eastern-nation-specific effect
concerning overbenefitting individuals displaying relationship-maintenance
behaviors at different levels than did individuals who viewed their relationships as equitable or as underbenefitting. The results of the study by Yum et al.
(2015) lead us to wonder to what extent Yum and Canary's (2009) earlier,
South Korea–specific findings, which had linked overbenefitting patterns and
relationship maintenance, were simply anomalous rather than indicative of a
broader trend across some Eastern nations.

In the aforementioned study by Yum and Li (2007), perceived equity
(Hatfield et al., 1978) was replaced by attachment style (Bartholomew &
Horowitz, 1991; see also Guerrero & Bachman, 2006) as a predictor of relationship maintenance behaviors (Stafford & Canary, 1991). Unlike the impact of
perceived equity on relationship maintenance behaviors, it is not clear why
(from the standpoint of the self-expansion model; Aron & Aron, 1986)
national group membership should be relevant to the impact of attachment
style on relationship maintenance behaviors. Indeed, Yum and Li found that
the main effect of attachment style (i.e., securely attached individuals displayed significantly higher levels of all relationship maintenance behaviors
except tasks compared with insecurely attached individuals) did not differ
significantly between individuals from the USA (including the mainland and
Hawaii) and South Korea.

The null results by Yum and Li (2007) concerning the would-be moderation effect of national group membership on links between attachment styles
and relationship maintenance behaviors deserves further comment.
Influenced by Bowlby's (1977) attachment theory, Yum and Li operationalized
attachment style in terms of a secure–insecure dichotomy. However, influenced by Bartholomew's (1990) typology of secure, preoccupied, fearful-
avoidant, and anxious-avoidant individuals, Yum and Li measured attachment style in terms of one secure attachment style and *three* insecure attachment styles (using the Relationship Questionnaire, or RQ; Bartholomew &
Horowitz, 1991). One could argue that three of Bartholomew's attachment
styles are compatible with Hatfield, Traupmann, Sprecher, Utne, and May's
(1985) three equity categories (i.e., secure attachment style overlaps with
individuals' perception of their relationships as equitable, preoccupied

attachment style overlaps with individuals' perception of underbenefitting, and fearful-avoidant attachment style overlaps with individuals' perception of overbenefitting; the dismissing-avoidant attachment style reflects disengagement with close relationships and, thus, does not map neatly onto components of an equity typology; see Hazan & Shaver, 1994a, b). However, Yum and Li did not suggest such a synthesis of attachment theory (Bowlby, 1969/1997; 1973/1998; 1980/1998) and equity theory (Hatfield & Rapson, 1996; Hatfield et al., 1978; 1985) in mind. Thus, the secure–insecure dichotomy that Yum and Li applied to their attachment style data might have interfered with their goal of examining a moderation effect for national group membership.

All in all, results provide limited support for the moderating role of national group membership regarding links between relationship maintenance behaviors and other relationship-related variables. The best-documented moderation effect is the impact of perceived equity on relationship maintenance behaviors (i.e., individuals who perceive themselves as overbenefitting or underbenefitting tend to engage in fewer relationship maintenance behaviors compared with individuals who perceive their relationships as equitable) – an effect that is limited to Western nations, and primarily limited to the USA. More evidence is needed regarding a counteracting moderation effect in one Eastern nation (i.e., overbenefitting individuals engaging in higher levels of relationship maintenance behaviors than do individuals who either perceive their relationships as equitable or report underbenefitting within South Korea).

Ethnic group membership, within a given nation, as a moderator. To our knowledge, unless specific comparisons are made between European-descent and Asian-descent persons within a particular nation, neither the suffocation model (Finkel et al., 2015; Finkel, Hui, et al., 2014; Finkel, Larson, et al., 2014) nor the self-expansion model (Aron & Aron, 1986) would lead one to expect ethnic group membership to moderate covariance between relationship maintenance behaviors and other relationship-relevant variables. Consistent with the null hypothesis, in the aforementioned study by Yum and Li (2007), individuals in the US mainland did not differ significantly from individuals in Hawaii regarding the impact of attachment styles (Bartholomew & Horowitz, 1991) on relationship maintenance behaviors (Stafford & Canary, 1991). Among both groups (which one could view as "ethnic" if region of country counts as a basis for classifying individuals' ethnic group membership; e.g., Cohen, 2009; 2010), securely attached individuals generally engaged in relationship-maintenance behaviors at significantly higher levels than did insecurely attached individuals.

One additional study that includes within-nation data on covariance between relationship maintenance and other relationship-relevant variables is Ballard-Reisch et al.'s (1999) aforementioned study of couples in Russian-only, Tartar-only, and Russian–Tartar marriages within Russia. Alongside measures of relationship maintenance variables (Canary & Stafford, 1992), Ballard-Reisch et al. included measures of two key variables from the interdependence theory of Thibaut and Kelley (1959; Kelley, 1979; Kelley & Thibaut, 1978) and the investment model (Rusbult, 1980; 1983) – namely, marital satisfaction (Schumm et al., 1986) and marital commitment (Lund, 1985). Ballard-Reisch et al. did not comment on a main effect from relationship maintenance behaviors to interdependence variables (or vice versa, given that interdependence theory likely would frame relationship maintenance variables as *consequences*, rather than antecedents, of relationship maintenance variables; see Le & Agnew, 2003). Furthermore, Ballard-Reisch et al. did not comment on a moderating effect for couples' ethnic group membership (s). Therefore, we cannot speculate on ethnic group membership as a moderator in Ballard-Reisch et al.'s study.

CONCLUDING THOUGHTS

Like any literature review, the present chapter is necessarily selective in terms of the studies that we have included or excluded concerning relationship maintenance (a multifaceted construct; Dindia, 2000) among cultural groups. Perhaps the most notable omissions come from the interdependence literature, in which relationship maintenance tends to be viewed as a special instance of interdependence rather than the other way around (e.g., Kelley et al., 1983/2002; 2003). For example, we did not explore Lin and Rusbult's (1995) finding that the investment model (i.e., significant positive impact of satisfaction, significant negative impact of perceived alternatives, and significant positive impact of investments on commitment; Rusbult, 1980; 1983) generalizes across US and Taiwanese samples (thus signifying a null effect for national group membership as a moderator across Western and Eastern nations). Also, we did not explore Gaines and Ramkissoon's (2008) finding that the negative impact of personal value orientation (operationalized in terms of individualism; Gaines et al., 1997) and the positive impact of social group orientation (operationalized in terms of collectivism, familism, romanticism, and spiritualism; Gaines et al., 2005) on accommodation (operationalized in terms of exit, voice, loyalty, and neglect; Rusbult et al., 1991) generalizes across the USA, Jamaica, and the UK (thus signifying a null effect for national group membership as a moderator across two Western nations and one nation that does not fit neatly within the East–West dichotomy). Granted that we focused on studies that utilized the RMSM (Canary & Stafford, 1992; Stafford & Canary, 1991) in measuring relationship maintenance behaviors (an indication of the dominance of that particular survey in research on relationship maintenance; see Ogolsky & Bowers, 2013), we believe that the present review provides a representative portrait of the relevance versus nonrelevance of cultural group membership to relationship maintenance behaviors and their covariates (see also Ogolsky et al., 2017).

At the beginning of the present chapter, we noted that Coontz (2005) credited Maslow (1954) with anticipating the increased strain that spouses' heightened expectations had placed upon marriage in the USA after World War II. Part of the strain, Coontz (2007) subsequently argued, was due to the fact that traditional gender roles (i.e., husbands as wage-earners and wives as homemakers) were inadequate for enabling spouses to simultaneously meet those growing expectations for themselves or to enable each other to meet those expectations. Guided by Maslow's self-actualization theory, as interpreted by Finkel and colleagues' (Finkel et al., 2015; Finkel, Hui, et al., 2014; Finkel, Larson, et al., 2014) suffocation model and augmented by Aron and Aron's (1986) self-expansion model, our review of the literature on relationship maintenance among cultural groups suggests that – even before Americans enter into marriage – their romantic relationships bear the unique marks of a double-edged sword: individuals in the USA (frequently, but not always, compared with individuals in South Korea) are less constricted by gender role demands than was the case for previous generations but are working especially hard to maintain relationships that are especially fragile by historical standards. We hope that the present review will encourage relationship scientists to redouble their efforts toward examining links between culture and relationship maintenance.

REFERENCES

Agnew, C. R., van Lange, P. A. M., Rusbult, C. E., & Langston, C. A. (1998). Cognitive interdependence: Commitment and the mental representation of close relationships. *Journal of Personality and Social Psychology, 74*, 939–954.

Aron, A., & Aron, E. N. (1986). *Love and the expansion of self: Understanding attraction and satisfaction.* Washington, DC: Hemisphere.

Aron, E. N., & Aron, A. (1996). Love and expansion of the self: The state of the model. *Personal Relationships, 3*, 45–58.

Aron, A., Aron, E. N., & Smollan, D. (1992). Inclusion of Other in the Self Scale and the structure of interpersonal closeness. *Journal of Personality and Social Psychology, 63*, 596–612.

Aron, A., Lewandowski, G. W., Jr., Mashek, D., & Aron, E. N. (2013). The self-expansion model of motivation and cognition in close relationships. In J. A. Simpson & L. Campbell (Eds.), *The Oxford handbook of close relationships* (pp. 90–115). Oxford: Oxford University Press.

Aron, A., Norman, C. C., & Aron, E. N. (2001). Shared self-expanding activities as a means of maintaining and enhancing close romantic relationships. In J. Harvey & A. Wenzel (Eds.), *Close romantic relationships: Maintenance and enhancement* (pp. 47–66). Mahwah, NJ: Erlbaum.

Ballard-Reisch, D., Weigel, D., & Zaguidoulline, M. (1999). Relational maintenance behaviors, marital satisfaction, and commitment in Tatar, Russian, and mixed Russian-Tatar marriages. *Journal of Family Issues, 20,* 677–697.

Bartholomew, K. (1990). Avoidance of intimacy: An attachment perspective. *Journal of Social and Personal Relationships, 7,* 147–178.

Bartholomew, K., & Horowitz, L. M. (1991). Attachment styles among young adults: A test of a four-category model. *Journal of Personality and Social Psychology, 61,* 226–244.

Bowlby, J. (1977). The making and breaking of affectional bonds. *British Journal of Psychiatry, 130,* 201–210.

Bowlby, J. (1997). *Attachment and loss* (Vol. 1: Attachment). London: Pimlico. (Original work published 1969)

Bowlby, J. (1998). *Attachment and loss* (Vol. 2: Separation: Anxiety and anger). London: Pimlico. (Original work published 1973)

Bowlby, J. (1998). *Attachment and loss* (Vol. 3: Loss: Sadness and depression). London: Pimlico. (Original work published 1980)

Braithwaite, V. A., & Scott, W. A. (1991). Values. In J. P. Robinson, P. R. Shaver, & L. S. Wrightsman (Eds.), *Measures of personality and social psychological attitudes* (pp. 661–753). San Diego: Academic Press.

Canary, D. J., & Stafford, L. (1992). Relational maintenance strategies and equity in marriage. *Communication Monographs, 59,* 243–267.

Cho, J. H., & Gilgen, A. R. (1980). Performance of Korean medical and nursing students on the East-West Questionnaire. *Psychological Reports, 47,* 1093–1094.

Cohen, A. B. (2009). Many forms of culture. *American Psychologist, 64,* 194–204.

Cohen, A. B. (2010). Just how many different forms of culture are there? *American Psychologist, 65,* 59–61.

Coontz, S. (2005). *Marriage, a history: How love conquered marriage.* New York: Penguin.

Coontz, S. (2007). The origins of modern divorce. *Family Process, 46,* 7–16.

Diener, E., Oishi, S., & Lucas, R. E. (2003). Personality, culture, and subjective well-being: Emotional and cognitive evaluations of life. *Annual Review of Psychology, 54,* 403–425.

Dindia, K. (2000). Relational maintenance. In C. Hendrick & S. S. Hendrick (Eds.), *Close relationships: A sourcebook* (pp. 287–300). Thousand Oaks, CA: Sage.

Dindia, K., & Canary, D. S. (1993). Definitions and theoretical perspectives on maintaining relationships. *Journal of Social and Personal Relationships, 10,* 163–173.

Drigotas, S. M., Whitney, G. A., & Rusbult, C. E. (1995). On the peculiarities of loyalty: A diary study of responses to dissatisfaction in everyday life. *Personality and Social Psychology Bulletin, 21,* 596–609.

Ewen, R. B. (1998). *An introduction to theories of personality* (5th ed.). Mahwah, NJ: Erlbaum.

Finkel, E. J., Cheung, E. O., Emery, L. F., Carswell, K. L., & Larson, G. M. (2015). The suffocation model: Why marriage in America is becoming an all-or-nothing institution. *Current Directions in Psychological Science, 24,* 238–244.

Finkel, E. J., & Eastwick, P. E. (2015). Interpersonal attraction: In search of a theoretical Rosetta stone. In M. Mikulincer & P. R. Shaver (Eds.), *APA handbook of personality and social psychology* (Vol. 3: Interpersonal relations, pp. 179–210). Washington, DC: American Psychological Association.

Finkel, E. J., Hui, C. M., Carswell, K. L., & Larson, G. M. (2014). The suffocation of marriage: Climbing Mount Maslow without enough oxygen. *Psychological Inquiry, 25,* 1–41.

Finkel, E. J., Larson, G. M., Carswell, K. L., & Hui, C. M. (2014). Marriage at the summit: Response to the commentaries. *Psychological Inquiry*, 25, 120–145.

Fiske, A. P., Kitayama, S., Markus, H. R., & Nisbett, R. E. (1998). The cultural matrix of social psychology. In D. T. Gilbert, S. T. Fiske, & G. Lindzey (Eds.), *The handbook of social psychology* (4th ed., Vol. 2, pp. 915–981). New York: McGraw-Hill.

Gaines, S. O., Jr. (with Buriel, R., Liu, J. H., & Rios, D. I.) (1997). *Culture, ethnicity, and personal relationship processes*. New York: Routledge.

Gaines, S. O., Jr. (2016). *Personality and close relationship processes*. Cambridge, UK: Cambridge University Press.

Gaines, S. O., Jr., & Hardin, D. P. (2013). Interdependence revisited: Perspectives from cultural psychology. In L. Campbell & J. A. Simpson (Eds.), *Oxford handbook of close relationships* (pp. 553–572). Oxford: Oxford University Press.

Gaines, S. O., Jr., Henderson, M. C., Kim, M., Gilstrap, S., Yi, J., Rusbult, C. E., Hardin, D. P., & Gaertner, L. A. (2005). Cultural value orientations, internalized homophobia, and accommodation in romantic relationships. *Journal of Homosexuality*, 50, 97–117.

Gaines, S. O., Jr., & Ketay, S. (2013). Positive psychology, culture, and personal relationship processes. In M. Hojjat & D. Cramer (Eds.), *Positive psychology of love* (pp. 218–231). Oxford: Oxford University Press.

Gaines, S. O., Jr., Marelich, W. D., Bledsoe, K. L., Steers, W. N., Henderson, M. C., Granrose, C. S., … Page, M. S. (1997). Links between race/ethnicity and cultural values as mediated by racial/ethnic identity and moderated by gender. *Journal of Personality and Social Psychology*, 72, 1460–1476.

Gaines, S. O., Jr., & Ramkissoon, M. W. (2008). US/Caribbean relationships. In T. A. Karis & K. D. Killian (Eds.), *Cross-cultural couples: Transborder relationships in the 21st century* (pp. 227–250). Binghamton, New York: Taylor & Francis.

Gilgen, A. R., & Cho, J. H. (1979a). Performance of Eastern- and Western-oriented college students on the Value Survey and Ways of Life Scale. *Psychological Reports*, 45, 263–268.

Gilgen, A. R., & Cho, J. H. (1979b). Questionnaire to measure Eastern and Western thought. *Psychological Reports*, 44, 835–841.

Goldstein, K. (1939). *The organism: A holistic approach to biology derived from pathological data in man*. New York: American Book Company.

Goldstein, K. (1940). *Human nature in the light of psychopathology*. Cambridge, MA: Harvard University Press.

Goodwin, R. (1999). *Personal relationships across cultures*. London: Routledge.

Goodwin, R., & Pillay, U. (2006). Relationships, culture, and social change. In A. L. Vangelisti & D. Perlman (Eds.), *The Cambridge handbook of personal relationships* (pp. 695–708). Cambridge: Cambridge University Press.

Guerrero, L. K., & Bachman, G. F. (2006). Associations among relational maintenance behaviors, attachment-style categories, and attachment dimensions. *Communication Studies*, 57, 341–361.

Hall, C. S., & Lindzey, G. (1970). *Theories of personality* (2nd ed.). New York: Wiley & Sons.

Hatfield, E., & Rapson, R. L. (1996). *Love and sex: Cross-cultural perspectives*. Needham Heights, MA: Allyn & Bacon.

Hatfield, E., Traupmann, J., Sprecher, S., Utne, M., & Hay, J. (1985). Equity and intimate relations: Recent research. In W. Ickes (Ed.), *Compatible and incompatible relationships* (pp. 1–27). New York: Springer-Verlag.

Hatfield, E., Walster, G. W., & Berscheid, E. (1978). *Equity: Theory and research*. Boston: Allyn and Bacon.

Hayes, A. F. (2013). *Introduction to mediation, moderation, and conditional process analysis: A regression-based approach.* New York: Guilford.

Hazan, C., & Shaver, P.R. (1994a). Attachment as an organizational framework for research on close relationships. *Psychological Inquiry, 5,* 1–22.

Hazan, C., & Shaver, P. R. (1994b). Deeper into attachment theory: Reply to commentaries. *Psychological Inquiry, 5,* 68–79.

Heine, S. J. (2010). Cultural psychology. In S. T. Fiske, D. T. Gilbert, & G. Lindzey (Eds.), *Handbook of social psychology* (5th ed., Vol. 2, pp. 1423–1464). Hoboken, NJ: Wiley.

Hofstede, G. (2001). *Culture's consequences: Comparing values, behaviors, institutions, and organizations across nations.* Thousand Oaks, CA: Sage.

Hofstede, G., Hofstede, G. J., & Minkov, M. (2010). *Cultures and organizations: Software of the mind.* New York, NY: McGraw-Hill.

Inglehart, R. (1997). *Modernization and postmodernization: Cultural, economic, and political change in 43 societies.* Princeton, NJ: Princeton University Press.

Inglehart, R., & Baker, W. E. 2000. Modernization, cultural change, and the persistence of traditional values. *American Sociological Review, 65,* 19–51.

Inglehart, R., & Welzel, C. (2005). *Modernization, cultural change and democracy.* New York: Cambridge University Press.

Kelley, H. H. (1979). *Personal relationships: Their structures and processes.* Hillsdale, NJ: Erlbaum.

Kelley, H. H., Berscheid, E., Christensen, A., Harvey, J. H., Huston, T. L, Levinger, G., … Peterson, D. R. (2002). *Close relationships.* New York: Percheron Press. (Original work published 1983)

Kelley, H. H., Holmes, J. G., Kerr, N. L., Reis, H. T., Rusbult, C. E., & Van Lange, P. A. M. (2003). *An atlas of interpersonal situations.* New York: Cambridge University Press.

Kelley, H. H., & Thibaut, J. W. (1978). *Interpersonal relations: A theory of interdependence.* New York: Wiley.

Le, B., & Agnew, C. R. (2003). Commitment and its theorized determinants: A meta-analysis of the investment model. *Personal Relationships, 10,* 37–57.

Le, B., Dove, M. I., Agnew, C. R., Korn, M. S., & Mutso, A. A. (2010). Predicting nonmarital romantic relationship dissolution: A meta-analytic synthesis. *Personal Relationships, 17,* 377–390.

Lin, Y. H. W., & Rusbult, C. E. (1995). Commitment to dating relationships and cross-sex friendships in America and China: The impact of centrality of relationship, normative support, and investment model variables. *Journal of Social and Personal Relationships, 12,* 7–26.

Lund, M. (1985). The development of investment and commitment scales for predicting continuity of personal relationships. *Journal of Social and Personal Relationships, 2,* 3–23.

Lydon, J. E., & Quinn, S. K. (2013). Relationship maintenance processes. In L. Campbell & J. A. Simpson (Eds.), *Oxford handbook of close relationships* (pp. 573–588). Oxford: Oxford University Press.

Markus, H. R. (2008). Pride, prejudice, and ambivalence: Toward a unified theory of race and ethnicity. *American Psychologist, 63,* 651–670.

Markus, H. R., & Kitayama, S. (1991). Culture and the self: Implications for cognition, emotion, and motivation. *Psychological Review, 98,* 224–253.

Markus, H. R., & Kitayama, S. (1994). A collective fear of the collective: Implications for selves and theories of selves. *Personality and Social Psychology Bulletin, 20,* 568–579.

Markus, H. R., & Kitayama, S. (2010). Cultures and selves: A cycle of mutual constitution. *Perspectives on Psychological Science, 5*, 420–430.

Maslow, A. H. (1943). A theory of human motivation. *Psychological Review, 50*, 370–396.

Maslow, A. H. (1954). *Motivation and personality.* New York: Harper & Row.

Maslow, A. H. (1962). *Toward a psychology of being.* Princeton, NJ: van Nostrand.

Maslow, A. H. (1968). *Toward a psychology of being* (2nd ed.). New York: van Nostrand Reinhold.

Maslow, A. H. (1970). *Motivation and personality* (2nd ed.). New York: Harper & Row.

Maslow, A. H. (1971). *The farther reaches of human nature.* Harmondsworth, UK: Penguin.

Matsumoto, D. (1999). Culture and self: An empirical assessment of Markus and Kitayama's theory of independent and interdependent self-construals. *Asian Journal of Social Psychology, 2*, 289–310.

McClelland, D. C. (1987). *Human motivation.* New York: Cambridge University Press. (Original work published 1985)

Ogolsky, B., & Bowers, J. (2013). A meta-analytic review of relationship maintenance and its correlates. *Journal of Social and Personal Relationships, 30*, 343–367.

Ogolsky, B., Monk, J., Rice, T., Theisen, J., & Maniotes, C. (2017). Relationship maintenance: A review of research on romantic relationships. *Family Theory and Review, 9*, 275–306.

Oishi, S., Diener, E., Lucas, R. E., & Suh, E. M. (1999). Cross-cultural variations in predictors of life satisfaction: Perspectives from needs and values. *Personality and Social Psychology Bulletin, 25*, 980–990.

Phinney, J. S. (1996). When we talk about American ethnic groups, what do we mean? *American Psychologist, 51*, 918–927.

Pietromonaco, P. R., & Perry-Jenkins, M. (2014). Marriage in whose America? What the suffocation model misses. *Psychological Inquiry, 25*, 1–6.

Rusbult, C. E. (1980). Commitment and satisfaction in romantic associations: A test of the investment model. *Journal of Experimental Social Psychology, 16*, 172–186.

Rusbult, C. E. (1983). A longitudinal test of the investment model: The development (and deterioration) of satisfaction and commitment in heterosexual involvements. *Journal of Personality and Social Psychology, 45*, 101–117.

Rusbult, C. E., & Buunk, B. P. (1993). Commitment processes in close relationships: An interdependence analysis. *Journal of Social and Personal Relationships, 10*, 175–204.

Rusbult, C., Verette, J., Whitney, G., Slovik, L., & Lipkus, I. (1991). Accommodation processes in close relationships: Theory and preliminary evidence. *Journal of Personality and Social Psychology, 60*, 53–78.

Ryan, R. M., & Deci, E. L. (2001). On happiness and human potentials: A review of research on hedonic and eudaimonic well-being. *Annual Review of Psychology, 52*, 141–166.

Schumm, W., Paff-Bergen, L., Hatch, F., Obiorah, J., Copeland, J., Meens, L., & Bugaighis, M. (1986). Concurrent and discriminant validity of the Kansas Marital Satisfaction Scale. *Journal of Marriage and the Family, 48*, 381–387.

Stafford, L., & Canary, D. J. (1991). Maintenance strategies and romantic relationship type, gender, and relational characteristics. *Journal of Social and Personal Relationships, 8*, 217–242.

Tabachnick, B. G., & Fidell, L. S. (2007). *Using multivariate statistics* (5th ed.). Boston: Allyn and Bacon.

Thibaut, J. W., & Kelley, H. H. (1959). *The social psychology of groups*. New York: Wiley.

Ullman, A. D. (1965). The framework. In A. D. Ullman (Ed.), *Sociocultural foundations of personality* (pp. 1–6). Boston: Houghton Mifflin.

Yum, Y-O., & Canary, D. J. (2003). Maintaining relationships in the U.S. and Korea. In D. J. Canary & M. Dainton (Eds.), *Maintaining relationships through communication: Relational, contextual, and cultural variations* (pp. 277–296). Mahwah, NJ: Erlbaum.

Yum, Y.-O., & Canary, D. J. (2009). National and cultural differences in equity theory predictions of relational maintenance strategies. *Human Communication Research*, 35, 384–406.

Yum, Y.-O., Canary, D. J., & Baptist, J. (2015). The roles of culture and fairness in maintaining relationships: A comparison of romantic partners from Malaysia, Singapore, and the United States. *International Journal of Intercultural Relations*, 44, 100–112.

Yum, Y.-O., & Li, H. Z. (2007). Associations among attachment style, maintenance strategies, and relational quality across cultures. *Journal of Intercultural Communication Research*, 36, 71–89.

16

Relationship Maintenance in the Age of Technology

JOHN P. CAUGHLIN[1] AND NINGXIN WANG[2]

Computers and smartphones have become ubiquitous, and these technologies enable many forms of technologically mediated communication (TMC), including texting, social media, instant messaging, and e-mail. With the increased availability of TMC, it is perhaps inevitable that communication technologies are used to help maintain relationships. The current chapter examines the literature on how TMC is used with (and occasionally instead of) face-to-face (FtF or F2F) interactions for relationship maintenance. First, we explicate two different definitions of the phrase "relationship mainte-nance." Second, we summarize research that examines the role of particular technologies in relationship maintenance. Then, we argue that much con-temporary relationship maintenance, particularly in romantic relationships, occurs in mixed-media relationships, which are relationships that the "parties conduct in whole or in part through the use of multiple media, including F2F" (Parks, 2017, p. 506) and thus, utilize various communication technologies along with FtF interactions for relationship maintenance. The primary focus of this chapter is on the maintenance of romantic relationships, yet we also review research on other types of relationships when the processes examined seem applicable to close relationships more broadly. We conclude with some broad directions for future research.

TWO FORMS OF RELATIONSHIP MAINTENANCE

There is a longstanding recognition that relationship maintenance can be defined in a variety of ways, including maintaining the mere existence of a relationship, keeping a relationship in a particular state, maintaining the well-being of the relationship, or rejuvenating a relationship (Dindia & Canary, 1993). Although such categories of maintenance are clearly important, an even

[1] Department of Communication, University of Illinois at Urbana-Champaign, caughlin@illinois.edu
[2] Department of Management and Organization, National University of Singapore, nwang@nus.edu.sg

broader distinction is apparent in the literature on technologies and relationship maintenance: preserving contacts with a network of people versus sustaining a particular close relationship. Both forms of relationship maintenance are prevalent, yet very little research specifies a particular definition, which is problematic because they are quite different and potentially have distinct predictors and consequences. We therefore consider each separately in the following.

Maintaining one's network of contacts. A number of studies examine how communication technologies help establish or maintain social ties generally (e.g., LaRose, Connolly, Lee, Li, & Hales, 2014; Seo, Kim, & Yang, 2016) or with various social circles (e.g., Baym, Zhang, & Lin, 2004). Mobile phones, for example, can be crucial for maintaining a sense of belongingness and connectedness among youth (Walsh, White, & Young, 2009). Ellison, Steinfield, and Lampe (2007) found that Facebook played a role in individuals' success in building and maintaining social capital, which refers to the "resources accumulated through the relationships among people" (p. 1145).

From the network perspective, relationship maintenance behaviors are not aimed at any particular relationship. Instead, maintenance refers to patterns of behaviors in which technologies are used to foster or preserve network connections. Some work emphasizes how communication technologies allow people to be in constant contact with others (e.g., Pettegrew & Day, 2015). Additionally, Ellison, Vitak, Gray, and Lampe (2014) focused explicitly on network maintenance by creating the Facebook Relational Maintenance Behaviors measure, which assesses individuals' behavioral and motivational tendencies on Facebook (e.g., sample item: "When I see someone asking for advice on Facebook, I try to respond," p. 860).

Many of the studies taking a network perspective on technologies and maintenance examine links to individual well-being. Importantly, the implications for personal well-being depend on how a particular communication technology is used. Burke and Kraut (2016), for instance, examined Facebook usage and personal well-being in a panel study with three waves over a three-month period. Burke and Kraut framed relationship maintenance as important, because "social ties are causally related to improvements in mental health" (p. 267), and argued that "online communication can influence psychological well-being by helping people maintain their stock of friendships" (p. 267). They found that messages specifically tailored to participants (i.e., comments, messages, and wall posts received) predicted personal well-being over time, particularly when those messages came from people they had identified as close friends. In contrast, well-being was not significantly related to receiving one-click messages (i.e., likes and pokes) or simply viewing other people's content.

Maintaining a particular relationship. In contrast to the network perspective, some scholarship conceptualizes relationship maintenance in a way that is more like the majority of the literature on relationship maintenance in close relationships (e.g., Dindia & Canary, 1993). Laliker and Lannutti (2014), for example, asked married and cohabiting couples to log all their electronic communication with their partner (e.g., texts, instant messages, and Facebook messages) for a one-week period. The messages from randomly selected days were coded using the relationship maintenance behavior categories developed by Alberts, Yoshimura, Rabby, and Loschiavo (2005). Laliker and Lannutti found that even when using the new communication technologies, the content of the messages was largely consistent with what had been found in past studies of relationship maintenance in person. Additionally, Ledbetter (2010) found that Stafford and Canary's (1991) relationship maintenance measure showed sound measurement properties when individuals were asked about maintenance in friendships via instant messaging. Such findings suggest that what is known about maintenance behaviors from past research is pertinent to new communication technologies.

Although there is evidence that traditional relationship maintenance strategies are still important with contemporary communication technologies, there is also some evidence that additional mediated maintenance behaviors are prominent in at least some instances. Vitak (2014), for instance, found that strategies such as passively viewing another person's Facebook content and using Facebook to keep up with the other person's daily activities can be important maintenance strategies in geographically distant relationships, including in long-distance romantic relationships.

SCHOLARSHIP FOCUSING ON PARTICULAR TECHNOLOGIES

Much research on technologies and maintaining relationships has focused on a particular medium or platform. For example, in a study of home e-mail use toward the end of the last century, Stafford, Kline, and Dimmick (1999) found in interviews of 112 people that the most widespread use of email was to maintain interpersonal relationships (e.g., "to keep in touch with friends," p. 664). Such studies, and many others, provide glimpses into how particular technologies play a role in relationship maintenance, but they also have the potential to become dated if a particular mode of communication becomes less prominent. Thus, rather than trying to comprehensively catalog maintenance via every particular mode, we focus primarily on the communication technologies that are currently most prevalent: social media and mobile communication.

Maintenance on social media. At least some scholars have argued that "Social networking sites have profoundly changed the way in which romantic relationships are experienced" (Van Ouytsel, Van Gool, Walrave, Ponnet, &

Peeters, 2016, p. 76). There are, of course, a variety of different platforms that fall under the rubric of social media, and differences among them likely afford different relationship maintenance activities. Mobile message apps such as WhatsApp and WeChat, for example, are a type of social media that primarily use smartphones to facilitate multiparty interactions (Ling & Lai, 2016). Such forms of social media have become increasingly popular, but Facebook is the most popular social networking site in North America and much of the world (Greenwood, Perrin, & Duggan, 2016), and Facebook constitutes the most frequently examined site for research on relationship maintenance and social networking (Tong & Walther, 2011). Studies examining Facebook and relationships have certain common foci, such as an interest in relationship-related outcomes linked to Facebook use, but the specific questions asked and the assumptions about mechanisms underlying the impacts of Facebook vary widely. In this section, we review three approaches used to study relationship maintenance on Facebook: (a) research from a network perspective, (b) research that foregrounds the communication-based behaviors on Facebook, and (c) research that stresses norms and needs in relationships.

First, from a social network perspective, Facebook provides an important means to maintain social relationships that often exist in people's offline network (e.g., Ellison et al., 2007; Steinfield, Ellison, & Lampe, 2008; Valenzuela, Park, & Kee, 2009). Relationships are referred to as *ties* between people, and a distinction has to be made between strong ties and weak ties (Putnam, 2000). *Strong ties* are close, intimate relationships with family and close friends that are located in the core of people's social network, whereas *weak ties* encompass casual acquaintances. As noted earlier, social networks are important because they help people accumulate *social capital* – resources embedded in social networks (Bourdieu, 1986; Coleman, 1988). Specifically, *bonding social capital* is available through strong ties (e.g., emotional and financial support), and *bridging social capital* is usually provided by weak ties (e.g., information and resources unavailable through strong ties, or new perspectives; Putnam, 2000). Focusing on these key concepts, research has established associations between Facebook use and these two forms of social capital (e.g., Ellison et al., 2007; Valenzuela et al., 2009). For example, the intensity of Facebook use was positively associated with college students' bonding and bridging social capital above and beyond the amount of internet use, suggesting that Facebook is useful for maintaining strong ties and cultivating weak ties (Ellison et al., 2007).

Second, building upon earlier research on social networking sites and social capital, some studies delved into the more specific communication-based behaviors and demonstrated that certain types of Facebook communication could result in more desirable relationship outcomes than the others (e.g., Ellison, Steinfield, & Lampe, 2011; Ellison et al., 2014; McEwan, Summer, Eden, & Fletcher, 2018; Sosik & Bazarova, 2014; Wendorf & Yang, 2015). On

Facebook, people can choose to engage in different forms of communication, ranging from undemanding transactions, such as "liking" a post, writing "happy birthday" on someone's Facebook wall, and tagging someone in a photo, to communication requiring more effort, such as providing substantive comments to a post. In addition, Facebook provides one-on-one private messaging between users and thus, allows communication of varying levels of publicness (Bazarova, Taft, Choi, & Cosley, 2013).

Ellison et al.'s (2014) aforementioned Facebook relationship maintenance behavior (FRMB) scale is one specific measure that assesses social grooming activities signaling attention to friends through "small but meaningful actions" (p. 860), such as responding to a friend's or acquaintance's good or bad news shared on Facebook. The authors found that adults' FRMB was positively associated with bridging social capital, even after controlling for the number of Facebook friends and time spent on Facebook (Ellison et al., 2014). Additionally, McEwan and colleagues (2018) showed that whereas social contact behaviors on Facebook (e.g., sending private messages to this person and coordinating future interactions) was positively associated with relational markers including satisfaction, closeness, and commitment of friendships, response-seeking behaviors (e.g., broadcasting status updates or implicit support requests in hopes of getting a response from someone) were associated with lower levels of liking and satisfaction. This implies that the mass distribution of personal information on social media may be perceived as impersonal and unable to facilitate effective relationship maintenance (McEwan, 2013). It is important to note that although Facebook provides an additional means for relationship maintenance, scholars have noted that people tend to maintain their more established relationships using more personal channels (e.g., phone calls and texting) and the relatively more private forms of communication on Facebook (e.g., private messaging; Sosik & Bazarova, 2014). In short, increasing research shows the merits of delineating between different types of communication on Facebook when examining relational outcomes of Facebook maintenance behaviors.

Third, a handful of studies aimed to understand the role of Facebook in relationship maintenance while paying focal attention to the norms and needs of relational partners (e.g., Brody, LeFebvre, & Blackburn, 2016; Fox, Osborn, & Warber, 2014). This line of research suggests that what are considered appropriate or effective maintenance behaviors are subject to interpretations of partners. Analyzing focus group discussions that involved college Facebook users, Fox and colleagues (2014) revealed that whereas one partner may think public displays of affection on Facebook (e.g., writing affectionate posts on the other's wall) strengthen the relationship, the other partner may think that this hurts the relationship. Fox and colleagues argued that when it comes to relationship maintenance on Facebook, sociocultural norms are less dominant than interpersonal or individual-level beliefs, perhaps because such norms are still emerging. Further complicating this issue, people's needs and the norms surrounding Facebook maintenance behaviors change throughout the lifespan of relationship development (Brody et al., 2016; see also Rauer & Proulx, Chapter 17). Hence, it seems that a fuller understanding of relationship maintenance on Facebook and other social media entails considering not only the technology-enabled communication and its impacts on relationships but also relational partners' goals and needs, which motivate them to adopt technologies in different ways.

Mobile communication. In addition to social networking sites, mobile technologies such as texting, instant messaging (IM), and phone calls are important technologies for people to maintain social relationships, particularly close relationships (Baym, 2015). Mobile communication affords people the ability to quickly exchange messages on a frequent basis (Ramirez & Broneck, 2009; Reid & Reid, 2010; Wei & Lo, 2006), which is helpful for maintaining a sense of psychological connection and propinquity (Tong & Walther, 2011). There are some empirical findings in support of the relationship maintenance function of mobile technologies; for instance, Valkenburg and Peter (2009) conducted a six-month-long panel study and found that IM use predicted increases in the quality of Dutch adolescents' friendships (whereas friendship quality did not predict increases in IM usage).

However, the use of mobile technologies in romantic relationships is not consistently associated with positive relational outcomes. In two experimental studies that were designed to show that positive texting can enhance romantic relationships, Luo and Tuney (2015) found that such messaging had a positive impact on individuals' own satisfaction, but only when they crafted the messages themselves (instead of sending scripted messages). Luo and Tuney also found no evidence that the positive texts had any impact on the partners' satisfaction, which raises questions about the scope of the effects of texting. Other work suggests that texting may be less consequential than other forms of mobile communication. In a survey of individuals in dating relationships, Jin and Peña (2010) found that mobile voice calling was associated with high love and commitment and low relational uncertainty, but they found no evidence that texting was associated with any relationship outcomes. A potential explanation for why texting may have different implications than mobile voice calls in romantic relationships is that a heavy reliance on texting for interactions may be a sign of problems. Luo (2014) found that the share of texting in the overall amount of communication between romantic couples was inversely associated with relationship satisfaction. Texting and IM appear to be most beneficial to close relationships when they are used in conjunction with other channels (including FtF communication) instead of being used alone (Luo, 2014; Ramirez & Broneck, 2009). Further, enacting the relationship maintenance strategy of "openness" via texting was negatively associated with satisfaction in romantic relationships, suggesting that texting may not be deemed appropriate for serious discussions about relationship status (Brody & Peña, 2015). Hence, the effects of texting or IM in terms of relationship maintenance likely depend on the content of communication as well as the extent to which texting or IM dominates communication between the partners.

Although mobile communication enables relational accessibility and a sense of continuity (Licoppe, 2004), mobile technologies may create pressure for too much connection (Baym, 2015; LaRose et al., 2014; Stafford & Hillyer, 2012). Romantic partners reported experiencing a tension between connection and autonomy because of mobile phone use, and such tension was a source of conflict as couples argued about the frequency and timing of texting or phone calls (Duran, Kelly, & Rotaru, 2011). In friendships, increased mobile phone use contributed to higher expectations for maintenance behaviors through mobile communication, which in turn, was positively associated with interdependence, over-interdependence, and a feeling of entrapment (Hall & Baym, 2012).

MAINTENANCE IN MIXED-MEDIA RELATIONSHIPS

Although it is at times useful to examine how a particular communication technology is used within relationships, there is growing recognition that most of our relationships – especially close ones – routinely utilize multiple modes of interacting (Baym et al., 2004; Pettegrew & Day, 2015). A romantic couple may begin the day with an FtF conversation but send texts later that same day. Friends might first learn about each other's new job on social media, and may even comment on the news online, but then they can also talk in person about the news in more detail later. The potential combinations are infinite, but the broader point is that if one focuses on the question of how relationships are maintained in a contemporary communication ecosystem (rather than asking how a communication channel is implicated in relationship maintenance), it becomes clear that most close relationships are maintained as "mixed-media relationships" (Parks, 2017). That is, rather than maintaining relationships via any particular channel, people use "a rapidly evolving portfolio" (Parks, 2017, p. 505) of communication modes, including technology and FtF conversations.

To date, most of the literature has not taken an explicit mixed-media perspective on maintenance, yet there is emerging consensus surrounding two key conclusions that suggest the importance of adopting a mixed-media perspective. First, there is now compelling evidence that when people adopt new communication media, those media typically do not replace existing ones for communication in close relationships (e.g., using mobile phones and social media does not mean romantic partners talk to each other less FtF).

In fact, there is a tendency in close relationships for frequent use of one channel to be positively associated with frequent use of other modes (Caughlin & Sharabi, 2013; Ramirez & Broneck, 2009; Ruppel, Burke, & Cherney, 2018). Baym and colleagues (2004), for example, found that more communication via the internet was associated with more FtF and more telephone communication.

Second, scholars examining multiple media within interpersonal interactions have begun showing that it is important to examine the connections and interplay among various media and FtF interaction (e.g., Caughlin & Sharabi, 2013; Ling & Lai, 2016). For example, people often use technologies to engage in *microcoordination*, which involves using communication technologies (e.g., smartphones) to help negotiate scheduling in-person encounters and everyday activities between people (Ling & Lai, 2016). Interestingly, such microcoordination can occur between dyads, but the recent expansion of mobile messaging has led to increased microcoordination among groups (Ling & Lai, 2016), suggesting that microcoordination is not only important to maintaining particular relationships but also may function to maintain social networks.

Another prominent example of the interplay between modes of communication is the notion of *multicommunicating*, which occurs when technologies allow people to engage in more than one conversation at the same time (e. g., Seo, Kim, & Prabu, 2015). A person having an FtF conversation with a dating partner, for example, might use a mobile device to carry out a simultaneous interaction with a friend in another location. Although the notion of multicommunicating has not been prominent in the relationships literature to date, there is evidence that one manifestation of problematic mobile phone usage is frequent multicommunication (Seo et al., 2015).

THEORIES OF MIXED-MEDIA RELATIONSHIPS

The emerging understanding that close relationships involve interaction via a mixture of media (including FtF interaction) has begun to lead to theoretical work aimed at understanding the importance of a mixed-media environment. The most prominent theory in this vein is *media multiplexity theory* (MMT; Haythornthwaite, 2005). The original formulation of MMT examined the strength of network ties and argued that the number of communication channels is a reflection of the strength of a link in a network. This perspective has been adapted by relationship scholars to explain variations in the closeness of relationships. Consistent with MMT, there is evidence that the frequency of communication via various channels (Caughlin & Sharabi, 2013; Ledbetter, 2009) and the number of channels used (e.g., Ruppel et al., 2018) are both associated with relational closeness.

Whereas the MMT focuses primarily on the frequency of communication and/or the number of channels, the *communication interdependence perspective* (CIP; Caughlin & Sharabi, 2013) concerns the interconnections among various channels, especially between those that are FtF and mediated. There are a number of different potential indicators of interdependence among communication modes. *Integration* refers to the extent that people engage in the same conversation using various channels (e.g., talking in person about information they previously shared via text). *Segmentation* is a marker of low communication interdependence, and it involves reserving certain topics for certain channels (e.g., waiting to have a conflict using FtF communication). Another indicator of low communication interdependence is *difficulty transitioning* between TMC and FtF communication (e.g., finding it awkward to talk in person after discussing something via texting). This perspective suggests that high communication interdependence in general is an indicator of relational closeness that goes beyond frequency of communication (Caughlin & Sharabi, 2013). Of course, interdependence in relationships can have a downside when negative aspects of communication become intensified by the interdependence. Indeed, Pusateri, Roaché, and Wang (2015) found that the extent of integration of TMC and FtF communication when discussing serial arguments (i.e., partners' conflicts carrying over across channels) was negatively associated with relational satisfaction and overall relational closeness. Work on the CIP is still in its nascent stage, but borrowing from interdependence theory generally (e.g., Kelley et al., 1983; see also VanderDrift & Agnew, Chapter 2), Caughlin, Basinger, and Sharabi (2017) argued that an important distinction to make when considering communicative interdependence is whether using one channel *facilitates* communication by another channel or whether it *interferes*. For example, if microcoordination were used to facilitate the maintenance of positive FtF interactions, it should enhance relationship maintenance. In contrast, multicommunicating that involves texting other friends while one's partner attempts to engage in FtF relationship maintenance would likely reduce the effectiveness of the maintenance.

   Although theorizing in this area is still in its infancy, there is enough evidence that people use multiple modes in maintaining relationships and that it is worth conceptualizing relationships from a mixed-media perspective. An implication of this perspective is that rather than focusing on particular channels (e.g., instant messaging) or devices, the focus should be on how individuals in relationships utilize the variety of technological and non-technological means available to them to maintain their relationships. Thus, our following review of relationships cuts across specific technologies, even though many of the specific studies do not take a mixed-media perspective. Because there is evidence that relationship maintenance processes differ meaningfully in geographically close versus long-distance relationships (Johnson, Haigh, Becker, Craig, & Wigley, 2008), we distinguish between these two broad categories.

MAINTAINING GEOGRAPHICALLY CLOSE RELATIONSHIPS

Although communication technologies allow people to communicate at a distance, they are extremely prominent in proximal relationships as well. Ruppel (2014), for example, found that more than half of daily conversations between geographically close relational partners occurred via communication technologies. Also, the primary use of communication technologies for many people is in relationships with people they see on a routine basis. In Ishii's (2006) study in Japan, for example, mobile phones primarily supplemented FtF connections and were not often used to expand one's social network. Although some websites and apps (e.g., Match.com and eHarmony) are specifically designed for relationship initiation, the internet and mobile devices are used frequently for maintaining existing relationships (see Ogolsky, Monk, Rice, Theisen, & Maniotes, 2017). It is much more common, for instance, to use Facebook to connect with people with whom one already has an offline relationship than it is to use Facebook to connect with new people (Ellison et al., 2007). In short, communication technologies are an important way that people communicate in proximal relationships, and such relationships are a main context in which communication technologies are used. There are, of course, a number of different types of proximal relationships, including romantic couples, friendships, and family relationships. Although research has been conducted in each of these contexts, the majority of studies focus on romantic relationships; thus, rather than discussing each type of relationship, we first summarize general processes that appear to cut across the relationship types, then specify some findings that seem specific to romantic relationships.

General processes. Communication technologies, especially mobile, enhance the ability to be connected even when people are apart (Seo et al., 2015). This ability to be connected at any time obviously can facilitate relationship maintenance, but it can also interfere in at least two ways. First, Seo and colleagues (2015) note that being "always-on-and-connected" (p. 667) can be problematic for one's FtF interactions as one multicommunicates (i.e., carries on interactions with other nonpresent individuals during an FtF conversation). Second, the possibility of constant contact with a particular person can become burdensome. As Su (2016) found in interviews with Chinese adults about romantic relationships, new technologies can create a "mediated togetherness that is characterized by immediacy, but it also makes a high demand on lovers' management of time and attention" (p. 5). Duran and colleagues' (2011) findings among college students in the USA show that the potential burden of perpetual contact extends transnationally. Similarly, Hall and Baym's (2012) findings that friends can feel entrapped when expectations for mobile phone contact become excessive provide another example of the potential relational burdens of communication technologies.

The potential burden of expectations for contact may be exacerbated by platforms, such as WhatsApp and Facebook Messenger, that indicate when messages have been read (Ling & Lai, 2016). Some adolescents in Van Ouytsel and colleagues' (2016) focus groups indicated that they expected quick responses from their dating partners and that they felt they were being ignored when they were aware a message had been read but there was not a prompt response. This phenomenon can even happen in workplace relationships; at least one participant in Ling and Lai's (2016) study reported choosing to communicate with a boss via texting rather than WhatsApp because the boss knowing when messages had been read seemed to violate a desire for privacy.

Thus, in general terms, communication technologies can facilitate maintenance, can interfere with FtF maintenance, and can create a sense of burden that relationships require too much maintenance. In addition to those general functions of technologies, it is also important to recognize that what people say via technologies still matters. Brody and Peña (2015), for example, found that in both friendships and romantic relationships, the kinds of maintenance strategies associated with satisfaction in the FtF maintenance literature also typically predicted satisfaction when sent via text (although an exception was that openly talking about the relationship via text was inversely related to satisfaction in romantic relationships). Coupled with evidence that maintenance messages are similar in TMC and FtF (e.g., Laliker & Lannutti, 2014), this suggests that much of what is known about variations in maintenance behaviors and relational outcomes will be applicable to, albeit influenced by, the use of technologies in relationships.

Processes specific to romantic relationships. Although many aspects of relationship maintenance via technology are likely applicable to various types of relationships, some are specifically geared toward romantic relationships. For example, the notion of changing one's relational status to indicate that the relationship is "Facebook Official" is a sign of relational escalation, but it also is used as an attempt to promote relational stability, such as when it serves as a signal to others not to pursue one's partner (Fox et al., 2014). Interestingly, declaring a relationship "Facebook Official" may be culturally specific as well. A study of romantic relationships and social media in Belgium (Van Ouytsel et al., 2016) found no evidence that Facebook Official was salient to participants; instead, other signs of relational closeness and trust (e.g., sharing passwords with each other) were used. Additionally, although TMC may enable burdensome maintenance in any type of relationship, one form of intrusive maintenance that is probably primarily linked to romantic relations is negative relationship maintenance (Tokunaga, 2016). Negative relationship maintenance involves surveilling a partner to guard against relational threats such as potential alternative relationships for one's partner. People who are less satisfied with or secure in their romantic relationships tend to spend more time than other people do scrutinizing their partner's social networking pages, perhaps looking for reassurance that their investments in the relationship are not at risk (Tokunaga, 2016).

MAINTAINING LONG-DISTANCE RELATIONSHIPS

Communication technologies play a vital role in relationship maintenance of long-distance relationships (Arditti & Kauffman, 2004; Jiang & Hancock, 2013; Johnson, Bostwick, & Bassick, 2017; Johnson, Haigh, Becker, Craig, & Wigley, 2008). When partners are not physically copresent, TMC facilitates partners' perceptions of each other's presence (Maguire & Connaughton, 2011). Indeed, long-distance dating partners' frequency of TMC is positively related to relationship satisfaction and trust (Dainton & Aylor, 2002).

In families with extended geographical separations (e.g., transnational families and military couples), TMC helps members maintain emotional connections and enact family roles across a distance (Baldassar, 2007; Chen & Katz, 2009; Madianou & Miller, 2011). Wilding (2006) used the term *virtual intimacies* to indicate how technologies have helped long-distance family members develop "a strong sense of shared space and time that overlooked – even if only temporarily – the realities of geographic distance and time zones" (p. 133). Immigrants often receive emotional support from their families in countries of origin via technologies, which may help them cope with the stress of adapting to a new culture (Baldassar, 2007). Moreover, individuals may fulfill family responsibilities through mediated interactions; for instance, Filipina migrant mothers utilized mobile phones to "parent" their left-behind children (Madianou & Miller, 2011). It is important to note that contemporary communication technologies allow people to do much more than simply convey information at a distance. In a study of deployed service members and their spouses or fiancées, for instance, Rossetto (2012) noted that "several women used technology to participate in joint activities with their husbands ... Using the Internet and web cameras, women and their husbands talked, but also conducted house searches, shopped, read, and even played games" (p. 574).

Given that people in long-distance relationships employ multiple TMC modes as well as (FtF) communication for relationship maintenance (Dainton & Aylor, 2002; Jiang & Hancock, 2013; Stafford & Merolla, 2007), and that most partners transition between being separate and together (Merolla, 2010; Sahlstein, 2004), research has begun to look beyond the frequency of FtF contact (Guldner & Swensen, 1995) and the use of particular TMC modes between long-distance partners (Luo, 2014; Neustaedter & Greenberg, 2012) to focus on interconnection (or the lack thereof) and transition between multiple modes (e.g., Wang, Roaché, & Pusateri, 2017). Based on the communicative interdependence perspective (Caughlin & Sharabi, 2013), Wang and colleagues (2018) found that among a sample of college students in long-distance dating relationships, segmentation of TMC modes (i.e., relying on technologies for communication about certain topics) was negatively associated with relational closeness and relationship satisfaction. Such negative associations were stronger in individuals who had relatively less FtF contact with their partner than in those who had more frequent FtF communication. Further, difficulty in transitioning between TMC and FtF communication was related to lower levels of relationship satisfaction (Wang et al. 2018). In sum, it is important to note that most long-distance relationships are mixed-media relationships because the relationships continue across different TMC modes and FtF interactions. A more nuanced understanding of the role of TMC in maintenance of close relationships across a distance, therefore, requires examining TMC modes in relation to, instead of in isolation from, FtF communication.

CONCLUSION

This chapter examines the burgeoning scholarly literature on communication technologies and relationship maintenance. Our review suggests several important points for future work in this area. First, it is clear that technologies can help people maintain their relationships, but it is also clear that technologies can create burdens and problems, such as expectations for perpetual contact (Su, 2016) and the potential for "Partner phubbing," which occurs when mobile phones lead people (either intentionally or unintentionally) to be less than fully engaged with FtF interaction with their relational partner (Roberts & David, 2016, p. 134). Future research should recognize the varying impacts that technologies have and work toward a better understanding of when and how communication technologies facilitate maintenance and when they interfere with maintenance.

Second, there is now clear evidence that the way technologies are used matters; for instance, simply being connected on Facebook is not the same as engaging in targeted communication with someone via Facebook (Burke & Kraut, 2016). This fact means that questions about how new technologies affect relationships can only be understood fully if scholars also examine how individuals are using new technologies and the messages they exchange with each other using these technologies.

Additionally, given that the manner of technology use matters for relationship maintenance, greater attention needs to be paid to the conceptualization of mediated relational behaviors, particularly across modes. For example, rather than focusing on the specifics of a particular platform (e.g., examining the maintenance functions of e-mail; Stafford et al., 1999), a more productive long-term approach will likely be to conceptualize relational behaviors in ways that cut across modes of communication, including those that have yet to become prominent. Burke and Kraut's (2016) notion of targeted, composed communication was specific to Facebook, but it also could be relevant to distinguishing relationally relevant behaviors via other media and on other platforms (e.g., a group chat versus targeted chat on WhatsApp or WeChat, or a directed email versus a blast to many people). Hall's (2018) recent articulation of what constitutes social interaction on social media is another potentially useful distinction. Most of what people do on social media is actually scanning (i.e., viewing other people's content without actually interacting) or broadcasting (i.e., posting to a general audience rather than tailoring a message to a particular interactant), and only a small percentage of social media usage involves true social interaction (Hall, 2018). When two people use technologies to interact specifically with each other, it probably has different maintenance implications than when they use the same technologies for other purposes.

Finally, although this chapter focused on how communication technologies have become implicated in relationship maintenance, it is important to recognize that mixed-media relationships retain a central role for FtF communication. Indeed, there is evidence that even contemporary undergraduate students in the USA, who are generally very accustomed to using communication technologies, still often rate FtF communication as preferable to – and higher in quality than – other mediated forms of communication (e.g., Baym et al., 2004; Ruppel, 2014; Sharabi & Caughlin, 2017). Thus, even while considering how technologies are used to maintain relationships, relationship scholars must also consider maintenance that occurs face-to-face to be part of what it means to view "relationships as maintained through multiple media" (Baym et al. 2004).

REFERENCES

Alberts, J. K., Yoshimura, C. G., Rabby, M., & Loschiavo, R. (2005). Mapping the topography of couples' daily conversation. *Journal of Social and Personal Relationships, 22,* 299–322. doi:10.1177=0265407505050941

Arditti, J. A., & Kauffman, M. (2004). Staying close when apart: Intimacy and meaning in long-distance dating relationships. *Journal of Couple & Relationship Therapy, 3,* 27–51. doi:10.1300/J398v03n01_03

Baldassar, L. (2007). Transnational families and the provision of moral and emotional support: The relationship between truth and distance. *Identities: Global Studies in Culture and Power, 14,* 385–409. doi:10.1080/10702890701578423

Baym, N. K. (2015). *Personal connections in the digital age* (2nd ed.). Malden, MA: Polity Press.

Baym, N. K., Zhang, Y. B., & Lin, M. (2004). Social interactions across media. *New Media & Society, 6,* 299–318. doi:10.1177/1461444804041438

Bazarova, N. N., Taft, J. G., Choi, Y. H., & Cosley, D. (2013). Managing impressions and relationships on Facebook: Self-presentational and relational concerns revealed through the analysis of language style. *Journal of Language and Social Psychology, 32,* 121–141. doi:10.1177/0261927X12456384

Bourdieu, P. (1986). The forms of capital. In J. G. Richardson (Ed.), *Handbook of theory and research for the sociology of education* (pp. 241–258). New York, NY: Greenwood.

Brody, N., LeFebvre, L. E., & Blackburn, K. G. (2016). Social networking site behaviors across the relational lifespan: Measurement and association with relationship escalation and de-escalation. *Social Media + Society, 2,* 1–16. doi:10.1177/2056305116680004

Brody, N., & Peña, J. (2015). Equity, relationship maintenance, and linguistic features of text messaging. *Computers in Human Behavior, 49,* 499–506. doi:10.1016/j.chb.2015.03.037

Burke, M., & Kraut, R. E. (2016). The relationship between Facebook use and well-being depends on communication type and tie strength. *Journal of Computer Mediated Communication, 21,* 265–281. doi:10.1111/jcc4.12162

Caughlin, J. P., Basinger, E. D., & Sharabi, L. L. (2017). The connections between communication technologies and relational conflict: A multiple goals and communication interdependence perspective. In J. A. Samp (Ed.), *Communicating interpersonal conflict in close relationships: Contexts, challenges and opportunities* (pp. 57–72). New York: NY: Routledge.

Caughlin, J. P., & Sharabi, L. L. (2013). A communicative interdependence perspective of close relationships: The connections between mediated and unmediated interactions matter. *Journal of Communication, 63,* 873–893. doi:10.1111/jcom.12046

Chen, Y-F., & Katz, J. E. (2009). Extending family to school life: College students' use of the mobile phone. *International Journal of Human-Computer Studies, 67,* 179–191. doi:10.1016/j.ijhcs.2008.09.002

Coleman, J. S. (1988). Social capital in the creation of human capital. *The American Journal of Sociology, 94,* 95–120. doi:10.1086/228943

Dainton, M. & Aylor, B. (2002). Patterns of communication channel use in the maintenance of long-distance relationships. *Communication Research Reports, 19,* 118–129. doi:10.1080/08824090209384839

Dindia, K., & Canary, D. J. (1993). Definitions and theoretical perspectives on maintaining relationships. *Journal of Social and Personal Relationships, 10,* 163–173. doi:10.1177/026540759301000201

Duran, R. L., Kelly, L., & Rotaru, T. (2011). Mobile phones in romantic relationships and the dialectic of autonomy versus connection. *Communication Quarterly, 59,* 19–36. doi:10.1080/01463373.2011.541336

Ellison, N. B., Steinfield, C., & Lampe, C. (2007). The benefits of Facebook "friends:" Social capital and college students' use of online social network sites. *Journal of Computer-Mediated Communication, 12,* 1143–1168. doi:10.1111/j.1083-6101.2007.00367.x

Ellison, N. B., Steinfield, C., & Lampe, C. (2011). Connection strategies: Social capital implications of Facebook-enabled communication practices. *New Media & Society, 13,* 873–892. doi:10.1177/1461444810385389

Ellison, N. B., Vitak, J., Gray, R., & Lampe, C. (2014). Cultivating social resources on social network sites: Facebook relationship maintenance behaviors and their role in social capital processes. *Journal of Computer-Mediated Communication, 19,* 855–870. doi:10.1111/jcc4.12078

Fox, J., Osborn, J. L., & Warber, K. M. (2014). Relational dialectics and social networking sites: The role of Facebook in romantic relationship escalation, maintenance, conflict, and dissolution. *Computers in Human Behavior, 35,* 527–534. doi:10.1016/j.chb.2014.02.031

Greenwood, S., Perrin, A., & Duggan, M. (2016). *Social media update 2016*. Pew Research Center. Retrieved from www.pewinternet.org/2016/11/11/social-media-update-2016/

Guldner, G. T., & Swensen, C. H. (1995). Time spent together and relationship quality: Long-distance relationships as a test case. *Journal of Social and Personal Relationships, 12*, 313–320. doi:10.1177/0265407595122010

Hall, J. A. (2018). When is social media use social interaction? Defining mediated social interaction. *New Media & Society, 20*(1), 162–179. doi:10.1177/1461444816660782

Hall, J. A., & Baym, N. K. (2012). Calling and texting (too much): Mobile maintenance expectations, (over) dependence, entrapment, and friendship satisfaction. *New Media & Society, 14*, 316–331. doi:10.1177/1461444811415047

Haythornthwaite, C. (2005). Social networks and Internet connectivity effects. *Information, Communication & Society, 8*, 125–147. doi:10.1080/13691180500146185

Ishii, K. (2006). Implications of mobility: The uses of personal communication media in everyday life. *Journal of Communication, 56*, 346–365. doi:10.1111/j.1460-2466.2006.00023.x

Jiang, C. L., & Hancock, J. T. (2013). Absence makes the communication grow fonder: Geographic separation, interpersonal media, and intimacy in dating relationships. *Journal of Communication, 63*, 556–577. doi:10.1111/jcom.12029

Jin, B., & Peña, J. F. (2010). Mobile communication in romantic relationships: Mobile phone use, relational uncertainty, love, commitment, and attachment styles. *Communication Reports, 23*, 39–51. doi:10.1080/08934211003598742

Johnson, A. J., Bostwick, E., & Bassick, M. (2017). Long-distance versus geographically close romantic relationships: The effects of social media on the development and maintenance of these relationships. In N. Punyanunt-Carter & J. S. Wrench (Eds.), *The impact of social media in modern romantic relationships* (pp. 113–129). Lanham, MD: Lexington Books.

Johnson, A. J., Haigh, M. M., Becker, J. A. H., Craig, E. A., & Wigley, S. (2008). College students' use of relational management strategies in email in long-distance and geographically close relationships. *Journal of Computer-Mediated Communication, 13*, 381–404. doi:10.1111/j.1083-6101.2008.00401.x

Kelley, H. H., Berscheid, E., Christensen, A., Harvey, J. H., Huston, T. L., Levinger, G., … Peterson, D. R. (1983). *Close relationships*. New York, NY: Freeman.

Laliker, M. K., & Lannutti, P. J. (2014). Remapping the topography of couples' daily interactions: Electronic messages. *Communication Research Reports, 31*, 262–271. doi:10.1080/08824096.2014.924336

LaRose, R., Connolly, R., Lee, H., Li, K., & Hales, K. D. (2014). Connection overload? A cross cultural study of the consequences of social media connection. *Information Systems Management, 31*, 59–73. doi:10.1080/10580530.2014.854097

Ledbetter, A. M. (2009). Patterns of media use and multiplexity: Associations with sex, geographic distance and friendship interdependence. *New Media & Society, 17*, 1187–1208. doi:10.1177/1461444809342057

Ledbetter, A. M. (2010). Assessing the measurement invariance of relationship maintenance behavior when face-to-face and online.*Communication Research Reports, 27*, 30–37. doi:10.1080/08824090903526620

Licoppe, C. (2004). "Connected" presence: The emergence of a new repertoire for managing social relationships in a changing communication technoscape. *Environment and Planning D: Society and Space, 22*, 135–156. doi:10.1068/d323t

Ling, R., & Lai, C. (2016). Microcoordination 2.0: Social coordination in the age of smartphones and messaging apps. *Journal of Communication, 68*, 834–856. doi:10.1111/jcom.12251

Luo, S. (2014). Effects of texting on satisfaction in romantic relationships: The role of attachment. *Computers in Human Behavior, 33*, 145–152. doi:10.1016/j.chb.2014.01.014

Luo, S., & Tuney, S. (2015). Can texting be used to improve romantic relationships? – The effects of sending positive text messages on relationship satisfaction. *Computers in Human Behavior, 49*, 670–678. doi:10.1016/j.chb.2014.11.035

Madianou, M., & Miller, D. (2011). Mobile phone parenting: Reconfiguring relationships between Filipina migrant mothers and their left-behind children. *New Media & Society, 13*, 457–470. doi:10.1177/1461444810393903

Maguire, K., & Connaughton, S. L. (2011). A cross-contextual examination of technologically mediated communication and presence in long distance relationships. In L. Webb & K. Wright (Eds.), *Computer-Mediated Communication in Personal Relationships* (pp. 244–265). New York, NY: Peter Lang.

McEwan, B. (2013). Sharing, caring, and surveilling: An actor-partner interdependence model investigation of Facebook relationship maintenance. *Cyberpsychology, Behavior, and Social Networking, 16*, 863–869. doi:10.1089/cyber.2012.0717

McEwan, B., Sumner, E., Eden, J., & Fletcher, J. (2018). The effects of Facebook relationship maintenance on friendship quality: An investigation of the Facebook relationship maintenance measure. *Communication Research Reports, 35*(1), 1–11. doi:10.1080/08824096.2017.1361393

Merolla, A. J. (2010). Relationship maintenance and noncopresence reconsidered: Conceptualizing geographic separation in close relationships. *Communication Theory, 20*, 169–193. doi:10.1111/j.1468-2885.2010.01359.x

Neustaedter, C., & Greenberg, S. (2012). Intimacy in long-distance relationships over video chat. Proceedings of the 2012 ACM Annual Conference on Human Factors in Computing Systems – CHI'12, 753–762. New York, NY. doi:10/1145/2207676.2207785

Ogolsky, B. G., Monk, J. K., Rice, T. M., Theisen, J. C., & Maniotes, C. R. (2017). Relationship maintenance: A review of research on romantic relationships. *Journal of Family Theory & Review, 9*(3), 275–306.

Parks, M. R. (2017). Embracing the challenges and opportunities of mixed-media relationships. *Human Communication Research, 43*, 505–517. doi:10.1111/hcre.12125

Pettegrew, L. S., & Day, C. (2015). Smart phones and mediated relationships: The changing face of relational communication. *The Review of Communication, 15*, 122–139. doi:10.1080/15358593.2015.1044018

Pusateri, K. B., Roaché, D. J., & Wang, N. (2015). The role of communication technologies in serial arguments: A communication interdependence perspective. *Argumentation and Advocacy, 52*, 44–60. www.questia.com/library/journal/1G1-443059657/the-role-of-communication-technologies-in-serial-arguments

Putnam, R. (2000). *Bowling alone: The collapse and revival of American community*. New York, NY: Simon & Schuster.

Ramirez, A., & Broneck, K. (2009). "IM me": Instant messaging as relationship maintenance and everyday communication. *Journal of Social and Personal Relationships, 26*, 291–314. doi:10.1177/0265407509106719

Reid, F. J. M., & Reid, D. J. (2010). The expressive and conversational affordances of mobile messaging. *Behaviour & Information Technology, 29*, 3–22. doi:10.1080/01449290701497079

Roberts, J. A., & David, M. E. (2016). My life has become a major distraction from my cell phone: Partner phubbing and relationship satisfaction among romantic partners. *Computers in Human Behavior, 54*, 134–141. doi:10.1016/j.chb.2015.07.058

Rossetto, K. R. (2012). Relational coping during deployment: Managing communication and connection in relationships. *Personal Relationships*, *20*, 568–586. doi:10.1111/pere.12000

Ruppel, E. K. (2014). Use of communication technologies in romantic relationships: Self-disclosure and the role of relationship development. *Journal of Social and Personal Relationships*, *32*, 667–686. doi:10.1177/0265407514541075

Ruppel, E. K., Burke, T. J., & Cherney, M. R. (2018). Channel complementarity and multiplexity in long-distance friends' patterns of communication technology use. *New Media & Society*, *20*, 1564–1579. doi:10.1177/1461444817699995

Sahlstein, E. M. (2004). Relating at a distance: Negotiating being together and being apart in long-distance relationships. *Journal of Social and Personal Relationships*, *21*, 689–710. doi:10.1177/0265407504046115

Seo, M., Kim, J., & Prabu, D. (2015). Always connected or always distracted? ADHD symptoms and social assurance explain problematic use of mobile phone and multicommunicating. *Journal of Computer-Mediated Communication*, *20*, 667–681. doi:10.1111/jcc4.12140

Seo, M., Kim, J., & Yang, H. (2016). Frequent interaction and fast feedback predict perceived social support: Using crawled and self-reported data of Facebook users. *Journal of Computer-Mediated Communication*, *21*, 282–297. doi:10.1111/jcc4.12160

Sharabi, L. L., & Caughlin, J. P. (2017). Usage patterns of social media across stages of romantic relationships. In N. Punyanunt-Carter & J. S. Wrench (Eds.), *The impact of social media in modern romantic relationships* (pp. 15–29). Lanham, MD: Lexington Books.

Sosik, V. S., & Bazarova, N. N. (2014). Relationship maintenance on social network sites: How Facebook communication predicts relational escalation. *Computers in Human Behavior*, *35*, 124–131. doi:10.1016/j.chb.2014.02.044

Stafford, L., & Canary, D. J. (1991). Maintenance strategies and romantic relationship type, gender and relational characteristics. *Journal of Social and Personal Relationships*, *8*, 217–242. doi:10.1177/0265407591082004

Stafford, L., & Hillyer, J. D. (2012). Information and technologies in personal relationships. *Review of Communication*, *14*, 290–312. doi:10.1080/15358593.2012.685951

Stafford, L., Kline, S., & Dimmick, J. (1999). Home e-mail: Relationship maintenance and gratification opportunities. *Journal of Broadcasting & Electronic Media*, *43*, 659–669. doi:10.1080/08838159909364515

Stafford, L., & Merolla, A. J. (2007). Idealization, reunions, and stability in long-distance dating relationships. *Journal of Social and Personal Relationships*, *24*, 37–54. doi:10.1177/0265407507072578

Steinfield, C., Ellison, N. B., & Lampe, C. (2008). Social capital, self-esteem, and use of online social network sites: A longitudinal analysis. *Journal of Applied Developmental Psychology*, *29*, 434–445. doi:10.1016/j.appdev.2008.07.002

Su, H. (2016). Constant connection as the media condition of love: Where bonds become bondage. *New Media & Society*, *38*, 232–247. doi:10.1177/0163443715594037

Tokunaga, R. S. (2016). Interpersonal surveillance over social network sites: Applying a theory of negative relationship maintenance and the investment model. *Journal of Social and Personal Relationships*, *33*, 171–190. doi:10.1177/0265407514568749

Tong, S. T., & Walther, J. B. (2011). Relationship maintenance and CMC. In K. B. Wright & L. M. Webb (Eds.) *Computer-mediated communication in personal relationships* (pp. 98–118). New York, NY: Lang.

Valenzuela, S., Park, N., & Kee, K. F. (2009). Is there social capital in a social network site?: Facebook use and college students' life satisfaction, trust, and participation.

Journal of Computer-Mediated Communication, 14, 875–901. doi:10.1111/j.1083-6101.2009.01474.x

Valkenburg, P. M., & Peter, J. (2009). The effects of instant messaging on the quality of adolescents' existing friendships: A longitudinal study. *Journal of Communication*, 59, 7–97. doi:10.1111/j.1460-2466.2008.01405.x

Van Ouytsel, J., Van Gool, E., Walrave, M., Ponnet, K., & Peeters, E. (2016). Exploring the role of social networking sites within adolescent romantic relationships and dating experiences. *Computers in Human Behavior*, 55, 76–86. doi:10.1016/j.chb.2015.08.042

Vitak, J. (2014). Facebook makes the heart grow fonder: Relationship maintenance strategies among geographically dispersed and communication-restricted connections. CSCW'14 Proceedings of the 17th ACM conference on Computer supported cooperative work & social computing, 842–853. New York, NY. doi:10.1145/2531602.2531726

Walsh, S. P., White, K. M, & Young, R. M. (2009). The phone connection: A qualitative exploration of how belongingness and social identification relate to mobile phone use amongst Australian youth. *Journal of Community & Applied Social Psychology*, 19, 225–240. doi:10.1002/casp.983

Wang, N., Roaché, D. J., & Pusateri, K. B. (2018). *Interconnection of multiple communication modes in long-distance dating relationships.* Online first publication. *Western Journal of Communication.* doi: 10.1080/10570314.2018.1552986

Wei, R., & Lo, V.-H. (2006). Staying connected while on the move: Cell phone use and social connectedness. *New Media & Society*, 8, 53–72. doi:10.1177/1461444806059870

Wendorf, J. E., & Yang, F. (2015). Benefits of a negative post: Effects of computer-mediated venting on relationship maintenance. *Computers in Human Behavior*, 52, 271–277. doi:10.1016/j.chb.2015.05.040

Wilding, R. (2006). "Virtual" intimacies? Families communicating across transnational contexts. *Global Networks*, 6, 125–142. doi:10.1111/j.1471-0374.2006.00137.x

17

Relationship Maintenance across the Life Course

AMY RAUER[1] AND CHRISTINE PROULX[2]

Relationship maintenance encompasses the cognitive and behavioral dynamics that assist in preserving or strengthening a relationship (Dindia, 2000). By its very definition, relationship maintenance implies development within intimate relationships. Whether couples are engaging in activities that keep relationships in good repair, in a satisfactory state, or even just in existence (Dindia, 2003), the underlying assumption is clear – the natural state of relationships, if left unattended to, is to deteriorate (Goldberg, Smith, & Kashy, 2010; VanLaningham, Johnson, & Amato, 2001). Thus, romantic partners must engage in a broad array of relationship-enhancing behaviors and threat-mitigation strategies, both individually and together, to preserve their relationships (Ogolsky, Monk, Rice, Theisen, & Maniotes, 2017). Given that relationship maintenance takes place between the start of a romantic relationship and its end (Montgomery, 1993), partners therefore spend the bulk of their time together engaging in relationship maintenance efforts, though their form and function are likely to change as the partners themselves develop across the life course.

Despite the clearly developmental – and in fact, lifespan – concept of relationship maintenance, scholars have argued that the approach to its study has remained relatively static and disproportionately focused on younger, less established couples (Ogolsky et al., 2017; Weigel & Ballard-Reisch, 1999a). Embedded in a literature more concerned with the bookends of romantic relationships (i.e., relationship initiation and dissolution) than their rich middle, it is not surprising that scholars tend to underestimate the dynamic nature of stability. Montgomery (1993), however, suggests that "[s]tability is but an illusion, caused by looking at relationships through too narrow a window of observation and seeing but a mere moment ... in the larger flux

[1] Department of Child and Family Studies, University of Tennessee, arauer@utk.edu
[2] Department of Human Development and Family Science, University of Missouri, proulxc@missouri.edu

and flow of time and space" (p. 213). Thus, the goal of our chapter is to broaden this window of observation by considering the extent to which relationship maintenance behaviors and strategies vary according to the developmental stage of both the relationship and the individuals within it, as well as to explore whether the antecedents and consequences of relationship maintenance may change across the life course.

To capture this moving target, we use life course theory to organize our review of the literature around how relationship maintenance is manifested at different points across the life course (e.g., young adulthood, middle adulthood, and older adulthood), while acknowledging that such developmental distinctions were often absent from the studies themselves and that many tended to conflate individual and relationship development. Where possible, we draw from Ogolsky and colleagues' (2017) integrative model of relationship maintenance to elucidate whether the behaviors occurred at the individual level or as an interactive dyadic process, and the underlying motives (threat mitigation versus relationship enhancement).

THEORETICAL BACKGROUND

Elder's (1998) life course theory frames this chapter, as its tenets elucidate why relationship maintenance needs to be both conceptualized and captured more dynamically over the life course. There is variability not only in how it is enacted across the life course (e.g., moving from threat mitigation to relationship enhancement as the relationship matures; Ogolsky et al., 2017) but also in its very definition (e.g., goals change from keeping the relationship in good repair to keeping it in existence to helping it flourish). Also fitting with this analysis is life course theory's concern with the sociohistorical context in which individuals and relationships develop. From a sociohistorical standpoint, the idea and study of relationship maintenance are relatively new, emerging in the 1980s (Stafford & Canary, 1991). Romantic or love-based relationships and marriages are, relatively speaking, also a fairly new phenomenon. Prior to the industrial revolution in the USA, marriage was a pragmatic arrangement that helped guarantee the survival of family units by providing food, shelter, and protection (Coontz, 2005; Finkel, 2017). It was not until the second half of the twenty-first century that mate selection and partnership formation became focused on finding a "soul mate" with whom one falls in love (Cherlin, 2009). Even more ambitiously, social psychologists now argue that not only must love exist in a marriage, but spouses must also assist one another in realizing their full potential as human beings (Finkel, 2017). As the field of relationship science emerged and developed, the emphasis was primarily on what brought couples together or what prompted them to dissolve the relationship (Berscheid, 1999). Such a focus shed little light on how couples maintained or enhanced their relationship. It was not until relatively recently that relationship health, or flourishing, became a focus of research and, subsequently, of the partners within the relationship.

As to why this focus has broadened, employing a sociohistorical perspective highlights multiple factors that may explain why relationship maintenance has gained momentum. First, the types of relationships people are trying to maintain have both grown more numerous and evolved over the past century. Numerous relationship forms have gained researchers' attention (e.g., stayover or visiting relationships, cohabitation, living apart together [LAT]), and their roles and functions across the life course continue to be examined (e.g., Connidis, Borell, & Karlsson, 2017; Jamison & Proulx, 2013). Second, theoretical notions of the ideal marriage have also evolved. For example, Finkel and colleagues (Finkel, Hui, Carswell, & Larson, 2014) suggest that now the goal in marriage is to maintain an optimal state of the relationship, in which individuals can come to realize their optimal self with the assistance of their spouse, whereas before the stakes were lower. Further, much of the literature to date has focused on the negative side of romantic relationships (Fincham & Beach, 2010), emphasizing threat mitigation rather than relationship enhancement (Ogolsky et al., 2017). Lastly, the tools available for engaging in maintenance behaviors have changed considerably over the last 50 years, with e-mail, texting, sexting, and social media, among others, being routinely used to achieve relationship maintenance goals (see also Caughlin & Wang, Chapter 16).

Life course theory also emphasizes timing within lives and relationships. The meaning, manifestation, antecedents, and consequences of maintenance are likely to change over the life course and over the course of a relationship (Montgomery, 1993), which requires an elasticity to thinking about relationship maintenance. For this reason, focusing on key life course transitions might be one way to identify the various processes that encompass maintenance over the individual and relational life course. Longitudinal studies of relationships as they unfold over the life course are also particularly useful, as they help researchers further understand the needs relationships fill at various points in the individual and relationship life course (Pietromonaco & Perry-Jenkins, 2014).

Life course theory's emphasis on linked lives is particularly relevant to the study of interpersonal relationships, especially from a dyadic or family perspective. The concept of linked lives highlights not only the co-occurring developmental trajectories of those who share an intimate relationship with one another, but also the developmental trajectories of their family members (or other significant persons). These additional trajectories might have direct or indirect effects on the individuals or their relationship, and on the maintenance strategies they might use at a given point in the course of a relationship. These multiple developmental trajectories thus shape what individuals need in, and can contribute to, a relationship (Parke, 1998).

The last life course concept we see as critical to the understanding of maintenance over the life course is human agency, since individuals are seen as active agents of change. Although human agency is inherent in relationship maintenance, given its proactive and reactive behavioral manifestations, it is important to note that factors across the life course might influence the extent to which partners can exercise agency. Some of these might be individual factors, such as limitations due to illness or aging, and some might be cultural, such as limitations on perceptions of socially acceptable behavior in specific relationship forms.

Although our primary theoretical framework is life course, we acknowledge that other theories might be helpful in understanding relationship maintenance over the life course, especially in later life. Socioemotional selectivity theory (Carstensen, 1992) might help explain why older adults would continue to invest in relationship maintenance from an age, if not relationship duration, perspective. Carstensen's theory suggests that as people age, they invest more heavily in meaningful relationships and less so in those that cause pain or grief. This suggests a potentially greater investment in relationship enhancement over threat mitigation. Other research suggests that older adults are better at many of the processes seen as key to relationship maintenance (e.g., forgiveness, sacrifice, generosity, and gratitude; Ogolsky et al., 2017). Across these theoretical frameworks, it is clear that relationship maintenance is sensitive to issues of timing – historical, individual, and relational.

DISENTANGLING THE EFFECTS OF AGE VERSUS MARITAL DURATION

Perhaps this complexity related to issues of timing is best illustrated when considering the challenges associated with disentangling the effects of age versus marital duration in the study of relationship maintenance. The tension between partners' ages and relationship duration is not new, nor is it uniquely a problem for research on relationship maintenance. Given that age and relationship duration are highly correlated (Cooney, Proulx, & Snyder-Rivas, 2016), it is often difficult to account for both age and relationship duration simultaneously in analytic procedures. Relatedly, the distinction between intra-individual change in relationship behaviors and preferences versus intra-relational change in behaviors and preferences remains unknown. That is, do differences that emerge in mid- and later-life relationships when compared with relationships earlier in life result from individual development or relational development, or both? In their meta-analysis on the correlates of relationship maintenance (as defined by the five factors of the Relational Maintenance Strategies Measure [RMSM]; Stafford & Canary, 1991), Ogolsky and Bowers (2013) report mixed findings regarding whether relationship duration is linked to maintenance behaviors. For some behaviors (positivity, openness, and assurances), there was a small, negative association with relationship duration. For social networks and sharing tasks, there was no association with relationship duration. Perhaps one of the most relevant studies included in the meta-analysis came from Dindia and Baxter (1987), who found that marital duration was associated with engaging in fewer relationship maintenance strategies. To our knowledge, however, no studies to date have examined the development of these processes within a sample of continuously partnered dyads over a substantial amount of time.

Such an inquiry is warranted, as Ogolsky's (2009) work indicates that the antecedents and consequences of maintenance may depend on how long couples have been together. Even the process of maintenance itself may vary based on relationship duration, as Weigel and Ballard-Reisch (1999a) suggest that communication should become more unconscious the longer a couple are together, and thus, relationship maintenance might be enacted less frequently in longer-term relationships. In their study of 143 married couples, they found that husbands' use of all five maintenance strategies was negatively associated with marital duration, particularly openness. Wives' use of positivity, openness, assurances, and networks negatively correlated with duration, particularly assurances, but wives' use of tasks was uncorrelated with length of marriage. Using unevenly spaced marital duration groupings, (i.e., 0–2, 3–6, 7–14, 15–23, and 24+ years), they found what they called a curvilinear pattern in maintenance behaviors, such that maintenance is high up to 6 years of marital duration, drops to its lowest from 15 to 23 years of duration, and then rebounds. These findings suggest that there might be some fluctuation in the use of maintenance behaviors over the course of a relationship. It is important to note, however, that the lowest observed maintenance value for those in the shortest relationships (0–2 years) was still 3.57 on a 5-point scale (openness for husbands), and this was a cross section of marriages of various lengths rather than a continuous examination of the same marriages over time. Using hierarchical linear regressions, the authors did not find evidence that including marital duration in the models changed the links between maintenance strategies and relationship functioning. The mixed findings regarding the role of relationship duration as a potential moderator again underscore the importance of examining couples over an extended period to reveal how maintenance develops and its associations with relationship functioning over time.

CONSIDERING RELATIONSHIP DEVELOPMENT IN DEPTH: A FOCUS ON RELATIONSHIP TYPES

Consistent with life course theory's focus on heterogeneity within a population, one strength of the relationship maintenance literature worth highlighting is that it has examined a variety of relationship types, although the literature as a whole has focused primarily on different-sex relationships (for exceptions, see Haas & Stafford, 1998; 2005; Ogolsky, 2009). In their early work on the topic, Stafford and Canary (1991) found that *seriously* dating, engaged, and married people perceived more assurances than dating people; engaged and seriously dating people perceived their partners as more open than dating or married people; and married people reported their partners using social networks more than seriously dating people. Perceptions of relationship-maintenance behaviors appear to vary across relationship stages or types, whereby relational partners may rely on some types of maintenance more at the beginning of relationships or premaritally. Thus, relational motivations, such as progressing the relationship to the next stage versus keeping a marriage intact, might influence relationship maintenance behaviors differentially across the relational life course.

Although it is likely that many of the maintenance behaviors that have been identified in the literature thus far would apply to those couples in more marginalized relationships (Ogolsky et al., 2017), they might be differentially influential, and it is important to note that maintenance behaviors that have yet to be identified may occur in these relationships. For example, for long-distance relationships or couples who choose to live apart together (LAT), limited face-to-face interaction (when compared with coresidential relationships) might influence the maintenance strategies used or the tools used to engage in maintenance behaviors (Merolla, 2010). Alternatively, for same-sex couples, stigma may heighten the importance of being "out" as a couple and drawing upon same-sex supportive environments (Haas & Stafford, 1998). We see this as a critical avenue for future research to explore, particularly as these types of relationships may be more common at certain points of the lifespan (e.g., later in life when one spouse is institutionalized due to failing health; Walker & Luszcz, 2009).

RELATIONSHIP MAINTENANCE IN YOUNG ADULTHOOD

Although considerations of how relationship maintenance manifests across the life course are difficult to disentangle from how it is experienced over the course of a single relationship, we focus here on young adults (ages 18–35). Although they tend to be in less established relationships in comparison with their older counterparts, young adults still engage in high levels of relationship maintenance. In fact, some scholars suggest that individuals just beginning their relationships – as most young adults are (Rauer, Pettit, Lansford, Bates, & Dodge, 2013) – have to engage more strategically in maintaining their relationships and may face more threats from the wider perceived availability of alterative partners, whereas those in established relationships often display more routinized and potentially less intentional efforts (Dindia, 2003). Such concerted efforts at relationship maintenance are possible in young adulthood, as the achievement of a committed intimate relationship is theorized to be the critical task of this developmental period (Erikson, 1968; Rauer et al., 2013).

As to the nature of these relationship maintenance efforts, much of the literature has focused on young adults' communicative strategies due to the heavy utilization of Stafford and Canary's (1991) RMSM. Originally comprised of the aforementioned five maintenance behaviors (positivity, openness, assurances, networks, and sharing tasks), it was later expanded to also include relationship talk, self-disclosure, advice, and conflict management (Stafford, 2010; Stafford, Dainton, & Haas, 2000; see also Stafford, Chapter 7). Across these studies, young adults appear to engage in all of these behaviors to enhance their relationships, though with decidedly mixed success (Dainton, 2013; Dainton & Aylor, 2002; Guerrero, Eloy, & Wabnik, 1993). For example, Guerrero and colleagues (1993) found that young adults (21 years old and in relationships of 1.5 years on average) who reported greater positivity, assurances, and task sharing were more likely to be in relationships that remained stable or even increased in commitment, but few differences in relationship outcomes emerged for networking or openness. Even accounting for more modern forms of networking via technology (i.e., Facebook) appeared to provide little boost to the importance of this maintenance behavior for relationship satisfaction (Dainton, 2013), despite young adults in longer-term relationships perceiving networking to be a more important behavior than young adults in less established relationships (Dainton, 2000).

As to why positivity, assurances, and task sharing may be more beneficial for romantic relationships, scholars suggest that even young adults tend to perform these behaviors more routinely than strategically (Dainton & Aylor, 2002). Routine relationship maintenance behaviors are theorized to require less cognitive effort, thus putting less strain on individuals while enabling the same potential benefits to the couple as more strategic behaviors (Dainton & Stafford, 1993). Routine maintenance behaviors may be especially effective at enhancing romantic relationship stability in young adulthood due to differences in how families and friends are perceived at this stage of life. A longitudinal study from Roberts and Dunbar (2011) of young adults' (18 years old on average) relationships with family and friends suggests that friendships – even the closest ties – required greater maintenance to sustain emotional intensity than did kin relationships, whereas the emotional closeness of family appeared to be self-sustaining. As young adults perceive their romantic relationships requiring less intentional effort, they may consider romantic partners as more similar to their family than to their friends. Given that recent cohorts of young adults see their families as especially stable and supportive (Fingerman, Cheng, Tighe, Birditt, & Zarit, 2012; Jensen, Rauer, Rodriquez, &

Brimhall, 2018), this perception may yield additional benefits for the romantic relationship.

Although the benefits of routinization suggest that maintenance behaviors may be more difficult to capitalize on for young adults in newer relationships, broadening the scope of relationship maintenance reveals that certain maintenance behaviors may in fact be easier to achieve earlier in a relationship. For example, positive illusions and benevolent cognitions may be easier to access as a young adult in a newly established relationship due to limerence and may perhaps be just as beneficial as other maintenance behaviors (McNulty, O'Mara, & Karney, 2008; Neff & Karney, 2005). Drawing upon two longitudinal studies of newlyweds in their 20s, McNulty and colleagues (2008) found that spouses who interpreted negative events (e.g., being criticized or ignored) in a way that allowed them to maintain a positive view of each other reported higher levels of initial marital satisfaction. Unfortunately, the benefits of these benign attributions appeared to be reserved for those in higher-quality marriages, as this reframing of negative experiences weakened more troubled marriages. Such complexity underscores the importance of taking a life course perspective when studying relationship maintenance, as the benefits and costs of relationship-maintenance behaviors may depend largely on their specific developmental and relational contexts.

RELATIONSHIP MAINTENANCE IN MIDDLE ADULTHOOD

As individuals enter middle adulthood, their focus expands beyond their intimate relationships to include many other ties as well (e.g., children, other family members, and coworkers; Erikson, 1968; Levinson, 1986). These competing demands for partners' time and energy may explain the importance of more routinized relationship-maintenance behaviors during middle adulthood (Dindia, 2003). This explanation is consistent with work by Goldberg and colleagues (2010) on lesbian, gay, and heterosexual couples in their late 30s who transitioned to parenthood. Utilizing Braiker and Kelley's (1979) measure of maintenance, which focuses on self-disclosure, they found that those who engaged in greater relationship maintenance prior to adoption reported more love, less ambivalence, and less conflict at the time of the adoption. However, engaging in more maintenance also predicted increases in marital conflict. Their interpretation of these seemingly contradictory findings highlights the importance of considering both individual and relationship context, as the authors concluded that the benefits of maintenance may be limited to the initial transition to parenthood. When the parental demands facing spouses increase over time, sustaining such high levels of maintenance may become impossible and lead to arguments over the lack of intimate communication. Furthermore, an individual may perceive their partner's openness about his or her needs quite differently when experienced in the context of limited resources. Given that openness has been less strongly correlated with relationship outcomes than other maintenance behaviors (e.g., positivity; Guerrero et al., 1993; Ogolsky & Bowers, 2013), it may be that the effects of openness are particularly sensitive to not only an individual's developmental context but also that of the larger family unit in which the couple is embedded.

Unfortunately, such developmental considerations are largely absent from the literature on middle-aged adults' use of relationship maintenance, as much of the literature on this population is characterized by samples in which the average age of the participants is in the late 30s to early 40s, but the full range is significantly broader. For example, work from the leading relationship maintenance experts includes samples with age ranges from 24 to 68 (Dainton, 2008), 19 to 74 (Canary & Stafford, 1992), and 21 to 83 (Weigel & Ballard-Reisch, 1999a,b). Although diverse age representation has advantages depending on the research question, it is difficult to capture what normative relationship maintenance is during middle adulthood with age ranges that span anywhere from 44 to 62 years of development. It would be similarly challenging to interpret the effects of marital duration across these aforementioned studies, as the span of relationship duration often ranges from newly-formed relationships of a few months up to four or more decades. Moving forward, scholars may need to contemplate collecting more homogeneous samples along both the individual and relationship development dimensions, since developmental methodologists have advocated this method as a way to aid in the interpretation of effects (Jager, Putnick, & Bornstein, 2017).

Keeping this caution in mind, one consequence of these wide age and relationship duration ranges is that they appear to encourage speculation about the development of relationship maintenance over time (Canary & Stafford, 1992; Dainton, 2008). For example, Weigel and Ballard-Reisch (1999b) suggest that spouses can in fact change their marital quality by deliberately engaging in more or less of certain maintenance behaviors, and "these changes may very well change how their partners feel about the relationships and their partners' subsequent use of maintenance behaviors" (p. 268). Such a heavy emphasis on an individual's ability to affect their relationships through their own actions may reflect key developmental changes, as individuals' sense of agency grows in young adulthood and peaks during middle adulthood (Diehl, Owen, & Youngblade, 2004). A somewhat more cynical take on the importance of this sense of agency in middle adulthood comes from Ragsdale and Brandau-Brown (2005), who found that couples in their late 30s who had been married for an average of 14 years (ranges not provided) engaged in maintenance quite strategically. For example, individuals, particularly men, who endorsed more negatively slanted characteristics (e.g., cynicism and Machiavellianism) reported utilizing

more maintenance strategies. Whether the underlying motivations for engaging in relationship maintenance are self-serving or something nobler, it is
clear that – despite the importance of routinized maintenance behaviors
(Dainton & Aylor, 2002; Dindia, 2003) – middle-aged adults may also be
uniquely poised to benefit from taking a more deliberate approach to the
maintenance of their romantic relationships.

RELATIONSHIP MAINTENANCE IN OLDER ADULTHOOD

If relationship maintenance in young and middle adulthood can be characterized by a developing sense of agency within romantic relationships, older
adulthood could be conversely thought of as working to maintain one's
romantic relationship in the face of shrinking resources, both internal and
external. To note, although a small number of older adults were included in
the studies described earlier for middle adulthood (Canary & Stafford, 1992;
Dainton, 2008; Weigel & Ballard-Reisch, 1999a,b), most studies examining
relationship maintenance later in life focus on those who are struggling with
declining health (Badr & Taylor, 2008; Korporaal, Broese van Groenou, &
Tilburg, 2013; Walker & Luszcz, 2009). Such a slant is understandable given
the increases in the incidence of chronic illness, disability, and dependency
that characterize older adulthood (Hodes & Suzman, 2007).

One consistent theme emerging from this work is that the routines that
may have enhanced relationships earlier in life no longer suffice when
couples are dealing with illnesses, particularly when spouses' health problems are dissimilar (Korporaal et al., 2013). Instead, older spouses must take
a more active role by communicating positively, sharing tasks, and increasingly relying on their social networks in order to maintain marital satisfaction when confronted with health challenges (e.g., lung cancer; Badr &
Taylor, 2008). Whether these health issues are more severe or more common
(e.g., hearing impairments; Yorgason, Piercy, & Piercy, 2007), couples are
described as having to develop new relationship strengths in order to
rebalance "the emotional ledgers between spouses" (p. 223). Such a task
may be particularly difficult, as strategies that worked earlier in the life
course may be less effective or even detract from relationship functioning
later in life. For example, Jensen and Rauer (2015) found that although
talking about your relationship to your partner – considered an interactive
relationship-enhancing approach (Ogolsky et al., 2017) – may benefit
younger adults' romantic relationships (Jensen & Rauer, 2016), doing so
later in life was linked to poorer marital outcomes. Older adults' desire to
avoid conflictual interactions in order to maximize emotional intimacy may
explain why the benefits of marital problem solving wane later in life (Jensen
& Rauer, 2015).

Although the task of maintaining one's relationship later in life sounds insurmountable in the face of such health challenges, older adults appear to be inimitably up to the task. In fact, socioemotional selectivity theory suggests that the very thing that puts older adults in this tenuous position (e.g., poor health) is the same thing that enables them to engage in relationship maintenance behaviors more easily (Carstensen, 1992; Carstensen, Fung, & Charles, 2003). As older adults become aware of their mortality, this awareness motivates them to engage in more positive relationship maintenance behaviors (Birditt & Fingerman, 2005; Carstensen, 1992). For example, older couples tend to use conflict-resolution strategies that focus on collaborating and preserving relationship quality rather than on winning the argument (Hoppmann & Blanchard-Fields, 2011; Rauer, Williams, & Jensen, 2017). Furthermore, the very tasks that older adults consider to be a part of care provision when their spouse is ailing fall cleanly within the definition of relationship maintenance (e.g., assurances, positivity, and sacrifice; Lee & Montelongo, 2016). Finally, older adults' developmental need to engage in reminiscence may also serve as relationship maintenance to the extent that couples bond over their shared histories (Butler, 2002; McCoy, Rauer, & Sabey, 2017) – a strategy that has been successfully used by interventionists to enhance couples' relationships and their well-being even in the face of dementia (Ingersoll-Dayton, Spencer, Campbell, Kurokowa, & Ito, 2013). Thus, although working to "re-frame the notion of 'couplehood'" sounds daunting later in life (Walker & Luszcz, 2009, p. 463), older adults' position in the life course and in their relationships appears to confer distinct advantages that enable them to successfully maintain their unions.

FUTURE DIRECTIONS AND CONCLUSIONS

Our review of maintenance across the life course suggests several fruitful areas for future research. The first is to determine the importance of relationship maintenance over the life course – is it equally important over time to partners, does it decline linearly over time, or does it fluctuate, and if so, based on what factors? Critical to understanding change over time is increasing the number of longitudinal studies on relationship development and maintenance using samples of couples whose duration represents a small range of years (i.e., is relatively homogeneous) within studies. This will help address the criticism raised earlier about the difficulty in isolating factors that are important at relatively understudied time points such as midlife.

To accompany such research, the field will need developmentally appropriate theories and measures of relationship maintenance. Given normative contextual and developmental changes as individuals and their relationships age, it appears that the time has come to question whether traditional indicators of maintenance apply equally well across the life course. For example,

Impett, Muise, & Rosen (Chapter 12) highlight the role of sex as relationship maintenance, but it may be that this maintenance behavior is less critical, or takes on a notably different form, in late-life relationships. Socioemotional selectivity theory suggests that maintenance behaviors such as positivity might be of increasing importance in later life, but research has yet to confirm this. Of the theories that characterize the literature on relationship maintenance, interdependence theory (see VanderDrift & Agnew, Chapter 2) might be best poised to help researchers and practitioners understand the development of maintenance behaviors in longer-term relationships, particularly as they progress toward caregiving needs of one or both partners. Further, theoretical constructs such as relational uncertainty (Theiss, Chapter 5) might shift in their focus from uncertainty about the viability of a relationship to uncertainty about the time remaining with a given partner due to illness or old age, and little is known about how this type of uncertainty might influence relationship maintenance behaviors. Engaging with social support networks changes over the lifespan, and although high engagement with social networks might be linked to positive relational trajectories early in relationships (Ogolsky, Surra, & Monk, 2016), couples in later life derive less of their well-being from social networks outside the relationship (Ermer & Proulx, 2017). Even more concerning is that this social support might actually be perceived as undermining in later life (Rauer, Sabey, & Jensen, 2014).

From a sociohistorical perspective, it will be critical to continue to explore how various contexts influence relationship maintenance throughout both the individual and the relational life course. For example, because androgyny increases later in life, might we see fewer differences between men and women later in the life course when examining relational maintenance and how it links to relationship outcomes (see Fiori & Rauer, Chapter 14)? In addition, Baltes (1997) suggests that culture becomes more salient later in life, but culture exists within a larger sociohistorical frame that is not static. Further, age at first marriage continues to rise in the USA (although it is less clear whether age at first coresidence [i.e., cohabitation] is similarly rising; Kuperberg, 2014), which allows adults more time for engaging in relationship maintenance behaviors premaritally. Will such engagement lend itself to better maintenance skills in marriage? As technology progresses and "digital natives" age, will technology take a more central role in relationship maintenance, or will we experience a backlash to more "old school" methods of engaging in maintenance (see Caughlin & Wang, Chapter 16)?

In sum, the questions raised here point to the need for more research on relationship maintenance across the life course – of both individuals and relationships – and for that research to be better situated in the actual contexts in which couples are engaging in maintenance. Such a body of research would advance theory on not only what relationship maintenance entails but also why, when, and how partners engage in it.

REFERENCES

Badr, H., & Taylor, C. L. C. (2008). Effects of relationship maintenance on psychological distress and dyadic adjustment among couples coping with lung cancer. *Health Psychology, 27*(5), 616–627.

Baltes, P. B. (1997). On the incomplete architecture of human ontogeny: Selection, optimization, and compensation as foundation of development theory. *American Psychologist, 52,* 366–380.

Berscheid, E. (1999). The greening of relationship science. *American Psychologist, 54,* 260–266.

Birditt, K. S., & Fingerman, K. L. (2005). Do we get better at picking our battles?: Age group differences in descriptions of behavioral reactions to interpersonal tensions. *The Journals of Gerontology Series B: Psychological Sciences and Social Sciences, 60,* 121–128.

Braiker, H. B., & Kelley, H. H. (1979). Conflict in the development of close relationships. In L. Burgess & T. L. Huston (Eds.), *Social exchange in developing relationships* (pp. 135–168). New York: Academic Press.

Butler, R. N. (2002). Age, death, and life review. In K. J. Doka (Ed.), *Living with grief: Loss in later life* (pp. 3–11). Washington, DC: Hospice Foundation of America.

Canary, D. J., & Stafford, L. (1992). Relational maintenance strategies and equity in marriage. *Communication Monographs, 59*(3), 243–267.

Carstensen, L. L. (1992). Social and emotional patterns in adulthood: Social support for socioemotional selectivity theory. *Psychology and Aging, 7,* 331–338.

Carstensen, L. L., Fung, H. H., & Charles, S. T. (2003). Socioemotional selectivity theory and the regulation of emotion in the second half of life. *Motivation and Emotion, 27*(2), 103–123.

Cherlin, A. J. (2009). *The marriage-go-round: The state of marriage and the family in America today.* New York, NY: Alfred A. Knopf.

Connidis, I. A., Borell, K., & Karlsson, S. G. (2017). Ambivalence and Living Apart Together in later life: A critical research proposal. *Journal of Marriage and Family, 79*(5), 1404–1418.

Cooney, T. M., Proulx, C. M., & Snyder-Rivas, L. A. (2016). A profile of later life marriages: Comparisons by gender and marriage order. In G. Gianesini & L. Blair (Eds.), *Divorce, separation, and remarriage: The transformation of family* (Contemporary Perspectives in Family Research, Volume 10) (pp. 1–37). London: Emerald Group Publishing Limited.

Coontz, S. (2005). *Marriage, a history: From obedience to intimacy or how love conquered marriage.* New York, NY: Viking.

Dainton, M. (2000). Maintenance behaviors, expectations for maintenance, and satisfaction: Linking comparison levels to relational maintenance strategies. *Journal of Social and Personal Relationships, 17*(6), 827–842.

Dainton, M. (2008). The use of relationship maintenance behaviors as a mechanism to explain the decline in marital satisfaction among parents. *Communication Reports, 21*(1), 33–45.

Dainton, M. (2013). Relationship maintenance on Facebook: Development of a measure, relationship to general maintenance, and relationship satisfaction. *College Student Journal, 47*(1), 113–121.

Dainton, M., & Aylor, B. (2002). Routine and strategic maintenance efforts: Behavioral patterns, variations associated with relational length, and the prediction of relational characteristics. *Communication Monographs, 69*(1), 52–66.

Dainton, M., & Stafford, L. (1993). Routine maintenance behaviors: A comparison of relationship type, partner similarity and sex differences. *Journal of Social and Personal Relationships, 10*(2), 255–271.

Diehl, M., Owen, S., & Youngblade, L. (2004). Agency and communion attributes in adults' spontaneous self-representations. *International Journal of Behavioral Development, 28*(1), 1–15.

Dindia, K. (2000). Relational maintenance. In Hendrick, C. & Hendrick, S. S. (Eds.), *Close relationships: A sourcebook* (pp. 287–299). Thousand Oaks, CA: Sage.

Dindia, K. (2003). Relationship maintenance communication. In D. J. Canary & M. Dainton (Eds.), *Maintaining relationships through communication: Relational, contextual, and cultural variations* (pp. 1–28). New York, NY: Psychology Press.

Dindia, K., & Baxter, L. A. (1987). Strategies for maintaining and repairing marital relationships. *Journal of Social and Personal Relationships, 4*(2), 143–158.

Elder, G. H. (1998). The life course as developmental theory. *Child Development, 69*, 1–12.

Erikson, E. H. (1968). *Identity: Youth and crisis.* New York, NY: Norton.

Ermer, A., & Proulx, C.M. (2017, November). Well-being among older adult couples: The role of social networks and neighbors. Paper presented at the annual meeting of the National Council of Family Relations, Orlando, FL.

Fincham, F. D., & Beach, S. R. (2010). Of memes and marriage: Toward a positive relationship science. *Journal of Family Theory and Review, 2*, 4–24.

Fingerman, K. L., Cheng, Y., Tighe, L. A., Birditt, K. S., & Zarit, S. H. (2012). Relationships between young adults and their parents. In A. Booth, S. L. Brown, N. Landale, W. Manning, & S. M. McHale (Eds.), *Early adulthood in a family context* (pp. 59–85). New York, NY: Springer.

Finkel, E. J. (2017). *The all-or-nothing marriage: How the best marriages work.* New York, NY: Dutton.

Finkel, E. J., Hui, C. M., Carswell, K. L., & Larson, G. M. (2014). The suffocation of marriage: Climbing Mount Maslow without enough oxygen. *Psychological Inquiry, 25*, 1–41.

Goldberg, A. E., Smith, J. Z., & Kashy, D. A. (2010). Preadoptive factors predicting lesbian, gay, and heterosexual couples' relationship quality across the transition to adoptive parenthood. *Journal of Family Psychology, 24*(3), 221–232.

Guerrero, L. K., Eloy, S. V., & Wabnik, A. I. (1993). Linking maintenance strategies to relationship development and disengagement: A reconceptualization. *Journal of Social and Personal Relationships, 10*(2), 273–283.

Haas, S. M., & Stafford, L. (1998). An initial examination of maintenance behaviors in gay and lesbian relationships. *Journal of Social and Personal Relationships, 15*(6), 846–855. doi:10.1177/0265407598156008

Haas, S. M., & Stafford, L. (2005). Maintenance behaviors in same-sex and marital relationships: A matched sample comparison. *The Journal of Family Communication, 5*(1), 43–60. doi:10.1207/s15327698jfc0501_3

Hodes, R. J., & Suzman, R. (2007). *Growing older in America: The Health and Retirement Study.* Bethesda, MD: US Department of Health and Human Services.

Hoppmann, C. A., & Blanchard-Fields, F. (2011). Problem-solving variability in older spouses: How is it linked to problem-, person-, and couple-characteristics? *Psychology and Aging, 26*, 525–531.

Ingersoll-Dayton, B., Spencer, B., Campbell, R., Kurokawa, Y., & Ito, M. (2014). Creating a duet: The couples life story approach in the United States and Japan. *Dementia, 15*, 481–493. doi:10.1177/1471301214526726

Jager, J., Putnick, D. L., & Bornstein, M. H. (2017). More than just convenient: The scientific merits of homogeneous convenience samples. *Monographs of the Society for Research in Child Development, 82*(2), 13–30.

Jamison, T., & Proulx, C. M. (2013). Stayovers in emerging adulthood: Who stays over and why? *Personal Relationships, 20*, 155–169.

Jensen, J., & Rauer, A. (2015). Marriage work in older couples: Disclosure of marital problems to spouses and friends over time. *Journal of Family Psychology, 29*, 732–743.

Jensen, J., & Rauer, A. (2016). Young adults' relationship work over time: The impact of disclosing romantic problems to partners and friends. *Journal of Social and Personal Relationships, 33*, 687–708.

Jensen, J., Rauer, A., Rodriquez, Y., & Brimhall, A. (2018). Whom should I talk to? Emerging adults' romantic relationship work. *Journal of Social, Behavioral, and Health Sciences, 12*, 17–39.

Korporaal, M., Broese van Groenou, M. I., & Tilburg, T. G. V. (2013). Health problems and marital satisfaction among older couples. *Journal of Aging and Health, 25*, 1279–1298.

Kuperberg, A. (2014). Age at coresidence, premarital cohabitation, and marriage dissolution: 1985–2009. *Journal of Marriage and Family, 76*, 352–369.

Lee, J. Y., & Montelongo, R. (2016). Caregiving and care-receiving in transition to older adulthood: Integrating an attachment theory perspective. *Journal of Religion, Spirituality & Aging, 28*(3), 200–218.

Levinson, D. J. (1986). A conception of adult development. *American Psychologist, 41*, 3–13.

McCoy, A., Rauer, A., & Sabey, A. (2017). The meta marriage: Links between older couples' relationship narratives and marital satisfaction. *Family Process, 56*, 900–914.

McNulty, J. K., O'Mara, E. M., & Karney, B. R. (2008). Benevolent cognitions as a strategy of relationship maintenance: "Don't sweat the small stuff" .... but it is not all small stuff. *Journal of Personality and Social Psychology, 94*(4), 631–646.

Merolla, A. J. (2010). Relational maintenance and non-co-presence reconsidered: Conceptualizing geographic separation in close relationships. *Communication Theory, 20*, 169–193.

Montgomery, B. M. (1993). Relationship maintenance versus relationship change: A dialectical dilemma. *Journal of Social and Personal Relationships, 10*(2), 205–223.

Neff, L. A., & Karney, B. R. (2005). To know you is to love you: The implications of global adoration and specific accuracy for marital relationships. *Journal of Personality and Social Psychology, 88*(3), 480–497.

Ogolsky, B. G. (2009). Deconstructing the association between relationship maintenance and commitment: Testing two competing models. *Personal Relationships, 16*(1), 99–115.

Ogolsky, B. G., & Bowers, J. R. (2013). A meta-analytic review of relationship maintenance and its correlates. *Journal of Social and Personal Relationships, 30*(3), 343–367. doi:10.1177/0265407512463338

Ogolsky, B. G., Monk, J. K., Rice, T. M., Theisen, J. C., & Maniotes, C. R. (2017). Relationship maintenance: A review of research on romantic relationships. *Journal of Family Theory & Review, 9*(3), 275–306.

Ogolsky, B. G., Surra, C. A., & Monk, J. K. (2016). Pathways of commitment to wed: The development and dissolution of romantic relationships. *Journal of Marriage and Family, 78*, 293–310.

Parke, R. D. (1998). A developmentalist's perspective on marital change. In T. N. Bradbury (Ed.), *The developmental course of marital dysfunction* (pp. 393–409). New York, NY: Cambridge University Press.

Pietromonaco, P. R., & Perry-Jenkins, M. (2014). Marriage in whose America? What the suffocation model misses. *Psychological Inquiry*, *25*, 108–113.

Ragsdale, J. D., & Brandau-Brown, F. E. (2005). Individual differences in the use of relational maintenance strategies in marriage. *Journal of Family Communication*, *5* (1), 61–75. doi:10.1207/s15327698jfc0501_4

Rauer, A., Pettit, G., Lansford, J., Bates, J., & Dodge, K. (2013). Romantic relationship patterns in young adulthood and their developmental antecedents. *Developmental Psychology*, *49*, 2159–2171.

Rauer, A. J., Sabey, A., & Jensen, J. F. (2014). Growing old together: Compassionate love and health in older adulthood. *Journal of Social and Personal Relationships*, *31*(5), 677–696.

Rauer, A., Williams, L., & Jensen, J. (2017). Finer distinctions: Variability in satisfied older couples' problem-solving behaviors. *Family Process*, *56*, 501–517.

Roberts, S. G., & Dunbar, R. I. (2011). The costs of family and friends: An 18-month longitudinal study of relationship maintenance and decay. *Evolution and Human Behavior*, *32*(3), 186–197.

Stafford, L. (2010). Measuring relationship maintenance behaviors: Critique and development of The Revised Relationship Maintenance Behavior Scale. *Journal of Social and Personal Relationships*, *28*(2), 278–303.

Stafford, L., & Canary, D. J. (1991). Maintenance strategies and romantic relationship type, gender and relational characteristics. *Journal of Social and Personal Relationships*, *8*(2), 217–242.

Stafford, L., Dainton, M., & Haas, S. (2000). Measuring routine and strategic relational maintenance: Scale revision, sex versus gender roles, and the prediction of relational characteristics. *Communication Monographs*, *63*(3), 306–323.

VanLaningham, J., Johnson, D. R., & Amato, P. (2001). Marital happiness, marital duration, and the U-shaped curve: Evidence from a five-wave panel study. *Social Forces*, *79*(4), 1313–1341.

Walker, R. B., & Luszcz, M. A. (2009). The health and relationship dynamics of late-life couples: A systematic review of the literature. *Ageing & Society*, *29*(3), 455–480.

Weigel, D. J., & Ballard-Reisch, D. S. (1999a). The influence of marital duration on the use of relationship maintenance behaviors. *Communication Reports*, *12*(2), 59–70.

Weigel, D. J., & Ballard-Reisch, D. S. (1999b). How couples maintain marriages: A closer look at self and spouse influences upon the use of maintenance behaviors in marriages. *Family Relations*, *48*(3), 263–269.

Yorgason, J. B., Piercy, F. P., & Piercy, S. K. (2007). Acquired hearing impairment in older couple relationships: An exploration of couple resilience processes. *Journal of Aging Studies*, *21*(3), 215–228.

18

Relationship Maintenance in Couple Therapy and Relationship Education

AMBER VENNUM[1], JEREMY B. KANTER[2],
AND JOYCE BAPTIST[3]

The term "relationship maintenance" has been used to describe a broad range of processes within romantic relationships (Ogolsky, Monk, Rice, Theisen, & Maniotes, 2017). Historically, clinicians and relationship educators have promoted maintenance behaviors for the purpose of "enhancing the quality of marital relationships and … preventing distress and dissolution" (Wadsworth & Markman, 2012, p. 99). Ogolsky and colleagues (2017) label the two motivational categories of relationship maintenance strategies as threat mitigation and relationship enhancement. Relationship enhancement is characterized by maintenance strategies that foster and sustain positive aspects of relationships, whereas threat-mitigation processes occur in response to some sort of relational concern but can become long-term enhancement strategies. Additionally, Ogolsky and colleagues explain that relationship maintenance strategies within these two motivational categories can either stem "from individuals or from an interactive dyadic process," aligning with current calls to target both intrapersonal and interpersonal processes in intervention models (e.g., Kanter & Schramm, 2018). In this chapter, we start with a brief discussion of current cultural forces impacting relationships, followed by a description of the general definition of maintenance within the applied field, theories of change used within these interventions, and example interventions that have effectively facilitated specific maintenance processes, and end with future directions for the field.

CONTEMPORARY CONTEXTUAL INFLUENCES ON RELATIONSHIP MAINTENANCE

Although there are common themes, there are subtle differences in what maintains a stable romantic relationship based on the intersections of gender,

[1] School of Family Studies and Human Services, Kansas State University, avennum@ksu.edu
[2] Department of Family and Consumer Sciences, Illinois State University, Jbkante@ilstu.edu
[3] School of Family Studies and Human Services, Kansas State University, jbaptist@k-state.edu

sexual orientation, cultural norms, social class, and point in the relational life course of each couple (e.g., Fiori & Rauer, Chapter 14; Rauer & Proulx, Chapter 17), a point we return to later in this chapter. Despite the nuances in relationship maintenance, individuals from a young age report a desire for a flourishing romantic relationship in the future (Anderson, 2016). As such, there is a growing need to help couples develop and sustain behaviors that support healthy relationship development. However, definitions of what constitutes a "healthy" relationship have varied throughout history, and the values individuals in Western cultures draw from to evaluate whether their relationship is worth maintaining may be shifting.

Cherlin (2010) suggests that contemporary couples are expecting more from their romantic relationships than previous generations. Finkel (2017) elaborates on this notion, positing that these expectations are skewed toward higher-order needs (e.g., self-expansion) than lower needs (e.g., safety and security) compared with previous generations. Indeed, not only are partners expected to fill a multitude of roles, but there has also been an emphasis on communication, responsiveness, and support as qualities a partner *must* display for a satisfying relationship (Finkel, Hui, Carswell, & Larson, 2014). The growing instrumental view of relationships in which people assess their relationships as they would any consumer product ("Is the relationship meeting my personal needs?") may place couples at increased risk for instability in times of hardship (Doherty, 2013). Doherty (2013) posits that partners with a high instrumental perspective may more readily choose to exit a relationship than choose to put in the work to maintain it. In contrast, partners may be more likely to sustain their relationship if they view relationships as a context in which partners can grow together through hard times in ways that are mutually beneficial. This latter perspective illustrated by Doherty (2013) is considered a "companionate view," in which partners consider the benefits of maintaining the relationship within larger societal and moral values such as loyalty, generosity, commitment, and friendship that encourage relationship maintenance even when relationship satisfaction is low (Bellah, Madsen, Sullivan, Swidler, & Tiptont, 1996).

Unfortunately, as socioeconomic demands in Western societies shift, couples are expected to manage increasing demands from careers and other familial obligations (e.g., parenting and caregiving; see Finkel et al., 2014) while receiving progressively less help from community and familial support systems due to high mobility, decreased civic engagement, and increasing urbanization (Amato, Booth, Johnson, & Rogers, 2007). Whereas marriage was once a central, organizing institution of society, shifts in Western countries have increased options for coupling, uncoupling, and recoupling throughout the lifespan. This variability in coupling practices is reflected in a later average age at first marriage and decreasing overall marriage rate; greater fluidity in gender roles; and increases in nonmarital cohabitation and child-rearing, heterogamy in partner characteristics, and acceptance of divorce, repartnering, and remarriage (Amato et al., 2007). The increased emphasis on personal choice coupled with decreases in the structural supports for couples makes the decision to maintain, and the act of maintaining, a relationship more and more challenging, but increasingly necessary.

This task of maintaining a "mutually beneficial" relationship may be further complicated by dominant gender roles in heterosexual relationships, in which women are tasked with the emotional work (Erickson, 2005) while being unequivocally burdened with other familial responsibilities (Pietromonaco & Perry-Jenkins, 2014). Although inequality in gender roles may be declining and egalitarianism increasing as a value for contemporary couples (Kornich, Brines, & Leupp, 2012), many couples still perform traditional gender roles during normative transitions (e.g., transition to parenthood; Dew & Wilcox, 2011), and women are more likely than men to engage in a multitude of relationship maintenance behaviors in heterosexual relationships (Ogolsky & Bowers, 2013). As a result, the expectations associated with relationship maintenance might be gendered in heterosexual relationships, resulting in relationship inequalities that need to be addressed in therapy and relationship education.

As members of society, therapists and educators, without conscious effort, can become reinforcers of these social narratives, which make it harder for partners of all genders to choose to maintain their relationships (Doherty, 2015). For example, when therapists hold more individualistic societal values, they are more likely to advocate for the needs of individual partners than to advocate for partners to invest in the relationship as a potential way to fulfill companionate needs in the long term (Bridges, 2017). In referring to Discernment Counseling, which helps couples decide whether or not to try couples therapy before filing for divorce, Doherty (2015) argues that choosing to work through challenges in a relationship by owning one's own contribution provides an opportunity for personal growth that would be missed if partners left their unions when times were challenging. In this way, investing in relationships has the potential to be in the best long-term interest of each partner as well as any children involved (Doherty, 2015). According to ideas first presented in interdependence theory (Rusbult & Van Lange, 2003; Thibaut & Kelley, 1959), as people invest in their relationship and have positive interpersonal exchanges, a couple identity is formed, and long-term stability and quality are maintained by partners occasionally choosing to sacrifice immediate self-interest for the long-term benefits to themselves and their partner (Rusbult, Martz, & Agnew, 1998; see also VanderDrift & Agnew, Chapter 2).

Of course, at the other end of the spectrum, a strict adherence to societal and moral values such as commitment may result in keeping the union intact despite abusive or highly destructive patterns. Scholars argue that interventions to support relationship maintenance or enhancement may encourage people to stay in unhealthy or unsafe relationships if care is not taken to explicate when relationships need to change or end for the good of both partners and any involved children (see Sparks, 2008; see Johnson, 2012, for other criticisms). The safe ending of relationships with ongoing violence or emotional abuse may lead to fewer mental health barriers to partners being able to successfully maintain future relationships and is thus considered a potential positive outcome of intervention (Vennum, Monk, Pasley, & Fincham, 2017; Whiting, Bradford, Vail, Carlton, & Bathje, 2009). To facilitate the best outcomes, therapists and relationship educators must be consciously attuned to how their own values may influence the tone of their interventions to create the space necessary for partners to consider how their own values and circumstances influence their decisions to actively maintain or safely leave their romantic relationships.

CHOOSING TO MAINTAIN THE RELATIONSHIP

Relationship maintenance requires an ongoing decision to sustain or improve the relationship. Forces that keep relationships stable are not always the same forces that keep them functional (e.g., Rhoades, Stanley, & Markman, 2010). For example, Stanley and Markman (1992) discuss various factors (e.g., a shared lease, children, a marriage certificate) that may make dissolving a relationship more difficult (i.e., constraint commitment) regardless of partners' commitment to making the relationship work (i.e., dedication commitment). Although constraint commitment may benefit the relationship by increasing stability during normal ebbs and flows of relationship functioning, it can be detrimental when it keeps partners in an unhealthy relationship (e.g., Vennum, Lindstrom, Monk, & Adams, 2013). Therefore, long-term maintenance of a healthy relationship also requires a conscious and ongoing decision by partners to be dedicated to improving or maintaining the quality of their relationship (e.g., Doherty, 2015). In this context, relationship maintenance means consciously choosing to behave in ways that are beneficial for the relationship in the long term.

In many cases, there are subtle differences between how relationship maintenance is conceptualized in therapy and relationship education (although some have argued that the distinction has converged over time; Markman & Ritchie, 2015). Therapy for couples in distress is a process tailored to the needs of each unique couple (Markman & Ritchie, 2015) and first requires assessment of the extent to which both partners are committed to working on the relationship (Doherty, Harris, & Wilde, 2016). In the case that both partners are invested in making their relationship work, therapy is focused on addressing current barriers to improving or maintaining the relationship (e.g., communication skills and patterns, past attachment injuries, inequality, reconnecting and finding common interests, emotion regulation, and external stressors).

When one or both partners are ambivalent about the future of their relationship, therapy must first focus on helping partners decide whether to keep the union in its current state, invest further in the relationship in an effort to improve it, or exit the relationship in the least damaging way possible (Doherty et al., 2016).

Couple relationship education (CRE), on the other hand, is seen as a more universal preventive intervention providing "education, skills, and principles" for couples who want to improve "their chances of having healthy and stable relationships" often in a generalizable, curriculum-based group format (Markman & Rhoades, 2012, p. 169; Markman & Ritchie, 2015). CRE programs have been developed for individuals and couples in a variety of situations (premarital, coparenting, stepfamilies, etc.) and cultural contexts. Although CRE is often viewed as enrichment, recent research has emphasized the benefits of relationship education to couples who report high distress and instability in their relationship (e.g., Carlson, Rappleyea, Daire, Harris, & Liu, 2017; McGill et al., 2016), and CRE and therapy services may be used in tandem to address the needs of couples (Markman & Ritchie, 2015).

THEORIES OF CHANGE

There are many theoretical models of change in couple therapy and CRE that are used to decrease risk for, and increase protective factors against, further distress and/or instability. These models and the interventions within them predominantly differ in the degree to which they target behavior, emotion, cognitions, or context (e.g., Sprenkle, Davis, & Lebow, 2009) as the primary change mechanism(s). Several common approaches are outlined in the following section, along with example interventions used in CRE and/or clinical settings.

COGNITIVE BEHAVIORAL APPROACHES

Cognitive behavioral approaches are grounded in social learning theory, which primarily focuses on cognitions and behaviors as driving forces in maintaining relationships. The premise that these changes will improve relational outcomes is a long-held, but currently debated, hypothesis in both therapeutic and prevention settings (Johnson & Bradbury, 2015; Karney, Bradbury, & Lavner, 2018). According to strictly behavioral models of intervention, factors such as socioeconomic status or personality are viewed as largely static (Markman & Floyd, 1980); thus, problem behaviors can be alleviated by changing the consequences of those behaviors (Cluxton-Keller, 2011). Specifically, when positive behaviors are reinforced and dysfunctional behaviors minimized, relationship quality will improve, ultimately leading to stability (Johnson & Bradbury, 2015). Cognitive behavioral models of change incorporate ideas from social exchange theory to include cognitive, in addition to behavioral, strategies that help partners positively shift their evaluation of the cost–reward ratio in their relationships (Cluxton-Keller, 2011), potentially leading to increased desire to maintain the relationship.

Cognitive behavioral change models gained support in the 1990s as research on the impact of couple communication and conflict processes on relationship quality and stability (e.g., Gottman, Coan, Carrere, & Swanson, 1998; Markman, Rhoades, Stanley, Ragan, & Whitton, 2010) grew in prominence (Johnson & Bradbury, 2015; Lavner, Karney, & Bradbury, 2016). Accordingly, many CRE programs focus on communication behaviors between couples, such as scripted statements (e.g., "I" statements) and activities to provide structure during conflict discussions. For example, one heavily used tactic is the speaker-listener technique, which attempts to provide skills for the speaker (e.g., distinguishing a criticism from a complaint or request) and the listener (e.g., active listening) to help partners avoid negative interactions when having a disagreement (for a review, see Stanley, Markman, & Blumberg, 1999). Ultimately, these exercises are meant to ensure that positive communication patterns are established in the relationship in hopes of mitigating potentially destructive behaviors during a disagreement.

Arguably the most widely used cognitive behavioral CRE approach is the Prevention and Relationship Enhancement Program (PREP; Stanley et al., 1999) which focuses on communication and self-regulation knowledge and exercises (including those mentioned earlier) to change maladaptive communication patterns. Early evaluations of PREP have shown improvements in marital satisfaction and decreased rates of dissolution (Markman, Floyd, Stanley, & Storaasli, 1988; Markman, Renick, Floyd, Stanley, & Clements, 1993). In addition, most couples report significant improvements in communication skills (e.g., Allen, Rhoades, Markman & Stanley, 2015; Rhoades, Stanley, Markman, & Allen, 2015; Loew et al., 2012). However, some evaluations of PREP using experimental methods have found mixed results in the long term (see Johnson & Bradbury, 2015), a point we return to in our limitations section.

Aligning with the cognitive emphasis in cognitive behavioral approaches, other interventions take a strengths-based approach to help partners address maladaptive cognitions. For instance, in order to enhance positive illusions and idealization, Solution-Focused Brief Therapy helps couples identify and express to each other what is going well in the relationship, visualize a positive future, set small goals to get there, and identify the solution-finding abilities and resources they already possess to overcome future problems (e.g., Kim, 2008; Zimmerman, Prest, & Wetzel, 1997). Solution-focused interventions with couples have been found to increase dyadic adjustment (Zimmerman et al., 1997) self-esteem, and positive behaviors (Marigold, Holmes, & Ross, 2007; 2010). In CRE, Gottman and Gottman (2017) promote positive sentiment override (the ability to hold a generally positive view of one's partner) through interventions that encourage partners to think about and share what they appreciate about each other and plan time daily to reflect and engage in activities that highlight positive aspects of their relationship (e.g., Gottman & Silver, 1999). Outcomes of a randomized controlled study with distressed spouses found that the combination of interventions aimed at building positivity and admiration in the couple along with conflict-management techniques had a stronger positive impact on marital satisfaction in the long term than either component alone (Babcock, Gottman, Ryan, & Gottman, 2013).

INSIGHT- AND PRINCIPLE-BASED APPROACHES

Due to the limited effectiveness of models emphasizing behavioral skills training, interest has increased throughout the past decade in the potential effectiveness of insight- or principle-based approaches (Schramm, Galovan, & Goddard, 2017). Whereas the cognitive component of the cognitive behavioral models focuses primarily on changing the maladaptive thoughts themselves, insight- and principle-based approaches seek to help people understand the source behind those maladaptive beliefs in order to facilitate change in how individuals think about themselves in relationships. The primary assertion of these models is that changing a person's understanding of themselves, their behaviors and beliefs, and the world around them will create greater change than simply changing the thought, belief, or behavior in the present; it will change how people *are* versus simply changing how they behave (see Schramm et al., 2017, for a review). Therapeutic and CRE models using this approach include Bowen Family Systems Therapy (e.g., Titleman, 1998) and David Schnarch's Crucible Therapy (Schnarch, 1991), Kim Halford's Couple CARE program (Halford, 2011), and Blaine Fowers's virtue-based approach to therapy and CRE (Fowers, 2000; 2001). Interventions in these models focus on increasing partners' ability to act in ways that support their relationship goals by highlighting each partner's responsibility for maintaining the relationship (Halford, 2011) and may include strategies such as prompting partners to explore their values and expectations, where their ideas about relationships come from, how each partner handles stress, and their commitment to making the relationship work.

The Couple CARE program, for example, seeks to promote self-regulation by providing relationship information followed by reflective exercises that culminate with each partner articulating a vision for their relationship and identifying self-change goals in specific domains such as communication, intimacy, and caring (Halford, 2011). The Couple CARE program has been found to be effective at helping couples reduce negative communication and maintain relationship satisfaction over time compared with purely educational approaches to relationship education (Halford, Wilson, Watson, Verner, & Larson, 2010) and parenting education (Halford, Petch, & Creedy, 2010). Additional research is needed into insight- and principle-based approaches with regard to fostering relationship maintenance in general.

EXPERIENTIAL AND EMOTION-BASED APPROACHES

Experiential and emotion-based approaches focus on helping couples experience new ways of processing and organizing their emotions in order to prompt new insight into self and other, change rigid patterns of interaction (Martinez, Hollingsworth, Stanley, Shepard, & Lee, 2011), self-actualize their growth potential, and connect more authentically with others (e.g., Banmen, 2002; Brubacher, 2006; Wetchler & Piercy, 1996). Models that take this approach include Satir's Transformational Systemic Therapy (Satir, Banmen, Gerber, & Gomori, 1991), Emotion Focused Therapy (EFT; Johnson, 2004), and Symbolic-Experiential Family Therapy (Smith, 1998).

Research on the effectiveness of EFT supports the theoretical tenet that helping couples deeply explore core emotions may lead to long-term positive changes such as increases in relationship and sexual satisfaction, emotional connection, and forgiveness. Forgiveness may be a particularly important factor for promoting emotional recovery (Worthington, 2001) and facilitating later closeness and commitment (Tsang, Mccullough, & Fincham, 2006) in response to a relationship event that caused hurt between partners (see also McNulty & Dugas, Chapter 8). Accordingly, with its focus on processing emotional experiences, EFT has demonstrated effectiveness in promoting trust and forgiveness following a betrayal or violation of trust (e.g., an affair; Greenberg, Warwar, & Malcolm, 2010). Specific processes found to facilitate forgiveness in EFT include the injuring individual nondefensively accepting responsibility, and expressing feelings of shame and distress, for the pain they have caused their partner (Meneses & Greenberg, 2011). The extent to which these facilitators of forgiveness can be promoted in relationship education has yet to be explored, as little integration of experiential and emotion-based theories of change into relationship education programs with couples has occurred up to this point (Schramm et al., 2017).

ADDITIONAL CONSIDERATIONS TO ENHANCE EFFECTIVENESS

Although numerous interventions show promising results for promoting maintenance processes, families are contending with numerous and diverse challenges over the life course (e.g., Finkel et al., 2014; see also Rauer & Proulx, Chapter 17). The vulnerability adaptation model (VSA; Karney & Bradbury, 1995) posits that the contextual stressors occurring outside the relationship (see Neff & Karney, 2016) and vulnerabilities (Bradbury & Karney, 2004) that partners bring into the relationship influence their ability to enact and sustain the maintenance behaviors (i.e., adaptive processes) necessary for long-term marital quality. Therefore, Johnson & Bradbury (2015) speculate that without accounting for stressors and vulnerabilities, positive changes in maintenance processes will be considerably harder to achieve.

ATTENDING TO CONTEXTUAL STRESSORS

Research indicates that a sole focus on behavioral maintenance processes in relationships may be less effective at promoting relationship satisfaction when couples are contending with stressful circumstances. For example, Neff and Karney (2016) illustrate that external stress and maintenance behaviors covary over time (i.e., stress spills over into interactions). That is, couples dealing with multiple stressors are more likely to exhibit maladaptive maintenance behaviors. Although over 1 billion dollars in US federal funding (i.e., The Healthy Marriage Initiative) has been used to promote healthy relationships for low-income couples (primarily through targeting behavioral changes), to date, the results of these programs provide mixed findings (Johnson & Bradbury, 2015; Randles, 2016). Compared with more affluent couples, maintenance behaviors are not as strongly associated with relationship satisfaction in low-income couples, who experience unique stressors such as financial strain (Lavner et al., 2016; Nguyen, Williamson, Karney, & Bradbury, 2017; Williamson, Altman, Hsueh, & Bradbury, 2016). Therefore, only promoting behavioral changes without accounting for stressful circumstances may be insufficient to ensure long-term, satisfying relationships.

As such, relationship researchers have begun to explore the influence of contextual stressors on maintenance processes and overall global satisfaction (e.g., Cutrona et al., 2003) and to target the reduction of contextual stressors (e.g., financial strain, discrimination, and chronic illness) as a mechanism to promote relationship maintenance (Williamson, Karney, & Bradbury, 2017). The Couple Coping Enhancement Training (Bodenmann & Shantinath, 2004), for example, includes ideas from stress and coping research in an attempt to improve both individual and dyadic coping and prevent relationship distress (see also Randall & Messerschmitt-Coen, Chapter 10). In order to successfully promote maintenance strategies, educators and therapists may be most effective by not only including exercises on how to cope with contextual stressors (e.g., strengthening positive attributions about stressful circumstances) but also including interventions to reduce stressors (e.g., job skills training to reduce financial strain; Boss, 2002).

Unfortunately, few studies have examined how distinct stressors influence relational functioning. Rather, previous work has generally summed diverse stressors to create an overall stress variable. While warranted, because stressors tend to covary (Rauer, Karney, Garvan, & Hou, 2008), this conceptualization may overlook how distinct stressors impact relationships (Clavél, Cutrona, & Russell, 2017; Kanter & Proulx, 2018). Three topics that have received more specific attention in regard to their influence on relationship maintenance and functioning are financial strain, physical health challenges, and minority stress.

Financial strain. Results of numerous studies indicate that financial strain is associated with more destructive relationship dynamics and potentially lower relationship quality and stability (Lavner, Karney, & Bradbury, 2015). Accordingly, financial management skills and knowledge have been integrated into both clinical (e.g., Relational Financial Therapy; Kim, Gale, Goetz, & Bermudez, 2011) and CRE approaches (Administration for Children and Families, 2015) to working with couples. Of note, this integration into CRE has largely been focusing on money-management skills, which may help some low-income couples, but may be insufficient for couples who do not have sufficient financial resources to manage (e.g., Randles, 2016). As a result, scholars suggest that improving people's ability to manage financial stress through diverse strategies (e.g., career training or childcare subsidies; Hardoy & Schøne, 2008; Karney et al., 2018) is needed to help reduce financially stressful circumstances and potentially improve their relationship-maintenance behaviors and stability (e.g., Lavner et al., 2015). Evaluation of these CRE programs is needed to examine whether this more direct focus on economic stability leads to greater relationship maintenance, satisfaction, quality, and stability.

Health challenges. Various health diagnoses have been studied in relation to relationship maintenance strategies (e.g., Berg & Upchurch, 2007). For instance, following diagnosis of a health condition, the support provided by a partner and changes in leisure activities can largely dictate how the dyad manages and adjusts (Berg & Upchurch, 2007). Similarly, other maintenance strategies (e.g., relationship talk or positivity) have been linked to individual and couple well-being during initial treatment of, and subsequent functioning during, specific health challenges (e.g., Badr, Acitelli, & Taylor, 2008; Badr & Taylor, 2008). An example of an intervention to improve health and relationship maintenance, *Exercising Together* (Lyons, Winters-Stone, Bennett, & Beer, 2015), provides structured opportunities for couples to support one another as they complete a physical activity. For couples in which the husband was diagnosed with prostate cancer, wives reported increases in their own affectionate behavior following completion of the program (Lyons et al., 2015). The success of this intervention demonstrates how the effectiveness of an intervention may be improved by addressing dyadic processes within the context of a joint stressor the couple is experiencing (e.g., health). Further work is needed to explore how the effectiveness of interventions may differ as a function of role (i.e., patient or partner).

Minority stress. The minority stress perspective suggests that the experience of structural societal prejudice and discrimination by members of minority groups negatively impacts individuals' maintenance behaviors (e.g., Clavél et al., 2017) through detrimental effects on their self-concept (e.g., Trail, Goff, Bradbury, & Karney, 2012) and mental and physical health (e.g., Meyer, 2003). For example, researchers have found positive associations between discrimination experiences and adverse relationship maintenance, quality, and stability outcomes for sexual (e.g., Balsam & Szymanski, 2005; Otis, Rostosky, Riggle, & Hamrin, 2006), gender (e.g., Gamarel, Reisner, Laurenceau, Nemoto, & Operario, 2014), and ethnic-racial minority couples (e.g., Trail et al., 2012).

Inherent in systemic stressors, such as discrimination, is an absence of a simple intervention to remove this stressor. Pepping and Halford (2014) suggest that increased relationship maintenance (dyadic coping and caregiving, specifically) could serve as a protective factor in the presence of adversity. For example, research has shown that Black–White mixed-race couples are especially subject to discrimination (Dainton, 1999), and while Black partners experience direct discrimination, White partners may be discriminated against by virtue of their marriage to a Black person. The ability for mixed-race couples to confide in each other and develop strategies to counter such discrimination can influence the strength and longevity of their marriage. Maintenance behaviors, such as openly sharing and encouraging one's partner to express their feelings (Stafford & Canary, 1991), could contribute to buffering the effects of discrimination (see Fiori & Rauer, Chapter 14, for potential drawbacks and racial disparities in certain maintenance behaviors). Similarly, reframing stigmatizing experiences together (see Frost, 2014) and highlighting equity within the relationship (Haas & Stafford, 2005) may be beneficial in mitigating minority stress for marginalized couples. Pepping and Halford further suggest that relationship education programs include examples of what positive dyadic coping in the face of discrimination may look like and provide couples with space to discuss what this could look like for themselves. Similarly, in a therapy context, it may also be important for clinicians to provide space for couples to practice dyadic coping skills while discussing experiences of discrimination (see Monk & Ogolsky, 2019).

ATTENDING TO CULTURE

It is important to reinforce that some maintenance behaviors may function differently across cultures and contexts (see Fiori & Rauer, Chapter 14; Gaines & Ferenczi, Chapter 15). Although behaviors that promote positivity (e.g., verbal acknowledgement or praise, positive affirmations, being respectful and polite, and being optimistic about the relationship), for example, can be beneficial to relationships (Stafford & Canary, 1991) and are appreciated in both individualist and collectivist cultures (e.g., Yum & Canary, 2009; Yum, Canary, & Baptist, 2015), it is important to ensure that positive affirmations are genuine and not excessive to the point that their meaning and value are lost, especially in cultures where praise needs to be earned. Indeed, in some cultures, praise and acknowledgement for work well done are only valued and appropriate when the achievement is well beyond what is ordinarily expected of the person (Alston & Takei, 2005). Bringing attention to the fact that the person has fulfilled obligatory responsibilities can imply that there were doubts about the person's capabilities and, therefore, be deemed insulting. Such is the case within Japanese culture, where highlighting positive behaviors may do more harm than good (Alston & Takei, 2005). Culturally appropriate positive affirmation could include one partner highlighting the achievements of the couple's children, which indirectly recognizes the other partner's successful parenting.

Another consideration would be the extent to which cultures place importance on equity in relationships. In individualistic cultures, equity influences the amount of effort expended by partners to build and maintain relationships (e.g., Yum et al., 2015). In such cultures, avoiding conflict may be interpreted as a partner being disinterested or lacking concern (Rahim, 1983); thus, ensuring that problem solving produces win–win solutions through collaboration is valued. Same-sex couples are also more likely to work collaboratively; compared with heterosexual couples, same-sex couples were found to be more likely to share laundry (44% vs. 31%) and house repair (33% vs. 15%) tasks (Matos, 2015; see also Haas & Stafford, 2005). In cultures that are patriarchal, conflict in heterosexual couples may arise from the expectation for women to continually "do the sacrificing" for the overall good of the relationship. In such cases, and especially for younger couples that are influenced by, and embrace, modern values of equality, balancing the scale by facilitating sacrifice on the part of men may be necessary. Men, too, need to understand the value of sacrificing individually focused desires and goals for the overall good of their relationships. To facilitate this process, it would be important for couples to identify their threshold or limit of sacrifice (i.e., at what point sacrifice would be more destructive than reparative to their personal and couple well-being). Sacrifice would be contraindicated if it meant compromising anyone's physical and/or emotional safety (see Gaines & Ferenczi, Chapter 15, for more on relationship maintenance across cultures).

In collectivist cultures, solving problems by compromising one's own needs in order to accommodate the needs of the family or couple system (Ting-Toomey, 2017) is normative and is often a role expectation. Accordingly, nonconfrontational methods of problem solving are often preferred. Further, conflict-management strategies appropriate in cultures that embrace individualism and value self-expression (e.g., freedom of choice and pursuit of happiness; Inglehart, 1997; Inglehart & Welzel, 2005) may not work as well within collectivist cultures that value face maintenance (i.e., "saving face"), which has to do with ensuring that shame is not brought on oneself or another in times of conflict. This cultural preference to avoid conflict in order to maintain face is particularly prominent in Asian collectivist cultures that embrace Confucianism, such as Chinese, Korean, and Japanese cultures (Ting-Toomey, 2017). Interventions that encourage open and direct communication of relational conflict and problems can be replaced by less direct interventions such as externalizing the problem, a technique used in Narrative Therapy (White & Epston, 1990). Externalizing the problem treats the problem as an objective entity outside the couple or either partner, thus helping with the process of depersonalization, which in turn prevents the natural tendency to place blame; the couple can develop strategies to address the problem together (i.e., as "co-problem solvers" vs. adversaries) without carrying the burden of blame and shame. Such an intervention would further suit cultures where respect for authority by virtue of one's gender or age is valued, or help partners who come from different cultural backgrounds and see the problem differently develop a common understanding of the problem and its solution (Kim, Prouty, & Roberson, 2012).

ATTENDING TO RELEVANCE AND ACCESSIBILITY

Increasing relevance. Although incorporating general strategies to help couples address contextual stressors is important, it is also vital to account for individual variability in vulnerabilities and context. Many scholars suggest moving away from a one-size-fits-all approach (e.g., Barton, Futris, & Bradley, 2014) and toward an adaptive model to ensure that interventions are meeting the diverse needs of contemporary couples (Vennum et al., 2017). In adaptive interventions, components that are thought to be universally effective may be provided to everyone, but in cases where the effects of a fixed intervention are expected to vary significantly for individuals who differ on certain characteristics or circumstances, tailored components may greatly increase effectiveness (Collins, Murphy, & Bierman, 2004). Screening for the strengths and risks of the individual or couple prior to attending the first session would allow CRE program developers (and therapists) to create particular orderings of content (or therapeutic techniques) shown to be most effective for improving relationship maintenance based on the particular risk or resiliency factors that participants present.

Some practitioners have met the challenge of individual variability by developing *wise interventions* that target specific processes within relationships (see Walton, 2014, for a review) and focusing on tailoring variables within interventions. At a time when researchers are gaining a more nuanced understanding of variation in relational experiences over time (e g , Proulx, Ermer, & Kanter, 2017), practitioners are better able to create profiles of couples that may be most likely to benefit from specific intervention sequences and protocols. For example, Proulx and colleagues (2017) found that a substantial proportion of couples do not experience an inevitable decline in marital quality over time. Thus, it may be that couples who are able to sustain marital quality would benefit from a focus on relationship-enhancement maintenance processes to sustain the positive interactions within their relationship. In contrast, couples who experience marital decline over time may need more intensive assistance with threat-mitigation relationship maintenance processes to minimize the deterioration of marital quality. Additionally, many clinicians have suggested a life-course perspective to match interventions with specific couple circumstances (e.g., Cowan & Cowan, 2014). A couple who is transitioning to parenthood, for instance, may need different skills to promote aspects of relationship maintenance than those raising children who are in middle childhood (see Rauer & Proulx, Chapter 17, for more on relationship maintenance across the life course).

Increasing accessibility. Clinicians have theorized that distressed couples wait an average of six years before seeking clinical help (Gottman, 1999). In response, traditional CRE was initially thought to be an excellent preventative service to educate couples in a less threatening environment compared with therapy (Stanley, 2001). Most CRE programs, however, still fail to reach broad audiences. These programs demand a considerable amount of time, which many couples cannot afford (Cordova, 2009). As a result, many couples may first seek help from social circles and books before research-based workshops (Bradford, Mock, & Stewart, 2016). To increase the reach of CRE, Hawkins and Ooms (2010) recommend low-cost and easily accessible delivery methods. Thus, many have developed nontraditional delivery methods to overcome this barrier (McAllister, Duncan, & Hawkins, 2012), including online programs (Braithwaite & Fincham, 2009), e-mail-based interventions (Coulter & Malouff, 2013), and mobile applications (Bortz, 2016; Conner & Vennum, 2016). Similarly, technology has also been harnessed to increase access to therapy through secure telehealth (e.g., Haregu, Chimeddamba, & Islam, 2015) and video-conferencing (e.g., Berger, 2016) modalities, although more research is needed on working clinically with couples and families through these formats (Jensen & Mendenhall, 2018; see also Caughlin & Wang, Chapter 16, for more discussion of technology and relationship maintenance). Ultimately, though, as competing time constraints continue to mount for couples, investing in brief and targeted relationship maintenance interventions may ensure that research-based information is attainable for individuals and couples (e.g., Kanter & Schramm, 2018).

DIRECTIONS FOR FUTURE RESEARCH AND THEORY

To build on previous efforts to facilitate romantic relationship maintenance, we have several suggestions for future research and theory development. Specifically, we suggest that further attention be given to gaining a deeper understanding of the effect of *specific* maintenance strategies and theories of change throughout the life-course, the influence of cultural context and resilience on maintenance processes, unintended consequences of relationship maintenance interventions, and the evaluation process for interventions promoting maintenance behaviors.

Explicate the Impact of Diverse Maintenance Activities

Ogolsky and colleagues (2017) outline two types of maintenance motivations, threat mitigation and relationship enhancement within a relationship, but little is known about how they differentially promote relationship stability and growth. As illustrated theoretically (Fincham & Rogge, 2010) and empirically (e.g., Bradbury & Lavner, 2012), reducing deficits and promoting flourishing may not be achieved by targeting the same maintenance processes. That is, a couple may be able to *sustain* their relationship with poor threat-mitigation maintenance behaviors (e.g., conflict management) if they have few other challenges (e.g., depressive symptoms or an unsafe environment; Lavner & Bradbury, 2012); however, it is unclear whether sustainment or improvement is feasible without enacting enhancement strategies over time. More research is needed on how couples successfully use different ratios of threat mitigation and relationship enhancement depending on their context and the stage of their relationship development (such as couples experiencing military deployment; e.g., Cordova et al., 2017) in order to best tailor interventions by couples' context and time in the relational life course.

Further, the association of relationship maintenance behaviors with partners' global evaluations of relationships may not be as straightforward as once theorized, especially for diverse samples. Not only have observed communication behaviors not been associated with improvements in relationship satisfaction in a multistate behaviorally focused CRE program (Williamson et al., 2016), but longitudinal research suggests that the association between observed communication behaviors and satisfaction is inconsistent, or moderated by contextual factors, for many low-income couples (Lavner et al., 2016; Nguyen et al., 2017; Ross, Karney, Nguyen, & Bradbury, 2019). It may be that partners' subjective appraisals of behaviors (e.g., attributions; Bradbury & Fincham, 1990) are more critical to relationship functioning than the behaviors themselves in low-resource environments. Because cognitions may be difficult to alter within a brief CRE program, future intervention work should focus on shifting attributions or increasing understanding of specific behaviors, promoting a "team" mentality when facing stressors, and reducing stressors that inhibit adaptive attributions (e.g., Karney et al., 2018; Neff & Karney, 2016).

Accordingly, although there is much research behind behavioral theories of change, more research is needed to understand the utility of insight/principle-based and experiential/emotion-focused approaches in enhancing relationship maintenance and how to combine multiple approaches for optimal short- and long-term impacts. Combined approaches may be conceptualized as targeting both intrapersonal and interpersonal maintenance processes (see Ogolsky et al., 2017). In therapy and basic research, intrapersonal relationship maintenance processes have often been operationalized with terms such as attributions (e.g., Bradbury & Fincham, 1990), schemas (e.g., Ledbetter, 2016), and attachment models (e.g., Overall, Girme, Lemay, & Hammond, 2014) that are based on value and belief systems, learned coping strategies, and past relationship experiences (e.g., Schramm et al., 2017; Stafford, 2016; Weiser & Weigel, 2016). Future research should examine the malleability and effectiveness of different intrapersonal and interpersonal processes across time in different contexts to discern optimal combinations of interventions for promoting both quick and lasting changes in relationship maintenance strategy use.

Increase Understanding of the Impact of Context

As noted by Ogolsky and colleagues (2017), many maintenance processes have not been examined while accounting for the context in which these processes manifest. Accordingly, it is important for researchers to continue identifying the ways social and environmental context may promote or hinder maintenance processes, how diverse contextual stressors may differentially impact partners' ability to both learn and implement new maintenance strategies (e.g., Lee, 2015), and when it is important to include efforts to positively influence couples' contexts in addition to efforts to enhance partners' ability to cope with contextual stressors (Boss, 2002). Thus, more research on specific moderators of relationship maintenance interventions is needed, including the impact of larger sociocultural messages clients receive about relationships and gender roles; discrimination experiences at the individual, community, and couple level; values and traditions around coupling; socioeconomic stressors; acute versus long-term stressors; and partners' life stages as well as the developmental stage of the relationship. It would also be important to understand how to influence relationship-maintenance behaviors during diverse relationship statuses, including singlehood. For example, which maintenance processes are best addressed through individual CRE to increase a single person's own resilience to contextual stressors and improve later relationship outcomes, and which maintenance processes are more effective when addressed during dating or marriage?

Additionally, the majority of research to date on stress and maintenance behaviors has taken a deficit approach, examining how stress negatively influences maintenance behaviors within a relationship, yet numerous couples who experience adversity are able to sustain their marital functioning over time (e.g., Neff & Broady, 2011). While researching the impact of stress on relationships is important (as stress is a key predictor of diverse marital outcomes over time; Lavner & Bradbury, 2010), this deficit approach does not focus on couples who are flourishing despite these stressors (i.e., a strength-based approach). For example, when experiencing marginalization, some couples are able to grow from the discrimination they experience, present a unified front, and cope with marginalization-related stressors (e.g., Clavél et al., 2017; Frost, 2014; Seshadri & Knudson-Martin, 2013). It will be important for future research to examine when maintenance behaviors sustain flourishing relationships within a stressful context in order to better promote resilience in maintenance processes (see Monk & Ogolsky, 2019).

Identify Unintended Effects

It is also vital to examine the unintended effects relationship maintenance interventions may have on individual well-being and couple dynamics. Unintended effects may occur in three primary avenues: curricula content, curricula examples, and clinicians' own values and beliefs. First, more research is needed on the potential adverse outcomes of relationship maintenance interventions on partners' views of their relationship. For example, interventions to improve communication behaviors may unintentionally raise individuals' expectations beyond what is possible for their partner to reasonably meet (e.g., Bradbury & Lavner, 2012). Further, more research is needed on when relationship-maintenance strategies may be harmful due to abusive dynamics within the relationship. Along these same lines, more research is needed to understand under what circumstances ending an unhealthy relationship may improve a person's capacity for healthy relationship maintenance in subsequent relationships by decreasing the detrimental impacts of the current relationship on their well-being (Hawkins & Booth, 2005).

Second, the majority of relationship education curricula are based on White, middle-class, heterosexual samples (Johnson, 2012), so scholars need to account for the indirect effects of specific curricula content and delivery methods on participants' beliefs and behaviors about what is "normal" or "preferred." Broadly, clinicians and educators need to attend to cultural norms of a specific vision of relationship health, trajectories, or gender that are inadvertently promoted in presentation materials. Interventions that are based on heteronormative relational expectations may result in same-sex couples feeling ostracized and unconnected to interventions (see Randles, 2016). Similarly, gender roles presented in CRE relationship vignettes or examples may not adequately match the experiences of many participants and may unintentionally fortify traditional gender stereotypes that could be harmful to some couples' relationship functioning (Randles, 2016). Future research should continue to examine best practices in teaching relationship maintenance to diverse couples (e.g., labeling and coping with the effects of minority stress).

Last, practitioners must be not only aware of, but invested in, how their work influences dominant societal discourses. For example, while in the therapeutic field, there has been awareness of the balance between promoting the maintenance of unions and aiding in the dissolution of unhealthy unions (e.g., Bridges, 2017; Monk, Ogolsky, & Oswald, 2018), there has been less balance in the field of CRE (cf. Vennum et al., 2017). That is, in CRE, there has been an overt focus on promoting marriage and the benefits of marriage by facilitators (Randles & Avishai, 2018). This one-sided approach to marriage has been a major focus in the continued goals of federal policy (e.g., Healthy Marriage Initiative) but may ignore contextual barriers to marriage and do a disservice to participants who would benefit from exiting an unhealthy relationship. In fact, the rhetoric around the *causal* benefits of becoming and remaining married has been vastly overstated in colloquial narratives about marriage (e.g., Lee, 2015). Taken together, the attitudes that therapists and educators bring to interventions may impact not only individuals and couples, but also the societal narrative surrounding general beliefs about romantic relationships.

Advance Evaluation Methodology

To extend knowledge on the impact of interventions and inform basic research, we advocate for therapeutic and CRE evaluations to utilize longitudinal and randomization designs with active control groups that test potential moderators of effectiveness. In a recent review of marital quality over time, Proulx and colleagues (2017) present evidence that, on average, initial levels of marital quality are rarely surpassed over time ("honeymoon-as-ceiling effect"), which is problematic for couples who enter marriage at greater levels of distress. Longitudinal relationship maintenance intervention studies could examine under what circumstances, if any, strengthening maintenance behaviors can "break through" this observed ceiling effect and potentially mitigate a decline of marital quality.

Additionally, basic research evaluating the effectiveness of specific relationship-maintenance strategies that couples use and applied research evaluating the effectiveness of interventions aimed at improving couples' use of maintenance strategies need to test the potential moderating effects of contextual stressors and individual vulnerabilities (e.g., cultural attitudes, discrimination experiences, trauma history, and relationship status). This would further enable practitioners to identify key variables by which interventions can be adapted to maximize effectiveness for diverse couples in diverse circumstance (Collins et al., 2004). Once these potential tailoring variables are identified, different decision rules can be tested to assess which combinations of components (e.g., by using expanded factorial designs), as well as which sequences and intensities of components (e.g., by using SMART designs; see Nahum-Shani et al., 2012, for an overview), are most effective given specific situations.

Finally, although many interventions discussed in this chapter evaluated interventions by randomly assigning couples to treatment and control groups, a critical future direction for strengthening evaluation is using active control groups (i.e., having individuals or couples participate in some sort of activity; see Rogge et al., 2013, for an example) compared with just a passive control condition (e.g., waitlist control). By using active control groups, researchers can better understand whether it is specific exercises that promote relationship maintenance or whether it is simply focusing on the relationship that has positive outcomes for couples. For example, Rogge and colleagues (2013) found similar results in divorce rates for a time-intensive intervention (a popular CRE program) and an active control group (watching and discussing relationship-themed movies together). Indeed, by using various active and control conditions during the evaluation process, clinicians and relationship educators will have a clearer understanding of the mechanisms of change that lead to increases in maintenance strategies (e.g., Rauer et al., 2014).

CONCLUSION

Scholars have theorized that relationships may be more rewarding, but simultaneously more fragile, than ever before (Coontz, 2004). Thus, improving the effectiveness of interventions aimed at promoting maintenance behaviors is critical. The movement toward increased reciprocity between basic and applied research (Gottfredson et al., 2015), coupled with the integration of various models of change being used in applied settings, makes the present time ripe for reevaluating the various approaches to promoting relationship maintenance strategies with diverse individuals and couples. As technological advances have made it easier to provide adaptive and accessible interventions and to conduct more rigorous and nuanced assessments of these interventions, our hope is that future research will be able to increase our understanding of which theories of change and interventions are most effective in enhancing maintenance strategies throughout the life course and in diverse contexts.

REFERENCES

Administration for Children and Families. (2015). *Healthy Marriage and Relationship Education Grants* (No. HHS-2015- ACF-OFA-FM-0985). Retrieved from https://ami.grantsolutions.gov/files/HHS-2015-ACF-OFA-FM-0985_0.htm

Allen, E. S., Rhoades, G. K., Markman, H. J., & Stanley, S. M. (2015). PREP for Strong Bonds: A review of outcomes from a randomized clinical trial. *Contemporary Family Therapy*, *37*, 232–246. doi:10.1007/s10591-014-9325-3

Amato, P. R., Booth, A., Johnson, D. R., & Rogers, S. J. (2007). *Alone together: How marriage is changing in America*. Cambridge, MA: Harvard University.

Anderson, L. R. (2016). *High School Seniors' Expectations to Marry*. Family Profiles, FP-16-14, OH: National Center for Family & Marriage Research. Retrieved from https://scholarworks.bgsu.edu/cgi/viewcontent.cgi?article=1056&context=ncfmr_family_profiles

Alston, J. P., & Takei, I. (2005). *Japanese business culture and practices: A guide to twenty-first century Japanese business*. Lincoln, NE: iUniverse.

Babcock, J. C., Gottman, J. M., Ryan, K. D., & Gottman, J. S. (2013). A component analysis of a brief psycho-educational couples' workshop: One-year follow-up results. *Journal of Family Therapy*, *35*, 252–280. doi:10.1111/1467-6427.12017

Badr, H., & Taylor, C. L. C. (2008). Effects of relationship maintenance on psychological distress and dyadic adjustment among couples coping with lung cancer. *Health Psychology*, *27*, 616–627. doi:10.1037/0278-6133.27.5.616

Badr, H., Acitelli, L. K., & Taylor, C. L. C. (2008). Does talking about their relationship affect couples' marital and psychological adjustment to lung cancer? *Journal of Cancer Survivorship*, *2*, 53–64. doi:10.1007/s11764-008-0044-3

Balsam, K. F., & Syzmanski, D. M. (2005). Relationship quality and domestic violence in women's same-sex relationships: The role of minority stress. *Psychology of Women Quarterly*, *29*, 258–269. doi:10.1111/j.1471-6402.2005.00220.x

Banmen, J. (2002). The Satir model: Yesterday and today. *Contemporary Family Therapy*, *24*, 7–22. doi:10.1023/A:1014365304082

Barton, A. W., Futris, T. G., & Bradley, R. C. (2014). Changes following premarital education for couples with differing degrees of future marital risk. *Journal of Marital and Family Therapy*, *40*, 165–177. doi:10.1111/jmft.12006

Bellah, R. N., Madsen, R., Sullivan, W. M., Swidler, A., & Tipton, S. M. (1996). *Habits of the heart: Individualism and commitment in American life*. Los Angeles, CA: University of California Press.

Berg, C. A., & Upchurch, R. (2007). A developmental-contextual model of couples coping with chronic illness across the adult life span. *Psychological Bulletin*, *133*, 920–954. http://dx.doi.org/10.1037/0033-2909.133.6.920

Berger, T. (2016). The therapeutic alliance in internet interventions: A narrative review and suggestions for future research. *Psychotherapy Research*, *27*, 511–524. doi:10.1080/ 10503307.2015.1119908

Bodenmann, G., & Shantinath, S. D. (2004). The Couple Coping Enhancement Training (CCET): A new approach to prevention of marital distress based upon stress and coping. *Family Relations*, *53*, 477–484. doi:10.1111/j.0197-6664.2004.00056.x

Bortz, P. R. (2016). *A formative evaluation of a smartphone application for couples: The affectionate gesture planner* (Master's thesis). Retrieved from University of Kentucky UKnowledge. doi:10.13023/ETD.2016.260

Boss, P. (2002). Coping, adapting, being resilient … or is it managing? *In Family stress management: A contextual approach* (pp. 71–91). Thousand Oaks, CA: Sage.

Bradbury, T. N., & Fincham, F. D. (1990). Attributions in marriage: Review and critique. *Psychology Bulletin, 107*, 3–33. doi:10.1037/0033- 2909.107.1.3

Bradbury, T. N., & Karney, B. R. (2004). Understanding and altering the longitudinal course of marriage. *Journal of Marriage and Family, 66*, 862–879. doi:10.1111/j.0022-2445.2004.00059.x

Bradbury, T. N., & Lavner, J. A. (2012). How can we improve preventive and educational interventions for intimate relationships? *Behavior Therapy, 43*(1), 113–122. doi:10.1016/j.beth.2011.02.008

Bradford, K., Mock, D. J., & Stewart, J. W. (2016). It takes two? An exploration of processes and outcomes in a two-session couple intervention. *Journal of Marital and Family Therapy, 42*(3), 423–437. doi:10.1111/jmft.12144

Braithwaite, S. R., & Fincham, F. D. (2009). A randomized clinical trial of a computer based preventive intervention: replication and extension of ePREP. *Journal of Family Psychology, 23*, 32–38. doi:10.1037/a0014061

Bridges, J. G. (2017). *Instrumentalism and couple's therapy: Influential impacts on therapist's values, neutrality, and perceived role in couple's therapy* (Master's thesis). Retrieved from http://krex.k-state.edu/dspace/handle/2097/38271

Brubacher, L. (2006). Integrating emotion-focused therapy with the Satir model. *Journal of Marital and Family Therapy, 32*, 141–153. doi:10.1111/j.1752-0606.2006.tb01596.x

Carlson, R. G., Rappleyea, D. L., Daire, A. P., Harris, S. M., & Liu, X. (2015). The effectiveness of couple and individual relationship education: Distress as a moderator. *Family Process, 56*, 91–104. doi:10.1111/famp.12172

Cherlin, A. J. (2010). *The marriage-go-round*. New York, NY: Vintage.

Clavél, F. D., Cutrona, C. E., & Russell, D. W. (2017). United and divided by stress: How stressors differentially influence social support in African American couples over time. *Personality and Social Psychology Bulletin, 43*(7), 1050–1064. doi:10.1177/0146167217704195

Cluxton-Keller, F. (2011). Cognitive behavioral models of family therapy. In L. Metcalf (Ed.), *Marriage and family therapy: A practice-oriented approach* (pp. 91–128). New York: Springer.

Collins, L. M., Murphy, S. A., & Bierman, K. L. (2004). A conceptual framework for adaptive preventive interventions. *Prevention Science, 5*, 185–193. doi:10.1023/b:prev.0000037641.26017.00

Conner, S., & Vennum, A. (2016, April). *Exploring young adults' preferences for mobile relationship education*. Poster presented at the International Society for Research on Internet Interventions Annual Conference in Seattle, WA.

Coontz, S. (2004). The world historical transformation of marriage. *Journal of Marriage and Family, 66*(4), 974–979. doi:10.1111/j.0022-2445.2004.00067.x

Cordova, J. V. (2009). *The marriage checkup: A scientific program for sustaining and strengthening marital health*. Lanham, MD: Rowman and Littlefield.

Cordova, J. V., Cigrang, J. A., Gray, T. D., Najera, E., Havrilenko, M., Pinkley, C., ... Redd, K. (2017). Addressing relationship health needs in primary care: Adapting the marriage checkup for use in medical settings with military couples. *Journal of Clinical Psychology in Medical Settings, 24*(3–4), 259–269. doi:10.1007/s10880-017-9517-8

Coulter, K., & Malouff, J. M. (2013). Effects of an intervention designed to enhance romantic relationship excitement: A randomized-control trial. *Couple and Family Psychology: Research and Practice, 2*, 34–44. doi:10.1037/a0031719

Cowan, P. A., & Cowan, C. P. (2014). Controversies in couple relationship education (CRE): Overlooked evidence and implications for research and policy. *Psychology, Public Policy, and Law, 20*, 361–383. doi:10.1037/law0000025

Cutrona, C. E., Russell, D. W., Abraham, W. T., Gardner, K. A., Melby, J. N., Bryant, C., & Conger, R. D. (2003). Neighborhood context and financial strain as predictors of marital interaction and marital quality in African American couples. *Personal Relationships, 10*, 389–409. doi:10.1111/14/5-6811.00056

Dainton, M. (1999). African American, European American, and biracial couples' meanings for and experiences in marriage. In R. C. Diggs & T. J. Socha (Eds.), *Communication, race, and family: Exploring communication in black, white, and biracial families* (pp. 147–165). Mahwah, NJ: Erlbaum.

Dew, J., & Wilcox, W. B. (2011). If momma ain't happy: Explaining declines in marital satisfaction among new mothers. *Journal of Marriage and Family, 73*(1), 1–12. doi:10.1111/j.1741-3737.2010.00782.x

Doherty, W. J. (2013). *Take back your marriage: Sticking together in a world that pulls us apart.* (2nd ed.). New York, NY: The Guilford Press.

Doherty, W. J. (2015, July/August). The divorce revolution: Assessing our impact. *Psychotherapy Networker.* Retrieved from www.psychotherapynetworker.org.

Doherty, W. J., Harris, S. M., & Wilde, J. L. (2016). Discernment counseling for "mixed-agenda" couples. *Journal of Marital and Family Therapy, 2*, 246–255. doi:10.1111/jmft.12132

Erickson, R. J. (2005). Why emotion work matters: Sex, gender, and the division of household labor. *Journal of Marriage and Family, 67*, 337–351. doi:10.1111/j.0022-2445.2005.00120.x

Fincham, F. D., & Rogge, R. (2010). Understanding relationship quality: Theoretical challenges and new tools for assessment. *Journal of Family Theory & Review, 2*(4), 227–242. doi:10.1111/j.1756-2589.2010.00059.x

Finkel, E. J. (2017). *The all-or-nothing marriage.* New York: Penguin Random House.

Finkel, E. J., Hui, C. M., Carswell, K. L., & Larson, G. M. (2014). The suffocation of marriage: Climbing Mount Maslow without enough oxygen. *Psychological Inquiry, 25*, 1–41. doi:10.1080/1047840X.2014.863723

Fowers, B. J. (2000). *Beyond the myth of marital happiness.* San Francisco, CA: Jossey-Bass.

Fowers, B. J. (2001). The limits of a technical concept of a good marriage: Exploring the role of virtue in communication skills. *Journal of Marital and Family Therapy, 27*, 327–340. doi:10.1111/j.1752-0606.2001.tb00328.x

Frost, D. M. (2014). Redemptive framings of minority stress and their association with closeness in same-sex relationships. *Journal of Couples & Relationship Therapy, 13*, 219–239. doi:10.1080/15332691.2013.871616

Gamarel, K. E., Reisner, S. L., Laurenceau, J.-P., Nemoto, T., & Operario, D. (2014). Gender minority stress, mental health, and relationship quality: A dyadic investigation of transgender women and their cisgender male partners. *Journal of Family Psychology, 28*, 437–447. doi:10.1037/a0037171

Gottfredson, D. C., Cook, T. D., Gardner, F. E. M., Gorman-Smith, D., Howe, G. W., Sandler, I. N., & Zafft, K. M. (2015). Standards of evidence for efficacy, effectiveness, and scale-up research in prevention science: Next generation. *Prevention Science, 7*, 893–926. doi:10.1007/s11121-015-0555-x

Gottman, J. M. (1999). *The marriage clinic: A scientifically-based marital therapy.* New York: WW Norton & Company.

Gottman, J. M., Coan, J., Carrere, S., & Swanson, C. (1998). Predicting marital happiness and stability from newlywed interactions. *Journal of Marriage and the Family, 60*, 5–22. doi:10.2307/353438

Gottman, J., & Gottman, J. (2017). The natural principles of love. *Journal of Family Theory and Review, 9*, 7–26. doi:10.1111/jftr.12182

Gottman, J. M., & Silver, N. (1999). *The seven principles for making marriage work.* New York: Three Rivers Press.

Greenberg, L., Warwar, S., & Malcolm, W. (2010). Emotion-focused couples therapy and the facilitation of forgiveness. *Journal of Marital and Family Therapy, 36,* 28–42. doi:10.1111/j.1752-0606.2009.00185.x

Haas, S. M., & Stafford, L. (2005). Maintenance behaviors in same-sex and marital relationships: A matched sample comparison. *Journal of Family Communication, 5,* 43–60.

Halford, W. K. (2011). *Marriage and relationship education: What works and how to provide it.* New York: Guilford Press.

Halford, W. K., Petch, J., & Creedy, D. K. (2010). Promoting a positive transition to parenthood: A randomized clinical trial of couple relationship education. *Prevention Science, 11,* 89–100. doi:10.1007/s11121-009-0152-y

Halford, W. K., Wilson, K., Watson, B., Verner, T., & Larson, J. (2010). Couple relationship education at home: Does skill training enhance relationship assessment and feedback? *Journal of Family Psychology, 24,* 188–196. doi:10.1037/a0018786

Hardoy, I., & Schøne, P. (2008). The family gap and family friendly policies: The case of Norway. *Applied Economics, 40,* 2857–2871. doi:10.1080/00036840600993981

Haregu, T. N., Chimeddamba, O., & Islam, M. R. (2015). Effectiveness of telephone-based therapy in the management of depression: A systematic review and meta-analysis. *SM Journal of Depression Research and Treatment, 1*(2), 1006–1012.

Hawkins, A. J., & Ooms, T. (2010). What works in marriage and relationship education? A review of lessons learned with a focus on low-income couples. *National Healthy Marriage Resource Center.*

Hawkins, D. N., & Booth, A. (2005). Unhappily ever after: Effects of long-term, low-quality marriages on well-being. *Social Forces, 84*(1), 451–471. doi:10.1353/sof.2005.0103

Inglehart, R. (1997). Modernization, postmodernization and changing perceptions of risk. *International Review of Sociology, 7*(3), 449–459. doi:10.1080/03906701.1997.9971250

Inglehart, R., & Welzel, C. (2005). *Modernization, cultural change, and democracy: The human development sequence.* New York: Cambridge University Press.

Jensen, E. J., & Mendenhall, T. (2018). Call to action: Family therapy and rural mental health. *Contemporary Family Therapy, 40*(4), 309–317.

Johnson, M. D. (2012). Healthy marriage initiatives: On the need for empiricism in policy implementation. *American Psychologist, 67,* 296–308. doi:10.1037/a0027743

Johnson, M. D., & Bradbury, T. N. (2015). Contributions of social learning theory to the promotion of healthy relationships: Asset or liability? *Journal of Family Theory & Review, 7,* 13–27. doi:10.1111/jftr.12057

Johnson, S. M. (2004). *The practice of emotionally focused couples therapy: Creating connection* (2nd ed.). New York: Brunner-Routledge.

Kanter, J. B., & Proulx, C. M. (2019). The longitudinal association between maternal parenting stress and spousal supportiveness. *Journal of Family Psychology, 33*(1), 121–131. doi:10.1037/fam0000478

Kanter, J. B., & Schramm D. G.(2018). Brief interventions for couples: An integrative review. *Family Relations, 67,* 211–226. doi:10.1111/fare.12298

Karney, B. R., & Bradbury, T. N. (1995). The longitudinal course of marital quality and stability: A review of theory, methods, and research. *Psychological Bulletin, 118,* 3–34. doi:10.1037/0033-2909.118.1.3

Karney, B. R., Bradbury, T. N., & Lavner, J. A. (2018). Supporting healthy relationships in low-income couples: Lessons learned and policy implications. *Policy Insights from the Behavioral and Brain Sciences, 5,* 33–39. doi:10.1177/2372732217747890

Kim, J. S. (2008). Examining the effectiveness of solution-focused brief therapy: A meta-analysis. *Research on Social Work Practice, 18,* 107–116. doi:10.1177/1049731507307807

Kim, J., Gale, J., Goetz, J., & Bermudez, M. (2011). Relational financial therapy: An innovative and collaborative treatment approach. *Contemporary Family Therapy, 33,* 229–241. doi:10.1007/s10591-011-9145-7

Kim, H., Prouty, A. M., & Roberson, P. N. (2012). Narrative therapy with intercultural couples: A case study. *Journal of Family Psychotherapy, 23*(4), 273–286. doi:10.1080/08975353.2012.735591

Kornrich, S., Brines, J., & Leupp, K. (2012). Egalitarianism, housework, and sexual frequency in marriage. *American Sociological Review, 78,* 26–50. doi:10.1177/0003122412472340

Lavner, J. A., & Bradbury, T. N. (2010). Patterns of change in marital satisfaction over the newlywed years. *Journal of Marriage and Family, 72*(5), 1171–1187. doi:10.1111/j.1741-3737.2010.00757.x

Lavner, J. A., & Bradbury, T. N. (2012). Why do even satisfied newlyweds eventually go on to divorce? *Journal of Family Psychology, 26*(1), 1.

Lavner, J. A., Karney, B. R., & Bradbury, T. N. (2015). New directions for policies aimed at strengthening low-income couples. *Behavioral Science and Policy, 1,* 1–12.

Lavner, J. A., Karney, B. R., & Bradbury, T. N. (2016). Does couples' communication predict marital satisfaction, or does marital satisfaction predict communication? *Journal of Marriage and Family, 78,* 680–694. doi:10.1111/jomf.12301

Ledbetter, A. (2016). Relational maintenance behavior and shared TV viewing as mediators of the association between romanticism and romantic relationship quality. *Communication Studies, 68,* 95–114. doi:10.1080/10510974.2016.1263804

Lee, G. R. (2015). *The limits of marriage: Why getting everyone married won't solve all our problems.* Lexington Books.

Loew, B., Rhoades, G., Markman, H., Stanley, S., Pacifici, C., White, L., & Delaney, R. (2012). Internet delivery of PREP-based relationship education for at-risk couples. *Journal of Couple & Relationship Therapy, 11,* 291–309. doi:10.1080/15332691.2012.718968

Lyons, K. S., Winters-Stone, K. M., Bennett, J. A., & Beer, T. M. (2016). The effects of partnered exercise on physical intimacy in couples coping with prostate cancer. *Health Psychology, 35*(5), 509–513. doi:10.1037/hea0000287

Marigold, D. C., Holmes, J. G., & Ross, M. (2007). More than words: Reframing compliments from romantic partners fosters security in low self-esteem individuals. *Journal of Personality and Social Psychology, 92,* 232–248. doi:10.1037/0022-3514.92.2.232

Marigold, D. C., Holmes, J. G., & Ross, M. (2010). Fostering relationship resilience: An intervention for low self-esteem individuals. *Journal of Experimental Psychology, 46,* 624–630. doi:10.1016/j.jesp.2010.02.011

Markman, H. J., & Floyd, F. (1980). Possibilities for prevention of marital discord: A behavioral perspective. *American Journal of Family Therapy, 8,* 29–40. doi:10.1080/01926188008250355

Markman, H. J., Floyd, F. J., Stanley, S. M., & Storaasli, R. D. (1988). Prevention of marital distress: A longitudinal investigation. *Journal of Consulting and Clinical Psychology, 56,* 210–217. doi:10.1037/0022-006X.56.2.210

Markman, H. J., Renick, M. J., Floyd, F. J., Stanley, S. M., & Clements, M. (1993). Preventing marital distress through communication and conflict management training: A 4-and 5-year follow-up. *Journal of Consulting and Clinical Psychology, 61,* 70–77. doi:10.1037/0022-006X.61.1.70

Markman, H. J., & Rhoades, G. K. (2012). Relationship education research: Current status and future directions. *Journal of Marital and Family Therapy, 38*, 169–200. doi:10.1111/j.1752-0606.2011.00247.x

Markman, H. J., Rhoades, G. K., Stanley, S. M., Ragan, E. P., & Whitton, S. W. (2010). The premarital communication roots of marital distress and divorce: The first five years of marriage. *Journal of Family Psychology, 24*, 289–298. doi:10.1037/a0019481

Markman, H. J., & Ritchie, L. L. (2015). Couples relationship education and couples therapy: Healthy marriage or strange bedfellows? *Family Process, 54*, 655–671. doi:10.1111/famp.12191

Martinez, J., Hollingsworth, B., Stanley, C., Shephard, R., & Lee, L. (2011). Satir human validation process model. In L. Metclaf (Ed.), *Marriage and family therapy: A practice-oriented approach* (pp. 175–199). New York: Springer.

Matos, K. (2015). Modern families: Same- and different-sex couples negotiating at home. Retrieved from Families and Work Institute website: www.familiesandwork .org/downloads/modern-families.pdf

McAllister, S., Duncan, S. F., & Hawkins, A. J. (2012). Examining the early evidence for self-directed marriage and relationship education: A meta-analytic study. *Family Relations, 61*, 742–755. doi:10.1111/j.1741-3729.2012.00736.x

McGill, J., Adler-Baeder, F., Bradford, A. B., Kerpelman, J., Ketring, S. A., & Sollie, D. (2016). The role of relational instability on individual and partner outcomes following couple relationship education preparation. *Family Relations, 65*, 407–423. doi:10.1111/fare.12201

Meneses, C. W., & Greenberg, L. (2011). The construction of a model of the process of couples' forgiveness in emotion-focused therapy for couples. *Journal of Marital and Family Therapy, 37*, 491–502. doi:10.1111/j.1752-0606.2011.00234.x

Meyer, I. H. (2003). Prejudice, social stress, and mental health in lesbian, gay, and bisexual populations: Conceptual issues and research evidence. *Psychological Bulletin, 129*, 674–697. doi:10.1037/0033-2909.129.5.674

Monk, J. K., & Ogolsky, B. G. (2019). Contextual relational uncertainty model: Understanding ambiguity in a changing legal context of marriage. *Journal of Family Theory & Review, 11*(2), 243–261.

Monk, J. K., Ogolsky, B. G., & Oswald, R. F. (2018). Coming out and getting back in: Relationship cycling and distress in same-and different-sex relationships. *Family Relations, 67*, 523–538. doi:10.1111/fare.12336

Nahum-Shani, I., Qian, M., Almirall, D., Pelham, W. E., Gnagy, B., Fabiano, G. A., … Murphy, S. A. (2012). Experimental design and primary data analysis methods for comparing adaptive interventions, *Psychological Methods, 17*, 457–477. doi:10.1037/a0029372

Neff, L. A., & Broady, E. F. (2011). Stress resilience in early marriage: Can practice make perfect? *Journal of Personality and Social Psychology, 101*(5), 1050. doi:10.1037/a0023809

Neff, L. A., & Karney, B. R. (2016). Acknowledging the elephant in the room: How stressful environmental contexts shape relationship dynamics. *Current Opinion in Psychology, 13*, 107–110. doi:10.1016/j.copsyc.2016.05.013

Nguyen, T. P., Williamson, H. C., Karney, B. R., & Bradbury, T. N. (2017). Communication moderates effects of residential mobility on relationship quality among ethnically diverse couples. *Journal of Family Psychology, 31*, 753–764. doi:10.1037/fam0000324

Ogolsky, B. G., & Bowers, J. R. (2013). A meta-analytic review of relationship maintenance and its correlates. *Journal of Social and Personal Relationships, 30*, 343–367. doi:10.1177/0265407512463338

Ogolsky, B. G., Monk, J. K., Rice, T. M., Theisen, J. C., & Maniotes, C. R. (2017). Relationship maintenance: A review of research on romantic relationships. *Journal of Family Theory and Review, 9,* 275–306. doi:10.1111/jftr.12205

Otis, M. D., Rostosky, S. S., Riggle, E. D. B., & Hamrin, R. (2006). Stress and relationship quality in same-sex couples. *Journal of Social and Personal Relationships, 23,* 81–99. doi:10.1177/0265407506060179

Overall, N. C., Girme, Y. U., Lemay Jr., E. P., & Hammond, M. D. (2014). Attachment anxiety and reactions to relationship threat: The benefits and costs of inducing guilt in romantic partners. *Journal of Personality and Social Psychology, 106,* 235–256.

Pepping, C. A., & Halford, W. K. (2014). Relationship education and therapy for same-sex couples. *Australian and New Zealand Journal of Family Therapy, 35,* 431–144. doi:10.1002/anzf.1075

Pietromonaco, P. R., & Perry-Jenkins, M. (2014). Marriage in whose America? What the suffocation model misses. *Psychological Inquiry, 25,* 108–113. doi:10.1080/1047840X.2014.876909

Proulx, C. M., Ermer, A. E., & Kanter, J. B. (2017). Group-based trajectory modeling of marital quality: A critical review. *Journal of Family Theory and Review, 9,* 307–327. doi:10.1111/jftr.12201

Rahim, M. A. (1983). A measure of styles of handling interpersonal conflict. *Academy of Management Journal, 26*(2), 368–376. doi:10.5465/255985

Randles, J. M. (2016). *Proposing prosperity?: Marriage education policy and inequality in America.* New York: Columbia University Press.

Randles, J., & Avishai, O. (2018). Saving marriage culture "one marriage at a time": Relationship education and the reinstitutionalization of marriage in an era of individualism. *Qualitative Sociology, 41,* 21–40. doi:10.1007/s11133-018-9375-1

Rauer, A. J., Adler-Baeder, F., Lucier-Greer, M., Skuban, E., Ketring, S. A., & Smith, T. (2014). Exploring processes of change in couple relationship education: Predictors of change in relationship quality. *Journal of Family Psychology, 28*(1), 65. doi:10.1037/a0035502

Rauer, A. J., Karney, B. R., Garvan, C. W., & Hou, W. (2008). Relationship risks in context: A cumulative risk approach to understanding relationship satisfaction. *Journal of Marriage and Family, 70,* 1122–1135. doi:10.1111/j.1741-3737.2008.00554.x

Rhoades, G. K., Stanley, S. M., & Markman, H. J. (2010). Should I stay or should I go? Predicting dating relationship stability from four aspects of commitment. *Journal of Family Psychology, 24,* 543–550. doi:10.1037/a0021008

Rhoades, G. K., Stanley, S. M., Markman, H. J., & Allen, E. S. (2015). Can marriage education mitigate the risks associated with premarital cohabitation? *Journal of Family Psychology, 29*(3), 500. doi:10.1037/fam0000081

Rogge, R. D., Cobb, R. J., Lawrence, E., Johnson, M. D., & Bradbury, T. N. (2013). Is skills training necessary for the primary prevention of marital distress and dissolution? A 3-year experimental study of three interventions. *Journal of Consulting and Clinical Psychology, 81*(6), 949–961. doi:10.1037/a0034209

Ross, J. M., Karney, B. R., Nguyen, T. P., & Bradbury, T. N. (2019). Communication that is maladaptive for middle-class couples is adaptive for socioeconomically disadvantaged couples. *Journal of Personality and Social Psychology, 116*(4), 582–597. doi:10.1037/pspi0000158

Rusbult, C. E., Martz, J. M., & Agnew, C. R. (1998). The investment model scale: Measuring commitment level, satisfaction level, quality of alternatives, and investment size. *Personal Relationships, 5,* 357–391. doi:10.1111/j.1475-6811.1998.tb00177.x

Rusbult, C. E., & Van Lange, P. A. (2003). Interdependence, interaction, and relationships. *Annual Review of Psychology, 54*, 351–375. http://dx.doi.org/10.1146/annurev.psych.54.101601.145059

Satir, V., Banmen, J., Gerber, J., & Gomori, M. (1991). *The Satir model: Family therapy and beyond.* Palo Alto, CA: Science and Behavioral Books.

Schnarch, D. M. (1991). *Constructing the sexual crucible: An integration of sexual and marital therapy.* New York: Norton & Company.

Schramm, D. G., Galovan, A. M., & Goddard, H. W. (2017). What researchers and relationship practitioners wished the other knew: Integrating discovery and practice in couple relationships. *Family Relations, 66*, 696–711. doi:10.1111/fare.12270

Seshadri, G., & Knudson-Martin, C. (2013). How couples manage interracial and intercultural differences: Implications for clinical practice. *Journal of Marital and Family Therapy, 39*, 43–58. doi:10.1111/j.1752-0606.2011.00262.x

Smith, G. L. (1998). The present state and future of symbolic-experiential family therapy: A post-modern analysis. *Contemporary Family Therapy, 20*, 147–161. https://doi.org/10.1023/A:1025073324868

Sparks, A. (2008). Implementation of "Within My Reach:" Providing a relationship awareness and communication skills program to TANF recipients in Oklahoma (National Poverty Center Working Paper Series #08-11). Retrieved from www.npc.umich.edu/publications/working_papers/

Sprenkle, D. H., Davis, S. D., & Lebow, J. L. (2009). *Common factors in couple and family therapy: The overlooked foundation for effective practice.* New York: Guilford Press.

Stafford, L. (2016). Marital sanctity, relationship maintenance, and marital quality. *Journal of Family Issues, 37*, 119–131. doi:10.1177/0192513X13515884

Stafford, L., & Canary, D. J. (1991). Maintenance strategies and romantic relationship type, gender and relational characteristics. *Journal of Social and Personal Relationships, 8*, 217–242. doi:10.1177/0265407591082004

Stanley, S. M. (2001). Making a case for premarital education. *Family Relations, 50*(3), 272–280. doi:10.1111/j.1741-3729.2001.00272.x

Stanley, S. M., & Markman, H. J. (1992). Assessing commitment in personal relationships. *Journal of Marriage and the Family, 54*(3), 595–608. doi:10.2307/353245

Stanley, S. M., Markman, H. J., & Blumberg, S. L. (1999). *Helping couples fight for their marriages: The PREP approach.* New York: Routledge.

Thibaut, J. W., & Kelley, H. H. (1959). *The social psychology of groups.* Oxford, UK: Wiley.

Ting-Toomey, S. (2017). Conflict face-negotiation theory. In X. Dia & G. Chen (Eds.), *Conflict management and intercultural communication: The art of intercultural harmony.* New York: Routledge.

Titelman, P. (Ed.) (1998). *Clinical applications of Bowen Family Systems Theory.* New York: Haworth Press.

Trail, T. E., Goff, P. A., Bradbury, T. N., & Karney, B. R. (2012). The costs of racism for marriage: How racial discrimination hurts, and ethnic identity protects, newlywed marriages among Latinos. *Personality and Social Psychology Bulletin, 38*, 454–465. doi:10.1177/0146167211429450

Tsang, J., Mccullough, M. E., & Fincham, F. D. (2006). The longitudinal association between forgiveness and relationship closeness and commitment. *Journal of Social and Clinical Psychology, 25*, 448–472. https://doi.org/10.1521/jscp.2006.25.4.448

Vennum, A., Lindstrom, R., Monk, J. K., & Adams, R. (2013). It's complicated: The continuity and correlates of cyclicality in cohabiting and marital relationships. *Journal of Social and Personal Relationships, 31*, 410–430. doi:10.1177/0265407513501987.

Vennum, A., Monk, J. K., Pasley, B. K., & Fincham, F. D. (2017). Emerging adult relationship transitions as opportune times for tailored interventions. *Emerging Adulthood, 5*, 293–305. doi:10.1177/2167696817705020

Wadsworth, M. E., & Markman, H. J. (2012). Where's the action? Understanding what works and why in relationship education. *Behavior Therapy, 43*, 99–112. doi:10.1016/j.beth.2011.01.006

Walton, G. M. (2014). The new science of wise psychological interventions. *Current Directions in Psychological Science, 23*, 73–82. doi:10.1177/0963721413512856

Weiser, D. A., & Weigel, D. J. (2016). Self-efficacy in romantic relationships: Direct and indirect effects on relationship maintenance and satisfaction. *Personality and Individual Differences, 89*, 152–156. doi:10.1016/j.paid.2015.10.013

Wetchler, J. L., & Piercy, F. P. (1996). Experiential family therapies. In F. P. Piercy, D. H. Sprenkel, J. L. Wetchler & Associates (Eds.), *Family therapy sourcebook* (2nd ed.) (pp. 79–105). New York: Guilford Press.

White, M., & Epston, D. (1990). *Narrative means to therapeutic ends*. New York: W. W. Norton & Company.

Whiting, J. B., Bradford, K., Vail, A., Carlton, E. T., & Bathje, K. (2009). Developing a domestic violence protocol for marriage education: Critical components and cautions. *Journal of Couple and Relationship Therapy, 8*, 181–196. doi:10.1080/15332690902813844

Williamson, H. C., Altman, N., Hsueh, J., & Bradbury, T. N. (2016). Effects of relationship education on couple communication and satisfaction: A randomized controlled trial with low-income couples. *Journal of Consulting and Clinical Psychology, 84*(2), 156–166. doi:10.1037/ccp0000056

Williamson, H. C., Karney, B. R., & Bradbury, T. N. (2017). Education and job-based interventions for unmarried couples living with low incomes: Benefit or burden? *Journal of Consulting and Clinical Psychology, 85*, 5–12. doi:10.1037/ccp0000156

Worthington, E. L., Jr. (2001). *Five steps to forgiveness: The art and science of forgiving*. New York: Crown.

Yum, Y. O., & Canary, D. J. (2009). Cultural differences in equity theory predictions of relational maintenance strategies. *Human Communication Research, 35*(3), 384–406. doi:10.1111/j.1468-2958.2009.01356.x

Yum, Y. O., Canary, D. J., & Baptist, J. (2015). The roles of culture and fairness in maintaining relationships: A comparison of romantic partners from Malaysia, Singapore, and the United States. *International Journal of Intercultural Relations, 44*, 100–112. doi:10.1016/j.ijintrel.2014.12.003

Zimmerman, T. S., Prest, L. A., & Wetzel, B. E. (1997). Solution-focused couples therapy groups: An empirical study. *Journal of Family Therapy, 19*, 125–144. https://doi.org/10.1111/1467-6427.00044

PART V

CONCLUSION

19

Relationship Maintenance Reprise and Reflections: Past, Present, and Future

DANIEL PERLMAN[1]

After it is started one is still faced with having to make the friendship *work*.

Rom Harre, 1977, p. 341

Many relationships, including ones of great importance to us, last a long time. It is often said that sibling relations are our long-lasting relations. In the USA circa 2016, the average life expectancy was 78.6 years (Kochanek, Murphy, Xu, & Arias, 2017). With spacing on average of about three years between siblings (Buckles & Munnich, 2012), sisters and brothers can easily have relationships of 75 years' duration. Despite images of the USA as a divorce-prone society, a 2011 US Census Bureau report showed that over 50% of marriages formed in the early 1960s were still intact in 2009 some 40 plus years later (Kreider & Ellis, 2011), and other data show that of married individuals over 70, roughly two-thirds had been married 50 or more years (Wu & Brown, 2016). Even friendships can last a long time. In a study of midlife married fathers ages 35 to 50, the median duration of their closest friendships was about 13 years (Stueve & Gerson, 1977). In an analysis of the social networks of older adults (55+) living in the USA and the Netherlands, the participants reported having known their significant friends for 18 and 28.5 years, respectively (de Jong Gierveld & Perlman, 2006). Relationships begin and end, but what happens in between to keep them going is a major, key part of the significant social bonds we have in our lives.

The current volume is devoted to the exploration of what maintains relationships over time. My goal in this chapter is to reflect on the other chapters in the book, doing some synthesizing, placing the volume's contents in context, and adding my own views. I proceed by first discussing what maintenance is and then examining the past, the present, and the future of scholarship on maintenance. In discussing the past, I map the growth of work on maintenance and reflect on a few comparisons between early and current

---

[1] University of North Carolina at Greensboro

contributions. Turning to the present, I identify who's who in the area, compare theories, and offer a broad-stroke synthesis of antecedents and consequences of maintenance. Looking forward to the future, I highlight what authors in the volume recommend as future directions and add my own thoughts.

Scattered throughout the chapter, I report some objective data (e.g., citation counts) and results from a survey of relationship scholars. This grounds parts of the chapter in objective evidence. Also, of course, the other chapters themselves are the foundation on which the current chapter is built. So, there is a clear reference point. Nonetheless, this, like most concluding chapters, is necessarily selective and has elements of subjectivity stemming from my interests and skills as an author. Before reading on, you might use my preview as a template to think briefly about what you see as key features of the book, and after reading this chapter, judge how closely our visions correspond.

WHAT IS RELATIONSHIP MAINTENANCE?

Several contributors to the relationship maintenance literature, including the authors in this volume, have offered various definitions of relationship maintenance (see Ogolsky & Monk, Chapter 1). In this volume, multiple chapter authors either used or built on Dindia's (2003) definition, which centered on keeping relationships in existence; in a specified state or condition; in a satisfactory condition; and in repair. The emphasis of this definition was implicitly on preventing relationships from deteriorating. More explicitly than Dindia, other definitions state that maintenance combats threats to relationships (see Young & Simpson, Chapter 3). Still other definitions go beyond the defensive and steady-state notions of maintenance to include enhancing relationships. For instance Stafford (Chapter 7) writes: "A fifth definition is ... to keep a relationship growing, i.e., in a state and process of growth." Lee, Karantzas, Gillath, and Fraley (Chapter 4); Xu, Lewandowski, and Aron (Chapter 6); and Rauer and Proulx (Chapter 17) each also included efforts to strengthen relationships in their conceptualizations of maintenance.

What should we make of the variability in definitions of relationship maintenance? Such variability is common in actively pursued areas of research. It often stems from the focus of investigators' interests or their theoretical perspective (e.g., Young and Simpson's concern with threats versus Xu, Lewandowski, and Aron's interest in growth). Diversity can lead to seeming contradictions in findings, but when findings based on different definitions converge, it adds robustness to what we know. Although there have been rich discussions of definitions of maintenance (e.g., Stafford, Chapter 7), it is likely that subtle differences in the way investigators define maintenance will persist. One prescription for those studying maintenance is to think carefully about how they define the concept and to make it explicit in their publications.

One can use the term "maintenance" as condition or a stage between initial development and the decline of relationships. Gaines and Ferenczi (Chapter 15) explicitly define maintenance as "a state of interdependence" influenced by commitment and relationship satisfaction. Leo, Leifker, Baucom, and Baucom (Chapter 11) talk about strategies leading to maintenance, presumably seeing it as a condition. Many of the contributors to this book, however, see relationship maintenance as various processes or enactments that partners do. Stafford (1994, p. 300) resolved the state versus process conundrum by saying that "maintenance is the process of maintaining a given state." Thus, another way to know what the study of maintenance is all about is to enumerate maintenance processes. Ogolsky and Monk (2018) have identified over 40 different ways in which maintenance processes have been operationalized (see Table 19.1). Their list is admirable for its comprehensiveness and its connections to measuring instruments.

There have been various ways of grouping maintenance strategies. For example, Theiss (Chapter 5) and Stafford (Chapter 7) talk about positive and negative maintenance strategies. Positive strategies are much more common, but negative ones (e.g., jealousy induction or communicating that partners are not liked) have been identified. A second distinction, between routine (less mindful, habitual) and strategic (tactics to achieve specific goals) maintenance, is found in several chapters (e.g., Fiori & Rauer, Chapter 14; Rauer & Proulx, Chapter 17; Sprecher, Felmlee, Stokes, & McDaniel, Chapter 9; Stafford, Chapter 7; Theiss, Chapter 5). Following an earlier chapter by Rusbult, Olsen, Davis, and Hannon (2001), Sprecher and colleagues (Chapter 9) distinguish between cognitive and behavioral strategies. Caughlin and Wang (Chapter 16) differentiate maintaining one's network of relationships from one's close relationships. Multiple authors in this volume (Chapters 4, 7, 17, and 18), use Ogolsky, Monk, Rice, Theisen, and Maniotes's (2017) categories of threat mitigation and relationship enhancement, which can each occur at the individual or interactive levels. These various category schemes have been based on logical assessments of the similarity within each category rather than, as is done in other research areas, on the basis of such techniques as cluster analysis. More effort to derive and test empirically based typologies would be a worthwhile future direction for research.

Ogolsky and colleagues (2017) reflect that "the boundaries of the concept of relationship maintenance are quite nebulous" (p. 275). In focusing on maintenance processes, it does seem that the concept of maintenance has a nebulous quality. Does any process that prevents deterioration, sustains the level of relationships, and/or enhances the relationship qualify as a

TABLE 19.1 *Forty-one operationalizations of relationship maintenance*

Accommodating
Advice-giving
Allowing control
Antisocial acts
Assurances
Avoidance
Benevolent cognitions
Cards-calls-letters
Conflict management
Deep talk
Destructive conflict
Expressing gratitude and appreciation
Facilitative behaviors
Forgiveness
Generosity
Sacrifice and willingness to sacrifice
Self-disclosure
Sharing tasks
Social networks
Tasks
Time together
Transformation of motivation (cognitive interdependence)
Understanding
Verbal affection
Humor
Inattentiveness to or derogation of alternatives
Infidelity
Informal talk
Joint activities
Media
Monitoring/spying
Negative maintenance: jealousy induction
Networks
Openness
Partner-focused prayer (spiritual behaviors)
Physical affection
Positive illusions
Positivity
Providing support (supportive behaviors)
Relational talk
Resources

Source: Ogolsky and Monk, 2018.

maintenance phenomenon? Or does this apply only to some interpersonal processes (e.g., habitual or conscious processes as opposed to unconsciously motivated ones)? Also, the identification of individual maintenance strategies is the product of a labeling process. The identification of strategies via labeling can be done differently by different researchers and new strategies added. For example, Leo and colleagues (Chapter 11) describe soft emotional expression and "we" requests (akin to cognitive interdependence; VanderDrift & Agnew, Chapter 2); Randall and Messerschmitt-Coen (Chapter 10) emphasize dyadic coping; and Impett, Muise, and Rosen (Chapter 12) explore sex as maintenance strategies that go beyond Ogolsky and Monk's (2018) list, for which there are extant measures. The number of strategies has been growing and undoubtedly will continue to grow in the future.

THE PAST

Scholarly interest in interpersonal attraction (who likes whom) and the demise of relationships (e.g., divorce) can be traced back over 100 years to roughly 1900. For much of the twentieth century, maintenance was the neglected aspect in the arc of relation development. In 1994, Steve Duck wrote:

Relationship maintenance refers generally to the vast unstudied void in relational research – that large area where relationships continue to exist between the point of their initial development (which has been intensively studied) and their possible decline (which has also been studied but somewhat less intensively) (Duck, 1994, p. 45)

In the current volume, Laura Stafford credits Murray Davis (1973) with compiling the first "list of actions or activities intended to maintain relationships." This can be used as a marker of the beginning of more focused interest in a topic labeled maintenance.

The Growth of Publications on Relationship Maintenance

Using standard bibliographic techniques for mapping the growth of the area is challenging for various reasons (e.g., its somewhat nebulous form; the term "relationship" is used in other ways in titles). Ogolsky and colleagues (2017) carefully compiled a comprehensive bibliography in conjunction with their review. They used multiple search sources, they not only used relationship maintenance as a search term but also used 29 other maintenance-related terms, and finally, they had judges decide which articles should be retained. They only included studies involving romantic relationships, so their results underestimate the total pool, perhaps by 40% or so. From over 15,000 potentially relevant items they generated in total, they compiled a final bibliography of 1,149 items. The first article they found was published in 1971.

Using Ogolsky et al.'s bibliography, Figure 19.1 shows the 1976 to 2015 growth curve of articles on relationship maintenance in romantic relationships. Considering key annual data points, the curve climbed steadily and

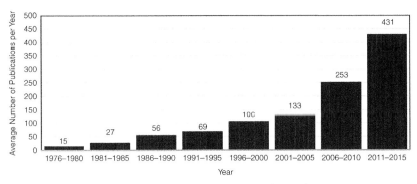

FIGURE 19.1 Growth of publications on romantic relationship maintenance 1976–2015.

fairly gradually from the early 1970s through the 1990s, hit a peak in 1999, dropped until 2003, and then began a steeper climb through 2014. (A modest drop in 2015 may partially be due to the exact timing of when the bibliography was compiled.) At its 2014 peak, Ogolsky and colleagues identified 100 sources. The growth does indicate that maintenance has become a topic getting attention in the relationship literature. Consistently with this assessment, in a 2016 poll of 210 members of the International Association of Relationship Research, relationship maintenance ranked 12th among the 21 most frequently mentioned topics currently being investigated (Perlman, Duck, & Hengstebeck, 2018). Relationship maintenance had fewer mentions than topics such as attachment, social support, and commitment. Complementing the polling data, these more frequently mentioned topics also were the subject of a larger number of 2014 publications as revealed via a simple title word search in the *PsycInfo* database, the results being as follows: attachment (1,074), social support (623), and commitment (505).

In perusing Ogolsky et al.'s bibliography and related sources, there are certain publications after Davis's 1973 book that also stand out as signs of the area's development. Quantitative research requires measuring instruments. Earlier ones were created, but Stafford and Canary's (1991) index of five relationship strategies (and its descendants) is one, if not the, dominant measurement tradition for this concept (see Stafford, Chapter 7). This was followed shortly thereafter by a special issue of the *Journal of Social and Personal Relationships* that Kathryn Dindia and Daniel Canary edited in 1993. It was the first of several noteworthy edited collections focused on (Canary & Dainton, 2003; Canary & Stafford, 1994; Stafford, 2005; and the current volume), or partially focused on (Harvey & Wenzel, 2001; 2002), relationship maintenance. There have also been a series of handbook chapters (Agnew & VanderDrift, 2015; Canary & Dainton, 2006; Dindia, 2000; Lydon & Quinn, 2013; Ogolsky & Monk, 2018) and reviews (Ogolsky & Bowers, 2013;

Ogolsky et al., 2017). Most recently, Finkel, Simpson, and Eastwick (2017), in their *Annual Review of Psychology* assessment of the field, include maintenance as one of 14 core principles or focal topics of our knowledge about relationships.

Collectively, the growth of publications, the survey data, and the publication markers of development indicate that relationship maintenance is no longer a "vast unstudied void." It is a topic in good standing among relationship scholars.

Three Phases of Concept Development

Stephen Margulis (1977) articulated three progressive, albeit sometimes overlapping, stages in concept development. The first stage involves justifying interest in the concept. Sociologist Murray Davis's (1973) treatment of what he called reintegrative mechanisms (preventive and corrective maintenance) illustrates this stage. He believed that these mechanisms were important because without them, relationships would fall apart. Characteristically of first-stage steps, he used logical analysis, described maintenance mechanisms, and cited cases such as from movies and literature (e.g., Tristan and Iseult). The first stage began using the concept, specifying processes within the maintenance domain, and implying its potential importance.

The second stage is exploration. Margulis (1977) saw this as a stage in which researchers are accepting of the concept. During this stage, investigators endeavor to identify similarities and differences between concepts as well as the types and functions of the phenomenon. I see this as a stage in which measures need to be developed, providing a foundation for establishing the prevalence of the phenomenon's occurrence and conducting initial studies of its correlates. A 1983 report by Joe Ayres (Ayres, 1983) is an early example of this stage. He first identified 38 potential maintenance factors, asked 359 students the likelihood they would use each strategy, factored analyzed the results, extracted three types of maintenance factors, and created a scale score for each. In a second phase of his research, he tested whether these maintenance factors would be used more or less by males versus females, in different types of relationships (e.g., friend versus coworker), or at different points in a relationship's development (developing, stable, or deteriorating). The one significant result was that different types of maintenance were used at different stages of relationship development. Ayres conducted the second phase of his study without any hypotheses, although in this stage of research development, often some rationale for predictions is advanced.

Margulis (1977) identifies the third stage of concept development as characterized by theorizing. In his words, it is when there are "systematically related sets of statements some of whose logical implications are empirically testable" (p. 6). He sees such theories as explicating the "whys and hows" of the phenomenon. A chapter by Rusbult, Drigotas, and Verette (1994) is an early example of Margulis's third stage. They put relationship maintenance behaviors within Rusbult's investment model version of interdependence theory. Working with the concepts of that theory, this group explicitly addressed the how (e.g., via accommodative behaviors) and the why (maintenance behaviors promote healthy relationships that are beneficial to individuals) of relationship maintenance. Part II of the current volume testifies that research on relationship maintenance has now reached a stage where it has a variety of theories currently being used as conceptual guides.

Yesterday and Today: Reflections on Changes

A striking difference between the influential early collections edited by Daniel Canary and associates (e.g., Canary & Dainton, 2003; Canary & Stafford, 1994; Dindia & Canary, 1993) and the current volume is the disciplinary affiliations of the authors involved. In Canary's collections, 72% were communications scholars, 24% psychologists, and 3% family scientists. In the current volume, 9% of the authors are communication scholars, 60% are psychologists, 21% are family scientists, and 4% are sociologists. In the prefaces to Canary's books, he and his coeditors make clear that their focus was on the communicative aspects of maintenance: "as the title suggests, this book highlights the role of communication in the maintenance of relationships" (Canary & Stafford, p. 1994, p. xiii); "the present volume focuses on communicative processes that have been found critical in the maintenance and enhancement of social and personal relationships" (Canary & Dainton, 2003, p. xiv). In the current volume, psychological processes and social psychological models have a considerably larger presence.

In looking backward, it appears that Canary and other communication scholars especially deserve credit for starting to use the concept of relationship maintenance in the late 1980s and 1990s in communication journals and the *Journal of Social and Personal Relationships*. In 2001, Harvey and Wenzel published a volume whose authors were primarily (80%) psychologists. In the 1970s, 1980s, and 1990s, psychologists and others had published on a variety of topics (e.g., positive illusions, network and social support, joint activities, the investment model, willingness to sacrifice, interdependence theory, destiny vs. growth beliefs, and derogation of potential alternative partners) as they related to variables associated with maintenance, such as the development or continuation of relationships. Descendants of these publications exist in what is now seen as the relationship maintenance area, but at the time they were published, their authors were not necessarily using the vocabulary of relationship maintenance or linking them together as part of a larger whole.

As noted by Dainton (2003), five theoretical perspectives were used in the 2003 Canary and Dainton volume: interdependence theory (aka the investment model), equity theory, dialectical perspectives, uncertainty reduction theory, and systems approaches. Interdependence and relational dialectics theory were also frameworks salient in the 1993 *Journal of Social and Personal Relationships* special issue (Dindia & Canary, 1993). The current volume overlaps with the earlier communications collections in devoting chapters to the interdependence (VanderDrift & Agnew, Chapter 2) and uncertainty reduction (Theiss, Chapter 5) perspectives. Neither relational dialectics nor equity nor systems theories are treated as main perspectives in the current volume, although some chapters (e.g., Stafford, Chapter 7) briefly discuss equity theory, and Randall and Messerschmitt-Coen (Chapter 10) discuss Bodenmann's work on couple stress and coping, which draws on a systematic perspective.

The current volume, which offers considerable coverage of theoretical treatments, adds the following approaches: life history, an analysis within the broader evolutionary tradition (Young & Simpson, Chapter 3), self-expansion (Xu, Lewandowski, & Aron, Chapter 6), and attachment (Lee et al., Chapter 4). In the more psychologically oriented early work on relationship maintenance represented in Harvey and Wenzel's (2001) book, both Aron's self-expansion and an evolutionary theoretical approach were presented (Aron, Norman, & Aron, 2001; Wu, 2001). Research relating attachment styles and maintenance strategies appeared as early as 1993 (Simon & Baxter, 1993), and Mikulincer and Shaver discussed relationship maintenance in their 2007 book (Mikulincer & Shaver, 2007). Nonetheless, the current chapter (Lee et al., Chapter 4) appears to be the first effort devoted to advancing an attachment perspective on relationship maintenance.

The selection of theoretical perspectives in the current volume reflects the demographics of who studies close relationships (psychologists being the largest group) more accurately than the early Canary and associates publications. The five theories represented in this volume also reflect current trends in the field. In a recent commentary on theories of close relationships, Clark (2018) identified attachment, interdependence, and evolution as the dominant broad theories in the field along with some narrower theories, including self-expansion and uncertainty reduction. Perlman and colleagues' (2018) survey of relationship researchers found results complementing Clark's viewpoint.

Another noteworthy shift between the early research done from a communication perspective and research referenced in the present volume has to do with methodology. Early researchers used two key ways of collecting data on maintenance behaviors: they asked participants to describe the techniques they used to maintain their behaviors, or they presented them with various strategies and asked them to indicate the frequency or likelihood of use of each strategy (Burleson & Samter, 1994, p. 64). As research on maintenance progressed, other techniques have been added (e.g., experiments, daily diary studies, consideration of actor and partner effects, and longitudinal studies) and are being further advocated (see Future Directions in Methodology section).

Having identified some of the historical roots of more current scholarship on relationship maintenance and a few ways in which work today differs from work in the past, what does looking at the current volume's contents suggest about the state of relationship maintenance scholarship today? Three vantage points for doing this are the currently influential scholars, theories, and a collage of visions of the antecedents and consequences of relationship maintenance.

A Current Who's Who of Relationship Maintenance Scholarship

Table 19.2 lists the 50 most-mentioned scholars identified via an analysis of prepublication drafts of Chapters 2 through 18 of this volume. The text of each chapter, not including the reference list, was put into a single file, and a word frequency search was performed using DataBasic.io's WordCounter (https:// databasic.io/en/wordcounter/). Authors' names were then identified, and an effort was made to distinguish between different authors with the same name (e.g., Brooke vs. Judy Feeney). In the case of chapter authors, their citation count was the total number of times other authors in the book cited them plus the average number of times the chapter author was cited in other chapters. Chapter authors' self-citations were not included in their citation count.

As a group, the gender and disciplinary breakdowns of the most cited scholars were as follows: 63% males and 37% females; 63% psychologists, 24% communication scholars, and 12% family studies. These breakdowns are relatively similar to those found among currently eminent scholars in the broader field of personal relationships as found in a survey of members of the International Association of Relationship Research members (Perlman et al., 2018). The corresponding percentages were 58.5% males, 41.5% females; 60% psychologists, 26% communication scholars. Twenty-three of the 50 most frequently cited scholars in the current volume were also identified as currently eminent in the broader area of personal relationships.

Looking at the top half of the individuals most cited in this volume, multiple points stand out. First, the four most cited scholars (Canary, Stafford, Rusbult, and Dainton) were all early pioneers. Menard (1971) has argued that such early contributors often have considerable impact on the field. They tend to deal with broad questions, sometimes offer key measures (e.g., Stafford & Canary, 1991), and shape the way later researchers think about the phenomena. Second, many of the most mentioned scholars have offered

TABLE 19.2 *Most cited scholars*

Scholar	Citations
Daniel Canary	176
Laura Stafford[a]	146
Marianne Dainton	89
Carol Rusbult	76
Brian Ogolsky	66
Guy Bodenmann	62
Thomas Bradbury	50
Harold Kelley	45
Phillip Shaver	45
Frank Fincham	42
Kathryn Dindia	39
James McNulty[a]	30
Denise Solomon	29
Jeffry Simpson[a]	29
Benjamin Karney	27
Mario Mikulincer	26
Sandra Murray	25
Nancy Collins	24
John Thibaut	24
Jill Bowers	24
Leanne Knobloch	24
Daniel Weigel	23
Howard Markman	23
Arthur Aron[a]	22
Christopher Agnew[a]	22
Margaret Clark	22
John Gottman	22
Brent Mattingly	22
John Holmes	21
Deborah Ballard-Reisch	21
Scott Stanley	21
Nicole Ellison	21
Stephen Haas	20
Paul van Lange	19
Eli Finkel	19
Brooks Aylor	19
Mariana Falconier	19
Jesse Fox	16
Steven Beach	16
Andrew Christensen	15
Susan Sprecher[a]	15
Robert Milardo	14
Harry Reis	14
Cindy Hazan	14
Brooke Feeney	13

TABLE 19.2 *(cont.)*

Scholar	Citations
Jay Belsky	13
Charles Berger	13
John Lydon	13
Danielle Mitnick	13

[a] Score adjusted for self-citations.

valuable theoretical or conceptual analyses. For example, Rusbult, Kelley, Thibaut, and Agnew are associated with the interdependence position; Shaver, Mikulincer, Collins, and J. Feeney with the attachment viewpoint; Solomon, Knobloch, and Theiss with uncertainty perspectives; Aron with self-expansion; and Simpson with both the evolutionary and the attachment perspective.

Third, despite the influence of pioneers, there is a newer generation of scholars gaining considerable influence. Ten of the most mentioned scholars in this volume received their doctoral degrees after 2000; four in 2001–2002 (McNulty, Weigel, Knobloch, and Finkel); and six in 2005 or later (Ogolsky, Bowers, Mattingly, Falconier, Fox, and Mitnick). Of these, the two most frequently mentioned are editor Brian Ogolsky and James McNulty. One can easily see how each has opened new territory in the study of relationship maintenance. Ogolsky has advanced the field by synthesizing major aspects of the current state of knowledge about relationship maintenance by doing groundbreaking meta-analyses and narrative reviews (e.g., Ogolsky & Bowers, 2013; Ogolsky et al., 2017). He identified the importance of the perception of one's partner's maintenance efforts. In his 2009 article, he offered a sophisticated analysis of the association between the perception of the receipt of maintenance and commitment, finding that a cognitive model of maintenance leading to commitment held for early-stage relationships, whereas a motivational model of commitment leading to maintenance better fitted established relationships (Ogolsky, 2009). In his 2017 review, he offered a model for organizing work on relationship maintenance that considers relationship partners' motives (threat mitigation vs. relationship enhancement), their interactions, and the social context in which individuals and relationships exist.

As described in Chapter 8, McNulty and Dugas have taken well-established principles and identified limiting conditions (i.e., moderator variables), indicating when they do and do not operate to promote maintenance. This analysis builds on a more general contextual model of interpersonal relationships previously advanced by James McNulty (2016). In that model, McNulty identified three classes of factors as moderating variables: qualities of the individual, qualities of the relationship, and external factors such as stress.

Both Ogolsky and McNulty are starting with a larger, more advanced body of knowledge, yet one with inconsistencies that they are trying to better understand and/or organize. Both are trying to make sense of extensive bodies of literature considering the importance of individual, dyadic, and contextual factors.

Theoretical Viewpoints

In thinking about the theories identified in the current volume, I have identified eight dimensions on which to compare them (see Table 19.3). Naturally, constructing the table involves making judgments and simplifying details. Nonetheless, the table is useful in organizing information and seeing similarities and differences.

Each of the five theories largely has its own intellectual heritage, although in holding the premise that attachment serves an evolutionary function, attachment theorists have some overlap with evolutionary theorists. For the most part, each of these theories traces its roots back to relatively recent (mid- and late-twentieth-century) ideas generated within the social sciences. Life history, with its ancestry going back to Darwin, is the clearest exception.

The theorists generally agree that maintenance is salutary, but they differ in terms of the type of well-being that maintenance fosters. For advocates of the life history perspective, reproductive success is a fundamental goal. For attachment theory, feeling secure and surviving, also key to the species, is important. Interdependence and self-expansion theorists see maintenance, in enhancing relationships, as also helping to fulfill personal needs or motives. From the uncertainty perspective, maintenance reduces (or manages) the individual's uncertainty about their relationships.

Each of the theorists has their own key concepts. Arguably, the self-expansion theorists, working primarily with two principles, have the most parsimonious perspective for analyzing maintenance.

Most of the theorists see maintenance as both mitigating deterioration and enhancing relationships. Young and Simpson (Chapter 3) focus primarily on maintenance preventing deterioration.

In terms of their temporal perspectives, interdependence, uncertainty, and self-expansion theorists focus most on what is happening at present in relationships and people's lives. Life history and attachment theorists attribute importance to earlier life events.

TABLE 19.3 *Dimensions of relationship maintenance theories*

Dimension	Interdependence (VanderDrift and Agnew)	Life history (Young and Simpson)	Attachment (Lee, Karantzas, Gillath, and Fraley)	Uncertainty (Theiss)	Self-expansion (Xu, Lewandowski, and Aron)
Intellectual heritage	Thibaut and Kelley, Rusbult	Darwin, Trivers, Belsky, Gangestad, and Simpson	Bowlby, Shaver and Hazan, Shaver and Mikulincer	Bradac and associates; Solomon, Knobloch, and associates	Aron and Aron
Why maintenance	Maintenance fosters well-being	Maintenance fosters reproductive fitness	Proximate goal of felt security (feeling safe), ultimate goal survival in times of danger	To reduce relational uncertainty and improve relationship quality	The self-expansion motive (i.e. to expand self-efficacy and the ability to accomplish goals)
Illustrative key concepts	Commitment, investments, payoffs (costs, benefits), cognitive interdependence, transformation of motivation, accommodation, transitions lists, derogation of alternatives, willingness to sacrifice	Reproductive fitness, conditional reproductive strategies, sensitization, faster versus slower reproductive strategies, initial obligatory investment in reproduction, biparental care, adaptation, current environmental stress	Attachment; attachment styles: secure, anxious, avoidant; proximity seeking; safe base; safe haven; hyperactivating; deactivating; broaden and build cycle	Relational uncertainty; types of relational uncertainty (e.g., behavioral, cognitive, partner, self, episodic), relational turbulence, interference from a partner, negative maintenance behavior	Self-expansion, motivational principle, nonrelational self-expansion, inclusion of other in self principle

Prevent deterioration vs. promote enhancement	Persistence in the face of forces pulling partners apart	Emphasis on preventing deterioration	Mitigate threats and enhance relationship quality	Maintenance is intertwined with both enhancement and deterioration	Enhancement and preventive strategies
Temporal perspective	The present	Evolutionary development, childhood, and later conditions	Strategies and attachment styles developed in childhood tend to persist	The present	The present
Key factors that foster maintenance	Commitment	Predictable environments (past and present), slower reproductive strategies, where biparental care is beneficial, being female	Attachment bonds (involving proximity seeking, safe haven, secure base); secure attachment style; support, effective communication, commitment	Relationship uncertainty (inversely related to + maintenance behaviors, directly related to – maintenance)	Self-expansion
Illustrative maintenance processes	Transformation of motivation, derogation of alternatives, willingness to sacrifice	Inattention or devaluation of alternatives, benign attributions or accommodation, sacrifice, idealization and affirmation	Describes pro-relational behaviors in three domains: (a) support, (b) communication, and (c) commitment (e.g., sensitive, responsive support; asking for support when needed)	Positivity, openness, assurances, giving advice, managing conflicts, sharing tasks, and enjoying social networks	Novel, exciting self-expanding dyadic activities

TABLE 19.3 (cont.)

Dimension	Interdependence (VanderDrift and Agnew)	Life history (Young and Simpson)	Attachment (Lee, Karantzas, Gillath, and Fraley)	Uncertainty (Theiss)	Self-expansion (Xu, Lewandowski, and Aron)
Emphasis on individual, interaction, or context	The interaction of partners, although commitment can be within an individual	The context (including partner as a contextual element) and recognition of evolved human nature	Individual differences with acceptance of normative patterns	Relational uncertainty is a state within the individual	Focus on dyadic activities, considers individual differences and individual self-expansion

In terms of the maintenance processes, several theorists draw on a pool of mechanisms that have been identified in the literature. At the time Rusbult developed her model, communication strategies were prominent in the literature. Rusbult drew attention to other processes (e.g., cognitive). Aron has emphasized novel activities.

Theorists see maintenance as influenced by individual, dyadic, and contextual factors. Attachment and relational uncertainty theorists place more emphasis on individual processes; interdependence and self-expansion theorists place more emphasis on dyadic influences, and Young and Simpson (Chapter 3), espousing a life history evolutionary perspective, emphasize contextual factors.

Looking to the future, the past suggests there is both persistence and change in the influence of specific theories. Ellen Berscheid (1995) called for a grand, unifying theory of close relationships that would encompass anthropological, psychological, and sociological perspectives. At the same time, she acknowledged that grand theories were not faring well in psychology. Will a grand relationship theory drawing on multiple disciplinary pillars emerge? I am skeptical.

What does seem plausible to me is that influential theories, falling short of Berscheid's prescription but nonetheless covering multiple other aspects of close relationships, will be used to address maintenance. Finkel and colleagues (2017) encourage relationship theorists to extend their conceptual frameworks to explain as many of the core aspects of relationships as possible. I believe that this has happened (e.g., in this volume's theoretical chapters) and probably will continue to occur. Taken to a next step, Finkel et al.'s viewpoint implies that it would be beneficial not only to see how each theory treats maintenance but to close the circle as much as possible by theorizing on how maintenance relates to other key relational phenomena. Collectively, the theories in this volume do connect maintenance to most of the phenomena Finkel and colleagues identify, but there is variability among the theories in the specific phenomenon with which they connect. For example, attachment theory links maintenance with responsiveness and individual dispositions, whereas interdependence theory links maintenance with standards and alternatives.

There are numerous forces that contribute to the progression of science. These include methodological advances (e.g., diary studies; Lemay & Teneva, Chapter 13), funding opportunities, the effect of findings as well as seeming inconsistences between findings (e.g., McNulty & Dugas, Chapter 8; see also Fiori & Rauer, Chapter 14), clashes as well as the integration of ideas (Lee et al., Chapter 4, draw on interdependence work), historical changes in society (e.g., Caughlin & Wang, Chapter 16), and the changing varieties of relational patterns common in society, personal relationships among members of the scientific community, and the like. We anticipate that such forces will impact the rise and fall of theories as well as research directions to be discussed later.

A Schematic View of Contemporary Maintenance Research

In this volume, both Young and Simpson and Lemay and Teneva have schematic diagrams to encapsulate their ideas. Along these lines, I hope to provide a gestalt of contemporary maintenance research with a more general picture, illustrated with a small sampling of findings.

A common pattern in social science investigations of a phenomenon is to look for antecedents that lead to the phenomenon as well as consequences of it. There are various ways to cluster theoretical as well as empirical antecedents: distal (or ultimate) versus proximal; predisposing versus triggering; and Instigation, Impellance, and Inhibition (Finkel & Hall, 2018). With the phenomenon of maintenance, there are types and numerous processes (discussed earlier). Mediating or intervening variables are often inserted in path diagrams, and moderators are often identified that can alter the relationships between two variables depending on the level of some third condition. Akin to others (e.g., McNulty & Dugas, Chapter 8; Ogolsky et al., 2017), I believe it is useful to think of variables at three levels – individual, dyadic, and external or environmental factors.

In moving into a schematic examination of maintenance and its correlates, some complexities should be noted. First, often, what we have is the association between variables, which are conceptually put into the antecedent and consequence categories, although this is often done on a logical basis rather than on the basis of firm causal evidence. Obviously, as Theiss (Chapter 5) makes clear in discussing relational uncertainty and maintenance as well as VanderDrift and Agnew (Chapter 2) do in discussing commitment, there can be bidirectional influences; ergo, variables can be both antecedents and consequences. Second, given the multiple maintenance strategies, correlates of one type of maintenance may not be antecedents of all maintenance behaviors, and strategies that work well in the short term may not be beneficial in the long term (Leo et al., Chapter 11). Third, although my review is skewed toward empirically demonstrated points, some of the propositions about antecedents of maintenance in this volume are speculative rather than empirically confirmed.

Figure 19.2 represents my attempt at a schematic diagram. Mediating and moderating relationships are implied but not shown. They could occur at multiple points in the diagram.

The figure starts with distal antecedents. These are largely of concern to evolutionary psychologists, who believe that much of our behavior has roots in humans' evolutionary history. Young and Simpson (Chapter 3) discuss reproductive fitness, the survival and reproductive success of our ancestors, as

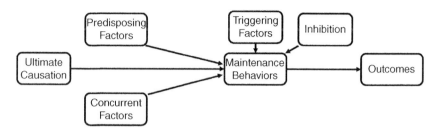

Maintenance: Antecedent and Consequences

FIGURE 19.2 Maintenance: antecedents and consequences.

an ultimate cause. They talk about fast and slow reproductive strategies. Fast reproductive strategies involve less investment in offspring but have adaptive value in harsh, unpredictable environments. Slow reproductive strategies involve greater investment in offspring and have adaptive value in stable, predictable environments. They postulate that in stable environments, where biparental care can benefit a child's long-term prospects, relationship-maintenance behaviors should be high to sustain parental pair-bonds.

The second box is predisposing, relatively stable, factors, including childhood factors, one's cultural background, individual differences, personality traits, and the like. In terms of background, Gaines and Ferenczi (Chapter 15) report that the country or region where one lives (and presumably grew up) has an impact, with Spaniards and Americans being relatively high in relational maintenance. Young and Simpson (Chapter 3) postulate that growing up in a harsh and unpredictable environment suppresses relationship maintenance. Turning to individual differences, attachment styles influence engagement in relationship maintenance, with a secure style generally fostering it (Lee et al., Chapter 4). Individuals with higher levels of depressive symptomology engage in fewer maintenance behaviors, and husbands' depressive symptoms also limited their wives' level of relationship maintenance (see Stafford, Chapter 7). Beliefs matter, too: individuals with growth beliefs (e.g., that relationships take work) as opposed to those with destiny beliefs (i.e., that relations are, or are not, meant to be) engage in more maintenance behavior (Stafford, Chapter 7). Believing in the sacred nature of marriage is also associated with engaging in more maintenance (Stafford, Chapter 7). In terms of sex, women perform more maintenance behaviors than men, and femininity is an even stronger predictor than sex per se (Fiori & Rauer, Chapter 14).

The third box is current factors, things that may fluctuate or be active in brief spurts that are associated with maintenance behaviors. In discussing theories, we have already seen that interdependence (VanderDrift & Agnew, Chapter 2), the uncertainty perspective (Theiss,

Chapter 5), and the self-expansion model (Xu et al., Chapter 6) focus on contemporaneous influences on relationship maintenance. Young and Simpson (Chapter 3) see the harshness of current environments combining with early childhood environments to impact maintenance. From another theoretical position, Stafford (Chapter 7) and her associates have argued that when people see their relationships as being in an equitable state, they are more motivated to maintain them.

Lemay and Teneva (Chapter 13) are concerned with biases in people's judgments. They see Partner A's perception of their partner's benevolent motivation (caring about Partner A) as a prime factor in relationship motivation. Lemay and Teneva go through various cognitive biases and goals that can influence engagement in maintenance behaviors, either amplifying it or diminishing it. For example, they talk about the impact of confirmation biases (i.e., interpreting information in a way that supports one's existing beliefs). Their analysis is that anxiously attached individuals, who fear rejection and abandonment, see their partner's behaviors as less supportive and more upsetting, which in turn, leads them to be less supportive of their partners. In terms of possible maintenance-enhancing processes, Lemay and Teneva discuss how the desire or goal of developing a relationship can bias Person A to see Person B's benevolence as greater than it really is and thereby fuel A's engagement in maintenance activities.

Other examples of current influences come from Sprecher and colleagues' (Chapter 9) social network chapter. For instance, via providing childcare or other resources, network members can facilitate partners having time together. By their reactions or words, network members can affect whether victims forgive their transgressing partners.

Vennum, Kanter, and Baptist (Chapter 18) present a number of interventions used in therapy and relationship education to facilitate relationship maintenance. For instance, these include writing exercises, communication skills development (I-statements and active listening), and encouraging couples to exercise together.

Triggers, the fourth box, are things that prompt engagement in maintenance behaviors but do not necessarily influence the type of maintenance process activated. Young and Simpson discuss four broad types of relationship threats: (a) one's partner having an attractive alternative to oneself, (b) the partner enacting transgressions, (c) goal conflicts between relationship partners, and (d) that one could judge a partner's attributes as merely average compared with the attributes of attractive other potential partners. Attachment theorists (Lee et al., Chapter 4) point to more general challenges and threats as activating the attachment system and thereby activating maintenance activities. Theiss (Chapter 5) casts relational uncertainty as a trigger. Lemay and Teneva (Chapter 13) point to negative events engaging maintenance behaviors.

Inhibiting forces might be classified as antecedents, but rather than fostering behavior, they are forces against it. Often, we think of predictive dimensions, of which one end is associated with the increased likelihood of a maintenance behavior, and the other end is associated with the improbability of that maintenance behavior. It is possible, however, that the things that inhibit a behavior do not promote maintenance action in their absence. Furthermore, some authors refer to factors in terms of what blocks maintenance. Reflecting inhibition, Lemay and Teneva (Chapter 13) discuss how low self-esteem, anxious attachment, rejection sensitivity, and the sense of not being valued by one's partner interfere with maintenance behaviors. Fiori and Rauer (Chapter 14) report a study by Ogolsky and Gray (2016) in which higher daily levels of negative emotion were associated with lower levels of maintenance.

Turning to what Ogolsky (2007) classified as the outcomes of maintenance, Ogolsky and Bowers's (2013) meta-analysis demonstrated that maintenance is associated with key relationships characteristics, including liking/love, satisfaction, mutuality (consensus on the partners' decision-making power structure), and commitment (at least for couples still in the early stages of their relationship; Ogolsky, 2009). Discussion of these, especially commitment and relationship satisfaction, is found extensively in this volume. There are also mentions of the stability of relations (or divorce) (e.g., Randall & Messerschmitt-Coen, Chapter 10; Sprecher et al., Chapter 9) as well as more specific outcomes, such as those used in research on the efficacy of psychoeducational and therapeutic interventions (e.g., healthy communication and more positive expectations about conflict; Vennum et al., Chapter 18).

Finally, turning to variables as mediators and moderators, there is relatively sparse discussion in the present volume of empirically confirmed mediation. An example is the Ogolsky and Gray (2016) study reported by Fiori and Rauer (Chapter 14), which demonstrated that negative emotion mediated the relationship between conflict and lower levels of relationship maintenance.

Within this volume, examples of moderation are more frequent. In trying to resolve seeming inconsistencies in earlier findings, McNulty and Dugas (Chapter 8) make moderation a key part of their approach to bringing order into the evidence. For example, making benevolent attributions for a partner's negative behaviors has been shown to have mixed long-term implications for relationship satisfaction. With colleagues, McNulty has found that making benign attributions buffered against declines in relationship satisfaction if the negative behaviors were relatively minor but did not buffer against declines if the negative behaviors were substantial. Similarly, with forgiveness and declines in marital satisfaction, if the offenses were rare, forgiveness served as a buffer against decline, but if the offences were frequent, forgiveness did not protect against a decline in relationship satisfaction.

Obviously, this schematic representation is only a skeleton. It is designed to reflect a somewhat sprawling literature, not the essence of a compact conceptual model of key variables. Nonetheless, hopefully, it provides some categories in which to place a good deal of what has been written about maintenance and to spur your own recollection about additional key points made in this volume.

Many contributors to this volume discuss future directions for research. Arguably, the prototypical call for more research focuses on possible next steps springing from the ideas and evidence presented in the chapter. Many authors in the current volume proceed in that manner (e.g., Caughlin & Wang, Chapter 16; Impett et al., Chapter 12; Leo et al., Chapter 11; McNulty & Dugas, Chapter 8; Rauer & Proulx, Chapter 17; Sprecher et al., Chapter 9; Vennum et al., Chapter 18; Xu et al., Chapter 6). Others more simply call for more research on the topic of their chapter (e.g., Fiori & Rauer, Chapter 14; Gaines & Ferenczi, Chapter 15).

Cutting across chapters, there were themes in the directions authors feel research should take. Two major clusters of these themes center on methodology and change over time.

Future Directions in Methodology

Methodology involves sampling, measurement, research designs, the types of data collected, and statistical analysis. A first methodological theme that echoes across chapters is the need for more diverse samples, whether this is a generic call for more diverse samples (e.g., Vennum et al., Chapter 18; Xu et al., Chapter 6) or calls for more specific types of diversity, such as race/ethnicity (e.g., Fiori & Rauer, Chapter 14) or sexual orientation (Randall & Messerschmitt-Coen, Chapter 10). Nonetheless, studying homogeneous groups such as midlife adults can also illuminate maintenance within designated populations, as Rauer and Proulx (Chapter 17) note. Both comparative analysis of different subsamples within a given study and in-depth examination of different homogeneous samples across studies are pathways to achieving a more comprehensive and inclusive picture of maintenance.

Turning to a different form of sampling diversity, virtually all maintenance studies take an insider's view, asking the partners themselves. Sprecher and colleagues (Chapter 9) see value in collecting data from outsiders, onlookers to relationships, in the hope that they will see things that are invisible to the partners themselves. Along these general lines, MacDonald and Ross (1999) demonstrated that roommates and parents were more accurate than partners themselves in predicting the longevity of dating relationships.

Contributors to this volume also recommended future work on measuring maintenance. Rauer and her coauthors (Fiori and Proulx) see value in determining what aspects of maintenance, such as having a supportive spouse, mean in different groups (Fiori & Rauer, Chapter 14) and call for creating developmentally appropriate measures (Rauer & Proulx, Chapter 17). Assessment of the equivalence of measures in different populations is now fairly common in other domains and could profitably be used for traditional self-report maintenance scales (Vandenberg & Lance, 2000). As Impett and colleagues (Chapter 12) argue, greater use could also be made of observational and psychophysiological assessments.

Studies of maintenance frequently use correlational designs. Calls for the use of other types of designs are scattered throughout the chapters. These include conducting experiments to enhance confidence in causal inference (Sprecher et al., Chapter 9; Xu et al., Chapter 6), clinical trial–type studies to enhance the generalizability and practical application of findings (Xu et al., Chapter 6), and daily diary and experience sampling studies that obtain reports on events and experiences in their context and in the moment (Sprecher et al., Chapter 9). As will be discussed later, several contributors recommend greater use of longitudinal designs or designs requiring the collection of data at multiple time points (Impett et al., Chapter 12; McNulty & Dugas, Chapter 8; Rauer & Proulx, Chapter 17; Sprecher et al., Chapter 9; Vennum et al., Chapter 18).

Statistical analysis is another facet of methodology. Since the early 1980s, statistical procedures in the study of relationships have become increasingly sophisticated. A relatively early breakthrough was dealing with yoked data such as partners in a relationship via techniques such as Kenny's (1996) Actor-Partner Interaction Model (APIM). In this volume, McNulty and Dugas (Chapter 8) recommend its use, thus testifying to its continuing value. More recently, advances have been made in dyadic growth models that examine systematic change in outcome scores over time as well as the similarity between partners in their change patterns (Kashy, Ackerman, & Donnellan, 2018). Consistently with this march forward in quantitative analysis, authors in this volume advocate techniques including growth curve analysis (Impett et al., Chapter 12; Vennum et al., Chapter 18) for seeing change over time, and person-centered, group-based analysis (Vennum et al., Chapter 18).

In addition to adding to the generality and applicability of findings, employing more diverse samples and evolving, sophisticated methods can enhance the validity of the conclusions reached and add to the questions that can be addressed. These advances have enriched and undoubtedly will continue to enrich what is known about maintenance.

Maintenance in a Developmental Perspective

This volume benefits from providing some elaboration of a developmental perspective on relationship maintenance. Rauer and Proulx's chapter on maintenance across the life course (Chapter 17) is the centerpiece of that. In addition, there was discussion of uncertainty reduction in emerging relations (Theiss, Chapter 5), the transition to parenthood (Impett et al., Chapter 12), stressful events (Randall & Messerschmitt, Chapter 10), and life stages (Fiori & Rauer, Chapter 14; Sprecher et al., Chapter 9).

Examining maintenance over time and the life course as a profitable future direction for investigation is another theme in multiple chapters in this volume and elsewhere (Ogolsky & Monk, 2018). Obviously, this thrust overlaps with the methodological call for longitudinal designs and various types of related statistical analyses. Contributors to this volume hope that research will proceed along the following avenues.

- In their future directions section, Rauer and Proulx (Chapter 17) focus on life-course possibilities such as:

  - Does the importance maintenance has for relationships fluctuate over the life course?
  - Is positivity as a maintenance strategy more important in later life?
  - Will life course–related historical changes such as cohabitation foster better marital maintenance skills?

- Young and Simpson (Chapter 3) articulate a model in which one's early and current environments combine to influence one's maintenance and destabilizing behaviors. They recommend ontogenetic research to see the impact of early environments as well as studies on ultimate causation (i.e., distal cause due to evolutionary history).
- McNulty and Dugas (Chapter 8) want studies that examine how maintenance behaviors impact relationship satisfaction both immediately and over time as well as how the maintenance strategies themselves change over time in relationships. They entertain the idea that some maintenance strategies can be beneficial in the short run but undermine relationships in the long run.
- Sprecher and colleagues (Chapter 9) want further evidence on whether, over time, network interference affects partners' maintenance behaviors and the dissolution of relationships.
- Randall and Messerschmitt-Coen (Chapter 10) suggest work to determine the long-term effects of dyadic coping as a maintenance strategy.
- Impett and colleagues (Chapter 12) advocate for studies of how different sexual trajectories help or interfere with relationship maintenance and satisfaction over time, plus studies of life transitions such as having children.

- Fiori and Rauer (Chapter 14) want research on whether the effects of race and gender vary across the life cycle.
- Vennum and colleagues (Chapter 18) call for research demonstrating the long-term impact (e.g., on marital quality) of interventions designed to promote maintenance strategies.

Even looking at this set of suggestions, I see other gaps that could be filled. For example, there has been relatively little discussion of maintenance processes during important life transitions (e.g., graduating from high school and starting college, starting work, getting married, moving, getting divorced, and retiring). These are times when relationships can be taxed, and adjustments often need to be made. Thus, I see a place for more research on maintenance during life transitions and how that contributes to posttransition relationship outcomes.

It is also noteworthy to me that Rauer and Proulx (Chapter 17), in covering stages of the life course, start with young adulthood. Given that the scope of this volume is primarily focused on romantic relationships, they ignore maintenance in children and adolescents. The early elementary years, as well as early adolescence, however, are periods when friendships are relatively low in stability: first graders only keep about 50% of their friendships across the school year; this increases during the elementary years but then drops again in early adolescence (Poulin & Chan, 2010). Friendships instability among children and adolescents has been linked with internalizing problems (e.g., depression), externalizing problems (e.g., antisocial behaviors; Poulin & Chan, 2010). Furthermore, friendship stability has been associated with better school adjustment (more involvement, less disruptive behavior in class, and higher grades; Berndt, 1999). Additional research could profitably be conducted on the maintenance strategies of children/youths, the association between the use of maintenance processes and friendship stability, and testing interventions to foster the use of maintenance processes in younger people.

Clearly, there is still much work that can be done on maintenance over time and the life course.

A Few Final Suggestions for Future Directions

In what other directions might maintenance research go? I have four suggestions. First, Young and Simpson (Chapter 3) talk about how maintenance research examines the ways that relationship partners deal with threats to their relationships, including the occurrence of goal conflicts. Presumably, this means that conflicts trigger maintenance processes. Ogolsky and Gray (2016), however, reported data showing that conflict suppressed relationship maintenance. This is a seeming contradiction that is worth better illuminating.

Second, I see one of life's dialectical choices as being the extent to which to seek novelty and change versus constancy and stability. Following Aron's self-expansion model, this volume gives more attention to novelty and change. A key word search of Ogolsky and colleagues' (2017) bibliography suggests that the maintenance literature more generally gives scant attention to the place of ritual in relationship maintenance. Scholars such as Barbara Fiese (2006) have emphasized the general value of routines and rituals. I feel that they warrant more attention and should lead to coming to an understanding of when each side of the dialectic is most beneficial.

Third, Catrin Finkenauer organized a 2015 mini-conference on self-regulation and relationships sponsored by the International Association for Relationship Research (see www.iarr2015amsterdam.nl/). I was impressed by the work being done in that area. Going back to the classic children's delay of gratification studies (Mischel, Shoda, & Peake, 1988), the benefits of self-regulation-type processes have been documented. What is the role of self-regulation in relationship maintenance?

Finally, I was impressed with Ogolsky's (2009) efforts to identify causal directions between commitment and relationship maintenance. There have also been efforts to find moderators and mediators among maintenance and the variables associated with it. We have made progress in specifying causal directions as well in identifying mediating and moderating variables, but I feel there is still work along these lines to be done.

CONCLUSION

I accepted with enthusiasm the invitation to write this concluding chapter. In the developmental arc of our key relationships, maintaining existing relationships is often the longest of the development, maintenance, and decline segments. It may not be as exciting or turbulent as other phases, but I see maintenance as a crucial element in the science of relationships.

In this chapter, I have tried to place current maintenance scholarship in a broader historical context, focusing on the past, the present, and the future. I have tried to draw heavily on the chapters in the volume to highlight commonalities and differences among them. Seventeen years ago, I authored a similar concluding chapter (Perlman, 2001). Since that time, maintenance has gone from a fledgling topic gaining a toehold in the scholarly examination of personal relationships to now having a more significant place. The number of publications has grown, and the methods used to study maintenance have expanded. In terms of Margulis's (1977) three stages of concept development, Stage 1 (establishing the importance of the concept) has passed. The first main section of this volume testifies that Stage 3 (theorizing) of concept development is now fully alive.

Clearly, research on relationship maintenance has come a long way during the first two decades of the twenty-first century. But, as the contributors to this volume have identified, there are still avenues to explore. Hopefully, they or others will follow those suggestions and blaze exciting trails not yet envisioned. Seventeen years ago, I ended my commentary on a note that is still germane:

> I hope in the next decade and beyond that those involved in the research decision-making process … will use strategies to maintain and enhance research on relationship maintenance. Sharing Baumeister and Leary's (1995) view of the centrality of relationships to our existence, I am convinced that maintaining relationship maintenance research will contribute to human well-being. (Perlman, 2001, p. 373)

REFERENCES

Agnew, C. R., & VanderDrift, L. E. (2015). Relationship maintenance and dissolution. In M. Mikulincer, P. R. Shaver, J. A. Simpson, & J. F. Dovidio (Eds.), *APA handbooks in psychology. APA handbook of personality and social psychology, Vol. 3. Interpersonal relations* (pp. 581–604). Washington, DC: American Psychological Association.

Aron, A., Norman, C. C., & Aron, E. N. (2001). Shared self-expanding activities as a means of maintaining and enhancing close romantic relationships. In J. M. Harvey & A. E. Wenzel (Eds.), *Close romantic relationships: Maintenance and enhancement* (pp. 47–66). Mahwah, NJ: Lawrence Erlbaum.

Ayres, J. (1983). Strategies to maintain relationships: Their identification and perceived usage. *Communication Quarterly, 31,* 62–67.

Baumeister, R. F., & Leary, M. R. (1995). The need to belong: Desire for interpersonal attachments as a fundamental human motivation. *Psychological Bulletin, 117,* 497–529.

Berndt, T. J. (1999). Friends' influence on students' adjustment to school. *Educational Psychologist, 34,* 15–28.

Berscheid, E. (1995). Help wanted: A grand theorist of interpersonal relationships, sociologist or anthropologist preferred. *Journal of Social and Personal Relationships, 12,* 529–533.

Buckles, K. S., & Munnich, E. L. (2012). Birth spacing and sibling outcomes. *Journal of Human Resources, 47,* 613–642.

Burleson, B. R., & Samter, W. (1994). A social skills analysis of relationship maintenance: How individual differences in communication skills affect the achievement of relationship functions. In D. J. Canary & L. Stafford (Eds.), *Communication and relational maintenance* (pp. 61–90). New York, NY: Academic Press.

Canary, D. J., & Dainton, M. (Eds.). (2003). *Maintaining relationships through communication: Relational, contextual, and cultural variations.* Mahwah, NJ: Lawrence Erlbaum.

Canary, D. J., & Dainton, M. (2006). Maintaining relationships. In A. L. Vangelisti & D. Perlman (Eds.), *The Cambridge handbook of personal relationships* (pp. 727–743). New York, NY: Cambridge University Press.

Canary, D., & Stafford, L. (Eds.). (1994). *Communication and relational maintenance.* New York, NY: Academic Press.

Clark, M. S. (2018). What is good and what is missing in relationship theory and research. In A. Vangelisti & D. Perlman (Eds.), *Cambridge handbook of personal relationships* (pp. 28–38). New York, NY: Cambridge University Press.

Dainton, M. (2003). Framing the maintenance of relationships through communication: An epilogue. In D. J. Canary & M. Dainton (Eds.), *Maintaining relationships through communication: Relational, contextual, and cultural variations* (pp. 299–321). Mahwah, NJ: Lawrence Erlbaum.

Davis, M. S. (1973). *Intimate relations.* New York, NY: Free Press.

de Jong Gierveld, J., & Perlman, D. (2006). Long-standing nonkin relationships of older adults in the Netherlands and the U.S.A. *Research on Aging, 28,* 730–748.

Dindia, K. (2000). Relational maintenance. In C. Hendrick & S. S. Hendrick (Eds.), *Close relationships: A sourcebook* (287–299). Thousand Oaks, CA: Sage.

Dindia, K. (2003). Relationship maintenance communication. In D. J. Canary & M. Dainton (Eds.), *Maintaining relationships through communication: Relational, contextual, and cultural variations* (pp. 1–28). New York, NY: Psychology Press.

Dindia, K., & Canary, D. J. (Eds.). (1993). Special issue on relational maintenance [Special issue]. *Journal of Social and Personal Relationships, 10*(2).

Duck, S. (1994). Steady as (s)he goes: Relational maintenance as a shared meaning system. In D. J. Canary & L. Stafford (Eds.), *Communication and relational maintenance* (pp. 45–60). New York, NY: Academic Press.

Fiese, B. H. (2006). *Family routines and rituals.* Yale University Press.

Finkel, E. J., & Hall, A. N. (2018). The I³ Model: A metatheoretical framework for understanding aggression. *Current Opinion in Psychology, 19,* 125–130.

Finkel, E. J., Simpson, J. A., & Eastwick, P. W. (2017). The psychology of close relationships: Fourteen core principles. *Annual Review of Psychology, 68,* 383–411.

Harre, R. (1977). Friendship as an accomplishment: An ethnogenic approach to social relationships. In S. Duck (Ed.), *Theory and practice in interpersonal attraction* (pp. 339–354). New York, NY: Academic Press.

Harvey, J. H., & Wenzel, A. (Eds.). (2001). *Close romantic relationships: Maintenance and enhancement.* Mahwah, NJ: Lawrence Erlbaum.

Harvey, J. H., & Wenzel, A. (Eds.). (2002). *A clinician's guide to maintaining and enhancing close relationships.* Mahwah, NJ: Lawrence Erlbaum.

Kashy, D. A., Ackerman, R. A., & Donnellan, M. B. (2018). Analyzing cross-sectional and longitudinal data in close relationships (pp. 49–64). In A. L. Vangelisti & D. Perlman (Eds.), *Cambridge handbook of personal relationships.* New York, NY: Cambridge University Press.

Kenny, D. A. (1996). Models of non-independence in dyadic research. *Journal of Social and Personal Relationships, 13,* 279–294.

Kochanek, K. D., Murphy, S. L., Xu, J. Q., & Arias, E. (2017). *Mortality in the United States, 2016.* NCHS Data Brief, no 293. Hyattsville, MD: National Center for Health Statistics.

Kreider, R. M., & Ellis, R. (2011). Number, timing, and duration of marriages and divorces: 2009. *Current Population Reports,* p70–125, Washington, DC: US Census Bureau.

Lydon, J., & Quinn, S. (2013). Relationship maintenance processes. In J. Simpson & L. Campbell (Eds.), *The Oxford handbook of close relationships* (pp. 573–588). New York, NY: Oxford.

MacDonald, T. K., & Ross, M. (1999). Assessing the accuracy of predictions about dating relationships: How and why do lovers' predictions differ from those made by observers? *Personality and Social Psychology Bulletin, 25,* 1417–1429.

Margulis, S. T. (1977). Conceptions of privacy: Current status and next steps. *Journal of Social Issues, 33*(3), 5–21.

McNulty, J. K. (2016). Highlighting the contextual nature of interpersonal relationships. In J. M. Olson & M. P. Zanna (Eds.), *Advances in experimental social psychology* (Vol. 54, pp. 247–315). San Diego, CA: Academic Press.

Menard, H. W. (1971). *Science: Growth and change.* Cambridge, MA: Harvard University Press.

Mikulincer, M., & Shaver, P. R. (2007). *Attachment in adulthood: Structure, dynamics, and change.* New York, NY: Guilford Press.

Mischel, W., Shoda, Y., & Peake, P. K. (1988). The nature of adolescent competencies predicted by preschool delay of gratification. *Journal of Personality and Social Psychology, 54*(4), 687–696.

Ogolsky, B. G. (2007). Antecedents and consequences of relationship maintenance in intimate relationships. *Dissertation Abstracts International Section A: Humanities and Social Sciences, 68*(2-A), 746.

Ogolsky, B. G. (2009). Deconstructing the association between relationship maintenance and commitment: Testing two competing models. *Personal Relationships, 16*, 99–115.

Ogolsky, B. G., & Bowers, J. R. (2013). A meta-analytic review of relationship maintenance and its correlates. *Journal of Social and Personal Relationships, 30*, 343–367.

Ogolsky, B. G., & Gray, C. R. (2016). Conflict, negative emotion, and reports of partners' relationship maintenance in same-sex couples. *Journal of Family Psychology, 30*(2), 171–180.

Ogolsky, B. G., & Monk, J. K. (2018). Maintaining relationships. In A. Vangelisti & D. Perlman (Eds.), *Cambridge handbook of personal relationships* (pp. 523–537). New York, NY: Cambridge University Press.

Ogolsky, B. G., Monk, J. K., Rice, T. M., Theisen, J. C., & Maniotes, C. R. (2017). Relationship maintenance: A review of research on romantic relationships. *Journal of Family Theory and Review, 9*, 275–306.

Perlman, D. (2001). Maintaining and enhancing relationships: Concluding commentary. In J. M. Harvey & A. E. Wenzel (Eds.), *Close romantic relationships: Maintenance and enhancement* (pp. 357–377). Mahwah, NJ: Lawrence Erlbaum.

Perlman, D., Duck, S., & Hengstebeck, N. D. (2018). The seven seas of the study of personal relationships research: Historical and recent currents. In A. L. Vangelisti & D. Perlman (Eds.), *Cambridge handbook of personal relationships* (pp. 9–27). New York, NY: Cambridge University Press.

Poulin, F., & Chan, A. (2010). Friendship stability and change in childhood and adolescence. *Developmental Review, 30*, 257–272.

Rusbult, C. E., Drigotas, S. M., & Verette, J. (1994). The investment model: An interdependence analysis of commitment processes and relationship maintenance phenomena. In D. J. Canary & L. Stafford (Eds.), *Communication and relational maintenance* (pp. 115–139). New York, NY: Academic Press.

Rusbult, C. E., Olsen, N., Davis, J. L., & Hannon, P. A. (2001). Commitment and relationship maintenance mechanisms. In J. Harvey & A. Wenzel (Eds.), *Close romantic relationships: Maintenance and enhancement* (pp. 87–113). Mahwah, NJ: Lawrence Erlbaum.

Simon, E. P., & Baxter, L. A. (1993). Attachment-style differences in relationship maintenance strategies. *Western Journal of Communication, 57*, 419–430.

Stafford, L. (1994). Tracing the threads of spider webs. In D. J. Canary & L. Stafford (Eds.), *Communication and relational maintenance* (pp. 297–306). New York, NY: Academic Press.

Stafford, L. (Ed.). (2005). *Maintaining long-distance and cross residential relationships.* Mahwah, NJ: Lawrence Erlbaum.

Stafford, L., & Canary, D. J. (1991). Maintenance strategies and romantic relationship type, gender and relational characteristics. *Journal of Social and Personal Relationships, 8*, 217–242.

Stueve, C. A., & Gerson, K. (1977). Personal relations across the life-cycle. In C. S. Fischer, R. M. Jackson, C. A. Stueve, K. Gerson, L. McCallister Jones, & M. Baldassare (Eds.), *Networks and places: Social relations in the urban setting* (pp. 79–98). New York, NY: Free Press.

Vandenberg, R. J., & Lance, C. E. (2000). A review and synthesis of the measurement invariance literature: Suggestions, practices, and recommendations for organizational research. *Organizational Research Methods, 3*, 4–70.

Wu, H., & Brown. S. L. (2016). Long-term marriage among older adults. *Family Profiles*, FP-16–08. Bowling Green, OH: National Center for Family & Marriage Research. Retrieved from www.bgsu.edu/content/dam/BGSU/college-of-arts-and-sciences/NCFMR/documents/FP/wu-brown-longterm-marriage-older-adults-fp-16-08.pdf

Wu, K. D. (2001). Evolution and evolutionary psychology: Their application to close relationships. In J. Harvey & A. Wenzel (Eds.), *Close romantic relationships: Maintenance and enhancement* (pp. 215–233). Mahwah, NJ: Lawrence Erlbaum.

INDEX